SAP TOOLS, METHODOLOGIES AND TECHNIQUES

by

Sudipta Malakar

FIRST EDITION 2018

ISBN:978-93-87284-51-7

Distributors:

BPB PUBLICATIONS
20, Ansari Road, Darya Ganj
New Delhi-110002
Ph: 23254990/23254991

DECCAN AGENCIES
4-3-329, Bank Street,
Hyderabad-500195
Ph: 24756967/24756400

BPB PUBLICATIONS
376 Old Lajpat Rai Market,
Delhi-110006
Ph: 23861747

MICROMEDIA
Shop No. 5, Mahendra Chambers, 150 DN
Rd. Next to Capital Cinema, V.T.
(C.S.T.) Station, MUMBAI-400 001
Ph:22078296/22078297

Published by Manish Jain for BPB Publications, 20, Ansari Road, Darya Ganj, New Delhi-110002 and Printed by Repro India Ltd., Mumbai

PREFACE

Notice how SAP has changed the world now. Whether you are a newbie or an old-hat, you can learn to design & build simple and advanced SAP Data Medium Exchange (DME) graphical Tool, BAPI, Web services, MDM applications with ABAP/4, SAP UI5, Fiori, LSMW tool, ALE, IDOC, TabStrip control, SAP Query tool, SAP Quick viewer tool, Webdynpro, Object oriented ALV with SALV Factory method, SAP Report Painter tool by using this comprehensive artifact. You can also enrich your skillsets with the new object-oriented approach. Use this detailed programming referral guide to develop and optimize your applications. You'll be programming for SAP in no time. The goal of writing this book is to describe different SAP ABAP programming best practices, taken reference from different SAP & IBM blogs, books, articles, Global networks,Wikipedia, organizational forums, portals, etc.

The document explains what "Data conversion" is. What data needs to be converted and what method is used for this. It also explains cleansing the data and approach towards the historical data and its significance. The document gives an overview about the data conversion and can be consider as initial overview of the subject".

This book promises to be a very good starting point for beginners and an asset for those having insight towards programming.

It is said **"To err is human, to forgive divine"**. Although the book is written with sincerity and honesty but in this light, I wish that the shortcomings of the book will be forgiven. At the same the author is open to any kind of constructive criticisms and suggestions for further improvement. All intelligent suggestions are welcome and the author will try itsbest to incorporate such in valuable suggestions in the subsequent editions of this book.

Acknowledgement

No task is a single man's effort. Cooperation and Coordination of various peoples at different levels go into successful implementation of this book.
There is always a sense of gratitude, which everyone expresses others for their helpful and needy services they render during difficult phases of life and to achieve the goal already set.

At the outset I am thankful to the almighty that is constantly and invisibly guiding every body and helped me to work on the right path.

I am very much thankful to **my parents, spouse, son and family** for their guidance which motivated me to work for the betterment of consultants by writing the book with sincerity and honesty. Without their support, this book is not possible.

I wish my sincere thanks to colleagues who helped and kept me motivated for writing this text.

I also thank the Publisher and the whole staff at BPB Publication, especially **Mr. Manish Jain for motivation** and for bringing this text in a nice presentable form.

Finally, I thank everyone who has directly or indirectly contributed to complete this authentic work.

Table of Contents

CHAPTER 1

DME overview

DMEE is a graphical tool that enables you to define a format hierarchy and mapping rules for individual format fields without having to write ABAP code. This greatly simplifies the processes of creating new formats and maintaining existing ones. The Data Medium Exchange (DME) graphical tool enables you to define file formats that meet the requirements of your financial organization. By doing so, you model an externally defined bank format in the SAP R/3 System, which allows you to send or receive data in the form of Data Medium Exchange (DME) files in this format. The ability to effectively define these formats in the SAP R/3 System is extremely useful as there is no worldwide or regional standard format. In some cases, no country standard exists and the file must comply with bank-specific standards. Generally, covering such numerous and varied local / country specific format requirements is extremely difficult in standard software, without any ABAP programming knowledge or coding the Data Medium Exchange (DME) graphical tool enables you to define your local format yourself. With this Customizing graphical tool, in the form of an effective graphical editor, any user can define new formats flexibly and, as format requirements change, modify existing ones efficiently.

1.1 Transaction Code

DMEE

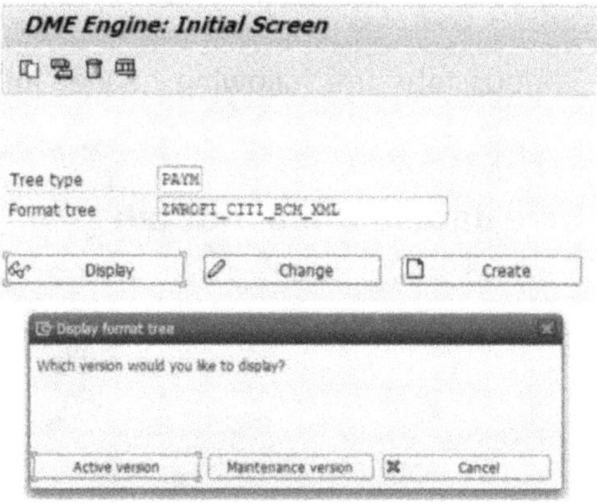

DME Engine: Initial Screen

Tree type PAYM
Format tree ZNROFI_CITI_BCM_XML

Display Change Create

Display format tree
Which version would you like to display?
Active version Maintenance version Cancel

This gives a user the flexible option to either open the already activated DMEE or the one which is only saved but not yet ready for use.

1.2 Main Components of DME File

- Header Data
- Nodes
- Data Mapping

Generally, there are some standard DME file formats, which can be changed as per country or bank requirements.
Acompletely new Data Medium Exchange (DME) graphical tool format can be created if business requirement is different from pre-existing formats.
Steps:

1. Go to Transaction code DMEE and Provide tree type from available ones.
2. DME files can be generated in flat files or XML format.
3. Provide short description and documentation.
4. Data Medium Exchange (DME) graphical tool contains three components as shown below.
5. Generally, there are some fields which are available for Data Medium Exchange (DME) graphical tool file as shown below.

1.3 DMEE Tree Nodes Creation Procedure

DMEE tree Nodes creation procedure:

Header Data:

Under header data in various tabs the following header information needs to be maintained:

Provide administrative data in node first tab

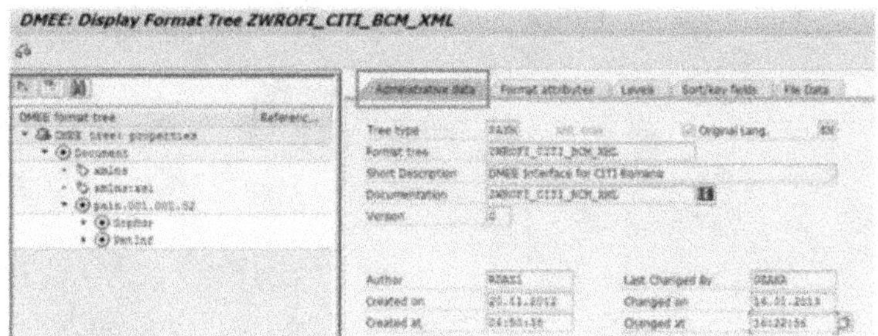

Format Attributes:

For flat files, you can enter delimiter information; for XML files, you can specify further processing (via exit module) for a file after its creation, by entering an XSLT program.

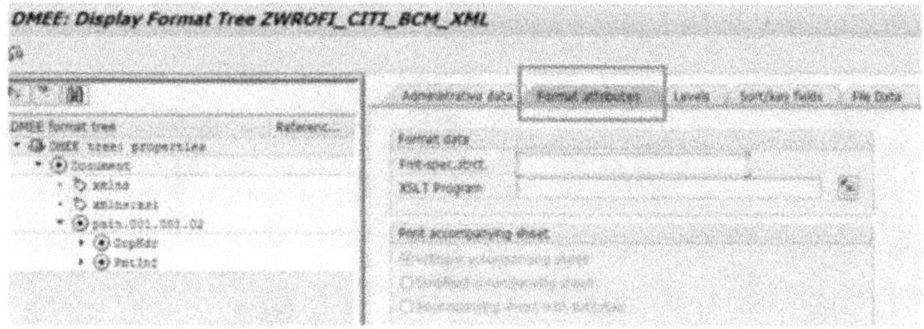

Levels

The number of levels defines the no of levels in a tree. The corresponding level cannot be output anymore if this number is exceeded. In case if the limit is reached for the uppermost level in the format tree and additional data is to be processed then a second file is generated. If the limit is reached for lower levels, the preceding level is repeated so that data can continue to be output for this level.

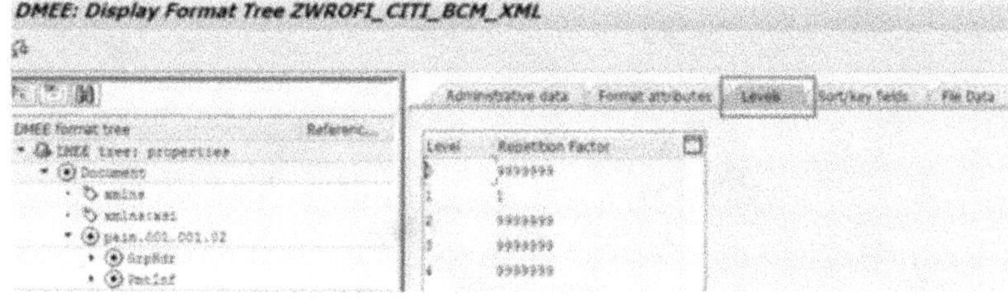

Sort Key Fields

File Data can be sorted based on given fields.

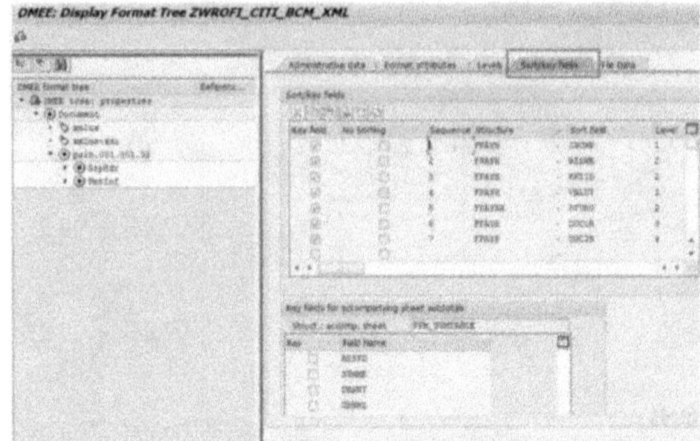

File Data

This tab provides the file row separator and segment ending indicator.

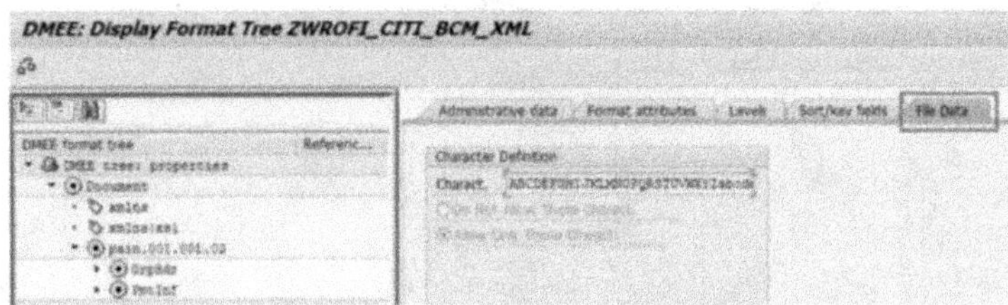

Please refer to the screenshot (excel sheet) for a requirement example view of DMEE segment, node creation. In the mapping file, the mention of the following should be provided:

1. Field/Node/Segment Name.
2. Type i.e. Parent Segment or XML Attribute or Technical Node or XML Element.
3. Mapping procedure.

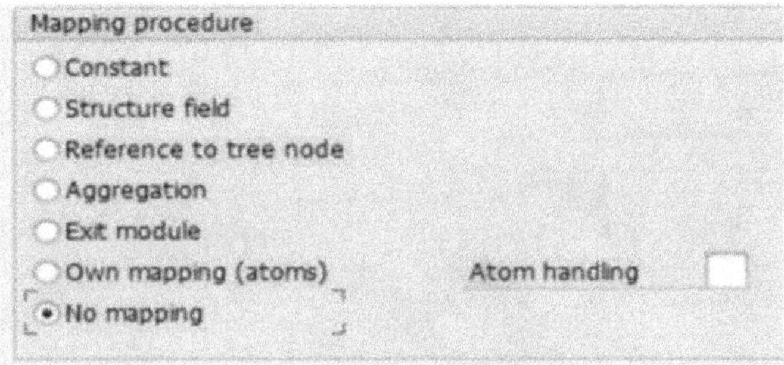

4. Length
5. Level
6. Detailed Mapping Logic

According to the above, segment will be created by right-clicking on

DMEE tree: properties

A tree can have multiple segments as well multiple nodes.

Header Filed in DMEE					
Level 1 in DMEE					
Level 2 in DMEE					
Level 3 in DMEE					
Level 4 in DMEE					
Field Name	Type	Mapping procedure	Length	Level	Detailed Mapping Logic
Document	Parent Segment	No Mapping		1	Header - No Mapping
xmlns	XML Attribute	Constant		1	urn:iso:std:iso:20022:tech:xsd:pain.001.001.02
xmlns:xsi	XML Attribute	Constant		1	http://www.w3.org/2001/XMLSchema-instance
<pain.001.001.02>	Parent Segment	No Mapping		1	Header - No Mapping

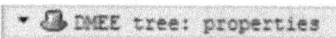

Node Info

Provide node information for output

1. **Attribute** –In this,feed in the information as requested in the mapping file. Please note that the mapping procedure mentioned here needs to be in line with the input in the next tab (Source).As shown in the below figurein mapping procedures, these elements may be of different types.

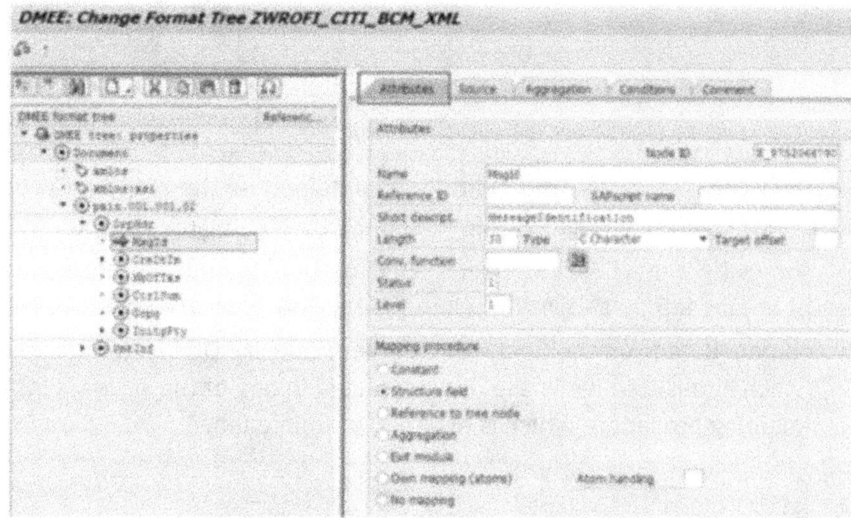

2. **Source**–Below figureshows the necessary data to be input in this Tab according to the mapping structure in Attributes Tab.
   - Here**'Constants'**is maintained as the mapping procedure in the 'Attributes' tab, one should input the constant value in this tab as shown below. This type of element is used to contain constant value like 'MIXD' (in this case) which is assigned in source tab.

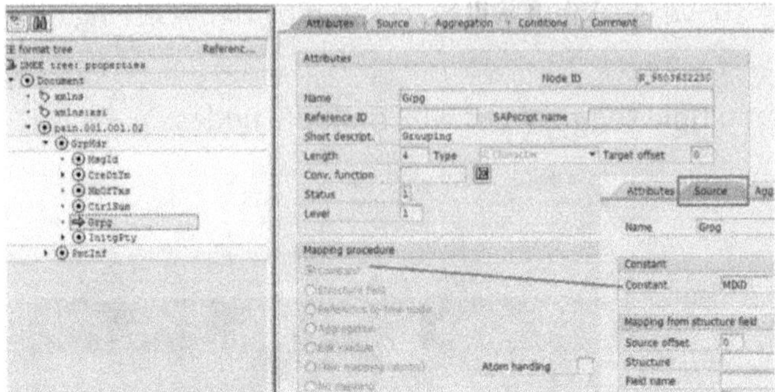

- Here **'Structure Field'** is maintained as the mapping procedure in the 'Attributes' tab.This node contains structure types which can have system fields. One should input the structure and the field name in this tab as shown in below figure. This type of element is used to contain data from the field in the structure like 'FPAYHX-RENUM' (in this case)which is assigned in source tab.

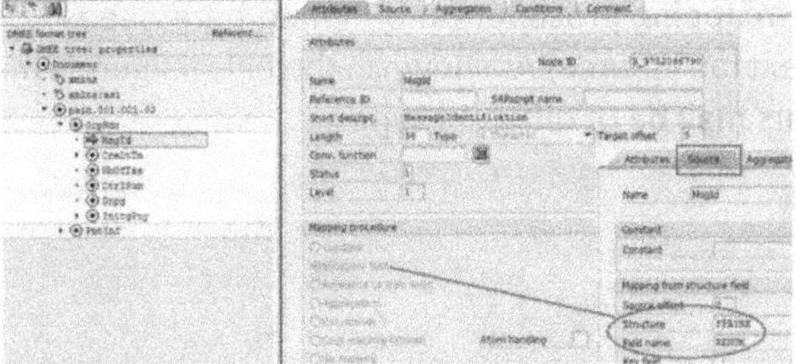

- Here **'Reference to Tree Node'** is maintained as the mapping procedure in the 'Attributes' tab. This node contains data whichis already captured somewhere in a DMEE node earlier. One should input the reference Node ID in this tab as shown in below figure. This type of element is used to contain data from the field in the earlier node like DOC1R (in this case) which in turn can well have data extracted in one of the six ways in the mapping procedure which is assigned in source tab.

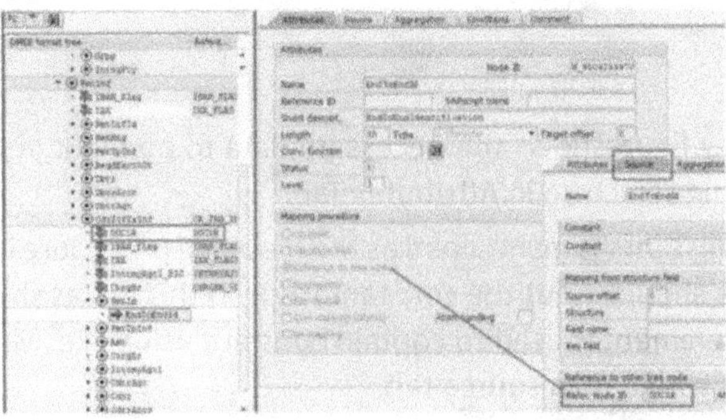

- Here **'Exit Module'** is maintained as the mapping procedure in the 'Attributes' tab. This node contains data which is a result of a Function Module. Within the FM one can write desired logic to derive the data required.One should input the Exit Function in this tab as shown in below figure. Z_W_DMEE_EXIT_BCM_UTILITIES (in this case)has a CASE-ENDCASE statement indicating the node name as illustrated below.

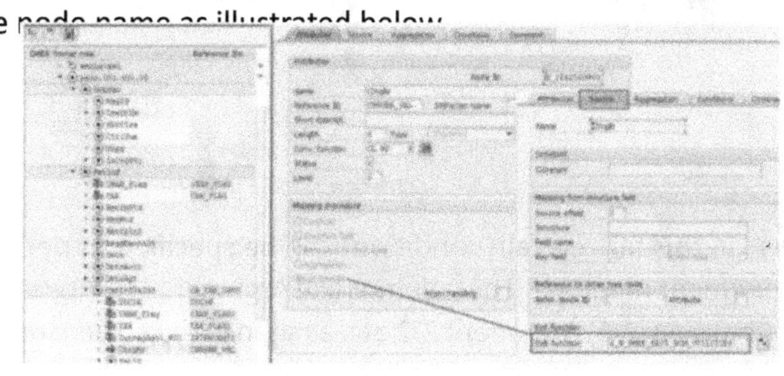

Click on the button to reach into the source code of the Function Module

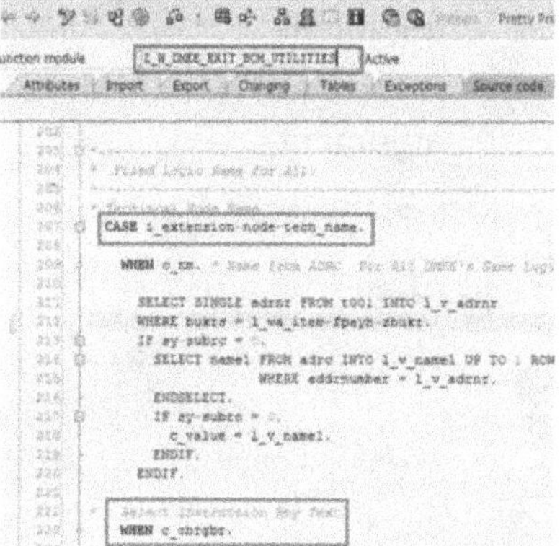

3. **Aggregation** – You can define an aggregation for elements oratoms. When you create either of these nodes, select the mappingprocedure Aggregation. You enter the reference IDs of thenodes you wish to aggregate and the aggregation type on the Aggregation tab, – how the aggregationnodes are to be totaled to the target node.

    - Here 'Aggregation' is maintained as the mapping procedure in the 'Attributes' tab. This function enables you to aggregate values for specified format tree nodes (called aggregation nodes) and it makes this number available to a defined field in the Data Medium Exchange (DME) graphical tool file. The aggregation function can be used at the end of a level or a file to:

i. Add the total value of specified nodes

ii. Add the number of nodes

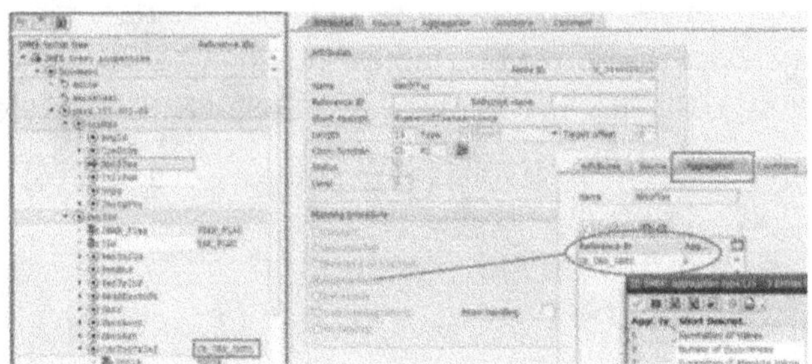

4. **Conditions**– In this tab, certain conditions can be specified as per logic provided in the requirement mapping. The columns like Argument1-1, Argument 1-2, Type, Operator, Argument2-1, Argument 2-2 etc. as seen in the screenshot below needs to be considered. There could be three types of Arguments

- Constant: A node with a constant value can be put as argument
- Structure-Field: A node with a Structure-Field value can be put as argument
- Ref ID: A Technical Node with Reference ID can be put as argument

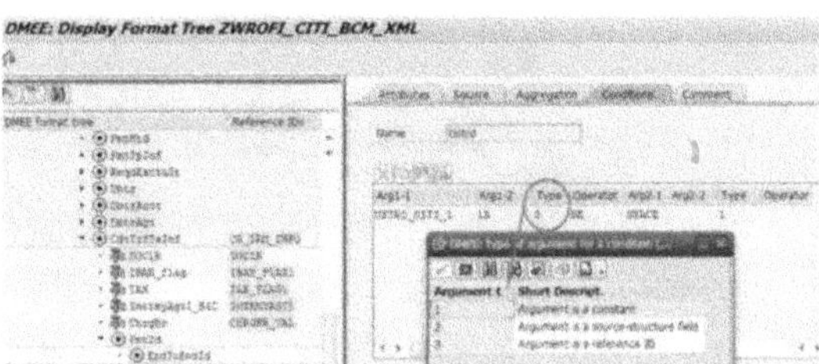

5. **Comment** – This column is used to contain comments for nodes. We can do maximum three lines of comments per node, this tab is visible for all nodes except the header.

Create Elements in Sub node as shown below:

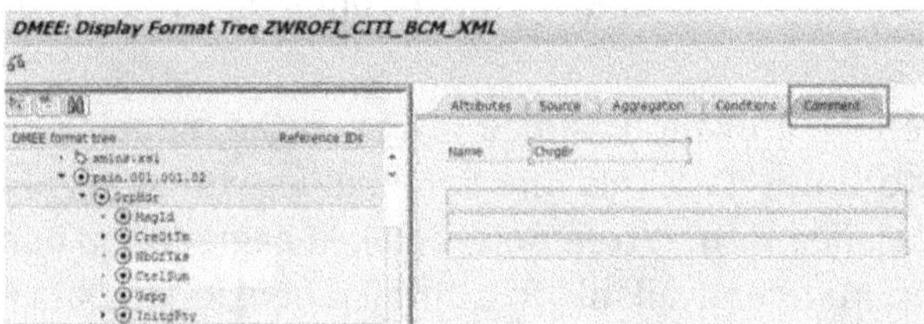

As per your need and requirement you may create a footer segment for footer data of the file which again contain any no. of elements as shown below.

1.4 Configuration of Data Medium Exchange (DME) graphical tool File

Configuration of Data Medium Exchange (DME) graphical tool File

After creation of Data Medium Exchange (DME) graphical tool file, next step is to configure the Data Medium Exchange (DME) graphical tool file for automatic payment run which requires below steps:

1. Go to Tcode FBZP and select 'pmnt methods in country'
2. Here different payment methods can be defined for country as shown below
3. Now select specific payment method and double click on the same. Following screen will be displayed. In payment medium workbench, Data Medium Exchange (DME) graphical tool tree can be assigned in Format column as shown below:
4. Click on Format settings.
5. Click on Data Medium Exchange (DME) graphical tool Engine, Data Medium Exchange (DME) graphical tool tree will be displayed.

Now Data Medium Exchange (DME) graphical tool tree format is being attached for a particular country and a particular payment method. You have to run the automatic payment program with this payment method in order to generate the Data Medium Exchange (DME) graphical tool file. After the payments have been successfully posted, you can go to Data Medium Exchange (DME) graphical tool administration and with the help of DME manager download files on your PC. Data Medium Exchange (DME) graphical tool can be attached to a print program and form for the creation of Payment Advices.

1.5 Conclusion

Data Medium Exchange (DME) graphical tool engine provides different layouts and readymade way to create flat files or XML files for external systems. It provides flexibility and speed over conventional ABAP Programs. Files can be modified based on country and regulations. The system can trigger the creation of a Data Medium Exchange (DME) graphical tool file from the payment program if, for example, you want to submit your vendor payments to your bank electronically.

1.6 Golden Rules

- Refer to the screenshot(s) of excel spreadsheet/Mapping file enclosed in CRF/RQI/RQT to have detailed info on Field/Node/Segment Name/Type/Mapping procedure/Length/Level/Sort/Key fields, Detailed Mapping logic/ Nodes Info/Exit Function Module Name etc. to be used in Data Medium Exchange (DME) graphical tool.
- Exit Function Module maintained in the 'Attributes/Source' tab of Data Medium Exchange (DME) graphical tool acts as data source. Logic should be written under CASE-ENDCASE statement within the Exit Function Module indicating the node name etc. as per current business requirement.

1.7 Quiz Sessions

1. The full form of DMEE is Data Medium Exchange Engine. (True / False)
2. DMEE is not a graphical Tool. (True / False)
3. Main components of Data Medium Exchange (DME) graphical tool File are Header Data, Nodes, Data Mapping. (True / False)
4. Exit Function Module maintained in the 'Attributes/Source' tab of Data Medium Exchange (DME) graphical tool acts as data source. (True / False)
5. Hard coding is allowed within Data Medium Exchange (DME) graphical tool Source Code. (True / False)

Ans

True, False, True, True, False.

CHAPTER 2

Purpose of SAP MDM Data Conversion document

The document explains what “Data conversion” is. What data needs to be converted and what method is used for this. It also explains cleansing the data and approach towards the historical data and its significance. The document gives an overview about the data conversion and can be consider as initial overview of the subject.

2.1. Activities in Data Conversion

Activity	Description of activity	System
Data Extraction	Data Extraction from legacy systems	Middleware
Cleansing in Source	Data Cleansing in legacy systems	Legacy
Cleansing in Data Services	Data Cleansing in Data services before loading	Middleware
Mapping	Map legacy data to SAP data	Middleware
Loading	SAP data loading with RTL/ETL	SAP and Middleware
Business Rules	Business Rules to be applied to various data elements	Middleware
Data Governance	Data Governance process definition	SAP
Data Governance Process Implementation	Implementation of Data Governance Process using MDG	SAP

2.2. Types of Systems

- COH, Siebel
- SARA
- MCSS
- MPSS
- GADD

2.3. Approach to SAP Data Loads

- **Data Cleansing**
  - o The legacy data needs to be cleansed before it is loaded into SAP systems- Development, Quality and Production. Ensure the data is up-to-date and as per the SAP parameters
  - o Data can be cleansed at three locations – in Legacy system – before transformation; Transformation/Enriching – while transforming in middleware; and in SAP- after transformation.

- **Test Conversions**
  - o Some data loads will be done automatically with the RTL tool and some will be done manually.
  - o Testing conversion Sequencing and Timing Prior to data load in SAP system.
  - o Validation of Data Loaded into SAP- Ensure data loaded is correct in SAP, perform unit testing.

2.4. Terms

- **Conversion** – Bringing Data into SAP for the first time as a starting point at go-live. In Scope for Conversion will be Master Data (i.e. Material Master, BOM, Customers, Vendors etc.), Transactional (i.e. Production order, Sales orders, Purchase Orders)
- **Data Cleansing** – Making the Data ready and to be used and harmonized for approved SAP data requirements. Remove unwanted part from the legacy data.

- **Enriching** – Fields are manipulated, systematically or manually, prior to load into SAP.
- **Validation** – Before the data is loaded in SAP, it is advisable to perform Unit testing and ensure what was loaded was as per the expectation in SAP. Validation can come in many forms – visually inspecting load extracts, entering SAP transactions to view data, or Excel or Access queries, ETL queries and reports to check field values. We will require validation prior and post to each load!
- **Test Loads** – Data loads will be tested in every SAP system like development , Quality and Pre-Production also as per the SAP system landscape there may be some dedicated clients (120, 130 etc.) in the systems(e.g. Development system) for checking the data loads.

2.5. Data Types to Be Converted

The three types of data are as follows:

1. **Configuration** - Data that is created at the time of configuration. Examples include Company Codes, Controlling Areas and Purchasing Organizations. This data must be established prior to Master Data being created and Transaction Data being processed. For data conversion purposes, it is necessary to identify the dependencies on this data. This data is mostly configured in SAP Development system and taken ahead by the Transport requests. Here it does not need any Data conversion. However, some configurations will need to be entered manually in SAP which may need data conversion.
2. **Master Data** - Data that is set up once and remains fairly static. Examples include the Material, BOM, Work Center, and Routing. For the data conversion purposes, it is necessary to identify dependencies with Configuration.
3. **Transaction Data** - Data that is continually changing. Examples include Production order, PO, invoices, checks, receipt of goods, issue of goods, etc. For data conversion purposes, it is necessary to identify the dependencies to the different types of Master Data and Configuration.

2.6. Data Not Be Converted

As with any data conversion, there will be some data that is decided to not be migrated which could be either master or transactional data. The below are some situations in which legacy data will not be migrated and the general strategy around how that data will be handled.

- **No Use** – This will exclusively cover master data. There will be data identified (via source data quality analysis) that has not been used in transactions nor will be it used in the future. This data will be left as is in the source system.
- **Old Data** – The scenario covers potentially either master or transaction data. On a case by case basis it will be determined how far back in time the data should be migrated. These criteria will represent a cutoff date after which users will be directed to the new solution. Data will still be made available in the source system prior to the cutoff until it is sunset.
- **Manual Migration** – Not all data needs to be subjected to the conversion process. This scenario usually arises when the size of data is relatively small and can be setup with little or no effort manually in the target system. This type of scenario should not be prevalent due to a higher susceptibility to human error during the migration process.
- **Out of Scope** – The legacy data may have certain information which is out of scope for the SAP Project. For example, The SAP project wants to have only the Order to cash scenario, i.e. SD module. Here the Material in legacy will be having the SD information and also some information of manufacturing the Material/Information about the BOM (example, Work scheduling views etc.). This information need not be converted.

2.7. Target Systems

Following SAP systems are going to be the target systems for converted data from various legacy systems:

1. SAP ECC – This is the central system which will hold most of the master and transactional(if needed) data related to SAP modules FI, CO, SD, MM
2. BI – Possible historical data may be moved to BI environment
3. SAP APO – Some data needs to be directly put into the APO system.

2.8. Migration Environment/Tools

We will be using RTL as our preferred tool to extract, transform and load data. The tool has the capability to extract data from various legacy systems with connectors like ODBC, JDBC ; extracted data will be stored in a staging server where various data validation, cleansing and transformation activities like field mapping, duplicate check, data translation, data quality check, data integration and manual/automated data correction; predefined SAP data structures are available for most of the master and transactional data; the tool primarily uses SAP IDOC loading technique to load data into SAP though it can also work with other methods like LSMW, BAPI, calling custom program etc. to load data as needed.

CHAPTER 3

Conversion Methodologies

There are three general strategies for migrating data from non-SAP to the SAP system. The recommended approach based on research is to use the best practices package for data migration (SAP AIO BP). The approach has fundamental "out of the box" templates for the majority of the SAP data structures. While that may be the best approach, there is some mention regarding higher volume data migration that the LSMW tool should be used. The least recommended approach (for time and cost purposes) is custom development.

3.1 SAP Data conversion landscape

Following Steps need to be followed in Conversion:

1. Identification of the Data to be converted – In this step the Data is identified like Material Master, BOM, Vendors, Customers etc. which is to be transferred.
2. In Legacy system this data is stored in certain Tables and Fields. These tables/fields are identified.
3. Corresponding Tables and Fields in SAP are identified.
4. These Tables are captured in BDR- Business Data Roadmap.
5. Further the one to one mapping of the Legacy and SAP Fields is done.
6. While mapping the conversion rules are taken into account. With this the data is filtered or conditioned to be taken over to SAP.
7. Execution of the data conversion.
8. Monitoring the IDOCs, ensure the data conversion is smooth.
9. Testing the data in SAP. Perform Unit testing.

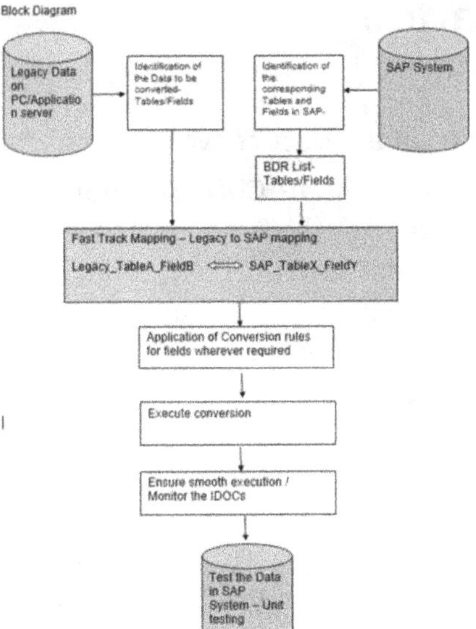

3.2 LSMW (Legacy Systems Migration Workbench)

This is a SAP R/3 based tool that is designed for periodic or one-time data migration from legacy non-SAP systems. Using this tool typical does NOT require coding in ABAP.

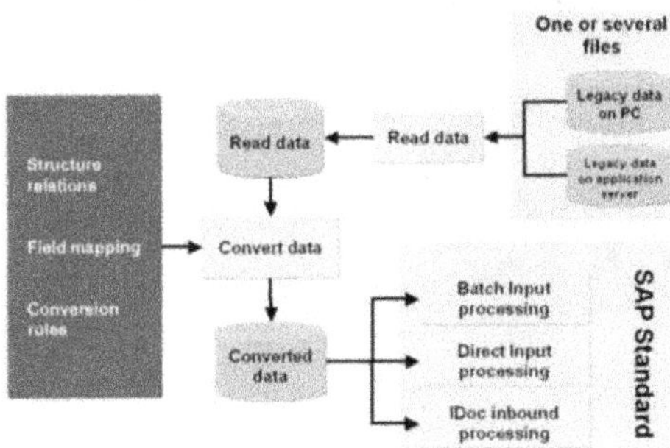

3.3 Custom Development

Custom Fields or tables can be used for accommodation of the Legacy data which cannot be fitted in Standard SAP.

3.4 Data conversion Approach

RTL will be used as our preferred tool to extract, transform and load data in SAP.

3.5 Documentation

The required documentation in the Data conversion activity is as follows-

1. **Conversion Definition Document**- CDD- This document is the outcome of the study and activity performed by the Functional consultant- Data team member. He participates in the workshops with the business legacy system users. Understands their business flow, Master data and Transaction data. He also participates in the Business workshops where the functional process in SAP would be discussed; here the functional consultant in the SAP functional team would explain the "To-Be" business flow in SAP. Co relating the two discussions the Data consultant would prepare the BDR list and Fast Track Mapping in RTL. All these activities would be documented in the CDD
2. **Technical design Document- TDD** – This document is prepared by the Technical team based on the Conversion definition document. It is more of technical stuff and contains the technical information as to how the data will be loaded into SAP. It will contain Formulas and commands etc. for loading data.

CHAPTER 4

Web services

4.1 What is Web services?

Web services can be processed through open internet standards and these are self-contained and self-describing application functionalities. We can create web Services on RFC FMs, function groups, or XI message interfaces.

Web Services act like a black-box that may require input and deliver a result:

- It works in synchronous and asynchronous scenarios,
- It facilitates integration within an enterprise as well as cross enterprises.

4.2 What is SAP Proxy?

During creation of Web services for RFC_Customer_get FM SAP Proxy is getting generated via SAP .NET Proxy generator.

4.3 What is .Net Web Service?

Web service is the way to publish application's function on web that can be accessible to the rest of the world.
Web services are the components that can be used by other applications
ASP.NET offers easy way to develop web services, just precede the functions with a special WebMethod ()> attribute in order them to work as Web Service.

Web services are built on XML standard and use SOAP protocol that allows them to communicate across different platforms and programming languages.
Web services easily manage to work across corporate firewalls as they use HTTP protocol which is firewall friendly.
Web services platform elements are
SOAP (Simple Object Access Protocol)
UDDI (Universal Description, Discovery and Integration)
WSDL (Web Services Description Language)
The web services are not platform or language specific and are built on internet standards.
The .Net framework provides in-built classes to build and consume web services.
The components offered by web services are reusable.
The examples of web service components can be shipment tracking, translation utility, weather forecasting, sports scores etc.

- **Is it possible to use User-Defined Types in Web** Services?

It is possible to process user-defined types (also known as custom types) in a Web service. These types can be passed to or returned from Web methods. They can use these user-defined types, because the proxy class created for the client contains these type definitions.

Custom types that are sent to or from a Web service are serialized, enabling them to be passed in XML format. This process is referred to as XML serialization.

4.4 Creating Web Services using Web Services wizard for a Function Module

Naming convention for Web Services:
For example:
FM name: ZBAPI_GET_EXPENSE_HISTORY
Virtual interface: ZVI_GET_EXPENSE_HISTORY
Web services definition: ZWS_GET_EXPENSE_HISTORY

From Function module, go to utilities -> More Utilities -> Create Web Services -> from the function module.

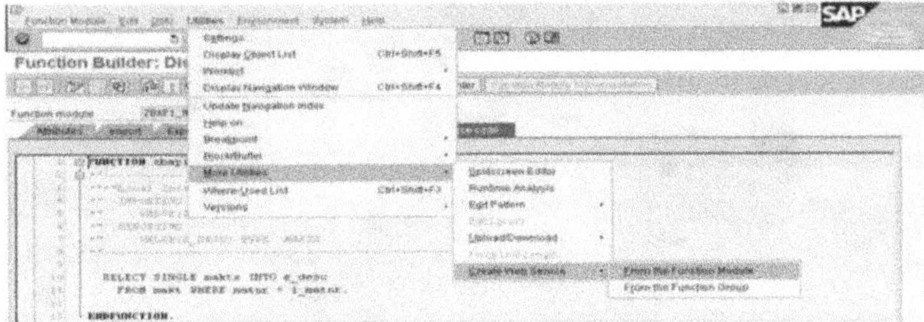

Web service wizard will open. Click on continue.

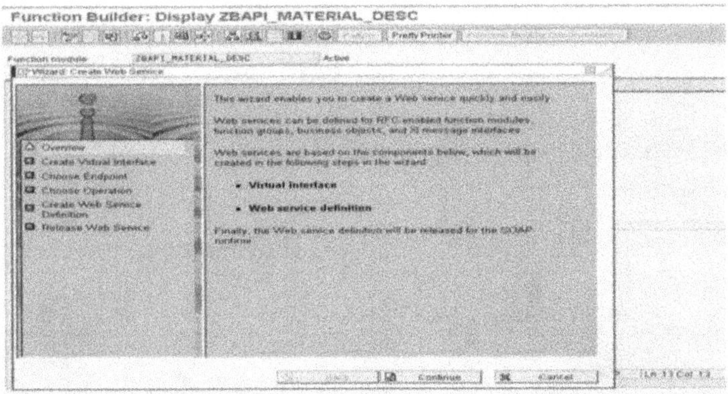

4.5.1 Creating Virtual Interface:

Enter the Virtual Interface name and description as shown below, End point will be "Function module" by default.

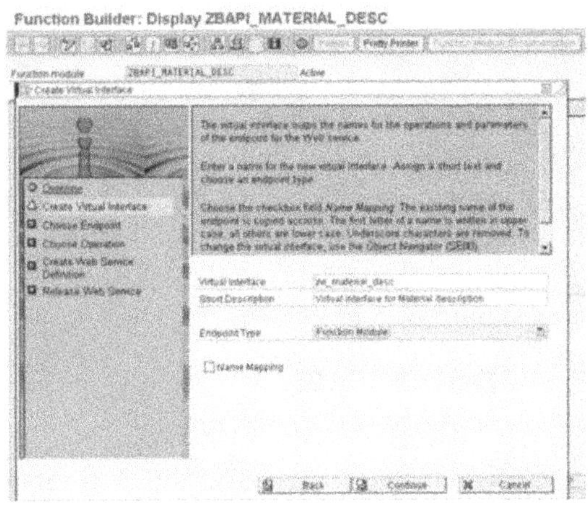

Function module name will be filled by default as shown below,

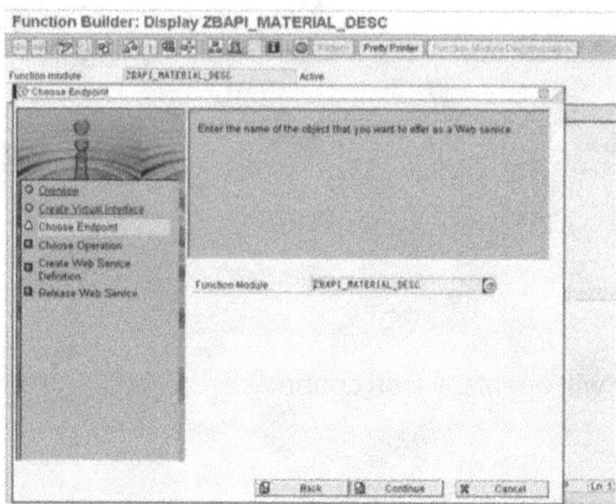

4.5.2 Creating web service definition:

Enter web service definition and description as shown below, and click on continue.

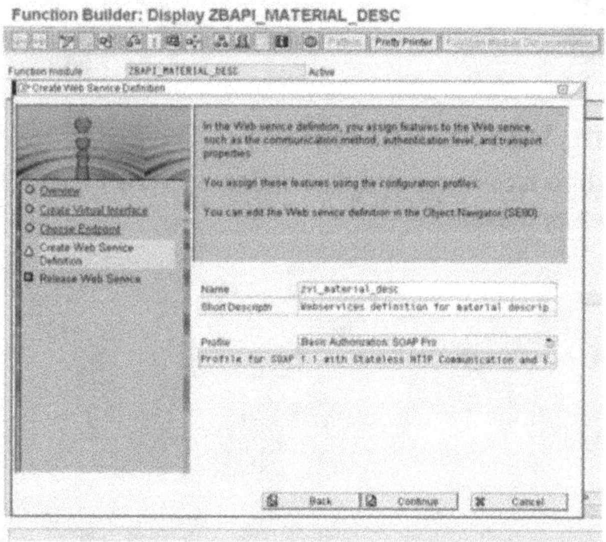

4.5.3 Releasing Web services:

Select complete in the following screen to release the web services.

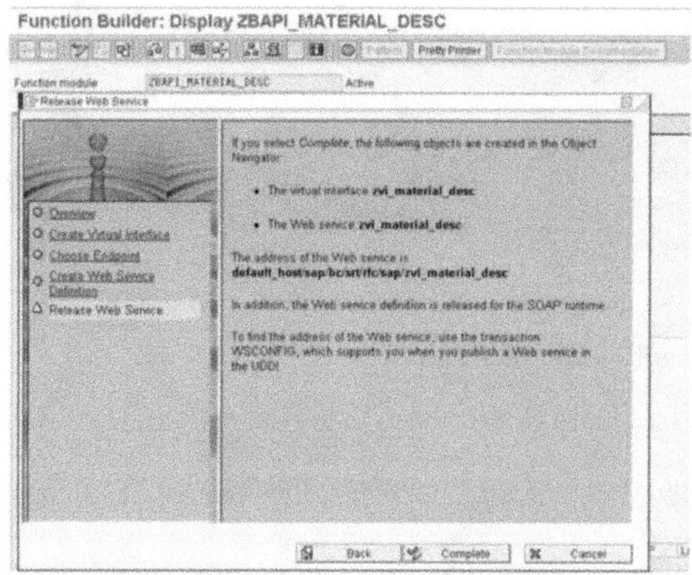

Assign the web services to the package and SAVE.

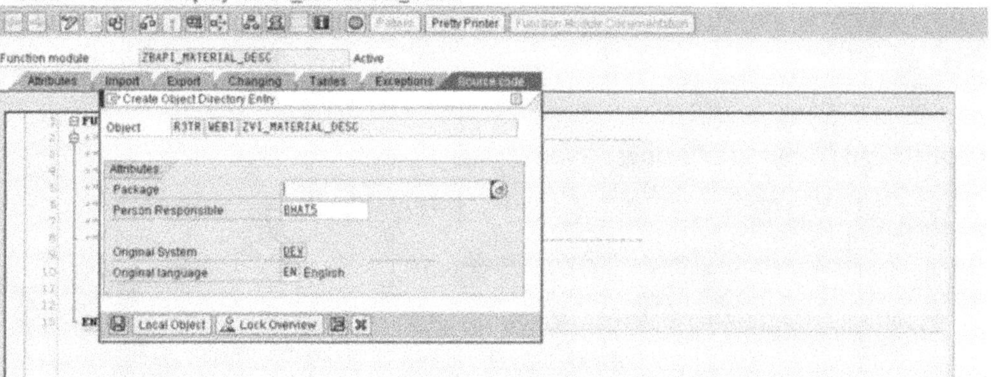

4.5.4 Testing Web services:

Got WSADMIN and select the Web Service that was created.

Click on WSDL button (ctrl + F1) or use menu path web Service->WSDL

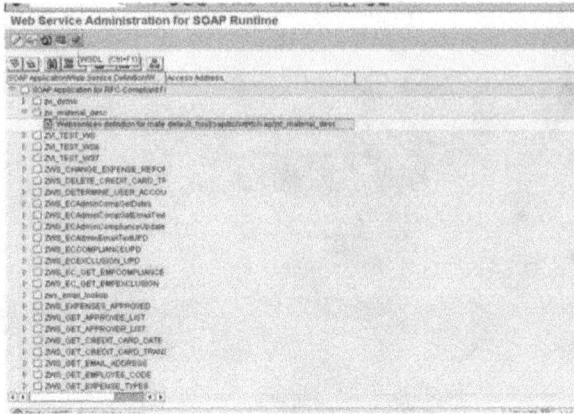

Select document style in below screen and continue.

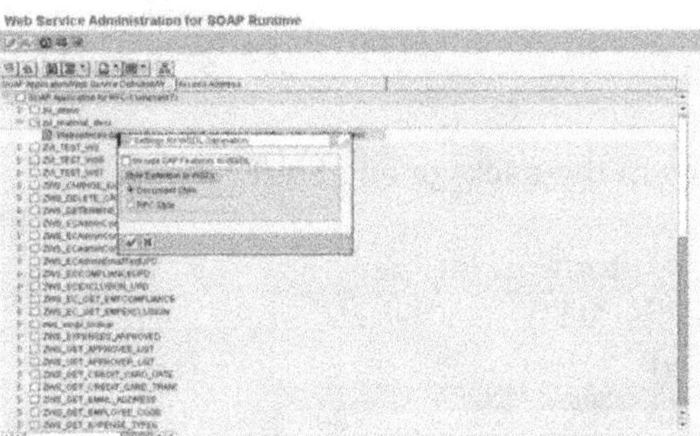

Copy the WSDL from the below screen.

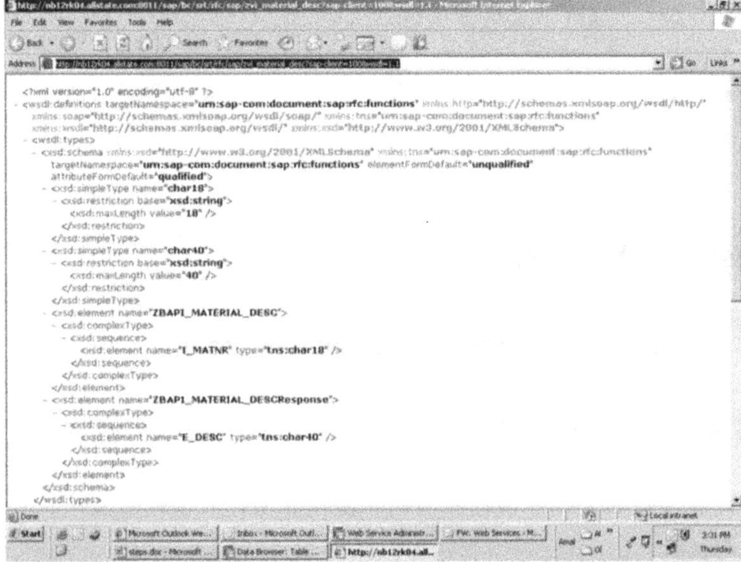

Goto web AS using http://nb12rk04.allstate.com:8011/index.html (This will be different depending on the system where you are testing the web service)

Provide user name and password (SAP-DEV). (Use the username/password provided if any)

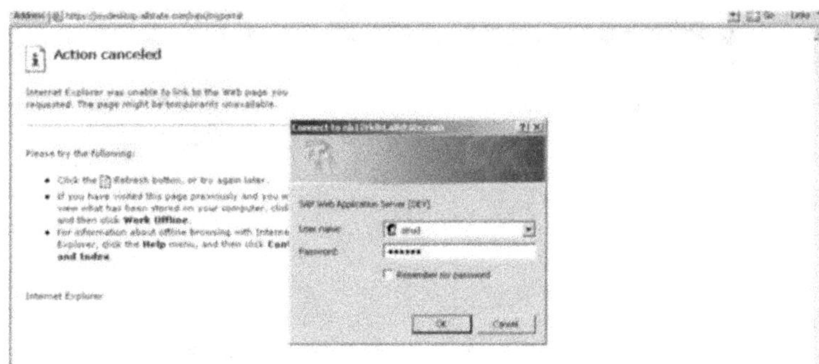

Select web services navigator

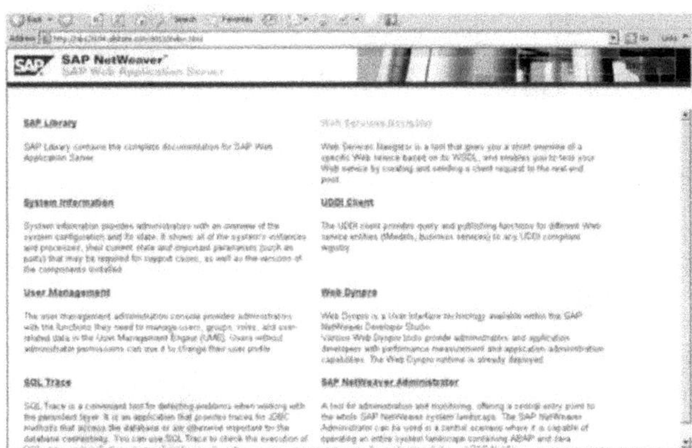

Provide the WSDL (copied above) in below screen and click next

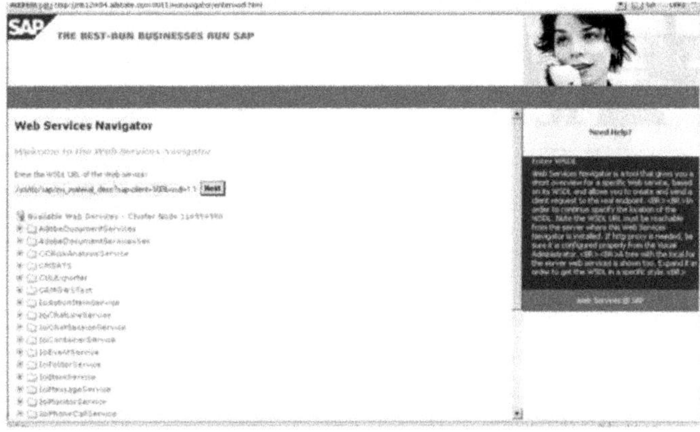

Provide logon credential.

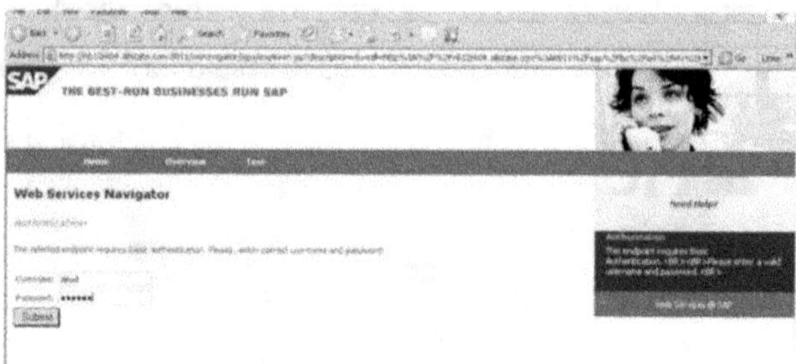

Click on test tab

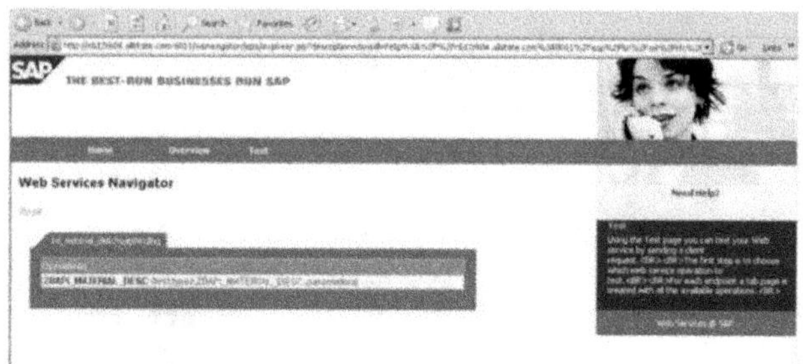

Enter the material number.

Material description will be shown as below,

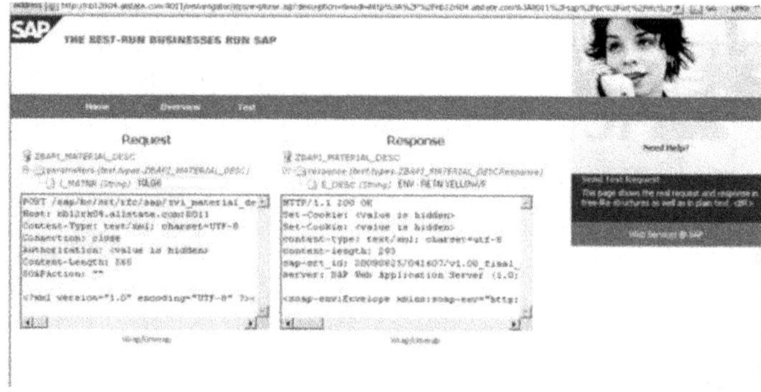

4.5.5 Procedure to re-create the Web services:

Web service Name: ZWS_GET_EXPENSES_FOR_APPRL

System: DEV 100

4.5.5.1 Requirement:

In case a particular source Function module undergoes a change in some or all parameters we need to re-create the web service after making the change.

Procedure to re-create the web service:

1. We first need to delete the web service and its components. Go to SE80 and locate the Enterprise web service via the package used.

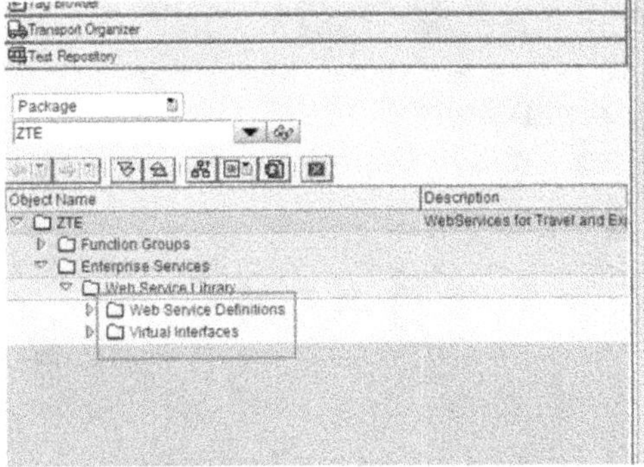

2. First delete the Virtual Interface of the web service.

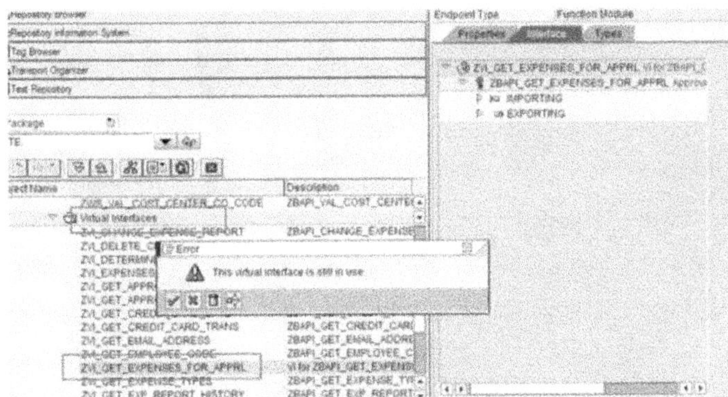

3. Then delete the web service definition itself.

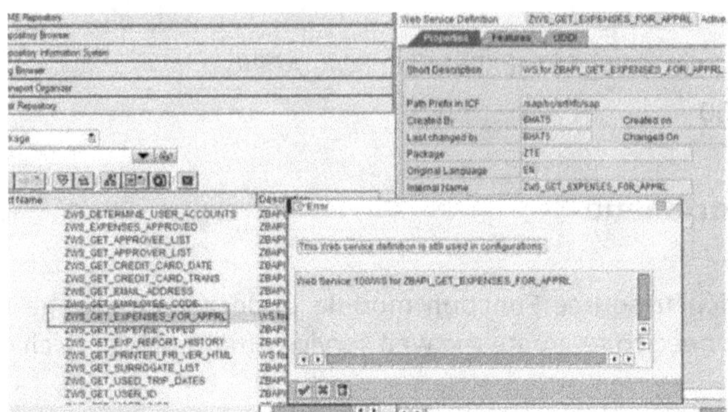

4. Go to WSCONFIG and delete the configuration entry for the web service

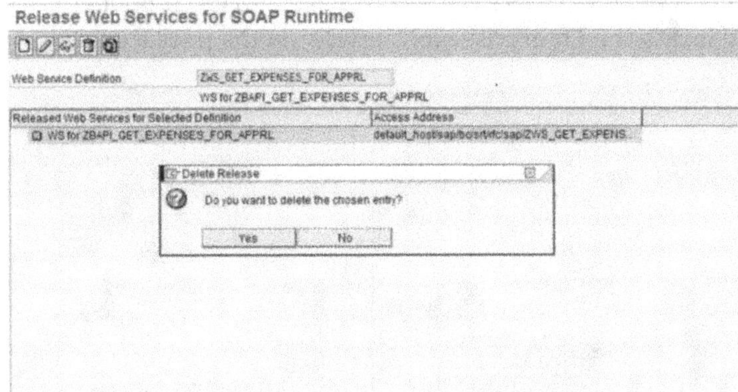

5. Now we can re-create the web service using the wizard.

CHAPTER 5

BAPI User Guide

5.1 Use

The prerequisite for the interoperabilitvof software components is SAP Business Obiects and thse are the heart of the Business Framework.

SAPBusiness Obiect are accessed through BAPIs(Businees SApplication Progromming Interfaces),which are stable, standardized methods. SAP Business Objects and their BAPIs provide an object-oriented view of R/3 business functionality.

There are about IOOO BAPIs enabling object•oriented access to the R/3System in Release 4.5.A

ThisUser Guide is an introduction to the technical concepts of BAPIs. We can use BAPIs to achieve a seamless integration between the R/3 System and external applications, legacy systems and add-ons

5.2 Prerequisites

Application developers wanting to create new integrated activities using SAP Business Objects and their BAPIs following the Use Guide.

- Integration of external applications with an R/3 System.
- Integration of existing business applications with an R/3 System.
- Alternative front-end Interfaces to R/3 Systems, for example, so that occasional users can access R/3.

  As Windows-based Client applications these front-ends can be implemented, for example, as Marcos for desktop applications (Microsoft Excel or Access), which are usually written in Visual Basic for Applications or implemented as applications in Visual Basic, Java or C++.

- Web-based access to an R/3 System through Internet or Intranet applications.
- Componentization within the R/3 System in the context of Business Framework.

5.3 Required Knowledge

You must be familiar with the basic concepts of object-oriented technology and programming in.order.to use BAPIs to access SAP Business Objects. Although you do not need to have a detailed knowledge of the R/3 System to work with BAPIs, you should have a basic understanding.

You must be familiar with the development environment used to access BAPIs.

BAPIs are available outside of R/3 from development platforms that support the Remote Function Call (RFC) protocol. You need to have RFC programming skills to call BAPIs via RFC in case if you are developing your application in a non-object-oriented programming language. You need to know how to perform RFC calls.

5.4 Introduction

5.4.1 Use

SAP has introduced object-oriented approach by making SAP R/3 processes and data available in the form of SAP Business Objects.

External applications can access SAP Business Objects through standardized, platform-independent interfaces - BAPIs.SAP Business Objects and their BAPIs provide an object-oriented view of R/3 business functionality.

This artifactarticulates an overview of the SAP Business Objects and SAP Interface Types, Business Framework and their BAPIs as well as the Business Object Repository in which business objects and BAPIs are defined and stored.

5.5 Business Framework

5.5.1 Use

The SAP R/3 Business Framework enables customers and partners to link their own components to the R/3 System.

5.5.2 Features

Business Framework architecture provides the basis for developing SAP Business Components. SAP R/3 Business Framework contains the below components:

- **Business Components**

  SAP Business Components provide autonomous business functions and consist of business objects. For example, the business objects Employee and Applicant are assigned to the Business Component Human Resources. Business processes are either implemented within a Business Component or across several Components (distributed business processes).

- **Business Objects**

  The object-oriented structure of the R/3 System is based on Business Objects. They define the functional scope and boundaries of a Business Component and encapsulate business data and functionality and Business Application Programming Interfaces (BAPI),

  BAPIs are interfaces for Business Objects. BAPIs define and document the interface standard at the business level together with the Business Objects.

- **Integration Sem.% Application Link Enabling (ALE)**

  The ALE Integration Service enables the integration of business processes that are carried out in different R/3 and non-SAP systems. It is based on the system-wide distribution of Business Objects using the ALE distribution model.

  The graphic below illustrates this architecture.

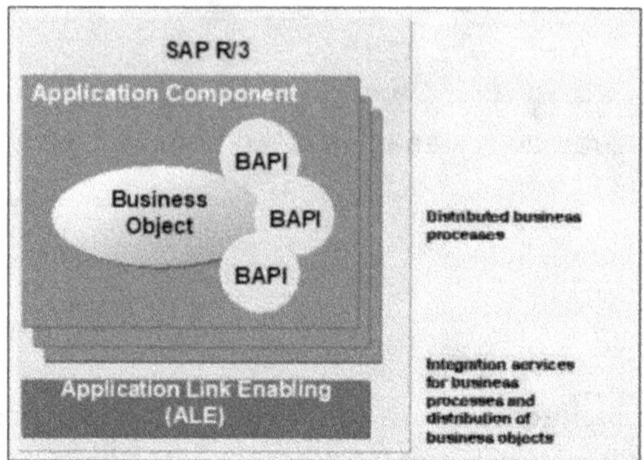

- **Communication Services**

  Communication Technologies use the Business Framework to access BAPIs, for example, Distributed Component Object Model (DCOM) and Remote Function Call (RFC).

  The graphic below illustrates this architecture.

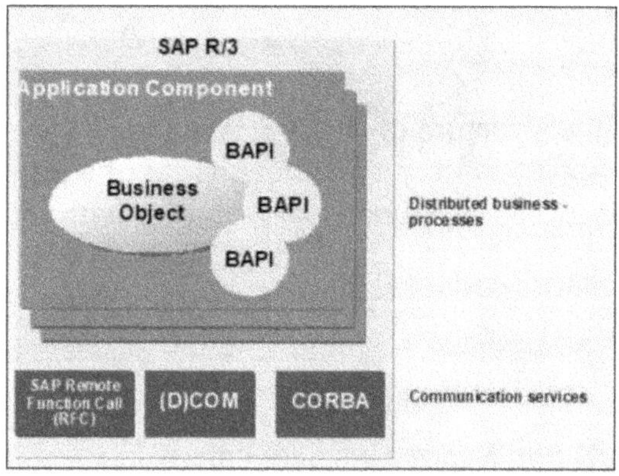

5.6 SAP Business Objects

5.6.1 Definition

On the concept of "business objects", business object technology and business object programming are based.

5.6.2 Structure

To achieve this encapsulation, the SAP Business Objects are constructed as entities from several layers:

- The object's inherent data can be represented by the kernel, core of an SAP Business Object
- The integrity layer, the second layer, represents the business logic of the object. The interface layer, the third layer, defines the object's interface to the outside world and it describes the implementation and structure of the SAP Business Object, and The fourth and outermost layer defines the technologies that can be used for external access to the object's data, for example, COM/DCOM (Component Object Model/Distributed Component Object Model).

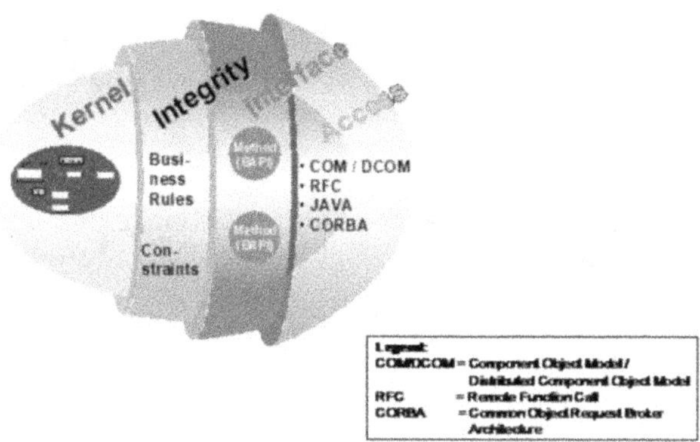

5.6.3 Integration

5.6.3.1 Accessing Business Objects

As the above graphic shows, the interface layer separates a business object's data and the applications and technologies that can be used to access it.

The set of methods that is associated with a business object represents the object's behavior.

5.6.3.2 Object Types and Object Instances

The object types can exist in R/3 and are descriptions of the actual SAP Business Objects; that is, each individual SAP Business Object is a representation, or instance, of its object type.

- **Object type**

  The object type describes the features common to all instances of that object type.
- **Key fields**

  The key fields allow an application to access a specific instance of the object type and determine the structure of an identifying key.
- **Methods**

  A method is an operation that can be performed on a business object and that provides access to the object data.A method is defined by a name and a set of parameters and exceptions, which can or must be provided by the calling program in order to use the method.BAPIs are examples of such methods.
- **Attributes**

  An attribute describes a particular object property and contains data about a business object.
- **Events**

  An event indicates the occurrence of a status change of a business object.

5.6.3.3 Inheritance and Polymorphism

One objective and the main benefit of object-oriented technology is software reusability.

The reuse of software code is achieved by deriving new object types from existing ones. When an object type is generated from an existing object type, the new object type is called the subtype and the existing object type is called the supertype.

When the same method triggers different types of behavior in different business object types, it is known as **Polymorphism.**

For further information on creating business objects refer to the documentation in SAP blogs, SDN blogs, SAP Easy Marketplace & wikis, professional portals.

5.7 Business Application Programming Interface (BAPI)

5.7.1 Use

A BAPI is defined as a method of an SAP Business Object.

For example, the functionality that is implemented with the SAP Business Object type Material includes a check for the material's availability.

Each function module underlying a BAPI:

- Supports the Remote Function Call (RFC) protocol
- Is processed without returning any screen dialogs to the calling application

5.7.2 Integration

Business Object with BAPIs and Associated Function Modules

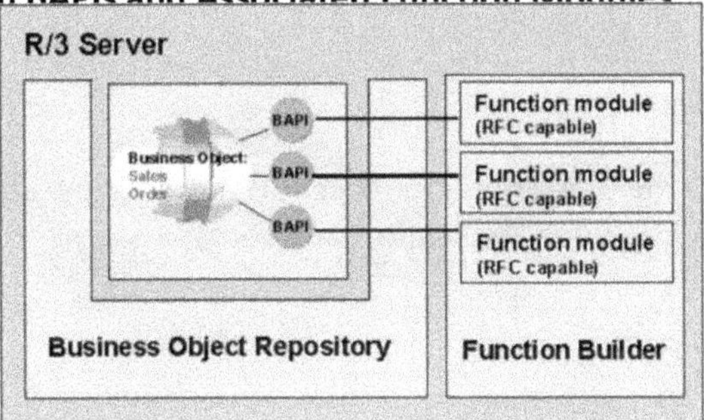

5.7.3 Prerequisites

An application program only needs to know how to call the method in order to use a BAPI method to access data in SAP Business Objects. Information required is:

- The name of the BAPI
- Details of the BAPI interface
  * From the calling program to the BAPI, import parameters data can be transferred
  * From the BAPI back to the calling program, export parameters datacan be transferred
  * Import/export (table) parameters for both importing and exporting data

5.8 Advantages of Using BAPIs

- SAP Business Objects and their BAPIs are the standard for the business functions in the R/3 System.They enable the R/3 System and other software products to be integrated on one business level.
- Once SAP has developed and released a BAPI, its interface definition and parameters remain stable for the long term.This ensures that application programs are not affected by changes to the underlying R/3 software and data.

5.9 Characteristics of BAPIs

5.9.1 Use

This section describes the BAPI characteristics you should know about before you begin integrating BAPI calls into your application programs.

5.9.1.1 No Dialog Orientation

BAPIs do not return dialog screens from the R/3 server system to the calling program.

5.9.1.2 Authorization

Any interaction with the R/3 System requires the user to have a certain set of authorizations.

5.9.1.3 Data Types and Data Display

BAPIs are programming interfaces for business applications.

BAPI parameters can use most of the supported SAP data types.The data types are documented in the individual parameter's structure entry in the ABAP Dictionary.

5.10 Standardized BAPIs

5.10.1 Features

This section provides an overview of the standardized BAPIs and how they are assigned to method types.

5.10.1.1 BAPIs for Reading Data

The following BAPIs provide you with read-only access to data in the associated business object:

- GetList
- GetDetail
- GetStatus
- ExistenceCheck

5.10.1.2 BAPIs for Creating or Changing Data

The following BAPIs can create, change or delete instances of a business object

- Create or CreateFromData
- Change
- Delete and Undelete
- Add<sub-object> and Remove<sub-object>

5.10.1.3 BAPIs for Replicating Business Object Instances

Replicate and Save Replica

They enable specific instances of an object type to be copied to one or more different systems.

5.11 Service BAPIs for Help Functions

5.11.1 Use

A number of service BAPIs provide basic help functions.

Service BAPIs are created in the BOR under the application component hierarchy shown below:

- o Cross-Application Components
- o Business Framework Architecture
- o BAPI Technology

5.11.2 Features

5.11.2.1 BAPIs for Accessing Interface Documentation

- **HelpValues.GetList**

  This method determines the allowed input values (F4 help) for a field in a BAPI parameter.The method displays valid input values for a specific BAPI parameter field, enabling end-users to enter a correct value in the input field.
- **BapiService.FieldHelpGetDocu**

  This method reads the documentation (F1 help) for the fields in a BAPI parameter.

  They provide end-users with the descriptions of the fields in a BAPI parameter.
- **BapiService.InterfaceGetDocu**

5.11.2.1.1 BAPIs for Interpreting Error Messages

- **BapiService.MessageGetDetail**

  Displays the short and long texts of BAPI error messages.
- **BapiService.ApplicationLogGetDetail**

  Reads the details of entries in the application log.

5.11.2.2 BAPIs for Controlling COMMIT and ROLLBACK

The commands used to commit changes to the database or to reset changes (COMMIT and ROLLBACK), must not be executed by the BAPI itself, they have to be called directly from the external application program.

External programs can use the following service BAPIs for these calls:

- **BapiService.TransactionCommit**

  This method executes a COMMIT WORK command.

- **BapiService.TransactionRollback**

  This method executes a ROLLBACK WORK command.

5.11.2.3 BAPIs for Converting Between Internal and External Data Formats (Domain Conversion)

BAPIs are programming interfaces, not end-user interfaces. For this reason a neutral data format (with some exceptions) must be used in BAPIs. Fields in BAPI parameters are displayed in the BAPI interface in the internal format used in the database, not in a formatted form.

When you call a BAPI in your program, you need to use the external data format, to display data on the screen, for example.You can use the following conversion BAPIs to display the data in the required format:

- **BapiService.DataConversionInt2Ext**

  This BAPI converts data from the internal format into the required external format.

- **BapiService.DataConversionExt2Int**

  This BAPI converts data from the external format into the required internal format.

These conversions can only be carried out provided that, the conversion routines for the domains underlying the data to be converted, are maintained in the ABAP Dictionary. Otherwise the data is returned unconverted.

5.11.2.4 Conversion BAPIs

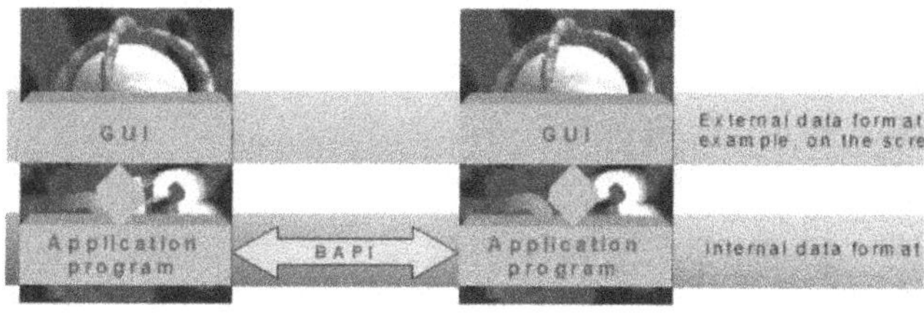

5.12 SAP Enhancements to BAPIs

5.12.1 Purpose

On the basis of SAP Release strategy and the strict rules for enhancing existing BAPIs, application developers can rely on the stability of BAPI interfaces.

BAPIs that are set to "obsolete" in an R/3 Release are listed in Note 0107644, "Collective Note for Obsolete BAPIs as of Release 4.5A" in the Online Software Service (OSS)

5.12.2 Process Flow

Expiry Phase of a BAPI

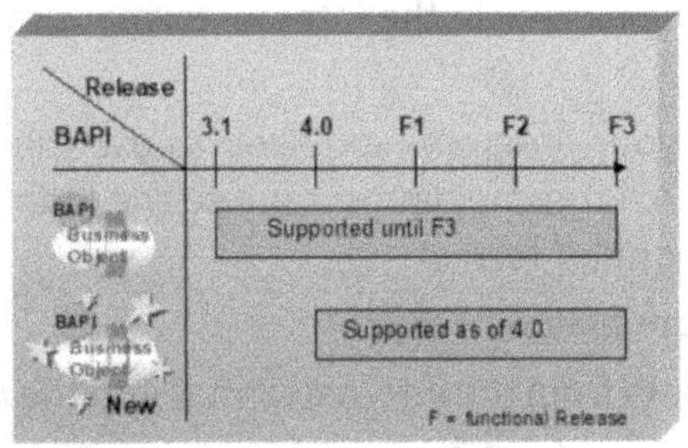

5.13 BAPIs of SAP Interface Types

5.13.1 Use

From Release 4.5A BAPIs can also describe interfaces implemented outside the R/3 System that an R/3 System can call in external systems.Such BAPIs are known as **BAPIs for outbound processing.**

BAPIs used for outbound processing are defined in the Business Object Repository as API methods **of SAP Interface Types**.

5.14 Business Object Repository

5.14.1 Definition

All SAP Business Object types and SAP Interface Types and their methods are defined and described in the R/3 Business Object Repository (BOR).

5.15 Programming with BAPIs

5.15.1 Use

In this section it is assumed that the application you developed is to use the data held in business objects in the R/3 System and that this data is to be accessed by calling one or more BAPIs. Your application can as simple or as complex as you like and can include calls for one or more BAPIs.

5.15.2 Integration

BAPIs are defined in the Business Object Repository (BOR) as methods of SAP Business Objects or SAP Interface Types and are implemented as function modules. The separation of a BAPI definition from its actual implementation enables you to access a BAPI in two ways:

- You can call the BAP1 in the BOR through object-oriented method
- You can make RFC calls to the function module on which the BAPI is based.

The two approaches are illustrated in the graphic below.

5.15.2.1 Ways of Accessing BAPIs

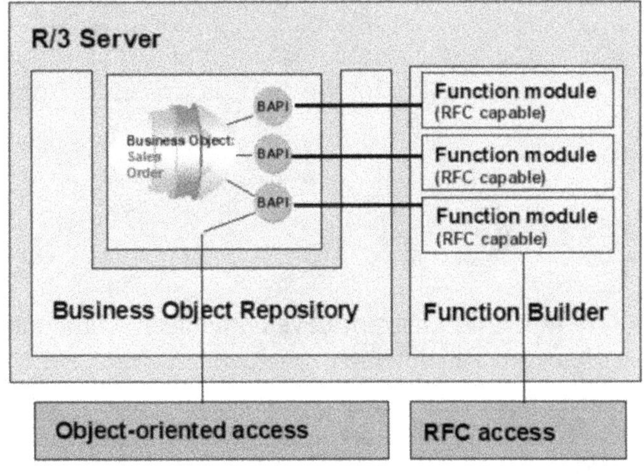

5.15.3 Features

Applications accessing BAPis can be broadly divided into two categories:

- **Dialog applications**
  With dialog applications the .1ler usually waits until the method call has been processed, for example, wait for the results of a GetList BAPI.
- **Distributed applications**
  BAPIs can also be used in Application Link Enabling (ALE) to exchange and replicate data between two distributed systems.

Activities Regardless of the technology used, you have to carry out the following steps to call BAPIs from your application program:

Task	For Further Information:
1. Identify the SAP Business Object Type or SAP Interface Type and the required BAPI.	Determining BAPIs of Business Objects or Determining BAPIs of Interface Types
2. Determine the parameter information for the BAPI interface.	Determining BAPIs of Business Objects or Determining BAPIs of Interface Types
3. Include the BAPI call or function call and the parameter declarations in your application program.	Programming Dialog Applications or Programming Distributed Applications For examples of calling BAPIs from various development platforms see Examples of BAPI Calls.

5.16 Object-oriented Access to BAPIs

5.16.1 Purpose

Object-oriented access to BAPIs in the BOR is possible from a number of platforms.

5.16.2 Process Flow

Applications run differently on different development environments and the steps required to invoke them are also different.

The example below illustrates the steps involved when the BAPI ActiveX Control is used to access BAPis. When the R/3 System is connected to, the client application accesses the SAP Business Objects at runtime by forwarding the OLE automation requests to the BAPI ActiveX Control.

The steps involved are:

- Creating a BAPI ActiveX Control object

  Set oBAPICtrl = CreateObject("SAP.BAPI.1")
- Creating a logon control object:

  Set oLogonCtrl = CreateObject("SAP.Logoncontro1.1")
- Creating a connection object to the R/3 System:

  Set oBAPICtrl.Connection = oLogonCtrl.NewConnection
- Logging on to .3 System by calling the logon method of the connection object:

  If oBAPICtrl.Connectionlogon(frmStart.hwnd,FALSE) = FALSE then

  MsgBox"R/3 Connection failed"

  End

  Endif

- Requesting the creation of a local instance of the SAP Business Object

  Before your application can call a BAPI of an SAP Business Object, it must first request that an instance of the object is created.

  The following command from a Visual Basic program shows the use of the BAPI ActiveX Control object and the GetSAPObject method to request the creation of an instance of the business object SalesOrder.

  Set boOrder = oBAPICtrl.GetSAPObject("SalesOrder")

- **'Creating the parameter objects**

  Set oOrderHeader = oBAPiCtrl.DimAs(boOrder, _

  "CreateFormatDat1",'OrderHeaderIn")

  Set otabItems = oBAPICtrl.DimAs(boOrder, _

  "CreateFromDat1, "OrderItemsIn")

  Set otabPartners = oBAPICtrl.DimAs(boOrder, _

  "CreateFromDat1, "OrderPartners")

  Then the relevant data must be entered in the parameter objects.

- Calling the BAPIs of the business objects

  Once the object instance has been created, the available BAPIs can be called.

The following command from a Visual Basic program illustrates a BAPI call:

```
oOrder.CreaterFromDat1 OrderHeaderIn=oOrderHeader, _
        OrderPartners:=otabPartners,_
        OrderItemsIn;=otabitems,_
        Return:=oReturn
```

- Releasing the SAP Business Object and releasing the BAPI ActiveX Control object.

The following figure illustrates the process of accessing SAP Business Objects and their BAPIs through the BAPI ActiveX Control.

5.16.2.1 Using the BAPI ActiveX Control

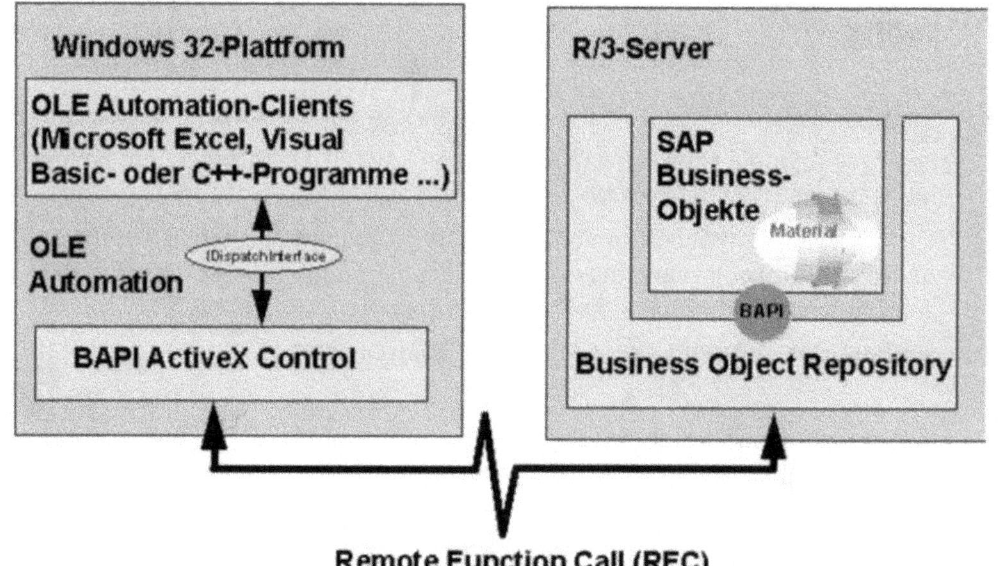

5.17 Function-oriented Access to BAPIs

5.17.1 Purpose

You can access BAPIs from platforms that do not provide direct object-oriented access to SAP Business Objects by making Remote Function Calls (RFC) to the function module that a BAPI is based on.

This approach can be used on Al development platforms supporting the RFC protocol, for example, ABAP or external platforms using C/C+4- Class Library.

5.17.2 Process Flow

During runtime your application program uses the RFC Library or the C/C++ Class Libretto to make an RFC call to the function module underlying the BAPI. The Library translates client calls into communication steps in accordance with the RFC protocol.

This is how client requests are forwarded to the relevant function module in the R/3 server system.

This approach is illustrated in the graphic below.

5.17.2.1 Accessing a BAPI Function Module Through RFC Calls

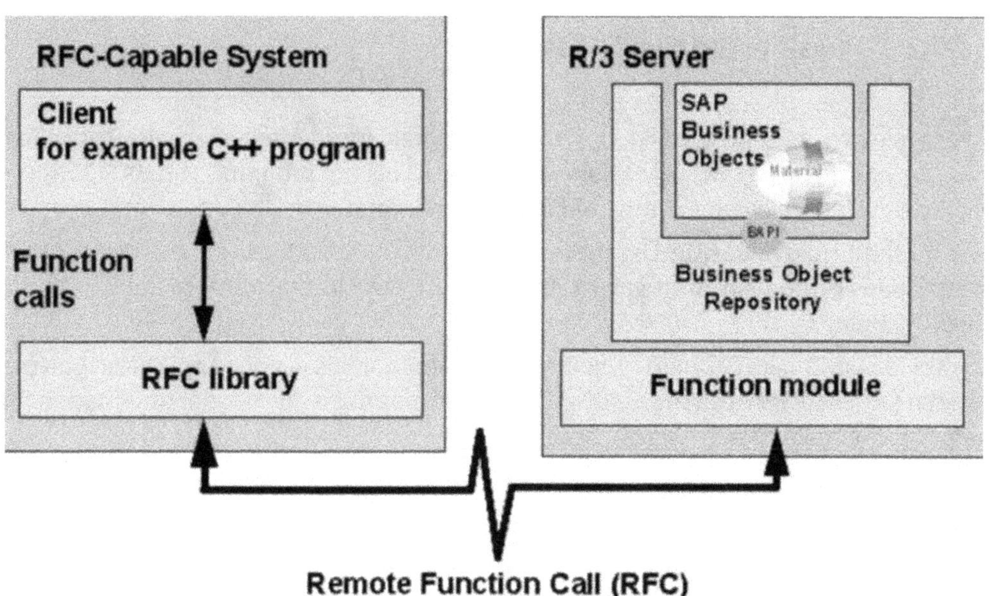

5.18 Programming Dialog Applications

5.18.1 Use

SAP provides various service functions to support dialog application programming.

5.18.2 Features

In dialog applications you can make use of the following help functions:

5.18.2.1 Transaction Control

Each dialog transaction using BAPIs to change data in one or more objects must directly execute the COMMIT WORK command to save the data. The BAPI BapiService. TransactionCommit is used for this and it writes the changes to the database.

If data is not to be written to the database, the BAPI BapiService.TransactionRollback can reset the changes, provided that the changes have not already been passed to the database with the BAPI

BapiService.TransactionCommit.

5.18.2.2 Possible Entries (F4 Help)

To provide possible entries (F4 help) for an input field forwarded when a BAPI is called, you can include the service BAPI HelpValues GetList in your program. This BAPI supplies the input values allowed for the field in a BAPI parameter.

The method HelpValues.GetList method refers to the help view for the check table, matchcodes or domain fixed values linked to the field in the ABAP Dictionary. Input Help (F1 Help)

To provide input help (F1 help or field help) for input fields in your application you can use the BAPI BapiService.ReldHelpGetDocu. This method reads the documentation (F1 help) for the fields in a BAPI parameter.

5.18.2.3 Interpreting Return Messages

Each BAPI contains a parameter named Return. This parameter returns exception messages or success messages to the calling program.

Two service BAPIs are provided to diagnose and process error messages from BAPI calls:

- BapiService.MessageGetDetail which displays the short and long texts of BAPI error messages.

- BapiService.ApplicationLogGetDefail, with which information in application logs can be displayed.

5.19 Programming Distributed Applications

5.19.1 Use

As of R/3 Release 4.0 BAPIs can also be used in Application Link Enabling (ALE) to exchange and replicate data between distributed systems. When data is exchanged between two distributed systems there is a difference between using synchronous and asynchronous BAPIs.

5.19.2 Features

5.19.2.1 Synchronous BAPIs

Synchronous BAPIs are used to read data from a remote logical system, for example, to display a list of customers.

You have to determine the RFC destination of the remote system or BAPI server before calling the BAPI. Application developers can use an API to determine the RFC destination of the BAPI.

5.19.2.2 Asynchronous BAPIs

Asynchronous BAPIs are used to replicate data on one or more logical systems, for example, to distribute article master data.

To transfer data asynchronously using BAPIs, an ALE IDoc interface must be generated. TEA interface handles the entire data exchange between the logical systems using IDoc technology. Thus, the application calls the generated ALE IDoc interface locally, instead of calling the BAPI.

As with synchronous BAPIs, the relevant logical systems of the BAPI must be specified before calling the ALE IDoc interface. These are transferred to the ALE !Doc interface as input parameters.

5.19.2.3 ALE Distribution Model

As with message types, synchronous and asynchronous BAPIs within the ALE framework are maintained in the ALE distribution model. The logical systems (in the case of asynchronous BAPIs) or the RFC destinations (in the case of synchronous BAPIs are determined at runtime using the distribution model.

5.20 Transaction Model for Developing BAPIs

5.20.1 Use

The transaction model in which BAPIs are used determines how you must program BAPIs.

5.20.1.1 Logical Unit of Work (LUW) and Statelessness

Within the context. of the transaction model used to develop BAPIs for R/3 Releases 3.1 and 4.0 a transaction represents one processing step or one logical unit of work (LUW). An R/3 LUW is all the steps involved in a transaction including updating the database.

The whole transaction must be programmed to be stateless.

The ACID principle applies to transaction models, meaning that transactions are:

- **Atomic**
  When a transaction is called, database operations are either fully executed or not at all Either all relevant data has to be changed in the database or none at all.
- **Consistent**
  If a transaction is called more than once. each call must have the same result. No data is imported that may indirectly affect the result.
- **Isolated**
  There must be no functional dependencies between two transactions, one transaction must not affect another transaction.
- **Durable**
  Changes cannot be reversed and transactions cannot be canceled.

5.20.2 Features

The following sections describe how the transaction model effects BAPI development:

In Release 3.1 the BAPIs themselves executed the COMMIT WORK command, BAPIs had the same purpose as an LUW or transaction. To integrate BAPIs into an LUW, the new BAPIs no longer execute COMMIT WORK commands as of Release 4.0.

The outcome is two transaction models:

BAPI Transaction Model with Commit (as of Release 3.1)

BAPI Transaction Model Without Commit (as of Release 4.0)

If a BAPI executes a COMMIT WORK command, this must be mentioned in the BAPI documentation. This is the only way users are abie to know that the BAPI contains a COMMIT WORK command.

5.21 BAPI Transaction Model with Commit

5.21.1 Use

The example below of an external program calling a BAPI to change data in an R/3 System, illustrates how the transaction model affects BAPI development in Release 3.1. For example, this could involve a transaction implemented with Visual Basic. Only data from the R/3 System is to be changed.

The RFC connection is live the whole time the external program is logged on to the R/3 System to avoid having to connect and disconnect repeatedly. When the RFC connection is already established, an RFC call does not essentially take up any more CPU time than a direct call to the function module from within the R/3 System.

There is one BAPI call for each transaction in the transaction model supported in 3.1. BAPIs can only be called synchronously. A BAPI call is essentially the call of the underlying RFC capable function module.

The process flow of the program consists of the following steps below (see graphic below):

Log on

----- Source code

Call BAPI to read and/or change data

----- Source code

Call BAPI to read and/or change data

Log off

5.21.1.1 Transaction Model for Release 3.1

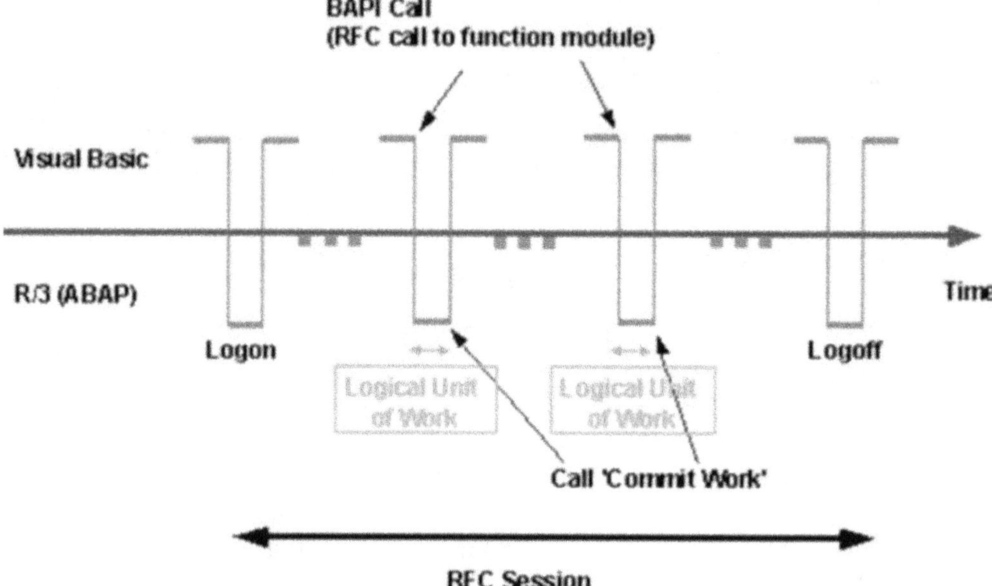

What do the terms "LOW" and "statelessness" mean to BAPIs that have been implemented in the framework of this transaction model?

If a transaction represents one Logical Unit of Work and in addition is supposed to be stateless, BAPIs are affected as follows:

- Initial state each time a BAPI is called

  A repeated call of one BAPI most produce the same result. Only data that is not affected by the execution of the BAPI, for example. Customizing data can be buffered.

  For BAPIs this means, for example, that due to transparency. Set and Get parameters and the global memory should not be used

However, you can keep Customizing data in a global memory as this data remains unchanged even if transaction calls are repeated.

- All or nothing principle

  A database change, for example, creating a new sales order, must be carried out completely or not at all (LUW).

  This is why BAPIs to be implemented in 3.1 are created with integrated commit control. The COMMIT WORK command is always invoked at the end of the function module of a BAPI that modifies data.

- No functional dependency between two BAPIs

  A BAPI call must not be negatively affected by an earlier call of another BAPI. A follow up call must not presuppose an earlier call. For this reason also, you should not use Set and Get parameters in the BAPI nor use the global memory.

  Make sure that a COMMIT WORK command only deletes the memory of the function module, and not the memory of the function group. The global data of the function group remains and could prevent another BAPI from being called, and thus impair the BAPI's functional independence.

- Other separate LUWs are not triggered

  The call of a BAPI must not trigger further LUWs that are independent of the BAPI.

  For this reason BAPIs must not contain the following commands:

  - CALL TRANSACTION
  - SUBMIT REPORT
  - SUBMIT REPORT AND RETURN

5.22 BAPI Transaction Model Without Commit

5.22.1 Use

In Release 4.0 the commit control must be taken out of write BAPIs, that is, those BAPIs that cause database changes. However, the existing transaction model used in Release 3.1 should not be changed. This is achieved by using the method TransactionCommit of the object BapiService which executes the command COMMIT WORK.

The process flow of the program consists of the following steps (see graphic below):

Call BAPI to read and/or change data

Log on

----- Source code

Call BAPI to read and/or change data

Call BAPI BapiService.TransactionCommit

----- Source code

Call BAPI to read and/or change data

Call BAPI BapiService.TransactionCommit

----- Source code

Log off

5.22.1.1 Extended Transaction Model

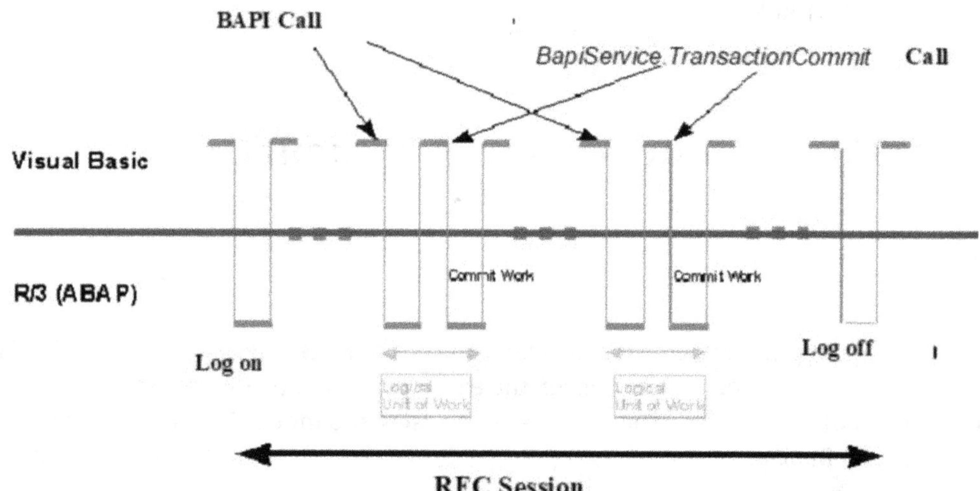

If termiantion message is displayed (message type A) in the Return parameter, a database rollback can be executed by the BAPI. This causes all the activities carried out since the last COMMIT WORK command to be canceled. This situation is described in the Return parameter documentation for the BAPI in question.

The same rules apply in this model as in the BAPI Transaction Model With Commit.

Operations that change the database can only be carried out through updating.

5.23 Determining BAPIs of Business Objects

5.23.1 Procedure

SAP Business Objects and their BAPIs are managed in the Business Object Repository (BOR) in a structure based on the R/3 Application Component hierarchy.

In the **BAPI Browser** you can display all the SAP Business Objects in the application hierarchy for which BAPIs have been implemented.

Follow the steps below:

1. Log on to the R/3 System.
2. Choose Tools Business Framework , BAP! Browser or enter the transaction code BAPI in the SAPgui command field. The BAPI Browser of the BOR is displayed in which all Business Objects with BAPIs are displayed in the R/3 application hierarchy.
3. Expand the nodes and the subordinate nodes of one of the application components until you get to the level where the SAP Business Objects are assigned. Only those business objects for which BAPIs have been implemented are displayed.
4. To open a business object, double-click on it The nodes Key fields and Methods are displayed.
5. Expand the node Methods to display a list of the BAPIs available for the selected SAP Business Object type. Select the information icon to display descriptions of individual BAPIs.
6. Expand the node Key fields, to list the key fields of the object. Select the information icon to display descriptions of individual key fields.

   Choose Utilities → Color Key to display a description of individual icons in the BAPI Browser.

After you have found the BAPI you want, you haye.to specify the information you have to forward to call the BAPI or function in your application program.

Information required is:

- They Key Fields of the SAP Business Object
- The Import, Export and Import/Export Parameters of the BAPI
- The Name of the Function Module, if you direct RFC calls to the function module underlying the BAPI.

Also refer to the Documentation, provided with each BAPI.

Once you have gathered all the necessary information, you can add the BAPI call to your application code.

5.24 Specifying the Key Fields of the Business Object

5.24.1 Prerequisites

The key fields of SAP Business Objects specify the identification structure with which client programs can uniquely access a specific instance of the object type.

The key fields of an SAP Business Object are required if the BAPI in question is using specific object type instances.

BAPIs can be divided into the following categories according to whether they access specific object instances:

- Instance-dependent BAPIs

  Instance-dependent BAPIs use specific instances of an object type which the client application must specify in the key fields of the Business Object. An example of an instacne-dependent BAPI is *CompanyCode.GetDetail* and when used the client applicaiton must specify the company code ID, for example, *GetSAPObject("CompanyCode","0001")*.
- Instance-independent BAPIs

  Instance-independent BAPIs do not use specific object instances. The usually return a list of object instances in tables to the calling program. Instance-independent BAPIs are also called class methods. An example of this BAPI is *CompanyCode.GetList*, which returns a list of company codes.

  Some instance-dependent BAPIs generate object instances and reports back information on the generated object instance to the calling application. An example of this type of BAPI is *SalesOrder.CreateFromData*, which creates a customer order and reports back information to the calling program.

5.24.2 Procedure

To display the key fields of an SAP Business Object, select the Business Object in the BAPI Browser and expand the node Key fields, as described in Determining BAPIs of Business Objects.

Select the relevant icon in the BAPI Browser to display further information about the individual key fields. Choose *Utilities* → *Color Key* to display a description of individual icons in the BAPI Browser.

After you have found the BAPI you want, you haye.to specify the information you have to forward to call the BAPI or function in your application program.

Information required is:

- They Key Fields of the SAP Business Object
- The Import, Export and Import/Export Parameters of the BAPI
- The Name of the Function Module, if you direct RFC calls to the function module underlying the BAPI.

Also refer to the Documentation, provided with each BAPI.

Once you have gathered all the necessary information, you can add the BAPI call to your application code.

5.25 Specifying the BAPI Parameters

5.25.1 Prerequisites

Once you have found the BAPI you want you to have to specify which parameters you can or must declare. BAPIs have import/export parameters (table parameters) as well as import parameters and export parameters for importing and exporting data.

5.25.2 Procedure

To display the parameters of the BAPI:

1. Open the Business Object and the node Methods in the BAPI Browser, as described in Displaying BAPIs in the BAPI Browser.
2. Expand the node for the relevant BAPI and then the node Parameters.

5.25.3 Result

A list of all the BAPI's parameters is displayed.

Select the relevant icon in the BAPI Browser to display further information about the individual parameters. Choose Mates → Color Key to display a description of individual icons in the BAPI Browser

5.26 Determining the Name of the Function Module

5.26.1 Prerequisites

If you want to call the BAPI by making an RFC call to the underlying function module, you should know the name of the function module.

5.26.2 Procedure

To determine the name of the function module implementing the BAPI:

1. Open the Business Object in the BAPI Browser, as described in Displaying BAPIs in the BAPI Browser.
2. Open the node Methods and position the cursor on the relevant BAPI.
3. To display the BAPI documentation select the information icon. The name of the function module is given at the start of the documentation.

   The names of BAPI function modules always begin with "BAPI".

Choose Utilities → Color Key to display a description of individual icons in the BAPI Browser.

5.26.2.1 Displaying the Function Module

You can display the BAPI function module in the Function Builder:

1. Choose Tools ABAP Workbench and then Function Builder. Alternatively enter the Transaction SE57 in the SAPgui command field
2. Display the BAPI function module by entering the names of the function module

in the field Function module and selecting Display.

5.27 Displaying BAPI Documentation

Documentation describing functionality and parameters is provided on each BAPI. To display documentation on a BAPII:

1. Open the Business Object in the BAPI Browser, as described in Displaying BAPIs in the BAPI Browser.
2. Open the node Methods and position the cursor on the relevant BAPI.
3. Select the information icon to display the documentation on the BAPI and its associated parameters.

Choose Utilities → Color Key to display a description of individual icons in the BAPI Browser

5.28 Determining BAPIs of Interface Types

5.28.1 Procedure

SAP Interface Types and their BAPIs are managed in the Business Object Repository (BOR) in a structure based on the R/3 Application Component hierarchy. In the Business Object Builder you can display all the SAP Interface Types in the application hierarchy.

Follow the steps below:

1. Log on to the R/3 System.
2. Choose Tools Business Framework BAPI Development Business Object Builder or enter the transaction code SWO1. in the SAPgui command field.
3. Select Business Object Repository.
4. In the next dialog box select the filter Other settings. In the field Type select the setting interface and deactivate the setting Object. in the field Type select the setting Others and mark all the settings in the field Status.

   The Business Object Repository Browser is displayed in which all the SAP Interface Types with BAPIs are displayed in the Ft/3 application hierarchy.

5. Expand the nodes and the subordinate nodes of one of the application components Until You get to the level where the SAP Interface Types are

assigned.

6. To open an SAP Interface Type, double-click on it. The nodes interfaces, Attributes,Methods and Events are displayed.
7. Expand the node Methods to display a list of the methods available for the selected SAP Interface Type. BAPIs are marked by a green circle ne. to the method name.

Once you have found the BAPI you want, you should retrieve the information on the BAPI interface which you need to implement and use the BAPI (see Specifying the BAPI Parameters). Also use the Documentation, provided with each BAPI.

Once you have gathered all the necessary information, you can implement the interface and use the BAPI in your application program.

5.29 Specifying the BAPI Parameters

5.29.1 Prerequisites

Once you have found the BAPI you want, you should specify the optional and mandatory parameters of the BAPI interface. BAPIs have import/export parameters (table parameters) as well as import parameters and export parameters for importing and exporting data.

5.29.2 Procedure

To display the parameters of a BAPI:

1. In the Business Object Repository Browser expand the node Methods, as described in Determining BAPIs of Business Objects.
2. Position the cursor on the relevant BAPI and select Parameters

5.30 Displaying BAPI Documentation

For each BAN of an interface type, documentation is available describing the BAPi's parameters and the functionality to be implemented.

To display documentation on a BAPI:

1. In the Business Object Repository Browser expand the node Methods, as described

in Determining

2. Position the cursor on the relevant BAR and choose Goto Documentation

5.31 Examples of BAPI Calls

The following examples illustrate how BAPIs are called from different development platforms.

- Calling BAPIs from Java
- Calling BAPIs from Visual Basic
- Calling BAPIs from ABAP

5.32 Calling BAPIs from Java

This is an example program for calling a BAPI from the IBM development platform, Access Builder for SAP R/3.

Detailed program examples are shipped with the Access Builder for R/3.

Access Builder for SAP R/3

```
            //Importing the required classes:

import com.sap.rfc. *;

import com.sap.rfc. exception. *;

import com.ibm.sap. bapi. *;

import com.ibm.sap.bapi.generated. *;

            //Connecting to the R/3 System:
```

```
import com.sap.rfc. *;
import com.sap.rfc. exception. *;
import com.ibm.sap. bapi. *;
import com.ibm.sap.bapi.generated. *;
```

5.32.1.1.1. //Connecting to the R/3 System:

```
static private IRfcConnection establishConnection (MiddlewareInfo aMiddlewareInfo)

        throws JRfcRemoteException

{

        IRfcConnection aConnection = null;

        ConnectInfo aConnectInfo = null;

        UserInfo aUserInfo = null;

        String orbServerName = aMiddlewareInfo.getOrbServerName();

        // Please adjust the values written in UPPERCASE LETTERS
        // in the lines below so that they fit to your needs!
        // If you don't know the correct values ask your system
        // administrator!
        // After correcting these values you should change the
        // <bAdjusted> variable in the following line
        // from "false" to "true".
        // Then you can re-compile ("javac SampleCompanyCode.java") and
        // re-run ("java SampleCompanyCode -conn JNI") this sample...

        boolean bAdjusted = true;
throw (new JRfcRfcConnectionException (
                        "Please adjust the Connection-Parameters to your
        needs! (See method \"establishConnection\")"));
        }
```

5.32.1.1.1 //Connection information:

```
        aConnectInfo = new ConnectInfo (
                3,              // int aRfcMode 3=R/3 or 2=R/2
                null,           // String aDestination
                "9.7.12.7",     // String aHostName YOUR HOSTNAME (e.g. IP-
        //address)
                0,          // int aSystemNo YOUR SYSTEM-NUMBER
                null,                           // String aGatewayHost
                null,                           // String aGatewayService
                null,                           // String aSystemName
                null,                           // String aGroupName
                null,                           // String aMsgServer
```

```
		false,				// Boolean isLoadBalancing
		true);				// Boolean isCheckAuthorization
```

5.32.1.1.2 //User information:

```
	aUserInfo = new UserInfo (
		"MUSTER",			// String aUserName,	YOUR USERID
		"IDES",		// String aPassword,	YOUR PASSWORD
		"800",		// String aClient, YOUR CLIENT NUMBER
		"e",			// String aLanguage, YOUR PREFERRED
		//LANGUAGE
		1103);		// int aCodePage YOUR REQUIRED CODEPAGE
```

5.32.1.1.3 //Technical conversion for the selected middleware;

```
  // Open connection:
	IRfcConnectionFactory aConnectionFactory = FactoryManager.getSingleIn-
stance().getRfcConnectionFactory() ;
	aConnection = aConnectionFactory.createRfcConnection(aConnectInfo, aU-
serInfo);
	aConnection.open();
  //Returning the connection:
	return aConnection;
}
```

5.32.1.1.4 //Calling the main method:

```
public static void main (java.lang.String[] args)
```

5.32.1.1.5 //Setting up the connection using the selected middleware:

```
{
	MiddlewareInfo aMiddlewareInfo = new MiddlewareInfo(args);
	FactoryManager aFactoryManager = FactoryManager.getSingleInstance();
	aFactoryManager.setMiddlewareInfo(aMiddlewareInfo);
```

5.32.1.1.6 //Initializing the connection object:

```
	IRfcConnection aConnection = null;
	try
```

```
        {
                aConnection = establishConnection(aMiddlewareInfo);
        }
        catch (Exception ex)
        {
                System.out.println("ERROR: Could not create connection : " + ex) ;
                System.exit(-1);
        }
        System.out.println("Connection established.");
 // --- TEST CODE (start) ------------------------------------
        try
        {
                printList(aConnection);
```

5.32.1.1.7 //Calling the BAPI:

5.32.1.1.8 //Declare an empty Object ID for the Business Object

```
 //CompanyCode:
                objectId = CompanyCode.getEmptyObjectId();
```

5.32.1.1.9 //Entering a value in the object ID:

```
                objectId.getKeyField("COMPANYCODEID").setString("1000");
```

5.32.1.1.10 //Instantiate the object Company Code with the object ID:

```
                companyCode = new CompanyCode(objectId) ;  // Create 2nd
     CompanyCode
                System.out.println ("Successfully created new CompanyCode: '" +
companyCode + "'") ;
                print Details (companyCode, aConnection) ;
        }
        // --- TEST CODE (end) ----------------------------------------
        catch (Exception ex)
        {
                System.out.println ("Unexpected exception occurred:");
                System.out.println (ex);
        }
}
```

```
private static void printDetails(CompanyCode companyCode, IRfcConnection con-
nection)
{
        try
        {
```

5.32.1.1.11 //Declare the parameters of the BAPI CompanyCode. GetDetail:

```
                CompanyCodeGetdetailParams aCompanyCodeGetdetailParams =
                        new CompanyCodeGetdetailParams () ;
```

5.32.1.1.12 //Aufruf des BAPIs CompanyCode.GetDetail auf die Object instanz:

```
                companyCode.getdetail(connection, aCompanyCodeGetdetail-
Params);
```

5.32.1.1.13 //Splitting the parameter object into its separate components

```
//(Struktur):
                Bapi0002_2Structure struct = aCompanyCodeGetdetailParams.get-
CompanycodeDetail();
                System.out.println ("The details of the companycode are: ") ;
```

5.32.1.1.14 //Splitting the structure into individual fields:

```
                System.out.println ("CompCode :        "" + struct.getCompCode() +
"""" );
                System.out.println ("CompName:        "" + struct.getCompName()
+ """" );
                System.out.println ("City1:          "" + struct.getCity()  + """" );
                System.out.println ("Country1:        "" + struct.getCountry() + """" );
                System.out.println ("Currency:        "" + struct.getCurrency() + """" );
                System.out.println ("Langu1:          "" + struct.getLangu() + """" );
                System.out.println ("ChrtAccts:        "" + struct.getChrtAccts() + """" );
                System.out.println ("FyVariant:        "" + struct.getFyVariant() + """" );
                System.out.println ("VatRegNo:        "" + struct.getVatRegNo() + """"
);
                System.out.println ("Company:         "" + struct.getCompany() + """"
```

```
);
        System.out.println ("AddrNo:        "" + struct.getAddrNo() + """
);
        System.out.println();
    }
    catch (Exception ex)
    {
        System.out.println("Exception in printDetails(): " + ex) ;
    }
    return;
}
private static void printList (IRfcConnection connection)
{
    try
    {
```

5.32.1.1.15 //Declaring the parameter object:

```
        CompanyCodeGetlistParams aCompanyCodeGetlistParams =
            new CompanyCodeGetlistParams();
```

5.32.1.1.16 //Actual BAPI call:

```
        CompanyCode.getlist(connection, aCompanyCodeGetlistParams);
```

5.32.1.1.17 //Splitting the parameter objects into its separate components

```
//(Table):
        Bapi0002_1Table table = aCompanyCodeGetlistParams.getCom-
panycodeList();
        int rowCount = table.getRowCount();
        System.out.println ("Returned table has " + rowCount + " lines.");
```

5.32.1.1.18 //Evaluating the table row by row:

```
        for (int i = 0; i < rowCount; i++)
        {
            Bapi0002_1TableRow row = table. getRow(i);
            System.out.println("\t" + row.getCompCode() + "\t" + row.
getCompName());
```

```
            }
            System.out.println();
        }
        catch (Exception ex)
        {
            System.out.println("Exception in printList(): " + ex) ;
        }
        return;
}
}
```

5.33 Calling BAPIs from Visual Basic

This is an example program for calling a BAPI from Visual Basic. This report uses the service BAPI BapiService.MessageGetDetail, to display the short text and the long text of error messages.

```
'
' Visual BASIC 5.0
' Copyright SAP AG Walldorf Juli 1998
'
' read a message short and long text using the BAPI
' BAPI_MESSAGE_GETDETAIL of the object BapiService

' constant for user identification
Const cstrMUsrClient      As String = "000"
Const cstrMUsrUser        As String = "MYUSER"
Const cstrMUsrPassword    As String = "MYPASS"
Const cstrMUsrLanguage    As String = "EN"

' constant for system identification
Const cstrMSysSystem      As String = "P45"
Const cstrMSysMessageServer As String = "p45main.wdf.sap-ag.de"
Const cstrMSysGroupName   As String = "PUBLIC"
'
' constant values for reading message texts
Const cstrMMsgId          As String = "SX"
Const cstrMMsgNumber      As String = "101"
Const cstrMMsgVariable1   As String = "var1"
Const cstrMMsgVariable2   As String = "var2"
```

```
Const cstrMMsgVariable3    As String = "var3"
Const cstrMMsgVariable4    As String = "var4"
Const cstrMMsgLanguage     As String = "DE"

' other constant
Const cstrMPathfile        As String = "D:\A\saptext.rtf"

' password for login in R/3
Dim strMUsrPassword        As String

' react on button START
Private Sub cmdMsgStart_Click()

'   define object for BAPI ActiveX control
    Dim oBAPICtrl       As Object
'   define object for R/3 logon control
    Dim oLogonCtrl      As Object
'   business object BapiService
    Dim boBapiSercice   As Object

'   for BAPI: BapiService.MessageGetDetail
    Dim oMsgReturn      As Object
    Dim oMsgText As Object
    Dim intCounter      As Integer
'   to open the file you need a file channel
    Dim intChannel      As Integer


'   create BAPI ActiveX control object
    Set oBAPICtrl           = CreateObject("SAP.BAPI.1")
'   create R/3 logon control object
    Set oLogonCtrl          = CreateObject("SAP.Logoncontrol.1")
'   connection object is part of the BAPI ActiveX Control object
    Set oBAPICtrl.Connection = oLogonCtrl.NewConnection

'   fill logon parameters for system to use
oBAPICtrl.Connection. System        = txtSysSystem
oBAPICtrl.Connection. MessageServer = txtSysMessageServer
    oBAPICtrl.Connection.GroupName     = txtSysGroupName
'   fill logon parameter for user
    oBAPICtrl.Connection.Client        = txtUsrClient
```

```
  oBAPICtrl.Connection.User        = txtUsrUser
  oBAPICtrl.Connection.Password     = strMUsrPassword
oBAPICtrl.Connection. Language     = txtUsrLanguage

' user logon to R/3
  If oBAPICtrl.Connection.Logon(frmStart.hWnd, False) = False Then
    MsgBox "R/3 connection failed"
    End
  End If

' create BAPI service object
  Set boBapiService = oBAPICtrl.GetSAPObject("BapiService")

' call method of BapiService
  boBapiService.MessageGetDetail id:=txtMsgId, _
                        Number:=txtMsgNumber, _
                        Language:=txtMsgLanguage, _
                        Textformat:=cboMsgTextformat.Text, _
                        message:=strMsgShorttext, _
                        Return:=oMsgReturn, _
                        Text:=oMsgText

' fill field in form
'  If txtMsgShorttext = "" Then
'     MsgBox "No message read"
'  End If

' user logoff from R/3
  oBAPICtrl.Connection.Logoff

' error handling check if RETURN parameter is not empty and react
  If oMsgReturn.Value("TYPE") <> "" Then
    lblReturn.Caption = oMsgReturn.Value("TYPE") + _
                " . " + _
                oMsgReturn.Value("ID") + _
                " . " + _
                oMsgReturn.Value("NUMBER") + _
                " . " + _
                oMsgReturn.Value("MESSAGE") + _
                " . " + _
                oMsgReturn.Value("MESSAGE_V1") + _
```

```
                " . " + _
                oMsgReturn.Value("MESSAGE_V2") + _
                " . " + _
                oMsgReturn.Value("MESSAGE_V3") + _
                " . " + _
                oMsgReturn.Value("MESSAGE_V4") + _
                " . " + _
                oMsgReturn.Value("LOG_NO") + _
                " . " + _
                oMsgReturn.Value("LOG_MSG_NO")

  Else

'   fill form fields
    txtMsgShorttext = strMsgShorttext
    arrayText       = oMsgText.Data

'   handling of non RTF texts
    If cboMsgTextformat.Text <> "RTF" Then
      For intCounter = 1 To oMsgText.RowCount
        If intCounter = 1 Then
          rtfMsgLongtext.Text = arrayText(intCounter, 1)
        Else
          rtfMsgLongtext.Text = rtfMsgLongtext.Text + _
                    Chr(13) + Chr(10) + _
                    arrayText(intCounter, 1)
        End If
      Next intCounter
    End If

'   handling of RTF texts
    If cboMsgTextformat.Text = "RTF" Then
'     save text as rtf file
      intChannel = FreeFile
      Open cstrMPathfile For Output As #intChannel
        For intCounter = 1 To oMsgText.RowCount
          Print #intChannel, arrayText(intCounter, 1)
        Next intCounter
      Close #intChannel
      rtfMsgLongtext.LoadFile cstrMPathfile, rtfRTF
    End If
```

```
  End If
End Sub
```

5.34 Calling BAPIs from ABAP

This report uses the service BAPI BapiService.MessageGetDetail, to display the short text and the long text of error messages.

```
*-------------------------------------------------------------------*
*      read a message short and long text using the BAPI            *
*      BAPI_MESSAGE_GETDETAIL of the object BapiService.            *
*-------------------------------------------------------------------*
```

5.34.1.1.1 * Data declaration

```
DATA: MY_ID         LIKE BAPIRET2-ID,
      MY_NUMBER     LIKE BAPIRET2-NUMBER,
      MY_TEXTFORMAT LIKE BAPITGA-TEXTFORMAT,
      MY_MESSAGE_V1 LIKE BAPIRET2-MESSAGE_V1,
      MY_MESSAGE    LIKE BAPIRET2-MESSAGE,
      MY_RETURN     TYPE BAPIRET2.
DATA BEGIN OF MY_TEXT OCCURS 1.
   INCLUDE STRUCTURE BAPITGB.
DATA END OF MY_TEXT.
```

5.34.1.1.2 * Enter values in object

```
MOVE 'FI'   TO MY_ID.            "message id of message to read
MOVE '024'  TO MY_NUMBER.        "message number of message to read
MOVE 'ASC'  TO MY_TEXTFORMAT.    "text format, here ASCII
MOVE '0001' TO MY_MESSAGE_V1.    "text to fill into message
```

5.34.1.1.3 *BAPI call

```
CALL FUNCTION 'BAPI_MESSAGE_GETDETAIL'
   EXPORTING
      ID         = MY_ID
      NUMBER     = MY_NUMBER
*      LANGUAGE   = SY-LANGU
      TEXTFORMAT = MY_TEXTFORMAT
      MESSAGE_V1 = MY_MESSAGE_V1
*      MESSAGE_V2 =
```

```
*       MESSAGE_V3 =
*       MESSAGE_V4 =
    IMPORTING
       MESSAGE    = MY_MESSAGE
       RETURN     = MY_RETURN
    TABLES
       TEXT       = MY_TEXT
       .
```

5.34.1.1.4 * Print results

```
WRITE: / 'Input' COLOR 5.
WRITE: / 'my_id............:', MY_ID.
WRITE: / 'my_number........:', MY_NUMBER.
WRITE: / 'my_textformat....:', MY_TEXTFORMAT.
WRITE: / 'my_message_v1....:', MY_MESSAGE_V1.
WRITE: / 'Output' COLOR 5.
WRITE: / 'my_message.........:', MY_MESSAGE.
WRITE: / 'my_return..........:', MY_RETURN.
WRITE: / 'Text output' COLOR 5.
LOOP AT MY_TEXT.
  WRITE: / MY_TEXT.
ENDLOOP.
```

5.35 Modifying BAPIs

5.35.1 Use

You can modify SAP Business Object types and their BAPIs, if you want, for example, to add a parameter to a BAPI or add a method to a business object type.

5.36 User Exits

5.36.1 Use

BAPIs can contain predefined user exits enabling application developers to enhance BAPI interfaces without modifications.

5.36.2 Features

User exits are implemented using specific standardized parameters which are used as containers to transfer the data.
BAPIs can provide standard or special user exits.

5.36.2.1 Standard User Exits

Standard user exits are enhancements to BAPI interfaces that allow customers to modify the program code in a CALL CUSTOMER FUNCTION command.

In this case the container parameter for transferring the data is called Extension X, where X is a number.Several extension parameters may be provided in one interface, so that the same parameters can be used for importing and exporting data, for example.

Through extension parameters appends as well as structured data and unstructured data can be incorporated into a BAPI.

An SAP BAPI with this type of user exits could look like this, for example:
Interface

```
BAPI_<Object>_<Method>
        Parameter1    LIKE   Structure1-Field1      Import  Field
        Parameter2    LIKE   Structure1-Field2      Import  Field
        Parameter3    LIKE   Structure2             Export  Structure
        Parameter4    LIKE   Structure2-Field3      Export  Field
        Parameter5    LIKE   Structure3             Imp/Ex. table
        ....
        EXTENSION1    LIKE   <Container structure>Import Structure
        EXTENSION2    LIKE   <Container Structure>Imp/Ex. table
...
```

Program code

```
Function BAPI_<Object>_<Method>
...
FormParam = Parameter1
...
FormTable = Parameter5
...
Parameter3= 'Content'
...
CALL CUSTOMER-FUNCTION '<three digit number>'
```

(Interface as above).

...

endfunction

5.36.2.1.1 Function Module Name

The customer-specific function is called using the command CALL CUSTOMER-FUNCTION. This function module must have the naming convention EXIT_<module pool name>_<three digit number>.

5.36.2.2 Special User Exits

These are standardized enhancements to BAPI interfaces for which customers do not have to change the program code. In this case the container parameter for the data transfer has the naming convention:
Extension<name>, where <Name> describes the type of enhancement.

For example, the container parameter ExtensionOrder could be used in the Table SALES (sales order master data) of the associated BAPI for the customer INCLUDE CLSALES.

5.36.2.3 Further Information

The standard Riles for user exits apply and maintenance with Transaction SMOD (SAP internal development) and CMOD (customer development). Refer also to the documentation on SAP Enhancement Management (SMOD) and to BC - Enhancing the SAP Standard (CMOD).

5.37 Customer Enhancements

5.37.1 Purpose

Customers can modify an existing BAPI or develop their own BAPIs, if required.

5.38 Enhancements Through Modification

5.38.1 Purpose

Customers can make modifications to existing BAPIs, for example, if new parameters or parameter fields are needed.

5.38.2 Process Flow

If a BAPI modification is needed, we recommend that you create a sub-type of the business object in question and make the changes to the sub-type. Then you should-lascertain the delegation relationship between the original SAP Business Object type (supertype) and the subtype.
In this way the SAP Standard delivered to customers is not changed and the modifications carried out are retained when the Release is upgraded. This procedure also enables BAPIs to be modified in steps because further subordinate sub-types of a business object can be created.

5.38.2.1 Creating and Redefining Subtypes

To create a subtype:

1. Choose Tools → Business Framework BAPI Development→Business Object Builder or enter the transaction code SWO1
2. In the field Object type enter the name of the subtype you want to create and sleet Create.
3. In the next diabg box, enter the required details:
   - In the field Supertype enter the name of the object type for which you want to create a subtype.
   - In the field Object type enter the name of the subtype you want to create and enter appropriate values in the remaining fields.

Then redefine the subtype.

1. Choose Tools Business Framework , BAPI Development Business Object Builder or enter the transaction code swol.
2. Display the subtype just created in the change mode.
3. Place the cursor on the BAPI you want to modify and choose Process Redefine.
4. Double-click on the BAPI and select the register ABAP/4.
5. In the field Name, enter the name of the modified function module.
6. Save your entries.

5.38.2.2 Defining the Delegation Relationship Between Object Type (Supertype) and Subtype

To define the delegation relationship between the supertype and subtype:

1. Choose Tools , Business Framework BAPI Development → Business Object Builder or enter the transaction code soot.
2. Choose Settings Delegate → System-wide.
3. Switch to the change mode and select New entries.
4. Enter the name of the original object type (supertype) in the field Object type and the name of the subobject type in the field Delegation type. Deactivate the check box GUI-specific.
5. Save your entries.

The BAPI Material.GetList for the Business Object Material should contain additional parameters. The function module associated with this BAPI is BAPI_MATERIAL_GETLIST.

Customers should first create a sub-type YMaterial of the existing business object Material in the BOR. They will also note that method calls of the business object YMaterial for the original object type Material are to be processed, provided that the associated method is implemented there. This is described as delegation. (For all methods that are not implemented for the sub-type Ymaterial, the method call is executed from the superordinate business object, Material.)

Customers make the necessary changes in the source code of the function module BAPI MATERIAL and makes changes to the interface by creating new, **optional** parameters. Next, customers create the method GetList for the sub-type YMaterial using the BOR/ BAPI Wizard. The method is linked to the function module BAPI_MATERIAL_GETLIST, where the new parameters are included as part of the method definition. If, on the other hand, the interface is enhanced with new, **mandatory** parameters, a new function module must be created and assigned to the method YMaterialGetList. (Customers can also copy the module BAPI_MATERIALGETLIST, for example, to Y_BAPI_MATERIAL_GETLIST, and then edit this copy.

At runtime the following process takes place:

- When the BAPI Material.GetList, the BAPI YMateriaLGetList is the one actually executed.
- In the case of all other method calls, the methods of the superordinate business object, Material are executed, because these are not implemented for the sub-type YMaterial

5.39 Customer Developments

5.39.1 Purpose

Using the information in these BAPI Programming guidelines you can create new methods for business objects.

5.39.2 Process Flow

Following on from the example in Enhancements Through Modification, an additional method Y GetDetail should be created for the sub-type Y Material of the business object type Material. The function module associated with this BAPI is Y BAPI_ MATERIAL_GETDETAIL.

Customers should create the new method YGetDetail of the business object YMaterial using the BOR/BAPI Wizard. This method is associated with the function module

Y _BAPI MATERIALGETDETAIL.

At runtime, when the BAPI MaterialY GetDetail is called. the BAPI YMaterial.YGetDetail is implemented' due to the delegation pointer in the business object Material.

5.40 Namespaces

5.40.1 Definition

The namespace concept describes how customers and partners have to name their development objects to avoid overlapping when SAP software is upgraded.

Customers and partners can create their own development objects, for example, to implement a new BAPI or to modify an existing BAPI. For further information see Customer Modifications and Developments.

In R/3 Release 3.1 the namespaces Y* and Z* were provided for customers, and the namespace .1<number> was reserved for partners.

In R/3 Release 4.0 a new namespace concept was introduced which, together with the longer development object names, made it easier to assign names to objects developed by customers and partners.

The Business Object Repository (BOB) introduced before R/3 Release 4.0 still uses the old namespace concept. For this reason, the limitations of the old namespace concept still apply to the namespaces for BAPI development objects.

5.40.1.1 Reserved Namespaces for the Various Application Groups

User	Prefix
Industrial Business Units (IBUs)	One of the options below: • "ISx", where "x" can be any letter. • Use your own unique namespace after agreeing it with the central BOR coordination. • Agree the name with standard development.
Other developments within SAP	For example, "JPN" for developments in the Japanese area.
Partners/software houses	• J_y" (where "y" is a single digit allocated namespace) for partners/software houses whose namespaces were assigned **before** Release 4.0. • "JJ<*Namespace*>" (where "<*Namespace*>" is the registered namespace) for partners/software houses whose namespaces were assigned **after** Release 4.0, for example, JJABC.
Customers	"Y" and "Z", for function modules matching "Y_" and "Z_".

If a customer or partner creates anew object type that is not a sub-type of another object type, the naming convention for this object type applies to all the sub-objects. In principle, therefore, SAP objects cannot overlap with each other, regardless of the names of the methods, attributes and so on.

Sub-object types split the namespace for methods, attributes and so on with the superordinate object type. You must follow the naming conventions for the sub-objects too.

5.40.1.2 Naming Conventions for BAPI Development Objects

Development Object	Created in...	Naming Convention
Domain	ABAP Dictionary	Standard in the respective R/3 Release
Data Element	ABAP Dictionary	Standard in the respective R/3 Release
Structure	ABAP Dictionary	*<Prefix>BAPI**
Field in structures	ABAP Dictionary	-
Append structure	ABAP Dictionary	Standard in the respective R/3 Release
Function group	Function Builder	Standard in the respective R/3 Release
Function Module	Function Builder	*<Prefix>BAPI_<Object>_<Method>*
Function module parameter	Function Builder	*<Präfix>**, except for parameters in customers' function modules
Object type	BOR	*<Prefix>**
Object name	BOR	*<Prefix>**
Attribute name	BOR	*<Prefix>**
Method	BOR	*<Prefix>**, except for modifications using delegation, otherwise delegation does not work.
Method parameters	BOR	<Function module parameter>

5.41 BAPI Creation

5.41.1 Technical Steps (from 0 – 16) for BAPI Creation

Step-0

The table ZBapiTable is created in the Data Dictionary as given in the below given Screen Shot:-0

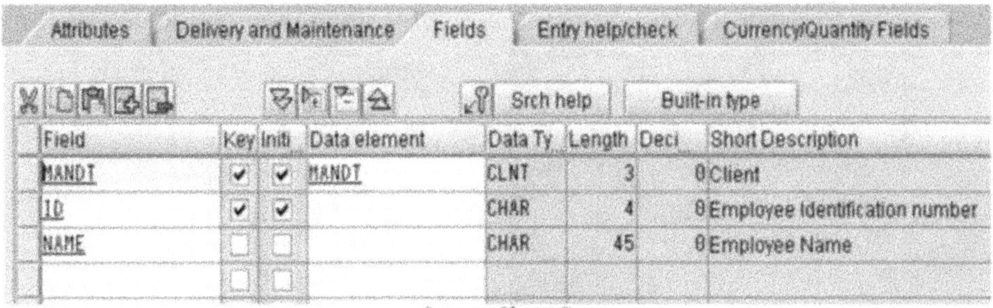

Attributes | Delivery and Maintenance | Fields | Entry help/check | Currency/Quantity Fields

Srch help | Built-in type

Field	Key	Initi	Data element	Data Ty	Length	Deci	Short Description
MANDT	✔	✔	MANDT	CLNT	3	0	Client
ID	✔	✔		CHAR	4	0	Employee Identification number
NAME	☐	☐		CHAR	45	0	Employee Name
	☐	☐					

Screen Shot:-0

Step-1

Run the transaction code SWO1. (see Screen Shot: 1)

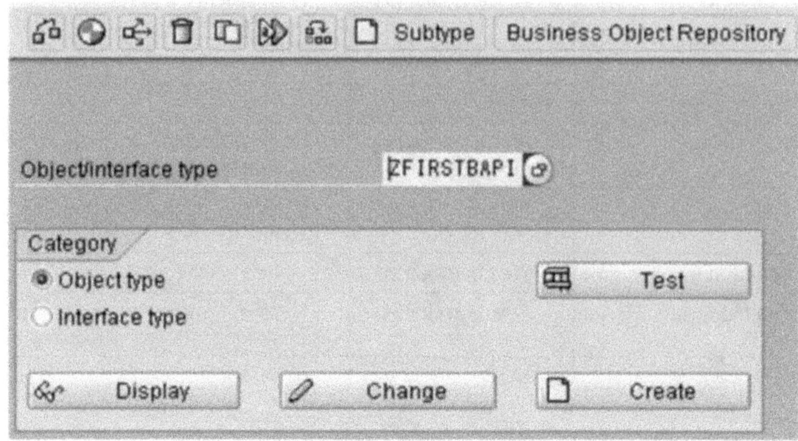

Screen Shot:-1

Now, we are in the process of creating a New Object Type (Business Object).

Note: There are 2 kinds of objects such as **Super-Type** and **Sub-Object Type**. Super-type is nothing but an object which has no inheritance from any other object. Whereas, an object which is inherited from other object is called Sub-Object Type.

Step-2

Click the button Create

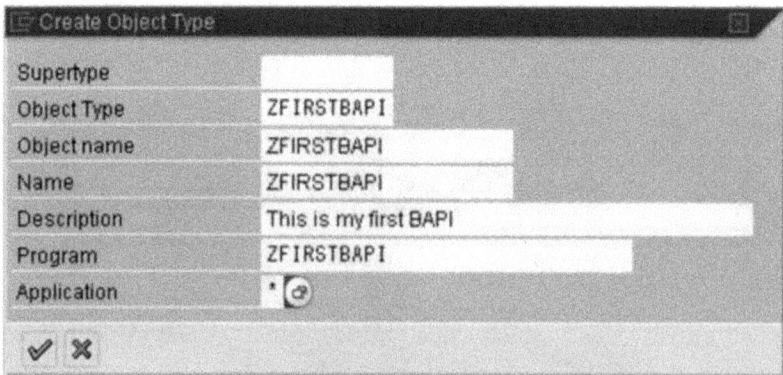

Create Object Type

Supertype	
Object Type	ZFIRSTBAPI
Object name	ZFIRSTBAPI
Name	ZFIRSTBAPI
Description	This is my first BAPI
Program	ZFIRSTBAPI
Application	*

Screen Shot:-2

Fill-in all the required fields as given in the Screen Shot: 2

Once the Tick Button ✔ is clicked, **Package Name**& Transport Request ID need to be entered and saved.

Step-3

The BAPI builder will look like as given in the Screen Shot:-3

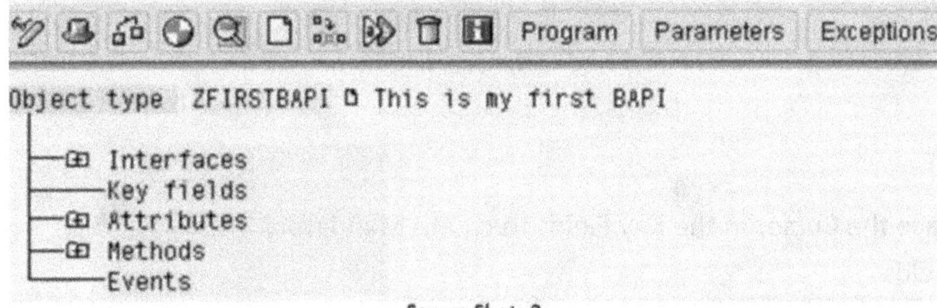

Screen Shot:-3

Now, we need to create Key Fields, Attributes, Methods & Events.

Step-4

Now this new Object Type need to be Implemented. The menu path is given in the Screen Shot:-4

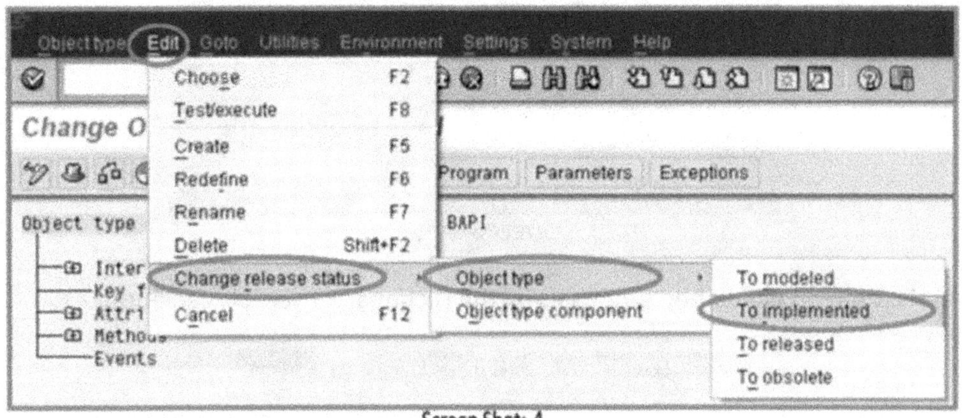

Screen Shot:-4

After implementing the Object Type, the screen will look like in the Screen Shot:-5:

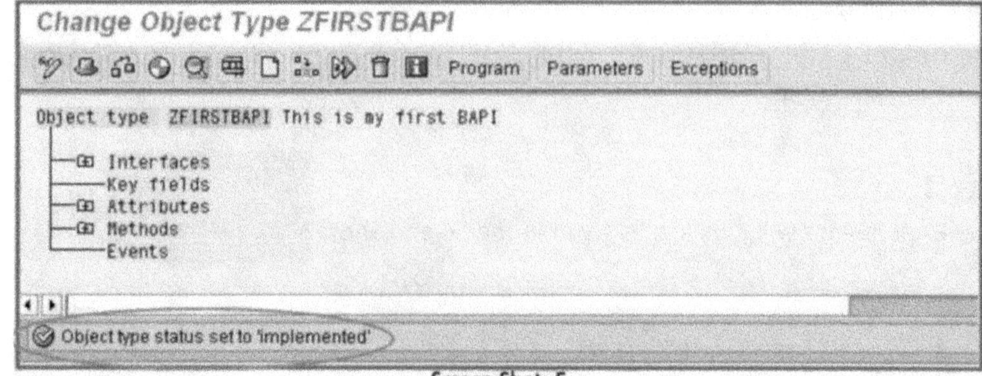

Screen Shot:-5

Step-5

5.1) Place the Cursor in the Key Fields to create Mandatory Fields

5.2) The popup:- "Create with ABAP Dictionary Proposals" would appear.

5.3) Click "Yes".
(see Screen Shot:-6)

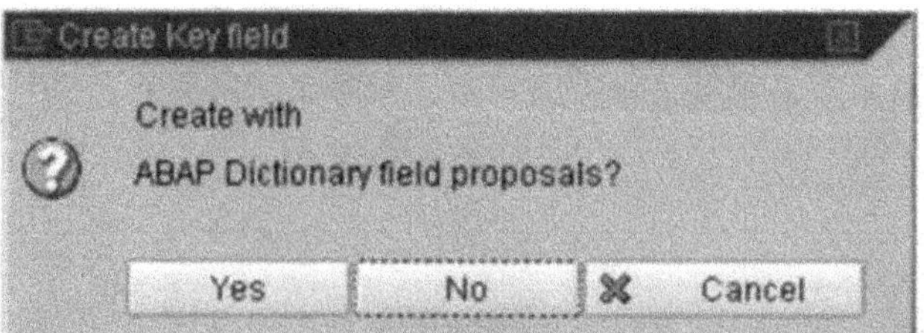

Screen Shot:-6

5.4) Next screen would be: Proposals by the Dictionary (see Screen Shot:-7)

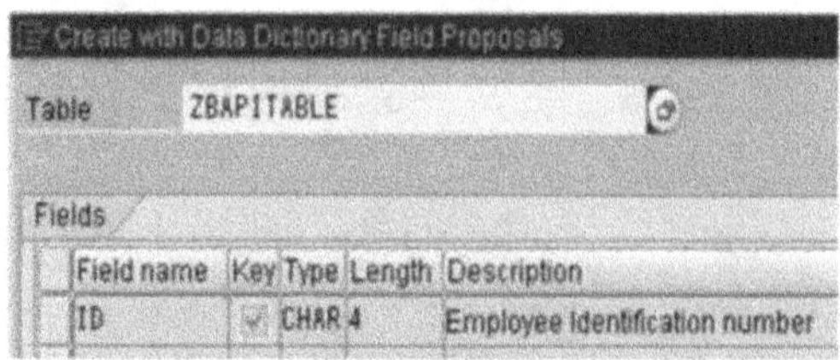

Screen Shot:-7

5.5) Select the row "ID"

Table ZBAPITABLE

Fields

Field name	Key	Type	Length	Description
ID	✓	CHAR	4	Employee Identification number

Screen Shot:-8

5.6) The next screen would be: (see Screen Shot:-9)

Fill in all the fields as given in the screen shot.

And, click the Create Icon.

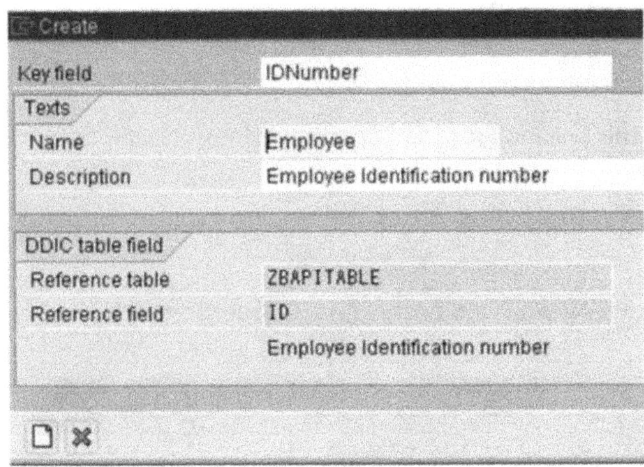

Screen Shot:-9

5.7) The Business Object Builder would like:Screen Shot:-10

The new Attribute "ID Number" is added to the Key fields Node.

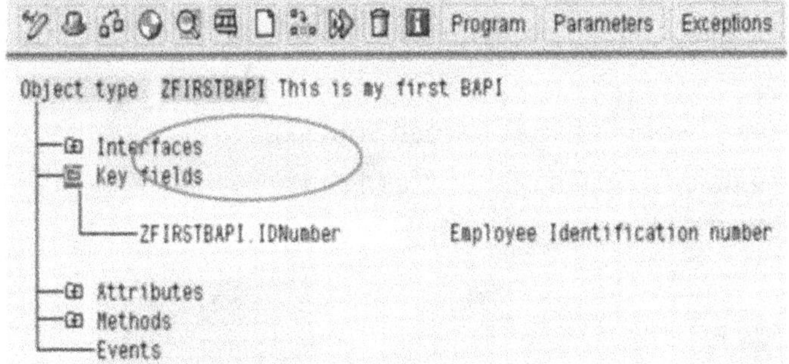

Screen Shot:-10

Step-6

Now, we are in the stage of creating "Attributes".

Here for an example, we are about to create an attribute "Name" with below given specificationand add the same into the Attribute Node of the Business Builder.

NAME	TYPE	ZBAPITABLE-NAME

6.1) Place the Cursor in the Attribute Node.

6.2) Click the Create Icon .

6.3) Once again this will look for the "Create with ABAP Dictionary Proposal Fields?".

6.4) Click "Yes".

6.5) Select the row "NAME" and press ENTER. (See Screen Shot:-11)

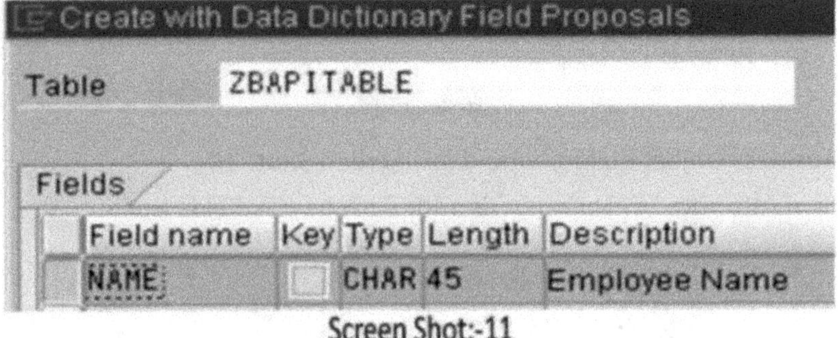

Screen Shot:-11

6.6) The next screen would be: (see Screen Shot:-12)

Fill in all the fields as given in the screen shot.

And, click the Create Icon.

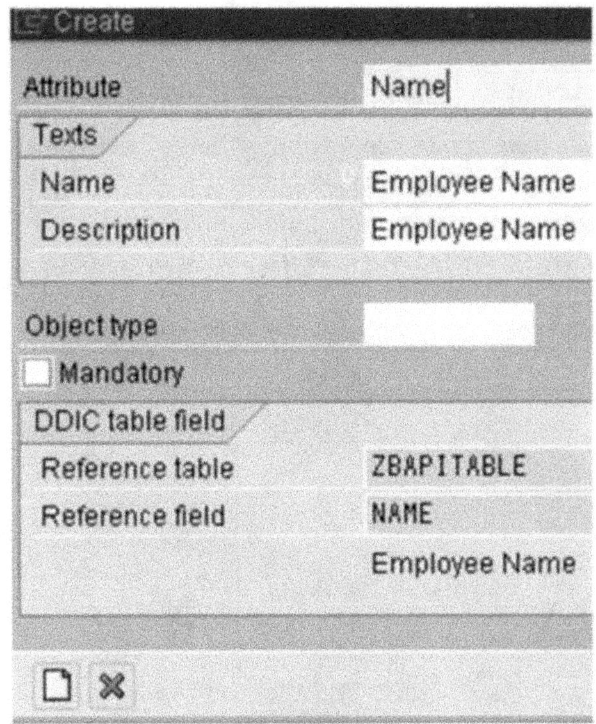

Screen Shot:-12

6.7) The Business Object Builder would like:Screen Shot:-13

The new Attribute "Name" is added to the Attribute Node.

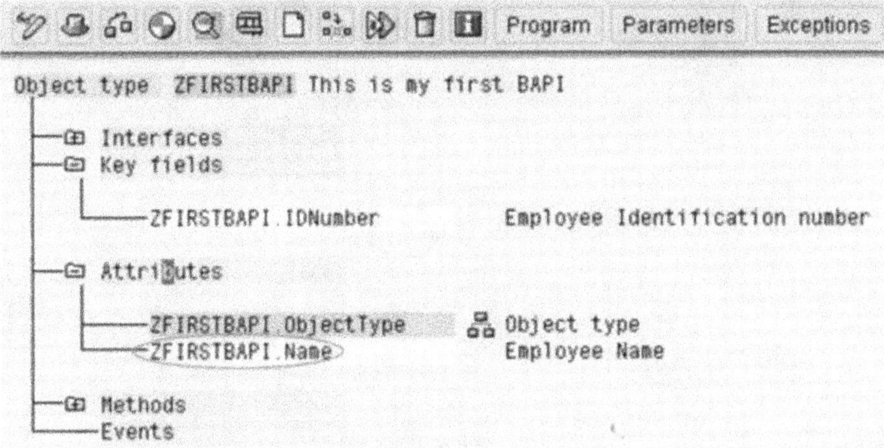

Screen Shot:-13

Step-7

7.1) Now all the "Attributes" need to be Declared

7.2) For our case, we have created an Attribute "Name" which is only to be declared. Below are the steps for doing the Declaration.

7.3) Place the cursor on the "Name" attribute.

7.4) Double Click on the attribute "Name". (see Screen Shot:-14)

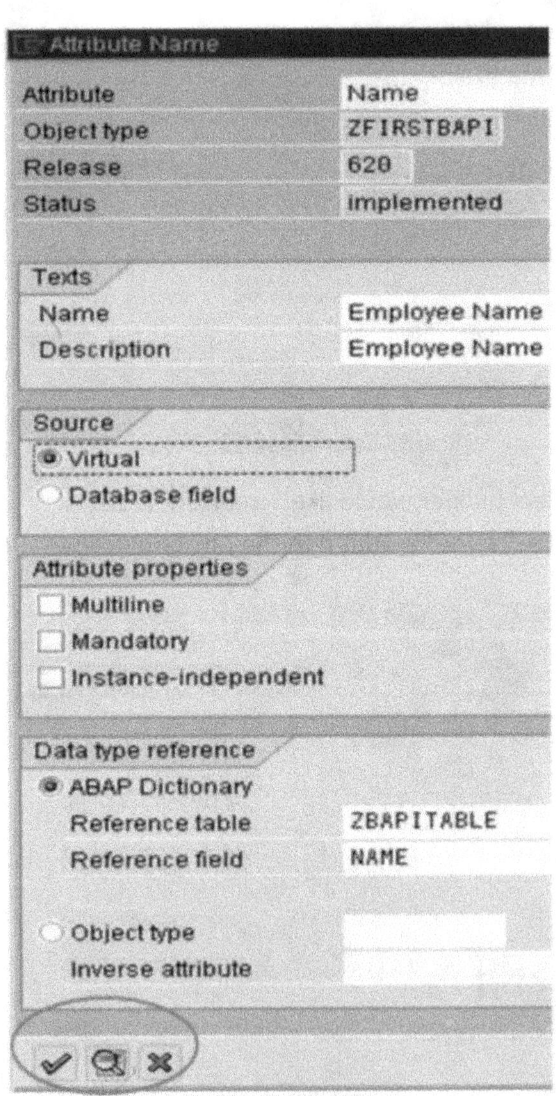

Screen Shot:-14

Select “Virtual” in the Source Tab. And press <ENTER>.

7.5) Click the button “**Program**” as seen in the Screen Shot:-15

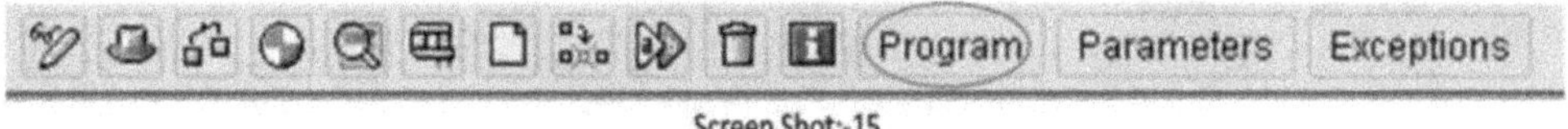

Screen Shot:-15

7.6) A popup would appear, where click “YES” (Screen Shot:-16)

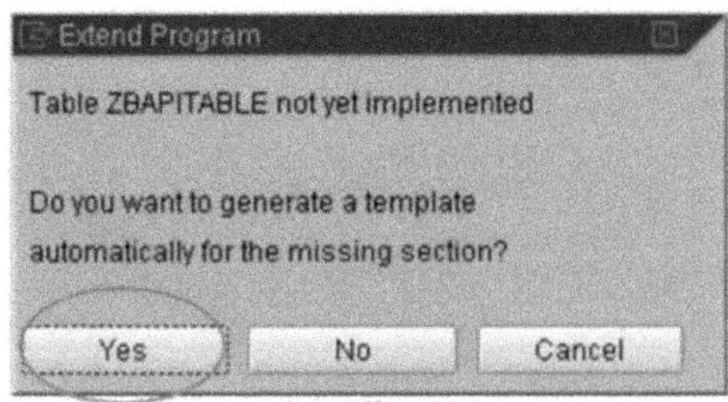

Screen Shot:-16

7.7) The Declaration is done automatically by the system. And the corresponding Declaration Code is written by the system. (see Screen Shot:-17)

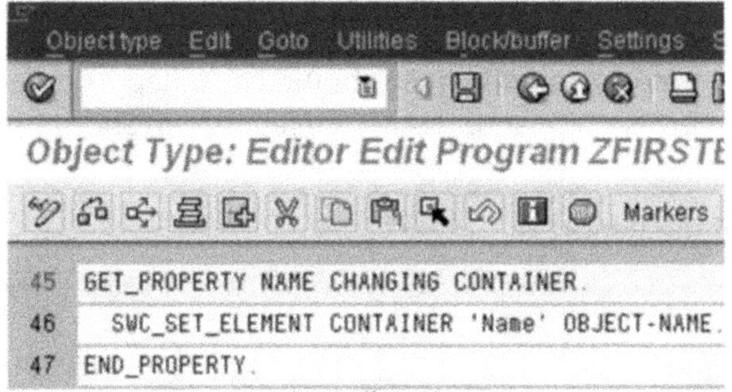

Screen Shot:-17

7.8) Now, this code need to be generated.

Path: **ObjectType>Generate**

Note: Here the Macros “**SWC_SET_ELEMENT CONTAINER ‘Name’ OBJECT-NAME.**” means, a new Container Attribute “NAME” is declared as OBJECT-NAME. Where, the OBJECT is automatically declared by the system at the beginning of the PROGRAM. See the Screen Shot:-18

Object Type: Editor Edit Program ZFIRSTBAPI

Markers Pattern Concatenate Doub

```
*****          Implementation of object type ZFIRSTBAPI          *****
INCLUDE <OBJECT>.
BEGIN_DATA OBJECT. " Do not change.. DATA is generated
* only private members may be inserted into structure private
DATA:
" begin of private,
"   to declare private attributes remove comments and
"   insert private attributes here ...
" end of private,
  BEGIN OF KEY,
      IDNUMBER LIKE ZBAPITABLE-ID,
  END OF KEY,
      NAME TYPE ZBAPITABLE-NAME.
END_DATA OBJECT. " Do not change.. DATA is generated

GET_PROPERTY NAME CHANGING CONTAINER.
  SWC_SET_ELEMENT CONTAINER 'Name' OBJECT-NAME.
END_PROPERTY.
```

Screen Shot:-18

Step-8

Now, we need to create a Method which should call a Report called "BAPI_REPORT" and pass the parameters "ID" and "NAME". (see Screen Shot:-19)

The Screen shot of the Report is:

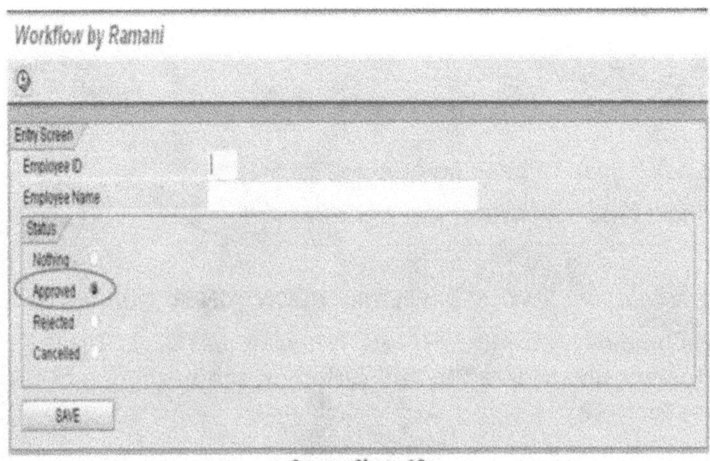

Screen Shot:-19

Step-9

Steps to create Methods and write Coding:

9.1) Place the cursor on the "Methods" node.

9.2) Click "Create ICON" 

9.3) A Pop-up would appear like: (see Screen Shot:-20)

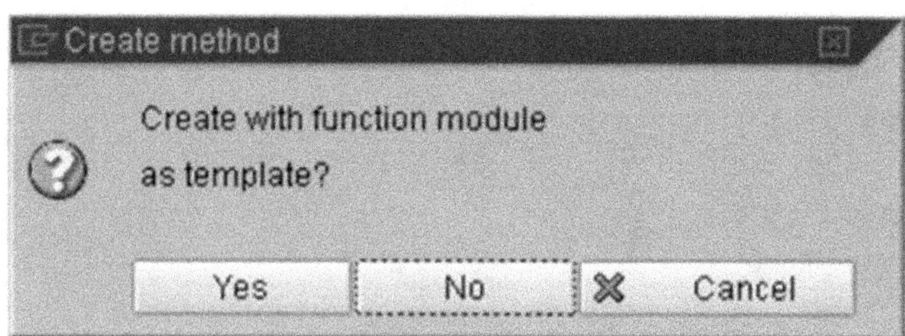

Screen Shot:-20

9.4) Click "Yes"

9.5) Create a Function Module "Z_BAPI_FIRST". Make it "Remote Enabled".
Coding done in the FM is given below.
After execution of this FM, the Export Parameter "EMPNAME" gets populated.
This EMPNAME value will later be assigned to the local BAPI-Attribute "Name" through Macros.

```
FUNCTION z_bapi_first1.
*"----------------------------------------------------------------------
*"*"Local interface:
*" IMPORTING
*"     VALUE(EMPID) LIKE ZBAPITABLE-ID
*" EXPORTING
*"     VALUE(RETURN) TYPE  BAPIRET2
*"     VALUE(EMPNAME) LIKE ZBAPITABLE STRUCTURE  ZBAPITABLE
*"----------------------------------------------------------------------
```

```
* Fetching Name for the given ID
 SELECT SINGLE name FROM zbapitable
      INTO   empname
WHERE id = empid.

* Assigning of Error Return Codes
* Table: T100 being used
   DATA par1 LIKE sy-msgv1.
   CALL FUNCTION 'BALW_BAPIRETURN_GET2'
      EXPORTING
         type   = 'E'
         cl     = 'BC_BOR'
         number = '107'
         par1   = par1
      IMPORTING
         return = return.

* Calling a Report
 SUBMIT zbapi_report VIA SELECTION-SCREEN
 WITH p_id = empid
 WITH p_nm = empname
 AND RETURN.
ENDFUNCTION.
```

9.6) Now the above Function Module need to be assigned as a Method in the Business Object.

Steps are given below:

9.6.1 Place the Cursor on the "Method" tab in the Business Object. (see Screen Shot:-21

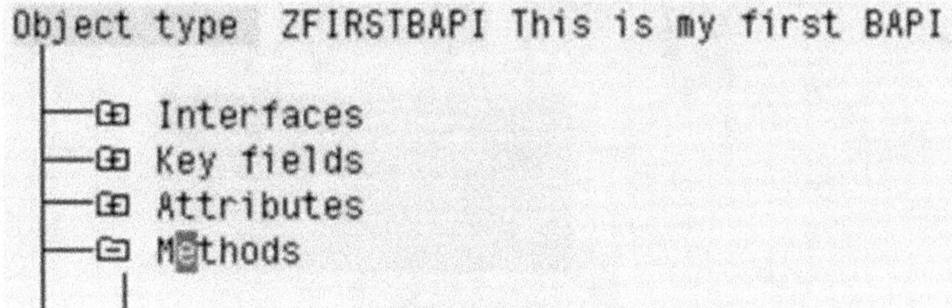

Screen Shot:-21

9.6.2 Click "Create ICON"

9.6.3 A Popup would appear as in the below screenshot. Click "YES" to continue as we are about to assign a Function Module.

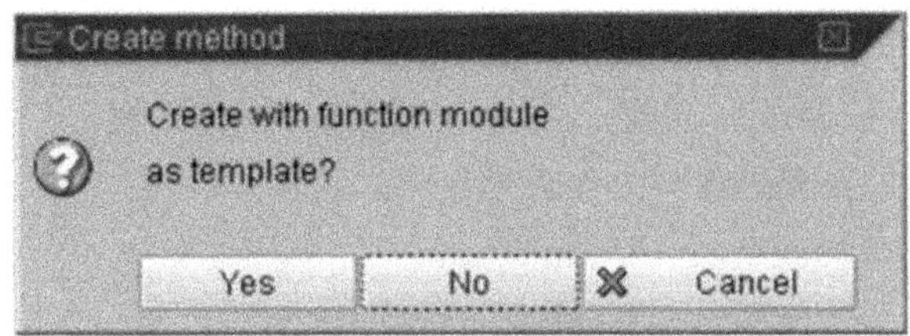

9.6.4 Continue & fill the values as given in the following slides:

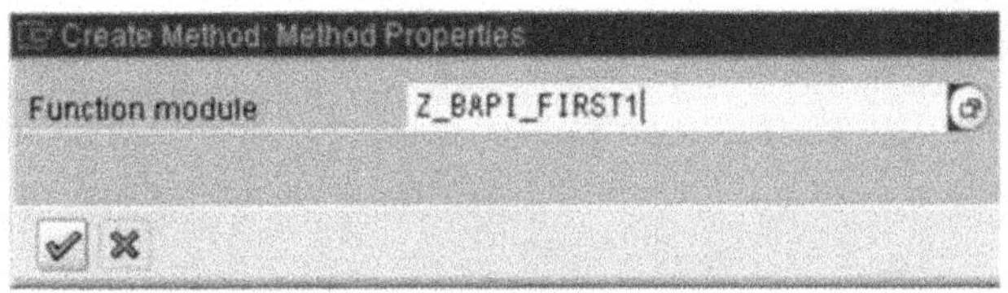

Screen Shot:-23

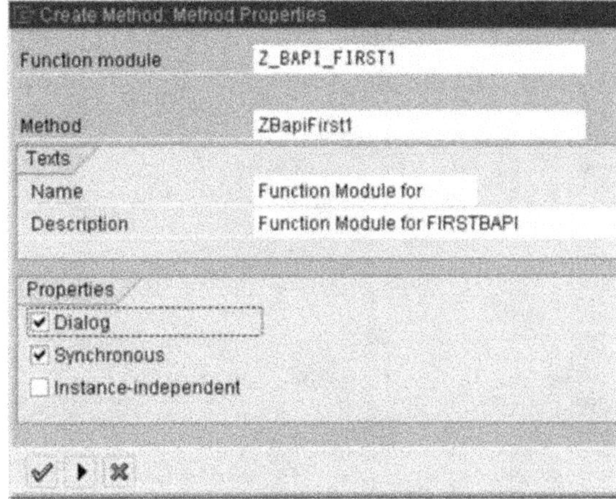

Screen Shot:-24

9.6.5 Now the Business Object Will Look like:

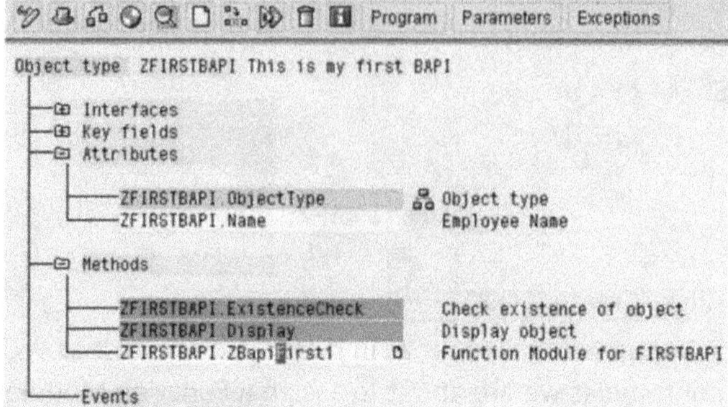

Screen Shot:-25

9.6.6 Now, double click on the Method: ZBapiFirst1.

- Go to "ABAP" tab.
- Make it an "API function"
- and press <ENTER>

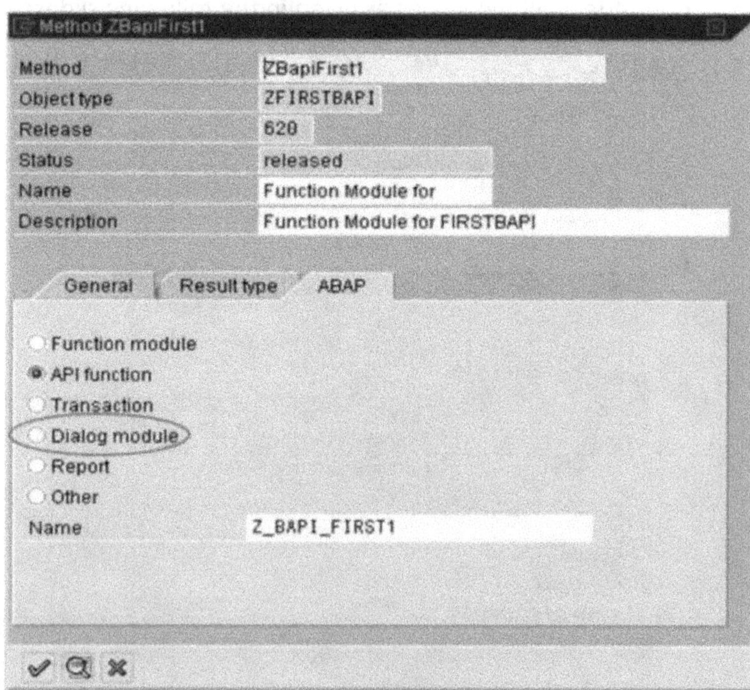

Screen Shot:-25A

9.6.7 Now look at the Business Object again:

Change Object Type ZFIRSTBAPI

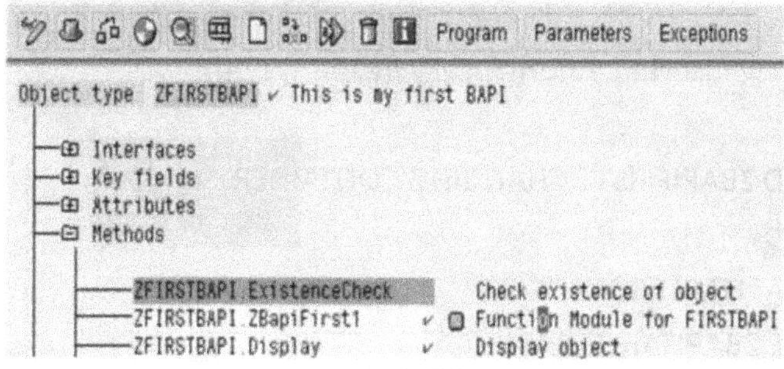

Screen Shot:-25B

9.6.8 Place the cursor on the method: ZFIRSTBAPI.ZBapiFirst1

9.6.9 Click "Program" Icon: Program Parameters Exceptions

9.7.0 Now, a popup would appear as given in the Screen Shot:-26

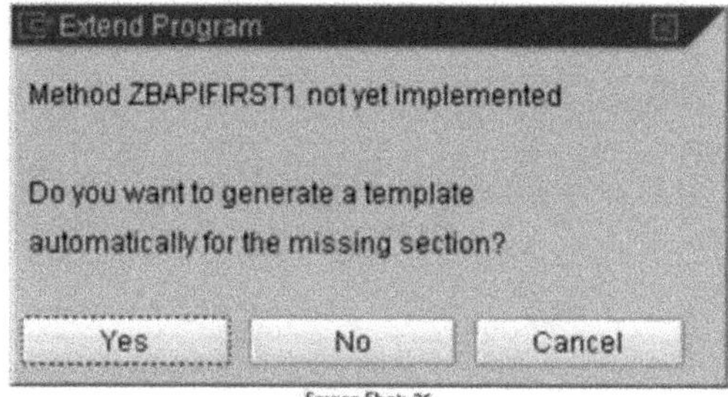

Extend Program
Method ZBAPIFIRST1 not yet implemented
Do you want to generate a template automatically for the missing section?
Yes
No
Cancel

Screen Shot:-26

9.6.7 Click "YES". We will get an Automatically Generated Template. (see Screen Shot:-27)

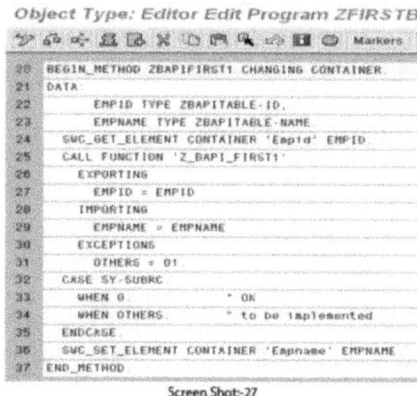

Object Type: Editor Edit Program ZFIRSTB

```
BEGIN_METHOD ZBAPIFIRST1 CHANGING CONTAINER.
DATA:
      EMPID TYPE ZBAPITABLE-ID,
      EMPNAME TYPE ZBAPITABLE-NAME.
  SWC_GET_ELEMENT CONTAINER 'Empid' EMPID.
  CALL FUNCTION 'Z_BAPI_FIRST1'
    EXPORTING
      EMPID = EMPID
    IMPORTING
      EMPNAME = EMPNAME
    EXCEPTIONS
      OTHERS = 01.
  CASE SY-SUBRC.
    WHEN 0.            " OK
    WHEN OTHERS.       " to be implemented
  ENDCASE.
  SWC_SET_ELEMENT CONTAINER 'Empname' EMPNAME.
END_METHOD.
```

Screen Shot:-27

Now, we see that the Function Module which we created is automatically programmed along with using Macro Commands.

Look at the coding inserted automatically by the system:

```
BEGIN_METHOD ZBAPIFIRST1 CHANGING CONTAINER.
DATA:
EMPID TYPE ZBAPITABLE-ID,
EMPNAME TYPE ZBAPITABLE-NAME.

SWC_GET_ELEMENT CONTAINER 'Empid' EMPID.
MOVE OBJECT-KEY-IDNumber TO EMPID.

CALL FUNCTION 'Z_BAPI_FIRST1'
EXPORTING
EMPID = EMPID
IMPORTING
EMPNAME = EMPNAME
EXCEPTIONS
OTHERS = 01.

CASE SY-SUBRC.
WHEN 0.          " OK
WHEN OTHERS.     " to be implemented
ENDCASE.

SWC_SET_ELEMENT CONTAINER 'Empname' EMPNAME.
END_METHOD.
```

Here,

1) Two Variables are declared
2) One Macro command is removed

3) Include MOVE OBJECT-KEY-IDNumber TO EMPID.
4) Function Module is called. Input Parameter <EMPIDID> is passed and Output Parameter is <ENAME> is returned.
5) Value of EMPNAME is set to the attribute 'Empname'.

Glimpse about Macros:

More Macros on page: 25

MACRO	USAGE
SWC_SET_ELEMENT CONTAINER 'Empname' EMPNAME.	Attribute: 'Empname' = EMPNAME
SWC_GET_ELEMENT CONTAINER 'Empname' EMPNAME.	EMPNAME = value of Attribute 'Empname'

9.7.1 Generate:

Menu Path: ObjectType > Generate

9.8 Method Definition gets Completed here.

Step-10: EVENTS CREATION

Now, we have to create EVENTS as given below:

- CREATED
- APPROVED

Step-11

Place cursor on the Events Tab in the Business Object Builder.

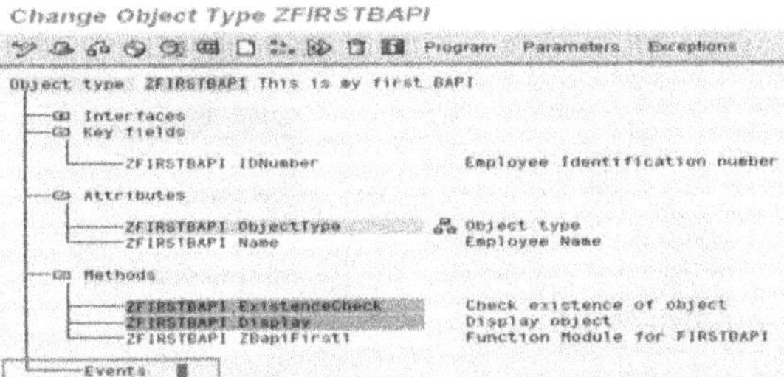

9.7.1 Generate:

Menu Path: ObjectType > Generate

9.8 Method Definition gets Completed here.

Step-10: EVENTS CREATION

Now, we have to create EVENTS as given below:

- CREATED
- APPROVED

Step-11

Place cursor on the Events Tab in the Business Object Builder.

Step-12

Click Create ICON from the Builder.

Step-13

Now, a dialog screen would appear. Fill in the values as given in the Screen Shot:-28

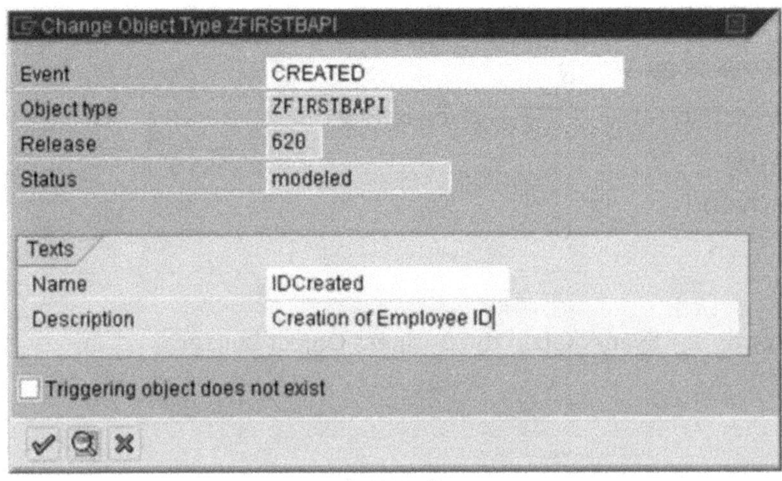

Screen Shot:-28

Press <ENTER>

The same way the Event 'APPROVED' also created.

Step-14

Now, total BAPI would appear as:

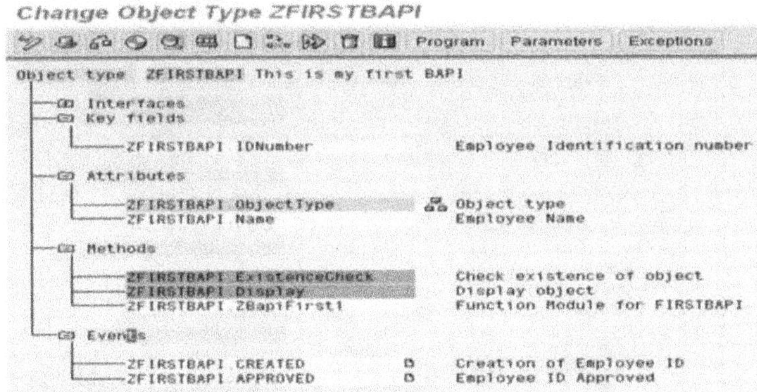

Step-15

Now, the object type need to be Implemented & Released. The steps are given below:

PLACE THE CURSOR AT	MENU
Object Type: ZFIRSTBAPI	Edit →Change Release Status → Object Type →To Implemented →To Released Object Type →Generate
Attribute: ZFIRSTBAPI.IDNumber	Edit →Change Release Status → Object Type Component →To Implemented →To Released
Methods: ZFIRSTBAPI.ZBapiFirst1	-do-
Events: ZFIRSTBAPI.CREATED	-do-
Events: ZFIRSTBAPI.APPROVED	-do-

Once the above activity is over, our BAPI will look like:

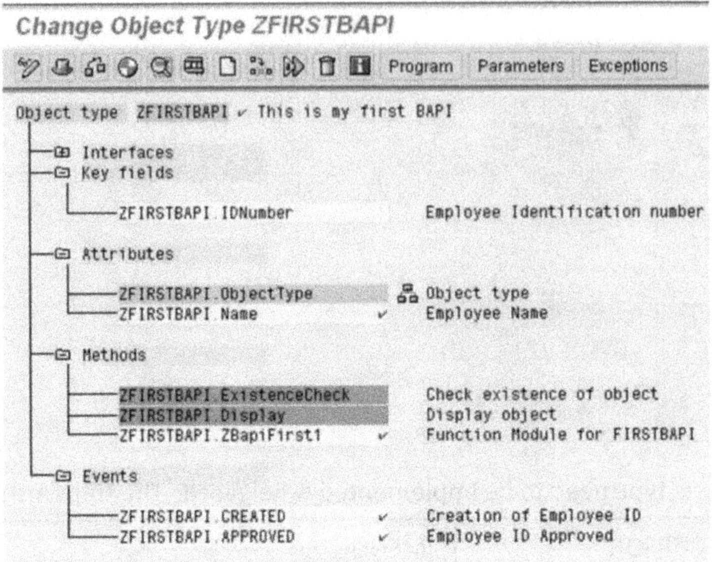

Step-16

Finally, ensure that the BAPI (ZBAPIFIRST) which we have created is available in the Business Object Repository (BOR).

Run the T/Code: BAPI

And, look at the BAPI Explorer:

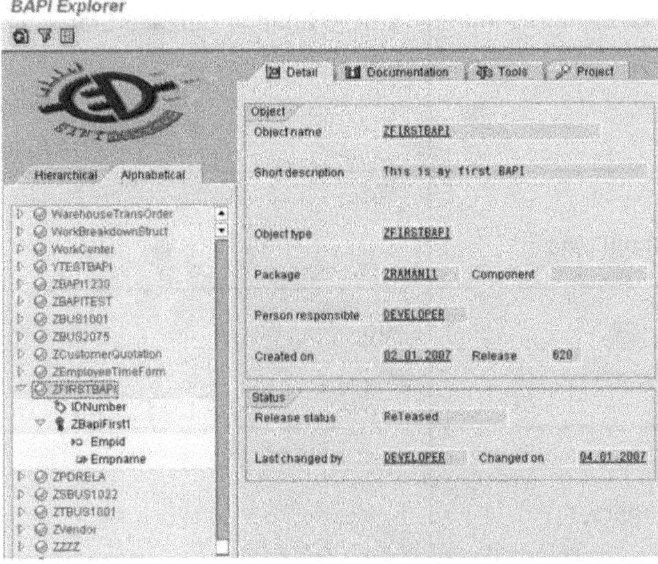

5.42 Frequently used BAPIs

⇒ **Sales and Distribution**

- Customer Material Info - BAPI_CUSTMATINFO_GETDETAILM
- Sales order - BAPI_SALESORDER_GETLIST
- Sales order - BAPI_SALESORDER_GETSTATUS

⇒ **Material Management**

- Purchase Req Item - BAPI_REQUIREMENT_GET_LIST
- Purchase order - BAPI_PO_GETDETAIL
- Purchase order - BAPI_PO_GETITEMS
- Purchase order - BAPI_PO_GETITEMSREL
- Purchase order - BAPI_PO_GET_LIST
- Purchasing info - BAPI_INFORECORD_GETLIST

⇒ **Production and Planning**

- Planned order - BAPI_PLANNEDORDER_GET_DETAIL
- Planned order - BAPI_PLANNEDORDER_GET_DET_LIST
- Planned Indep Reqmt - BAPI_REQUIREMENTS_GETDETAIL

⇒ **Finance**

- AP Account - BAPI_AP_ACC_GETOPENITEMS
- AP Account - BAPI_AP_ACC_GETOPENITEMS
- Debtor Credit Account - BAPI_CR_ACC_GETDETAIL
- AR Account - BAPI_AR_ACC_GETOPENITEMS
- AR Account - BAPI_AR_ACC_GETPERIODBALANCES
- AR Account - BAPI_AR_ACC_GETSTATEMENT

⇒ **Some Standard BAPI'S**

» **GetList**

Delivers a list of key fields objects that satisfies certain selection Criteria

» **GetDetail**

Delivers detailed information of an object, whose complete key has been Specified

» **CreateFromData**

Generates new objects in R3 from key fields and returns information.

The code to illustrate the steps involved when the BAPI ActiveX Control is used to access BAPIs.

- **Creating a BAPI ActiveX Control object**

Set oBAPICtrl = CreateObject("SAP.BAPI.1")

- **Creating a logon control object:**

Set oLogonCtrl = CreateObject("SAP.Logoncontrol.1")

- **Creating a connection object to the R/3 System:**

```
Set oBAPICtrl.Connection = oLogonCtrl.NewConnection
```

- **Logging on to R/3 System by calling the logon method of the connection object:**

```
If oBAPICtrl.Connection.Logon(frmStart.hwnd,FALSE) = FALSE then
  MsgBox"R/3 Connection failed"
  End
Endif
```

5.43 Definitions

⇒ **BOR Definition**

All SAP Business Object types and SAP Interface Types and their methods are defined and described in the R/3 Business Object Repository (BOR). The Business Object Repository was introduced in R/3 Release 3.0, at the same as time as SAP Business Objects and SAP Business Workflow. Presently, the BOR is mainly used by SAP Business Workflow.

The BOR has two essential functions:

» It defines and describes SAP Business Objects and SAP Interface Types and their BAPIs.

» It creates instances of SAP Business Objects

⇒ **BAPI programming**

BAPIs are defined in the Business Object Repository (BOR) as methods of SAP Business Objects or SAP Interface Types and are implemented as function modules. The separation of a BAPI definition from its actual implementation enables you to access a BAPI in two ways:

» You can call the BAPI in the BOR through object-oriented method calls

» You can make RFC calls to the function module on which the BAPI is based

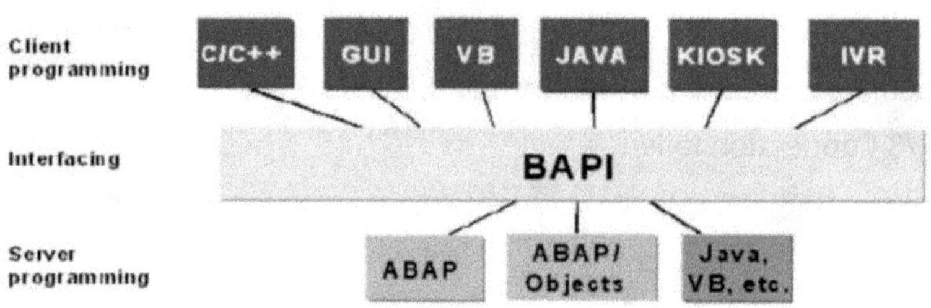

- BAPIs are language-independent interfaces.
- Basic software technology can be changed without having to reprogram applications.

5.44 List of BAPIs in SAP

LIST OF BAPIS IN QM MODULE

BAPI_INSPCHAR_GETREQUIREMENTS	Load Inspection Specifications for an Inspection Lot Charac.
BAPI_INSPCHAR_GETRESULT	Load Inspection Results
BAPI_INSPCHAR_SETRESULT	Confirm Inspection Results
BAPI_INSPLOT_GETDETAIL	Load Detail Data and Usage Decision for Inspection Lot
BAPI_INSPLOT_GETLIST	Select Inspection Lots
BAPI_INSPLOT_GETOPERATIONS	Select Inspection Operations for Inspection Lots
BAPI_INSPLOT_GETSTATUS	Get Current Status Information for Inspection Lot
BAPI_INSPLOT_SETUSAGEDECISION	Automatic Usage Decision
BAPI_INSPOPER_GETCHAR	Select Inspection Characteristics
BAPI_INSPOPER_GETLIST	Select Inspection Operations for Inspection Lots
BAPI_INSPPOINT_CHANGE	Change Inspection Point
BAPI_INSPPOINT_CREATEFROMDATA	Create Inspection Point
BAPI_INSPPOINT_GETLIST	Select Inspection Points
BAPI_INSPPOINT_GETREQUIREMENTS	Load Inspection Specifications and Inspection Points

BAPI_INSPPOINT_GETREQUIREMENTS	Load Inspection Specifications and Inspection Points
2078	BAPIs for quality notifications
BAPI_QNOTIFICAT_CREATE	Create Quality Notification
BAPI_QNOTIFICAT_GETCATALPROFIL	Determine Catalog Profile for Quality Notification
BAPI_QNOTIFICAT_GETKEYFIGURES	Determines Existing Quality Notifications
BAPI_QNOTIFICAT_GETLISTFORCUST	Select Quality Notifications for a Customer
BAPI_QNOTIFICAT_GETMATLISTFCUS	Select a Customer Material List for Quality Notifications

CTBP	BAPIs for Characteristics
BAPI_CHARACT_CHANGE	BAPI for Characteristics - Change
BAPI_CHARACT_CREATE	BAPI for Characteristics - Create
BAPI_CHARACT_DELETE	BAPI for Characteristics - Delete
BAPI_CHARACT_EXISTENCECHECK	BAPI for Characteristics - Check Existence
BAPI_CHARACT_GETDETAIL	BAPI for Characteristics - Read Attributes

QAALE	Distribution of QM Setup Data
BAPI_MATINSPCTRL_REPLICATE	Prepare Inspection Setup (Inspection Types) for Distribution
BAPI_MATINSPCTRL_SAVEREPLICA	Replication of QM Inspection Setup

QC08	BAPIs for Q-certificates on the Web
BAPI_CUSTOMER_GETSALESAREAS	Create List of Sales Areas for the Customer
BAPI_CUST_SAREAS_MATERIALS_GET	Create List of Materials for the Sales Areas of a Custome

QIST	QM Statistical Interface (QM-STI)
BAPI_INSPLOT_STATINTERFACE	QM STI Interface

LIST OF BAPIS IN PM MODULE

IWWW	BAPIs for Eqpt. + Service Notifications
BAPI_EQMT_CREATE	Create equipment
BAPI_EQMT_DETAIL	Read details for equipment
BAPI_EQMT_DISMANTLEFL	Dismantle equipment at functional location
BAPI_EQMT_DISMANTLEHR	Dismantle equipment from equipment hierarchy
BAPI_EQMT_GETCATALOGPROFIL	Determine catalog profile for equipment
BAPI_EQMT_GETLISTFORCUSTOMER	Select customer equipment
BAPI_EQMT_INSTALLFL	Install equipment at functional location
BAPI_EQMT_INSTALLHR	Install equipment in equipment hierarchy
BAPI_EQMT_MODIFY	Change equipment
BAPI_SERVICENOTIFICAT_CREATE	Create service notification
BAPI_SERVICENOTIFICAT_GETLIST	Select service notifications according to customer or contact person
J1BU	General Utilities
BAPI_BRANCH_GETDETAIL	Read Branch Data - for HR Use Only
BAPI_BRANCH_GETLIST	Read Branch List - for HR Use Only

LIST OF BAPIS IN FICO MODULE

	1	Express Delivery Company Interface
BAPI_CHARACT_GETLIST		BAPI for Characteristics - Find Name
	2	Company Code Business Object
BAPI_CCODE_GET_FIRSTDAY_PERIOD		For Company Code: First Day of Period
BAPI_CCODE_GET_LASTDAY_FYEAR		For Company Code: Last Day of Fiscal Year
BAPI_COMPANYCODE_EXISTENCECHK		Check if Company Code Exists
BAPI_COMPANYCODE_GETDETAIL		Company Code Details
BAPI_COMPANYCODE_GETLIST		List of Company Codes
BAPI_COMPANYCODE_GET_PERIOD		For Company Code: Posting Date -> Period, Fiscal Year

3	Business Area Business Object
BAPI_BUSINESSAREA_EXISTENCECHK	Check if business area exists
BAPI_BUSINESSAREA_GETDETAIL	Business area details
BAPI_BUSINESSAREA_GETLIST	List of business areas
4	Business Object Controlling Area
BAPI_CONTROLLINGAREA_GETDETAIL	List Detail Information for Controlling Area
|	
0004CORE	Business Object: Controlling Area (Core)
BAPI_COAREA_GETPERIODLIMITS	Controlling Area: First and Last Day of a Period
BAPI_COAREA_GET_RELATED_CCODES	Determine Company Codes Assigned to one Controlling Area
BAPI_CONTROLLINGAREA_FIND	Derive Controlling Area from Company Code
BAPI_CONTROLLINGAREA_GETLIST	Output List of Controlling Areas
BAPI_CONTROLLINGAREA_GETPERIOD	For Controlling Area: Posting Date -> Period, Fiscal Year
12	Business Object BUS0012 (Cost Center)
BAPI_COSTCENTER_CREATEMULTIPLE	Create One or More Cost Centers
BAPI_COSTCENTER_GETDETAIL	Detailed Information About Cost Center For Key Date
BAPI_COSTCENTER_GETDETAIL1	Detail Information for Cost Center on Key Date (1)
BAPI_COSTCENTER_GETLIST	List of Cost Centers Using Selection Criteria
BAPI_COSTCENTER_GETLIST1	List of Cost Centers for Selection Criteria (1)
BAPI_CTR_GETACTALLOCATIONTYPES	Checks Which IST-ILV Types are Possible According to Activity Type Cat
BAPI_CTR_GETACTIVITYPRICES	Read prices for cost center/activity type according to selection
BAPI_CTR_GETACTIVITYQUANTITIES	Rad plan activity/capacity/scheduled activity for cost center/acty typ
BAPI_CTR_GETACTIVITYTYPES	List of cost centers / activity types with control information
14	Company Business Object
BAPI_COMPANY_EXISTENCECHECK	Check if company exists
BAPI_COMPANY_GETDETAIL	Company details
BAPI_COMPANY_GETLIST	List of companies
15	Profit Center BAPI

BAPI_PROFITCENTER_CHANGE	Change Profit Center
BAPI_PROFITCENTER_CREATE	Create Profit Center
BAPI_PROFITCENTER_GETDETAIL	Display Profit Center Master Data
BAPI_PROFITCENTER_GETLIST	Display List of Profit Centers
23	Functional Area Business Object
BAPI_FUNC_AREA_EXISTENCECHECK	Check if functional area exists
BAPI_FUNC_AREA_GETDETAIL	Functional area details
BAPI_FUNC_AREA_GETLIST	List of functional areas
1021	Spec.Purpose Ledger BUS1021
BAPI_SL_GETTOTALRECORDS	Special Purpose Ledger: Select totals records for accounts
1022	BAPIs for BUS1022 (Fixed asset)
BAPI_FIXEDASSET_CHANGE	Changes an Asset
BAPI_FIXEDASSET_CREATE	Creates an Asset
BAPI_FIXEDASSET_CREATE1	Creates an Asset
BAPI_FIXEDASSET_GETDETAIL	Display Detailed Information on a Fixed Asset
BAPI_FIXEDASSET_GETLIST	Information on Selected Assets
BAPI_FIXEDASSET_OVRTAKE_CREATE	BAPI for Legacy Data Transfer

1021	Spec.Purpose Ledger BUS1021
BAPI_SL_GETTOTALRECORDS	Special Purpose Ledger: Select totals records for accounts
1022	BAPIs for BUS1022 (Fixed asset)
BAPI_FIXEDASSET_CHANGE	Changes an Asset
BAPI_FIXEDASSET_CREATE	Creates an Asset
BAPI_FIXEDASSET_CREATE1	Creates an Asset
BAPI_FIXEDASSET_GETDETAIL	Display Detailed Information on a Fixed Asset

BAPI_PROFITCENTER_CHANGE	Change Profit Center
BAPI_PROFITCENTER_CREATE	Create Profit Center
BAPI_PROFITCENTER_GETDETAIL	Display Profit Center Master Data
BAPI_PROFITCENTER_GETLIST	Display List of Profit Centers
23	Functional Area Business Object
BAPI_FUNC_AREA_EXISTENCECHECK	Check if functional area exists
BAPI_FUNC_AREA_GETDETAIL	Functional area details
BAPI_FUNC_AREA_GETLIST	List of functional areas

PBNK_NL	Business Object BankDetail (NL)
BAPI_BANKDETAILCREATESUCCESSNL	Create subsequent bank details record
BAPI_BANKDETAILGETDETAILEDLINL	Read instances with data
BAPI_BANKDETAILNL_APPROVE	Unlock bank details
BAPI_BANKDETAILNL_CHANGE	Change Bank Details
BAPI_BANKDETAILNL_CREATE	Create Bank Details
BAPI_BANKDETAILNL_DELETE	Delete Bank Details
BAPI_BANKDETAILNL_GETDETAIL	Read bank details
BAPI_BANKDETAILNL_GETLIST	Read Instances
BAPI_BANKDETAILNL_REQUEST	Create locked bank details record
PDATAR	Business object date type
BAPI_DATESPECS_GETDETAILEDLIST	Read instances with data

RWCL	Interface to Accounting
BAPI_ACC_DOCUMENT_DISPLAY	Accounting: Display Method for Follow-On Document Display
BAPI_ACC_DOCUMENT_RECORD	Accounting: Follow-on Document Numbers for Source Document

SZAK	BAPIs for BOR object BUS4001 (AddrOrg)
BAPI_ADDRESSORG_CHANGE	BAPI to change organization addresses
BAPI_ADDRESSORG_GETDETAIL	BAPI to read organization addresses
BAPI_ADDRESSORG_SAVEREPLICA	BAPI for inbound distribution of organizational addresses

BAPI_FIXEDASSET_GETLIST	Information on Selected Assets
BAPI_FIXEDASSET_OVRTAKE_CREATE	BAPI for Legacy Data Transfer
1024	Business Object ConsUnit
BAPI_CONSUNIT_GETCURRENCY	Procure Reporting Currency
BAPI_CONSUNIT_GETLIST	Display Consolidation Units
1025	Business Object ConsChartOfAccts
BAPI_CONSCHARTOFACCTS_GETITEMS	Display Financial Statement Items
BAPI_CONSCHARTOFACCTS_GETLIST	Display Consolidation Charts of Accounts
1026	Business Object ConsLedger
BAPI_CONSLEDGER_GETEQUITY	Display Changes in Investee Equity
BAPI_CONSLEDGER_GETINVESTMENT	Display Changes in Investments
BAPI_CONSLEDGER_GETTOTALS	Display Totals Records
1027	Business Object ConsGroup
BAPI_CONSGROUP_GETCONSUNITS	BAPI - Consolidation Group - Get Consolidation Units
BAPI_CONSGROUP_GETLIST	Display Consolidation Groups
1028	Business Object General Ledger
BAPI_GLX_GETDOCITEMS	Line item of document for ledger with summary table GLFLEXT
BAPI_GL_GETGLACCBALANCE	Closing balance of G/L account for chosen year
BAPI_GL_GETGLACCCURRENTBALANCE	Closing balance of G/L account for current year
BAPI_GL_GETGLACCPERIODBALANCES	Posting period balances for each G/L account
1030	Business Object BUS1030 (Cost Element)
BAPI_COSTELEM_CREATEMULTIPLE	Create One or More Cost Elements
BAPI_COSTELEM_GETDETAIL	Detail Information for Cost Element on Key Date
BAPI_COSTELEM_GETLIST	List of Cost Elements for Selection Criteria

1031	Business Object BUS1031 (Activity Type)
BAPI_ACTIVITYTYPE_GETDETAIL	Detail Information for Activity Type on Key Date
BAPI_ACTIVITYTYPE_GETLIST	List of Activity Types Using Selection Criteria
BAPI_ACTIVITYTYPE_GETPRICES	Output Activity Prices for Activity Types on Key Date
BAPI_ACTTYPE_CREATEMULTIPLE	Create One or More Activity Types
1057	Business Object Investment Program
BAPI_INVPROGRAM_CHECKEXISTENCE	Check Existence (of Sub-Tree) of Program
BAPI_INVPROGRAM_GET_LEAVES	Output End Nodes of an Investment Program
BAPI_INVPROGRAM_GET_REQUESTS	Output Appropriation Requests and End Nodes of an Investment Progra
BAPI_INVPROGRAM_SAVE_ENTITIES	Save Assigned Entities in Summarization Database
BAPI_INVPROGRAM_SAVE_VALUES	Save Summarized Values in Summarization Database
BAPI_INVPROGRAM_SELRE_ENTITIES	Select Assigned Entities and Replicate Them in Summarization DB
BAPI_INVPROGRAM_SELRE_VALUES	Select Values, Summarize Them and Replicate in Summarization DB
1079	BAPIs for General Cost Object/Cost Obj
BAPI_COSTOBJECT_GETDETAIL	Determine Details for a General Cost Object
BAPI_COSTOBJECT_GETLIST	Determine General Cost Objects for a Controlling Area
1120	Business Object ConsDimension
BAPI_CONSDIMENSION_GETLIST	Display Dimensions
1121	Business Object ConsSubitemCategory
BAPI_CONSSUBITEMCATEGORY_LIST	Display Subitem Categories
BAPI_CONSSUBITEMCATEGORY_SITEM	Display Subitems
1122	Business Object ConsDocumentType
BAPI_CONSDOCUMENTTYPE_GETADJ	Display Document Types for the Entry
BAPI_CONSDOCUMENTTYPE_GETLIST	Display Document Types

1137	Business Object 1137 BusProcStructureCO
BAPI_BUSPROCSTRUCTURECO_CREATE	BAPI for Creating Fixed Process Structures for Business Processes
1138	Business Object BUS1138 (Stat. Key Fig.)
BAPI_KEYFIGURE_CREATEMULTIPLE	Create One or More Statistical Key Figures
BAPI_KEYFIGURE_GETDETAIL	Detail Information for Statistical Key Figure on Key Date
BAPI_KEYFIGURE_GETLIST	List of Stat. Key Figures for Selection Criteria
1139	CO Resources: Business Object
BAPI_RESOURCECO_SAVE_REPLICA	Replicate individual CO resources (ALE)
1171	All Methods for PriceCatalog Object
BAPI_PRICECATALOGUE_EXISTCHECK	FM for ExistenceCheck method of BO PriceCatalogue
BAPI_PRICECATALOGUE_GETDETAIL	FM for GetDetail method of BO PriceCatalogue
BAPI_PRICECATALOGUE_SAVREPLICA	Store Price Catalog Instance
2027	Business Object 2027: Material Reval.
BAPI_M_REVAL_CREATEPRICECHANGE	BAPI: Material Revaluation - Generate Price Change
BAPI_M_REVAL_GETDETAIL	BAPI: Material Revaluation - Output Document
2044	BAPIs for Business Object Cost Estimate
BAPI_COSTESTIMATE_GETDETAIL	Determine detailed information for a cost estimate
BAPI_COSTESTIMATE_GETEXPLOSION	Determine BOM Explosion for a Cost Estimate
BAPI_COSTESTIMATE_GETLIST	Determine cost estimate lists
BAPI_COSTESTIMATE_ITEMIZATION	Determine itemization for a cost estimate
2073	BAPI profit center document
BAPI_PCA_BELEG_DELETE	Delete profit center documents (ALE)
BAPI_PCA_BELEG_REVERSE	Reversal of existing document line items (ALE)

BAPI_PCA_BELEG_SAVEREPLICA	Replicate PCA Line Items (ALE)
BAPI_PCA_PLANBELEG_SAVEREPLICA	Replicate EC-PCA Plan Line Items (ALE)
2075	FM for business object "Internal orders"
BAPI_INTERNALORDER_CREATE	Create Internal Order From Transferred Data
BAPI_INTERNALORDER_GETDETAIL	Display master data, status, and valid business trans. for internal or
BAPI_INTERNALORDER_GETLIST	Display list of internal orders according to various criteria
BAPI_INTERNALORDER_SAVEREPLICA	Replicate individual internal order (ALE)
2076	BAPIs for Cost Obj Hier/Cost Obj Node
BAPI_COSTOBJNODE_GETDETAIL	Determine Details for a Cost Object Node
BAPI_COSTOBJNODE_GETHIERARCHY	Determine Cost Object Hierarchy
BAPI_COSTOBJNODE_GETLIST	Determine Cost Object Nodes in a Controlling Area
2085	Allocation table: BAPIs
BAPI_MATALLOC_CONFIRMREQUEST	Report requested quantities for items and delivery phases (AllocTbl re
BAPI_MATALLOC_GETDETAILEDLIST	List of alloc tbls and items for a store
3006	Business Objekt General Ledger Account
BAPI_GL_ACC_EXISTENCECHECK	Check existence of G/L account
BAPI_GL_ACC_GETBALANCE	Closing balance of G/L account for chosen year
BAPI_GL_ACC_GETCURRENTBALANCE	Closing balance of G/L account for current year
BAPI_GL_ACC_GETLIST	List of G/L accounts for each company code
BAPI_GL_ACC_GETPERIODBALANCES	Posting period balances for each G/L account
3006_HRO	Business object G/L account
BAPI_GL_ACC_GETDETAIL	G/L account details
3033	Definition/Implementation BO BUS3033
BAPI_CUSTMATINFO_GETDETAILM	BAPI Public CustomerMaterialInfo getDetailMultiple()

BAPI_CUSTMATINFO_GETLIST	BAPI Public CustomerMaterialInfo getList()
4499	Business Object: Bank Statement
BAPI_ACCSTMT_CREATEFROMBALANCE	Store account balance/check debit information
BAPI_ACCSTMT_CREATEFROMLOCKBOX	Create lockbox data
BAPI_ACCSTMT_CREATEFROMPREVDAY	Create Bank Statement/Day-End Statement
BAPI_ACCSTMT_CREATEFROMSAMEDAY	Create Bank Statement/Today's Data
6003	Sales and distribution area
BAPI_SDAREA_EXIST	SD Area: Existence Check
BAPI_SDAREA_GET_LIST	SD Area: Possible Entries
6026	Costs and Activity Type Planning
BAPI_COSTACTPLN_CHECKACTINPUT	Activity Input Planning: Check
BAPI_COSTACTPLN_CHECKACTOUTPUT	Activity/Price Planning: Check
BAPI_COSTACTPLN_CHECKKEYFIGURE	Stat. Key Figure Planning: Check
BAPI_COSTACTPLN_CHECKPRIMCOST	Primary Cost Planning: Check
BAPI_COSTACTPLN_POSTACTINPUT	Activity Input Planning: Posting
BAPI_COSTACTPLN_POSTACTOUTPUT	Activity/Price Planning: Posting
BAPI_COSTACTPLN_POSTKEYFIGURE	Stat. Key Figure Planning: Postings
BAPI_COSTACTPLN_POSTPRIMCOST	Primary Cost Planning: Postings
6031	BusObj 6031: PlanDataTransferCO
BAPI_PDTRANSCO_CHECKACTINPUT	Plan data transfer: Check activity input
BAPI_PDTRANSCO_CHECKACTOUTPUT	Plan data transfer: Check activity planning
BAPI_PDTRANSCO_CHECKKEYFIGURE	Plan data transfer: Check stat. key figures
BAPI_PDTRANSCO_CHECKPRIMCOST	Plan Data Transfer: Check Primary Costs
BAPI_PDTRANSCO_GETSOURCEINFOS	Information About Settings for Plan Data Source
BAPI_PDTRANSCO_POSTACTINPUT	Planning Data Transfer: Post Activity Input
BAPI_PDTRANSCO_POSTACTOUTPUT	Planning Data Transfer: Post Activity Planning

BAPI_PDTRANSCO_POSTKEYFIGURE	Transfer of Planning Data: Post Stat. Key Figures
BAPI_PDTRANSCO_POSTPRIMCOST	Transfer of Planning Data: Post Primary Costs
ACC4	FI/CO: BAPIs for UPDATE
BAPI_ACC_BILLING_CHECK	Accounting: Check Billing Doc. (OAG: LOAD RECEIVABLE)
BAPI_ACC_BILLING_POST	Accounting: Post Billing Document (OAG: LOAD RECEIVABLE)
BAPI_ACC_GL_POSTING_CHECK	Accounting: General G/L Account Posting
BAPI_ACC_GL_POSTING_POST	Accounting: General G/L Account Posting
BAPI_ACC_GOODS_MOVEMENT_CHECK	Accounting: Check Goods Movement (OAG: POST JOURNAL)
BAPI_ACC_GOODS_MOVEMENT_POST	Accounting: Post Goods Movement (OAG: POST JOURNAL)
BAPI_ACC_INVOICE_RECEIPT_CHECK	Accounting: Check Invoice Receipt (OAG: LOAD PAYABLE)
BAPI_ACC_INVOICE_RECEIPT_POST	Accounting: Post Invoice Receipt (OAG: LOAD PAYABLE)
BAPI_ACC_PURCHASE_ORDER_CHECK	Accounting: Check Purchase Order
BAPI_ACC_PURCHASE_ORDER_POST	Accounting: Post Purchase Order
BAPI_ACC_PURCHASE_REQUI_CHECK	Accounting: Check Purchase Requisition
BAPI_ACC_PURCHASE_REQUI_POST	Accounting: Post Purchase Requisition
BAPI_ACC_SALES_ORDER_CHECK	Accounting: Check Sales Order
BAPI_ACC_SALES_ORDER_POST	Accounting: Post Sales Order
BAPI_ACC_SALES_QUOTA_CHECK	Accounting: Check Customer Quotation
BAPI_ACC_SALES_QUOTA_POST	Accounting: Post Customer Quotation
BAPI_ACC_TRAVEL_CHECK	Accounting: Check Trip
BAPI_ACC_TRAVEL_POST	Accounting: Post Trip
ACC5	FI/CO: BAPIs Asset Postings
BAPI_ACC_ASSET_ACQ_SETT_CHECK	ACC: Asset Acquisition - Synchronous Determination of Capitalization V
BAPI_ACC_ASSET_ACQ_SETT_POST	ACC: Asset Acquisition-Asynchronous Determination of Capitalization Va
BAPI_ACC_ASS_ACQUISITION_CHECK	Accounting: Post Asset Transfer
BAPI_ACC_ASS_INTRA_TRANS_CHECK	Accounting: Post Asset Transfer
BAPI_ACC_ASS_POSTCAP_CHECK	Accounting: Post Asset Transfer
BAPI_ACC_ASS_RETIREMENT_CHECK	Accounting: Post Asset Transfer

BAPI_ACC_ASS_TRANSFER_CHECK	Accounting: Post Asset Transfer
BAPI_ACC_ASS_TRANSFER_POST	Accounting: Post Asset Transfer
BAPI_ACC_ASS_TRANS_ACQ_CHECK	Accounting: Check Acquisition from Transfer
BAPI_ACC_ASS_TRANS_ACQ_POST	Accounting: Post Acquisition from Transfer
BAPI_ACC_ASS_TRANS_RET_CHECK	Accounting: Post Asset Transfer
BAPI_ACC_AUC_ACQUISITION_CHECK	Accounting: Asset Acquisition from Settlement
BAPI_ACC_AUC_ACQUISITION_POST	Accounting: Asset Acquisition from Settlement
AMFA	Fixed asset posting BAPIs
BAPI_ASSET_ACQUISITION_CHECK	Check asset acquisition
BAPI_ASSET_ACQUISITION_POST	Post asset acquisition
BAPI_ASSET_POSTCAP_CHECK	Check post-capitalization
BAPI_ASSET_POSTCAP_POST	Post post-capitalization
BAPI_ASSET_RETIREMENT_CHECK	Check asset retirement
BAPI_ASSET_RETIREMENT_POST	Post asset retirement
BUS1090	Business object currency
BAPI_CURRENCY_GETDECIMALS	Currency: Decimal places
BAPI_CURRENCY_GETLIST	Display All Currency Codes Existing in the SAP System
BUS1093	BAPIs to BO exchange rate
BAPI_EXCHANGERATE_CREATE	Insert an entry in table of exchange rates
BAPI_EXCHANGERATE_GETDETAIL	Exchange rate stored for exch.rate type, currency pair, value date
BAPI_EXCHANGERATE_GETFACTORS	Read exchange rate relationship for currency pair
BAPI_EXCHANGERATE_SAVEREPLICA	Replication of currency rates
BAPI_EXCHRATE_CREATEMULTIPLE	Insert one or more exchange rates in SAP tables
BAPI_EXCHRATE_GETCURRENTRATES	Output selected exchange rates and factors from the SAP system
BAPI_EXCHRATE_GETLISTRATETYPES	List of exchange rate types used for exchange rates
FTR_BUS2042	Financial Transaction: BUS2042

BAPI_FTR_CHANGE	Change Transaction
BAPI_FTR_COUNTERCONFIRM	Counterconfirm Transaction
BAPI_FTR_CREATEFROMDATA	Create Transaction
BAPI_FTR_GETDETAIL	Read Transaction Detailed Data
BAPI_FTR_GETLIST	Read Transaction List
BAPI_FTR_REVERSE	Reverse Transaction
BAPI_FTR_ROLLOVER	Roll Over Transaction
BAPI_FTR_SETTLE	Settle Transaction
BAPI_FTR_TERMINATE	Terminate Transaction
GLEX	Function modules for active EXCEL
BAPI_DUMMY	DUMMY
BAPI_F4_FORMOL	Selection of Line Layout Rules
BAPI_F4_RACCT	Selection of Item
BAPI_F4_RCOMP	Selection of Company
BAPI_F4_RMVCT	Selection of Transaction Type Group Texts
BAPI_F4_RSUBD	Selection of Subgroup
BAPI_F4_RVERS	Selection of Version
BAPI_GET_TABLE_HEADER	Get Column Headings for EXCEL_TAB* (Internal)
BAPI_READ_INDX_GESPOS	Read Gespos from INDX (internal)
BAPI_READ_INDX_GESVBUND	Read Imptab from INDX (internal)
BAPI_READ_INDX_IMPTAB	Read Imptab from MCDX (internal)
BAPI_READ_INDX_POSDATEN	Read Posdaten from INDX (internal)
BAPI_REP_GLI70	List of Companies
BAPI_SET_RACCT	Item Set acc. to Line Layout
BAPI_SET_RCOMP	Company Set acc. to Subgroup
BAPI_SET_RCOMP_SORT1	Company Set acc. to Sort Criterion 1
BAPI_SET_RCOMP_SORT2	Company Set acc. to Sort Criterion 2
BAPI_SET_RCOMP_SORT3	Company Set acc. to Sort Criterion 3
BAPI_SET_RMVCT	Transaction Type Groups-Set dissolved to TTy-Groups
BAPI_TAB_T880	General Company Data acc. to T880

BAPI_VALUE_GESPOS	L1P(L1) L2P(L2) G1P(L3) G2P(L4)	Company-FS Item Va
BAPI_VALUE_GESVBUND	L1B(L1) L2B(L2) G1B(L3) G2B(L4)	Company-Items-TTy-Va
BAPI_VALUE_IMPTAB	A2P(L2) A3P(L3)	Company Shares to FS I
BAPI_VALUE_IMPTAB_RMVCT	A2B(L2) A3B(L3)	Company Shares to
BAPI_VALUE_IMPTAB_RSUBD	K1B(L1) K2B(L2) K3B(L3)	Group-FS Items-TTy-Va
BAPI_VALUE_PIVOT	Group-Years-Company-FS Items-Values	
BAPI_VALUE_POSDATEN	K1P(LI) K2P(L2) K3P(L3)	Group FS Items Va
IF0002	Interface for Company Code BUS0002	
BAPI_IF_COMPANYCODE_GETDETAIL	Company code details	
ISBA	Solution Database BAPIs	
BAPI_SOLUTION_GETDETAIL	Get details about solution	
K40C	CO Actual Postings, Manual	
BAPI_ACC_ACTIVITY_ALLOC_CHECK	Accounting: Check Activity Allocation	
BAPI_ACC_ACTIVITY_ALLOC_POST	Accounting: Post Activity Allocation	
BAPI_ACC_ACT_POSTINGS_REVERSE	Accounting: Reverse CO Documents - Manual Actual Postings	
BAPI_ACC_MANUAL_ALLOC_CHECK	Accounting: Check Manual Cost Allocation	
BAPI_ACC_MANUAL_ALLOC_POST	Accounting: Post Manual Cost Allocation	
BAPI_ACC_PRIMARY_COSTS_CHECK	Accounting: Check Primary Costs	
BAPI_ACC_PRIMARY_COSTS_POST	Accounting: Post Primary Costs	
BAPI_ACC_REVENUES_CHECK	Accounting: Check Revenues	
BAPI_ACC_REVENUES_POST	Accounting: Post Revenues	
BAPI_ACC_SENDER_ACTIVITY_CHECK	Accounting: Check Sender Activities	
BAPI_ACC_SENDER_ACTIVITY_POST	Accounting: Post Sender Activities	
BAPI_ACC_STAT_KEY_FIG_CHECK	Accounting: Check Statistical Key Figures	
BAPI_ACC_STAT_KEY_FIG_POST	Accounting: Post Statistical Key Figures	
BAPI_CO_DOC_GET_ACT_POSTINGS	Read CO Documents: Manual Actual Postings	

KACG	Coding Block: FI/LO Part of KACB
BAPI_ACCSERV_CHECKACCASSIGNMT	BAPI: Object BUS6001 AccountingServices, Method CheckAccountAssignment
KEBAPI0017	BAPI CO-PA Operating Concern
BAPI_OPCONCERN_GETCHARACTS	BAPI CO-PA: Get Characteristics for Operating Concern
BAPI_OPCONCERN_GETDETAIL	BAPI Operating Concern GetDetail
BAPI_OPCONCERN_GETLIST	BAPI Operating Concern: Get All (F4)
BAPI_OPCONCERN_GETVALUEFIELDS	BAPI Operating Concern Value Fields
KEBAPI1161	BAPI CO-PA Characteristic
BAPI_COPACHARACT_GETDETAIL	BAPI CO-PA Characteristic GetDetail
BAPI_COPACHARACT_GETHIERARCH	BAPI CO-PA Characteristic: Get Hierarchies
BAPI_COPACHARACT_GETVALUES	BAPI CO-PA Characteristic: Get Master Data
KEBAPI1162	BAPI CO-PA User-Defined Characteristic
BAPI_COPACHARUDEF_ADDVALUES	BAPI CO-PA User-Defined Characteristic : Add Master Data
BAPI_COPACHARUDEF_REMOVEALLVAL	BAPI CO-PA User-Defined Characteristic: Delete All Master Data
BAPI_COPACHARUDEF_REMOVEVALUES	BAPI CO-PA User-Defined Characteristic: Delete Master Data
KEBAPI1164	BAPI CO-PA Hierarchy
BAPI_COPAHIERARCHY_GETDETAIL	Hierarchy GetDetail
BAPI_COPAHIERARCHY_GETTREE	Hierarchy GetValueTree
KE_BAPI_COPAPLANNING	BAPIs for CO-PA Planning Data
BAPI_COPAPLANNING_GETDATA	Read CO-PA Planning Data
BAPI_COPAPLANNING_POSTDATA	Write CO-PA Planning data
KE_BAPI_COPAQUERY	Modules for BOR Object COPAQuery
BAPI_COPAQUERY_GETACC_ACTDATA	BAPI COPAQuery.GetAccountBasedActualData

BAPI_COPAQUERY_GETACC_PLANDATA	BAPI COPAQuery.GetAccountBasedPlannningData
BAPI_COPAQUERY_GETCOST_ACTDATA	BAPI COPAQuery.GetCostingBasedActualData
BAPI_COPAQUERY_GETCOST_PLANDAT	BAPI COPAQuery.GetCostingBasedPlanningData
BAPI_OPCONCERN_GET_META_DATA	Do Not Use!
KGR2	External Access to CO Hierarchies
BAPI_ACTIVITYTYPEGRP_CREATE	Object BUS1115 (Activity type group) - Method Create
BAPI_ACTIVITYTYPEGRP_GETDETAIL	Object BUS1115 (Activity type group) - Method GetDetail
BAPI_ACTIVITYTYPEGRP_GETLIST	Object BUS1115 (Activity type group) - Method GetList
BAPI_BUSPROCESSCOGRP_ADDNODE	Object BUS1112 (Business process group) - Method AddNode
BAPI_BUSPROCESSCOGRP_CREATE	Object BUS1114 (Business process group) - Method Create
BAPI_BUSPROCESSCOGRP_GETDETAIL	Object BUS1114 (Business process group) - Method GetDetail
BAPI_BUSPROCESSCOGRP_GETLIST	Object BUS1114 (Business process group) - Method GetList
BAPI_COSTCENTERGROUP_ADDNODE	Object BUS1112 (Cost center group) - Method AddNode
BAPI_COSTCENTERGROUP_CREATE	Object BUS1112 (Cost center group) - Method Create
BAPI_COSTCENTERGROUP_GETDETAIL	Object BUS1112 (Cost center group) - Method GetDetail
BAPI_COSTCENTERGROUP_GETLIST	Object BUS1112 (Cost center group) - Method GetList
BAPI_COSTELEMENTGRP_CREATE	Object BUS1113 (Cost element group) - Method Create
BAPI_COSTELEMENTGRP_GETDETAIL	Object BUS1113 (Cost element group) - Method GetDetail
BAPI_COSTELEMENTGRP_GETLIST	Object BUS1113 (Cost element group) - Method GetList
KPLB	BAPIs: Plan data interface
BAPI_ACT_INPUT_CHECK_AND_POST	Activity Type Planning/Price Planning: Formal Parameter Check
BAPI_ACT_PRICE_CHECK_AND_POST	Activity Type Planning/Price Planning: Formal Parameter Check
BAPI_KEY_FIGURE_CHECK_AND_POST	Statistical Key Figures Planning: Formal Parameter Check
BAPI_PRIM_COST_CHECK_AND_POST	Primary Costs: Formal Parameter Check
KRHR	HR Interface to Bus. Place/Section Code
BAPI_BPLACE_GETDETAIL	Read Business Place Data - for HR Use Only
BAPI_BPLACE_GETLIST	Read Business Place List - for HR Use Only

BAPI_SECCODE_GETDETAIL	Read Section Code Data - for HR Use Only
BAPI_SECCODE_GETLIST	Read Section Code Place List - for HR Use Only
PBNK	Business Object BankDetail
BAPI_BANKDETAILCREATESUCCESSOR	Create subsequent bank details record
BAPI_BANKDETAILGETDETAILEDLIST	Read instances with data
BAPI_BANKDETAIL_APPROVE	Unlock bank details
BAPI_BANKDETAIL_CHANGE	Change bank details
BAPI_BANKDETAIL_CREATE	Create bank details
BAPI_BANKDETAIL_DELETE	Delete bank details
BAPI_BANKDETAIL_DELIMIT	Delimit bank details
BAPI_BANKDETAIL_GETDETAIL	Read bank details
BAPI_BANKDETAIL_GETLIST	Read instances
BAPI_BANKDETAIL_REQUEST	Create locked bank details record
PBNK_GB	Business Object BankDetail - GB
BAPI_BANKDETAILGBCREATESUCCESS	Create subsequent bank details record
BAPI_BANKDETAILGBGETDETAILLIST	Read instances with data
BAPI_BANKDETAILGB_APPROVE	Unlock bank details
BAPI_BANKDETAILGB_CHANGE	Change bank details
BAPI_BANKDETAILGB_CREATE	Create bank details
BAPI_BANKDETAILGB_DELETE	Delete bank details
BAPI_BANKDETAILGB_DELIMIT	Bankverbindung zeitlich abgrenzen
BAPI_BANKDETAILGB_GETDETAIL	Read bank details
BAPI_BANKDETAILGB_GETLIST	Read instances
BAPI_BANKDETAILGB_REQUEST	Create locked bank details record
PBNK_JP	Business Object BankDetail JP
BAPI_BANKDETAILJP_DETAILEDLIST	Bank Japan: Read instances with record
BAPI_BANKDETAILJP_GETDETAIL	Bank Japan: Read record

LIST OF BAPIS IN HR MODULE

7004	Display Payroll Results
BAPI_GET_PAYROLL_RESULT_LIST	Directory of payroll results for one personnel number
BAPI_GET_PAYSLIP	Selected remuneration statement for a personnel number
BAPI_GET_PAYSLIP_HTML	Payroll form for employees in HTML format
7023	Bapis for Business-Object BUS7023
BAPI_EXTPAYROLL_INSERT_LEGACY	Payroll Account Transfer
BAPI_EXTPAYROLL_INSERT_OUT	Payroll Result Update by a Third-Party Payroll Run
ABSE	Object Type "Absence"
BAPI_ABSENCE_APPROVE	Unlock absence
BAPI_ABSENCE_CHANGE	Change absence
BAPI_ABSENCE_CREATE	Create absence
BAPI_ABSENCE_DELETE	Delete absence
BAPI_ABSENCE_GETDETAIL	Read absence
BAPI_ABSENCE_GETDETAILEDLIST	Read instances with data
BAPI_ABSENCE_GETLIST	Read instances
BAPI_ABSENCE_REQUEST	Create locked absence
BAPI_ABSENCE_SIMULATECREATION	Simulation: Create absence

BAPI_ADDRESSPERS_GETDETAIL	BAPI to read person addresses
BAPI_ADDRESSPERS_SAVEREPLICA	BAPI for inbound distribution of private addresses
SZAM	BAPIs f. BOR obj. BUS4003 (AddrContPart)
BAPI_ADDRCONTPART_SAVEREPLICA	BAPI for inbound distribution of contact person addresses
BAPI_ADDRESSCONTPART_CHANGE	BAPI to change contact person addresses
BAPI_ADDRESSCONTPART_GETDETAIL	BAPI to read contact person addresses
TIQU	Time quota
BAPI_TIMEQUOTA_GETDETAILEDLIST	BAPI: Determines Quota Data for a Personnel Number
USR1	Business Object USR01DOHR
BAPI_USR01DOHR_GETEMPLOYEE	Determine employee from user name

BAPI_ACC_EMPLOYEE_EXP_CHECK	Accounting: Check G/L Acct Assignment for HR Posting (OAG: POS JOURNA
BAPI_ACC_EMPLOYEE_EXP_POST	Accounting: Post G/L Acct Assignment for HR Posting (OAG: POST JOURNAL
BAPI_ACC_EMPLOYEE_PAY_CHECK	Accounting: Check Vendor Acct Assignment for HR Posting (OAG:L PAYA
BAPI_ACC_EMPLOYEE_PAY_POST	Accounting: Post Vendor Acct Assignment for HR Posting (OAG: LC PAYA
BAPI_ACC_EMPLOYEE_REC_CHECK	Accounting: Check Cust. Acct Assignmt for HR Posting (OAG:LOAD RECEIVA
BAPI_ACC_EMPLOYEE_REC_POST	Accounting: Post Cust. Acct Assigt for HR Posting (OAG: LOAD RE
ACC7	CO: Check and Substitution for HR
BAPI_CODINGBLOCK_PRECHECK_HR	Check Module: CO Account Assignments in Personnel Settlement
BAPI_FIXACCOUNT_GETLIST	Read TKA30
ACC7CORE	CO: Check and Substitution for HR
BAPI_COST_ELEM_FIXACCOUNT_GET	Read Fixed Account Assignment for Company Code/Business Area Elem
BAPICATSRECORD	BAPIs for BUS TIMESHREC
BAPI_CATIMESHEETRECORD_GETLIST	Time Sheet: Data Record List
BAPIEMPLOYEECATS	BAPIs for BUS 7025
BAPI_EECATIMESHEET_GETWORKLIST	Time Sheet: Read Worklist
BAPIS1068	BAPIs for retail promotions
BAPI_PROMO_CHANGESITEPLANNING	Change of Quantities and Prices from Plants In a Promotion
BAPI_PROMO_CONFIRMREQUEST	Replies Containing Required Quantities of a Plant
BAPI_PROMO_CREATE	Create a Promotion
BAPI_PROMO_GETANNOUNCEDLIST	List of Promotions for a Plant
BAPI_PROMO_GETSITEPLANNING	Detailed Data for the Plants Involved in a Promotion
BAPI_PROMO_GETSITEPLANNING1	Detailed Data for the Plants Involved in a Promotion

BAPIS1073	BAPIs for Season Management
BAPI_PRICEMARKDOWNPLAN_CREATE	Create a markdown plan
BPAY	Basic pay object type
BAPI_BASICPAYEVALUATEWAGETYPES	Valuate Person-Specific Wage Types
BAPI_BASICPAY_APPROVE	Unlock basic pay
BAPI_BASICPAY_CHANGE	Change basic pay
BAPI_BASICPAY_CREATE	Create basic pay
BAPI_BASICPAY_CREATESUCCESSOR	Create subsequent basic pay record
BAPI_BASICPAY_DELETE	Delete Basic Pay
BAPI_BASICPAY_EVALUATEWAGETYPS	Create Basic Pay
BAPI_BASICPAY_GETDETAIL	Read basic pay
BAPI_BASICPAY_GETLIST	Read instances
BAPI_BASICPAY_REQUEST	Create locked basic pay record
BAPI_BASICPAY_SIMULATECREATION	Simulation: Create basic pay
BAPI_WAGETYPE_EMPLOYEEGETLIST	Read Wage Types
BAPI_WAGETYPE_GETLIST	Read Wage Types
BUBA	BAPIs for BOR Object BUS1006
BAPI_BP_REFERENCE_CREATE	Create BP/Logsys/GUID Reference Record in Target System
BAPI_BUSINESS_PARTNER_CHANGE	CBP: BAPI for Changing Business Partner
BAPI_BUSINESS_PARTNER_CREATE	CBP: BAPI for Creating Business Partner
BAPI_BUSINESS_PARTNER_MODIFY	CBP: BAPI for Modifying (Creating/Changing) Business Partner
BAPI_BUSINESS_PARTN_GET_DETAIL	CBP: Business Partner Detailed Information
HRBEN00BENADJREAS	Function group for object BENADJREAS
BAPI_BEN_BENADJREAS_CALC_ENDDA	Determination of the (new) end date of an existing adjustment reason
BAPI_BEN_BENADJREAS_DELIMIT	Delimitation of adjustment reason
BAPI_BEN_BENADJREAS_GET_LIST	Define adjustment reasons that are currently valid for an employee
HRBEN00BUS3029	Function Group for Business Object 3029

BAPI_BEN_BUS3029_CHECK_SELECT	Consistency Check
BAPI_BEN_BUS3029_CREATE_PLANS	Enroll employee
BAPI_BEN_BUS3029_DELETE_PLANS	Cancel EE enrollment
BAPI_BEN_BUS3029_GET_COREQ	Determine corequisite plans
BAPI_BEN_BUS3029_GET_EVT_LIST	Determine adjustment reasons that are currently valid for an employee
BAPI_BEN_BUS3029_GET_OFFER	Define benefits offer
BAPI_BEN_BUS3029_GET_OPEN_PERI	Check if open enrollment period exists and period is indicated
BAPI_BEN_BUS3029_GET_PARTICIP	Benefit participation of an employee
HRBEN00BUS302901	Function Group for Object BUS302901
BAPI_BEN_BUS302901_GET_DEP	Health plan dependents
BAPI_BEN_BUS302901_GET_POS_DEP	Possible health plan dependents
HRBEN00BUS302902	Function group for object BUS302902
BAPI_BEN_BUS302902_GET_BEN	Beneficiary for insurance
BAPI_BEN_BUS302902_GET_POS_BEN	Possible beneficiaries for insurance
HRBEN00BUS302903	Function group for object BUS302903
BAPI_BEN_BUS302903_GET_BEN	Beneficiaries for savings plan
BAPI_BEN_BUS302903_GET_INV	Investments for savings plan
BAPI_BEN_BUS302903_GET_POS_BEN	Possible beneficiaries for savings plans
BAPI_BEN_BUS302903_GET_POS_INV	Possible investments for savings plan
HRBEN00BUS302906	Function group for object BUS302906
BAPI_BEN_BUS302906_GET_BEN	Beneficiaries for miscellaneous plans
BAPI_BEN_BUS302906_GET_DEP	Health plan dependents
BAPI_BEN_BUS302906_GET_INV	Investments for miscellaneous plans
BAPI_BEN_BUS302906_GET_POS_BEN	Possible beneficiaries for misc. plans
BAPI_BEN_BUS302906_GET_POS_DEP	Possible dependents for miscellaneous plans
BAPI_BEN_BUS302906_GET_POS_INV	Possible investments for miscellaneous plans

HRBEN00BUS302907	Function group for object BUS302907
BAPI_BEN_BUS302907_GET_BEN	Beneficiaries for stock purchase plans
BAPI_BEN_BUS302907_GET_POS_BEN	Possible beneficiaries for stock purchase plans
HRBEN00GENBENINFO	Function group for object GENBENINFO
BAPI_BEN_GENBENINFO_GET_OPENP	Check if open enrollment period exists and period is indicated
HRIL	Incentive Wages: Integration w/Logistics
BAPI_CONFIRMATION_INPUT	BAPI: Transfer confirmations to Time Management/Incentive Wages
HROUT00BP	HR: Payroll Outsourcing BAPI's
BAPI_OUTEMPLOYEE_GETLIST	List of employees in a payroll area
HRPT	Transfer to accounting: 'Translate'
BAPI_PAYACCDOC_DISPLAY_AWKEY	Display posting document (from AC)
HRRW	HR-CA: Posting and CHECK BAPIs
BAPI_TRVACCDOC_DISPLAY_AWKEY	Display Trip Source Document (From RW)
HRTIM00ABSATTEXT	External interface for 2001/2002
BAPI_PTMGREXTATTABS_CHECK	BAPI: Checks External Attendance/Absence (w/o Account Assignment)
BAPI_PTMGREXTATTABS_CHECKCOLLI	Collision check
BAPI_PTMGREXTATTABS_CHECKQUOTA	Simulates Quota Deduction
BAPI_PTMGREXTATTABS_CHECKWACT	BAPI: Checks Attendance/Absence (with Activity Allocation)
BAPI_PTMGREXTATTABS_CHECKWCOST	BAPI: Checks Attendance/Absence (with Cost Assignment)
BAPI_PTMGREXTATTABS_INSERT	BAPI: Inserts External Abs./Atts. in Interface Table (w/o Acct Assignm
BAPI_PTMGREXTATTABS_INSERTWACT	BAPI: Inserts External Abs./Atts. in Interface Table (Activity Allocat
BAPI_PTMGREXTATTABS_INSWCOST	BAPI Ext. Att./Absence: Insert in IFT (Acct Assgnmnt)
HRTIM00ALP	Different Payment

BAPI_EETIMEVALSPEC_CHECK	BAPI: Checks Different Payment
BAPI_EETIMEVALSPEC_CHECKBONUS	BAPI: Checks Bonus
BAPI_EETIMEVALSPEC_CHECKCURR	BAPI: Checks Currency
BAPI_EETIMEVALSPEC_CHECKGRLEV	BAPI: Checks Payscale Group/Level
BAPI_EETIMEVALSPEC_CHECKPOS	BAPI: Checks Item
BAPI_EETIMEVALSPEC_GETCURR	BAPI: Determines Currency
BAPI_EETIMEVALSPEC_GETVALGRLEV	BAPI: Checks Payscale Group/Level
HRTIM00BAPIABSATT	BAPIs attendances/absences
BAPI_EMPATTABS_GETDETAIL	BAPI: Orginal and Derived Data from Attendances/Absences
BAPI_EMPATTABS_GETLIST	BAPI: List of Attendances/Absences for Online Interface
BAPI_PTMGRATTABS_MNGCHANGE	Change Attendances/Absences
BAPI_PTMGRATTABS_MNGCREATION	BAPI: Creates Attendances/Absences
BAPI_PTMGRATTABS_MNGDELETE	Delete Attendances/Absences
BAPI_PTMGRATTABS_MNGFROMWF	Create/Change/Delete Attendances/Absences from Workflow
HRTIM00BAPIPTWS	HR-TIM: Work Schedule, Time Data
BAPI_TIMEAVAILSCHEDULE_BUILD	Generate List of Employee Availability
HRTIM00BUS7013	BUS7013 PTimOverview
BAPI_PTIMEOVERVIEW_DELREPLICA	Delete employees' distributed time overviews
BAPI_PTIMEOVERVIEW_GET	BAPI 7013
BAPI_PTIMEOVERVIEW_REPLICATE	Trigger Distribution of Employee Time Overviews
BAPI_PTIMEOVERVIEW_SAVEREPLICA	Insert/Delete employee time overviews
HRTIM00REMINFO	Employee Remuneration Info
BAPI_PTMGREXTREMSPEC_CHECK	Check External Employee Remuneration Info (w/o Account Assignment)
BAPI_PTMGREXTREMSPEC_CHECKWACT	Check External Employee Remuneration Info (with Activity Allocation)
BAPI_PTMGREXTREMSPEC_CHECKWCOS	Check External Employee Remuneration Info (with Cost Assignment)
BAPI_PTMGREXTREMSPEC_INSERT	Inserts External EE Remuneraion Info in Table (w/o Account Assignmen

BAPI_PTMGREXTREMSPEC_INSWACT	Insert External EE Remuneration Info in Table (with Activity Allocatio
BAPI_PTMGREXTREMSPEC_INSWCOST	Inserts External EE Remuneration Info in Table (with Cost Assignment)
HRTL	HR TRV: FM Interfaces PAY
BAPI_PAYROLLTRAVELEXPNSESPOST	BAPI Transfer of trip costs results to payroll
HRTR	HR TRIP:Interface to Trip Costs
BAPI_TRIP_APPROVE	Approve trip
BAPI_TRIP_CANCEL	Cancel trip
BAPI_TRIP_CHANGE_STATUS	Change status of trip
BAPI_TRIP_CHECK_STATUS	Establish status of trip
BAPI_TRIP_COLLECT_MILEAGE	Determination of employee trip segments
BAPI_TRIP_CREATE_FROM_DATA	Create EmployeeTrip with CallTransaction on PR01
BAPI_TRIP_DELETE	Delete Trip
BAPI_TRIP_EXISTENCECHECK	ExistenceCheck object: EmployeeTrip (BAPI interface)
BAPI_TRIP_GET_DETAILS	Print detail tables for trip (receipt entry)
BAPI_TRIP_GET_FORM	Trip form as internal table / Display form
BAPI_TRIP_GET_FORM_HTML	Ouput of Travel Expense Form as HTML Table
BAPI_TRIP_GET_FORM_HTML_2	Ouput of Travel Expense Form as HTML Table
BAPI_TRIP_GET_OPTIONS	Import personal data and travel expense tables
BAPI_TRIP_REPORT_CREATE	Create simple weekly report (PR04)
BAPI_TRIP_REPORT_GET_DATA	Weekly report detail (Output of tables)
BAPI_TRIP_REPORT_INIT	Tables Needed for REPORT_CREATE (Local Workspace)
BAPI_TRIP_SET_ON_HOLD	Set trip status to "on hold"
HRW0	Internet Services (Who's Who)
BAPI_EMPLOYEE_GETLIST	Find Employees and Their Information on Basis of Search Criteria
PADR	Business object: AddressEmp
BAPI_ADDRESSEMPCREATESUCCESSOR	Create subs employee address record

BAPI_ADDRESSEMP_APPROVE	Unlock employee address
BAPI_ADDRESSEMP_CHANGE	Change Employee Address
BAPI_ADDRESSEMP_CREATE	Create Employee Address
BAPI_ADDRESSEMP_DELETE	Delete employee address
BAPI_ADDRESSEMP_DELIMIT	Delimit Employee Address Validity Period
BAPI_ADDRESSEMP_GETDETAIL	Read employee address
BAPI_ADDRESSEMP_GETLIST	Read Instances
BAPI_ADDRESSEMP_REQUEST	Create locked employee address record
PADR_CH	Business Object: AddressEmp
BAPI_ADDREMPCH_CREATESUCCESSOR	Create Subsequent Employee Address Record
BAPI_ADDREMPCH_GETDETAILEDLIST	Read Instances with Data
BAPI_ADDRESSEMPCH_CHANGE	Change Employee Address
BAPI_ADDRESSEMPCH_CREATE	Create Employee Address
BAPI_ADDRESSEMPCH_GETDETAIL	Read Employee Address
BAPI_ADDRESSEMPCH_REQUEST	Create Locked Employee Address Record
PADR_DE	Business Object AddressEmp (DE)
BAPI_ADDREMPDE_CREATESUCCESSOR	Create Next Employee Address Record
BAPI_ADDREMPDE_GETDETAILEDLIST	Read Instances with Data
BAPI_ADDRESSEMPDE_CHANGE	Change Employee Address
BAPI_ADDRESSEMPDE_CREATE	Create Employee Address
BAPI_ADDRESSEMPDE_GETDETAIL	Read Employee Address
BAPI_ADDRESSEMPDE_REQUEST	Create Locked Employee Address Record
PADR_DK	Business Object AddressEmp - DK
BAPI_ADDREMPDK_CREATESUCCESSOR	Create Subs Employee Address Record
BAPI_ADDREMPDK_GETDETAILEDLIST	Read Instances with Data
BAPI_ADDRESSEMPDK_CHANGE	Change Employee Address
BAPI_ADDRESSEMPDK_CREATE	Create Employee Address

BAPI_ADDRESSEMPDK_GETDETAIL	Read Employee Address
BAPI_ADDRESSEMPDK_REQUEST	Create Locked Employee Address Record
PADR_ES	Business Object AddrEmpE
BAPI_ADDREMPES_CREATESUCCESSOR	Create employee address next record
BAPI_ADDREMPES_GETDETAILEDLIST	Read instances with data
BAPI_ADDRESSEMPES_CHANGE	Change Employee Address
BAPI_ADDRESSEMPES_CREATE	Create Employee Address
BAPI_ADDRESSEMPES_GETDETAIL	Read employee address
BAPI_ADDRESSEMPES_REQUEST	Create locked employee address record
PADR_FR	
BAPI_ADDREMPFR_CREATESUCCESSOR	
BAPI_ADDREMPFR_GETDETAILEDLIST	
BAPI_ADDRESSEMPFR_CHANGE	
BAPI_ADDRESSEMPFR_CREATE	
BAPI_ADDRESSEMPFR_GETDETAIL	
BAPI_ADDRESSEMPFR_REQUEST	
PADR_IE	Business Object AddressEmp - Ireland
BAPI_ADDREMPIE_CREATESUCCESSOR	Create subs employee address record
BAPI_ADDREMPIE_GETDETAILEDLIST	Read instances with data
BAPI_ADDRESSEMPIE_CHANGE	Change Employee Address
BAPI_ADDRESSEMPIE_CREATE	Create Employee Address
BAPI_ADDRESSEMPIE_GETDETAIL	Read employee address
BAPI_ADDRESSEMPIE_REQUEST	Create locked employee address record
PADR_IT	HR Employee Self-Service: Address Italy
BAPI_ADDREMPIT_CREATESUCCESSOR	Create subsequent record personnel number
BAPI_ADDREMPIT_GETDETAILEDLIST	Read instances with data

BAPI_ADDRESSEMPIT_CREATE	Create employee's address
BAPI_ADDRESSEMPIT_GETDETAIL	Read employee's address
BAPI_ADDRESSEMPIT_REQUEST	Create blocked employee's address
PADR_JP	Business object: AddressEmpJP
BAPI_ADDRESSEMPJP_CHANGE	Address Japan: Change record
BAPI_ADDRESSEMPJP_CREATE	address Japan: Create record
BAPI_ADDRESSEMPJP_CRESUCCESSOR	Address Japan: Create succeeding record
BAPI_ADDRESSEMPJP_DETAILEDLIST	Address Japan: Read instances with record
BAPI_ADDRESSEMPJP_GETDETAIL	Address Japan: Read record
BAPI_ADDRESSEMPJP_REQUEST	Address Japan: Create locked record
BAPI_ADDRESSEMPJP_SIMUCREATION	Address Japan: Simulate Create record
PADR_NL	Business Object AddressEmp (NL)
BAPI_ADDREMPNL_CREATESUCCESSOR	Create subsequent employee address record
BAPI_ADDREMPNL_GETDETAILEDLIST	Read instances with data
BAPI_ADDRESSEMPNL_CHANGE	Change Employee Address
BAPI_ADDRESSEMPNL_CREATE	Create Employee Address
BAPI_ADDRESSEMPNL_GETDETAIL	Read employee address
BAPI_ADDRESSEMPNL_REQUEST	Create locked employee address record
PADR_US	Business Object AddressEmp (NL)
BAPI_ADDREMPUS_CREATESUCCESSOR	Create subs employee address record
BAPI_ADDREMPUS_GETDETAILEDLIST	Read instances with data
BAPI_ADDRESSEMPUS_CHANGE	Change Employee Address
BAPI_ADDRESSEMPUS_CREATE	Create Employee Address
BAPI_ADDRESSEMPUS_GETDETAIL	Read employee address
BAPI_ADDRESSEMPUS_REQUEST	Create locked employee address record
PAW4_US	Business Object W4W5InfoUS
BAPI_W4W5INFOUSGETDETAILEDLIST	Employee W4/W5 Information: Read Instances with Data
BAPI_W4W5INFOUS_APPROVE	Employee W4/W5 Information: Unlock Record

BAPI_W4W5INFOUS_CHANGE	Employee W4/W5 Information: Change Record
BAPI_W4W5INFOUS_CREATE	Employee W4/W5 Information: Create Record
BAPI_W4W5INFOUS_DELETE	Employee W4/W5 Information: Delete Record
BAPI_W4W5INFOUS_DELIMIT	Employee W4/W5 Information: Delimit Record
BAPI_W4W5INFOUS_GETDETAIL	Employee W4/W5 Information: Read Record
BAPI_W4W5INFOUS_GETLIST	Employee W4/W5 Information: Read Instances
BAPI_W4W5INFOUS_REQUEST	Employee W4/W5 Information: Create Locked Record
PERS	Business object: PersData
BAPI_PERSDATA_CHANGE	Change personal data
BAPI_PERSDATA_CREATE	Create personal data
BAPI_PERSDATA_CREATESUCCESSOR	Create subs.personal data record
BAPI_PERSDATA_DELETE	Delete personal data
BAPI_PERSDATA_DELIMIT	Delimit personal data validity period
BAPI_PERSDATA_GETDETAIL	Read personal data
BAPI_PERSDATA_GETDETAILEDLIST	Read instances with data
BAPI_PERSDATA_GETLIST	Read instances
BAPI_PERSDATA_SIMULATECREATION	Simulation: Create personal data
PERS_JP	Business object: PersDataJP
BAPI_PERSDATAJP_CHANGE	Personal data Japan: Change record
BAPI_PERSDATAJP_CREATE	Personal data Japan: Create record
BAPI_PERSDATAJP_CREATSUCCESSOR	Personal data Japan: Create succeeding record
BAPI_PERSDATAJP_GEDETAILEDLIST	Personal data Japan: Read instances with record
BAPI_PERSDATAJP_GETDETAIL	Personal data Japan: Read record
BAPI_PERSDATAJP_SIMULACREATION	Personal data Japan: Simulate Create record
PERS_NL	Business Object PersData (NL)
BAPI_PERSDANL_CREATESUCCESSOR	Create subs.personal data record
BAPI_PERSDANL_GETDETAILEDLIST	Read instances with data

BAPI_PERSDANL_SIMULATECREATION	Simulation: Create personal data
BAPI_PERSDATANL_CHANGE	Change Personal Data
BAPI_PERSDATANL_CREATE	Create Personal Data
BAPI_PERSDATANL_DELETE	Delete Personal Data
BAPI_PERSDATANL_GETDETAIL	Read Personal Data
BAPI_PERSDATANL_GETLIST	Read Instances
PFAM	Business Object Family
BAPI_FAMILY_APPROVE	Unlock family
BAPI_FAMILY_CHANGE	Change Family
BAPI_FAMILY_CREATE	Create Family
BAPI_FAMILY_CREATESUCCESSOR	Create subsequent family record
BAPI_FAMILY_DELETE	Delete Family
BAPI_FAMILY_DELIMIT	Delimit family validity period
BAPI_FAMILY_GETDETAIL	Read family
BAPI_FAMILY_GETDETAILEDLIST	Read instances with data
BAPI_FAMILY_GETLIST	Read Instances
BAPI_FAMILY_REQUEST	Create locked family record
BAPI_FAMILY_SIMULATECREATION	Simulation: Create family
PFAM_GB	Business Object Family - GB
BAPI_FAMILYGB_APPROVE	Unlock family
BAPI_FAMILYGB_CHANGE	Change family
BAPI_FAMILYGB_CREATE	Create family
BAPI_FAMILYGB_CREATESUCCESSOR	Create subsequent family record
BAPI_FAMILYGB_DELETE	Delete family
BAPI_FAMILYGB_DELIMIT	Delimit family
BAPI_FAMILYGB_GETDETAIL	Read family
BAPI_FAMILYGB_GETDETAILEDLIST	Read instances with data
BAPI_FAMILYGB_GETLIST	Read instances

BAPI_FAMILYGB_REQUEST	Create locked family record
BAPI_FAMILYGB_SIMULATECREATION	Simulation: Create family
PFAM_IE	Business Object Family - Ireland
BAPI_FAMILYIE_APPROVE	Unlock family
BAPI_FAMILYIE_CHANGE	Change family
BAPI_FAMILYIE_CREATE	Create family
BAPI_FAMILYIE_CREATESUCCESSOR	Create subsequent family record
BAPI_FAMILYIE_DELETE	Delete family
BAPI_FAMILYIE_DELIMIT	Delimit family
BAPI_FAMILYIE_GETDETAIL	Read family
BAPI_FAMILYIE_GETDETAILEDLIST	Read instances with data
BAPI_FAMILYIE_GETLIST	Read instances
BAPI_FAMILYIE_REQUEST	Create locked family record
BAPI_FAMILYIE_SIMULATECREATION	Simulation: Create family
PFAM_IT	IT family member Business object
BAPI_FAMILYIT_CHANGE	IT family member: change record
BAPI_FAMILYIT_CREATE	IT family members: create record
BAPI_FAMILYIT_CREATESUCCESSOR	IT family member: Create next record
BAPI_FAMILYIT_GETDETAIL	IT family member: detail
BAPI_FAMILYIT_GETDETAILEDLIST	IT family member: read instances with data
BAPI_FAMILYIT_REQUEST	IT family member: Create blocked record
BAPI_FAMILYIT_SIMULATECREATION	IT family member: Simulate creation
PFAM_JP	Business Object FamilyJP
BAPI_FAMILYJP_CHANGE	Family Japan: Change record
BAPI_FAMILYJP_CREATE	Family Japan: Create record
BAPI_FAMILYJP_CREATESUCCESSOR	Family Japan: Create succeeding record
BAPI_FAMILYJP_GETDETAIL	Family Japan: Read record

BAPI_FAMILYJP_GETDETAILEDLIST	Family Japan: Read instances with record
BAPI_FAMILYJP_REQUEST	Family Japan: Create locked record
BAPI_FAMILYJP_SIMULATECREATION	Family Japan: Simulate Create record
PFAM_NL	Business Object Family (NL)
BAPI_FAMILYNL_CHANGE	Change Family
BAPI_FAMILYNL_CREATE	Create Family
BAPI_FAMILYNL_CREATESUCCESSOR	Create subsequent family record
BAPI_FAMILYNL_GETDETAIL	Read family
BAPI_FAMILYNL_GETDETAILEDLIST	Read instances with data
BAPI_FAMILYNL_REQUEST	Create locked family record
BAPI_FAMILYNL_SIMULATECREATION	Simulation: Create family
PFAM_US	Business Object FamilyUS
BAPI_FAMILYUS_CHANGE	Family US: Change record
BAPI_FAMILYUS_CREATE	Family US: Create record
BAPI_FAMILYUS_CREATESUCCESSOR	Family US: Create subsequent family record
BAPI_FAMILYUS_GETDETAIL	Family US: Read Record
BAPI_FAMILYUS_GETDETAILEDLIST	Family US: Read instances with data
BAPI_FAMILYUS_REQUEST	Family US: Create locked record
BAPI_FAMILYUS_SIMULATECREATION	Family US: Simulate record creation
PFDC	Bus Object FISCDATACA : Fisc Data Canada
BAPI_FISCDATA_CA_GETDETAILLIST	Read the employee fiscal data - CANADA
RH65	HR-CA: Who is Who
BAPI_EMPLOYEE_GETDATA	Find Personnel Numbers for Specified Search Criteria
RHABAPI	HR-CA: Distribution Using BAPI
BAPI_HRMASTER_SAVE_REPL_MULT	BAPI for Replicating HR Master Data, HR Organizational Data

RHALMULT1	HR-CA: Distributed Org. Managemt (BAPIs)
BAPI_ORGMASTER_REPLICATE	HR-CA: Replication of HR Objects
BAPI_ORGMASTER_SAVE_ORIG_MULT	Save Replications of HR Organizational Objects as Originals
BAPI_ORGMASTER_SAVE_REPL_MULT	BAPI for Replication of HR Organizational Data
RHPE_JOBREQUIRE_BAPI	PA-PD: BAPI's for Requirements
BAPI_JOBREQUIRE_GETLIST	Read requirements profile
RHPE_JOBREQUIRE_PROF_BAPI	PA-PD: BAPIs for Requirements Profiles
BAPI_JOBREQUIREPROF_CHANGE	Create, Delete or Change Requirements Subprofile
RHPE_PDOTYPE_Q_BAPI	PA-PD: BAPI's for Qualification Type
BAPI_PDOTYPE_Q_GETDETAIL	Attributes of a qualification type
BAPI_PDOTYPE_Q_GETLIST	Read qualification types
RHPE_QUALIFIC_BAPI	PA-PD: BAPI's for Qualifications
BAPI_QUALIFIC_GETLIST	Read qualifications profile
RHPE_QUALI_DIR_BAPI	PA-PD: BAPIs for Qualifications Catalog
BAPI_QUALIDIRECTORY_LIST	Structure of qualifications catalog
BAPI_QUALIDIRECTORY_LIST_UP	Read qualification group for qualification
RHPE_QUALI_PROF_BAPI	PA-PD: BAPIs for Qualifications Profiles
BAPI_QUALIPROF_CHANGE	Create, delete, and change qualifications profile
RHVI	Training & Events: Internet, BAPI
BAPI_ATTENDEE_BOOK_LIST	Read Attendee Bookings
BAPI_ATTENDEE_CHANGEPASSWORD	Change attendee password
BAPI_ATTENDEE_CHECKEXISTENCE	Check existence of attendee
BAPI_ATTENDEE_CHECKPASSWORD	Check attendee password

BAPI_ATTENDEE_PREBOOK_LIST	Read attendee prebookings
BAPI_ATTENDEE_TYPE_LIST	Internet attendee types
BAPI_BOOK_ATTENDANCE	Book Attendance
BAPI_BUS_EVENTGROUP_LIST	Read Business Event Group Hierarchy
BAPI_BUS_EVENTTYPE_INFO	Read data for business event type
BAPI_BUS_EVENTTYPE_LIST	Read business event types in a business event group
BAPI_BUS_EVENT_INFO	Read Business Event Data
BAPI_BUS_EVENT_INIT	Read default values for creation of business event catalog
BAPI_BUS_EVENT_LANGUAGE	Business event languages
BAPI_BUS_EVENT_LIST	Read business event dates for event type
BAPI_BUS_EVENT_LOCATION	Business event locations
BAPI_BUS_EVENT_SCHEDULE	Read time schedule of a business event
BAPI_COMPANY_BOOK_LIST	Read all bookings of a group attendee
BAPI_COMPANY_PREBOOK_LIST	Read prebookings of a group attendee
BAPI_DELETE_ATTENDANCE	Cancel attendance
BAPI_GET_EVENTTYPE_FOR_QUALIF	Determine Business Event Types for Specified Qualifications
BAPI_GET_EVENTTYPE_FOR_TARGET	Determine Business Event Types via Target Group
BAPI_PREBOOK_ATTENDANCE	Prebook attendance
BAPI_SEARCH_EVENTTYPE_NAME	Find Business Event Types Using String in Object Text
BAPI_SEARCH_EVENTTYPE_TEXT	Find Business Event Types Using String in Object Description
BAPI_SUBTYPES_FOR_DESCRIPTION	Determine Subtypes of Description Infotype

RH_APPRAISAL_BAPI	PA-PD: BAPIs for Appraisals
BAPI_APPRAISAL_CHANGE	Change appraisals
BAPI_APPRAISAL_CREATE	Create appraisals
BAPI_APPRAISAL_DELETE	Delete appraisals
BAPI_APPRAISAL_GETDETAIL	Read appraisal
BAPI_APPRAISAL_GETLIST	Display appraisals
BAPI_APPRAISAL_STATUS_CHANGE	Change appraisal status

RH_APPRAISAL_MODEL_BAPI	PA-PD: BAPIs for Appraisal Models
BAPI_APPRAISAL_MODEL_GETDETAIL	Read appraisal model
BAPI_APPRAISAL_MODEL_GETLIST	Display Appraisal Model
BAPI_APPRAISAL_SCALE_GETDETAIL	Read proficiencies and texts for scale
BAPI_APPRAISEE_GETLIST	Read appraisees
BAPI_APPRAISER_GETLIST	Read appraisers
RH_ORGPUB_APP	OrgPublisher Integration/Application
BAPI_ORGUNITEXT_DATA_GET	Get data on organizational unit
RH_PDOTYPES	BAPI Function Modules
BAPI_PDOTYPES_GETDETAILEDLIST	Object List With Detailed Information
RPTC	HR-TIM: Connection to Time Rec. Systems
BAPI_CC1_DNLOAD_ATTABSREASON	HR-PDC: Download Attendance/Absence Reasons
BAPI_CC1_DNLOAD_BALANCES	HR-PDC: Download Employee Balances
BAPI_CC1_DNLOAD_COSTCENTER	HR-PDC: Download Cost Centers
BAPI_CC1_DNLOAD_EXTWAGETYPE	HR-PDC: Download Permitted Employee Expenditures
BAPI_CC1_DNLOAD_INTERNALORDER	HR-PDC: Download Internal Orders
BAPI_CC1_DNLOAD_MINIMASTER	HR-PDC: Download HR Mini-Master
BAPI_CC1_DNLOAD_OBJECTID	HRPDC: Download Objects (such as Positions)
BAPI_CC1_DNLOAD_TEVENTTGROUP	HR-PDC: Download Time Event Type Groupings
BAPI_CC1_DNLOAD_WBSELEMENT	HR-PDC: Download Work Breakdown Structure Element
BAPI_CC1_REQUEST_EXTWAGETYPE	HR-PDC: Upload Request for Employee Expenditures
BAPI_CC1_REQUEST_TIMEEVENT	HR-PDC: Upload Request for Time Events
BAPI_CC1_UPLOAD_EXTWAGETYPE	HR-PDC: Upload Employee Expenditures
BAPI_CC1_UPLOAD_TIMEEVENT	HR-PDC: Upload Time Events
SZAL	BAPIs for BOR object BUS4002 (AddrPers)

VBKA	Business Object IFVBKA Abstract Method
BAPI_SALESSUPDOCUMENT_ADD_ASGN	Abstract BAPI Sales Support Document Add to Assigned
BAPI_SALESSUPDOCUMENT_DELETE	Abstract BAPI Sales Support Document Delete
BAPI_SALESSUPDOCUMENT_GETLIST	Abstract BAPI Sales Support Document Get List
BAPI_SALESSUPDOCUMENT_REM_ASGN	Abstract BAPI Sales Support Document Remove from Assigned
BAPI_SALESSUPDOCUMENT_REPCH	Abstract BAPI Sales Support Document Replicate Changed Objects
BAPI_SALESSUPDOCUMENT_REPLIC	Abstract BAPI Sales Support Document Replicate Objects on Demand
BAPI_SALESSUPDOCUMENT_SAVE	Abstract BAPI Sales Support Document Save from Memory
BAPI_SALESSUPDOCUMENT_SETACT	Abstract BAPI Sales Support Document - Set simulated to active
VBRK	Methods for Object Type VBRK
BAPI_BILLINGDOC_CANCEL	Cancel Customer Individual Billing Document
BAPI_BILLINGDOC_CANCEL1	Cancel Customer Individual Billing Document
BAPI_BILLINGDOC_CONFIRM	Customer Individual Billing Document : Confirm Billing Document
BAPI_BILLINGDOC_CREATE	Custimer Individual Billing Document : Create Billing Document
BAPI_BILLINGDOC_CREATEFROMDATA	Create Customer Individual Billing Doc. Using Ext. Doc. from RH
BAPI_IBDLV_CREATE_FROM_OBDLV	BAPI Inbound Delivery from Outbound Delivery
BAPI_INB_DELIVERY_CONFIRM_DEC	BAPI for Inbound Delivery Confirmation from a Decentralized System
BAPI_INB_DELIVERY_SAVEREPLICA	BAPI Function Module for Replication of Inbound Deliveries
BAPI_OUTB_DELIVERY_CONFIRM_DEC	BAPI for Outbound Delivery Confirmation from a Decentralized System
BAPI_OUTB_DELIVERY_SAVEREPLICA	BAPI Function Module for Replication of Outbound Deliveries
V81ABAPI	SD Product Hierarchy: BAPI Impl.
BAPI_MATERIAL_GET_PRODUCTHIER	BAPI Material Get Product Hierarchy ()

V02D	Customer Master: Read/Block
BAPI_CUSTOMER_CHANGEFROMDATA	Customer: Change customer
BAPI_CUSTOMER_CHANGEFROMDATA1	Check personal data of a customer
BAPI_CUSTOMER_CREATEFROMDATA	Customer: Create customer
BAPI_CUSTOMER_CREATEFROMDATA1	BAPI Create customer for BO customer (KNA1) - with CAM features
BAPI_CUSTOMER_GETDETAIL	Customer: Read customer
BAPI_CUSTOMER_GETDETAIL1	BAPI Read customer to BO customer (KNA1) - with CAM features
BAPI_CUSTOMER_SEARCH	Customer: Find customer number
BAPI_CUSTOMER_SEARCH1	BAPI Search customer for BO customer (KNA1) - with CAM features
V02HBAPI	SD Customer Hierarchy: BAPI Implementn
BAPI_CUSTOMER_GET_CHILDREN	BAPI Customer Hierarchy GetChildren() Implementation
BAPI_CUSTOMER_GET_ROOT	BAPI Customer Hiearchy getRoot() Implementation
BAPI_CUSTOMER_GET_ROOT_LIST	BAPI Customer Hierarchy getRootList() Implementation
V10A	SD Customer-Material Info Record
BAPI_KTGRM_GETNAME	Existence Check and Text Determination for Account Assignment Group Ma
V46W	SD Functions: Incoming Orders WWW
BAPI_CUSTOMER_CHANGEPASSWORD	Change customer password
BAPI_CUSTOMER_CHECKEXISTENCE	Check valid customer number
BAPI_CUSTOMER_CHECKPASSWORD	Check customer password
BAPI_CUSTOMER_CREATEPWREG	Create entry for customer password
BAPI_CUSTOMER_DELETEPWREG	Delete entry for customer password
BAPI_CUSTOMER_GETPWREG	Read entry for customer password
BAPI_CUSTOMER_INITPASSWORD	Initialize customer password
V50I	Delivery BAPIs

BAPI_SALESORDER_PROXY_UPLOAD	Proxy BAPI for Request Upload in SFA Context: Create
IF1037SR	Partner sales activity - Receiver
BAPI_IFBUS1037SR_SAVEREPLICAM	BAPI Business Partner Sales Activity Receiver
LC01	Customer/Vendor Master: BAPIs
BAPI_BUSPARTNEREMPLOYE_GETLIST	Read contact persons and addresses (access via specified range)
BAPI_CUSTOMER_CHECKPASSWORD1	Check customer password
BAPI_CUSTOMER_CREATE	Create Customer Master Online
BAPI_CUSTOMER_DELETE	Delete Customer Master Online
BAPI_CUSTOMER_DISPLAY	Display Customer Master Online
BAPI_CUSTOMER_EDIT	Change Customer Master Online
BAPI_CUSTOMER_EXISTENCECHECK	Check Customer Existence
BAPI_CUSTOMER_FIND	Customer Matchcode
BAPI_CUSTOMER_GETCONTACTLIST	Read contact persons from customers
BAPI_CUSTOMER_GETDETAIL2	Customer Detail Information
BAPI_CUSTOMER_GETINTNUMBER	Provides internal customer numbers
BAPI_CUSTOMER_GETLIST	Reads customers and addresses
BAPI_PARTNEREMPLOYEE_CREATE	Create Contact Person Online
BAPI_PARTNEREMPLOYEE_DISPLAY	Display Contact Person Online
BAPI_PARTNEREMPLOYEE_EDIT	Display Contact Person Online
BAPI_PARTNEREMPLOYEE_GETINTNUM	Supplies new internal contact person numbers
TSPA	Division
BAPI_DIVISION_EXIST	Division: Existence Check
BAPI_DIVISION_GET_DETAIL	Division: Display Name
TVTW	Distribution channel
BAPI_DISTRIBCHANNEL_EXIST	Distribution Channel: Existence Check
BAPI_DISTRIBCHANNEL_GET_DETAIL	Distribution Channel: Display Name

BAPI_AR_ACC_GETKEYDATEBALANCE	Customer account balance at a key date
BAPI_AR_ACC_GETOPENITEMS	Customer account open items at a key date
BAPI_AR_ACC_GETPERIODBALANCES	Posting period totals per customer account in current fiscal year
BAPI_AR_ACC_GETSTATEMENT	Customer account statement for a given period
CPCM1	Mapping: Campaigns
BAPI_PCM_DELETE_MULTIPLE	Deleting Transferred Production Campaign
BAPI_PCM_SAVE_MULTIPLE	Storing Campaigns from APO
CRM3	SFA Interface Customers/Adresses
BAPI_CUSTOMERCRM_CHANGE	Proxy BAPI for Customer Upload in SFA Context: Customer Data Changes
BAPI_CUSTOMERCRM_CREATE	Proxy BAPI for Customer Upload in SFA Context (Create)
BAPI_CUSTOMERCRM_DELETE	Proxy BAPI to Delete Customers in SFA Context
CRM4	SFA Interface Contact Person
BAPI_CONTACTCRM_CHANGE	Proxy BAPI - Change Contact Person in SFA Context
BAPI_CONTACTCRM_CREATE	Proxy BAPI - Create Contact Person in SFA Context
BAPI_CONTACTCRM_DELETE	Proxy BAPI - Delete Contact Person in SFA Context
CRM8	SFA Interface Classification
BAPI_OBJCL_PROXY_CREATE	Proxy BAPI for Sales Order Upload in SFA Context: Create
CRMA	Sales Documents
BAPI_CREDITREQUES_PROXY_CREATE	Proxy BAPI for Credit Memo Upload in SFA Context: Create
BAPI_DEBITREQUEST_PROXY_CREATE	Proxy BAPI for Upload of Debit Memos in SFA Context: Create
BAPI_DELIVERYFREE_PROXY_CREATE	Proxy BAPI for Upload of Free Subsequent Delivery in SFA Context:
BAPI_INQUIRY_PROXY_CREATE	Proxy BAPI for Request Upload in SFA Context: Create
BAPI_QUOTATION_PROXY_CREATE	Proxy BAPI for Quotation Upload in SFA Context: Create
BAPI_RETURN_PROXY_CREATE	Proxy BAPI for Return Upload in SFA Context: Create

BAPI_PRODCAT_REPLICATEITEMS	Replicate Item Data of a Product Catalog (ALE Outbound)
BAPI_PRODCAT_SAVEHEADREPLICA	Replicate Basic and Structure Data of a Product Catalog (ALE Inbound)
BAPI_PRODCAT_SAVEITEMSREPLICA	Replicate Item Data of a Product Catalog (ALE Inbound)
2030	Business Object Inquiry
BAPI_CUSTOMERINQUIRY_CHANGE	Change Customer Inquiry
BAPI_INQUIRY_CREATEFROMDATA	Customer inquiry: Create customer inquiry
BAPI_INQUIRY_CREATEFROMDATA2	Customer Inquiry: Create Customer Inquiry
2031	Business Object Quotation
BAPI_CUSTOMERQUOTATION_CHANGE	Change Customer Quotation
BAPI_QUOTATION_CREATEFROMDATA	Customer quotation: Create customer quotation
BAPI_QUOTATION_CREATEFROMDATA2	Customer Quotation: Create Customer Quotation
2032	Business Object Sales Order
BAPI_SALESDOCU_CREATEFROMDATA	Creating a Sales Document
BAPI_SALESORDER_CHANGE	Sales Order: Change Sales Order
BAPI_SALESORDER_CREATEFROMDAT1	Sales Order: Create Sales Order
BAPI_SALESORDER_CREATEFROMDAT2	Sales Order: Create Sales Order
BAPI_SALESORDER_CREATEFROMDATA	Create sales order, no more maintenance
BAPI_SALESORDER_GETLIST	Sales order: List of all orders for customer
BAPI_SALESORDER_GETSTATUS	Sales order: Display status
BAPI_SALESORDER_SIMULATE	Sales Order: Simulate Sales Order
2034	Business Object Customer Contract
BAPI_CONTRACT_CREATEFROMDATA	Create Customer Contract
BAPI_CUSTOMERCONTRACT_CHANGE	Change Customer Contract
3007	Customer account business object

1037	Business object BUS1037
BAPI_BPCONTACT_ADD_TO_ASGN	BAPI Partner Sales Activity AddToAssigned
BAPI_BPCONTACT_CHANGE	BAPI Change Partner Sales Activity
BAPI_BPCONTACT_CREATEFROMDATA	BAPI Partner Sales Activity Create from Data
BAPI_BPCONTACT_CREATEWITHDIA	BAPI Partner Sales Activity - Create from Data Dialog
BAPI_BPCONTACT_DELETE	BAPI Delete Partner Sales Activity
BAPI_BPCONTACT_GETDETAIL	BAPI Partner Sales Activity - Get Details
BAPI_BPCONTACT_GETLIST	BAPI Partner Sales Activity - Get List
BAPI_BPCONTACT_REMOVEFROM_ASGN	BAPI Partner Sales Activity RemoveFromAssigned
BAPI_BPCONTACT_REPLICATE	BAPI Partner Sales Activity Replicate
BAPI_BPCONTACT_REPLICATECHANGE	BAPI Partner Sales Activity Replicate Changed Objects
BAPI_BPCONTACT_SAVEFROMMEMORY	BAPI Partner Sales Activity - Save from Memory
BAPI_BPCONTACT_SETTOACTIVE	BAPI Partner Sales Activity - Set simulated to active
1070	Business Object Assortment
BAPI_ASSORTMENT_MAINTAINDATA	Maintenance of Assortments
1071	Prod. cat. BAPIs
BAPI_ADV_MED_GET_ITEMS	Read Product Catalog Items
BAPI_ADV_MED_GET_LAYOBJ_DESCR	Read Long Text for Layout Area or Layout Area Item
BAPI_ADV_MED_GET_LAYOBJ_DOCS	Read Documents for a Layout Area or a Layout Area Item
BAPI_ADV_MED_GET_LAYOUT	Read Product Catalog Layout
BAPI_ADV_MED_GET_LIST	Read Product Catalog List
BAPI_ADV_MED_GET_PRICES	Read Product Catalog Item Prices
BAPI_ADV_MED_GET_SALES_AREA	Read Sales Area for a Product Catalog
BAPI_ADV_MED_GET_VARIANT_LIST	Read Product Catalog Variants
BAPI_PRODCAT_GETITEM	Read Individual Product Catalog Item
BAPI_PRODCAT_GETPRICES	Read Product Catalog Item Prices
BAPI_PRODCAT_GET_DETAIL	Read Header Data for a Product Catalog

LIST OF BAPIS IN HS & D MODULE

6	Sales organization
BAPI_SALESGROUP_GET_DETAIL	Sales Group: Display Name
BAPI_SALESOFFICE_GET_DETAIL	Sales Office: Display Name
BAPI_SALESOFFICE_GRP_EXIST	Sales Office / Sales Group: Existence Check
BAPI_SALESORG_EXIST	Sales Organization: Existence Check
BAPI_SALESORG_GET_DETAIL	Sales Organization: Display Data
BAPI_SALESORG_OFFICE_EXIST	Sales Organization / Sales Office: Existence Check
1007	Customer business object
BAPI_DEBTOR_CHANGEPASSWORD	Change Customer Password
BAPI_DEBTOR_CHECKPASSWORD	Check Customer Password
BAPI_DEBTOR_CREATE_PW_REG	Create Entry for Customer Password
BAPI_DEBTOR_DELETE_PW_REG	Delete Customer Password Entry
BAPI_DEBTOR_EXISTENCECHECK	Check Customer Existence
BAPI_DEBTOR_FIND	Customer Matchcode
BAPI_DEBTOR_GETDETAIL	Customer Detail Information
BAPI_DEBTOR_GET_PW_REG	Read Entry for Customer Password
BAPI_DEBTOR_INITPASSWORD	Initialize Customer Password
1010	Customer credit account business object
BAPI_CREDIT_ACCOUNT_GET_STATUS	Determine Credit Status of Credit Account
BAPI_CREDIT_ACCOUNT_REP_STATUS	Receive Credit Management Account Status and Send to Database
BAPI_CR_ACC_GETDETAIL	BAPI/BUS1010: Determine Master Record Data
BAPI_CR_ACC_GETHIGHESTDUNNINGL	BAPI/BUS1010: Determine Highest Dunning Level
BAPI_CR_ACC_GETOLDESTOPENITEM	BAPI/BUS1010: Determine Oldest Open Item
BAPI_CR_ACC_GETOPENITEMSSTRUCT	BAPI/BUS1010: Determine OI Structure

5.45. How to find BAPI for a transaction?

After knowing the Program name for the Transaction, search for the keyword **CL EX-ITHANDLER** in the main program of the transaction.

Go to transaction SE80 in a client where you can experiment with the transaction that you are interested in Go to class CL_EXITHANDLER. [**Select Class / Interface from the drop-down**; and put CL_EXITHANDLER for the class.]

Go to method get_instance. [Press RETURN to ensure that the contents of the Object Name frame are for CLEXITHANDLER. Expand the Methods node. Double-click on GETINSTANCE.]**Insert a breakpoint just after** = the call to the method cl_exit handler get_class_name_by_interface. **Use the transaction** in which you are BAPI-hunting.

Examine the contents of the field exit_name whenever the processing stops at the breakpoint.

After knowing the Application name for the Transaction, goto **TCode BAPI** to search for BAPI Function modules for it.

Goto the transaction and check the system->Status->Double Click on Transaction-> Double Click on Package-> Check out the app component (say SALES). Goto transaction Code **BAPI**, then check out sales and distribution->sales->sales order-> open any business method (Say, GetList OR GetStatus etc.) and there you can find the BAPI Function Module names and u can see them by Double Clicking on them

After knowing the Application name for the Transaction goto **TCode SE37** to search for BAPI Function modules for it.

Finding BAPIS for SD:

In SE37 in the Function Module name put *BAPI*SALES*-----> PRESS F4 or put "BAPI*. SALESORDER*-----> PRESS F4.

You will see a list of BAPIs for that particular Application.

Finding BAPIS for MM:

In SE37 in the Function Module name put *BAPI*GOODS*-----> PRESS F4 or put *BAPI*PURCHASE*-----> PRESS F4 or put *BAPI*VENDOR*-----> PRESS F4.

You will see a list of BAPIs for that particular Application.

Finding BAPIS for FI:

In SE37 in the Function Module name put *BAPI*ACC*----> PRESS F4.

You will see a list of BAPIs for that particular Application.

- Going to **SPRO**

5.46. BAPI Implementation Checklist

This checklist summarizes the individual steps you need to complete when implementing a BAPI.
Print this checklist and use the printout during the entire implementation phase of your BAPI. Ensure that you are can answer "yes" to each item on the list.

BAPI Implementation Checklist:

OK? Task(s)

Defining the scenario in which the BAPI will be used

Have you defined the scenario in which the BAPI is to be used?

Have you identified the SAP Business Object involved?

Have you defined the functional scope of the BAPI?

Have you defined the relationship between the BAPI you are planning to implement and other, related BAPIs?

Is the functionality to be implemented by the BAPI exclusively within the scope of the associated Business Object?

Is the BAPI assigned to the appropriate SAP Business Object?

Has there been a review of the BAPI concept and scenario?

Defining the BAPI

Have you identified the SAP Business Object in the Business Object Repository to

which the BAPI will be added as a method?
Have you identified the key fields of this Business Object?

Have you defined the interface of the BAPI?

Have you included the key fields of the SAP Business Object in the BAPI interface?

Have you included a Return parameter?

Have you identified the name of the function group or have you planned a name for a new function group to be created?

Have you planned the name of the function module on which the BAPI is based, using the format
BAPI_<Business Object name>_<method name>?

Defining the interface parameters in the function module

Have you defined the function module interface using only EXPORTING, IMPORTING and TABLES parameters?

Have you included the key fields of the SAP Business Object as parameters of the function module (i.e. depending on whether the BAPI is instance-dependent or instance-independent)?

Have you assigned correct names to the parameters in the function module?

Do the function module parameters for the Business Object's key fields have the same name as the key fields of the Business Object in the BOR?

Is the name of each parameter in the function module a maximum of 20 characters in length?

Are the names of the parameters in the function module in English?

Have you avoided the use of abbreviations in the names of function module parameters?

Did you ensure that none of the parameters in the function module is customizing-relevant or affects system settings in any other way?

Is the interface independent of the current customizing settings of the system?
Are all IMPORTING parameters independent from each other, i.e. did you ensure that none of the parameters is derived from another?

Have you defined the formats in which the values must be transferred in the function module interface?

Are you using the Dictionary structure BAPIRETURN1 or BAPIRET2 for the Return parameter (as of Release 4.0)?

Defining the structures and fields of the function module parameters

Have you assigned a corresponding currency code field to each field with currency amounts?

Have you assigned a field for the unit of measure to each quantity field?

Have you defined Dictionary structures for each function module parameter?

Do the names of the Dictionary structures start with BAPI?

Are these structures independent of the structures used in the R/3 application?

Have you defined the fields in the Dictionary structures?

Have you defined Help views or fixed values for the fields in order to enable your BAPI to provide input help (F4 help) for each field?

Are the field names a maximum of 10 characters in length?

Have you used English names for the fields, preferably those names that have been assigned to the corresponding data elements in the ABAP Dictionary?

Can the user of your BAPI access the values for each import field either by referring to the documentation, by obtaining input help (F4 help), or by using a GetDetail BAPI?

Have you used a structure with the fields SIGN, OPTION, LOW and HIGH for the corresponding BAPI parameter that selects values (for example, Material.GetList)?

Defining the BAPI in the Business Object Repository

Have you planned the name of the method in the BOR?
Have you defined the names of the parameters in the BOR?

Are the names of the parameters a maximum of 20 characters in length?

Did you choose English names for the parameters?

Are the names of the parameters of the method in the BOR and the names of the parameters in the function module the same?

Did you ensure that there are no underscores in the parameter names?

Did you start each new word in a method name with a capital letter?

Creating the objects in the R/3 System

Did you create the required Dictionary objects?

Did you create the function group, if required?

Did you create the function module?

Did you create the documentation for the BAPI in the Function Builder?

Did you use the program to map between internal and external data formats?

Did you write the program for your function module?

Did you use the BOR/BAPI wizard to define the BAPI as a method in the BOR?

Are the parameter names and types of the method in the BOR and of the function module in the Function Builder the same?

Documentation

Did you write appropriate documentation for the BAPI in the Function Builder?

Is the documentation complete?

Has the documentation been translated into the required languages?

Testing the BAPI

Did you test the function module using the test environment of the Function Builder?

Did you test the BAPI using the test environment of the Business Object Builder?

Did you test the BAPI by calling the method via the BAPI ActiveX Control?

Did you test the BAPI by making an RFC call to the underlying function module?

Did you test the documentation for its completeness, correctness and availability in the required logon languages?

Has the BAPI been released and frozen?

CHAPTER 6

SAP Report Painter

Report Painter is a powerful and easy **SAP** tool for **defining reports** in the SAP information system in the CO controlling and the FI financial accounting modules. With **Report Painter** you **define SAP reports** quickly and easily.

Report Painter & Report Writer is generally used for creating FI reports. The Transaction code to create report painter is GRR1 & for creating report writer it is GR31. So we can use GRR3 or GR33 to see the setting of the report.

Another simple way is use GR55 to display the setting of the report.

GR55:

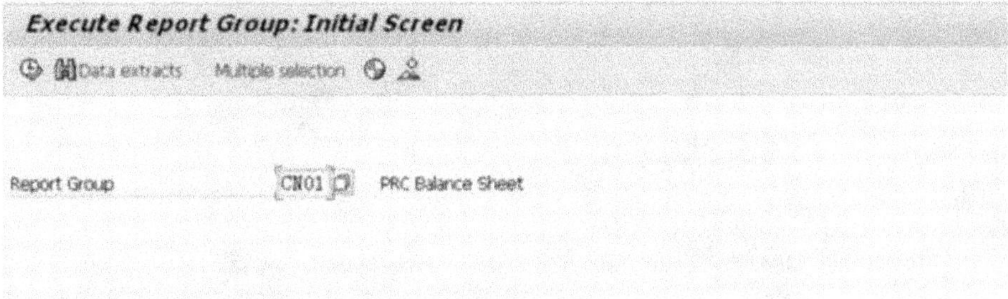

REPORT GROUP ->Displaypress the reports bottom

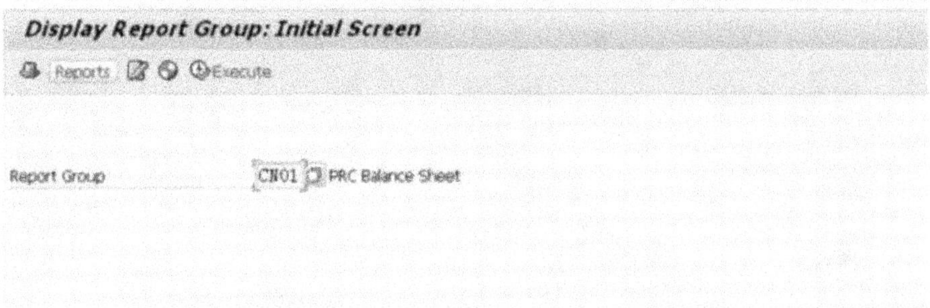

We can find all the report in this report group

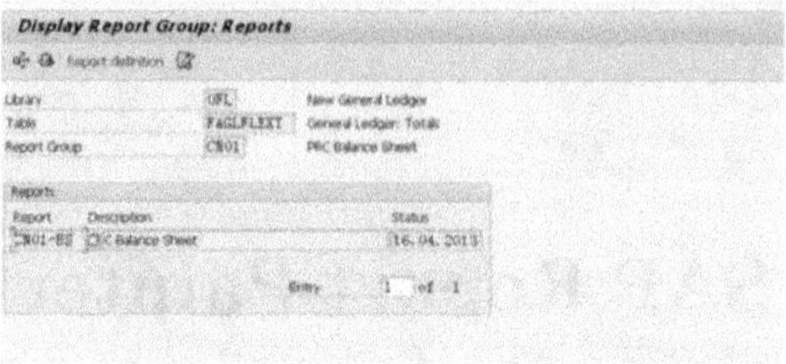

Double click reportand we can find the detailed setting for this report,it is defined by report painter.

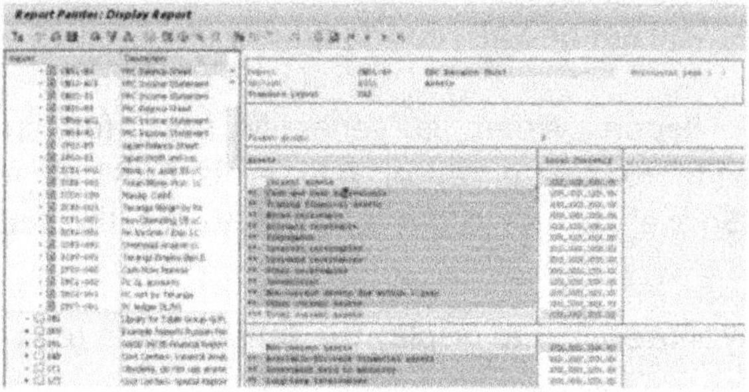

Take another report write report for example ,after display report by GR55 ,we can press sections,

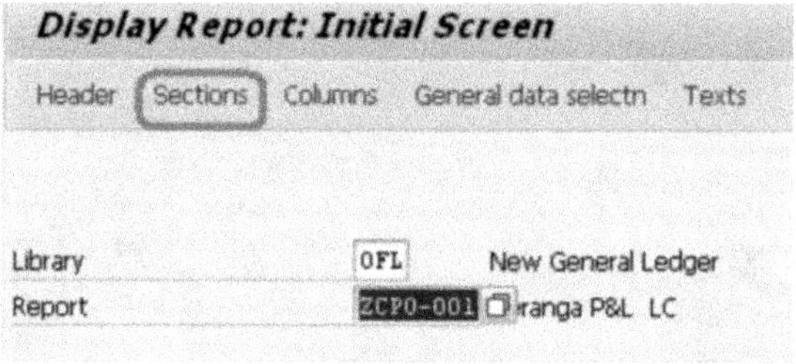

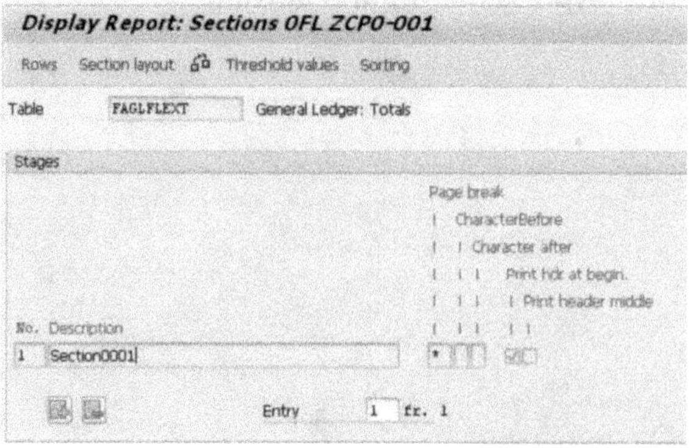

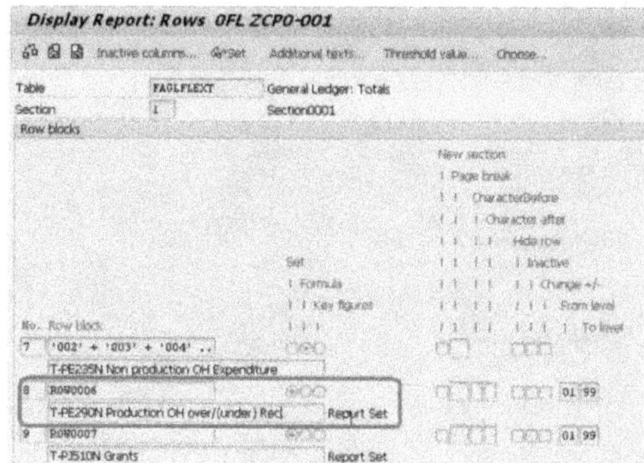

And the detailed setting such as GL and function area can be find.

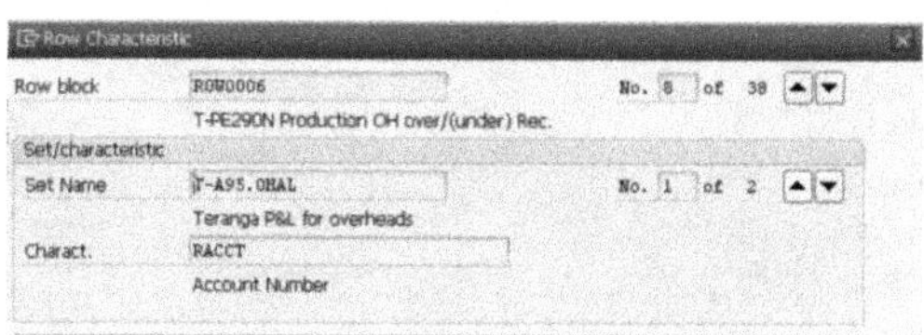

Use GS03 to see the set:

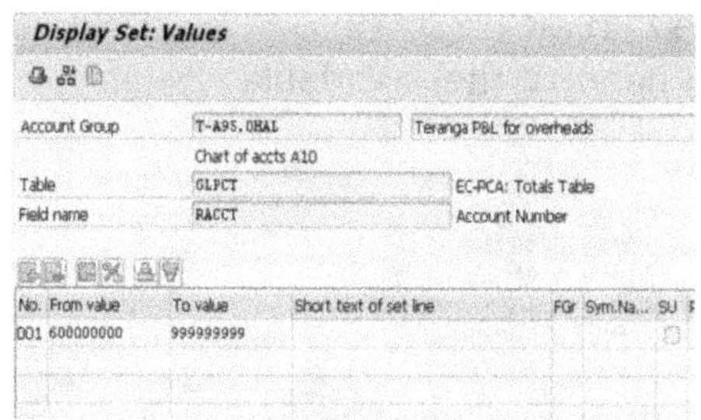

6.1 DEMO of SAP Report Painter

SAP Report Painter Steps

Pre-Requisites:

1. Create Account Groups for P/L Accounts in Profit Center Accounting
   TCODE: KDH1

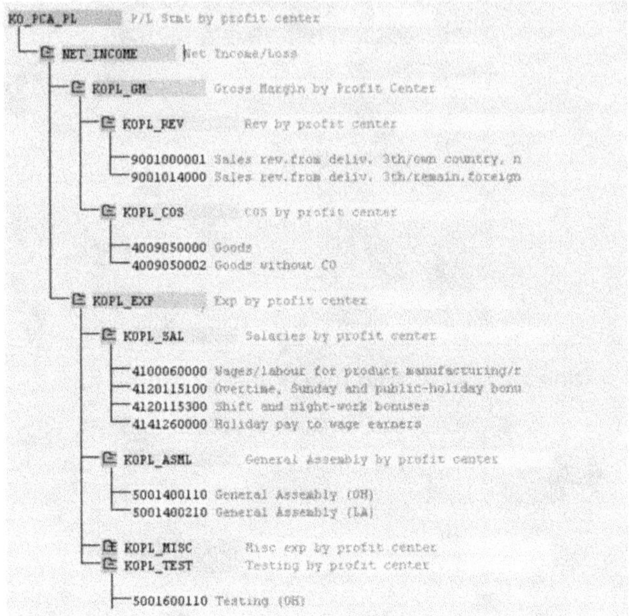

2. Create a variable Z_YEAR
Report Painter-> ReportWriter->Variable
TCODE: GS11

Change Formula Variable: Basic Data

Type change Value

Formula variable Z_YEAR

Table GLPCT EC-PCA Totals Table
Field name RYEAR Fiscal year

Description Current Fiscal Year

Proposal
Formula '#S001'

Variable
Formula exit
+ - * /

Entry fields on selection screens
Internal variable

Authorization group

3. Create library KA2 by copying from Library 8A2 Language s/b German
TCODE: GR21

PLEASE USE KA2 LIBRARY. (KA2 is already created once in this setup)
DO NOT CREATE A NEW ONE OR MORE COPIES.

Create the following reports

1. PCA-TB - Simple Trial Balance Report
2. PCA-P/L – Profit and loss Actual Plan Variance report

1 PCA-TB - Simple Trial Balance Report

If you enter the PCTR-GRP and GL-Acts group, it should generate following report

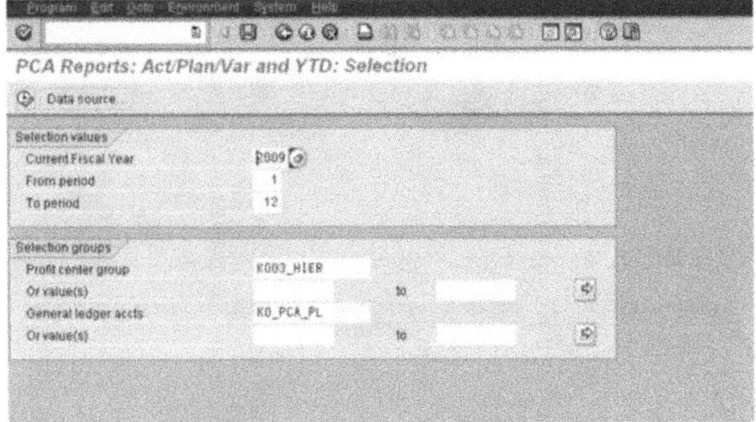

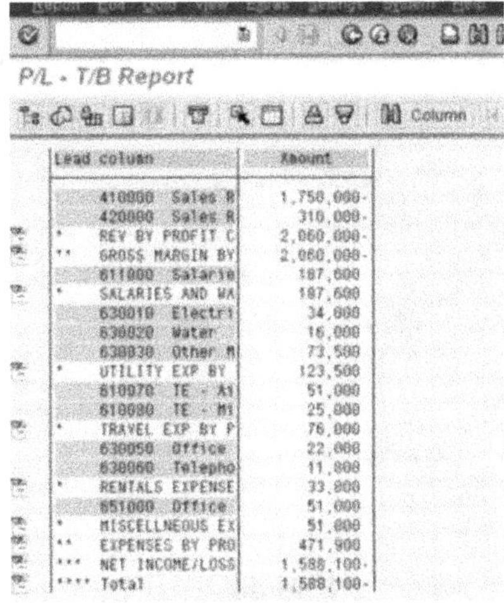

Lead column	Amount
410000 Sales R	1,750,000-
420000 Sales R	310,000-
* REV BY PROFIT C	2,060,000-
** GROSS MARGIN BY	2,060,000-
611000 Salarie	187,600
* SALARIES AND WA	187,600
630010 Electri	34,000
630020 Water	16,000
630030 Other M	73,500
* UTILITY EXP BY	123,500
610070 TE - A1	51,000
610080 TE - M1	25,000
* TRAVEL EXP BY P	76,000
630050 Office	22,000
630060 Telepho	11,800
* RENTALS EXPENSE	33,800
651000 Office	51,000
* MISCELLNEOUS EX	51,000
** EXPENSES BY PRO	471,900
*** NET INCOME/LOSS	1,588,100-
**** Total	1,588,100-

Here are the steps to create the above Report
Report Name: PCA-TB
TCODE –GRR1

SAP Menu-> Accounting->Controlling ->PCA->Information system->Tools -> Report Painter-> Create

Create PCA-TB under KA2 library

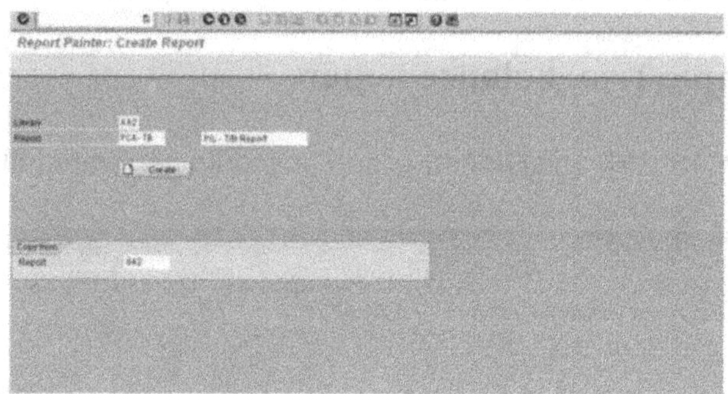

Click on Create table

(Note: EC-PCA standard Reports table: GLPCT)

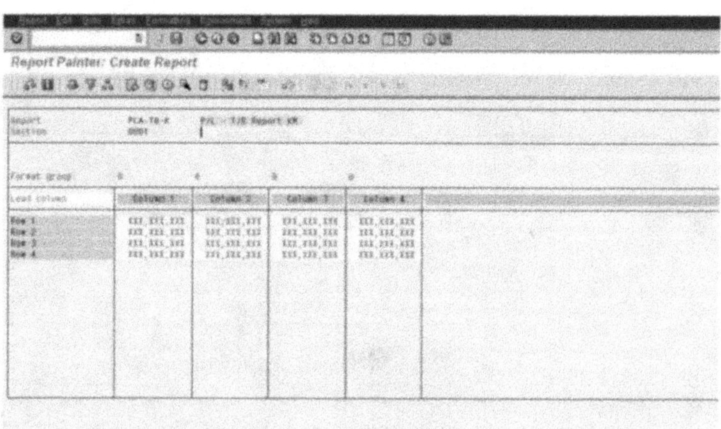

Get "Gen Data Selections":
Menu Path→Edit->Gen Data Selection

(General Data Selection for Header data)
(All properties are select for GLPCT table)

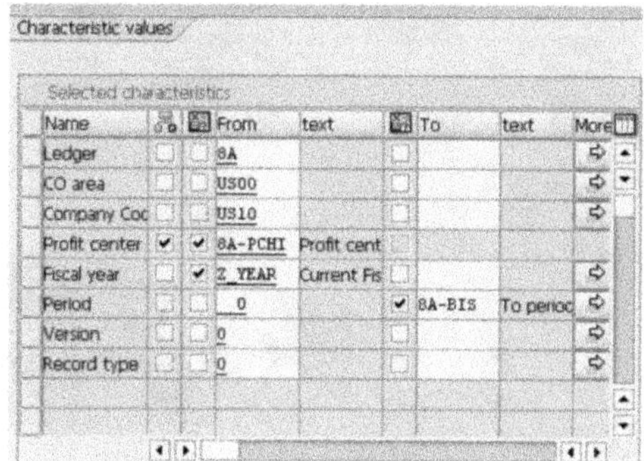

Double click on Row 1 then input row Element Definition (Row 1 is for line items properties)

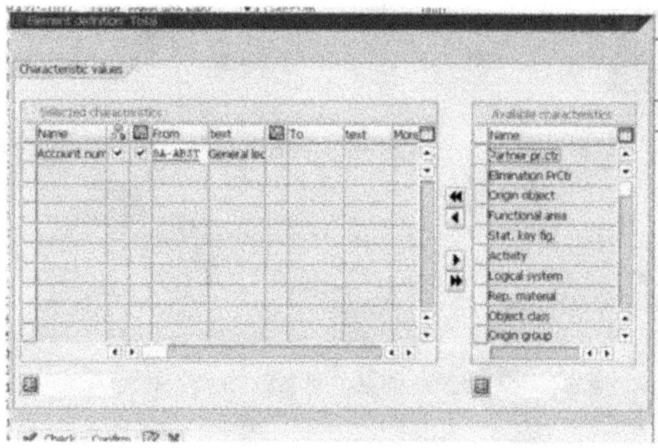

Double click on **Column 1** and Enter the **element Definition**

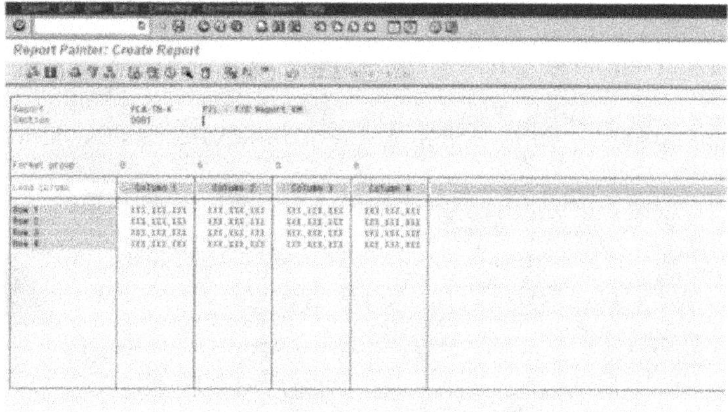

And select **Debit/credit**

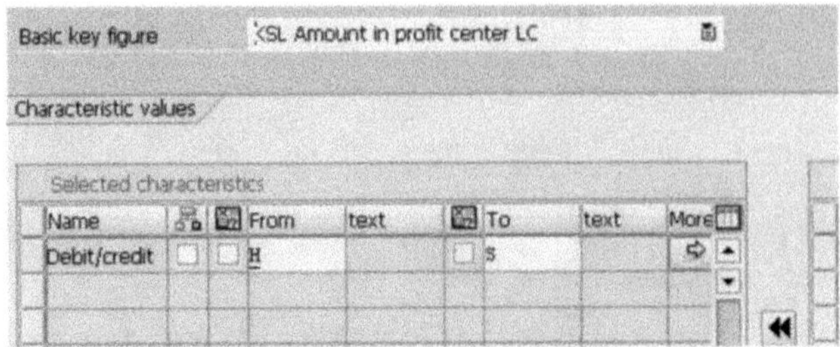

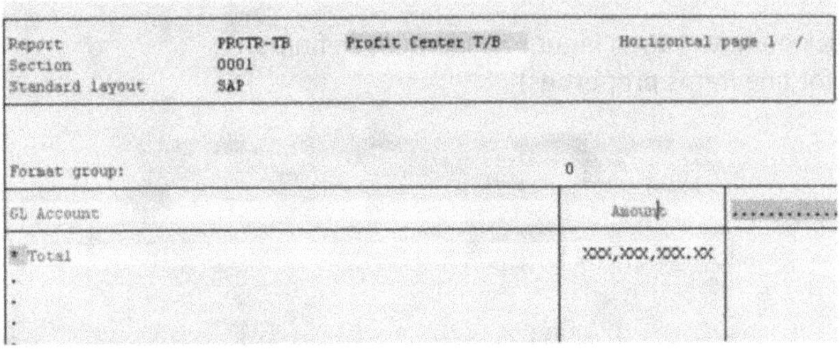

Report PRCTR-TB Profit Center T/B Horizontal page 1 /
Section 0001
Standard layout SAP

Format group: 0

GL Account Amount

* Total XXX,XXX,XXX.XX

Click on edit rows and explode

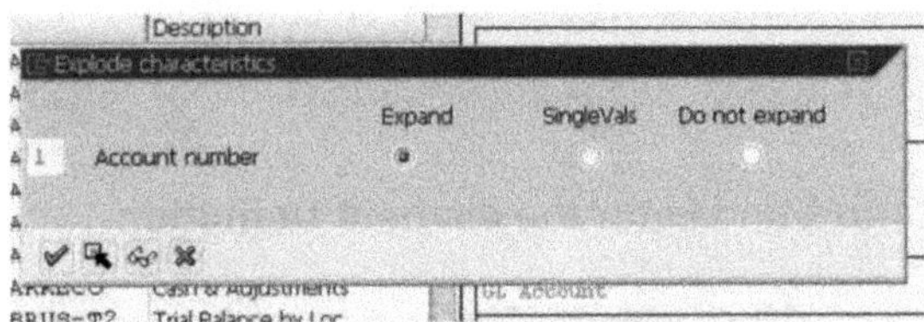

Increase the lead column length:

Click on Menu Path->formatting –>Report Layout and select lead column

Increase the lead column width to 60

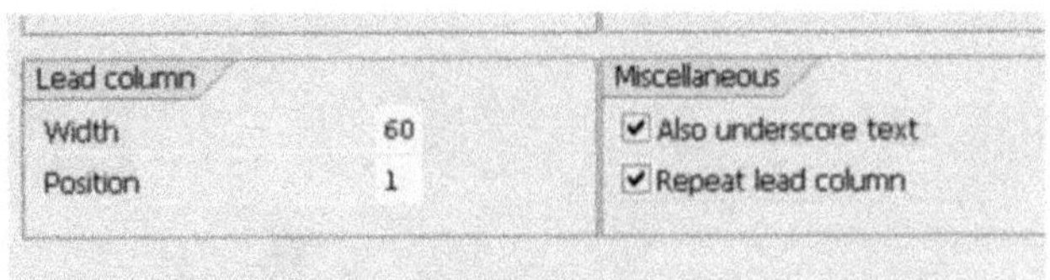

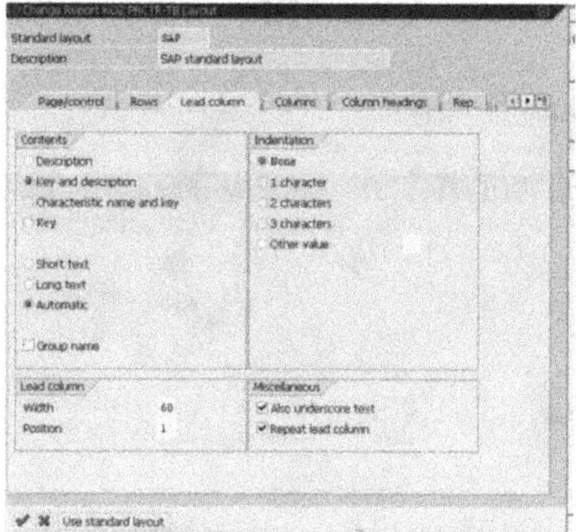

Save and execute the report by creating a report group KA26
Menu Path->Report->Execute F8

The output Looks

Lead column	Amount
113000 Bank - ban	268,000
121000 Customer r	1,500,000
217200 Other Liab	418,900-
410000 Sales Reve	1,750,000-
420000 Sales Reve	310,000-
610060 TE - Enter	32,000
610070 TE - Airfa	51,000
610080 TE - Misce	25,000
611000 Salaries -	187,600
630010 Electricit	34,000
630020 Water	11,200
630030 Other Main	73,500
630040 Insurance	96,800
630050 Office And	22,000
630060 Telephone	11,800
651000 Office Sup	51,000
800000 DAA- Machi	
801000 DAA-Labor	
850000 Allocation	
* Total	115,000-

2.PCA-P/L – Profit and loss Actual Plan Variance report

Create the following Report

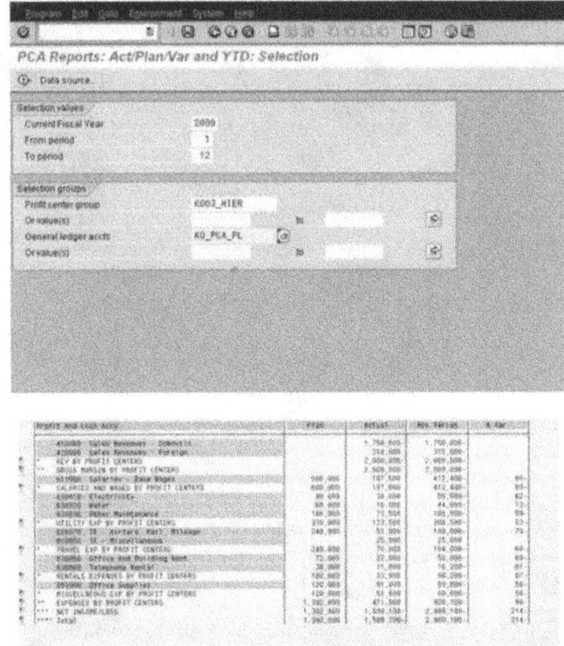

Step1. Create A report (GRR1)

Report Painter: Create Report

Library KA2

Report PCA-PL PCA - P/L Act Pln Vr

Create

Copy from

Report

Report Painter: Create Report

Report	PCA-PL1	PCA - P/L Act Pln Vr
Section	0001	PCA - P/L Act Pln Vr

Format group	0	0	0	0
Lead column	Column 1	Column 2	Column 3	Column 4
Row 1	XXX,XXX,XXX	XXX,XXX,XXX	XXX,XXX,XXX	XXX,XXX,XXX
Row 2	XXX,XXX,XXX	XXX,XXX,XXX	XXX,XXX,XXX	XXX,XXX,XXX
Row 3	XXX,XXX,XXX	XXX,XXX,XXX	XXX,XXX,XXX	XXX,XXX,XXX
Row 4	XXX,XXX,XXX	XXX,XXX,XXX	XXX,XXX,XXX	XXX,XXX,XXX

Step2. Click on Gen Data Selection

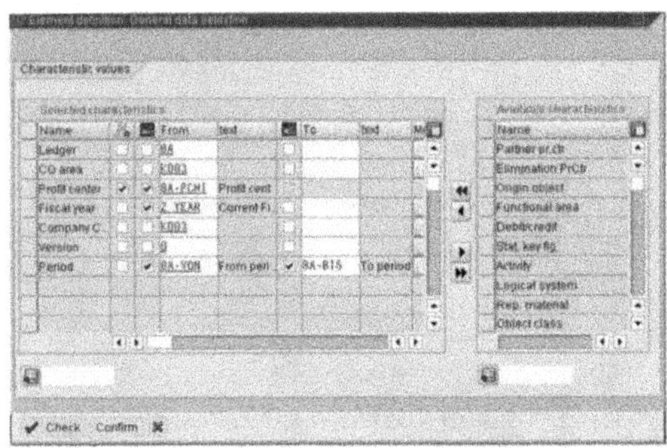

Step3: Double Click on Row1: Enter the row Definition

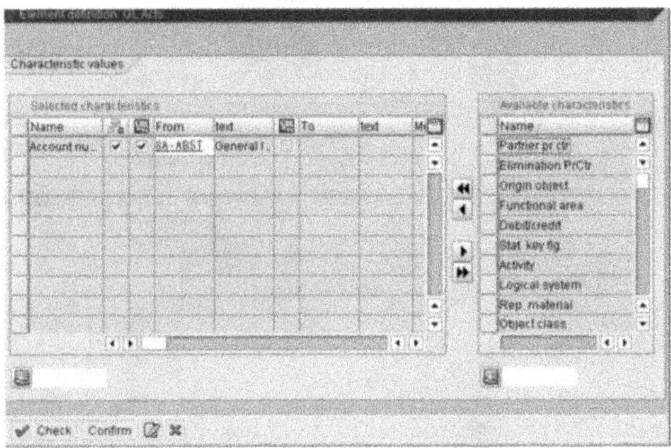

Step4: Double Click on Column 1 : Enter the Column Definition:PLAN

Note: Click on more to add second Row with Record Type

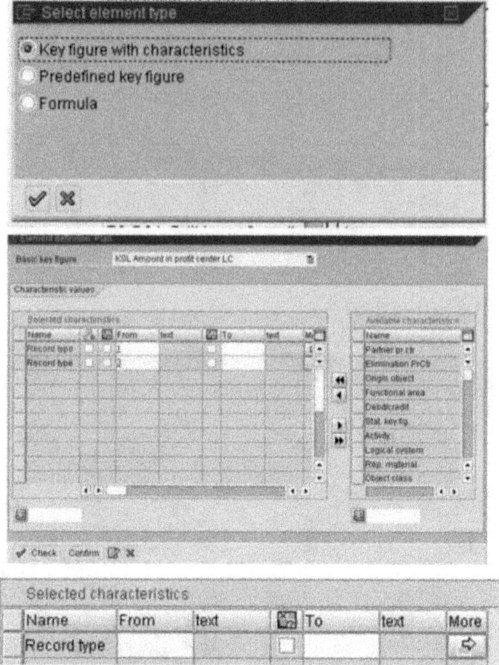

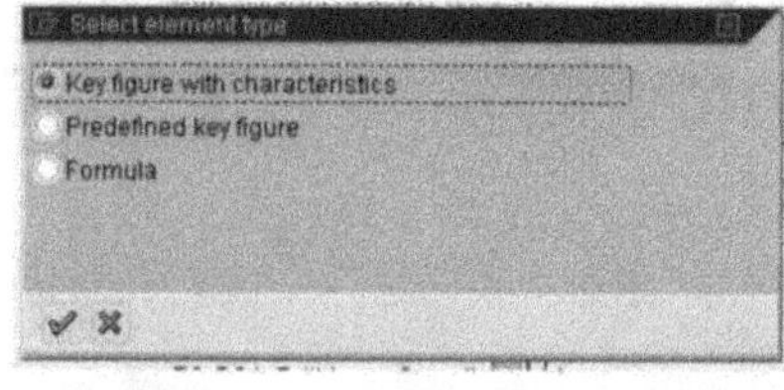

Step5: Double Click on Column 2: Enter the Column Definition : **Actual**

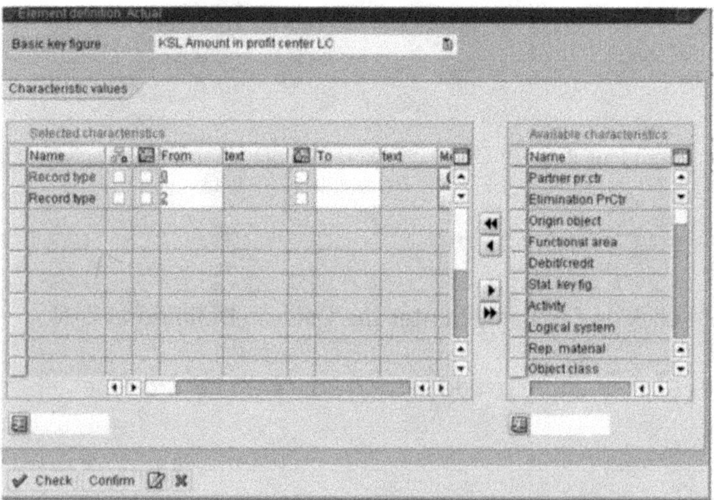

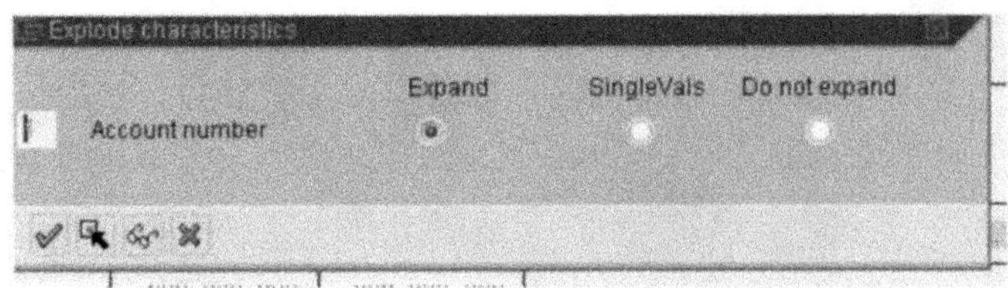

Step6: Double Click on Column 3: Enter the Column Definition : Abs Variance
Absolute Variance = Actual cost – Planed Cost
Use formula for Column definition.

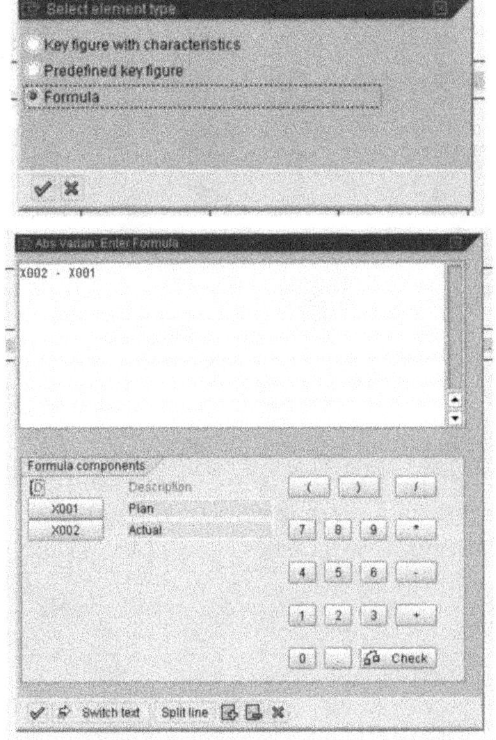

Step7: Double Click on Column 4:
Enter the Column Definition: % Variance
(Absolute Variance / Planned) * 100
(X003 / X001) * 100

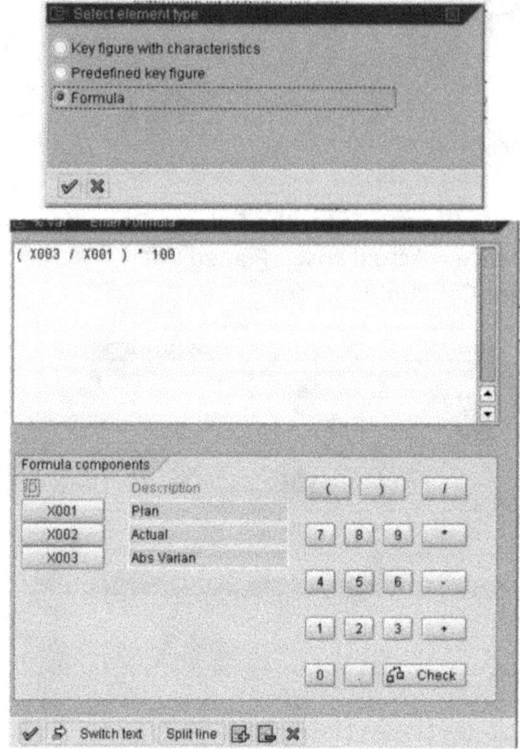

Final Step: Execute: Menu Path-> report -> Execute

The final Report:

(Note: in the test data there is no planned entries so we are getting blank in the Planned and % variance)

Profit And Loss Acco	Plan	Actual	Abs Varian	% Var
410000 Sales Revenues - Domestic		1,750,000-	1,750,000-	
420000 Sales Revenues - Foreign		310,000-	310,000-	
* REV BY PROFIT CENTERS		2,060,000-	2,060,000-	
** GROSS MARGIN BY PROFIT CENTERS		2,060,000-	2,060,000-	
611000 Salaries - Base Wages	600,000	187,600	412,400-	69-
* SALARIES AND WAGES BY PROFIT CENTERS	600,000	187,600	412,400-	69-
630010 Electricity	90,000	34,000	56,000-	62-
630020 Water	60,000	16,000	44,000-	73-
630030 Other Maintenance	180,000	73,500	106,500-	59-
* UTILITY EXP BY PROFIT CENTERS	330,000	123,500	206,500-	63-
670070 TE - Airfare, Rail, Mileage	240,000	51,000	189,000-	79-
610000 TE - Miscellaneous		25,000	25,000	
* TRAVEL EXP BY PROFIT CENTERS	240,000	76,000	164,000-	68-
630050 Office And Building Rent	72,000	22,000	50,000-	69-
630060 Telephone Rental	30,000	11,800	18,200-	61-
* RENTALS EXPENSES BY PROFIT CENTERS	102,000	33,800	68,200-	67-
651000 Office Supplies	120,000	51,000	69,000-	58-
* MISCELLANEOUS EXP BY PROFIT CENTERS	120,000	51,000	69,000-	58-
** EXPENSES BY PROFIT CENTERS	1,392,000	471,900	920,100-	66-
*** NET INCOME/LOSS	1,392,000	1,588,100-	2,980,100-	214-
**** Total	1,392,000	1,588,100-	2,980,100-	214-

Increase lead column width:

Formatting -> Report layout -> Lead Columns

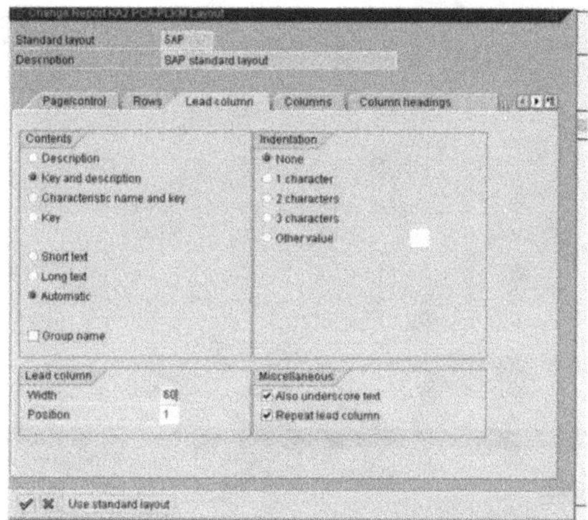

6.2 Create A Report Actual Planed Variance YTD report

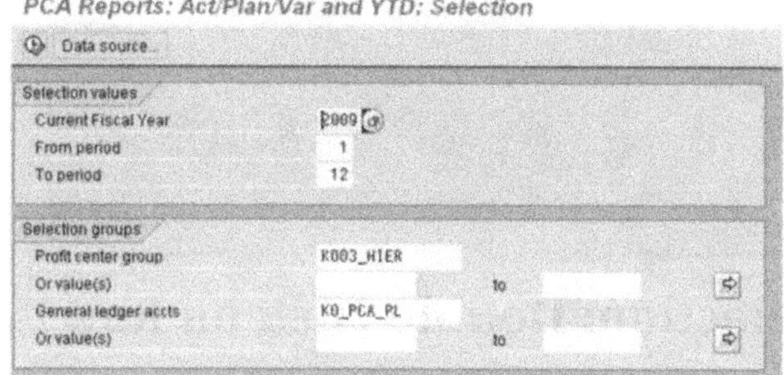


```
YTD Act Plan Var Report
  1
Report NamePCA-YTD
Report Desc: PCA - YTD APV Rep
Controlling Area:K003                    Company Code: K003
Report Changed By: KOSMANI
Current Fiscal Year: 2009
Date: 04/10/2009                 Time: 14:49:07
Client Name: Waltham Client            Cilent No: 110
Chart Of Account: CANA
Created By: KOSMANI                   Created On: *
```

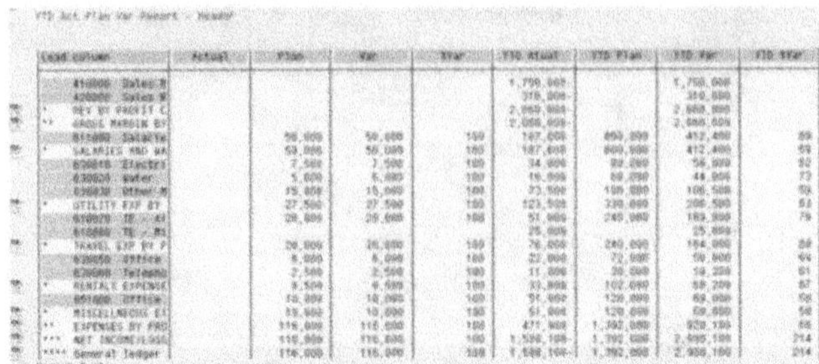

Gen data selection

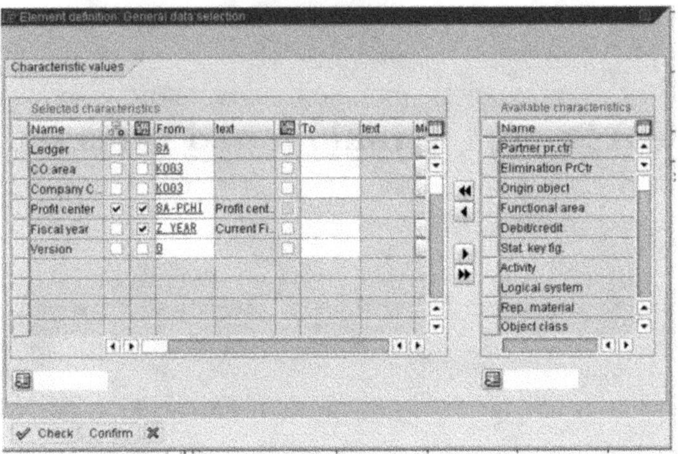

6.3 Row selection: Double click on Row1 and select the following properties.

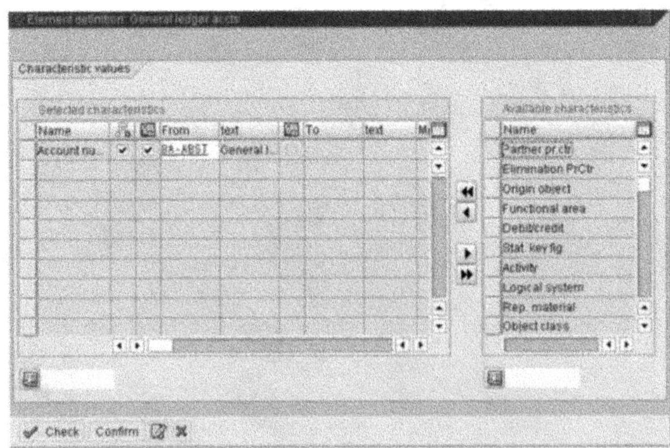

Enter the properties for

1. col1 – Actual 2.
2. Col2- Plan
3. Col3-Var 4.
4. Col4-%var
5. Col5 – YTD plan
6. Col6 – YTD actual
7. Col7 – YTD Var
8. Col8 – YTD %var

Actual

Name		From	text		To	text
Period	☐	✔	8A-VON	From peri...	☐		
Record type	☐	☐	0		☐		
Record type	☐	☐	2		☐		

Planned

Name		From	text		To	text
Period	☐	✔	8A-VON	From peri...	☐		
Record type	☐	☐	1		☐		
Record type	☐	☐	3		☐		

Variance:

Formula (Planned – Actual)

%Var

Formula (Varaince * 100/planned)

YTD Actual

(Note: here in the period you have to select from (1st period) and to (current Period)

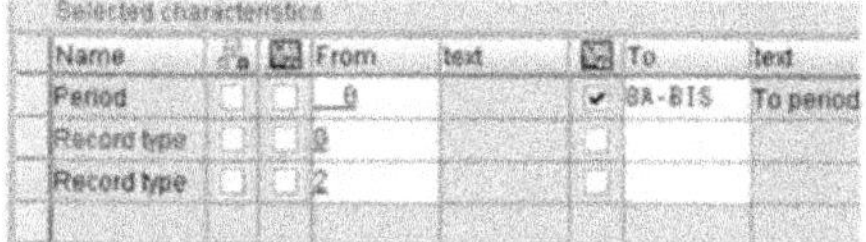

Selected characteristics

Name			From	text		To	text
Period	☐	☐	0		✔	8A-BIS	To period
Record type	☐	☐	0		☐		
Record type	☐	☐	2		☐		

6.4 YTD Planned

Selected characteristics

Name			From	text		To	text	M
Period	☐	☐	0		☑	8A-BIS	To period	
Record type	☐	☐	1		☐			
Record type	☐	☐	3		☐			

6.5 YTD Var

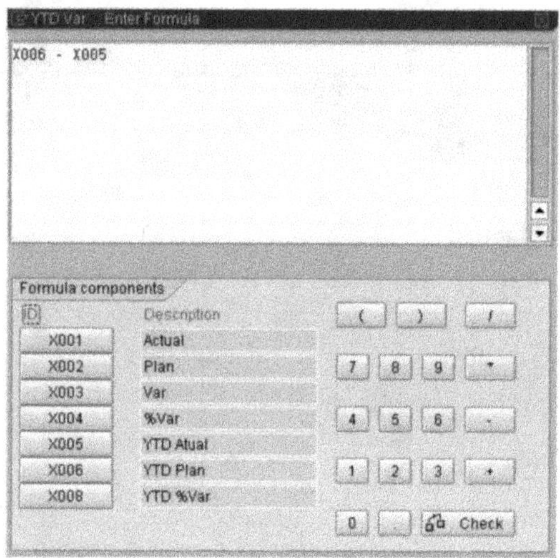

6.6 YTD %var

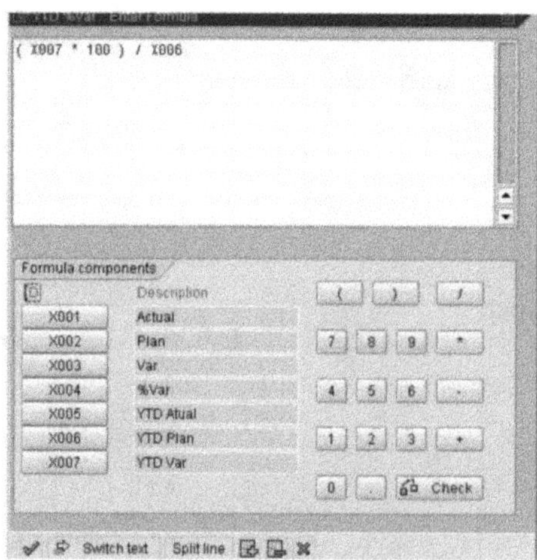

Final Step: Save/Generate and execute the report

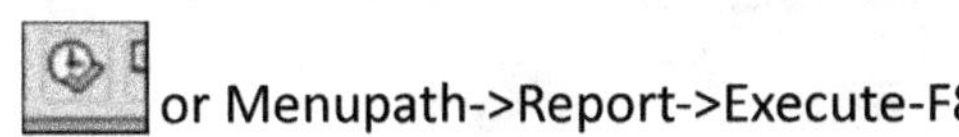
or Menupath->Report->Execute-F8

You can do the cosmetic changes to report by adding Header Footer Title etc.
Menu path->Extras-Report text

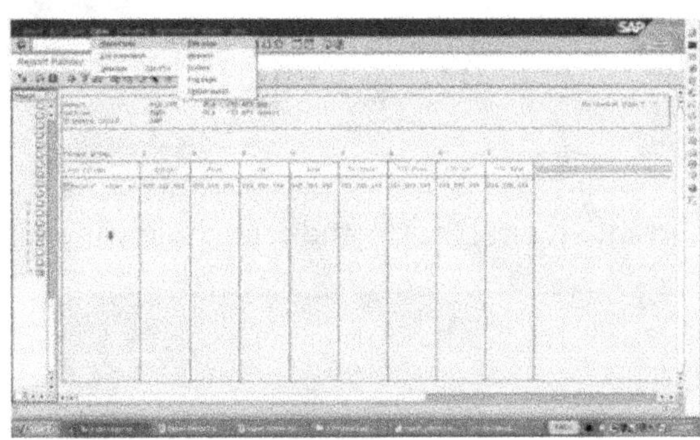

Select the following variables for the title

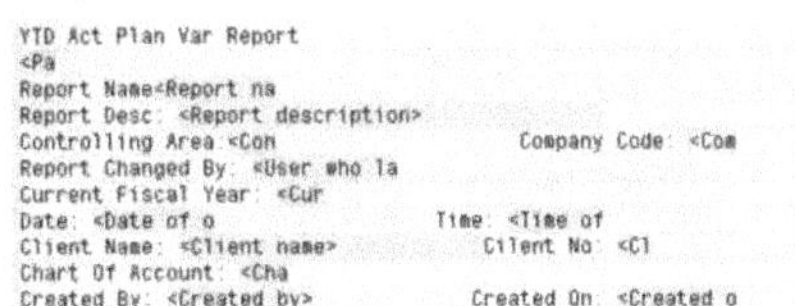

```
YTD Act Plan Var Report
<Pa
Report Name<Report na
Report Desc: <Report description>
Controlling Area:<Con                Company Code: <Com
Report Changed By: <User who la
Current Fiscal Year: <Cur
Date: <Date of o                Time: <Time of
Client Name: <Client name>        Client No: <Cl
Chart Of Account: <Cha
Created By: <Created by>          Created On: <Created o
```

For the above format, the output looks like this:

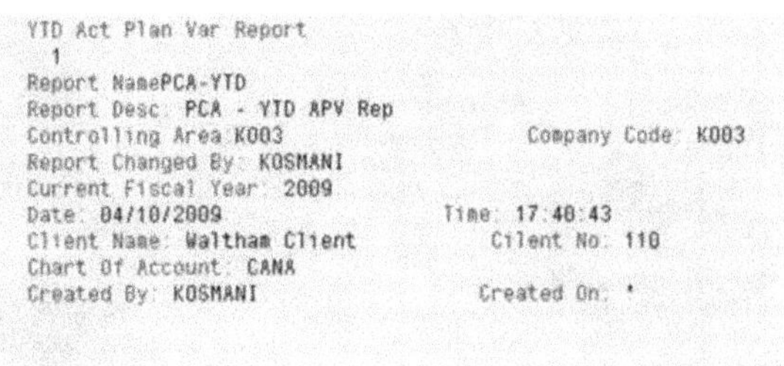

```
YTD Act Plan Var Report
  1
Report NamePCA-YTD
Report Desc: PCA - YTD APV Rep
Controlling Area:K003                Company Code: K003
Report Changed By: KOSMANI
Current Fiscal Year: 2009
Date: 04/10/2009                Time: 17:40:43
Client Name: Waltham Client        Client No: 110
Chart Of Account: CANA
Created By: KOSMANI               Created On: *
```

Example1: Print “Report Name:” and select the following variable

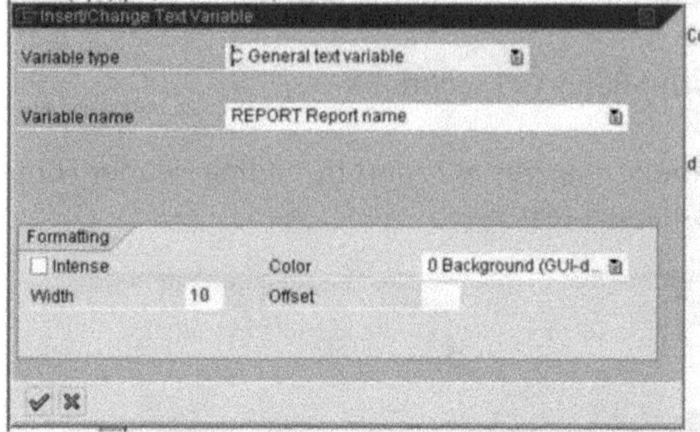

Example2: Print: "Current Physical year:" and select following variable

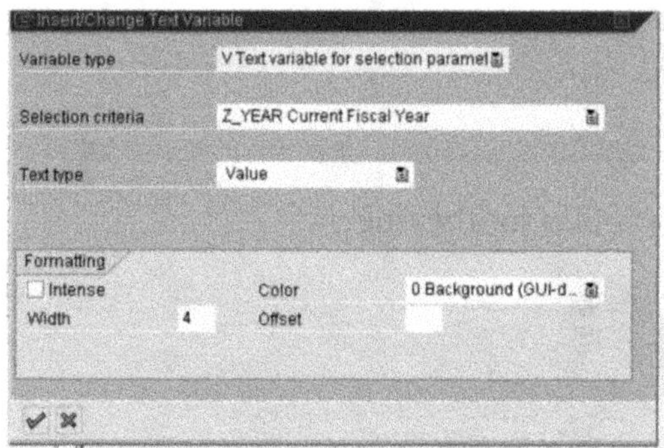

Example3: Print "Controlling Area:" and select the following variable

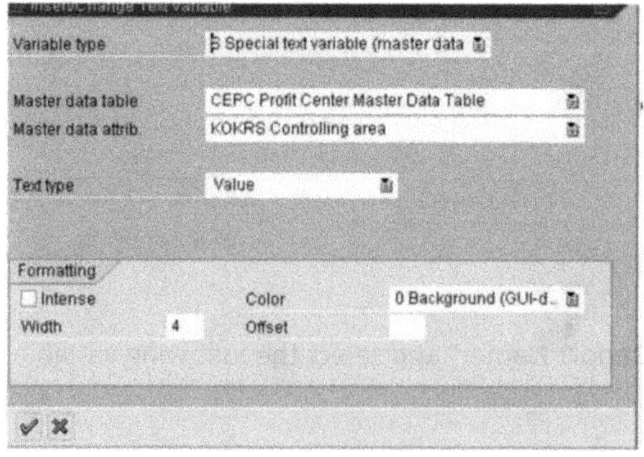

Create Report "Actual Costs by Cost Center"

Net Income/Loss by Profit Centers

P/L Accounts	CADILLAC	PONTIAC	SATURN	CORP	TOTAL
113000 Bank - bank statemt				265,200	265,200
121000 Customer receivables	700,000	530,000	270,000		1,500,000
217200 Other Liabilities				420,900-	420,900-
410000 Sales Revenues - Dom	910,000-	570,000-	270,000-		1,750,000-
420000 Sales Revenues - For	206,000-	104,000-			310,000-
610060 TE - Entertainment		12,000	20,000		32,000
610070 TE - Airfare, Rail,	12,000	19,000	20,000		51,000
610080 TE - Miscellaneous	20,000	5,000			25,000
611000 Salaries - Base Wage	118,600	39,000	30,000		187,600
630010 Electricity	15,000	12,000	7,000		34,000
630020 Water	16,000				16,000
630030 Other Maintenance	40,500	23,000	10,000		73,500
630040 Insurance	62,300	34,500			96,800
630050 Office And Building	12,000	4,000	6,000		22,000
630060 Telephone Rental	1,000		10,000		11,000
651000 Office Supplies	29,000	17,000	5,000		51,000
800000 DAA- Machine Hrs	13,600-	13,600			
801000 DAA-Labor Cost	2,520-	2,520			
850000 Allocation contract					
* GL Acts	104,920-	37,620	100,000	155,700-	115,000-

Report	PCA-PL3	Actuals by PCTRS
Section	0001	Actuals by PCTRS
Standard layout	SAP	

Format group	0	0	0	0	0
P/L Accounts	CADILLAC	PONTIAC	SATURN	CORP	TOTAL
GL Acts	XXX,XXX,XXX	XXX,XXX,XXX	XXX,XXX,XXX	XXX,XXX,XXX	XXX,XXX,XXX

Gen data selection:

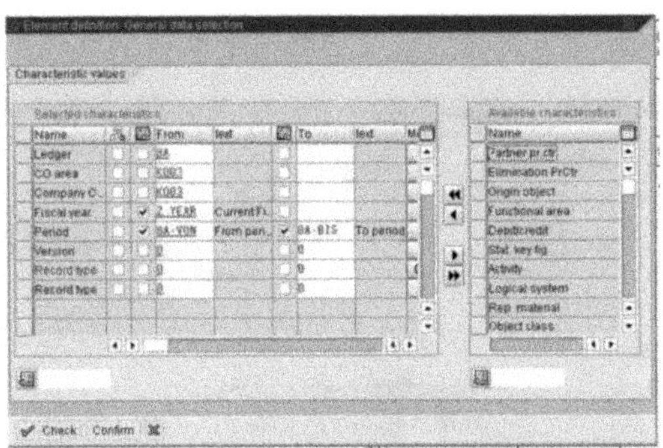

Row data selection:

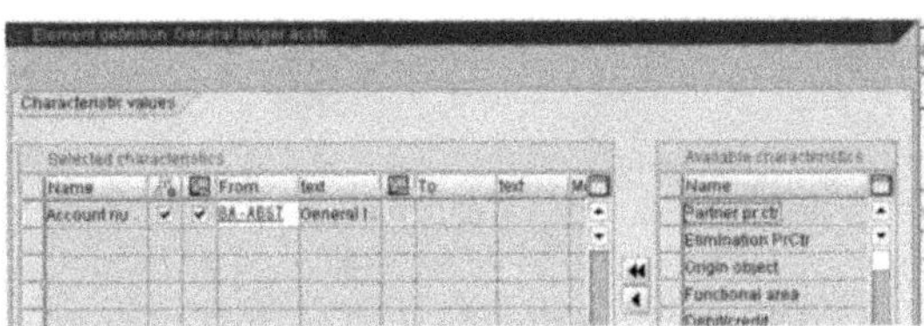

Coulmn1 – By Cadillac Profit Center

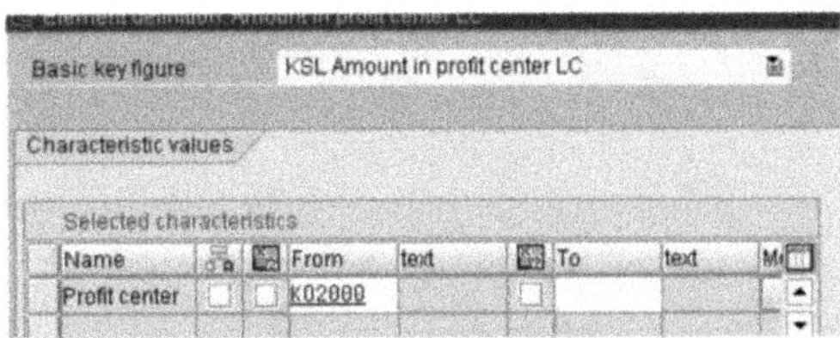

Coulmn3 – By Saturn Profit Center

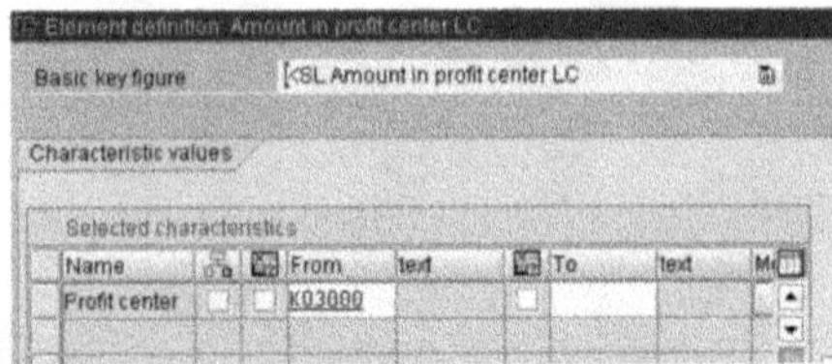

Coulmn4 – By GM Corporate

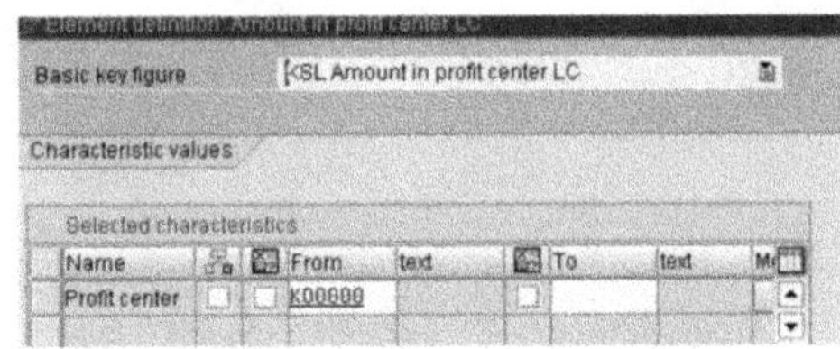

Coulmn5 – By Total
By formula

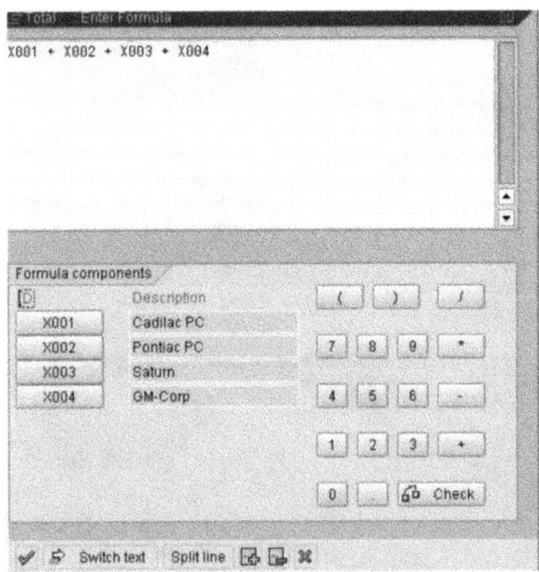

The final Report looks

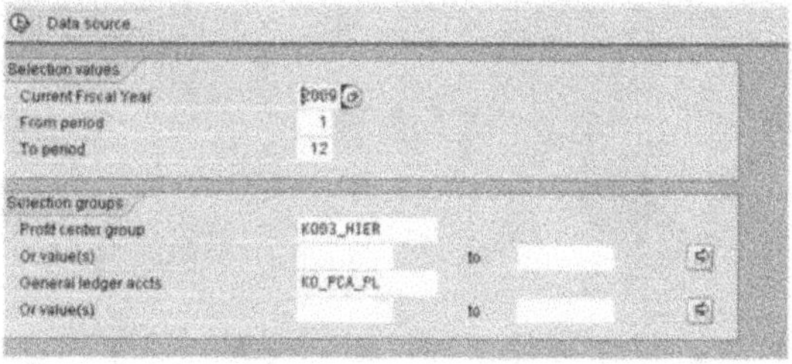

Data source

Selection values

Current Fiscal Year	2009
From period	1
To period	12

Selection groups

Profit center group	K093_HIER		
Or value(s)		to	
General ledger accts	KO_PCA_PL		
Or value(s)		to	

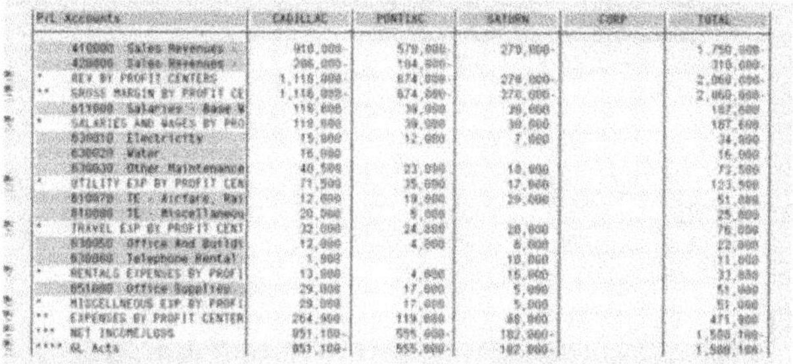

P/L Accounts	CADILLAC	PONTIAC	SATURN	CORP	TOTAL
410000 Sales Revenues -	910,000-	570,000-	270,000-		1,750,000-
420000 Sales Revenues -	206,000-	104,000-			310,000-
* REV BY PROFIT CENTERS	1,116,000-	674,000-	270,000-		2,060,000-
** GROSS MARGIN BY PROFIT CE	1,116,000-	674,000-	270,000-		2,060,000-
611000 Salaries - Base W	118,000	39,000	30,000		187,000
* SALARIES AND WAGES BY PRO	118,000	39,000	30,000		187,000
630010 Electricity	15,000	12,000	7,000		34,000
630020 Water	16,000				16,000
630030 Other Maintenance	40,500	23,000	10,000		73,500
* UTILITY EXP BY PROFIT CEN	71,500	35,000	17,000		123,500
610070 TE - Airfare, Rai	12,000	19,000	20,000		51,000
610080 TE - Miscellaneou	20,000	5,000			25,000
* TRAVEL EXP BY PROFIT CENT	32,000	24,000	20,000		76,000
630050 Office And Buildi	12,000	4,000	6,000		22,000
630060 Telephone Rental	1,000		10,000		11,000
* RENTALS EXPENSES BY PROFI	13,000	4,000	16,000		33,000
651000 Office Supplies	29,000	17,000	5,000		51,000
* MISCELLNEOUS EXP BY PROFI	29,000	17,000	5,000		51,000
** EXPENSES BY PROFIT CENTER	264,900	119,000	88,000		471,900
*** NET INCOME/LOSS	851,100-	555,000-	182,000-		1,588,100-
**** GL Accts	851,100-	555,000-	182,000-		1,588,100-

CHAPTER 7

Object Oriented ALV using SALV Factory method

Ref: Ashis Dey's artefact

Business Requirement

The output of a report can be displayed as a list or in grid. In most of the cases we use the grid display by calling the function module REUSE_ALV_GRID_DISPLAY or by calling the method set_table_for_first_display (). But utilizing the SALV factory method we can make the program more efficient to handle the grid display based on the object oriented methodology.
Report name ZREPORT_UPD
In this interactive ALV program the following requirements are met:

1. Display the final internal table output in a grid.
2. Display the Top of Page to provide the header information
3. Optimize the column settings
4. Include a customized PF Status having a new button in the Application toolbar named as – 'Deletion'
5. Get all the possible functions available in case of a ALV Grid display
6. Change the properties of a column (MANDT) to make the field hidden in the final output
7. Display the selection column at the extreme left for the selection of rows based on users' choice
8. 8. Activate the event ON_USER_COMMAND so that the records which are selected in the Step 7 can be deleted from the underlying database table after the user press the 'Deletion' button.
9. The final output is refreshed and the grid is populated with the new set of modified data after every user action is performed

10. The above functionalities are maintained in the program based on the OOPs methodology

The following is the table structure of the ZTVGT_6078_STOCK from which the data is fetched and the final output is displayed -

Advantages of utilizing the SALV Factory method

1. No need to create the Field catalog explicitly for the final internal table to be displayed as output.
2. The factory method creates the output structure for the grid dynamically just by passing the internal table name.
3. No need to fill the TOP-OF-PAGE event for display the header in the list
4. User actions can be handled just by registering the corresponding event which is generic for all the cases.
5. The volume of code is very less.

The below given screen shot for the final output is based on the customized table **ZTVGT_6078_STOCK**. But it can be any table based on the business requirement and can be displayed as final output dynamically.

The button  is added in the customized PF Status for the deletion of record

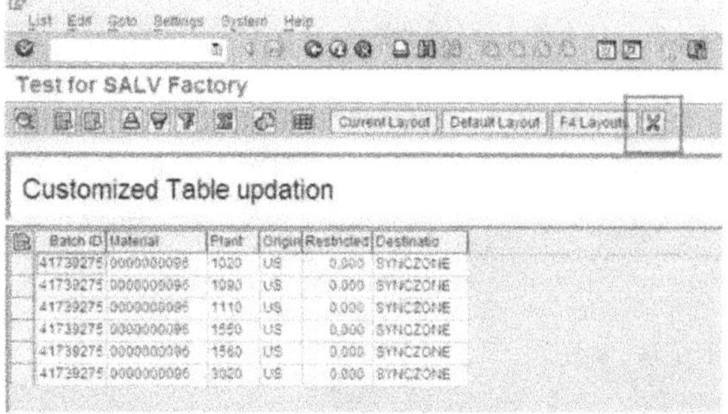

Based on the Material number 0000000096 the records are fetched from the ZTVGT_6078_STOCK table. Now let us select any record(s) and press the [delete button icon] button appeared on the Application toolbar.

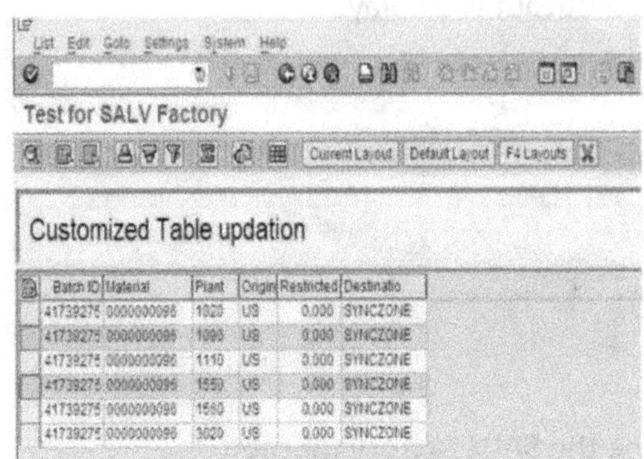

That selected records are deleted from the underlying database table level and the output will be refreshed accordingly.

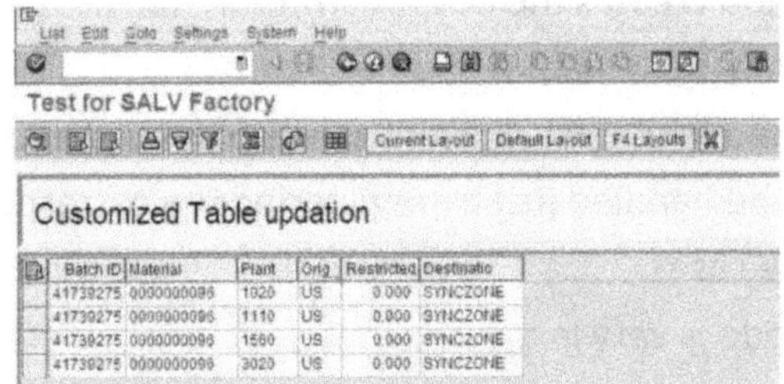

The entries for the Plant – 1090 and 1550 are deleted from the database table ZTVGT_6078_STOCK

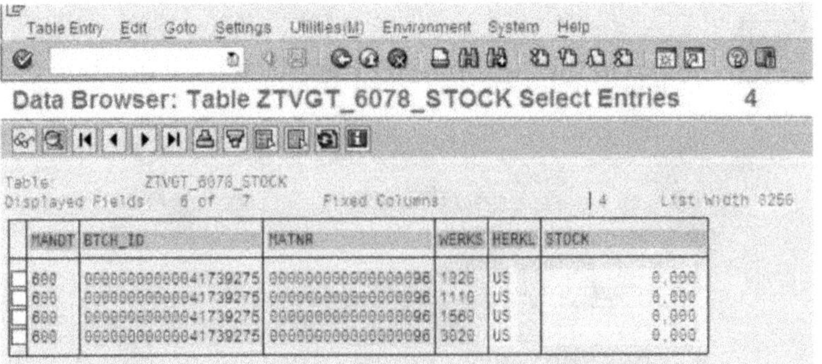

The code snippet is given below to achieve the above functionalities.

MAIN PROGRAM

```
*---------------------------------------------------------------------------          *
*ABAP Name     : Customized table Update
*Created       by       : XXXXX
*Created       on       : XXXXXX
*Request       Type     : Sample DEMO Report
*Request       No.      :
*Transport No.  :
*---------------------------------------------------------------------------          *
* This report will display the records from the customized table and user can        *
* delete        the entries from the same from table the display output.             *
*---------------------------------------------------------------------------          *

REPORT zreport_upd NO STANDARD PAGE HEADING.

*    Include for global data
     INCLUDE zreport_upd_top IF FOUND.      "Global Data Declaration
*    Include for selection          screen
     INCLUDE zreport_upd_sel  IF FOUND.     "Selection Screen
*    Include for subroutines
     INCLUDE zreport_upd_f00 IF FOUND.      "Subroutine

START-OF-SELECTION.

*    Start the processing based on the radio button selected PERFORM start_processing.

END-OF-SELECTION.

*    Display the final data for Summary OTS or the Settlement PERFORM display_
     output.
```

```
*&---------------------------------------------------------------------*
*& Include      ZREPORT_UPD_TOP        *
*&---------------------------------------------------------------------*
INCLUDE <icon>.
INCLUDE <symbol>.

* Definition is later

CLASS lcl_handle_events DEFINITION DEFERRED.

*---------------------------------------------------------------------          *
* Declaration of Global constants          *
*---------------------------------------------------------------------          *
CONSTANTS :
c_true  TYPE sap_bool  VALUE 'X',        "True value
c_false TYPE sap_bool  VALUE ' '.        "False value


*---------------------------------------------------------------------          *
* Declaration of Global structure types  *
*---------------------------------------------------------------------          *
TYPES :

* Structure for Customized table Update
BEGIN OF ty_upd          ,
mandt  TYPE mandt        ,       "Client
btch_id TYPE zbatch_id , "Data element for Batch ID
matnr  TYPE matnr        ,       "Material Number
werks  TYPE werks_d    ,       "Plant
herkl    TYPE herkl        , "Country of origin of the material
stock    TYPE einme       , "Total Stock of All Restricted Batches
dest TYPE zd_dest        ,       "Destination Application ID
flag  TYPE char1,        "Single-Character Indicator
END OF ty_upd.
```

```
*------------------------------------------------------------------------          *
* Declaration of Global table types       *
*------------------------------------------------------------------------          *
TYPES:
ty_t_upd TYPE STANDARD TABLE OF ty_upd INITIAL SIZE0.


*------------------------------------------------------------------------*
* Declaration of Global internal tables    *
*------------------------------------------------------------------------*
DATA:
i_upd    TYPE ty_t_upd  ,          "Customized table Upd
i_table  TYPE REF TO cl_salv_table         ,           "SALV table
i_events            TYPE REF TO lcl_handle_events. "Events table

*     ------------------------------------------------------------------------          *
*     CLASS lcl_handle_events DEFINITION          *
*     ------------------------------------------------------------------------          *
* Define a local class for handling events of cl_salv_table*
*     ------------------------------------------------------------------------          *
CLASS lcl_handle_events DEFINITION FINAL.
      PUBLIC SECTION.
      METHODS:
      on_user_command FOR EVENT added_function OF cl_salv_events
      IMPORTING e_salv_function.
ENDCLASS.       "lcl_handle_events DEFINITION

*     ------------------------------------------------------------------------          *
*     CLASS lcl_handle_events IMPLEMENTATION          *
*     ------------------------------------------------------------------------          *
* Implement the events for handling the events of cl_salv_table *
*     ------------------------------------------------------------------------          *
CLASS lcl_handle_events IMPLEMENTATION.
```

```
    METHOD on_user_command.
    PERFORM handle_user_command USING e_salv_function.
    ENDMETHOD.      "on_user_command
ENDCLASS.     "lcl_handle_events IMPLEMENTATION

*&  ---------------------------------------------------------------------------    *
*&  Include    ZREPORT_UPD_SUB            *
*&  ---------------------------------------------------------------------------    *
*&  ---------------------------------------------------------------------------    *
*&  Form       START_PROCESSING           *
*&  ---------------------------------------------------------------------------    *
*    Fetch data from the Customized Update table        *
*---------------------------------------------------------------------------    *
FORM start_processing.
    CLEAR : i_upd.
* Fetch records from Customized update table
    SELECT *              "All fields
    FROM ztvgt_6078_stock    "Customized table for updation
    INTO TABLE i_upd
WHERE matnr ='000000000000000096'. "Material number

IF sy-subrc =0.

*    Sort records by comparing the Client, Batch Id, Material number and the Plant
SORT i_upd BY mandt
btch_id
matnr
werks.
ELSE.

*    Provide Standard message if any exception occurred MESSAGE i072(sf).

LEAVE LIST-PROCESSING.
ENDIF."Record found
```

```
ENDFORM.      "start_processing

*&  ---------------------------------------------------------------------------
*
*&  Form      DISPLAY_OUTPUT                     *
*&  ---------------------------------------------------------------------------
*
*   Display the final output    *
*------------------------------------------------------------------------------
*
FORM display_output .
*------------------------------------------------------------------------------
*
* Declaration of Local constants *
*------------------------------------------------------------------------------   CONSTANTS    :
      *


    lc_mandt  TYPE lvc_fname VALUE 'MANDT',"Client
    lc_flag     TYPE lvc_fname VALUE 'FLAG'."Flag field
*------------------------------------------------------------------------------
*
* Declaration of Local reference variables          *
*------------------------------------------------------------------------------   DATA:
    *


* Reference     to ALV header info
    lv_header              TYPE REF TO cl_salv_form_header_info ,
* Reference     to ALV functions list
    lv_functions           TYPE REF TO cl_salv_functions_list       ,
* Reference     to columns selection
    lv_selections          TYPE REF TO cl_salv_selections  ,
* Reference     to ALV column list
    lv_columns                          TYPE REF TO cl_salv_columns    ,
* Reference     to ALV column
```

```
      lv_column          TYPE REF TO cl_salv_column_table       ,
* Reference    to Events table
      lv_events          TYPE REF TO cl_salv_events_table       ,
* Reference    to ALV message
      lv_msg             TYPE REF TO cx_salv_msg       ,
* Reference    to ALV not found
      lv_not_found       TYPE REF TO cx_salv_not_found ,
* Reference    to data error for manipulating cell
      lv_data_error      TYPE REF TO cx_salv_data_error,
*     Reference to create object error

lv_object_error TYPE REF TO cx_sy_create_object_error.


*----------------------------------------------------------------------------*

* Declaration of Local variables  *
*----------------------------------------------------------------------------*
DATA:
lv_text TYPE char255. "Text value


CLEAR: lv_text.

*     Generate the ALV table with the final data TRY.

cl_salv_table=>factory (

EXPORTING
list_display   = c_false
IMPORTING

r_salv_table   = i_table
CHANGING
```

```
t_table  = i_upd).

CATCH cx_salv_msg INTO lv_msg.

CLEAR lv_text.

lv_text = lv_msg->get_text().
MESSAGE i001(bl) WITH lv_text.
LEAVE LIST-PROCESSING.

ENDTRY.

*      Create header information CLEAR: lv_header,
lv_text.

lv_text = 'Customized Table updation'(001).

*      Create the object for ALV header TRY.

CREATE OBJECT lv_header
EXPORTING
text  = lv_text
tooltip = lv_text.

CATCH cx_sy_create_object_error INTO lv_object_error.

CLEAR lv_text.

lv_text = lv_object_error->get_text( ).
MESSAGE i001(bl) WITH lv_text.
LEAVE LIST-PROCESSING.

ENDTRY.            "Create the object
```

i_table->set_top_of_list(lv_header).

* Include own functions by setting customized PF status i_table->set_screen_status (

pfstatus= 'ZREPORT_UPD_ST'

report = sy-repid

set_functions = i_table->c_functions_all).

lv_columns = i_table->get_columns().

lv_columns->set_optimize(c_true).

* Get all the functions available for ALV output lv_functions = i_table->get_ functions(). lv_functions->set_all(c_true).

* Change the properties of the Column – MANDT (Hide field) TRY.

lv_column?= lv_columns->get_column(lc_mandt).
lv_column->set_visible(if_salv_c_bool_sap=>false).

CATCH cx_salv_not_found INTO lv_not_found.

CLEAR lv_text.

lv_text = lv_not_found->get_text().
MESSAGE i001(bl) WITH lv_text.
LEAVE LIST-PROCESSING.

CATCH cx_salv_data_error INTO lv_data_error.

lv_text = lv_data_error->get_text().
MESSAGE i001(bl) WITH lv_text.
LEAVE LIST-PROCESSING.

```
ENDTRY.
*     Change the properties of the Column – FLAG (Hide field) TRY.

lv_column?= lv_columns->get_column( lc_flag ).

lv_column->set_visible(if_salv_c_bool_sap=>false ).

CATCH cx_salv_not_found INTO lv_not_found.

CLEAR lv_text.

lv_text = lv_not_found->get_text().
MESSAGE i001(bl) WITH lv_text.
LEAVE LIST-PROCESSING.

CATCH cx_salv_data_error INTO lv_data_error.

lv_text = lv_data_error->get_text().
MESSAGE i001(bl) WITH lv_text.
LEAVE LIST-PROCESSING.

ENDTRY.

lv_events = i_table->get_event().

*     Create the object for ALV events TRY.

CREATE OBJECT i_events.
CATCH cx_sy_create_object_error INTO lv_object_error.

CLEAR lv_text.

lv_text = lv_object_error->get_text().
```

```
MESSAGE i001(bl) WITH lv_text.
LEAVE LIST-PROCESSING.

ENDTRY.          "Create the object

*     Register to the event USER_COMMAND

SET HANDLER i_events->on_user_command FOR lv_events.lv_selections = i_table->get_selections().
*     Set selection mode

lv_selections->set_selection_mode (
if_salv_c_selection_mode=>row_column).

*     Display the output table i_table->display().

CLEAR: lv_text.

ENDFORM.                    " DISPLAY_OUTPUT


*&  ----------------------------------------------------------------------
    *
*&  Form        HANDLE_USER_COMMAND                                      *
*&  ----------------------------------------------------------------------
    *
*     Handle user command       for the entry deletion    *
*-----------------------------------------------------------------------
    *
*     -->PV_SALV_FUNCTION      SALV user action command         *
*-----------------------------------------------------------------------
    *
FORM handle_user_command USING pv_salv_function TYPE salv_de_function.

*-----------------------------------------------------------------------
```

```
*
* Declaration of Global constants                              *
*---------------------------------------------------------------------------   CONSTANTS :
                *


    lc_delete   TYPE sap_bool VALUE 'L'.          "Deletion value
*---------------------------------------------------------------------------
    *
* Declaration of Local internal tables                 *
*---------------------------------------------------------------------------   DATA :
       *


    li_rows     TYPE salv_t_row,          "Selected rows
    li_temp     TYPE ty_t_upd.  "Customized update table
*---------------------------------------------------------------------------
    *
* Declaration of Local work areas                              *
*---------------------------------------------------------------------------   DATA :
       *


    lw_row      TYPE LINE OF salv_t_row."Selected row
*---------------------------------------------------------------------------
    *
* Declaration of Local variables                       *
*---------------------------------------------------------------------------   DATA :
       *


    lv_index    TYPE i."Currently selected rows
*---------------------------------------------------------------------------
    *
* Declaration of local reference variables                     *
*---------------------------------------------------------------------------   DATA:
       *


    lv_selections TYPE REF TO cl_salv_selections. "Selection reference
```

```
*----------------------------------------------------------------------------*

* Declaration of Global pointers *
*----------------------------------------------------------------------------*

FIELD-SYMBOLS:
<l_fs_upd>TYPE ty_upd. "Data table


* Clear the local variables

CLEAR: li_rows  ,
li_temp ,
lw_row ,
lv_index.

CASE pv_salv_function.

WHEN 'DELN'.

* Get the selected rows

lv_selections = i_table->get_selections().
li_rows = lv_selections->get_selected_rows().

IF li_rows [] IS NOT INITIAL.

CLEAR: li_temp,

lw_row.

*     Populate the rows which are selected from the display output LOOP AT li_rows
INTO lw_row.
```

```
CLEAR lv_index.

lv_index = lw_row.

*     Fetch the value for the currently selected row UNASSIGN <l_fs_upd>.

READ TABLE i_upd
INDEX lv_index
ASSIGNING <l_fs_upd>.

IF <l_fs_upd> IS ASSIGNED.

APPEND <l_fs_upd> TO li_temp.

<l_fs_upd>-flag = lc_delete. "Mark for deleteENDIF."Record found

CLEAR lw_row.

ENDLOOP.        "LOOP AT li_rows INTO lw_row



IF li_temp [] IS NOT INITIAL.

*     Delete the selected entries from the ZTABLE_UPD table PERFORM delete_entries
CHANGING li_temp
i_upd.



ENDIF.


ENDIF.
ENDCASE.
```

```
UNASSIGN <l_fs_upd>.

i_table->refresh().

*     Clear the local variables CLEAR: li_rows ,

li_temp , lw_row, lv_index.

ENDFORM.                 " HANDLE_USER_COMMAND

*&   ---------------------------------------------------------------------
*
*&      Form  DELETE_ENTRIES  *
*&   ---------------------------------------------------------------------
*
*     Delete the selected entries from the table and refresh the table display  *
*-----------------------------------------------------------------------
*
*     <  --C_T_TEMP     Customized update table
*     <  --C_T_UPD      Customized update table
*-----------------------------------------------------------------------
*
FORM delete_entries CHANGING c_t_temp       TYPE ty_t_upd
                   c_t_upd           TYPE ty_t_upd.
*-----------------------------------------------------------------------
*
* Declaration of Global constants            *
*-----------------------------------------------------------------------    CONSTANTS :
*


      lc_delete TYPE sap_bool VALUE'L'.  "Deletion value

*     Delete the entries which are marked for deletion DELETE c_t_upd WHERE flag =
lc_delete.
```

```
*      Lock the Error table for new insertion

CALL FUNCTION 'ENQUEUE_E_TABLES' EXPORTING

mode_rstable   = c_true
tabname           = 'ZTVGT_6078_STOCK'
EXCEPTIONS
foreign_lock      = 1
system_failure =            2
OTHERS=          3.

ELSE.

* Rollback the changes made

CALL FUNCTION 'BAPI_TRANSACTION_ROLLBACK'.

*      Append the records which are selected for deletion but failed from

*      actual update in database to reach at the previous stage
APPEND LINES OF c_t_temp TO c_t_upd.

*      Sort records by comparing the Client, Warehouse Number, Transfer

*      requirement number and item
SORT i_upd BY mandt
btch_id
matnr
werks.

ENDIF.
* Unlock the Error table

CALL FUNCTION 'DEQUEUE_E_TABLE'
```

```
EXPORTING
mode_rstable = c_true
tabname         = 'ZTVGT_6078_STOCK'.

ENDIF.

CLEAR: c_t_temp.

ENDFORM.        " DELETE_ENTRIES
```

Note: The above given example is the simpler form of SALV factory method. We can create checkboxes, cell color, row color, buttons, hyperlinks and lots of other functionalities using this method.

CHAPTER 8

Event Handling in 2 Grids simultaneously(ALV OOPS(SAP ABAP))

Purpose:

Handling Events in two grids simultaneously on the same Screen.
As being developed by OOPS, ALV grid control has some events that are triggered during interaction between the user.
These events are used to utilize some additional functionalities of the ALV grid.
For these types of functionalities, we require a class to be implemented to be the event handler for the ALV Grid instance.

Technical Information:

Handling Events in two grids at the same time using ALV with OOPS:

1. **Step 1:**

   First create a screen including two custom containers (CONT1 and CONT2) in it.

   On these two containers we are going to handle the data changes and capture them on any user interaction.

2. **Step 2:**

   In the **PBO(Process Before Output)** section of the screen, include a Module to display the ALV grid in the container.

   Ex: Module alv_display.

3. **Step 3:**

   In the **Module alv_display-**

   a.) **Create an object for the 1st custom container** exporting the name as parameter which links the program to the screen element.

```
CREATE OBJECT ob_custom1
EXPORTING
container_name = .CONT1.1
```

Where container_name is the name of the container given in the screen

b.) **Next create an object for the ALV Grid.1** exporting the parent container name.

```
CREATE OBJECT ob_grid1
EXPORTING
i_parent = ob_customl.
```

c.) **Create an object event receiver and then set a handler on all the cells of the grid** for handling any change in data in any of the cells of the grid.

```
CREATE OBJECT event_receiver.
SET HANDLER event_receiver->handle_data_changed FOR
ob_grid1.
```

d.) **Register the event you want to handle.** For ex:" Enter" event.

```
CALL METHOD ob_grid1->register_edit_event
EXPORTING
i_event_id = cl_gui_alv_grid=>mc_evt_enter.
```

This registers the enter event to all the cells present in the grid i.e. on changing any value in any of the cells and pressing enter will capture the value in the grid.

e.) **Build the field catalog and the Layout for the grid.**
And call the Method to display the data in the Grid passing the final internal table containing the values ,the field catalog and the layout for the first time when the container is empty.

```
If ob_custom1 is initial.
CALL METHOD ob_grid1->set_table_for_first_display
```

```
EXPORTING
is_layout = l_layout
CHANGING
it_fieldcatalog = t_fcat_final1
it_outtab = t_final1,
Endif.
```

f.) If the customcontainer is not empty (i.e. having some values and the grid needs to be populated with new values),a method to refresh the grid needs to be called.

```
If ob_custom1 is not initial.
CALL METHOD ob_grid1->refresh_table_display
 EXPORTING
 is_stable = l_lvc_s_stbl
 EXCEPTIONS
finished = 1
OTHERS   = 2.
IF sy-subrc <> 0.
 MESSAGE ID sy-msgid TYPE sy-msgty NUMBER sy-msgno
WITH sy-msgv1 sy-msgv2 sy-msgv3 sy-msgv4.
ENDIF.
End if.
```

Repeat the same steps for the 2nd container as well.

4. **Step 4:**

A class is implemented to handle the events in the two Grids.

In the class definition we call the event for controlling data changes when ALV grid is editable which invokes the class implementation on any interaction by the user when there is any change in the ALV grid..

```
CLASS lcl_event_receiver DEFINITION.
PUBLIC SECTION.
METHODS handle_data_changed
```

```
        FOR EVENT data_changed OF cl_gui_alv_grid
        IMPORTING
        er_data_changed
        sender.
    ENDCLASS.
```

Here Sender is an importing parameter which passes all the grids present on the screen to the class implementation.

5. **Step 5:**
   In the class implementation, handle the events that you want to be triggered i.e. the actual handling of event is done.

```
CLASS lcl_event_receiver IMPLEMENTATION.
  METHOD handle_data_changed.
    CASE sender.
      WHEN ob_grid1.
       TRY.
*populate all the changed data into ont table with their roww_ids*
          LOOP AT er_data_changed->mt_mod_cells INTO l_good .
CLEAR: w_error_flag.
           CASE l_good-fieldname.

* check if column 'F1' of this row was changed
            WHEN 'F1'.
             v_F1_flg = 'X'.
             "Flag set to indicate the row modification
             IF l_good-value IS NOT INITIAL.
               w_F1 = l_good-value.
             ENDIF.

* check if column 'F2' of this row was changed
            WHEN 'F2'.
             v_F2_flg = 'X'.
```

```
        "Flag set to indicate the row modification
        IF l_good-value IS NOT  INITIAL.
          w_F2 = l_good-value.
        ENDIF.
      ENDCASE.

* Populating t_changed_rows table with all the changed row ids *
      AT END OF row_id.

IF w_error_flag IS INITIAL.
   "if no error that row id is marked for further manipulation of data
        READ TABLE t_final2 ASSIGNING <fs_final> INDEX
        l_good-row_id.

        IF <fs_final> IS ASSIGNED.
          IF v_F1_flg IS NOT INITIAL.
<fs_final>-F1= w_F1.
          ENDIF.
 IF v_F2_flg IS NOT INITIAL.
<fs_final>-F2= w_F2.
          ENDIF.

          w_change_flag = abap_true.
      CLEAR:w_F1, v_F1_flg, w_F2 ,v_F2_flg,

UNASSIGN <fs_final>.
        ENDIF.
       ENDIF.
     ENDLOOP.

*& Get the cursor id from the cell on which data was modified&*
     CLEAR: l_row_no, l_col_id ,l_row_id.
     ob_grid2->get_current_cell (
    IMPORTING
```

```
          es_row_id = l_row_id
          es_col_id = l_col_id
          es_row_no = l_row_no
            ).

*& Refreshing the grid with modified data&*
          IF t_final1 IS NOT INITIAL.
          CALL METHOD ob_grid1->refresh_table_display
            EXPORTING
             is_stable = l_lvc_s_stbl
            EXCEPTIONS
finished = 1
             OTHERS    = 2.
           IF sy-subrc <> 0.
            MESSAGE ID sy-msgid TYPE sy-msgty NUMBER sy-msgno
                  WITH sy-msgv1 sy-msgv2 sy-msgv3 sy-msgv4.
           ENDIF.
          ENDIF.

*& Set the cursor to the cell on which data was modified&*
          ob_grid1->set_current_cell_via_id(is_row_id = l_row_id
                          is_column_id = l_col_id
                          is_row_no = l_row_no ).

        CATCH cx_sy_conversion_no_number INTO error_ref.
          err_text = error_ref->get_text().
          WRITE err_text.
        CATCH cx_root INTO oref.
          text = oref->get_text().
       ENDTRY.

      WHEN ob_grid2.
       TRY.
*populate all the changed data into ont table with their roww_ids*
```

```
    LOOP AT er_data_changed->mt_mod_cells INTO l_good.
     CLEAR: w_error_flag.
     CASE l_good-fieldname.

* check if column ‘G1’ of this row was changed
       WHEN ‘G1’.
        v_G1_flg = ‘X’.
        “Flag set to indicate the row modification
        IF l_good-value  IS NOT INITIAL.
         w_G1 = l_good-value.
        ENDIF.

* check if column ‘G2’ of this row was changed
       WHEN ‘G2’.
        v_G2_flg = ‘X’.
        “Flag set to indicate the row modification
        IF l_good-value IS NOT  INITIAL.
         w_G2 = l_good-value.
        ENDIF.
     ENDCASE.

*  Populating t_changed_rows table with all the changed row ids *
     AT END OF row_id.

       IF w_error_flag IS INITIAL.
  “if no error that row id is marked for further manipulation of data

        READ TABLE t_final2 ASSIGNING <fs_final> INDEX
        l_good-row_id.

        IF <fs_final> IS ASSIGNED.
         IF v_G1_flg IS NOT INITIAL.
<fs_final>-G1 = w_G1.
         ENDIF.
```

```
 IF v_G2_flg IS NOT INITIAL.
<fs_final>-G2 = w_G2.
            ENDIF.

            w_change_flag = abap_true.
        CLEAR:w_G1, v_G1_flg, w_G2 ,v_G2_flg,

 UNASSIGN <fs_final>.
          ENDIF.
         ENDIF.
       ENDLOOP.

*& Get the cursor id from the cell on which data was modified&*
       CLEAR: l_row_no, l_col_id ,l_row_id.

       ob_grid2->get_current_cell(
       IMPORTING
        es_row_id = l_row_id
        es_col_id = l_col_id
        es_row_no = l_row_no
          ).

*& Refreshing the grid with modified data&*
       IF t_final2 IS NOT INITIAL.
        CALL METHOD ob_grid2->refresh_table_display
         EXPORTING
          is_stable = l_lvc_s_stbl
         EXCEPTIONS
          finished = 1
          OTHERS    = 2.
        IF sy-subrc <> 0.
         MESSAGE ID sy-msgid TYPE sy-msgty NUMBER sy-msgno
               WITH sy-msgv1 sy-msgv2 sy-msgv3 sy-msgv4.
        ENDIF.
```

```
        ENDIF.

*& Set the cursor to the cell on which data was modified&*
        ob_grid2->set_current_cell_via_id(is_row_id = l_row_id
                                 is_column_id = l_col_id
                                 is_row_no = l_row_no).

      CATCH cx_sy_conversion_no_number INTO error_ref.
        err_text = error_ref->get_text().
        WRITE err_text.
      CATCH cx_root INTO oref.
        text = oref->get_text().
    ENDTRY.
  ENDCASE.
 ENDMETHOD.
ENDCLASS.
```

5. **Step 6:**

   Whenever there is any change in data in the grid and you press some Function Code it doesn't register the changes you made to the grid.

   For the Function Codes like SAVE etc. you need to call the method explicitly in the PAI(Process After Input) of the screen.

```
WHEN 'SAVE'.
   CLEAR: ok_code.
   CALL METHOD ob_grid1->check_changed_data.
   CALL METHOD ob_grid2->check_changed_data.
 ENDCASE.
```

Which triggers the class implementation if there is any change in data and any Func. Code button is pressed for both the grids.

CHAPTER 9

Creating ALV with Dynamic Columns

Ref: Harsh Vardhan Bhalla's artefact

Dynamic ALV is an extension to the ALV concept. It is used when the number of fields is **NOT** known at the design time or until compile time. It is only determined during **RUNTIME**. Take a look at this sample screenshot below. There are two static fields and five dynamic columns.

Steps involved to implement output with dynamic ALV are as below:

1. Create definition of fields to be displayed in output. This is equivalent to creating field catalog for ALV. Dynamic fields can be populated based on program logic.

Sample code is as below:

Internal **table gt**_temp contains the fields to be displayed in output.

Workarea **c_fieldname** is field name by which dynamic field is referred in program logic.

Internal table **gt_lvc_cat** is populated with definition of fields to be displayed and is field catalog.

```
*-- For dynamic fields in catalog
LOOP AT gt_temp INTO gwa_temp.

*-- Use counter to name dynamic fields
ADD 1 TO l_tabix.
```

```
CONDENSE l_tabix.
*-- Make name of field
CLEAR c_fieldname.
CONCATENATE cc_role l_tabix INTO c_fieldname SEPARATED BY
cc_underscore.
*-- Move to field catalog table
  gw_fieldcat-fieldname = c_fieldname.
  gw_fieldcat-seltext_l = gwa_temp-agr_name.
APPEND gw_fieldcat TO gt_fieldcat.
*-- Name
  gw_lvc_cat-fieldname = c_fieldname.
APPEND gw_lvc_cat TO gt_lvc_cat.

ENDLOOP.
```

2. Create dynamic internal table and work area based on this definition of fields or field catalog as below:

Dynamic Internal table created is **new_table** with workarea is **new_line** assigned to field symbol **g_table&g_line**, respectively.

```
*-- Create a new Table
CALL METHOD cl_alv_table_create=>create_dynamic_table
EXPORTING
   it_fieldcatalog = gt_lvc_cat
IMPORTING
   ep_table      = new_table.

*-- Create a new Line with the same structure of the table
ASSIGN new_table->* TO <g_table>.
CREATE DATA new_line LIKE LINE OF <g_table>.
ASSIGN new_line->* TO <g_line>.
```

3. Populate final table with resultant values based on program logic.

```
*-- Populate final table
LOOP AT gt_temp INTO gwa_temp.
*-----------------------------------------
*-- Program Logic to populate field values.
*-----------------------------------------
```

```
ASSIGN COMPONENT XXXXX OF STRUCTURE <g_line>TO <g_field>.
<g_field>= XXXXX_VALUE.

APPEND <g_line>TO <g_table>.
CLEAR <g_line>.

ENDLOOP.
```

4. Display final resultant table using function module 'REUSE_ALV_GRID_DISPLAY' as below:

```
*-- Call FM for ALV Grid Display
CALL FUNCTION 'REUSE_ALV_GRID_DISPLAY'
EXPORTING
    i_callback_program = sy-repid
    it_fieldcat      = gt_fieldcat
    is_layout        = gw_layout
TABLES
    t_outtab         = <g_table>
EXCEPTIONS
    program_error    = 1
OTHERS          = 2.
IF sy-subrc <>0.
MESSAGE 'Error in Displaying ALV'(001) TYPE 'E'.
ENDIF.
```

CHAPTER 10

Creation of Drop down in ALV in Web Dynpro ABAP

Ref: Naveesh Surapureddy's artefact

Creation of web Dynpro component

Transaction used: SE80

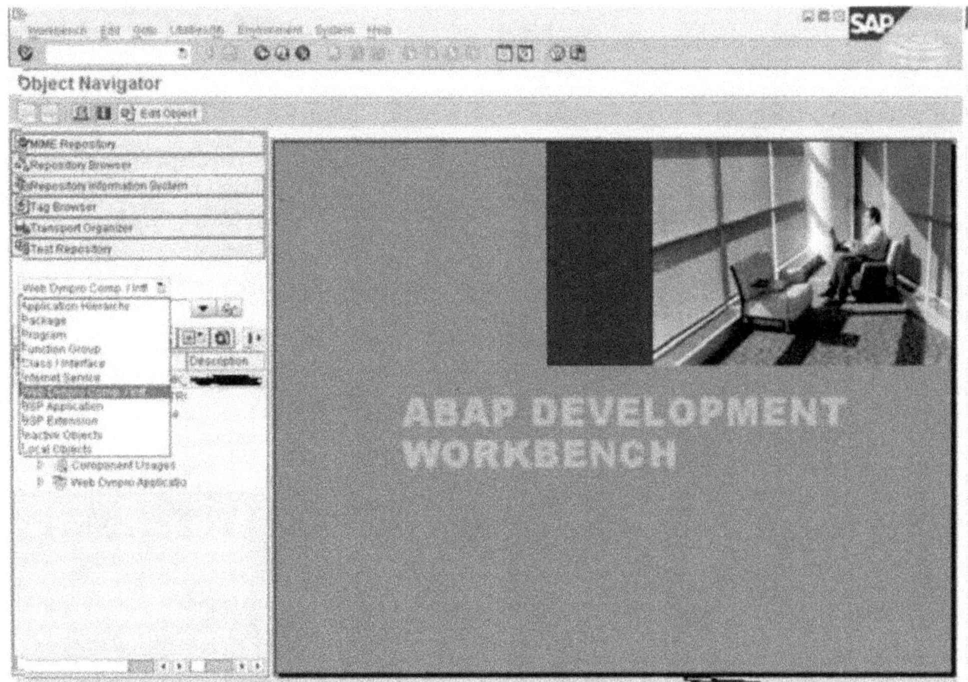

- Create a view for ALV and check whether alv is getting displayed or not. If the alv is not displayed kindly check and correct it to get the alv displayed.
- Now decide the column in which you want to display the drop down as per the

requirement given to you

- In the example here I have taken the column name as 'TYPES' Now add an attribute say VALUESET in the node of the ALV

Creation of Attribute Valueset for Dropdown in ALV

SAP ABAP Webdynpro

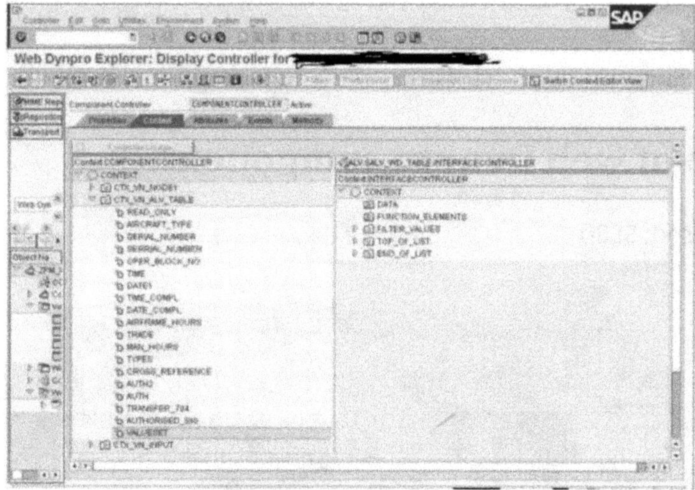

The Type of Value set must be WDR_CONTEXT_ATTR_VALUE_LIST

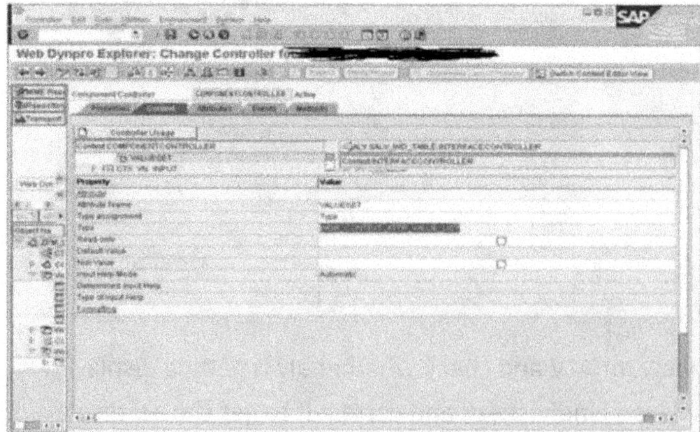

Method DOINIT

```
DATA: LT_VALUESET TYPE TABLE OF WDR_CONTEXT_ATTR_
VALUE,
LS_VALUESET TYPE WDR_CONTEXT_ATTR_VALUE.
DATA LV_VALUE TYPE REF
TO CL_SALV_WD_CONFIG_TABLE.
LV_VALUE->IF_SALV_WD_TABLE_SETTINGS~SET_DATA_CHECK
( IF_SALV_WD_C_TABLE_SETTINGS=>DATA_CHECK_ON_CELL_EVENT ).
DATA: LR_COL TYPE REF TO CL_SALV_WD_COLUMN,

LR_DROPDOWN TYPE REF TO CL_SALV_WD_UIE_
DROPDOWN_BY_KEY.
LO_VALUE = LO_INTERFACECONTROLLER->GET_MODEL( ).
LO_VALUE->IF_SALV_WD_TABLE_SETTINGS~SET_READ_ONLY( ABAP_FALSE ).
LR_COLUMN = LO_VALUE->IF_SALV_WD_COLUMN_SETTINGS~GET_
COLUMN( ID = 'TYPES' ).
CREATE OBJECT LR_DROPDOWN EXPORTING SELECTED_KEY_
FIELDNAME = 'TYPES'.
LR_COLUMN->SET_CELL_EDITOR( LR_DROPDOWN ).
DATA: LT_VALUESET TYPE TABLE OF WDR_CONTEXT_ATTR_
VALUE,
LS_VALUESET TYPE WDR_CONTEXT_ATTR_VALUE,
LR_NODE TYPE REF TO IF_WD_CONTEXT_NODE,

LR_NODEINFO TYPE REF TO IF_WD_CONTEXT_NODE_INFO.

LR_NODE = WD_CONTEXT->GET_CHILD_NODE( 'CTX_VN_ALV_
TABLE' ).
LR_NODEINFO = LR_NODE->GET_NODE_INFO( ).
* navigate from <CONTEXT> to <CTX_VN_ALV_TABLE> via lead
selection
    LO_ND_CTX_VN_ALV_TABLE = WD_CONTEXT->GET_CHILD_
NODE( NAME = WD_THIS-
>WDCTX_CTX_VN_ALV_TABLE ).
* get element via lead selection
```

```
LO_EL_CTX_VN_ALV_TABLE = LO_ND_CTX_VN_ALV_TABLE->GET_ELEMENT( ).
* @TODO handle
not set lead selection

IF LO_EL_CTX_VN_ALV_TABLE IS INITIAL.
ENDIF.

CALL METHOD LO_ND_CTX_VN_ALV_TABLE->GET_STATIC_ATTRIBUTES_TABLE
IMPORTING

TABLE = LT_ALV.

*append ls_valueset to lt_valueset.

LS_VALUESET-VALUE = 'FIRST'.
LS_VALUESET-TEXT = 'FIRST'.
APPEND LS_VALUESET TO LT_VALUESET.

LS_VALUESET-VALUE = 'SECOND' .
LS_VALUESET-TEXT = 'SECOND'.
APPEND LS_VALUESET TO LT_VALUESET.
LR_NODEINFO->SET_ATTRIBUTE_VALUE_SET(
EXPORTING
NAME = 'TYPES'
VALUE_SET = LT_VALUESET
```

Result

If the steps are correctly followed you will see the following result when you execute the code.

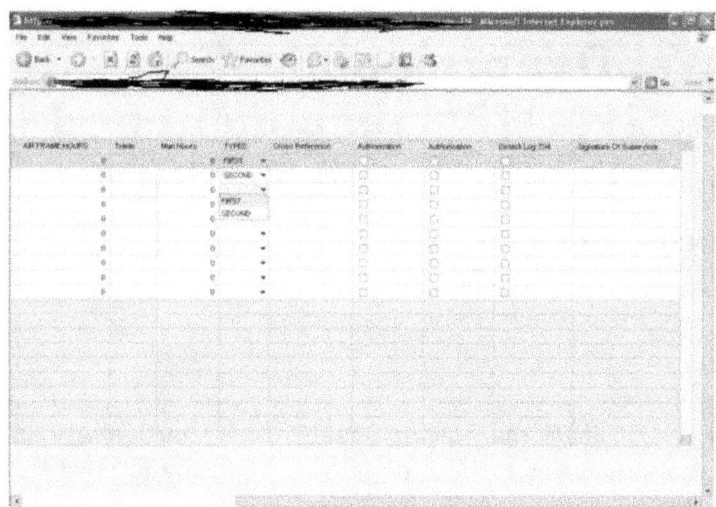

CHAPTER 11

WebDynpro application with Interactive ALV component and Use of Tabstrip and Tooltips

Ref: Ramandeep Gumbal's artefact

Document Scope

The Document explained the way to create an interactive ALV in webdynpro component. It also explains the Use of Tabstrip and How to create a Tooltips and column re-sizable functionality in the output ALV fields.

Overview - Description

Detail Information:

1. Reason for Development:

The requirement was to make a webdynpro application to be shown on portal screen. With 2 different Tabs. These Tabs will show data from a Custom table.

1) Tab 1: A summary View, which contains only few fields.
2) Tab 2: A detailed View, showing all the fields of custom table.

Next requirement was to make this ALV interactive i.e.

a) Columns should be resizable.
b) For longer length Fields a help popup or a tooltip should be provided so that User doesn't have to scroll the complete field to read its Value.
c) Export Button to download the Data into an Excel.

E.g. like below:

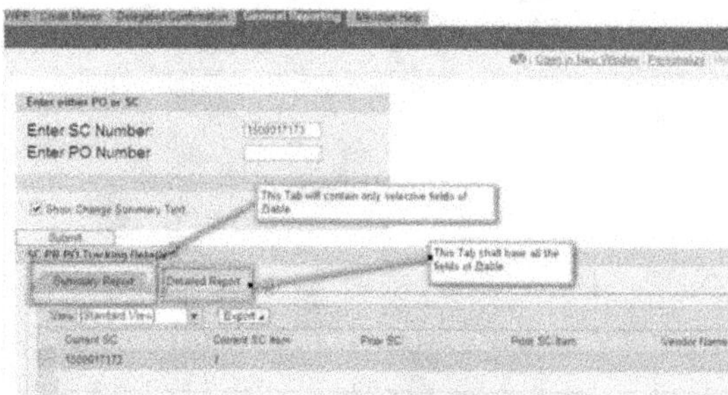

ALV features:

a) Field Tool tips:

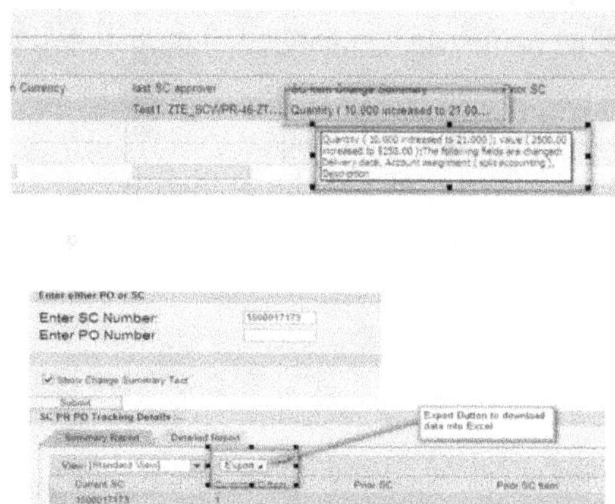

b)

Solution: Steps to create a web dynpro application with an ALV component in it.

Step 1: Open transaction SE80 and from the drop down list select WebDynpro Component.

Step 2: Enter the application name (Here ZQM_WD_ZQSCPRPO)

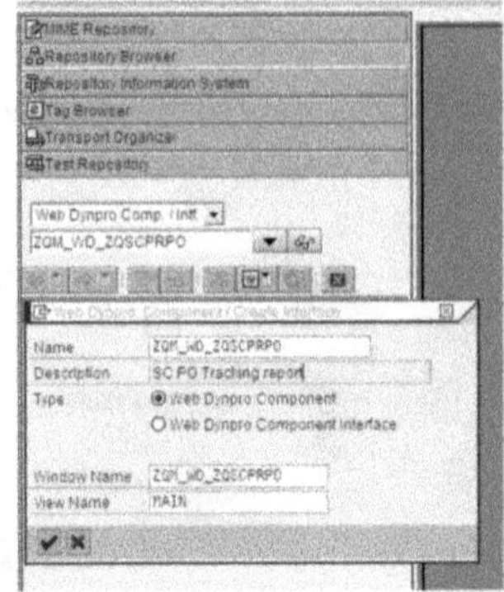

Step 3: You will get a pop up as shown above. Click YES.

Step 4: Enter the description on the next pop up as shown in the below screenshot. Here the Window name can be changed. It is defaulted to the name of the application.

Step 5: A Web Dynpro component will then be created. A COMPONENT CONTROLLER, WINDOW and INTERFACE COMPONENTS will be created automatically.

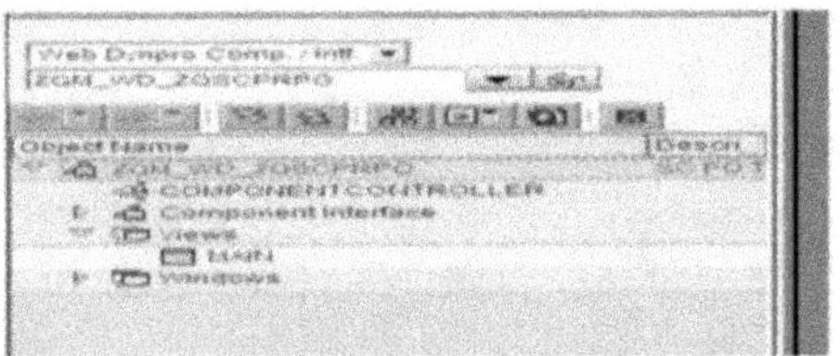

Step 6: Double click on the Component controller. You will see an empty context. Right click on the CONTEXT and click on create > node.

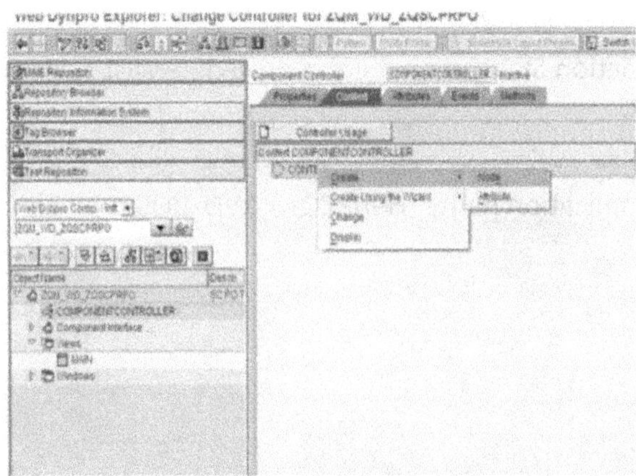

Step 7: Enter the details on the pop up as shown below. (Create NODE_SELECT)

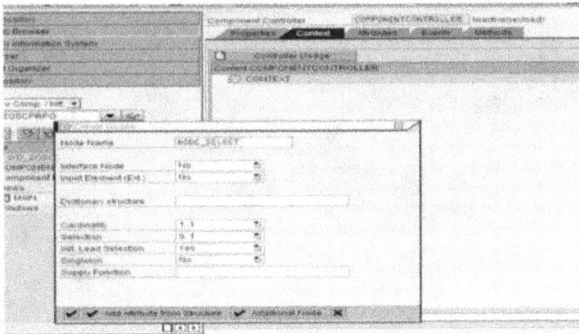

Step 8: Click on 'Add Attribute' for all input fields:

a) Shopping Cart Number

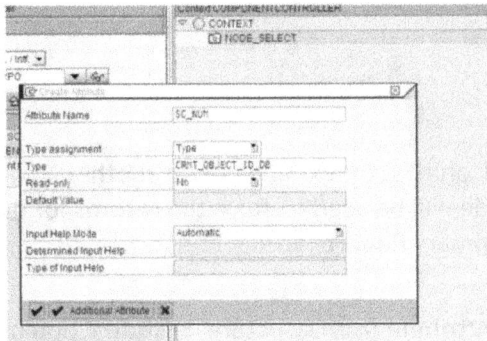

b) PO Number:

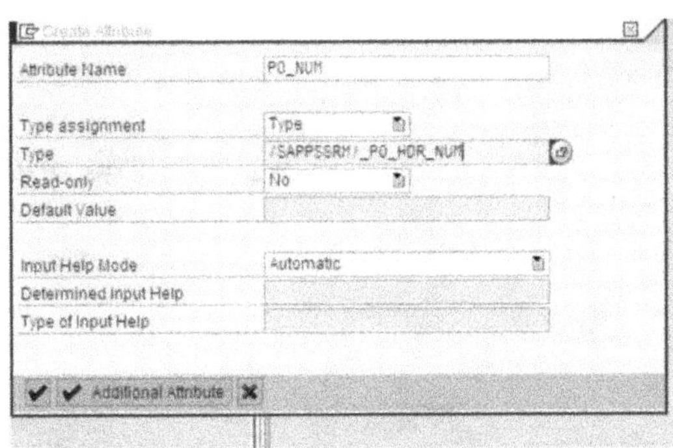

c) S_Text

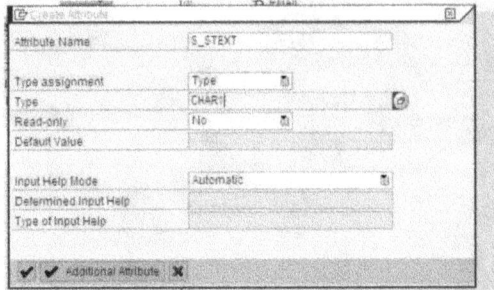

The Context Node will look like this:

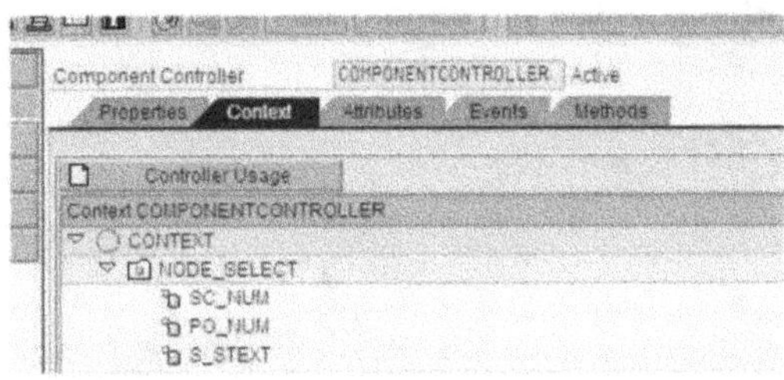

Step 9: Again right click on the context and create another Node called NODE_ALV_SHORT. This node will be used to store the records for displaying in the ALV output for "Summary Report Tab":

Step 10: Click on 'Add Attribute from structure' button. A pop up will be displayed on the screen, which will show the fields of the table. (Here ZQM_SHORT_VER_LINE):

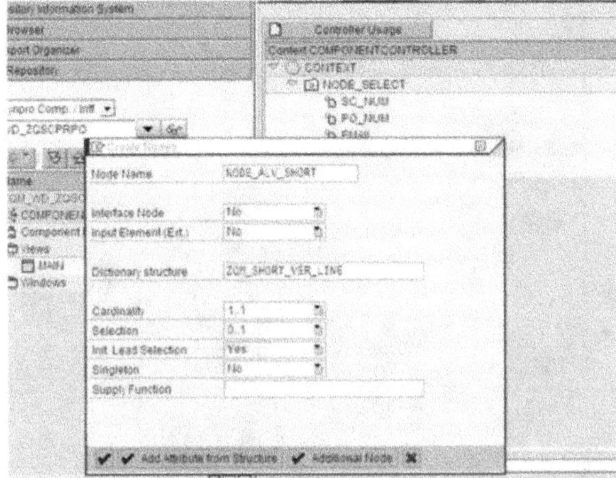

Step 11: Again click on 'Add attributes from structure' and select the following fields

Component	RTy	Component Type	Data Type	Length	Decim	Short
SC_CUR_NUM		CRMT_OBJECT_ID	CHAR	10	0	Tran
SC_CUR_ITM		BBP_ITEM_NO	NUMC	10	0	Item
SC_PRI_NUM		CRMT_OBJECT_ID	CHAR	10	0	Tran
SC_PRI_ITM		BBP_ITEM_NO	NUMC	10	0	Item
PO_ACT_VEN_NAME		AD_NAME1	CHAR	40	0	Nam
PO_SRC_NUM		/SAPPSSRM/_PO_HE	CHAR	10	0	Purc
PO_SRC_ITM		EBELP	NUMC	5	0	Item
SEQNUMBER		SEQNUMBER	CHAR	4	0	Appl
PO_ACT_NUM		/SAPPSSRM/_PO_HE	CHAR	10	0	Purc
PO_ACT_ITM		EBELP	NUMC	5	0	Item
PO_ACT_ITM_QTY		BBP_MNG	QUAN	13	3	Quar
PO_ACT_ITM_MEINS		MEINS	UNIT	3	0	Base
ALT_TEXT		BBP_CMS_XMLSTR	STRING	0	0	XML

Step 12: Again right click on the context and create another Node called NODE_ALV_LONG. This node will be used to store the records for displaying in the ALV output.

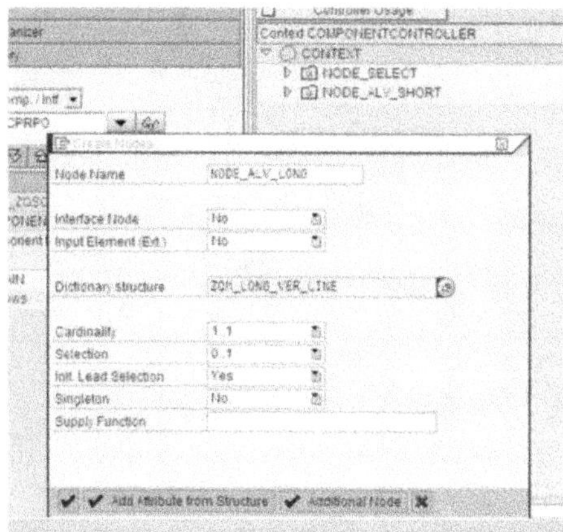

Step 13: Again click on 'Add attributes from structure' and select the following fields

1 / 31

Component	RTy	Component Type	Data Type	Length	Decim	Short
SC_CUR_NUM		CRMT_OBJECT_ID	CHAR	10	0	Tran
SC_CUR_ITM		BBP_ITEM_NO	NUMC	10	0	Item
SC_CUR_ITM_QTY		BBP_MNG	QUAN	13	3	Quar
SC_CUR_ITM_PRICE		BBP_PRICE	CURR	13	2	Net F
SC_PRI_NUM		CRMT_OBJECT_ID	CHAR	10	0	Tran
SC_PRI_ITM		BBP_ITEM_NO	NUMC	10	0	Item
PO_SRC_NUM		/SAPPSSRM/_PO_HE	CHAR	10	0	Purc
PO_SRC_ITM		/SAPPSSRM/_PO_IT	NUMC	10	0	Purc
SEQNUMBER		SEQNUMBER	CHAR	4	0	Appl
RECORD_CREATE		ZTRCOCRE	CHAR	14	0	Reco
RECORD_UPDATE		ZTRCOUPD	CHAR	14	0	Reco
PR_ACT_NUM		BANFN	CHAR	10	0	Purc
PR_ACT_ITM		BNFPO	NUMC	5	0	Item
PR_ACT_ITM_ROSTR		AFNAM	CHAR	12	0	Nam
PR_ACT_ITEM_QTY		BBP_MNG	QUAN	13	3	Quar
PR_ACT_ITEM_VAL		BBP_VALUE	CURR	15	2	Net V
PO_ACT_CREATE		AEDAT	DATS	8	0	Char
PO_ACT_NUM		/SAPPSSRM/_PO_HE	CHAR	10	0	Purc
PO_ACT_ITM		/SAPPSSRM/_PO_IT	NUMC	10	0	Purc
PO_ACT_ITM_ROTIN		AFNAM	CHAR	12	0	Nam
PO_ACT_ITM_CANUM		KONNR	CHAR	10	0	Num

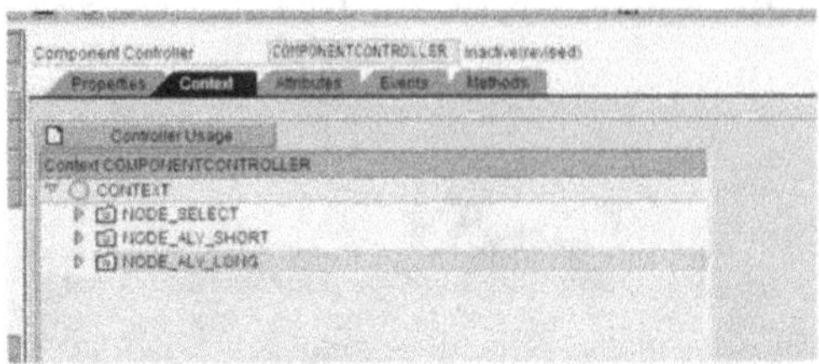

Step 14: Now save the component controller. Right click on the Component name (ZQM_WD_ZQSCPRPO) and click on create > View. Enter the following details on the pop up.

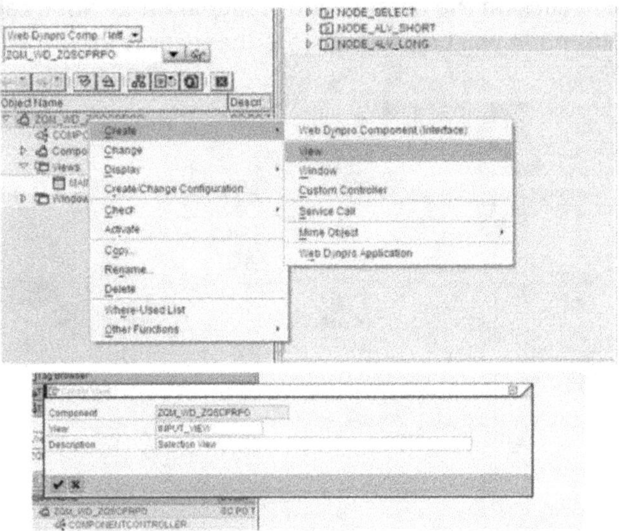

Step 15: We have now created a view where we will be displaying the input fields and which will accept values from the user. Now the LAYOUT of the view will be displayed. Navigate to the CONTEXT tab. You will see the following screen:

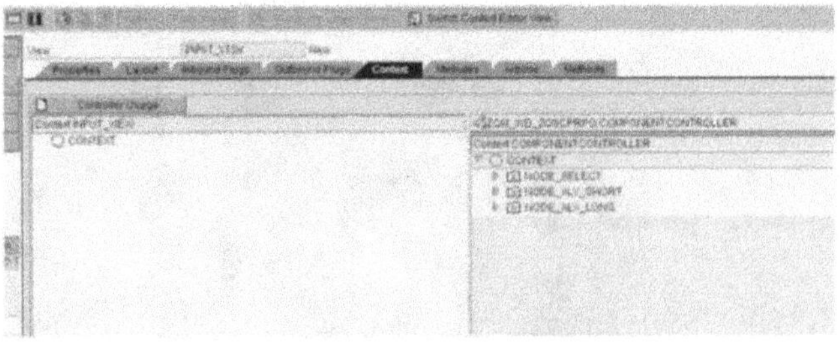

Step 16: Navigate to the LAYOUT tab on the input view. Right click on the ROOTELEMENTCONTAINER and click on create container form

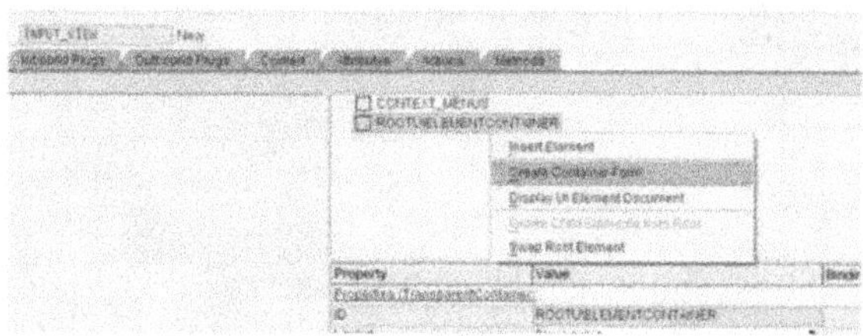

Step 17: A pop up will appear with a Create element, Enter ID as GROUP1 and select type Group.

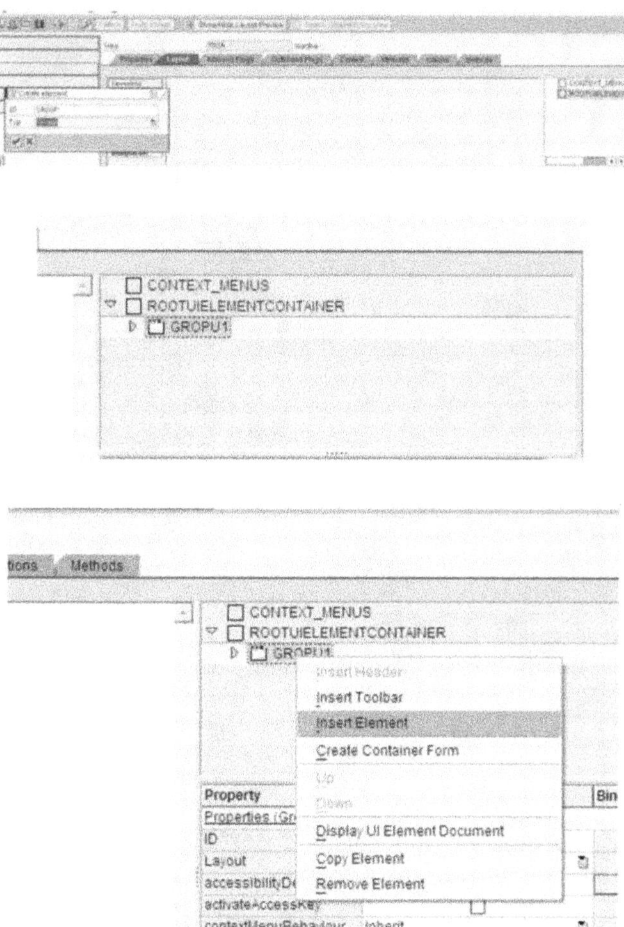

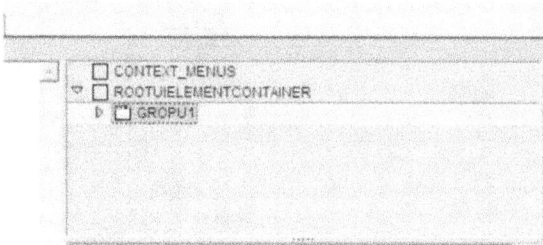

Step 18: Select type Group and right click to Insert Elements (to enter all input fields):

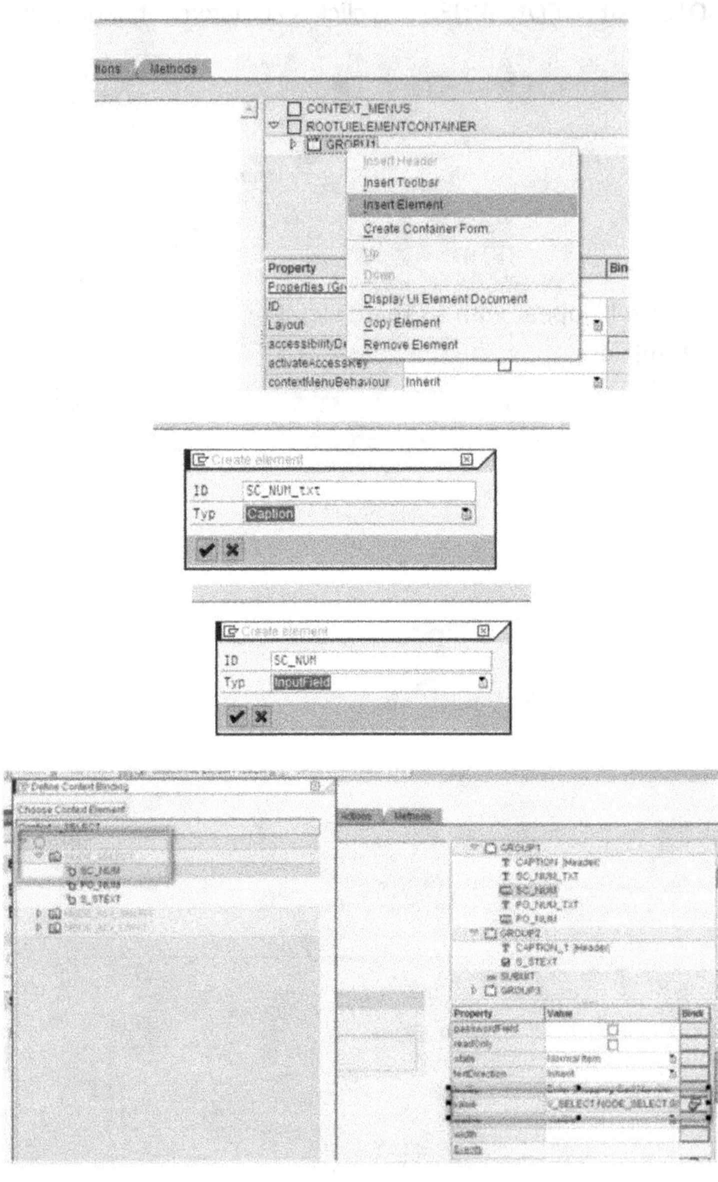

Step 19: Select type Group and right click to Insert Elements (to enter all input fields) and do the Binding with the Context:

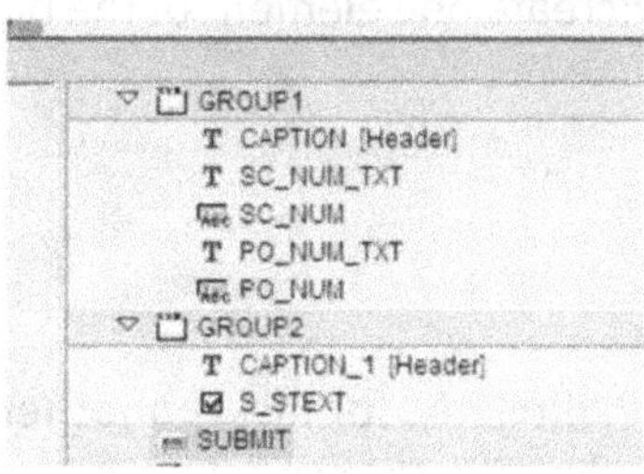

Step 20: For Submit Button-->

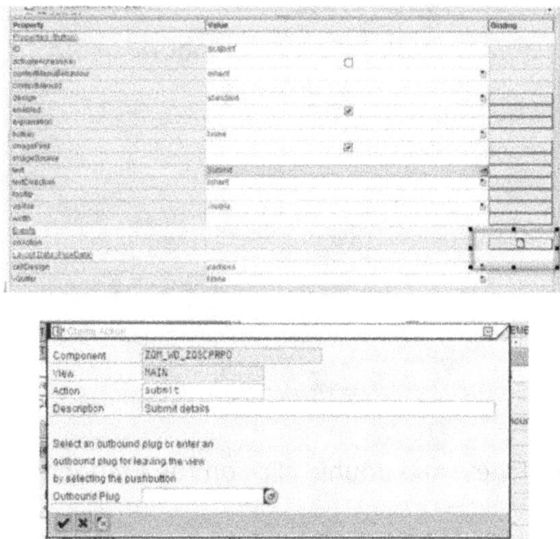

We have already renamed this MAIN view as V_SELECT for better visibility.

Step 21: Create a new Group 3, Select type Group and right click to Insert Element of type TABSTRIP:

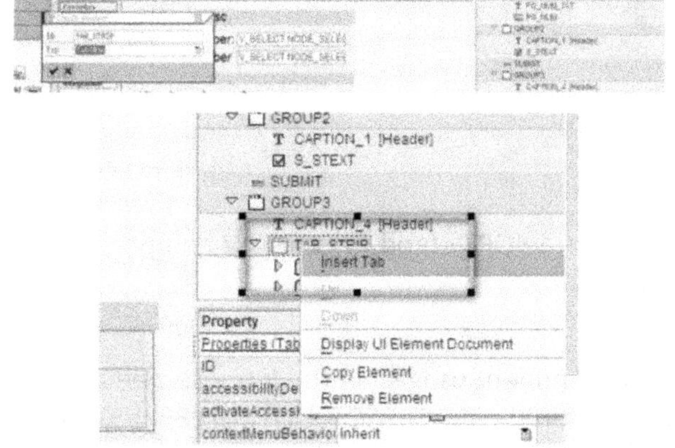

Step 22: Inside that TABSTRIP:create one element of the type ViewContainerUIelement:

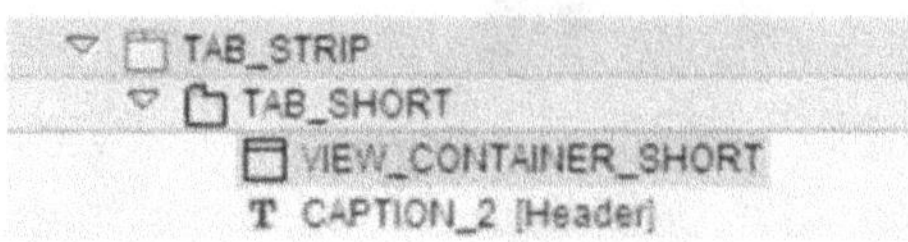

Step 23: Inside that TABSTRIP:Similarly, for Insert another Tab and further create one element of the type ViewContainerUIelement inside it:

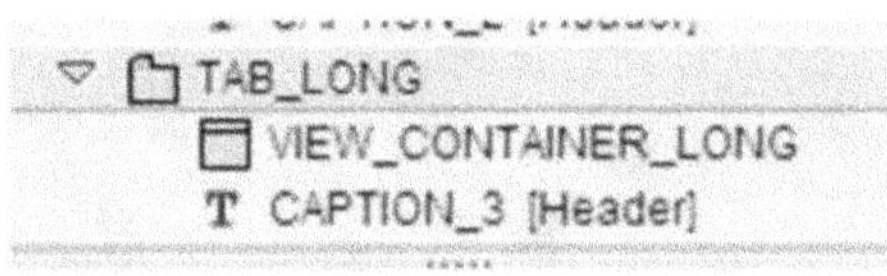

The Complete Tabstrip will look like:

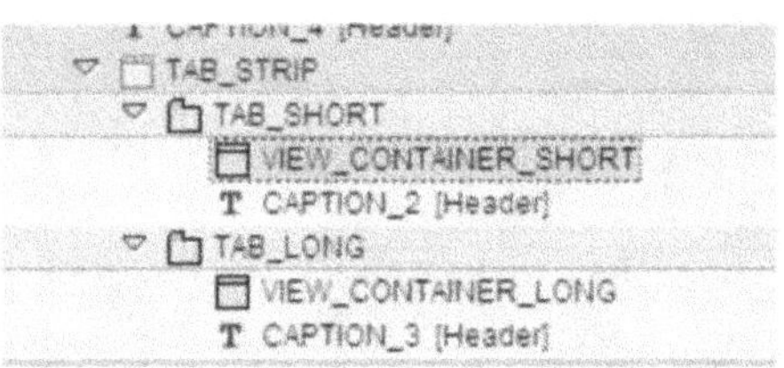

Step 24: Save V_SELECT view and double click on the Component name (ZQM_WD_ ZQSCPRPO).

Go to Properties tab of the component and declare the ALV component (one for Short view and another one for Full Version View) in it as shown below:

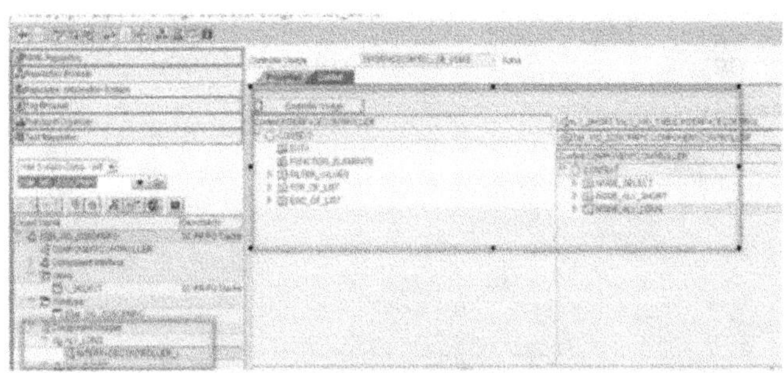

Here ALV_LONG and ALV_SHORT stand for the ALV component that we are going to use in the application.

Step 25: Now go to 'Component usages' in the left side tree and expand ALV_LONG and doubleclick on the INTERFACECONTROLLER_USAGE.

Step 26: You will see the screen as in the given picture, click on the CONTROLLER USAGE Button.

Now the component controller will open in the right side panel as shown above. Drag and drop the NODE_ALV_SHORT into the DATA node of the Interface Controller. This will declare a mapping. Meaning we have just declared which node is going to be displayed in the ALV.

Step 27: Repeat step 25 & 26 to create similarly for ALV_SHORT:

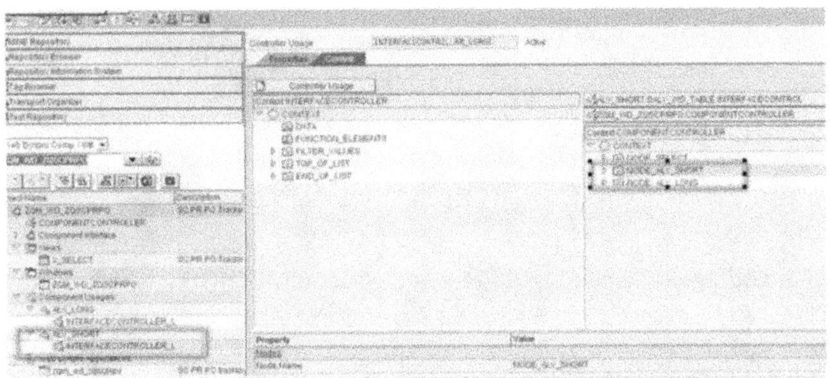

Step 28: SAVE everything. Double click the link, WINDOWS >ZQM_WD_ZQSCPRPO. Drag and drop V_SELECT view onto the Window. Now click on the arrow next to V_SELECT. Embed the view. The Window will look like:

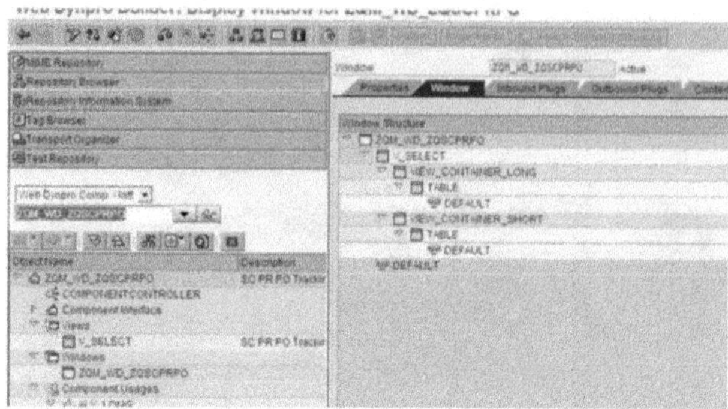

Step 29: Now save everything and right click on the Component (ZQM_WD_ZQSCPRPO).

Click the link Create > Application. Enter the following details.

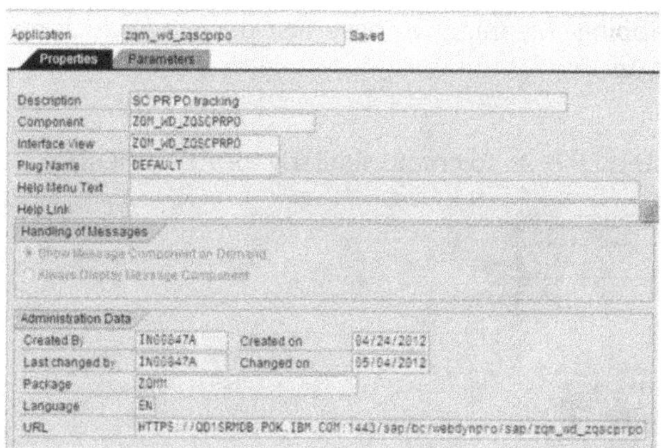

Step 30: For coding, go to the Input View and click on METHODS, which is the last tab.

There you will find a method ONACTIONSUBMITalready created. This is the event handler method ofthe action SUBMIT (associated with submit button).

```
method ONACTIONSUBMIT .
* Description        : Show report of tracking for reporting the       *
*                  links between SCs, PRs, and POs.             *
* Function          : WD will call function module                *
*                  FM (ZQM_FM_ZQSCPRPO) to report the links      *
*                  between SCs,PRs, and POs from table          *
*                  zqm_scpo_track, and output short and Full      *
```

```
*                version as ALV output              *
*&------------------------------------------------------------------*
*&      C H A N G E   H I S T O R Y                   *
*&------------------------------------------------------------------*
*& LVL  YYMMDD  USER ID   Programmer's Name     WR/CR/PTR: Transport  *
*&     Description                                  *
*&  0.0 08/May/2012 IN00847A   Ramandeep      CR P2P1847: QDSK901880  *
*&                        Show report of tracking for       *
*&                        links between SCs, PRs, and POs. *
*------------------------------------------------------------------*

* Data declaration to Read context Node
 data lo_nd_node_select type ref to if_wd_context_node.
 data lo_el_node_select type ref to if_wd_context_element.
 data ls_node_select type wd_this->element_node_select.
 data lv_sc_num type wd_this->element_node_select-sc_num.
 data lv_po_num type wd_this->element_node_select-po_num.
 data lv_s_stext type wd_this->element_node_select-s_stext.

 lo_nd_node_select = wd_context->get_child_node( name = wd_this->wdctx_node_
select ).
 lo_el_node_select = lo_nd_node_select->get_element( ).

*Data declarations for messages
data lo_api_controller     type ref to if_wd_controller.
data lo_message_manager    type ref to if_wd_message_manager.
lo_api_controller ?= wd_this->wd_get_api( ).
      call method lo_api_controller->get_message_manager
        receiving
          message_manager = lo_message_manager.



*Data declarations for Function module to fetch data
Data: it_long_ver type TABLE OF ZQM_LONG_VER_line,
```

```
    it_short_ver type TABLE OF ZQM_SHORT_VER_line.
 Data:   wa_SHORT type ZQM_SHORT_VER_line,
       wa_Long type ZQM_long_VER_line.
 Data: lv_sc_nump type CRMT_OBJECT_ID_DB,
      lv_po_nump type /SAPPSSRM/_PO_HDR_NUM,
      lv_s_stextp,
      lv_s_sall,
      email_sent,
      lv_EMAILp type BBP_EMAIL.

lv_s_sall = 'X'.

*Read User Input data from context
* get SC Num
  lo_el_node_select->get_attribute(
    exporting
      name =  `SC_NUM`
    importing
      value = lv_sc_num ).

lv_sc_nump = lv_sc_num.

*Get PO Number
  lo_el_node_select->get_attribute(
    exporting
      name =  `PO_NUM`
    importing
      value = lv_po_num ).

lv_po_nump = lv_po_num.

*Get checkbox STExt
  lo_el_node_select->get_attribute(
    exporting
```

```
    name = `S_STEXT`
  importing
    value = lv_s_stext ).

lv_s_stextp = lv_s_stext.
* Call FM to fetch Data.
*check if either PO or SC is provided, then fetch data
 if ( not lv_sc_num is initial
     and lv_po_num is initial )
  or ( lv_sc_num is initial and
     not lv_po_num is initial ).

call function 'ZQM_FM_ZQSCPRPO'
 EXPORTING
   SC_NUM                 = lv_sc_nump
   PO_NUM                 = lv_po_nump
   email               = lv_EMAILp
   S_STEXT               = lv_s_stextp
   S_ALL                = lv_s_sall
 IMPORTING
   EMAIL_SENT               = email_sent
  tables
   it_short_ver             = it_short_ver
   it_long_ver             = it_long_ver
 EXCEPTIONS
   ENTER_PO_OR_SC                = 1
   DOCUMENT_NOT_AVAILABLE           = 2
   NO_AUTHORISATION               = 3
   ERROR_CREATING_XLS_CONTENTS      = 4
   ERROR_OCCURRED_IN_BCS_CLASS      = 5
   EMAIL_NOT_SEND                = 6
   OTHERS                   = 7
       .
if sy-subrc = 0.
```

```
*write to context Node

  data: lo_nd_node_alv_short type ref to if_wd_context_node,
      lo_nd_node_alv_long type ref to if_wd_context_node.
  lo_nd_node_alv_short = wd_context->get_child_node( name = wd_this->wdctx_
node_alv_short ).
   lo_nd_node_alv_long = wd_context->get_child_node( name = wd_this->wdctx_
node_alv_long ).
 lo_nd_node_alv_short->bind_table( it_short_ver ).
 lo_nd_node_alv_long->bind_table( it_long_ver ).

 ENDIF.

end method.
```

11.1 Source code:

Step 31: Refer below code to create the Catalogue for both ALVs and it also explain the creationof Tooltips, Adjusting Length, Make the column size re-sizable, Give Column names, Wrapping the Texts in Columns, Give tool tips of fields of ALVs and so on....

On Component Controller method WDDOINIT:

```
method wddoinit .
*-------------------------------------------------------------------*
*-------------------------------------------------------------------*

* dynamic ALV
 data: l_ref_cmp_usage type ref to if_wd_component_usage.
 l_ref_cmp_usage =  wd_this->wd_cpuse_alv_short( ).
 if l_ref_cmp_usage->has_active_component( ) is initial.
   l_ref_cmp_usage->create_component( ).
 endif.
```

```
data l_salv_wd_table type ref to iwci_salv_wd_table.
l_salv_wd_table = wd_this->wd_cpifc_alv_short( ).

data l_table type ref to cl_salv_wd_config_table.
l_table = l_salv_wd_table->get_model( ).

l_table->if_salv_wd_table_settings~set_read_only( abap_false ).
l_table->if_salv_wd_std_functions~set_edit_check_available( abap_false ).
l_table->if_salv_wd_std_functions~set_edit_append_row_allowed( abap_false ).
l_table->if_salv_wd_std_functions~set_edit_delete_row_allowed( abap_false ).
l_table->if_salv_wd_std_functions~set_edit_insert_row_allowed( abap_false ).
l_table->if_salv_wd_std_functions~set_pdf_allowed( abap_false ).

*Code to change header text
data:  lt_columns          type      salv_wd_t_column_ref,
       ls_column          type      salv_wd_s_column_ref,
       lo_column          type ref to cl_salv_wd_column .

*below for tooltip/width
 data lr_input_field type ref to cl_salv_wd_uie_input_field. "RG02A
 data: lr_column_settings type ref to if_salv_wd_column_settings,
"RG02A
      lr_column type ref to cl_salv_wd_column,        "RG02A
      lr_column_cell_editor type ref to cl_salv_wd_uie, "RG02A
       lr_table_setting1 type ref to if_salv_wd_table_settings. "RG02A

case ls_column-id.  "set header to different string
   when 'SC_CUR_NUM'.
    lo_column->r_header->set_text( 'Current SC' ).
    lo_column->r_header->set_tooltip( 'Shopping cart number' ).
    lr_column = lr_column_settings->get_column( 'SC_CUR_NUM' ). "RG02A
    lr_column_cell_editor = lr_column->get_cell_editor( ). "RG02A
    lr_column->set_width( '150' ) .
```

```
when 'SC_CUR_ITM'.
  lo_column->r_header->set_text( 'Current SC Item' ).
  lo_column->r_header->set_tooltip( 'Shopping cart item number' ).
  lr_column = lr_column_settings->get_column( 'SC_CUR_ITM' ). "RG02A
  lr_column_cell_editor = lr_column->get_cell_editor( ). "RG02A
  lr_column->set_width( '150' ) .                "RG02A

when 'SC_CUR_ITM_QTY'.
  lo_column->r_header->set_text( 'SC Item Qty' ).
  lo_column->r_header->set_tooltip( 'Shopping cart item quantity ' ).
  lr_column = lr_column_settings->get_column( 'SC_CUR_ITM_QTY' ). "RG02A
  lr_column_cell_editor = lr_column->get_cell_editor( ). "RG02A
  lr_column->set_width( '150' ) .

when 'SC_PRI_NUM'.
  lo_column->r_header->set_text( 'Prior SC' ).
  lo_column->r_header->set_tooltip( 'Prior shopping cart number for the PO change
series ' ).
  lr_column = lr_column_settings->get_column( 'SC_PRI_NUM' ). "RG02A
  lr_column_cell_editor = lr_column->get_cell_editor( ). "RG02A
  lr_column->set_width( '150' ) .                "RG02A

when 'SC_PRI_ITM'.
  lo_column->r_header->set_text( 'Prior SC Item' ).
  lo_column->r_header->set_tooltip( 'Prior shopping cart item number for the PO
change series' ).
  lr_column = lr_column_settings->get_column( 'SC_PRI_ITM' ). "RG02A
  lr_column_cell_editor = lr_column->get_cell_editor( ). "RG02A
  lr_column->set_width( '150' ) .

when 'PO_ACT_VEN_NAME'.                          "Rg01A
  lo_column->r_header->set_text( 'Vendor Name' ).    "Rg01A
  lo_column->r_header->set_tooltip( 'Initiating PO vendor name ' ). "Rg01A
  lr_column = lr_column_settings->get_column( 'PO_ACT_VEN_NAME' ). "RG02A
```

```
lr_column_cell_editor = lr_column->get_cell_editor( ). "RG02A
lr_column->set_width( '150' ) .              "RG02A

when 'PO_SRC_NUM'.
 lo_column->r_header->set_text( 'Initiating PO' ).
 lo_column->r_header->set_tooltip( 'Initiating PO number for building Alteration
SC ' ).
 lr_column = lr_column_settings->get_column( 'PO_SRC_NUM' ). "RG02A
 lr_column_cell_editor = lr_column->get_cell_editor( ). "RG02A
 lr_column->set_width( '150' ) .              "RG02A

when 'PO_SRC_ITM'.
 lo_column->r_header->set_text( 'Initiating PO line Item' ).
 lo_column->r_header->set_tooltip( 'Initiating PO item number for building
Alteration SC ' ).
 lr_column = lr_column_settings->get_column( 'PO_SRC_ITM' ). "RG02A
 lr_column_cell_editor = lr_column->get_cell_editor( ). "RG02A
 lr_column->set_width( '150' ) .              "RG02A

when 'SEQNUMBER'.
 lo_column->r_header->set_text( 'Sequence' ).
 lo_column->r_header->set_tooltip( 'PO change series sequence number ' ).
 lr_column = lr_column_settings->get_column( 'SEQNUMBER' ). "RG02A
 lr_column_cell_editor = lr_column->get_cell_editor( ). "RG02A
 lr_column->set_width( '150' ) .              "RG02A

when 'PO_ACT_NUM'.
 lo_column->r_header->set_text( 'PO' ).
 lo_column->r_header->set_tooltip( 'Purchase order number ' ).
 lr_column = lr_column_settings->get_column( 'PO_ACT_NUM' ). "RG02A
 lr_column_cell_editor = lr_column->get_cell_editor( ). "RG02A
 lr_column->set_width( '150' ) .              "RG02A

when 'PO_ACT_ITM'.
```

```
    lo_column->r_header->set_text( 'PO Item' ).
    lo_column->r_header->set_tooltip( 'Purchase order item number ' ).
    lr_column = lr_column_settings->get_column( 'PO_ACT_ITM' ). "RG02A
    lr_column_cell_editor = lr_column->get_cell_editor( ). "RG02A
    lr_column->set_width( '150' ) .          "RG02A

   when 'PO_ACT_ITM_QTY'.
    lo_column->r_header->set_text( 'PO Item QTY' ).
    lo_column->r_header->set_tooltip( 'Purchase order item quantity ' ).
    lr_column = lr_column_settings->get_column( 'PO_ACT_ITM_QTY' ). "RG02A
    lr_column_cell_editor = lr_column->get_cell_editor( ). "RG02A
    lr_column->set_width( '150' ) .          "RG02A

   when 'ALT_TEXT'.
    lo_column->r_header->set_text( 'PO Item Change Summary' ).
   lo_column->r_header->set_tooltip( 'Shopping cart alteration summary. Generated
from Alteration SC item changes. ' ).

*add TOOLTIP attribute
    lr_column_settings ?= l_table.          "RG02A
    lr_column = lr_column_settings->get_column( 'ALT_TEXT' ). "RG02A
    lr_column_cell_editor = lr_column->get_cell_editor( ).   "RG02A
    lr_column_cell_editor->set_tooltip_fieldname( 'ALT_TEXT' ). "RG02A
    lr_column->set_width( '200' ) .          "RG02A

  endcase.

  lr_table_setting1 ?= l_table.          "RG02A
  lr_table_setting1->set_fixed_table_layout( abap_true ). "RG02A

 endloop.
*---------------------- Long tabstrip----------------------------------

 data: l_ref_cmp_usage2 type ref to if_wd_component_usage.
```

```
l_ref_cmp_usage2 =  wd_this->wd_cpuse_alv_long( ).
if l_ref_cmp_usage2->has_active_component( ) is initial.
  l_ref_cmp_usage2->create_component( ).
endif.
data l_salv_wd_table2 type ref to iwci_salv_wd_table.
l_salv_wd_table2 = wd_this->wd_cpifc_alv_long( ).
data l_table2 type ref to cl_salv_wd_config_table.
l_table2 = l_salv_wd_table2->get_model( ).
l_table2->if_salv_wd_table_settings~set_read_only( abap_false ).
l_table2->if_salv_wd_std_functions~set_edit_check_available( abap_false ).
l_table2->if_salv_wd_std_functions~set_edit_append_row_allowed( abap_false ).
l_table2->if_salv_wd_std_functions~set_edit_delete_row_allowed( abap_false ).
l_table2->if_salv_wd_std_functions~set_edit_insert_row_allowed( abap_false ).
l_table2->if_salv_wd_std_functions~set_pdf_allowed( abap_false ).
*Code to change header text
data:  lt_columns2            type      salv_wd_t_column_ref,
       ls_column2             type      salv_wd_s_column_ref,
       lo_column2             type ref to cl_salv_wd_column .

*below for tooltip/width
data lr_input_field2 type ref to cl_salv_wd_uie_input_field.
data: lr_column_settings2 type ref to if_salv_wd_column_settings,
      lr_column2 type ref to cl_salv_wd_column,
      lr_column_cell_editor2 type ref to cl_salv_wd_uie,
      lr_table_setting type ref to if_salv_wd_table_settings.

* Get the Columns of the ALV
call method l_table2->if_salv_wd_column_settings~get_columns
  receiving
    value = lt_columns2.

   lr_column_settings2 ?= l_table2.              "RG02A
```

```
* Get reference to each column and set the column heading.
 loop at lt_columns2 into ls_column2.
  lo_column2 = ls_column2-r_column.
    lo_column2->r_header->set_ddic_binding_field( if_salv_wd_c_column_
settings=>ddic_bind_none ).” use this line to hide ddic text
  case ls_column2-id.  “set header to different string
   when ‘SC_CUR_NUM’.
    lo_column2->r_header->set_text( ‘Current SC’ ).
    lo_column2->r_header->set_tooltip( ‘Shopping cart number’ ).
    lr_column2 = lr_column_settings2->get_column( ‘SC_CUR_NUM’ ). “RG02A
    lr_column_cell_editor2 = lr_column2->get_cell_editor( ). “RG02A
    lr_column2->set_width( ‘150’ ) .                    “RG02A

   when ‘SC_CUR_ITM’.
    lo_column2->r_header->set_text( ‘Current SC Item’ ).
    lo_column2->r_header->set_tooltip( ‘Shopping cart item number’ ).
    lr_column2 = lr_column_settings2->get_column( ‘SC_CUR_ITM’ ). “RG02A
    lr_column_cell_editor2 = lr_column2->get_cell_editor( ). “RG02A
    lr_column2->set_width( ‘150’ ) .                    “RG02A

*    when ‘SC_CUR_ITM_GUID’.                    “RG02A
*      lo_column2->r_header->set_text( ‘SC GUID’ ).  “RG02A
*      lo_column2->r_header->set_TOOLTIP( ‘Current SC Number’ ).    “RG02A
   when ‘SC_CUR_ITM_QTY’.
    lo_column2->r_header->set_text( ‘SC Item Qty’ ).
    lo_column2->r_header->set_tooltip( ‘Shopping cart item quantity’ ).
    lr_column2 = lr_column_settings2->get_column( ‘SC_CUR_ITM_QTY’ ). “RG02A
    lr_column_cell_editor2 = lr_column2->get_cell_editor( ). “RG02A
    lr_column2->set_width( ‘150’ ) .                    “RG02A

   when ‘SC_CUR_ITM_MEINS’.
    lo_column2->r_header->set_text( ‘SC Item UoM’ ).
    lo_column2->r_header->set_tooltip( ‘Shopping cart item unit of measure’ ).
   lr_column2 = lr_column_settings2->get_column( ‘SC_CUR_ITM_MEINS’ ). “RG02A
```

```
lr_column_cell_editor2 = lr_column2->get_cell_editor( ). "RG02A
lr_column2->set_width( '150' ) .                "RG02A

when 'SC_CUR_ITM_PRICE'.
lo_column2->r_header->set_text( 'SC Item Value' ).
lo_column2->r_header->set_tooltip( 'Shopping cart item value' ).
lr_column2 = lr_column_settings2->get_column( 'SC_CUR_ITM_PRICE' ). "RG02A
lr_column_cell_editor2 = lr_column2->get_cell_editor( ). "RG02A
lr_column2->set_width( '150' ) .                "RG02A

when 'SC_CUR_ITM_WAERS'.
lo_column2->r_header->set_text( 'SC Item Currency' ).
lo_column2->r_header->set_tooltip( 'Shopping cart item currency key' ).
lr_column2 = lr_column_settings2->get_column( 'SC_CUR_ITM_WAERS' ). "RG02A
lr_column_cell_editor2 = lr_column2->get_cell_editor( ). "RG02A
lr_column2->set_width( '150' ) .                "RG02A

when 'SC_CUR_APPROVER'.
lo_column2->r_header->set_text( 'last SC Approver' ).
lo_column2->r_header->set_tooltip( 'Shopping cart last approver first and last
name' ).
lr_column2 = lr_column_settings2->get_column( 'SC_CUR_APPROVER' ). "RG02A
lr_column_cell_editor2 = lr_column2->get_cell_editor( ). "RG02A
lr_column2->set_width( '150' ) .                "RG02A

when 'SC_PRI_NUM'.
lo_column2->r_header->set_text( 'Prior SC' ).
lo_column2->r_header->set_tooltip( 'Prior shopping cart number for the PO
change series' ).
lr_column2 = lr_column_settings2->get_column( 'SC_PRI_NUM' ). "RG02A
lr_column_cell_editor2 = lr_column2->get_cell_editor( ). "RG02A
lr_column2->set_width( '150' ) .                "RG02A

when 'SC_PRI_ITM'.
```

```
lo_column2->r_header->set_text( 'Prior SC Item' ).
lo_column2->r_header->set_tooltip( 'Prior shopping cart item number for the PO change series' ).
lr_column2 = lr_column_settings2->get_column( 'SC_PRI_ITM' ). "RG02A
lr_column_cell_editor2 = lr_column2->get_cell_editor( ). "RG02A
lr_column2->set_width( '150' ) .                "RG02A

when 'PO_ACT_VEN_NAME'.
lo_column2->r_header->set_text( 'Vendor Name' ).
lo_column2->r_header->set_tooltip( 'Initiating PO vendor name' ).
lr_column2 = lr_column_settings2->get_column( 'PO_ACT_VEN_NAME' ). "RG02A
lr_column_cell_editor2 = lr_column2->get_cell_editor( ). "RG02A
lr_column2->set_width( '150' ) .

when 'PO_SRC_NUM'.
lo_column2->r_header->set_text( 'Initiating PO' ).
lo_column2->r_header->set_tooltip( 'Initiating PO number for building Alteration SC' ).
lr_column2 = lr_column_settings2->get_column( 'PO_SRC_NUM' ). "RG02A
lr_column_cell_editor2 = lr_column2->get_cell_editor( ). "RG02A
lr_column2->set_width( '150' ) .                "RG02A


when 'PO_SRC_ITM'.
lo_column2->r_header->set_text( 'Initiating PO Item' ).
lo_column2->r_header->set_tooltip( 'Initiating PO item number for building Alteration SC' ).
lr_column2 = lr_column_settings2->get_column( 'PO_SRC_ITM' ). "RG02A
lr_column_cell_editor2 = lr_column2->get_cell_editor( ). "RG02A
lr_column2->set_width( '150' ) .                "RG02A

when 'SEQNUMBER'.
lo_column2->r_header->set_text( 'Sequence' ).
lo_column2->r_header->set_tooltip( 'PO change series sequence number' ).
lr_column2 = lr_column_settings2->get_column( 'SEQNUMBER' ). "RG02A
```

```
  lr_column_cell_editor2 = lr_column2->get_cell_editor( ). "RG02A
  lr_column2->set_width( '150' ) .                 "RG02A


when 'RECORD_CREATE'.
  lo_column2->r_header->set_text( 'Create Date Time' ).
lo_column2->r_header->set_tooltip( 'Shopping cart record create date and time' ).
  lr_column2 = lr_column_settings2->get_column( 'RECORD_CREATE' ). "RG02A
  lr_column_cell_editor2 = lr_column2->get_cell_editor( ). "RG02A
  lr_column2->set_width( '150' ) .                 "RG02A

when 'RECORD_UPDATE'.
  lo_column2->r_header->set_text( 'Change Date Time' ).
lo_column2->r_header->set_tooltip( 'Shopping cart record change date and time' ).
  lr_column2 = lr_column_settings2->get_column( 'RECORD_UPDATE' ). "RG02A
  lr_column_cell_editor2 = lr_column2->get_cell_editor( ). "RG02A
  lr_column2->set_width( '150' ) .                 "RG02A

when 'PR_ACT_NUM'.
  lo_column2->r_header->set_text( 'PR' ).
  lo_column2->r_header->set_tooltip( 'Purchase Requisition Number' ).
  lr_column2 = lr_column_settings2->get_column( 'PR_ACT_NUM' ). "RG02A
  lr_column_cell_editor2 = lr_column2->get_cell_editor( ). "RG02A
  lr_column2->set_width( '150' ) .                 "RG02A

when 'PR_ACT_ITM'.
  lo_column2->r_header->set_text( 'PR Item' ).
  lo_column2->r_header->set_tooltip( 'Purchase Requisition Item Number' ).
  lr_column2 = lr_column_settings2->get_column( 'PR_ACT_ITM' ). "RG02A
  lr_column_cell_editor2 = lr_column2->get_cell_editor( ). "RG02A
  lr_column2->set_width( '100' ) .                 "RG02A

when 'PR_ACT_ITM_DELET'.                           "Rg02A
  lo_column2->r_header->set_text( 'PR Deletion Indicator' ). "Rg02A
```

```
lo_column2->r_header->set_tooltip( 'Purchase requisition item deletion indicator' ). "Rg02A
lr_column2 = lr_column_settings2->get_column( 'PR_ACT_ITM_DELET' ). "RG02A
lr_column_cell_editor2 = lr_column2->get_cell_editor( ). "RG02A
lr_column2->set_width( '150' ) .              "RG02A

when 'PR_ACT_ITM_RQSTR'.
lo_column2->r_header->set_text( 'PR Requester' ).
lo_column2->r_header->set_tooltip( 'Purchase requisition item requester' ).
lr_column2 = lr_column_settings2->get_column( 'PR_ACT_ITM_RQSTR' ). "RG02A
lr_column_cell_editor2 = lr_column2->get_cell_editor( ). "RG02A
lr_column2->set_width( '150' ) .              "RG02A

when 'PR_ACT_ITM_QTY'.
lo_column2->r_header->set_text( 'PR Item Qty' ).
lo_column2->r_header->set_tooltip( 'Purchase requisition item quantity' ).
lr_column2 = lr_column_settings2->get_column( 'PR_ACT_ITM_QTY' ). "RG02A
lr_column_cell_editor2 = lr_column2->get_cell_editor( ). "RG02A
lr_column2->set_width( '150' ) .              "RG02A

when 'PR_ACT_ITM_MEINS'.
lo_column2->r_header->set_text( 'PR Item UoM' ).
lo_column2->r_header->set_tooltip( 'Purchase requisition item unit of measure' ).
lr_column2 = lr_column_settings2->get_column( 'PR_ACT_ITM_MEINS' ). "RG02A
lr_column_cell_editor2 = lr_column2->get_cell_editor( ). "RG02A
lr_column2->set_width( '150' ) .              "RG02A

when 'PR_ACT_ITM_VAL'.
lo_column2->r_header->set_text( 'PR Item Value' ).
lo_column2->r_header->set_tooltip( 'Purchase requisition item  value' ).
lr_column2 = lr_column_settings2->get_column( 'PR_ACT_ITM_VAL' ). "RG02A
lr_column_cell_editor2 = lr_column2->get_cell_editor( ). "RG02A
lr_column2->set_width( '150' ) .              "RG02A
```

```
when 'PR_ACT_ITM_WAERS'.
  lo_column2->r_header->set_text( 'PR Item Currency' ).
  lo_column2->r_header->set_tooltip( 'Purchase requisition item currency key' ).
lr_column2 = lr_column_settings2->get_column( 'PR_ACT_ITM_WAERS' ). "RG02A
  lr_column_cell_editor2 = lr_column2->get_cell_editor( ). "RG02A
  lr_column2->set_width( '150' ) .              "RG02A

when 'PO_ACT_CRDATE'.
  lo_column2->r_header->set_text( 'PO Create Date' ).
  lo_column2->r_header->set_tooltip( 'Purchase order create date' ).
  lr_column2 = lr_column_settings2->get_column( 'PO_ACT_CRDATE' ). "RG02A
  lr_column_cell_editor2 = lr_column2->get_cell_editor( ). "RG02A
  lr_column2->set_width( '150' ) .              "RG02A

when 'PO_ACT_NUM'.
  lo_column2->r_header->set_text( 'PO' ).
  lo_column2->r_header->set_tooltip( 'Purchase order number' ).
  lr_column2 = lr_column_settings2->get_column( 'PO_ACT_NUM' ). "RG02A
  lr_column_cell_editor2 = lr_column2->get_cell_editor( ). "RG02A
  lr_column2->set_width( '150' ) .              "RG02A

when 'PO_ACT_ITM'.
  lo_column2->r_header->set_text( 'PO Item' ).
  lo_column2->r_header->set_tooltip( 'Purchase order item number' ).
  lr_column2 = lr_column_settings2->get_column( 'PO_ACT_ITM' ). "RG02A
  lr_column_cell_editor2 = lr_column2->get_cell_editor( ). "RG02A
  lr_column2->set_width( '150' ) .              "RG02A

when 'PO_ACT_ITM_DELET'.                        "Rg02A
  lo_column2->r_header->set_text( 'PO Deletion Indicator' ). "Rg02A
    lo_column2->r_header->set_tooltip( 'Purchase order item deletion indicator' ).
"Rg02A
  lr_column2 = lr_column_settings2->get_column( 'PO_ACT_ITM_DELET' ). "RG02A
  lr_column_cell_editor2 = lr_column2->get_cell_editor( ). "RG02A
```

```
lr_column2->set_width( '150' ) .                "RG02A

when 'PO_ACT_ITM_RQTIN'.
 lo_column2->r_header->set_text( 'PO Requisitioner' ).
 lo_column2->r_header->set_tooltip( 'Purchase order item requisitioner' ).
lr_column2 = lr_column_settings2->get_column( 'PO_ACT_ITM_RQTIN' ). "RG02A
 lr_column_cell_editor2 = lr_column2->get_cell_editor( ). "RG02A
 lr_column2->set_width( '150' ) .                "RG02A

when 'PO_ACT_ITM_CNNUM'.
 lo_column2->r_header->set_text( 'PO Item Contract' ).
 lo_column2->r_header->set_tooltip( 'Purchase order item created from contract
number' ).
lr_column2 = lr_column_settings2->get_column( 'PO_ACT_ITM_CNNUM' ). "RG02A
 lr_column_cell_editor2 = lr_column2->get_cell_editor( ). "RG02A
 lr_column2->set_width( '150' ) .                "RG02A

when 'PO_ACT_ITM_CNITM'.
 lo_column2->r_header->set_text( 'PO Item Contract Item' ).
 lo_column2->r_header->set_tooltip( 'Purchase order item created from contract
item number' ).
lr_column2 = lr_column_settings2->get_column( 'PO_ACT_ITM_CNITM' ). "RG02A
 lr_column_cell_editor2 = lr_column2->get_cell_editor( ). "RG02A
 lr_column2->set_width( '150' ) .                "RG02A

when 'PO_ACT_ITM_GPS'.
 lo_column2->r_header->set_text( 'PO Item Contain Graduated Price Scales' ).
  lo_column2->r_header->set_tooltip( 'Purchase order item contain graduated
price scales' ).
 lr_column2 = lr_column_settings2->get_column( 'PO_ACT_ITM_GPS' ). "RG02A
 lr_column_cell_editor2 = lr_column2->get_cell_editor( ). "RG02A
 lr_column2->set_width( '200' ) .                "RG02A

when 'PO_ACT_ITM_FRGHT'.
 lo_column2->r_header->set_text( 'PO Item Is Freight From Buyer' ).
```

```
    lo_column2->r_header->set_tooltip( 'Purchase order item created by buyer for
freight' ).
   lr_column2 = lr_column_settings2->get_column( 'PO_ACT_ITM_FRGHT' ). "RG02A
    lr_column_cell_editor2 = lr_column2->get_cell_editor( ). "RG02A
    lr_column2->set_width( '200' ) .                "RG02A

   when 'PO_ACT_ITM_QTY'.
    lo_column2->r_header->set_text( 'PO Item QTY' ).
    lo_column2->r_header->set_tooltip( 'Purchase order item quantity' ).
    lr_column2 = lr_column_settings2->get_column( 'PO_ACT_ITM_QTY' ). "RG02A
    lr_column_cell_editor2 = lr_column2->get_cell_editor( ). "RG02A
    lr_column2->set_width( '150' ) .                "RG02A

   when 'PO_ACT_ITM_MEINS'.
    lo_column2->r_header->set_text( 'PO Item UOM' ).
    lo_column2->r_header->set_tooltip( 'Purchase order item unit of measure' ).
   lr_column2 = lr_column_settings2->get_column( 'PO_ACT_ITM_MEINS' ). "RG02A
    lr_column_cell_editor2 = lr_column2->get_cell_editor( ). "RG02A
    lr_column2->set_width( '130' ) .                "RG02A

   when 'PO_ACT_ITM_VAL'.
    lo_column2->r_header->set_text( 'PO Item Value' ).
    lo_column2->r_header->set_tooltip( 'Purchase order item value' ).
    lr_column2 = lr_column_settings2->get_column( 'PO_ACT_ITM_VAL' ). "RG02A
    lr_column_cell_editor2 = lr_column2->get_cell_editor( ). "RG02A
    lr_column2->set_width( '155' ) .                "RG02A

   when 'PO_ACT_ITM_GRQTY'.
    lo_column2->r_header->set_text( 'PO Item Received QTY' ).
    lo_column2->r_header->set_tooltip( 'Purchase order item received quantity' ).
   lr_column2 = lr_column_settings2->get_column( 'PO_ACT_ITM_GRQTY' ). "RG02A
    lr_column_cell_editor2 = lr_column2->get_cell_editor( ). "RG02A
    lr_column2->set_width( '150' ) .                "RG02A
```

```
when 'PO_ACT_ITM_GRVAL'.
 lo_column2->r_header->set_text( 'PO Item Received Value' ).
 lo_column2->r_header->set_tooltip( 'Purchase order item received value' ).
lr_column2 = lr_column_settings2->get_column( 'PO_ACT_ITM_GRVAL' ). "RG02A
 lr_column_cell_editor2 = lr_column2->get_cell_editor( ). "RG02A
 lr_column2->set_width( '155' ) .              "RG02A

when 'PO_ACT_ITM_WAERS'.
 lo_column2->r_header->set_text( 'PO Item Currency' ).
 lo_column2->r_header->set_tooltip( 'Purchase order item currency key' ).
lr_column2 = lr_column_settings2->get_column( 'PO_ACT_ITM_WAERS' ). "RG02A
 lr_column_cell_editor2 = lr_column2->get_cell_editor( ). "RG02A
 lr_column2->set_width( '150' ) .              "RG02A

when 'PO_ACT_ITM_INQTY'.
 lo_column2->r_header->set_text( 'PO Item Invoiced QTY' ).
 lo_column2->r_header->set_tooltip( 'Purchase order item invoiced quantity' ).
lr_column2 = lr_column_settings2->get_column( 'PO_ACT_ITM_INQTY' ). "RG02A
 lr_column_cell_editor2 = lr_column2->get_cell_editor( ). "RG02A
 lr_column2->set_width( '150' ) .              "RG02A

when 'PO_ACT_ITM_INVAL'.
 lo_column2->r_header->set_text( 'PO Item Invoiced Value' ).
 lo_column2->r_header->set_tooltip( 'Purchase order item invoiced value' ).
lr_column2 = lr_column_settings2->get_column( 'PO_ACT_ITM_INVAL' ). "RG02A
 lr_column_cell_editor2 = lr_column2->get_cell_editor( ). "RG02A
 lr_column2->set_width( '150' ) .              "RG02A

when 'SC_CUR_ITM_ALTXT'.
 lo_column2->r_header->set_text( 'PO Item Change Summary' ).
lo_column2->r_header->set_tooltip( 'Shopping cart alteration summary. Generated
from Alteration SC item changes.' ).

*add TOOLTIP attribute
```

```
    lr_column2 = lr_column_settings2->get_column( 'SC_CUR_ITM_ALTXT' ).
    lr_column_cell_editor2 = lr_column2->get_cell_editor( ).
    lr_column_cell_editor2->set_tooltip_fieldname( 'SC_CUR_ITM_ALTXT' ).
    lr_column2->set_width( '200' ) .               "RG02A

   when 'PR_ACT_ITM_ALTXT'.
    lo_column2->r_header->set_text( 'PO Item Change Log' ).
    lo_column2->r_header->set_tooltip( 'PO item change log from buyer.' ).

*add TOOLTIP attribute
    lr_column_settings2 ?= l_table2.
    lr_column2 = lr_column_settings2->get_column( 'PR_ACT_ITM_ALTXT' ).
    lr_column_cell_editor2 = lr_column2->get_cell_editor( ).
    lr_column_cell_editor2->set_tooltip_fieldname( 'PR_ACT_ITM_ALTXT' ).
    lr_column2->set_width( '200' ) .               "RG02A

  endcase.

 endloop.

 lr_table_setting ?= l_table2.
 lr_table_setting->set_fixed_table_layout( abap_true ).

endmethod.
```

11.2 Test Case @ Project S2P:

Got a chance to work on the same for one of my client S2P below is detailed Example with screen shot for the same.

1. Result

The above created Webdynpro was linked to be called Portal screen:

11.3 Portal Linking

11.4 Tool Tips and Help drop down got created as below:

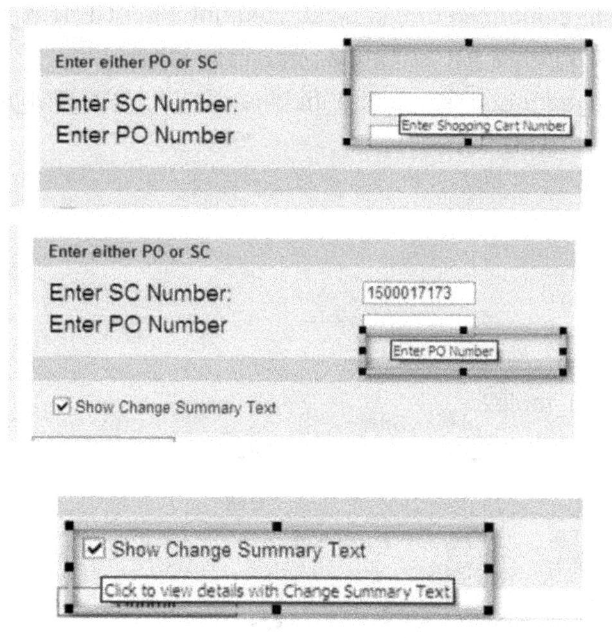

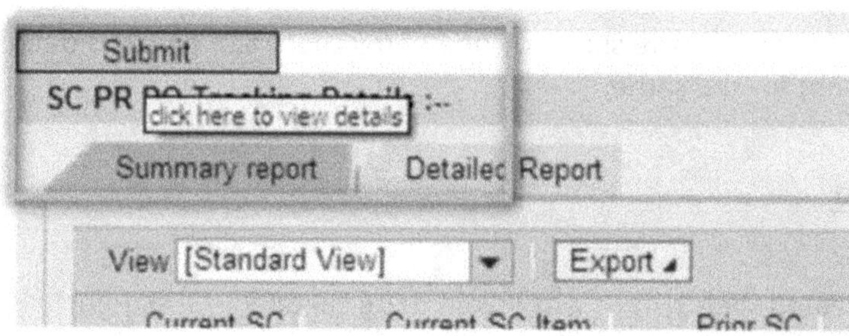

11.5. Scrollable Columns:

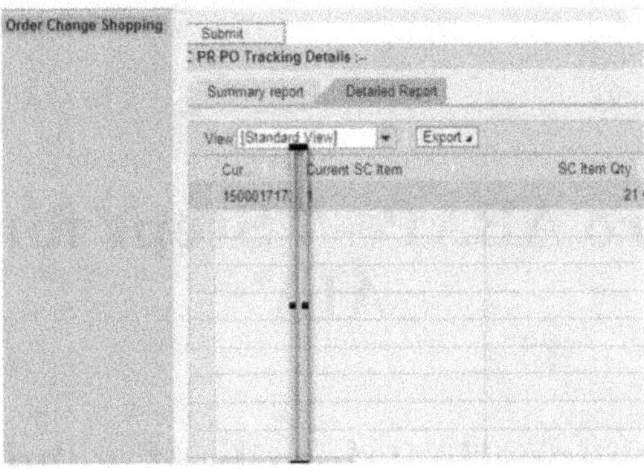

11.6. Text fields tooltip dropdowns:

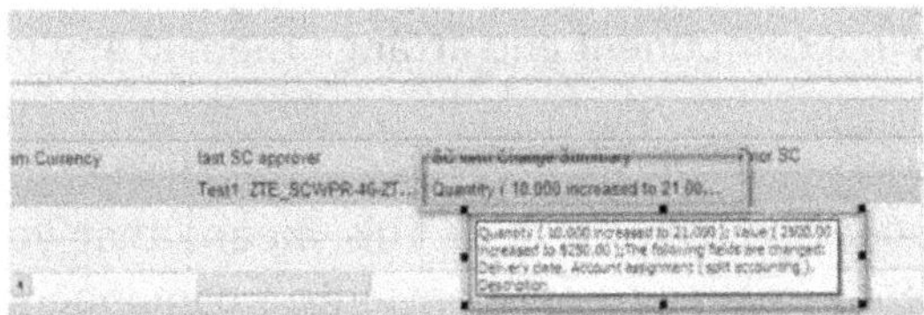

4. Additional Information/Key Assumptions (if any)

To make the columns of ALV re-sizable write below code:

```
lr_table_setting->set_fixed_table_layout( abap_true).
```

CHAPTER 12

Webdynpro ABAP - 7 Steps for Creating ALV

Some of the theoretical details of webdynpro:

Component:
The component is the central, reusable unit of the application project. You can create any number of views in a component and arrange them in any number of windows.

Component Usages:
Web Dynpro components can be nested. This means that you can integrate any number of other, already existing components into a component.

View:
The view is the smallest unit of a Web Dynpro application visible for the user. The layout elements and dialog elements - for example, tables, text fields, or buttons - required for the application are arranged in a view. The view contains a controller and a controller context in which the application data to be processed is stored in a hierarchical structure. This allows the linking of the graphical elements with the application data.

Window:
A window is used to group multiple views and to specify the navigation between the views. A view can only display by the browser if the view is embedded in a window.

First step is to create Webdynpro:

Go to SE80 and select Web Dynpro Comp and create. Enter the description and choose the type as Web Dynpro Component.

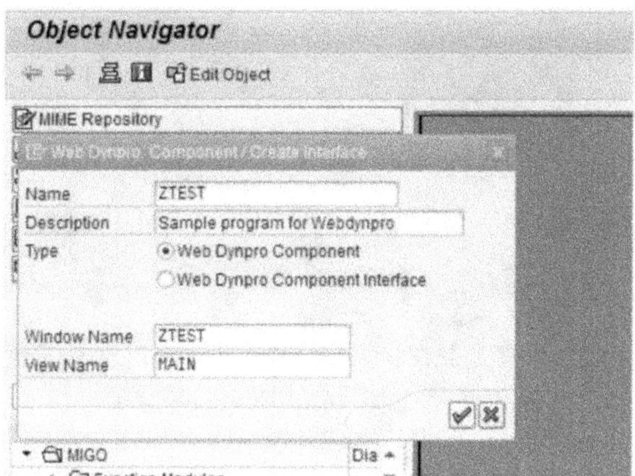

Click on Webdynpro.

Object Name	Description
ZTEST	Sample program for Webdynpro

Mention the Component Use as ALV and Component as SALV_WD_TABLE in the Used Components tab in Web Dynpro, this will create a Component Usages by name ALV_TEST

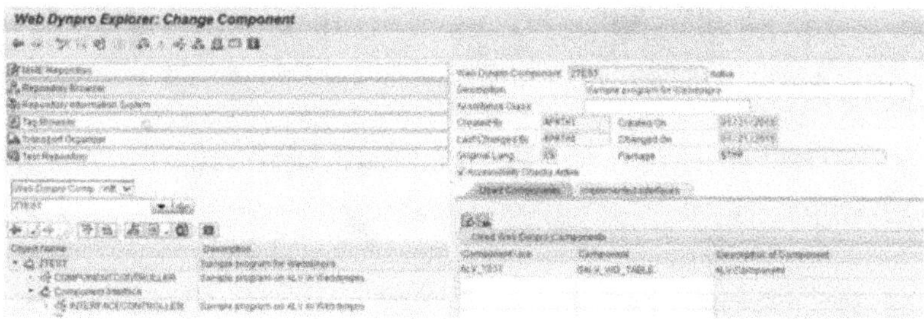

Second step to create Component Controller:

Go to Component Controller and Right click the context. Then select Create Node MAKT with dictionary structure MAKT and select the required attributes from MAKT by using Add Attribute from Structure.

Remove the dictionary structure MAKT from the node MAKT and set the properties as below (Cardinality, Lead selection, etc.,)

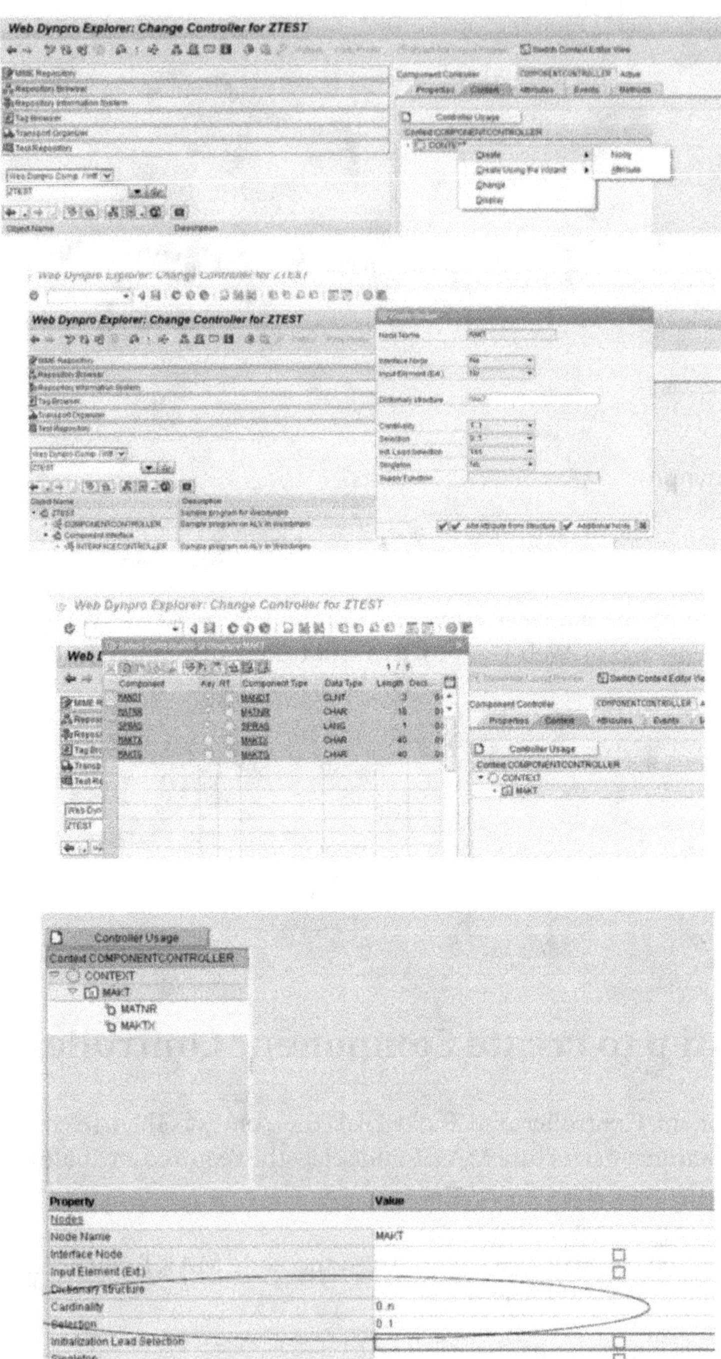

Third Step to create Component Usages:

Right click the component Usage (here with name ALV) and Click Controller Usage button for creating the same. Drag and drop the node(MAKT in right side) from Component Controller context to Data(in left side) in Controller Usage Context.

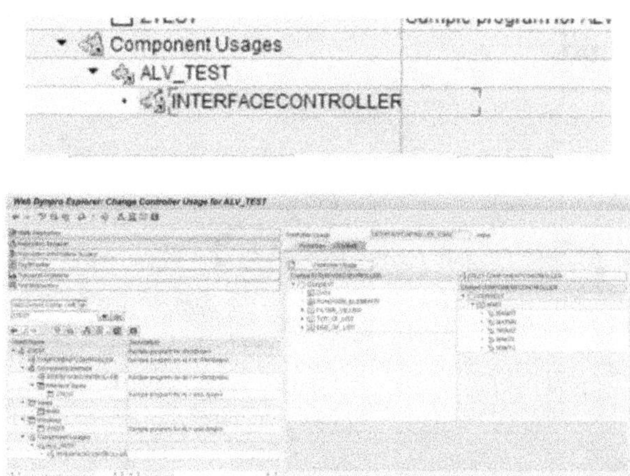

Once the data was mapped then the below message will be displayed.

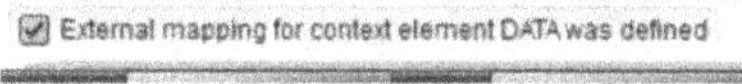

Fourth step is to create Designing view:

Go to the Context in the view and drag and drop the MAKT node which appears in Right side (Component Controller) to View.

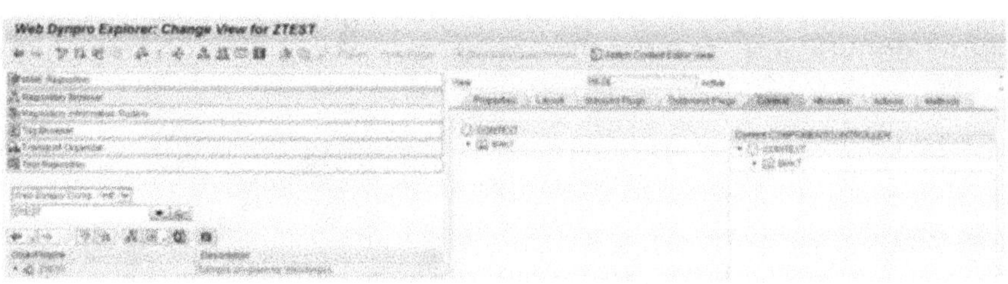

Mapping for context element CONTEXT is defined

Go to the layout in view and right click the ROOTUIELEMENTCONTAINER and then choose Insert element.

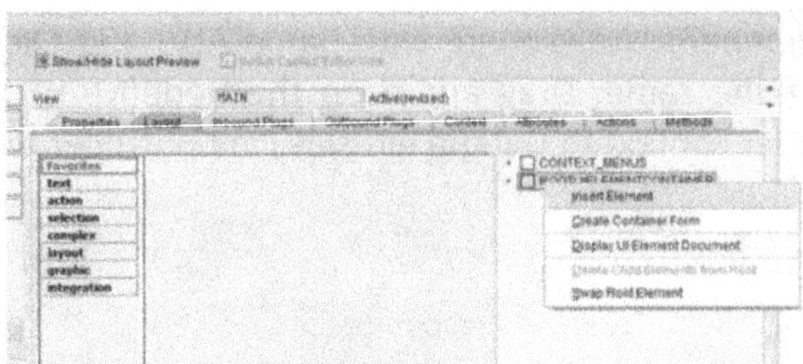

This will make the layout appear as below.

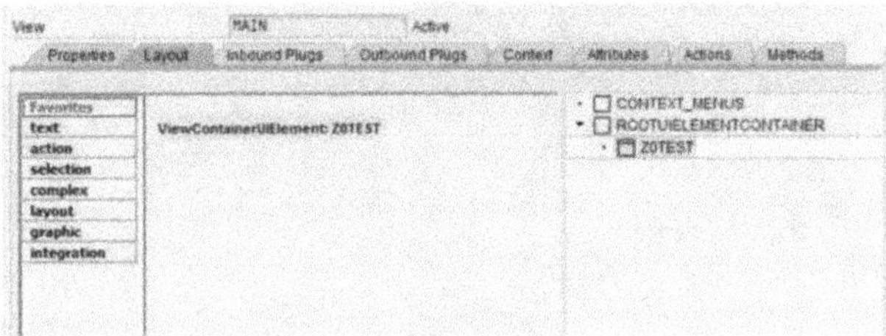

In the properties, use button create to define as below.

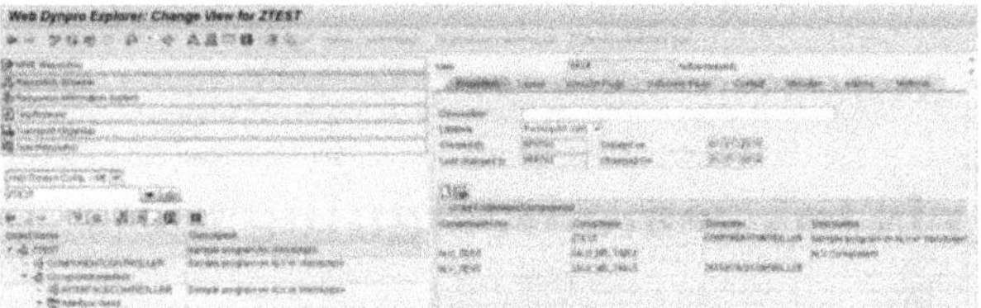

Fifth Steps is to write code:

Double click on WDDOINT to write the code.

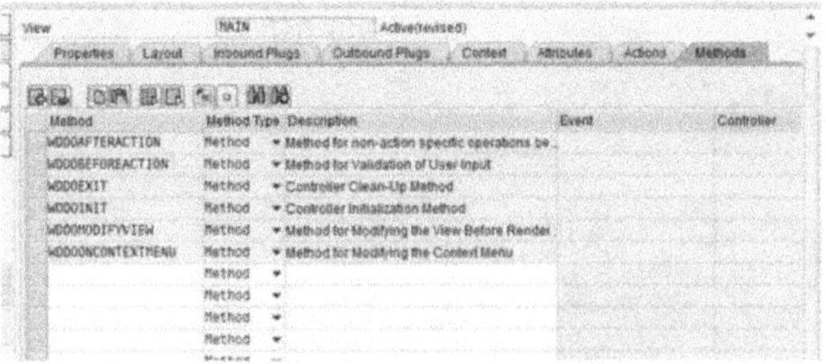

Click on the below icon to generate the code.

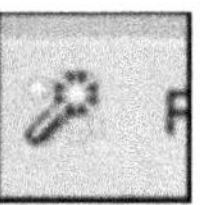

Then, select the read radio button.

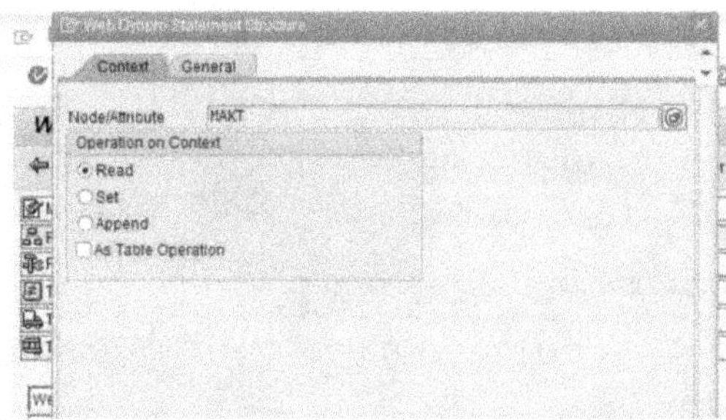

Keep the below two lines of code and keep the remaining code

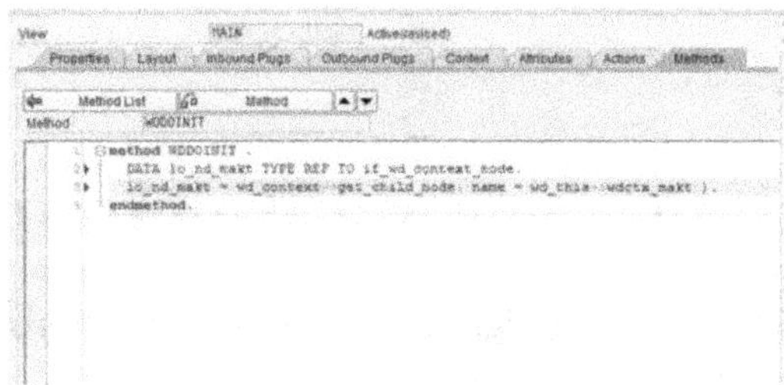

Sixth step is to create window:

Again double click on the below icon and select the general tab in pop-up and select instantiate used component.

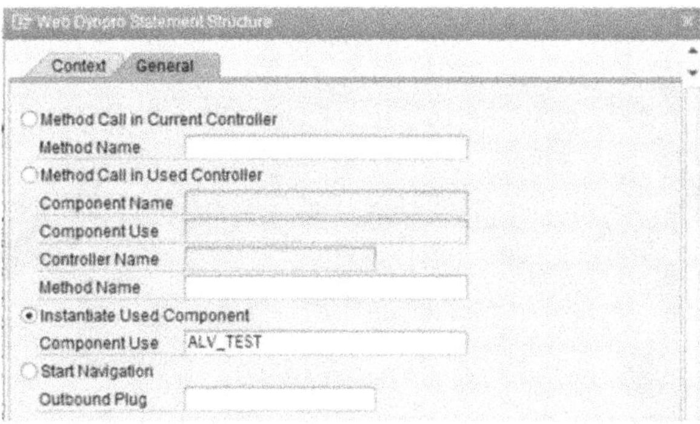

Then it will generate the below code:

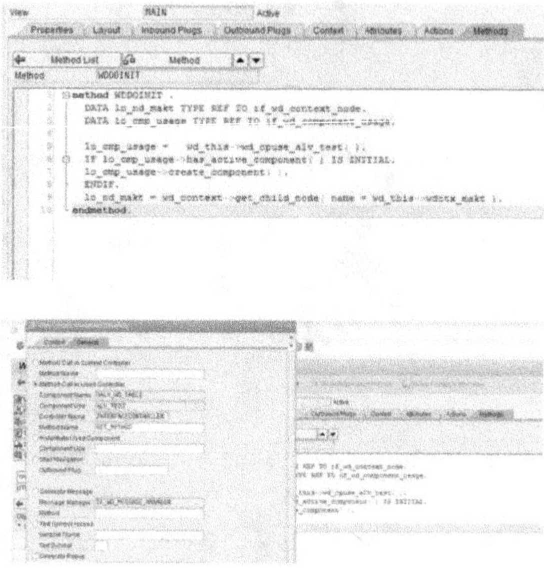

Seventh step is to create web dynpro application:

Create Web Dynpro Application by right clicking the Webdynpro (ZTest
Right click the Web Dynpro component and activate.

Output:
Double click the Web Dynpro Application and then Press F8 to execute.

CHAPTER 13

ALV Print Version Functionality

Print Version – SAP Notes

- SAP Note : 918236 - WD ABAP ALV - creating print version
  valid for SAP NetWeaver Releases 7.00, 7.01, 7.10, 7.11

- SAP Note: 1413938 - WD ABAP ALV - creating print version
  valid for SAP NetWeaver Releases 7.02, 7.30, and higher.

- SAP Note: 1882863 - WD ABAP ALV - Troubleshooting for print version

Prerequisites:

1. AS Java Release:

- 7.00 (at least Support Package 14)
- 7.01
- 7.02

The ALV print service is included in the usage type "BI Java". This usage type must be installed including its prerequisite usage types.
Therefore, at least the following usage types must be installed on your Application Server Java:

- AS Java
- EP/EPC (portal)
- BI Java

Note the following:

- The usage types must be installed completely, that is, all components for each usage type in each case.
- The dependent usage types must all have the same release and Support Package level.

The "SAP Installation Guide" describes how to additionally install a usage type for an existing system, and the components of the usage types are listed.

Note the following:

This concerns an installation only. You do not have to configure the portal or BI to be able to create the print version from the WD ABAP ALV.

2. AS Java Release:

- 7.30
- 7.31 and higher

The ALV print service is included in the usage type "PDF Export". This usage type must be installed including its prerequisite usage types.

Therefore, at least the following usage types must be installed on your Application Server Java:

- AS Java
- Adobe Document Services
- PDF Export

Note the following:

- The usage types must be installed completely, that is, all components for each usage type in each case.
- The dependent usage types must all have the same release and Support Package level.
- Since the usage type "Adobe Document Services" must be installed for the usage

type "PDF Export", it inherits the platform dependencies and restrictions of this usage type.

Note the following:

As of AS Java Release 7.30, the print service is still also contained in the usage type "BI Java". Therefore, customers who upgrade an existing Application Server Java with the usage types "EP/EPC" and "BI Java" to 7.30 or higher can still also use this Application Server Java to generate a print version from the WD ABAP ALV. The usage type "PDF Export" does not also have to be installed.

]To specify the service to generate the PDF document, it would be a transportable change, **if "BI Export Library" is to selected instead of Adobe Service Services, while setting up Web Dynpro ABAP-Specific settings.** (Step 1 mentioned in customizing steps below)

A transport would be created in Dev system and moved on to production for the change and hence moved through the landscape to production.

This would change the Value of PDF_GEN from "ADS" to "SAP" in table SALV_WD_ADMIN. By default, Value is maintained as ADS.

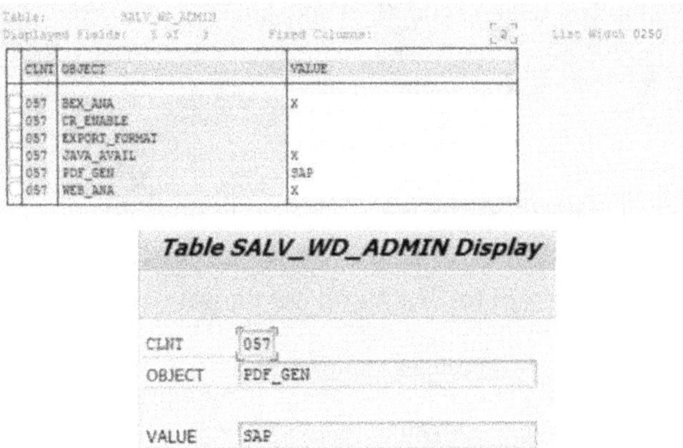

CLNT	OBJECT	VALUE
057	BEX_ANA	X
057	CR_ENABLE	
057	EXPORT_FORMAT	
057	JAVA_AVAIL	X
057	PDF_GEN	SAP
057	WEB_ANA	X

Technical Information

In a WD ABAP ALV, if we choose "Print Version", the following behavior occurs:

- The Application Server ABAP uses the RFC connection SALV_WD_EXPORT_PDF to call the registered print service on an Application Server Java. All data and metadata is transferred to the print service using XML.

- The print service dynamically calculates the column widths and the horizontal and vertical page breaks, and creates a PDF document using the Adobe Document Services (ADS) or the BI Export Library.

- The PDF document is returned to the WD ABAP ALV and displayed using the same RFC connection.

Service for generating the PDF document

As of Release 7.02, you have the following two options:

- ADS (default)
  If you use this option, you specify that the system is to use Adobe Document Services to generate the PDF document.

- SAP BI export library
  If you use this option, you specify that the system is to use the SAP BI export library to generate the PDF document. This is included in the usage type "BI Java", and as of 7.30, also in the usage type "PDF Export".

Here,

-- Using GRC ABAP system for the ABAP side configurations.

-- Using our BI portal system for JAVA end configuration, having the BI Usage type installed.

-- Print version test done from the Consumer portal.

System Details:
This can be checked through System Information.

Details about 01 (Instance ID135165)

Instance Number:	01
ID:	135165
Nodes Count:	1
Root Directory:	/usr/sap/[illegible]/J01
OS:	HP-UX (ia64) B.11.31
HTTP Port:	50100
HTTPS Port:	
Telnet Port:	50108
P4 Port:	50104
VM Name:	SAP Java Server VM
VM Vendor:	SAP AG
VM Java Version:	1.6.0_33
VM Runtime Version:	6.1.043 21.1-b02
Kernel Version:	7.30.3710.182851.20120113163657

Details about Database

Host:	sap[illegible]
Name:	[illegible]
Database:	Oracle (Oracle Database 11g Enterprise Edition Release 11.2.0.3.0 - 64bit Production With the Partitioning, OLAP, Data Mining and Real Application Testing options)
Driver Vendor:	Open SQL
Driver Version:	7.10

Usage Types

Information about Active Usage Types

Active Usage Types

Product Code	UT Code	Short Name	Description
NetWeaver	AS	Application Server Java Extensions	Application Server Java Extensions
NetWeaver	EP	Enterprise Portal	Enterprise Portal
NetWeaver	BI	BI Java	BI Java
NetWeaver	EPC	EP Core - Application Portal	EP Core - Application Portal
NetWeaver	CE-PROCESS	Guided Procedures	Guided Procedures
NetWeaver	CE-APPS	Composite Application Framework	Composite Application Framework
NetWeaver	COMP-ENV	Composition Environment Platform	Composition Environment Platform
NetWeaver	BASIC	Application Server Java	Application Server Java
NetWeaver	ADOBE	Adobe Document Services	Adobe Document Services
NetWeaver	NW-MODEL	NW-MODEL	NW Product Description
NetWeaver	EPCONTENT	EP Content	EP Content

Customizing steps as per SAP Note 1413938:

1) Transaction SPRO

Maintain Web Dynpro ABAP-Specific Settings.

Specify the service to generate the PDF document.

Branch to the following entry:

- Application Server.
- SAP List Viewer (ALV).
- Maintain Web Dynpro ABAP-specific Settings.

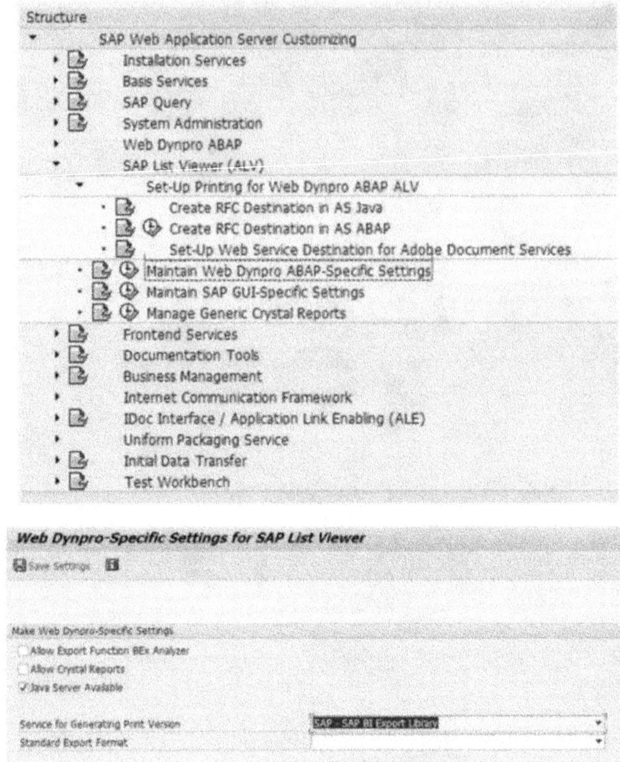

(Here when you select SAP – SAP BI Export Library and click on Save Settings, it will ask for a transport, a new one can be created here, which will then move to production.)

Configure the print version for Web Dynpro ABAP ALV.

Create RFC destination in AS Java

Until SAP NetWeaver 7.00, 7.01 or 7.02 (including SPs):
RFC will be created in Visual Admin.

Above 7.2 (including SPs):
RFC created in SAP NetWeaver Administrator.

Open nwa of the portal system.
Navigate to Configuration -> Infrastructure -> JCO RFC Provider.

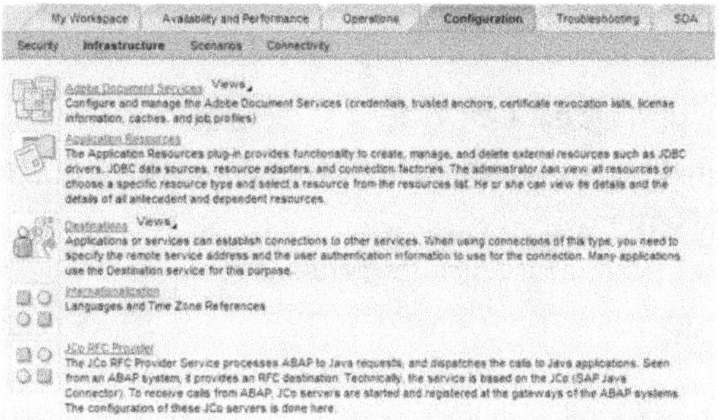

Choose Create.

Portal JCo can be created with the name as: <HOST>_PORTAL_<SID>

Enter the server configuration data.

- Program ID: <PORTAL_HOSTNAME>_PORTAL_<SID>

    Enter a unique program ID.

If it already exists, choose some other name. For eg. Here I have used as:

<HOST>_PORTAL_SID_Z (It should be a unique program ID).

- Gateway host: <GATEWAY_HOST>

    Specify the gateway of the AS ABAP on which your Web Dynpro applications run.
- Gateway service: sapgw<SYSTEM_NUMMER>
- Number of servers (1...20): 20

Enter the Repository configuration data in srep 2:

- Application server host: see Gateway host
- System number: <SYSTEM_NUMBER>
- Client: <CLIENT>
- User: <USER> (application system user with authorization S_RFC)
- Password: <PASSWORD>

- Language: EN

Enter the security settings data.

You can specify whether to use Secure Network Connection (SNC), and its data.

Choose additional options.

You can specify the instance on which the server is to run, and whether RFC traces are to be recorded.

Choose Complete, to confirm your entries.

The destination appears in the initial screen, in the table with the status Running.

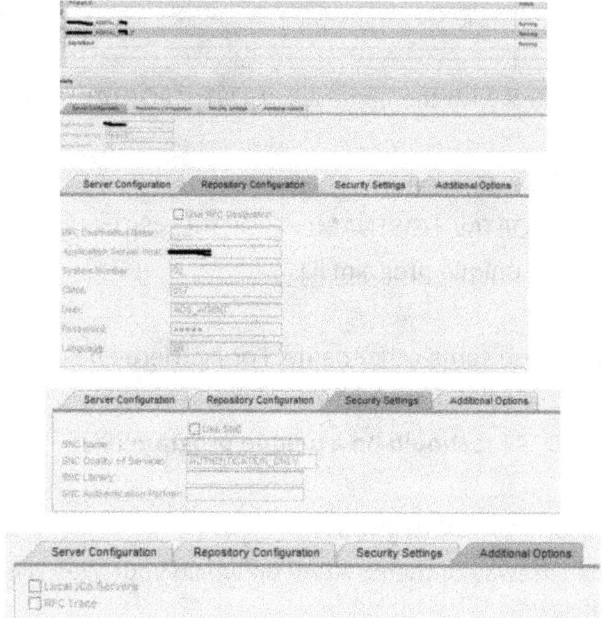

Create RFC destination in AS ABAP

Perform the following steps, to create an RFC connection to the AS Java, in the AS ABAP:

Start the transaction Configure RFC Connections (transaction code SM59).

Choose Create.

Maintain the RFC destination:

- RFC Destination: **SALV_WD_EXPORT_PDF**
- Connection Type: T

(for TCP/IP connection)

- Description: <DESCRIPTION>

Entries in the Technical Settings tab:

- Activation Type: Registered Server Program
- Program: <PORTAL_HOSTNAME>_PORTAL_<SID>

Enter the unique program ID which you used in the AS Java.

- Gateway Host: <GATEWAY_HOST>
- Gateway Service: sapgw<SYSTEM_NUMMER>

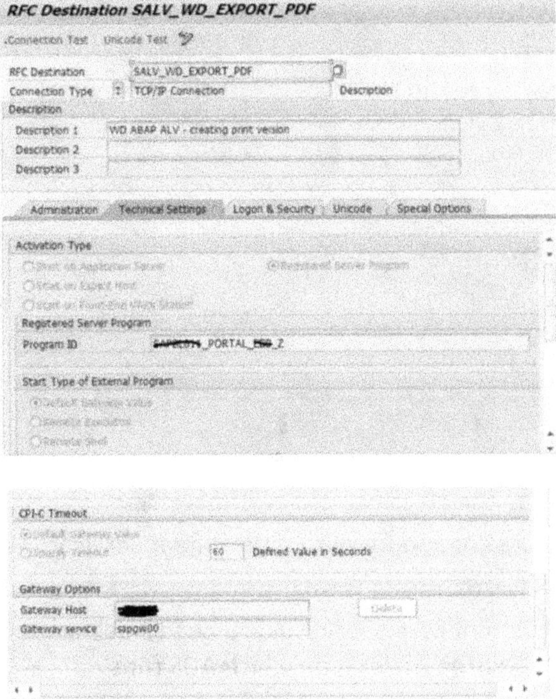

Click on the connection test, to check your data.

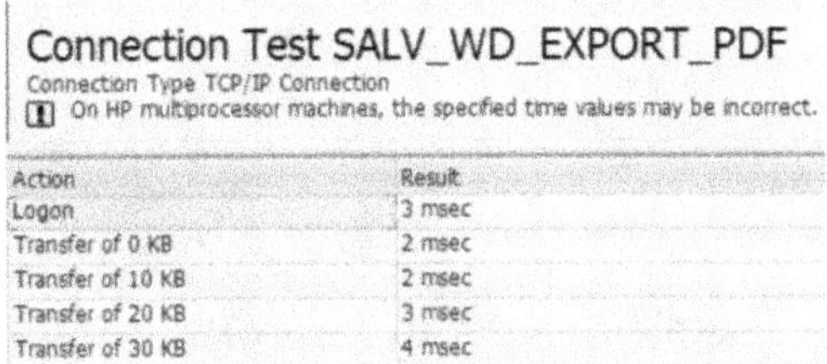

Connection Test SALV_WD_EXPORT_PDF

Connection Type TCP/IP Connection

On HP multiprocessor machines, the specified time values may be incorrect.

Action	Result
Logon	3 msec
Transfer of 0 KB	2 msec
Transfer of 10 KB	2 msec
Transfer of 20 KB	3 msec
Transfer of 30 KB	4 msec

Check whether the connection is to the correct system, choose: Extras -> System Information -> Target System and check the field **System ID**.

Verify, that target system is correctly pointing to the JAVA Portal, where you created the JCo.

RFC Destination: SALV_WD_EXPORT_PDF

Target System

System Name	<extern>	SAP Release	642
Host Name	sapbl011	Protocol Vers.	011
Database		Character Set	4102
Database Host		Integer	BIG
Database System		Floating Point	IE3
		Kernel Release	642
OS	HP-UX		
SAP Host ID			
Time Zone (s)	0		
System ID	sapbl011.am.hjheinz.net		
Network Address	10.196.130.76		

Set-Up Web Service Destination for Adobe Document Services

If you use Adobe Document Services (ADS), you need a destination for the connection between the AS Java and the AS JAVA on which ADS runs.

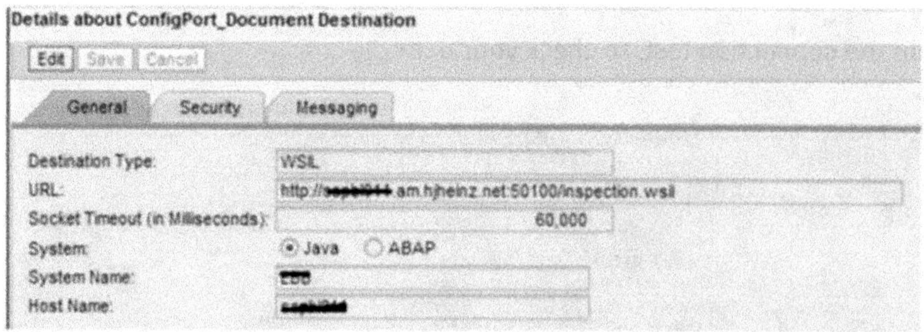

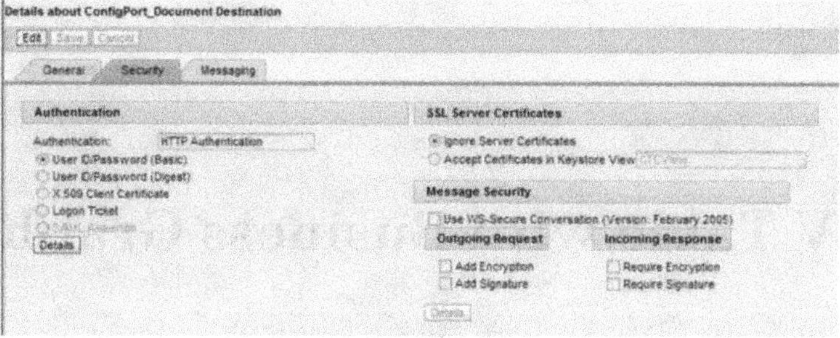

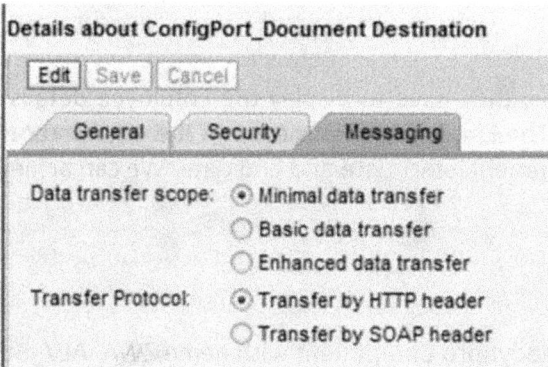

Details about ConfigPort_Document Destination

Edit Save Cancel

General Security Messaging

Data transfer scope: Minimal data transfer

Basic data transfer

Enhanced data transfer

Transfer Protocol: Transfer by HTTP header

Transfer by SOAP header

CHAPTER 14

ALV Table with Business Graphics

ALV Table with Business Graphics (WebDynpro for ABAP)

In one the Scenarios, they have to display the Employee details in a table with the Business Graphics. The Employee details contain the organization unit he is working, Percentage of Assignment, start date and end date. We can achieve this using the ALV.

Procedure:

1. Create one Webdynpro Component with name ZWA_ALV_BUSINESS_GRAPH.

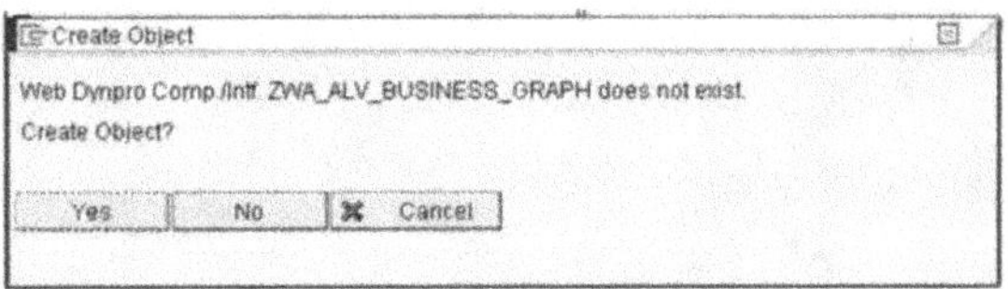

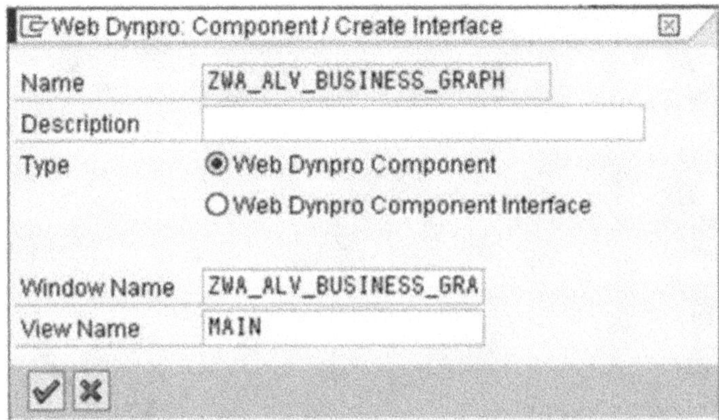

3. In the Component Controller, Go to the Context Tab, Right Click the Context and Select Create à Node.

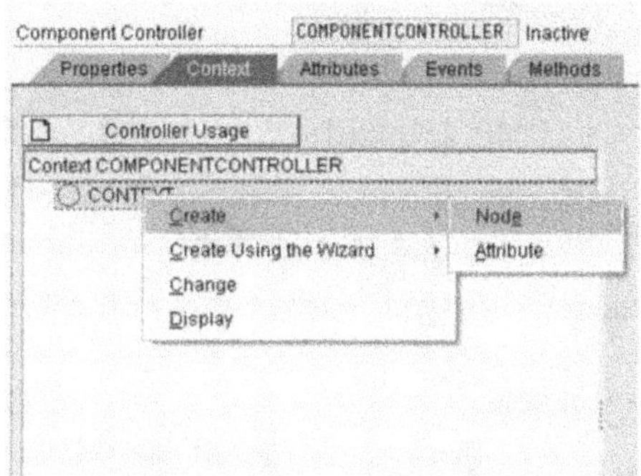

4. Give the Node Name as EMPLOYEE with Cardinality 0.n and Press Enter.
5. Create four Attributes inside that Node by Right Clicking the Employee and Select Create à Attribute.
6. The Attributes are of the Following Type.

ZZORGEH	- ORGEH
ZZ_PER_ASSG	- ZZASSG
BEGDA	- SYDATUM
ENDDA	- SYDATUM

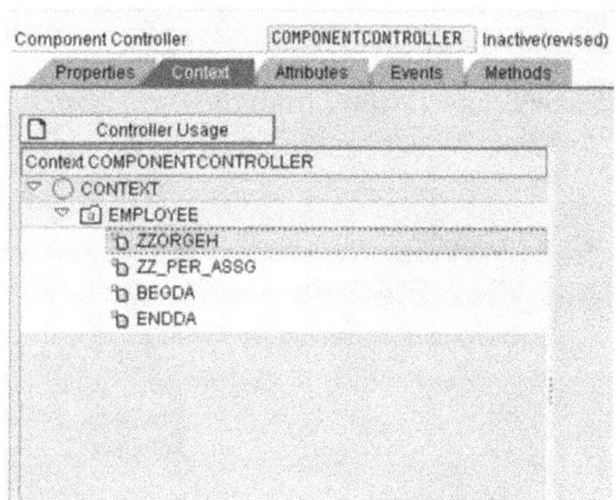

7. Go to the View Context, Drag and Drop the Node EMPLOYEE to the View Context.
8. Then Right Click the Context and Select Create à Attribute.

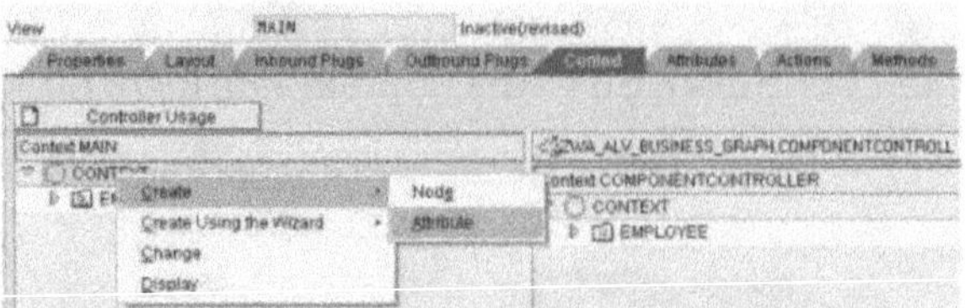

9. Give Attribute Name as EMP_NO with Type CHAR8 and Press Enter.
10. In the Layout Tab of the View, Right click the ROOT UIELEMENTCONTAINER and give Insert Element. It will open a Pop-Up for Creating an Element.
11. Enter Label in the Name Field and Select Label in the Type Field and Press Enter.

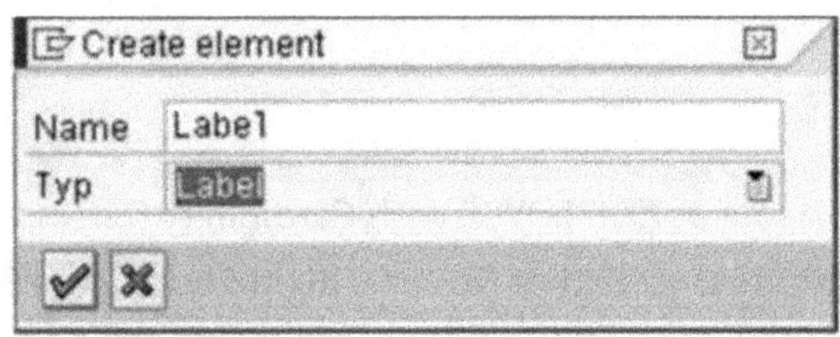

12. Create another UI Element with INPUT in the Name Field and Select Input Field in the Type Field and Press Enter.

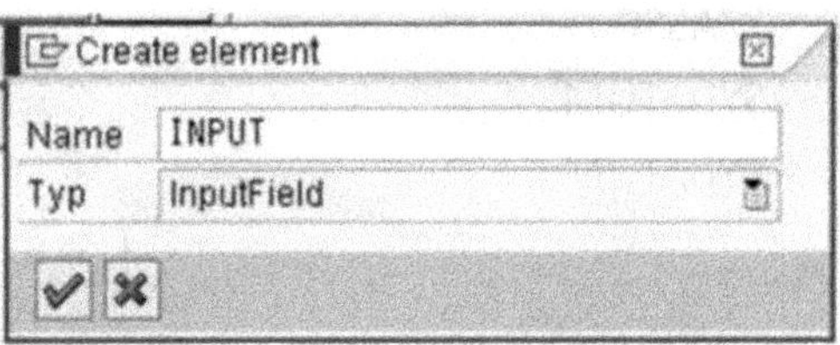

13. In the Label Properties, Select INPUT from the Dropdown for the labelfor Field and Enter 'Enter The Employee Number' in the Text Field.

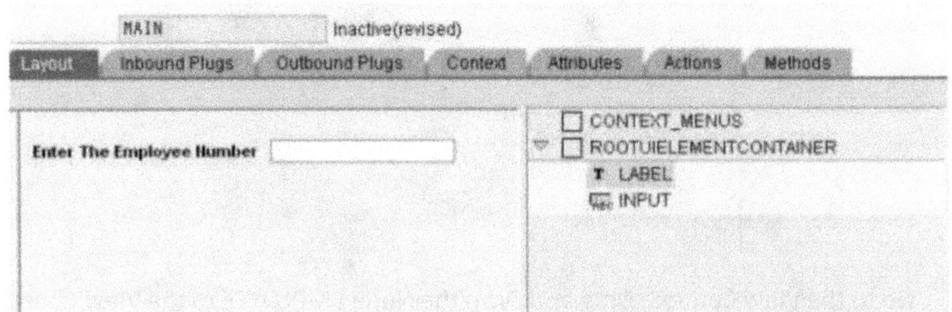

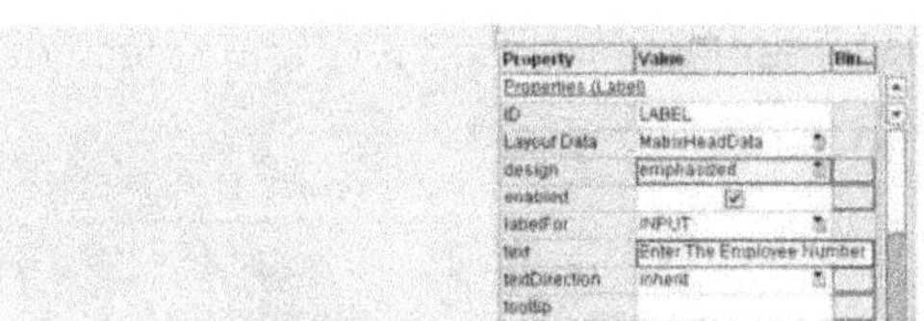

Create Context Binding for the INPUT by Clicking the Button in the Right Side of the value in the Properties. It will open a Popup with the Context Element. In that Select the Attribute EMP_NO AND Press Enter.

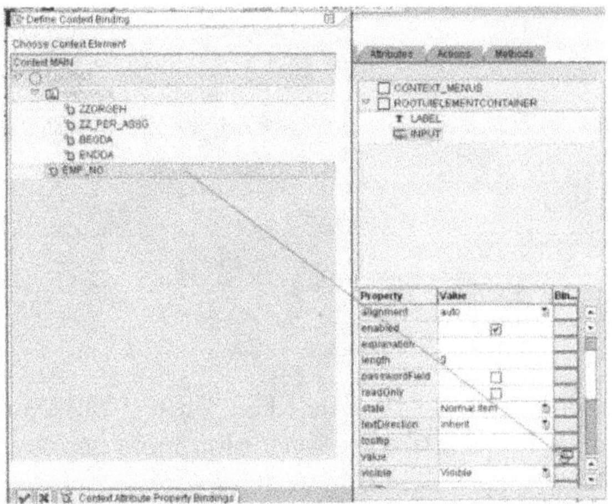

15. Create another Element by Right clicking the ROOTUIELEMENTCONTAINER and give Insert Element. It will open a Pop-Up for Creating an Element.
16. Enter BUTTON in the Name Field and Select Button in the Type Field and Press Enter.

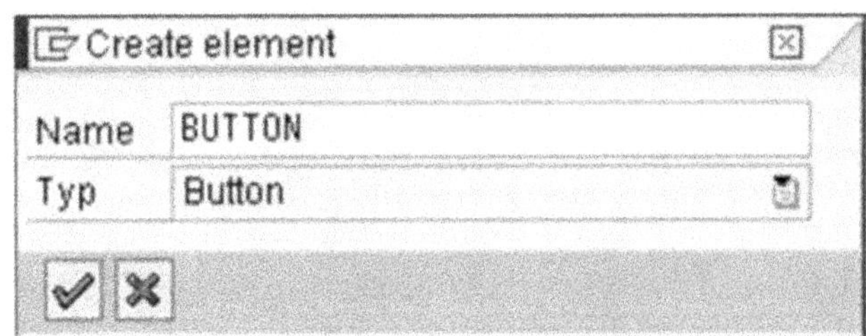

17. Then create one Action for on Action Event of the BUTTON by Clicking the Create Action Button. Then Give the Action Name as GET_EMPLOYEE_DETAILS and press Enter.

18. Create another UI Element with Name VIEW and Select ViewContainerUIElement from the Dropdown in the Type Field.

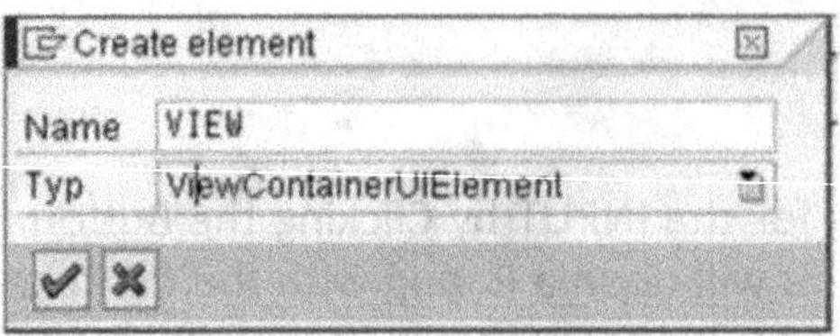

19. Go to the Outbound Plugs Tab in the View, and Enter TO_ALV_TABLE in the Plug Name.

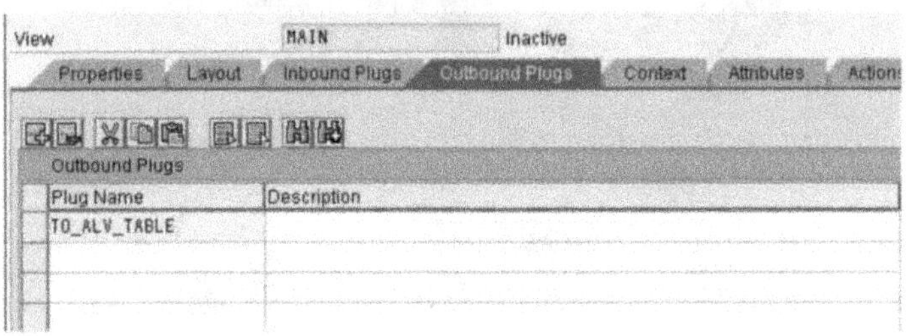

20. Go to the Component ZWA_ALV_BUSINESS_GRAPH and Double Click it. In the 'Used Component' Tab, declare the ALV Component as shown below and Press Enter.

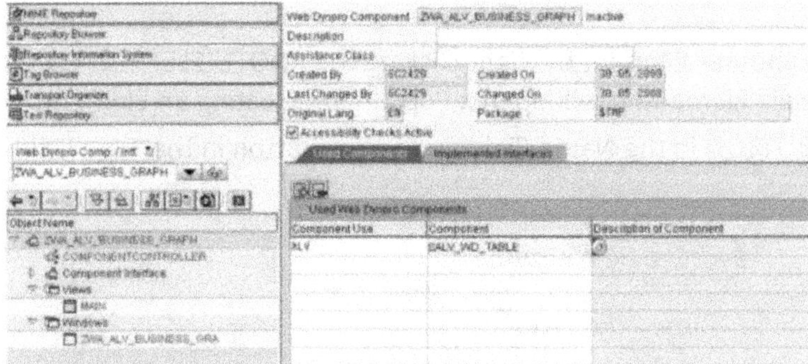

21. Now go to the View, in the Properties Tab click the Create Controller Usage Button as shown below.

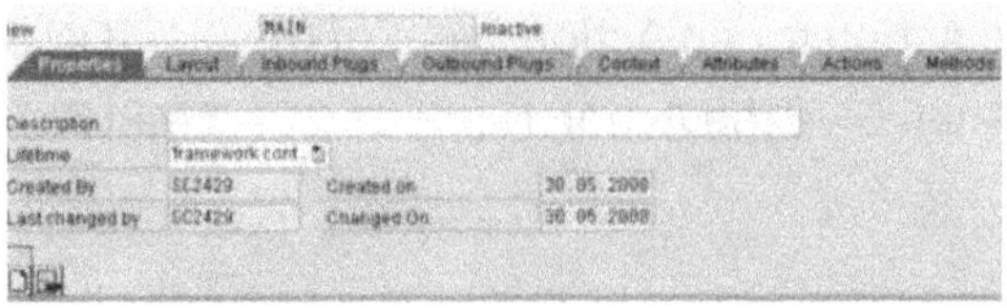

22. It will open a screen with Component Use Entries. There select the Component Use ALV with Interface Controller as shown below. Press Enter.

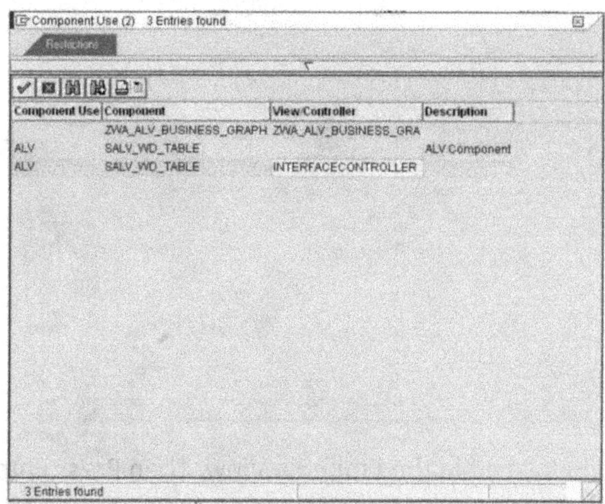

23. It will display as follows in the View Properties.
24. Then go to the Window ZWA_ALV_BUSINESS_GRA. Then Right Click the VIEW and Select Embed View.

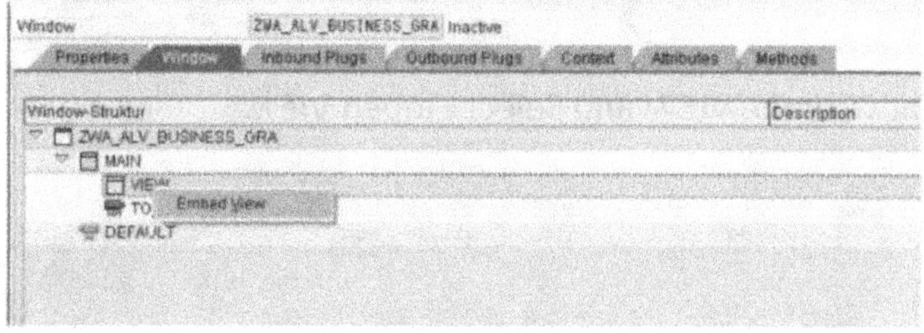

25. It will open a Pop-up for Embed View.
26. Click F4 by placing the Cursor in the 'View to Be Embedded' Field.

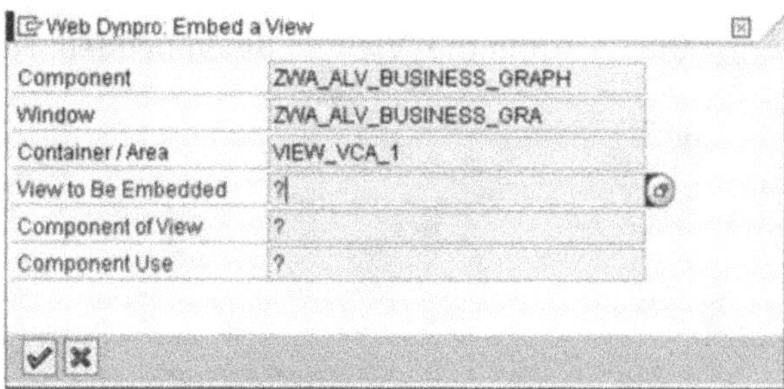

27. It will open a Screen for Selecting a View. Select EMPTYVIEW and Press Enter.

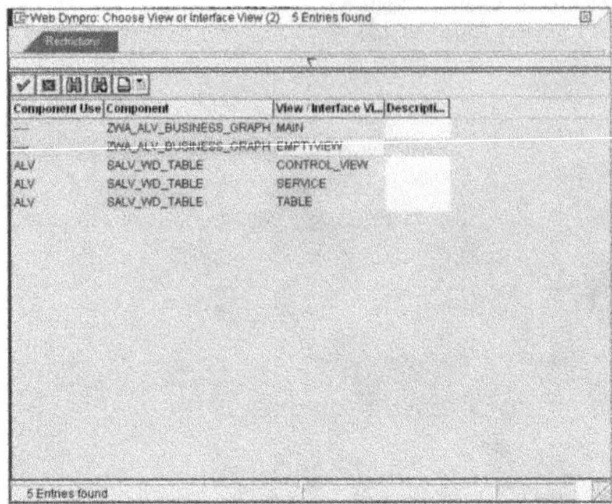

28. The Values will be placed in the Embed a View. Then Press Enter.

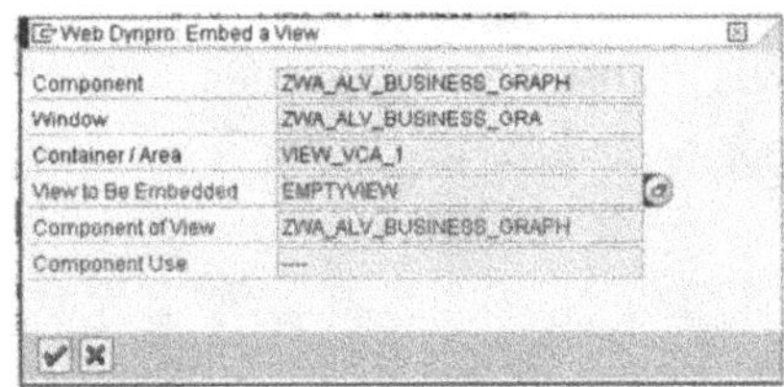

29. Again Right Click the VIEW and Select Embed View.

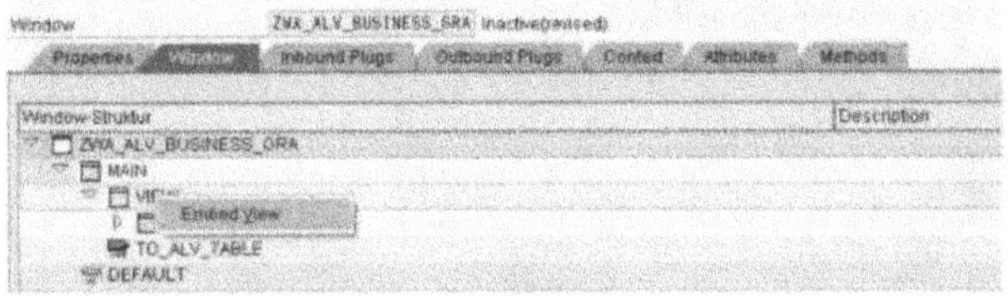

30. It will open a Pop-up for Embed View.
31. Click F4 by placing the Cursor in the 'View to Be Embedded' Field.

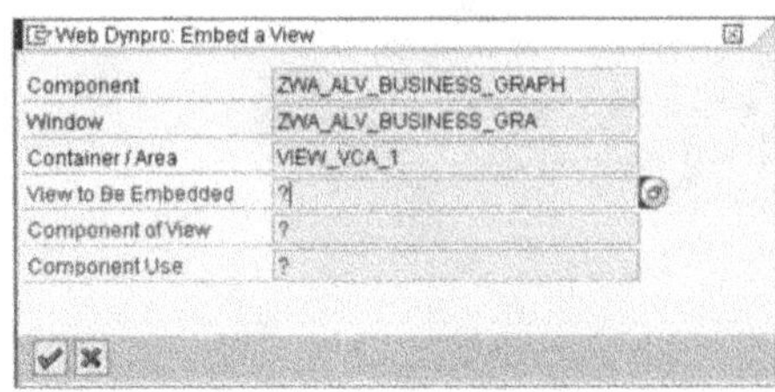

32. Select Component Use ALV with View/Interface View TABLE and Press Enter.

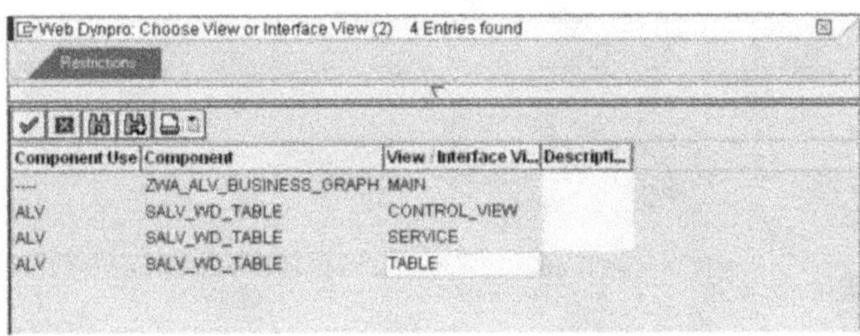

33. The Values will be placed in the Embed a View. Then Press Enter. (**Note**: The Empty View is placed before inside the View is to Hide the ALV Table at the Beginning).

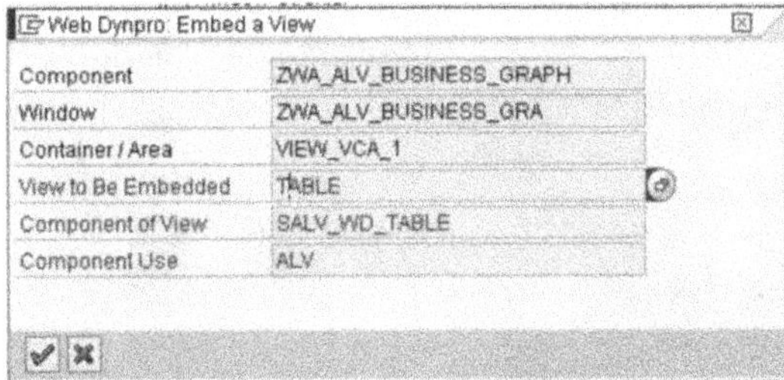

34. Right Click the Outbound Plug TO_ALV_TABLE and Select Create Navigation Link.

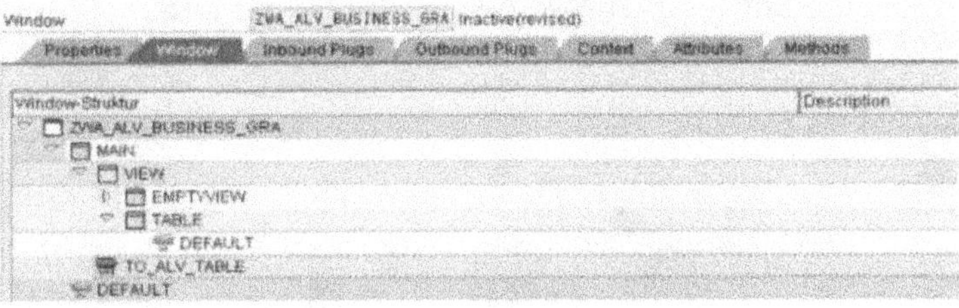

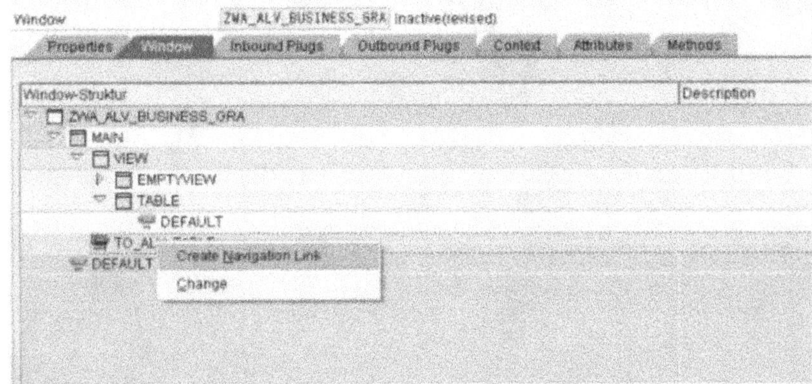

35. It will open a Pop-up for Choosing Destination for Navigation. Click F4 in the Dest. View Field.

Web Dynpro: Choose Destination for Navigation

Start Component	ZWA_ALV_BUSINESS_GRAPH
Start View	MAIN
Outbound Plug	TO_ALV_TABLE
Dest.View	
Embedding Position	
Inbound Plug	

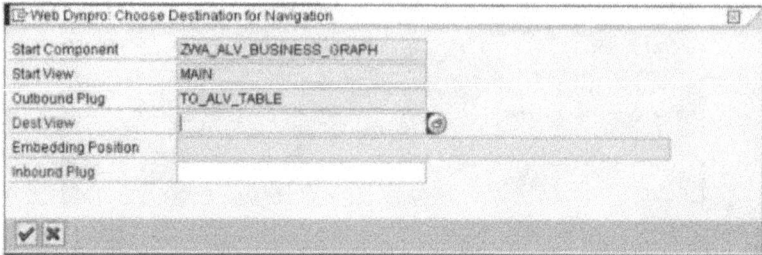

36. It will show the Destination Views. There select the Table in the View Column and Press Enter.

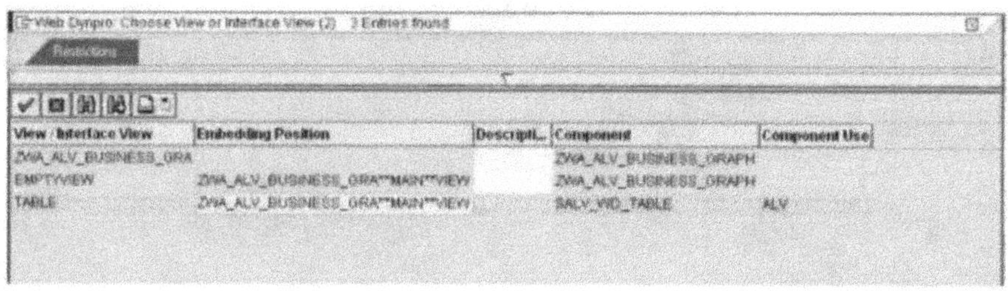

37. It will display the Entries as shown below. Then Press Enter.

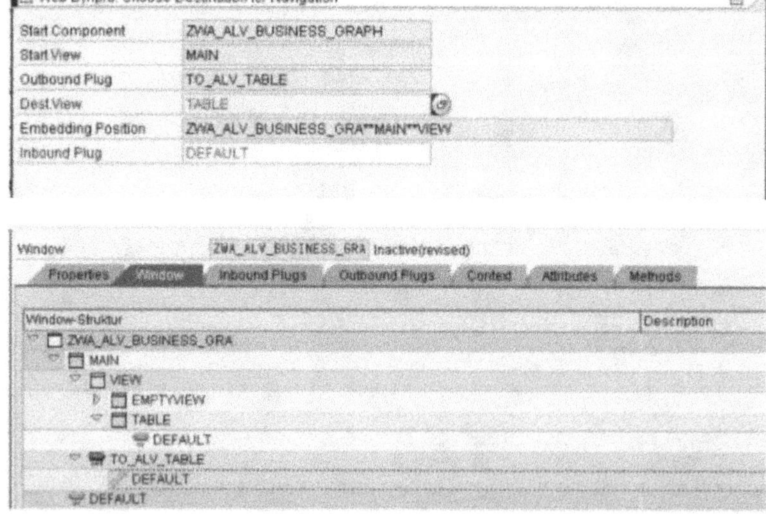

38. Now go to 'Component usages' in the left side tree and expand ALV and double click on the INTERFACECONTROLLER_USAGE. Then Click the Controller Usage Button in the Right Side Window.

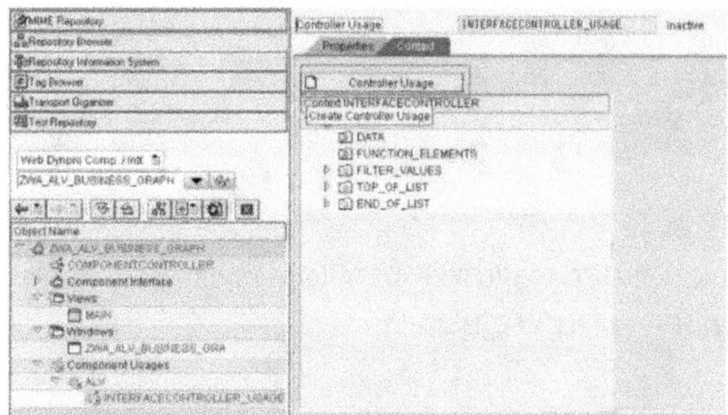

39. It will open a Screen for Selecting Component Use. There, select the COMPONENTCONTROLLER in the View/Controller. Then Press Enter.

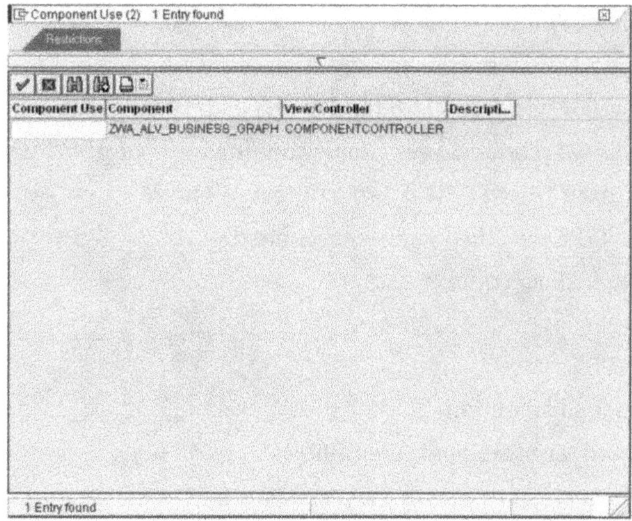

40. Then Drag and Drop the Node EMPLOYEE to the Node DATA in the Context INTERFACECONTROLLER.
41. Go to the View and Click the Tab Methods.

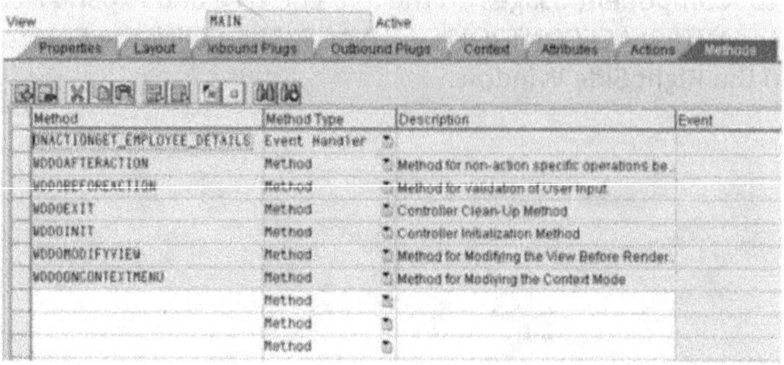

View MAIN Active

Properties | Layout | Inbound Plugs | Outbound Plugs | Context | Attributes | Actions | Methods

Method	Method Type	Description	Event
ONACTIONGET_EMPLOYEE_DETAILS	Event Handler		
WDDOAFTERACTION	Method	Method for non-action specific operations be...	
WDDOBEFOREACTION	Method	Method for validation of User Input	
WDDOEXIT	Method	Controller Clean-Up Method	
WDDOINIT	Method	Controller Initialization Method	
WDDOMODIFYVIEW	Method	Method for Modifying the View Before Render...	
WDDOONCONTEXTMENU	Method	Method for Modiying the Context Mode	
	Method		
	Method		
	Method		

42. In the ONACTIONGET_EMPLOYEE_DETAILS Method, Write the Following Coding. ONACTIONGET_EMPLOYEE_DETAILS:

```
method ONACTIONGET_EMPLOYEE_DETAILS.
  wd_this->fire_to_alv_table_plg( ).
  DATA lo_nd_employee TYPE REF TO if_wd_context_node.
  DATA lo_el_employee TYPE REF TO if_wd_context_element.
  DATA lt_employee TYPE wd_this->elements_employee.
  DATA ls_employee TYPE wd_this->element_employee.
* navigate from <CONTEXT> to <EMPLOYEE> via lead selection
 lo_nd_employee = wd_context->get_child_node(name = wd_this->wdctx_employee ).
  DATA lo_el_context TYPE REF TO if_wd_context_element.
  DATA ls_context TYPE wd_this->element_context.
  DATA lv_emp_no LIKE ls_context-emp_no.

  DATA lv_num TYPE I.
* get element via lead selection
  lo_el_context = wd_context->get_element( ).
* get single attribute
  lo_el_context->get_attribute (
    EXPORTING
      name = `EMP_NO`
    IMPORTING
      value = lv_emp_no).
 SELECT ZZORGEH ZZ_PER_ASSG BEGDA ENDDA INTO CORRESPONDING FIELDS OF TABLE
```

```
  lt_employeeFROM PA9027 WHERE PERNR EQ lv_emp_no AND ENDDA EQ '99991231'.
 DESCRIBE TABLE lt_employee LINES lv_num.
 lo_nd_employee->BIND_TABLE(lt_employee ).
 data lo_cmp_usage type ref to if_wd_component_usage.
 lo_cmp_usage =   wd_this->wd_cpuse_alv().

 if lo_cmp_usage->has_active_component() is initial.
   lo_cmp_usage->create_component().
 endif.
 DATA lo_INTERFACECONTROLLER TYPE REF TO IWCI_SALV_WD_TABLE.
 lo_INTERFACECONTROLLER =   wd_this->wd_cpifc_alv().
 DATA lo_value TYPE ref to cl_salv_wd_config_table.
 lo_value = lo_interfacecontroller->get_model().

* Set Visible Row Count as 5
 lo_value->if_salv_wd_table_settings~set_visible_row_count(lv_num ).
* The Config Table Setting to Display Table & Business Graphics
 DATA: l_ref_config_table TYPE REF TO if_salv_wd_table_settings,
     l_display_as TYPE salv_wd_constant VALUE '02'.
 l_ref_config_table?= lo_value.
 l_ref_config_table->set_display_as(value = l_display_as ).
endmethod.
```

43. Save the Application and Activate the Component.

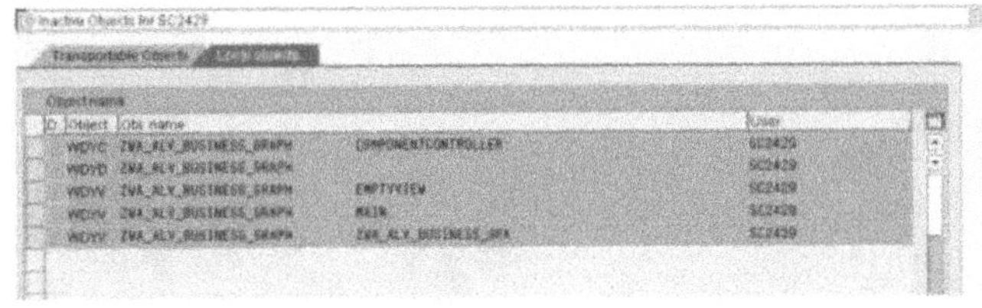

44. Create Webdynpro Application, save it and Test the Application.

Output:

1. Enter the Employee Number in the Input Field and Click the Button 'Get Details'.

Enter The Employee Number 82539 Get Details

2. The Output Will Display as shown below.

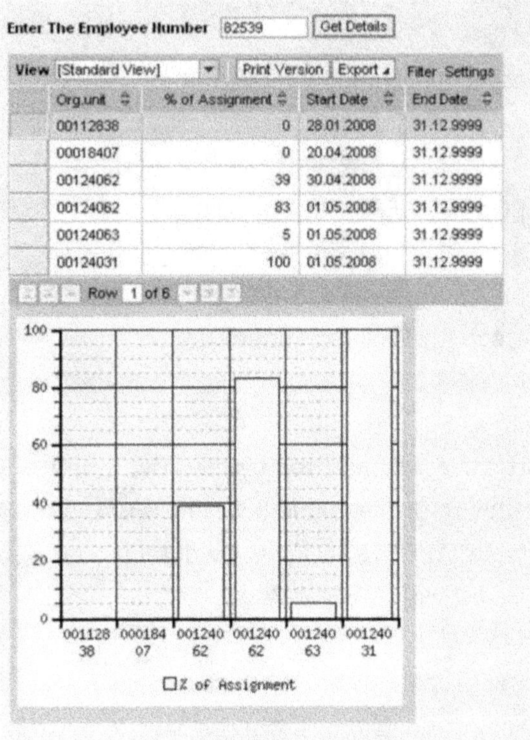

Enter The Employee Number 82539 Get Details

View [Standard View] Print Version Export Filter Settings

Org.unit	% of Assignment	Start Date	End Date
00112838	0	28.01.2008	31.12.9999
00018407	0	20.04.2008	31.12.9999
00124062	39	30.04.2008	31.12.9999
00124062	83	01.05.2008	31.12.9999
00124063	5	01.05.2008	31.12.9999
00124031	100	01.05.2008	31.12.9999

Row 1 of 6

CHAPTER 15

Sending the Multiple ALVs as PDF Attachment through Email

Ref: Bhawna Khosla's artefact

Brief Requirement Overview:

In this document, an email, with the PDF attachment of 3 ALV outputs, will be send to the Email addresses of multiple persons or single person as required. The principle is to print ALVs to spool directly, convert spool to PDF, and send the PDF toemail. It can be used in background as well as in foreground. The program must be executed in background to generate the spool request.

Scenario:

The program will display 3 ALV grids using Custom containers in foreground and will use FM REUSE_ALV_BLOCK_LIST_APPEND to generate spool. When the program is executed in foreground, the three ALV grids will be displayed and an email with PDF attachment of the ALV outputs will be send.When the program is executed in background, spool request will be generated containing the 3 ALV outputs and an email with PDF attachment of the ALV outputs will be send.

Challenge:

The challenge in this scenario is, the 3 ALV grids built using OOPS concept cannot be sent to Spool directly in foreground. For sending the 3 ALV grids to spool, FM REUSE_ALV_BLOCK_LIST_APPEND has been used. The foreground mode uses both the normal ALV grid display methods of OOPS to display the three ALVs in foreground and then uses REUSE_ALV_BLOCK_LIST_APPEND FM to send the report to spool as list. The background mode uses only REUSE_ALV_BLOCK_LIST_APPEND to send the report to spool.

Step1: Creating screen for foreground display

Go to Screen Painter Transaction Code SE51.

Create a screen with no 100.

Provide description for the screen and click on the Layout Button.

Place 3 Custom container UI elements and give names as 'G_CONTAINER1', 'G_CONTAINER2' and 'G_CONTAINER3' .The screen 100 will have 3 custom containers as shown below. Activate the Object.

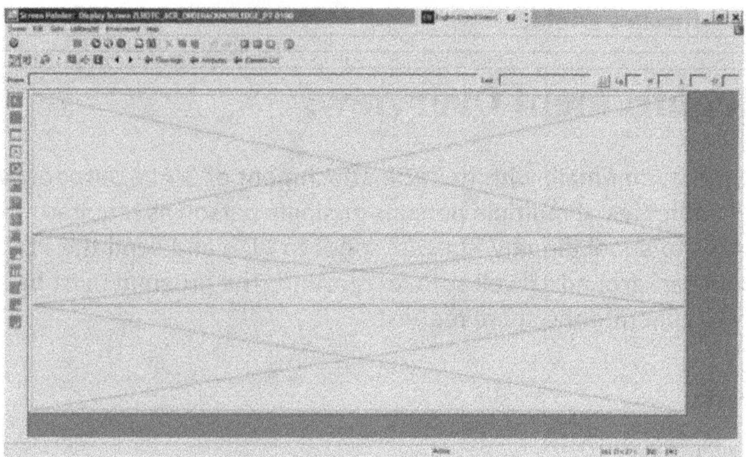

Step 2: Flow Logic

Go to the Flow Logic Tab to write coding for PBO & PAI.

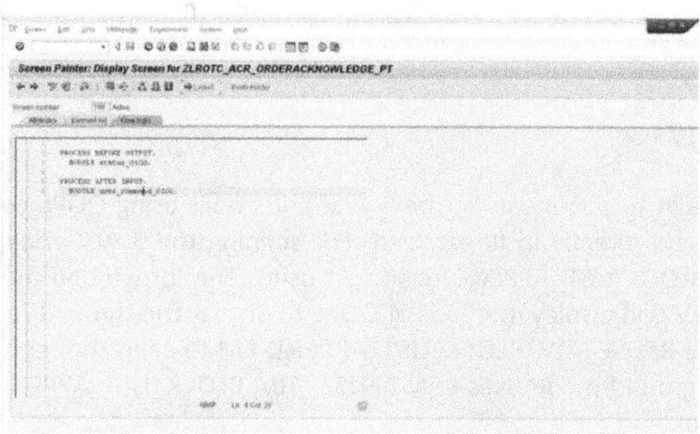

Step3: ABAP Editor

Create a Z program with the code as below:
The three internal tables for 3 ALVs are: I_ORDERS1, I_ORDERS2 and I_INVSTATUS.
The three field catalogs are built and the field catalog names are: I_FIELDCATALOG1, I_FIELDCATALOG2 and I_FIELDCATALOG3.

```
*&---------------------------------------------------------------------*
*&      Module STATUS_0100 OUTPUT
*&---------------------------------------------------------------------*
*       text
*----------------------------------------------------------------------*
MODULE status_0100 OUTPUT.

* PF status of the screen
PERFORM sub_pf_status.
*  Set the title of report
SET TITLEBAR 'TTL'.

* Display ALV Data
PERFORM sub_display_firstalv  USING  i_fieldcatalog1
                              i_orders1.

PERFORM sub_display_secondalv USING  i_fieldcatalog2
                              i_orders2.

PERFORM sub_display_thirdalv  USING  i_fieldcatalog3
                              i_invstatus.
* Send email to customers
PERFORM sub_send_mail.

*   Refresh the first display table
CALL METHOD g_grid1->refresh_table_display
EXCEPTIONS
   finished = 1
OTHERS   = 2.

*   Refresh the second display table
CALL METHOD g_grid2->refresh_table_display
EXCEPTIONS
   finished = 1
OTHERS   = 2.
```

```
*    Refresh the third display table
CALL METHOD g_grid3->refresh_table_display
EXCEPTIONS
   finished = 1
OTHERS   = 2.

ENDMODULE.              " STATUS_0100 OUTPUT

Subroutine to set the PF Status of the report
*&---------------------------------------------------------------------*
*&     Form sub_pf_status
*&---------------------------------------------------------------------*
*      text
*----------------------------------------------------------------------*
FORM sub_pf_status.

* Local data declaration
DATA: lt_excl TYPE ty_t_excl.

*Set PF status
SET PF-STATUS 'ZSTATUS_0100' EXCLUDING lt_excl.
ENDFORM.                "SUB_PF_STATUS
Subroutine to Display First ALV
*&---------------------------------------------------------------------*
*&     Form  SUB_DISPLAY_FIRSTALV
*&---------------------------------------------------------------------*
*      text
*----------------------------------------------------------------------*
*      -->P_I_FIELDCATALOG1  text
*      -->P_I_ORDERS1  text
*----------------------------------------------------------------------*
FORM sub_display_firstalv  USING    fp_i_fieldcatalog1 TYPE lvc_t_fcat
                          fp_i_orders1     TYPE ty_t_orders1.

DATA:     lx_print TYPE lvc_s_prnt.

* Local data declaration
DATA: li_layout TYPE lvc_s_layo.

* Layout for ALV
```

```
PERFORM sub_prepare_layout USING c_x
text-011
                          c_x
                          c_cellstyle
CHANGING li_layout.
* Use Flush
CALL METHOD cl_gui_cfw=>flush.

IF g_custom_container1 IS INITIAL.     "To ensure that object is created only once

CREATE OBJECT g_custom_container1
EXPORTING
     container_name = 'G_CONTAINER1'.

* Splitting the container
CREATE OBJECT g_split
EXPORTING
     parent       = g_custom_container1
     sash_position = 50 "Position of Splitter Bar (in Percent)
     with_border   = 0."With Border = 1 Without Border = 0

* Placing the containers in the splitter
   g_top_container = g_split->top_left_container.
   g_bottom_container = g_split->bottom_right_container.

*    Create an instance of ALV control
CREATE OBJECT g_grid1
EXPORTING
     i_parent = g_bottom_container.

*  Creating the document
CREATE OBJECT g_document
EXPORTING
     style = 'ALV_GRID'.

*Top of page
PERFORM sub_top_of_page.

CALL METHOD g_grid1->set_table_for_first_display
EXPORTING
     it_toolbar_excluding         = i_exclude
```

```
     is_layout                = li_layout
     is_print                 = lx_print
CHANGING
     it_outtab                = fp_i_orders1
     it_fieldcatalog          = fp_i_fieldcatalog1
EXCEPTIONS
     invalid_parameter_combination = 1
     program_error            = 2
     too_many_lines           = 3
OTHERS                   = 4.
IF sy-subrc <>0.
MESSAGE ID sy-msgid TYPE sy-msgty NUMBER sy-msgno
WITH sy-msgv1 sy-msgv2 sy-msgv3 sy-msgv4.
ENDIF.
ENDIF.


ENDFORM.                 "SUB_DISPLAY_FIRSTALV
```

Subroutine to Display Second ALV

```
*&---------------------------------------------------------------------*
*&     Form  SUB_DISPLAY_SECONDALV
*&---------------------------------------------------------------------*
*      text
*----------------------------------------------------------------------*
*     -->P_I_FIELDCATALOG2  text
*     -->P_I_ORDERS2  text
*----------------------------------------------------------------------*
FORM sub_display_secondalv  USING   fp_i_fieldcatalog2 TYPE lvc_t_fcat
                        fp_i_orders2     TYPE ty_t_orders2.

* Local data declaration
DATA: li_layout TYPE lvc_s_layo,
     lx_print TYPE lvc_s_prnt.


* Layout for ALV
PERFORM sub_prepare_layout USING c_x
text-012
                        c_x
```

```
                    c_cellstyle
CHANGING li_layout.
* Use Flush
CALL METHOD cl_gui_cfw=>flush.

IF g_custom_container2 IS INITIAL.     "To ensure that object is created only once

CREATE OBJECT g_custom_container2
EXPORTING
     container_name = 'G_CONTAINER2'.

*   Create an instance of ALV control
CREATE OBJECT g_grid2
EXPORTING
     i_parent = g_custom_container2.


CALL METHOD g_grid2->set_table_for_first_display
EXPORTING
     it_toolbar_excluding       = i_exclude
     is_layout                  = li_layout
     is_print                   = lx_print
CHANGING
     it_outtab                  = fp_i_orders2
     it_fieldcatalog            = fp_i_fieldcatalog2
EXCEPTIONS
     invalid_parameter_combination = 1
     program_error              = 2
     too_many_lines             = 3
OTHERS                     = 4.
IF sy-subrc <>0.
MESSAGE ID sy-msgid TYPE sy-msgty NUMBER sy-msgno
WITH sy-msgv1 sy-msgv2 sy-msgv3 sy-msgv4.
ENDIF.
ENDIF.

ENDFORM.              "SUB_DISPLAY_SECONDALV
```

Subroutine to Display Third ALV

```
*&---------------------------------------------------------------------*
```

```
*&     Form  SUB_DISPLAY_THIRDALV
*&---------------------------------------------------------------*
*      text
*----------------------------------------------------------------*
*     -->P_I_FIELDCATALOG3  text
*     -->P_I_INVSTATUS  text
*----------------------------------------------------------------*
FORM sub_display_thirdalv  USING    fp_i_fieldcatalog3 TYPE lvc_t_fcat
                        fp_i_invstatus TYPE ty_t_invstatus.

* Local data declaration
DATA: li_layout TYPE lvc_s_layo,
     lx_print TYPE lvc_s_prnt.


* Layout for ALV
PERFORM sub_prepare_layout USING c_x
text-013
                        c_x
                        c_cellstyle
CHANGING li_layout.
*  Use Flush
CALL METHOD cl_gui_cfw=>flush.

IF g_custom_container3 IS INITIAL.      "To ensure that object is created only once

CREATE OBJECT g_custom_container3
EXPORTING
     container_name = 'G_CONTAINER3'.

*    Create an instance of ALV control
CREATE OBJECT g_grid3
EXPORTING
     i_parent = g_custom_container3.


CALL METHOD g_grid3->set_table_for_first_display
EXPORTING
     it_toolbar_excluding        = i_exclude
     is_layout                  = li_layout
     is_print                  = lx_print
```

```
CHANGING
     it_outtab                   = fp_i_invstatus
     it_fieldcatalog              = fp_i_fieldcatalog3
EXCEPTIONS
     invalid_parameter_combination = 1
     program_error               = 2
     too_many_lines               = 3
OTHERS                  = 4.
IF sy-subrc <>0.
MESSAGE ID sy-msgid TYPE sy-msgty NUMBER sy-msgno
WITH sy-msgv1 sy-msgv2 sy-msgv3 sy-msgv4.
ENDIF.
ENDIF.
ENDFORM.                "SUB_DISPLAY_THIRDALV
```

Subroutine for ALV layout

```
*&---------------------------------------------------------------------*
*&     Form  SUB_PREPARE_LAYOUT
*&---------------------------------------------------------------------*
*      text
*----------------------------------------------------------------------*
*     <--P_LI_LAYOUT  text
*----------------------------------------------------------------------*
FORM sub_prepare_layout  USING fp_c_x        TYPE xfeld
                   fp_title      TYPE lvc_title
                   fp_smalltitle  TYPE xfeld
                   fp_stylename   TYPE lvc_fname
CHANGING fp_li_layout   TYPE lvc_s_layo.

  fp_li_layout-zebra     = fp_c_x.
  fp_li_layout-grid_title = fp_title.
  fp_li_layout-smalltitle = fp_smalltitle.
  fp_li_layout-stylefname = fp_stylename.

ENDFORM.                "SUB_PREPARE_LAYOUT
```

Subroutine for Report header, which will be created dynamically based on the fields selected by the User for a User selected report layout.

```
*&---------------------------------------------------------------------*
*&     Form SUB_TOP_OF_PAGE
*&---------------------------------------------------------------------*
```

```
*      text
*-------------------------------------------------------------------*
* --> p1       text
* <-- p2       text
*-------------------------------------------------------------------*
FORM sub_top_of_page.

* Local data Declaration
DATA: l_text TYPE sdydo_text_element,
      l_datel (10) TYPE c,
      l_dateh (10) TYPE c.

* Calling the methods for dynamic text
CALL METHOD g_document->add_text
EXPORTING
text         = text-014
    sap_emphasis = cl_dd_area=>strong " For bold
    sap_fontsize = cl_dd_area=>extra_large.

* Adding Line
CALL METHOD g_document->new_line.
* Adding Line
CALL METHOD g_document->new_line.

*  Sold-to customer
IF s_kunnr-high IS NOT INITIAL.
CONCATENATE  s_kunnr-low 'to' s_kunnr-high INTO l_text SEPARATED BY ' '.
ELSE.
  l_text = s_kunnr-low.
ENDIF.

CALL METHOD g_document->add_text
EXPORTING
text         = text-015
    sap_emphasis = cl_dd_area=>strong. "For bold.

CALL METHOD g_document->add_gap
EXPORTING
    width = '15'.

CALL METHOD g_document->add_text
```

```
EXPORTING
text = l_text.
CALL METHOD g_document->new_line.


CLEAR:l_text.
*  Change date
*  Converting date format
CALL FUNCTION 'CONVERT_DATE_TO_EXTERNAL'
EXPORTING
    date_internal = s_erdat-low
IMPORTING
    date_external = l_datel.


* Converting date format
CALL FUNCTION 'CONVERT_DATE_TO_EXTERNAL'
EXPORTING
    date_internal = s_erdat-high
IMPORTING
    date_external = l_dateh.

IF s_erdat-high IS NOT INITIAL.
CONCATENATE l_datel 'to' l_dateh INTO l_text SEPARATED BY ' '.
ELSE.
   l_text = l_datel.
ENDIF.

CALL METHOD g_document->add_text
EXPORTING
text        = text-016
    sap_emphasis = cl_dd_area=>strong. "For bold.

CALL METHOD g_document->add_gap
EXPORTING
    width = '24'.

CALL METHOD g_document->add_text
EXPORTING
text = l_text.
CALL METHOD g_document->new_line.
```

```
CLEAR:l_text.
IF NOT s_vkorg IS INITIAL.
*  Sales Organization
IF s_vkorg-high IS NOT INITIAL.
CONCATENATE  s_vkorg-low 'to' s_vkorg-high INTO l_text SEPARATED BY ' '.
ELSE.
   l_text = s_vkorg-low.
ENDIF.

CALL METHOD g_document->add_text
EXPORTING
text        = text-017
      sap_emphasis = cl_dd_area=>strong. "For bold.

CALL METHOD g_document->add_gap
EXPORTING
      width = '12'.

CALL METHOD g_document->add_text
EXPORTING
text = l_text.
CALL METHOD g_document->new_line.
ENDIF.

CLEAR : l_text.
IF NOT s_bsark IS INITIAL.
*  PO Type
IF s_bsark-high IS NOT INITIAL.
CONCATENATE  s_bsark-low 'to' s_bsark-high INTO l_text SEPARATED BY ' '.
ELSE.
   l_text = s_bsark-low.
ENDIF.

CALL METHOD g_document->add_text
EXPORTING
text        = text-018
      sap_emphasis = cl_dd_area=>strong. "For bold.

CALL METHOD g_document->add_gap
EXPORTING
```

```
    width = '32'.

CALL METHOD g_document->add_text
EXPORTING
text = l_text.
CALL METHOD g_document->new_line.
ENDIF.

* Display the data
CALL METHOD g_document->display_document
EXPORTING
    parent = g_top_container.
* Calling the method of ALV to process top of page
CALL METHOD g_grid1->list_processing_events
EXPORTING
    i_event_name = text-019
    i_dyndoc_id  = g_document.

ENDFORM.                "SUB_TOP_OF_PAGE
```

Step4: Sending an Email with PDF attachment of the output.

The ALV output is first send to spool request, then the spool is converted to PDF and then the PDF attachment is sent to Email.

a) Converting Spool to PDF

```
*&---------------------------------------------------------------*
*&    Form  SUB_CONVERT_SPOOL_TO_PDF
*&---------------------------------------------------------------*
*     text
*----------------------------------------------------------------*
* --> p1      text
* <-- p2      text
*----------------------------------------------------------------*
FORM sub_convert_spool_to_pdf CHANGING fp_size     TYPE i
fp_i_mess_att TYPE ty_t_mess_att.

TYPES: ty_t_pdf TYPE STANDARD TABLE OF tline.

DATA: lv_buffer    TYPE string,
```

```
      lv_spool_nr   TYPE tsp01-rqident,
      lw_mess_att   TYPE solisti1,
      li_pdf_output TYPE ty_t_pdf,
      lw_pdf_output TYPE tline.

* Get the spool number
MOVE sy-spono TO lv_spool_nr.
CALL FUNCTION 'CONVERT_ABAPSPOOLJOB_2_PDF'
EXPORTING
    src_spoolid         = lv_spool_nr "Spool Number
    no_dialog           = space
    dst_device          = 'LP01' "Printer Name
IMPORTING
    pdf_bytecount         = fp_size "Output Size
TABLES
    pdf                = li_pdf_output "Spool data in PDF Format
EXCEPTIONS
    err_no_abap_spooljob  = 1
    err_no_spooljob       = 2
    err_no_permission     = 3
    err_conv_not_possible = 4
    err_bad_destdevice    = 5
    user_cancelled        = 6
    err_spoolerror        = 7
    err_temseerror        = 8
    err_btcjob_open_failed = 9.

IF sy-subrc EQ 0.
LOOP AT li_pdf_output INTO lw_pdf_output.
TRANSLATE lw_pdf_output USING c_col1.
CONCATENATE lv_buffer lw_pdf_output INTO lv_buffer.
CLEAR :lw_pdf_output.
ENDLOOP.
TRANSLATE lv_buffer USING c_col2.
DO.
    lw_mess_att = lv_buffer.
APPEND lw_mess_att TO fp_i_mess_att.
SHIFT lv_buffer LEFT BY c_255 PLACES.
IF lv_buffer IS INITIAL.
EXIT.
ENDIF.
```

```
CLEAR lw_mess_att.
ENDDO.
ENDIF.

ENDFORM.                "SUB_CONVERT_SPOOL_TO_PDF
```

b) Sending PDF attachment to Email

The email addresses of the receivers are populated in table I_EMAIL which is passed in the below subroutine as FP_I_EMAIL.

```
*&---------------------------------------------------------------------*
*&    Form  SUB_SEND_PDF_TO_MAIL
*&---------------------------------------------------------------------*
*     text
*----------------------------------------------------------------------*
* --> p1      text
* <-- p2      text
*----------------------------------------------------------------------*
FORM sub_send_pdf_to_mail USING  fp_size      TYPE i
                        fp_i_mess_att TYPE ty_t_mess_att
                        fp_i_email    TYPE ty_t_email.



LOOP AT fp_i_email INTO lw_email.

TRY.
* Create persistent send request
     l_ref_bcs = cl_bcs=>create_persistent ( ).
* Mail subject
     lv_text = text-021.
APPEND text-021 TO lv_data.

* Create document
     l_ref_document = cl_document_bcs=>create_document (
     i_type = c_raw
     i_text = lv_data
     i_subject = lv_text).

* Create document reference
     lv_filesize = fp_size.
```

```
CALL METHOD l_ref_document->add_attachment
EXPORTING
        i_attachment_type    = c_pdf
        i_attachment_size    = lv_filesize
        i_attachment_subject = lv_text
        i_att_content_text   = fp_i_mess_att [].

* Set the document
     l_ref_bcs->set_document (l_ref_document).

* Get Recipient Object
       l_recipient = cl_cam_address_bcs=>create_internet_address (lw_email-smtp_
addr).
*


CATCH cx_bcs INTO l_ref_bcs_exception.
IF l_ref_bcs_exception IS NOT INITIAL.
CLEAR l_ref_bcs_exception.
ENDIF.
ENDTRY.
ENDLOOP.
COMMIT WORK.

ENDFORM.                  "SUB_SEND_PDF_TO_MAIL
```

Step 5: Report output in foreground

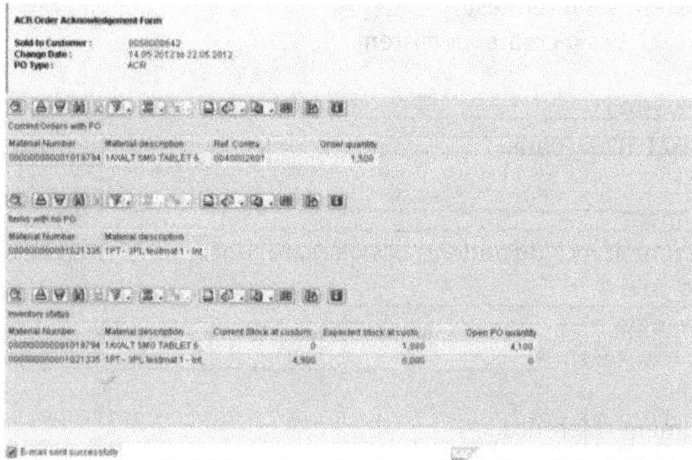

Step 6: Functionality for executing the report in Background.

When the report is executed in background, the single spool of three ALV grids will be created. For displaying the three ALV Grids in single spool, we will use the following FMs:

a) REUSE_ALV_BLOCK_LIST_INIT
b) REUSE_ALV_BLOCK_LIST_APPEND
c REUSE_ALV_BLOCK_LIST_DISPLAY

The three field catalogs are built for this and the field catalog names are: LI_FIELD-CAT1, LI_FIELDCAT2 and LI_FIELDCAT3.
The header of the three ALVs in the spool is created as follows by using the below code:

```
PERFORM sub_header_list CHANGING li_events_1
                                 li_events_2
                                 li_events_3.
*&---------------------------------------------------------------------*
*&      Form  SUB_HEADER_LIST
*&---------------------------------------------------------------------*
*       text
*----------------------------------------------------------------------*
*      <--P_LI_EVENTS_1  text
*      <--P_LI_EVENTS_2  text
*      <--P_LI_EVENTS_3  text
*----------------------------------------------------------------------*
FORM sub_header_list  CHANGING fp_li_events_1 TYPE slis_t_event
                               fp_li_events_2 TYPE slis_t_event
                               fp_li_events_3 TYPE slis_t_event.

DATA: lw_events   TYPE slis_alv_event.

  lw_events-name = 'TOP_OF_PAGE'.
  lw_events-form = 'TOP_OF_PAGE_1'."Subroutine name
APPEND lw_events TO fp_li_events_1.
CLEAR  lw_events.
  lw_events-name = 'TOP_OF_PAGE'.
  lw_events-form = 'TOP_OF_PAGE_2'."Subroutine name
APPEND lw_events TO fp_li_events_2.
CLEAR  lw_events.
  lw_events-name = 'TOP_OF_PAGE'.
```

```
  lw_events-form = 'TOP_OF_PAGE_3'."Subroutine name
APPEND lw_events TO fp_li_events_3.
CLEAR  lw_events.

ENDFORM.                "SUB_HEADER_LIST
```

Step 7:Displaying the three ALVs in background

```
lv_repid  = sy-repid.


CALL FUNCTION 'REUSE_ALV_BLOCK_LIST_INIT'
EXPORTING
    i_callback_program = lv_repid.

*call first ALV append list
CALL FUNCTION 'REUSE_ALV_BLOCK_LIST_APPEND'
EXPORTING
    is_layout              = lv_layout
    it_fieldcat            = li_fieldcat1
    i_tabname                = 'I_ORDERS1'
    it_events              = li_events_1[]
TABLES
    t_outtab               = i_orders1
EXCEPTIONS
    program_error            = 1
    maximum_of_appends_reached = 2
OTHERS               = 3.
IF sy-subrc <>0.
MESSAGE ID sy-msgid TYPE sy-msgty NUMBER sy-msgno
WITH sy-msgv1 sy-msgv2 sy-msgv3 sy-msgv4.
ENDIF.


CALL FUNCTION 'REUSE_ALV_BLOCK_LIST_APPEND'
EXPORTING
    is_layout              = lv_layout
    it_fieldcat            = li_fieldcat2
    i_tabname                = 'I_ORDERS2'
    it_events              = li_events_2
TABLES
```

```
    t_outtab              = i_orders2
EXCEPTIONS
    program_error            = 1
    maximum_of_appends_reached = 2
OTHERS                  = 3.
IF sy-subrc <>0.
MESSAGE ID sy-msgid TYPE sy-msgty NUMBER sy-msgno
WITH sy-msgv1 sy-msgv2 sy-msgv3 sy-msgv4.
ENDIF.

CALL FUNCTION 'REUSE_ALV_BLOCK_LIST_APPEND'
EXPORTING
    is_layout             = lv_layout
    it_fieldcat           = li_fieldcat3
    i_tabname               = 'I_INVSTATUS'
    it_events             = li_events_3
TABLES
    t_outtab              = i_invstatus
EXCEPTIONS
    program_error            = 1
    maximum_of_appends_reached = 2
OTHERS                  = 3.
IF sy-subrc <>0.
MESSAGE ID sy-msgid TYPE sy-msgty NUMBER sy-msgno
WITH sy-msgv1 sy-msgv2 sy-msgv3 sy-msgv4.
ENDIF.

* Get the print parameters
PERFORM sub_get_print_parameters.

NEW-PAGE PRINT ON PARAMETERS x_params
NO DIALOG.

  lx_print-print = ' '.
  lx_print-prnt_title = ' '.
  lx_print-prnt_info = ' '.
  lx_print-no_print_selinfos = 'X'. " Display no selection infos
  lx_print-no_print_listinfos = 'X'. " Display no listinfos
  lx_print-no_new_page = 'X'.

*display the data
```

```
CALL FUNCTION 'REUSE_ALV_BLOCK_LIST_DISPLAY'
EXPORTING
    i_interface_check = ' '
    is_print        = lx_print
EXCEPTIONS
    program_error    = 1
OTHERS          = 2.
IF sy-subrc <>0.
MESSAGE ID sy-msgid TYPE sy-msgty NUMBER sy-msgno
WITH sy-msgv1 sy-msgv2 sy-msgv3 sy-msgv4.
ENDIF.
COMMIT WORK.
NEW-PAGE PRINT OFF.
```

Subroutine to get print parameters

```
*&---------------------------------------------------------------------*
*&     Form SUB_GET_PRINT_PARAMETERS
*&---------------------------------------------------------------------*
*      text
*----------------------------------------------------------------------*
* --> p1       text
* <-- p2       text
*----------------------------------------------------------------------*
FORM sub_get_print_parameters.

DATA: lv_valid.

CALL FUNCTION 'GET_PRINT_PARAMETERS'
EXPORTING
    immediately    = 'X'
    no_dialog      = 'X'
    line_size      = '255'
    line_count     = '65'
    layout         = 'X_65_255'
    destination    = 'LP01'
IMPORTING
    out_parameters = x_params
    valid          = lv_valid
EXCEPTIONS
OTHERS        = 1.
```

```
IF sy-subrc <>0.
MESSAGE ID sy-msgid TYPE sy-msgty NUMBER sy-msgno
WITH sy-msgv1 sy-msgv2 sy-msgv3 sy-msgv4.
ENDIF.


ENDFORM.                "SUB_GET_PRINT_PARAMETERS
```

Step 8: Report output in background.

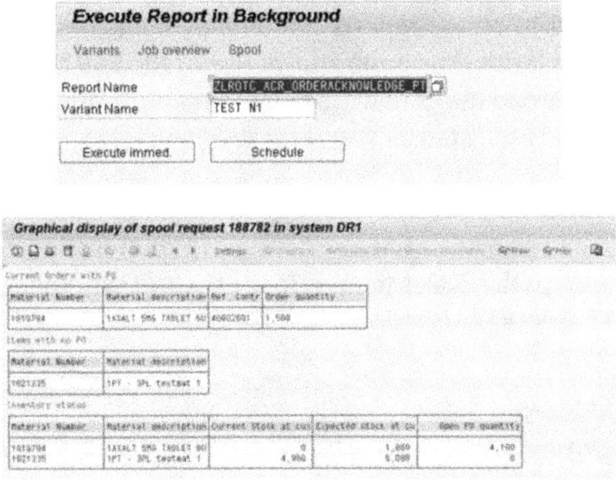

The above spool output is finally sent as a PDF attachment to email addresses of multiple persons.

CHAPTER 16

Query creation steps

The SAP Query is used to create reports not already contained in the default. It has been designed for users with little or no knowledge of the SAP programming language ASAP. It offers users a broad range of ways to define reports and create different types of reports such as basic lists, statistics, and ranked lists.

Step 1: Create User Group – SQ03

- Menu path – SAP Menu -> Tools -> ABAP Workbench -> Utilities -> SAP Query -> User Groups.

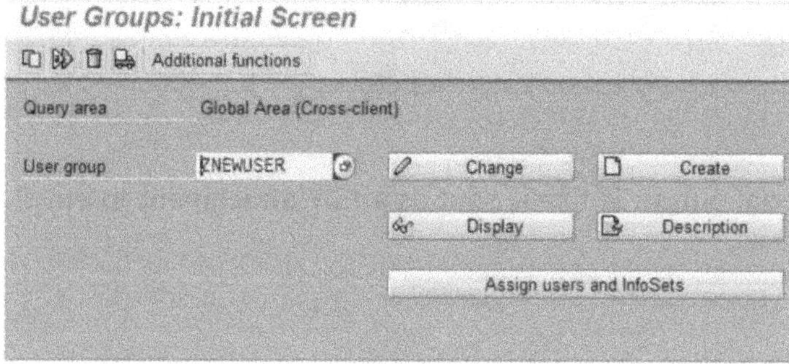

- In the User Group : Initial Screen
  - Enter User Group Code (Z****).
  - Click on “Create”.

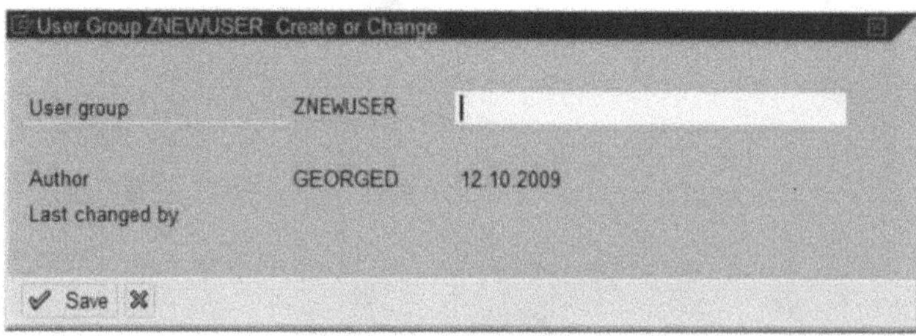

Step 2: Create User Group – SQ02

- Menu path – SAP Menu > Tools > ABAP Workbench > Utilities > SAP Query > Infosets.

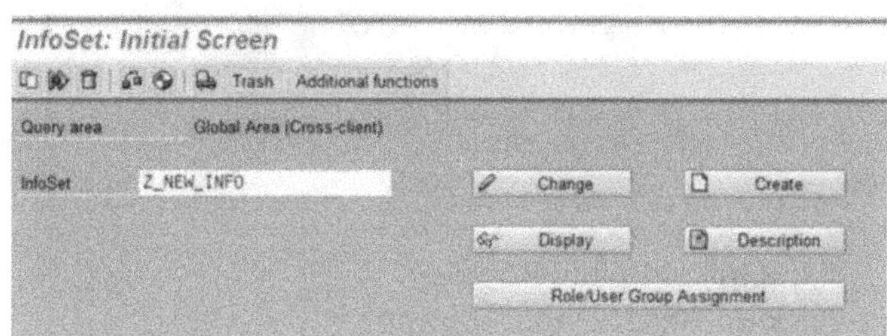

- In the Infoset : Initial screen:
  - Enter Infoset Code (Z****).
  - Click on "Create" button.
- In the Infoset : Title & Database Screen:
  - Enter Description of Infoset in the "Name" field.
  - In the Data Source selection: Select appropriate Data Source by clicking the radio button.

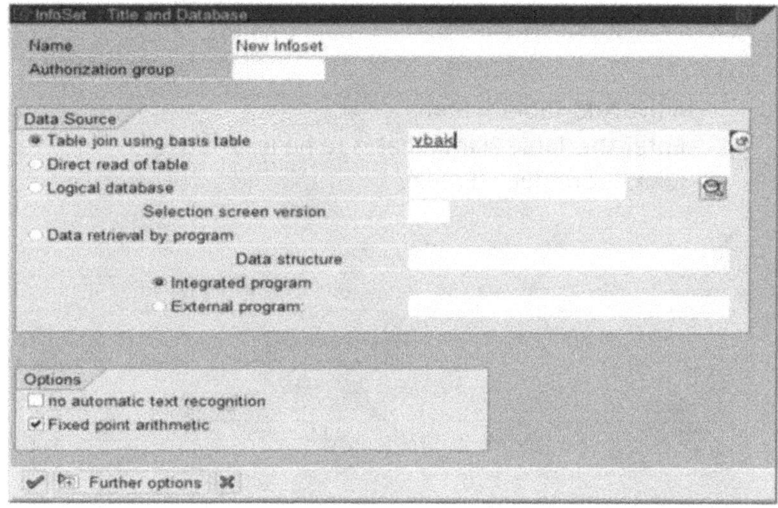

- Source the data can either be multiple tables OR single table. There are 4 options for the user to select from:
  - Click on "Continue" (Enter).
  - Selected Table gets displayed in the Infoset: Initial Screen.

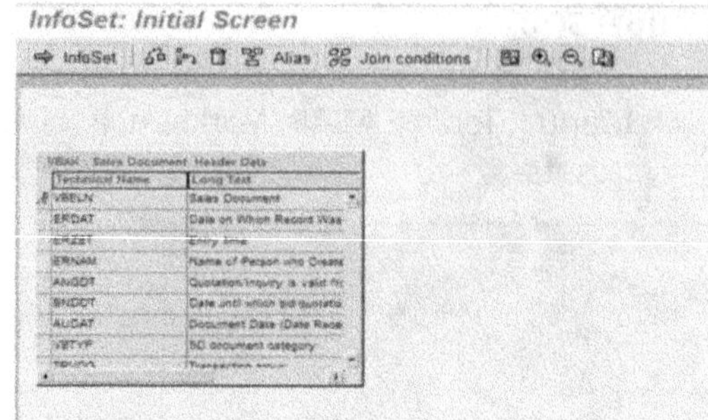

- In the Infoset : Initial Screen:
  - Click on “Insert Table” button.

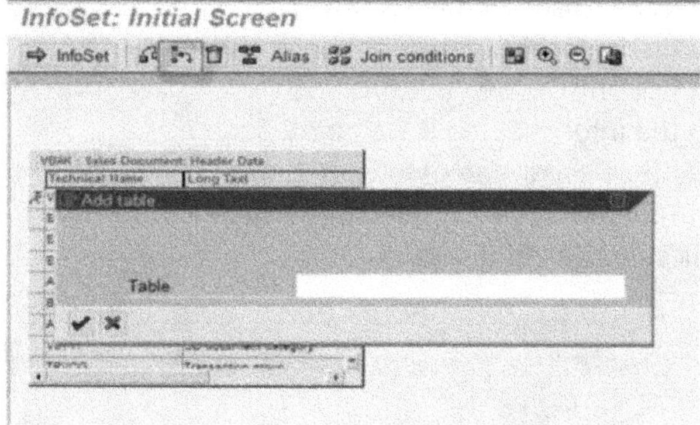

- In the Add Table Screen:
  - Enter the Table Name that is to be inserted.
  - Click “Continue” (Enter).

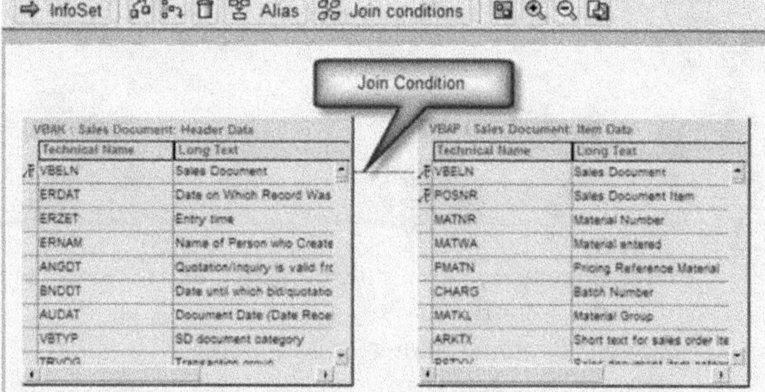

- In the Infoset: Initial Screen - Validate the join condition:
  - Click on "Back" button.

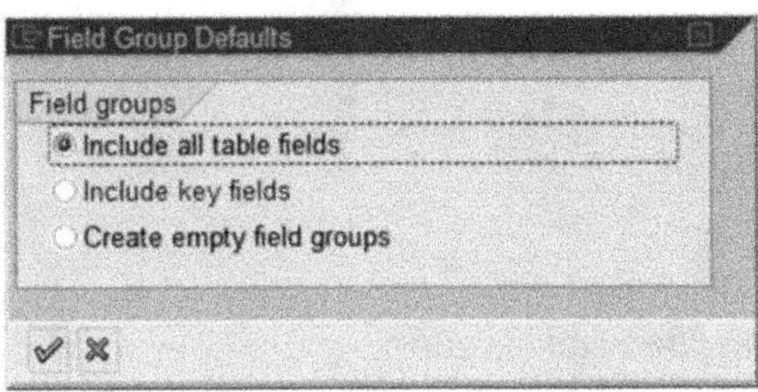

- In the Field Group Defaults pop-up Screen:
  - Select Appropriate Field Group Option by clicking on the radio button.

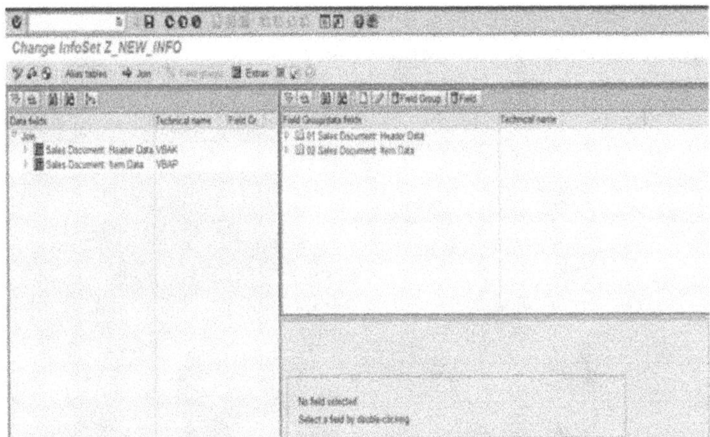

- In the Change Infoset Screen:
  The left side lists the Tables that the user has selected in previous steps.
  - In the right side, system creates field groups, one for each table listed in the left part.
- The field group will contain all the fields selected from the previous step.

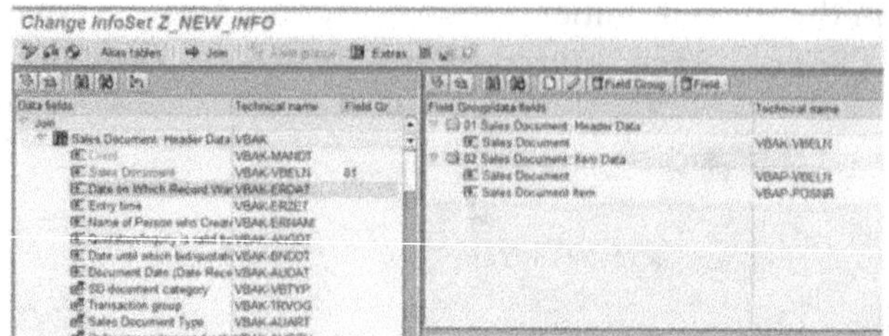

- Right click on a field in the left side and we can add the field to one of the provided Field groups.
- The query we create can only use the fields added to the Field groups.
- Once we pick up the Field groups, Generate the Infoset.

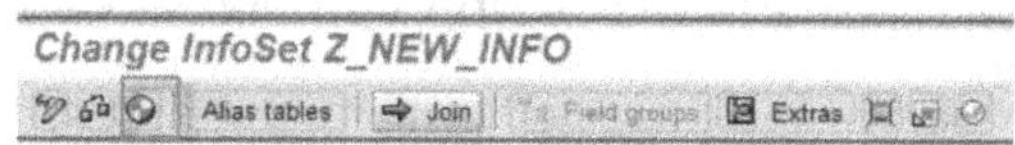

Assign the info set to a package and transport request.

The new infoset needs to be assigned to a user group before being used in a query.

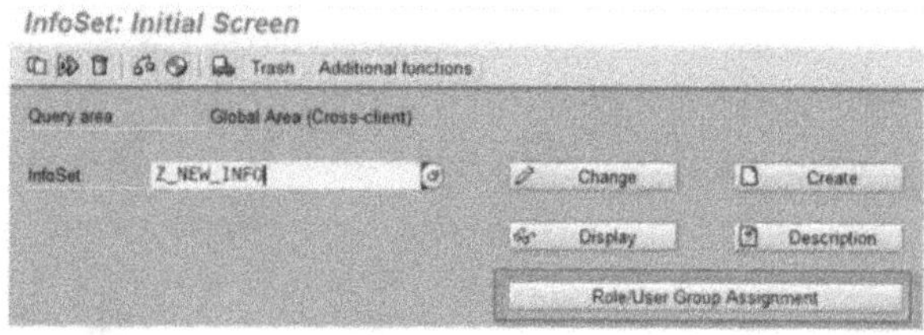

- Select Infoset. Click Role/User Group assignment.

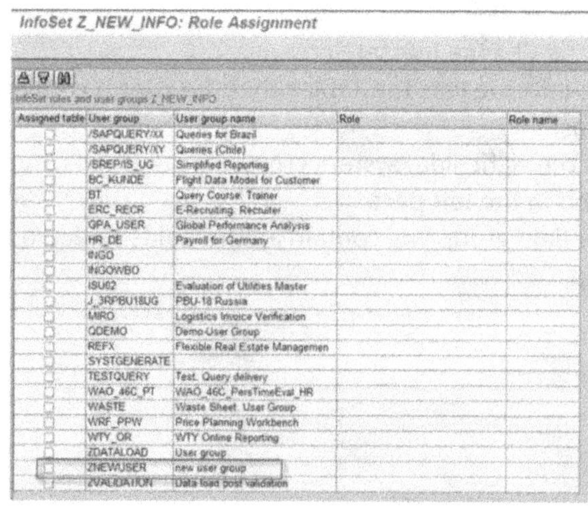

- Select User groups to which the Infoset needs to be added.

Step 3: Creating Query –SQ01

- Menu path – SAP Menu -> Tools -> ABAP Workbench -> Utilities -> SAP Query -> Queries.

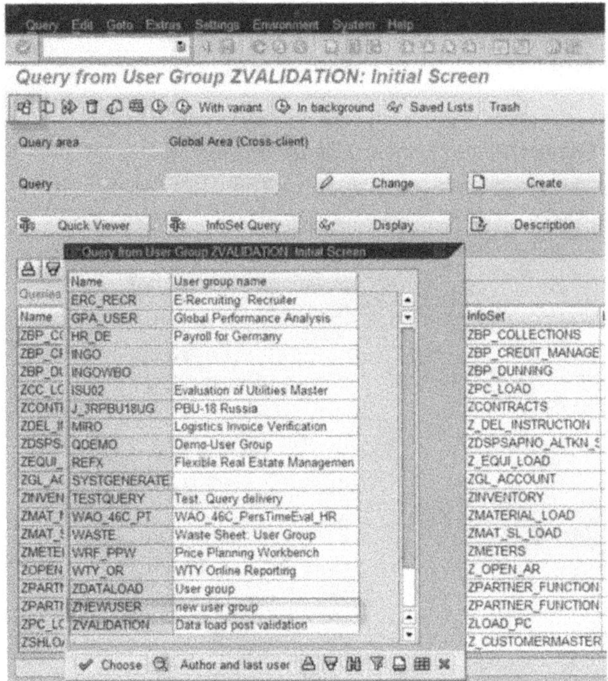

- In the "Query from User Group: Initial Screen:
  - Click on "Other User Groups" button.
  - In the pop-up screen, User Groups, select the User Group for which the Query has to created. The pop-up screen closes.
  - Enter the Query Code in the "Query" field.
  - Click on "Create" button.
- A pop up appears with the Infosets attached to the selected User groups.

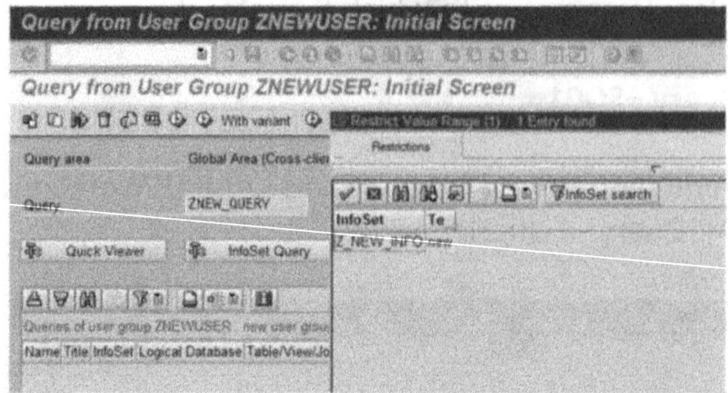

- In the new screen Create Query: Title, Format:
  - Enter the Description of the Query in the "Title" field.
- We will be able to determine the number of columns to be displayed, type of display and so on details.

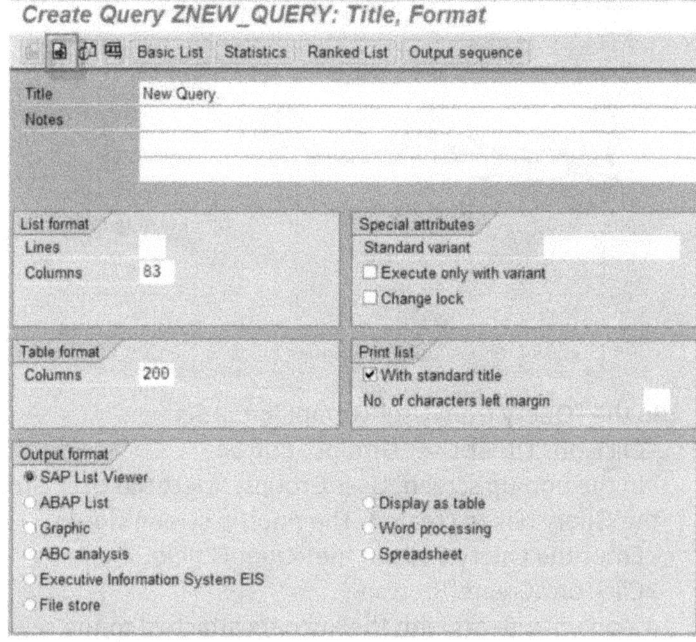

- Click on the "Next Screen" button.

- In the Select Field Group" screen:
  - Select the Field Groups from which Data Fields have to be selected for the Output.
  - Click on the "Next Screen" button.

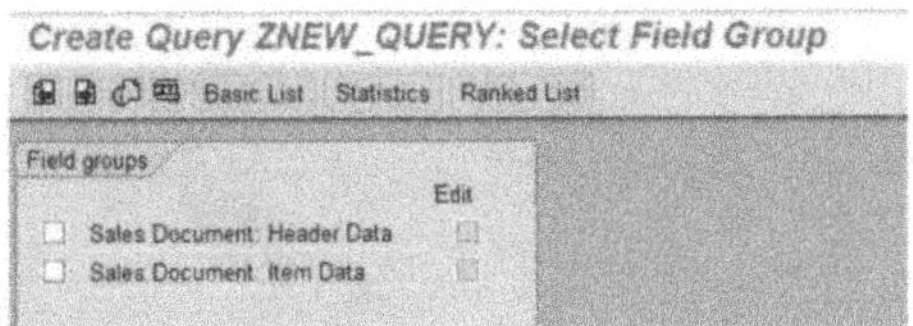

- In the "Select Field" screen:
  - Select the Data Fields which should appear in the output.
  - Click on the "Next Screen" button.

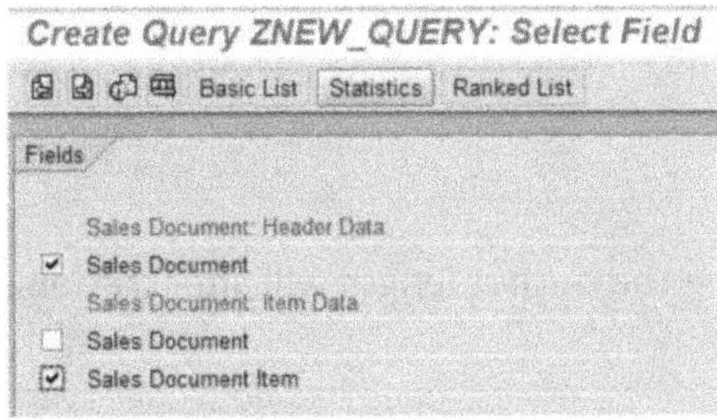

- In the Screen "Selection":
  - Select the Data Fields for the selection criteria.
  - Enter the sequence in which the selected fields would appear in the input screen of the query.
  - Define if the selection criteria should be Single Value or Multiple Value Rangeby clicking in the appropriate check boxes.

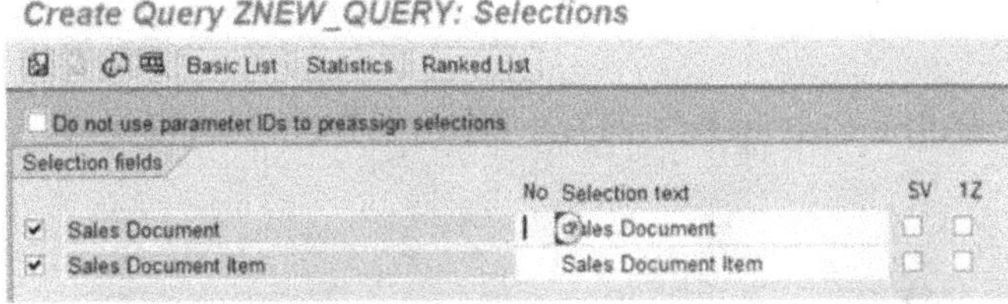

- Click on the "Basic List' button.
- In the screen "Query Layout Design":
  - Select the Output Fields from the Data Fields section by clicking the appropriate check box.
  - Change the sequence of Data Field columns if required.

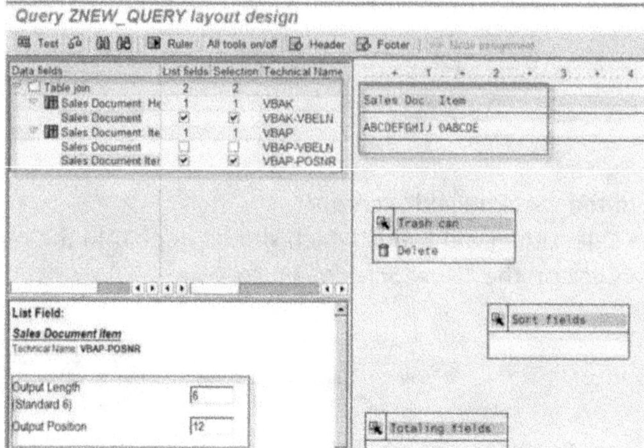

- Changing the output length will alter the length used for display on the list.

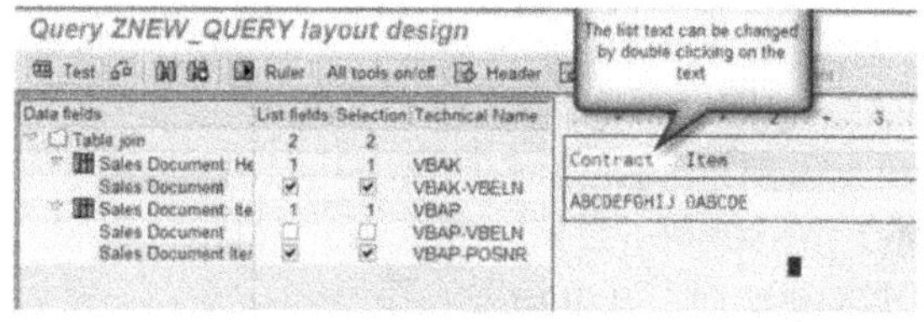

- Save the Query created.

We can test/Execute the query directly from SQ01 or we can use the Tcode SQ00.

- In the Query from User Group: Initial screen:

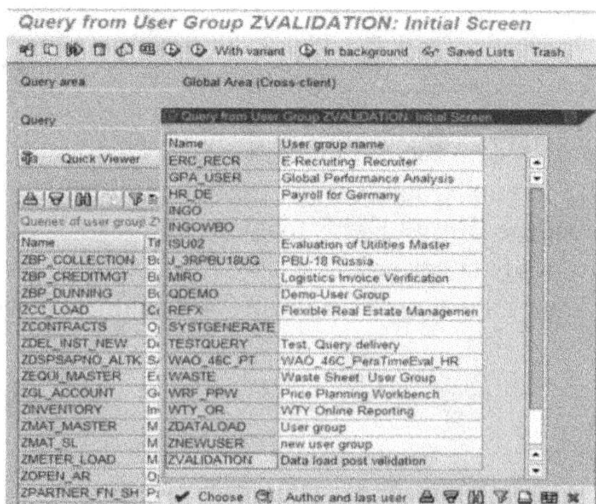

- Click on "Other User Groups" button to select the User Group:
  - In the pop-up screen "User Groups" select the User Group.
  - System lists all the queries created for the User Group.

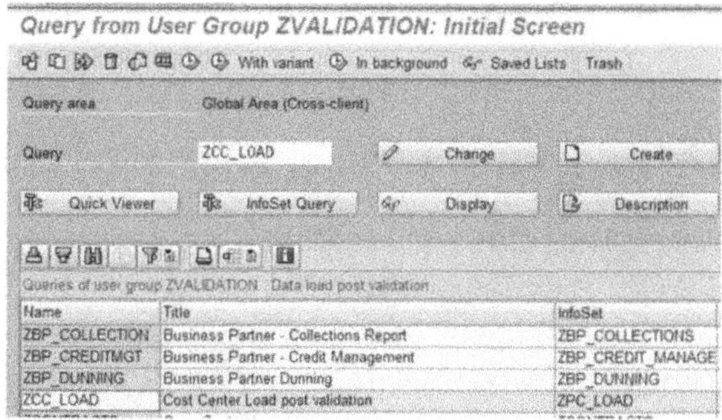

- Select the appropriate Query.
- Click on "Execute" button.

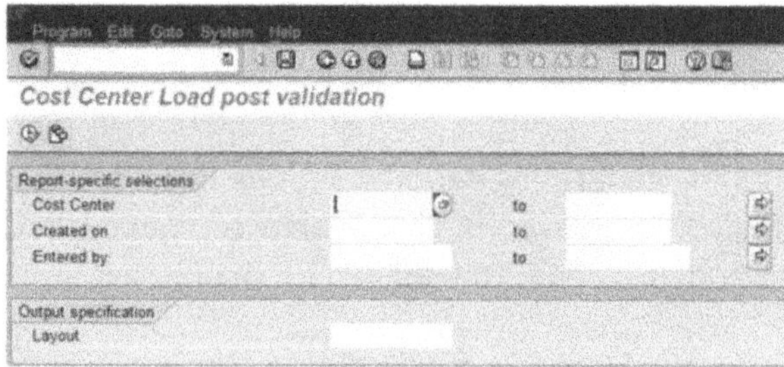

- User is taken to the Selection screen.
- Enter the selection criteria and click on "Execute" button.
- Keep your fingers crossed and the query and gives the output.

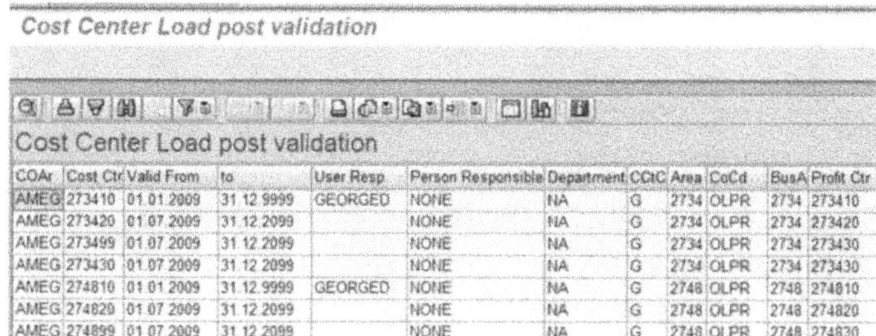
Cost Center Load post validation

COAr	Cost Ctr	Valid From	to	User Resp	Person Responsible	Department	CCtC	Area	CoCd	BusA	Profit Ctr
AMEG	273410	01.01.2009	31.12.9999	GEORGED	NONE	NA	G	2734	OLPR	2734	273410
AMEG	273420	01.07.2009	31.12.2099		NONE	NA	G	2734	OLPR	2734	273420
AMEG	273499	01.07.2009	31.12.2099		NONE	NA	G	2734	OLPR	2734	273430
AMEG	273430	01.07.2009	31.12.2099		NONE	NA	G	2734	OLPR	2734	273430
AMEG	274810	01.01.2009	31.12.9999	GEORGED	NONE	NA	G	2748	OLPR	2748	274810
AMEG	274820	01.07.2009	31.12.2099		NONE	NA	G	2748	OLPR	2748	274820
AMEG	274899	01.07.2009	31.12.2099		NONE	NA	G	2748	OLPR	2748	274830

CHAPTER 17

■ ■ ■

Simple report creation using SAP Quick Viewer Tool

Purpose of this document

This document will explain what SQVI is and how to create a query using QuickViewer. It will also include some important table queries. This will be rolled out to only supper users, who currently create reports in the legacy system.

What is QuickViewer (SQVI)?

QuickViewer is a tool for generating reports. It does not have the full capabilities of the SAP Query tool (SQ01) however; it allows relatively inexperienced users to create basic lists. It is quick and fairly easy to use.

Pros:

1. Quick and easy
2. One transaction
3. Create a query and see the results immediately.

Cons:

1. It is a personal view; other people cannot use it. Although you can convert the query to a standard SAP Query.
2. No Automatic text recognition, need to insert them into the table.
3. Less powerful than ABAP Query, cannot add code or logic.

17.1. DEMO 1:

This transaction is helpful for functional consultants to prepare simple report. This document details on how to prepare simple query using transaction SQVI. Some extent we can help ourself without seeking help from technical consultants.

Transaction Code: SQVI (Quick Viewer)

Example: To create a report this has following fields.

Input fields	Output fields
Purchase order	Purchase order
	Line item
	Created on
	Created by
	Material code
	Order quantity
	Order unit

By reading this requirement we can easily extract the data from table EKKO and EKPO.

- Go to transaction SQVI and provide "QuickView" name and click on create.
- Input "Title" and "Comments" and select "Data source" as Table join.
- Select "Basis mode" or "Layout mode" and hit Enter.

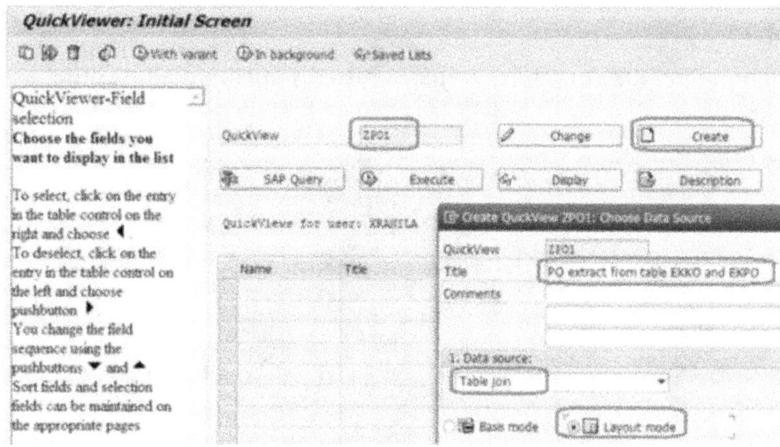

- Click on insert Table (Shift+F1)

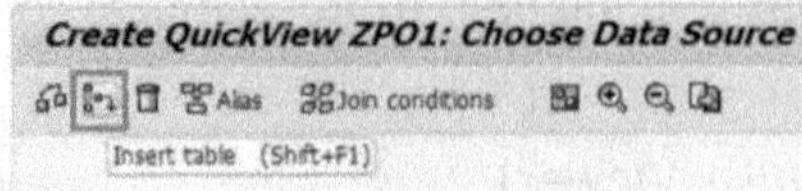

- Input table EKKO and hit continue.

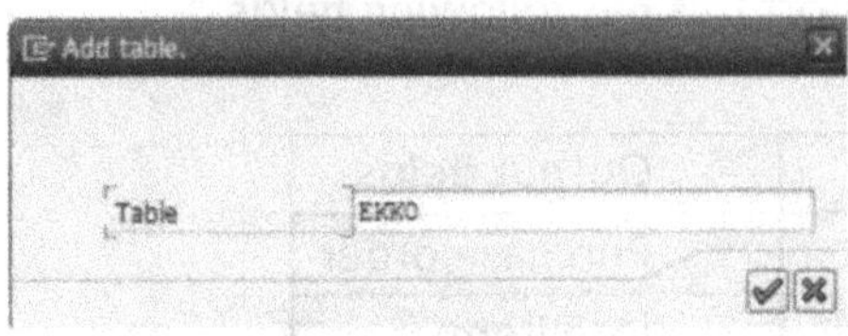

- You can see below screen shot:

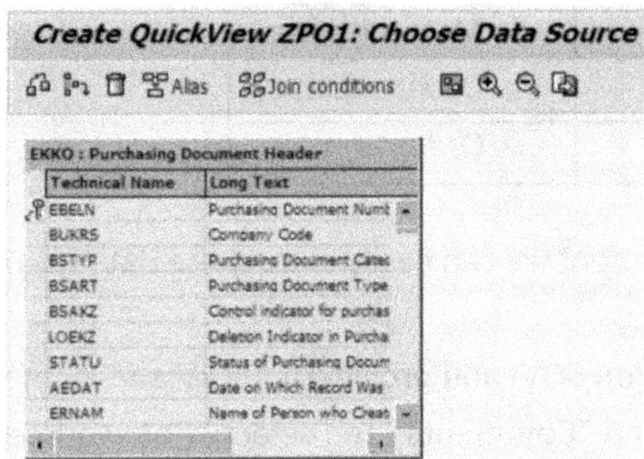

- Again click on "Insert table" and input table EKPO which should link to previous table.
- Example in EKKO purchase order number is linked to EKPO purchase order number.

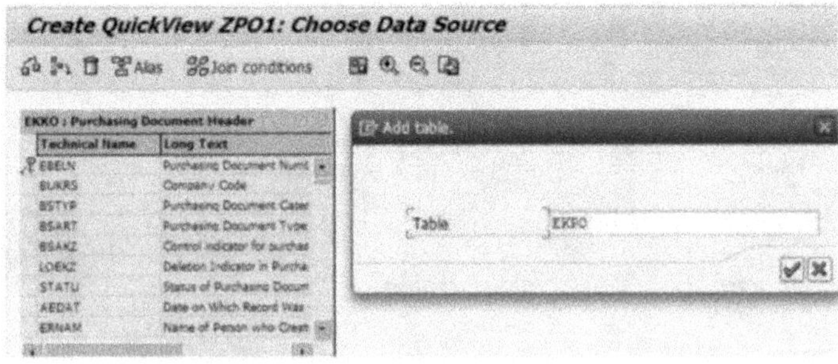

- You can see below screen shot.

- Similarly, we can link multiple tables.
- After completing all table linking then click on "Back" button (F3).

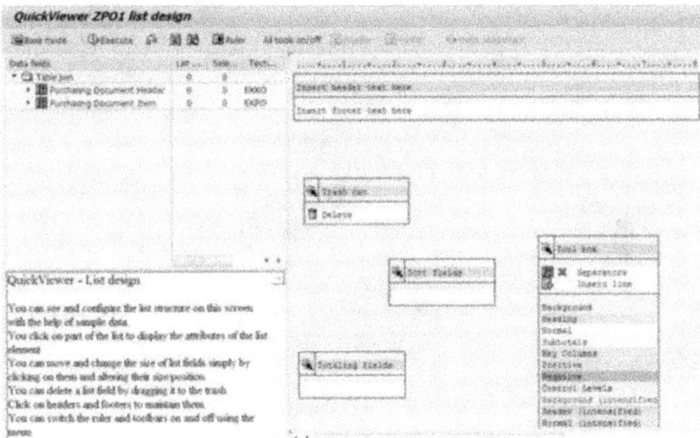

- Now extract the table which is in left side "Data fields".
- Here there are two columns showing 1) List fields and 2) Selection Fields

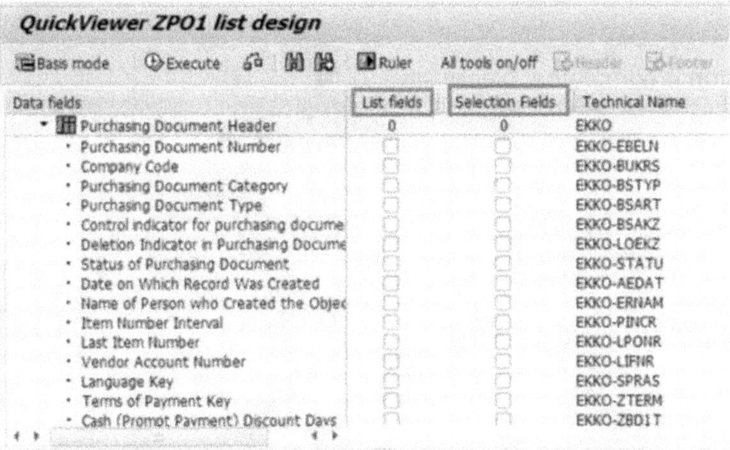

Selection fields: means fields appearing on the selection screen.

Ex: Purchase Order

List fields: means fields displayed in output.

Ex: Purchase order, Line item, Created on, Created by, Material code, Order quantity, Order unit

For our requirement, following check boxes needs to be ticked in EKKO and EKPO tables.

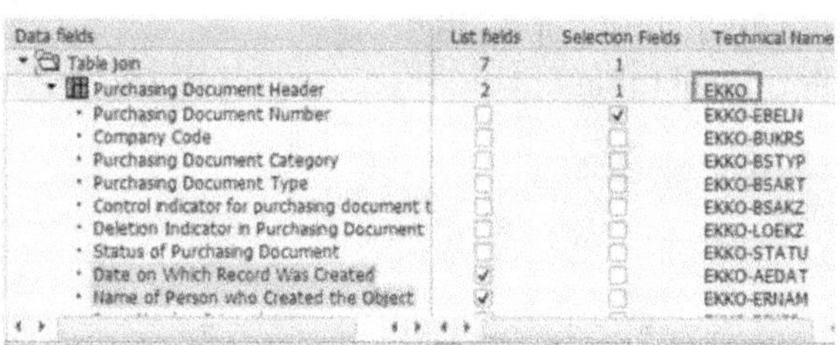

Data fields	List fields	Selection Fields	Technical Name
Table Join	7	1	
Purchasing Document Header	2	1	EKKO
Purchasing Document Number	☐	☑	EKKO-EBELN
Company Code	☐	☐	EKKO-BUKRS
Purchasing Document Category	☐	☐	EKKO-BSTYP
Purchasing Document Type	☐	☐	EKKO-BSART
Control indicator for purchasing document t	☐	☐	EKKO-BSAKZ
Deletion Indicator in Purchasing Document	☐	☐	EKKO-LOEKZ
Status of Purchasing Document	☐	☐	EKKO-STATU
Date on Which Record Was Created	☑	☐	EKKO-AEDAT
Name of Person who Created the Object	☑	☐	EKKO-ERNAM

Data fields	List fields	Selection Fields	Technical Name
Table Join	8	1	
Purchasing Document Header	3	1	EKKO
Purchasing Document Item	5	0	EKPO
Purchasing Document Number	☑	☐	EKPO-EBELN
Item Number of Purchasing Document	☑	☐	EKPO-EBELP
Deletion Indicator in Purchasing Docume	☐	☐	EKPO-LOEKZ
RFQ status	☐	☐	EKPO-STATU
Purchasing Document Item Change Dat	☐	☐	EKPO-AEDAT
Short Text	☐	☐	EKPO-TXZ01
Material Number	☑	☐	EKPO-MATNR
Material Number	☐	☐	EKPO-EMATN
Company Code	☐	☐	EKPO-BUKRS
Plant	☐	☐	EKPO-WERKS
Storage Location	☐	☐	EKPO-LGORT
Requirement Tracking Number	☐	☐	EKPO-BEDNR
Material Group	☐	☐	EKPO-MATKL
Number of Purchasing Info Record	☐	☐	EKPO-INFNR
Material Number Used by Vendor	☐	☐	EKPO-IDNLF
Target Quantity	☐	☐	EKPO-KTMNG
Purchase Order Quantity	☑	☐	EKPO-MENGE
Purchase Order Unit of Measure	☑	☐	EKPO-MEINS

Once selection is completed, please save it.

Log Display

InfoSet SYSTQV000000000000003196 (XRANILA:ZPO1)	Number
Warning Messages	7
Compare field group fields with Data Dictionary	6
Currency field WRF_POTB_CURRENCY_STY-OTB_CURR will not be filled	5
Affected currency amount fields:	1
EKKO-OTB_RES_VALUE	1
EKKO-OTB_SPEC_VALUE	1
EKKO-OTB_VALUE	1

Click "Continue" to save the Query

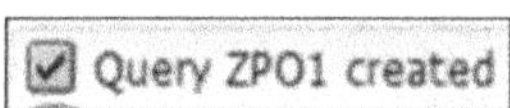

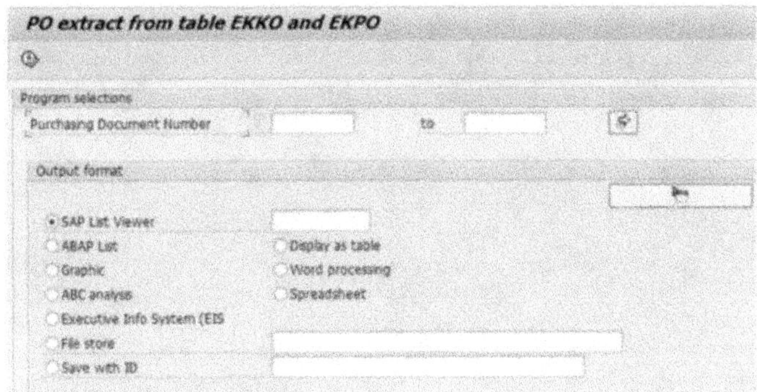

InfoSet SYSTQV000000000000003196 saved

To execute the report, go to SQVI and input "QuickView" ZPO1 and click on "Execute" button available just below.

Execute (F8) the report with PO 4506411252

Expected output from PO

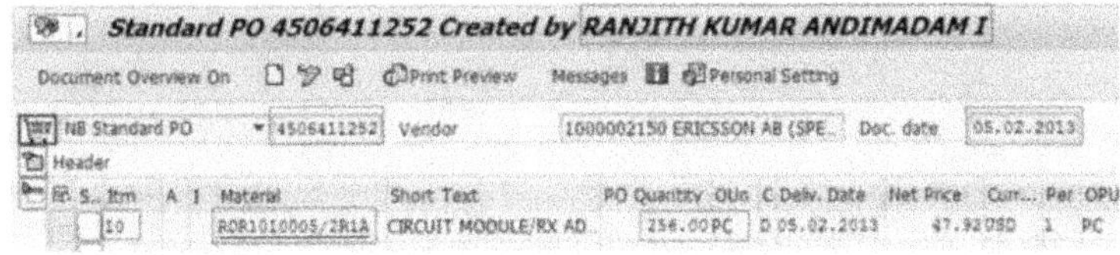

Obtained output from SQVI report ZPO1

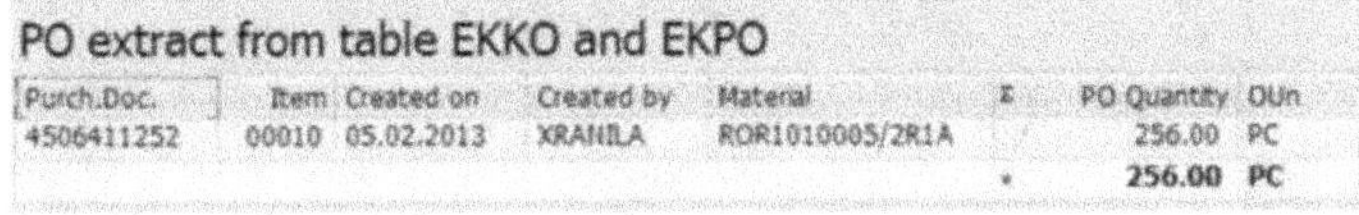

PO extract from table EKKO and EKPO

Purch.Doc.	Item	Created on	Created by	Material	Σ	PO Quantity	OUn
4506411252	00010	05.02.2013	XRANILA	ROR1010005/2R1A		256.00	PC
					•	**256.00**	**PC**

Assigning transaction code for SQVI report

Go to SQVI and input "QuickView" ZPO1 and click on "Execute" button available just below.

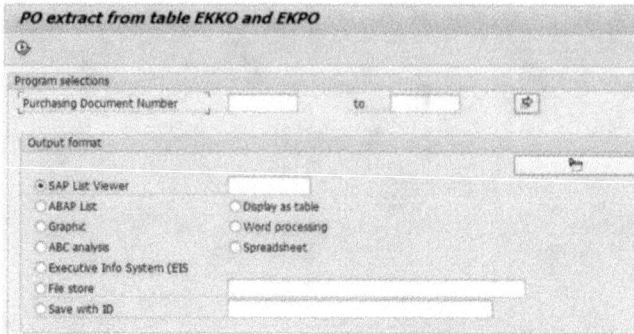

PO extract from table EKKO and EKPO

Program selections

Purchasing Document Number to

Output format

SAP List Viewer

ABAP List

Graphic

ABC analysis

Executive Info System (EIS

File store

Save with ID

Display as table

Word processing

Spreadsheet

Go to menu bar→System→Status→double click on program.

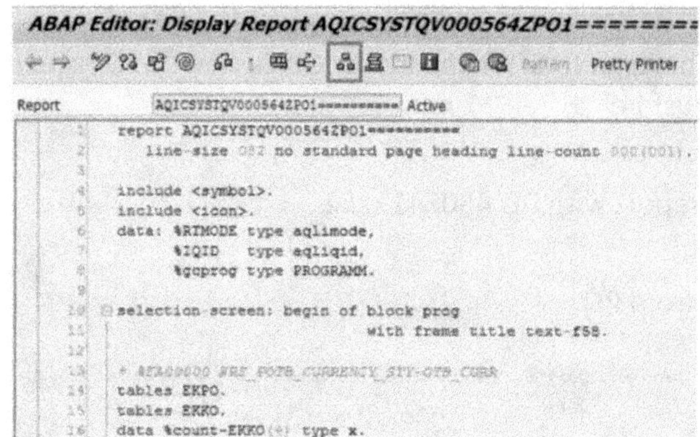

Click on Display object list (Ctrl+Shift+F5).

Select "Object Name" and right click and select "Create"→"Transaction".

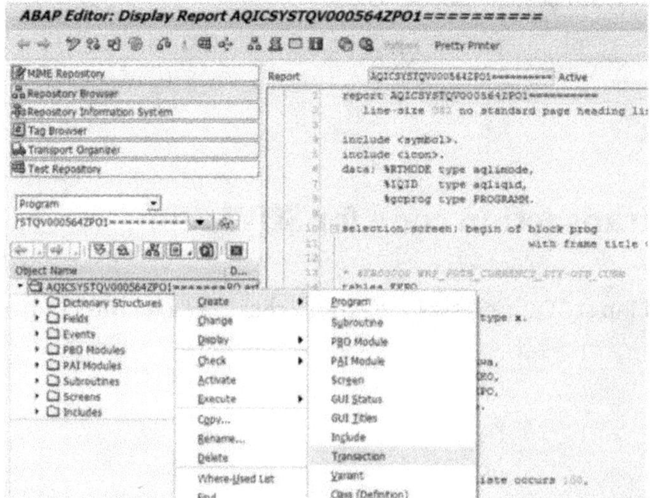

Input “Transaction Code” and “Short text”, select second option and “Continue” and save in local.

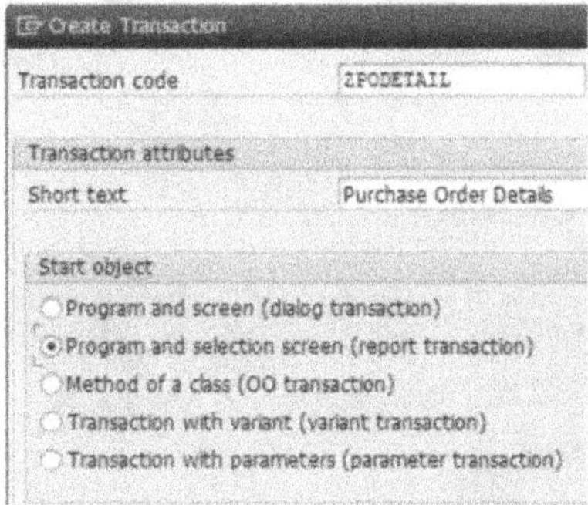

That’s end of assigning Transaction code to SQVI query.

Alternate way to assign transaction code is just select the query in SQVI and choose from menu Quick view → additional functions → display report name.

Then go to SE93 and create your own transaction code.

17.2. DEMO 2:

1. Execute transaction SQVI.

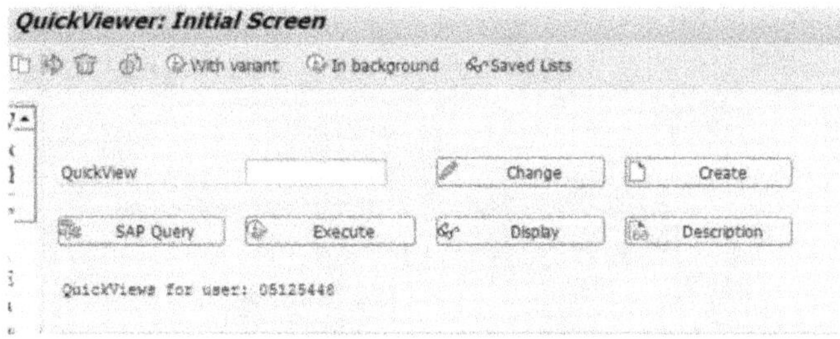

Enter the name of the Query.

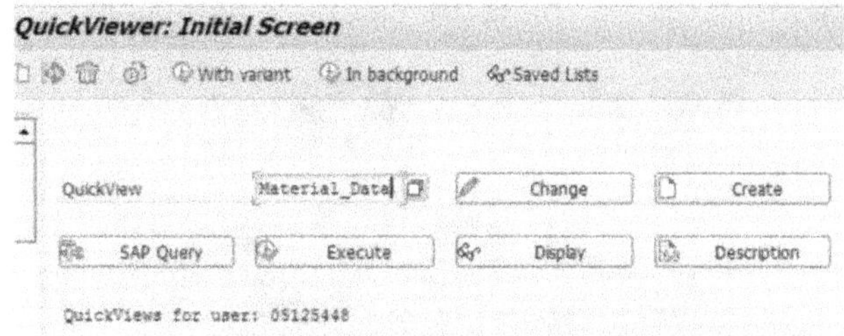

2. Press the Create button.

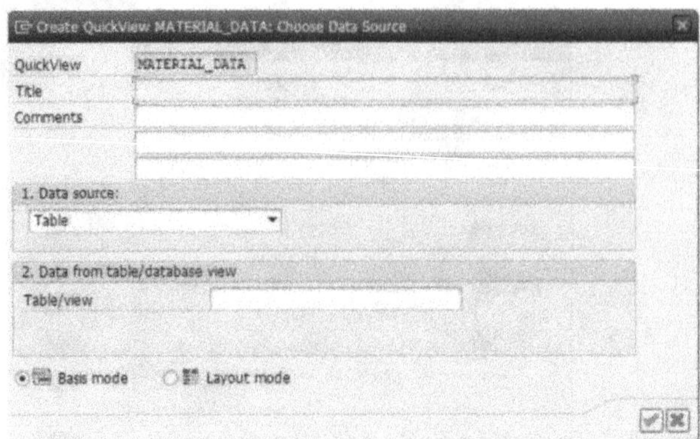

3. Enter the following data: Tittle and any comments. Select "Table Join" as the data source.

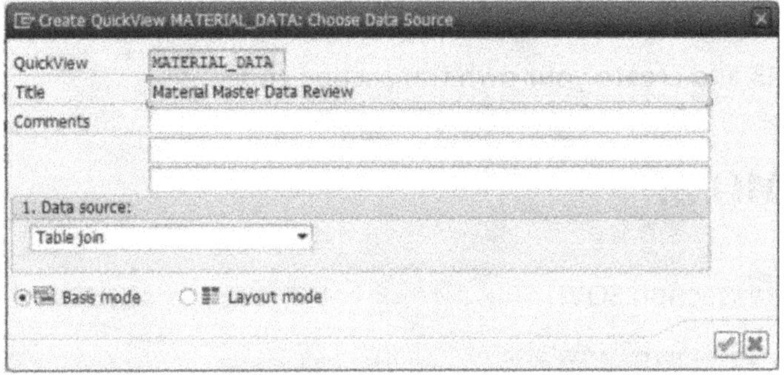

4. Press Enter.

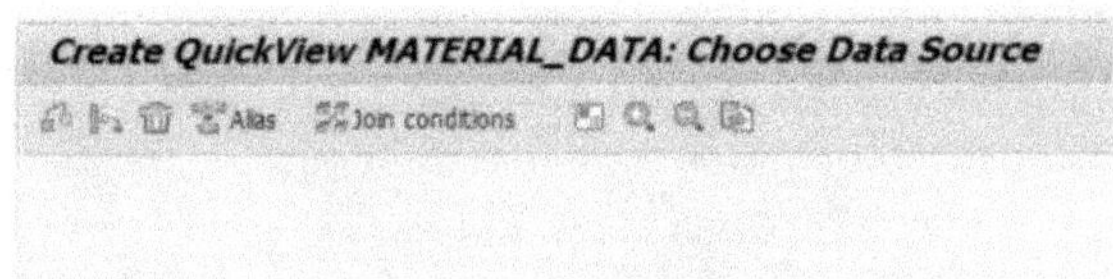

5. Press to insert tables. This is the first table in the join.

6. Enter MARA and click Enter.

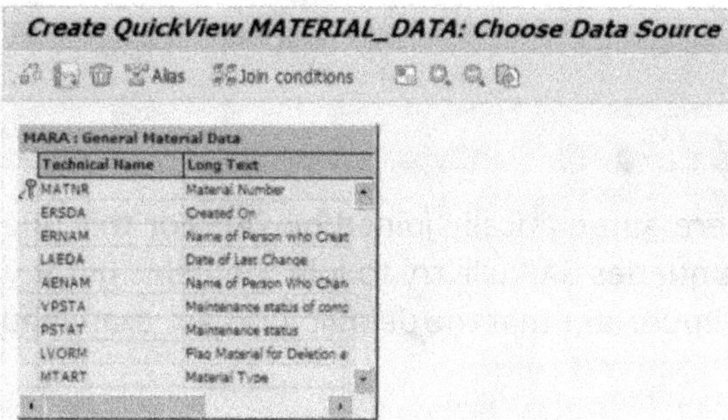

7. Press to insert tables. This will be the second table in the join.

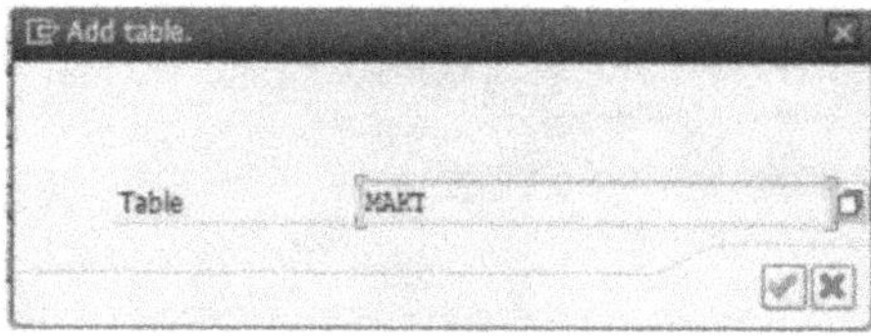

8. Enter MAKT and click Enter.

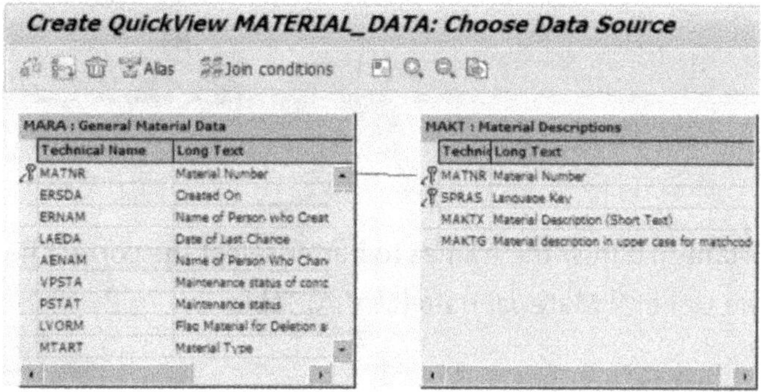

9. Press to insert tables. This will be the third table in the join.

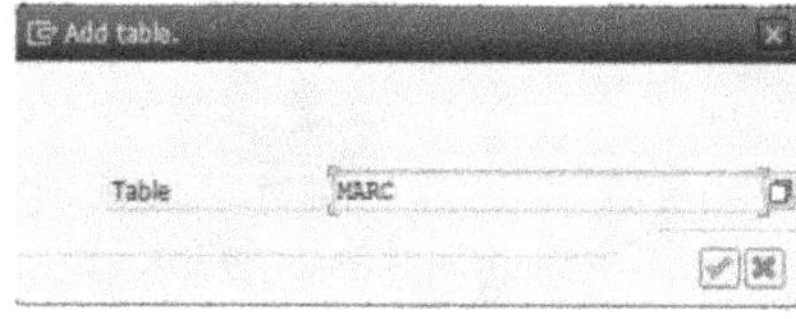

10. Enter MARC and click Enter.

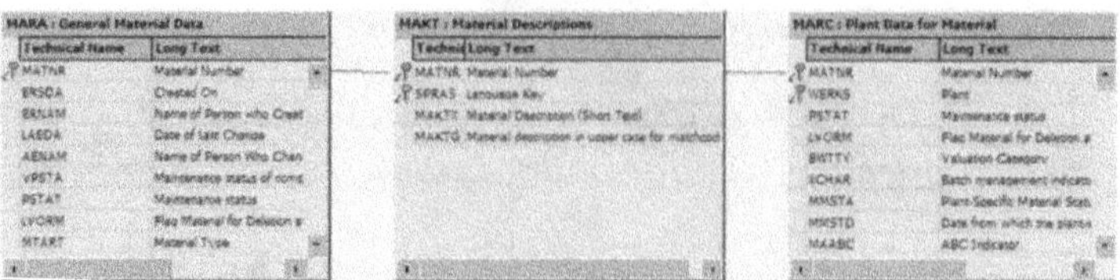

Notice the tables were automatically joined by SAP. For this query the default joins are correct. In some queries SAP will try to join the fields but it will result in no data being returned. It is important that the default joins are examined and determined to be correct.

11. Click on the green arrow 

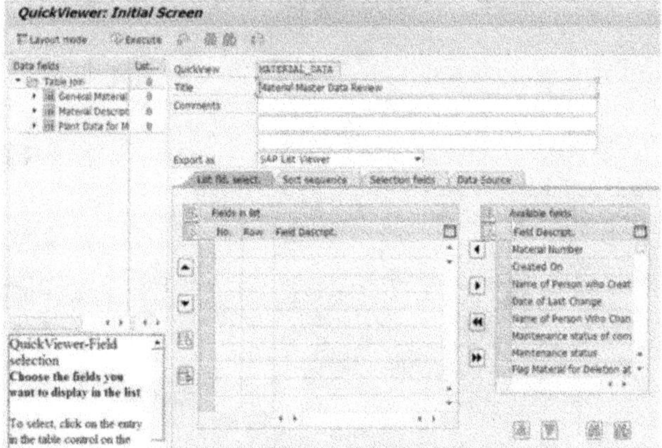

12. It is important to adjust the frames to better select the correct fields for the join. Expand the General Material Data (MARA) Table.

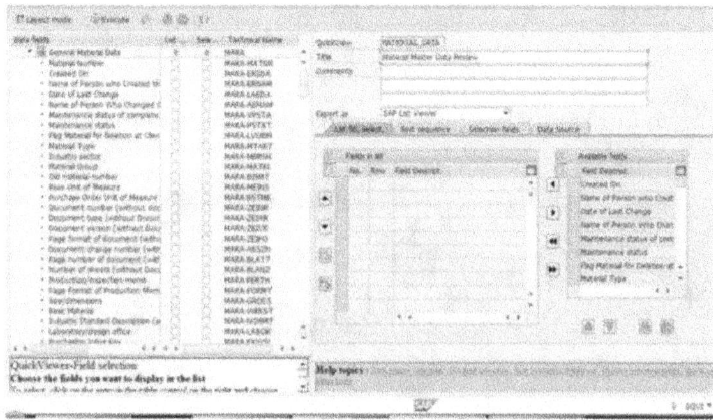

13. Select the fields which will be used as selection parameters and displayed in the report. The material number will be a selection parameter and also displayed in the report.

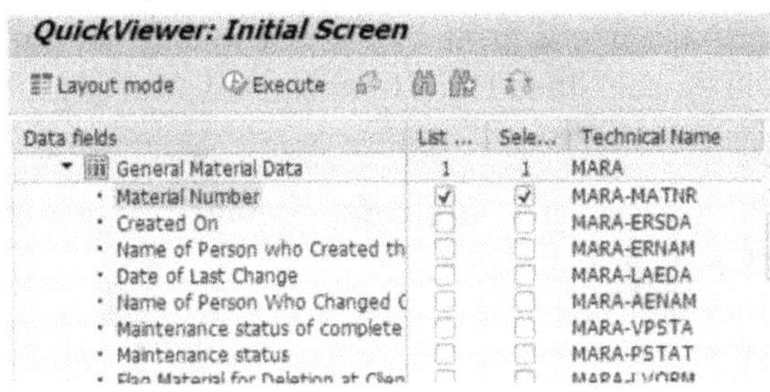

14. Expand the Material Description (MAKT) Table. The material description will only be in the list and not a selection parameter.

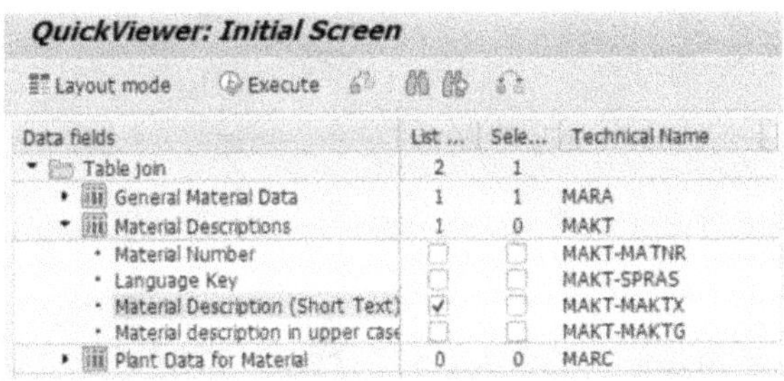

15. Expand the Material Description (MARC) Table. The description will only be in the list.

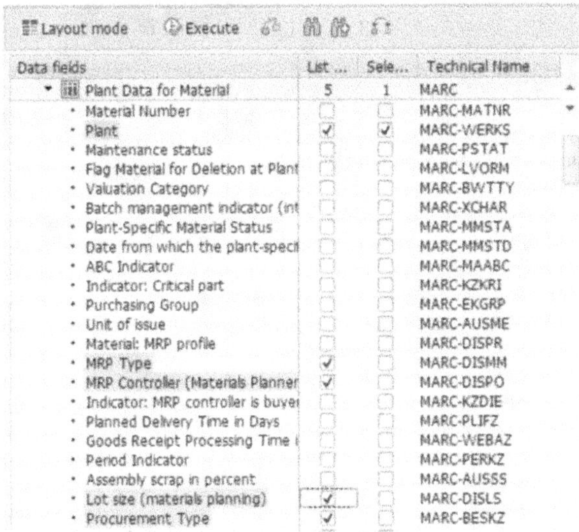

At a minimum the plant must be a selection parameter and should be in the report.

The report list will consist of those fields which the user wishes to review. It is important to know that the length of a line is finite and if you select too many fields to appear in the list, then there will be two lines which can cause some confusion.

16. When the selection parameters are complete and the report list is finished the collapse the tables

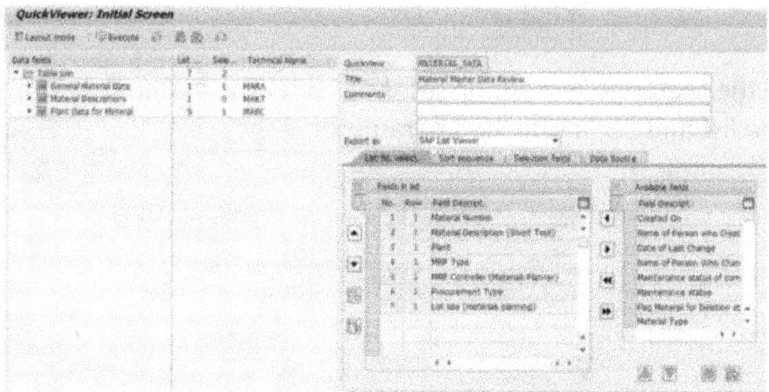

The list fields show 7 fields for the report. The left side of the frame shows 1 from MARA, 1 from MAICT and 5 from MARC. The display order may be changed using the arrows on the left, the standard SAP row selection process.

17. Click Execute

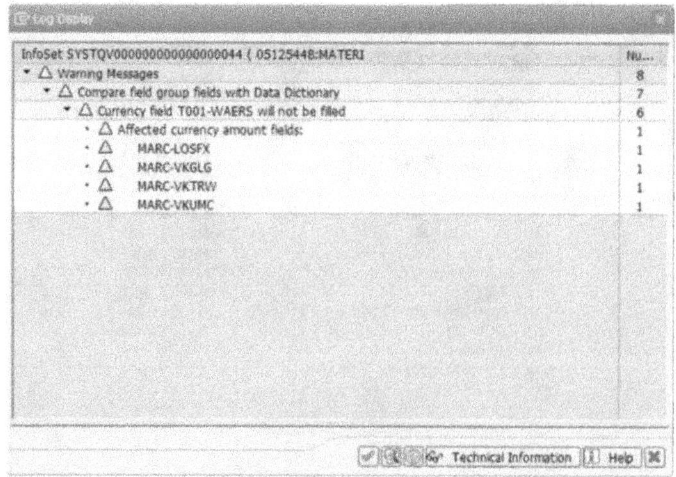

18. Click ✔

Material Master Data Review

Execute

Report-specific selections

Material Number ___ to ___

Plant ___ to ___

Output specification

Layout ___

19. Enter Data and click Execute.

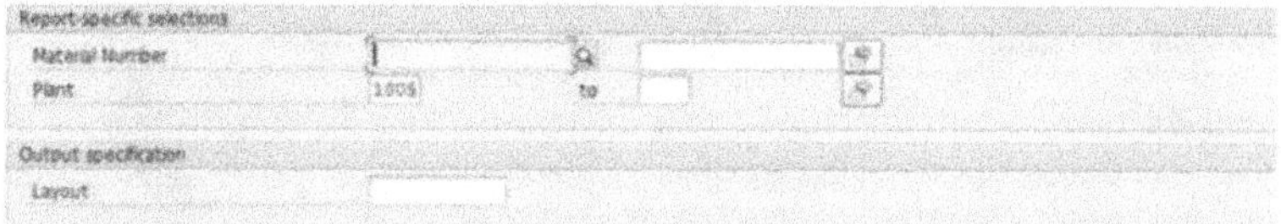

20. Read Results. Can be downloaded into Excel.

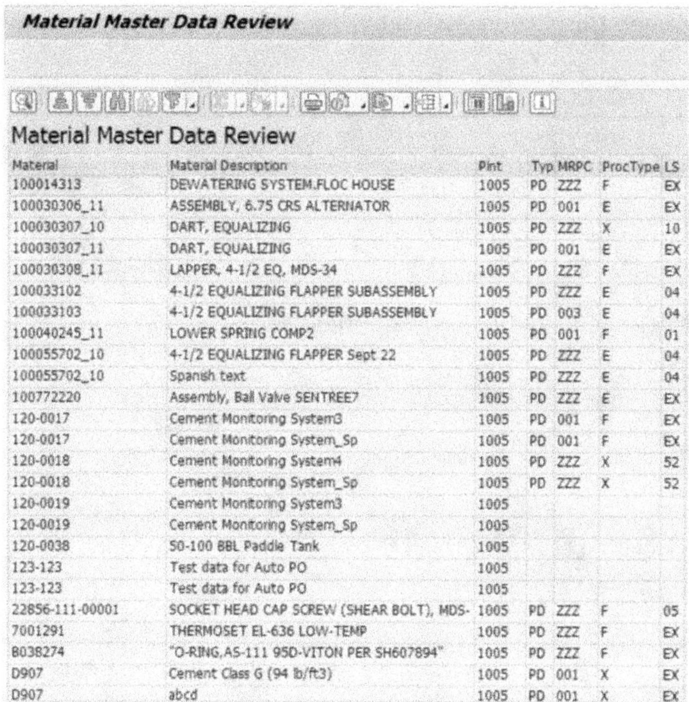

Material Master Data Review

Material Master Data Review

Material	Material Description	Plnt	Typ	MRPC	ProcType	LS
100014313	DEWATERING SYSTEM.FLOC HOUSE	1005	PD	ZZZ	F	EX
100030306_11	ASSEMBLY, 6.75 CRS ALTERNATOR	1005	PD	001	E	EX
100030307_10	DART, EQUALIZING	1005	PD	ZZZ	X	10
100030307_11	DART, EQUALIZING	1005	PD	001	E	EX
100030308_11	LAPPER, 4-1/2 EQ, MDS-34	1005	PD	ZZZ	F	EX
100033102	4-1/2 EQUALIZING FLAPPER SUBASSEMBLY	1005	PD	ZZZ	E	04
100033103	4-1/2 EQUALIZING FLAPPER SUBASSEMBLY	1005	PD	003	E	04
100040245_11	LOWER SPRING COMP2	1005	PD	001	F	01
100055702_10	4-1/2 EQUALIZING FLAPPER Sept 22	1005	PD	ZZZ	E	04
100055702_10	Spanish text	1005	PD	ZZZ	E	04
100772220	Assembly, Ball Valve SENTREE7	1005	PD	ZZZ	E	EX
120-0017	Cement Monitoring System3	1005	PD	001	F	EX
120-0017	Cement Monitoring System_Sp	1005	PD	001	F	EX
120-0018	Cement Monitoring System4	1005	PD	ZZZ	X	52
120-0018	Cement Monitoring System_Sp	1005	PD	ZZZ	X	52
120-0019	Cement Monitoring System3	1005				
120-0019	Cement Monitoring System_Sp	1005				
120-0038	50-100 BBL Paddle Tank	1005				
123-123	Test data for Auto PO	1005				
123-123	Test data for Auto PO	1005				
22856-111-00001	SOCKET HEAD CAP SCREW (SHEAR BOLT), MDS-	1005	PD	ZZZ	F	05
7001291	THERMOSET EL-636 LOW-TEMP	1005	PD	ZZZ	F	EX
8038274	"O-RING,AS-111 95D-VITON PER SH607894"	1005	PD	ZZZ	F	EX
D907	Cement Class G (94 lb/ft3)	1005	PD	001	X	EX
D907	abcd	1005	PD	001	X	EX

21. Green arrow back to the QuickViewer: Initial Screen.

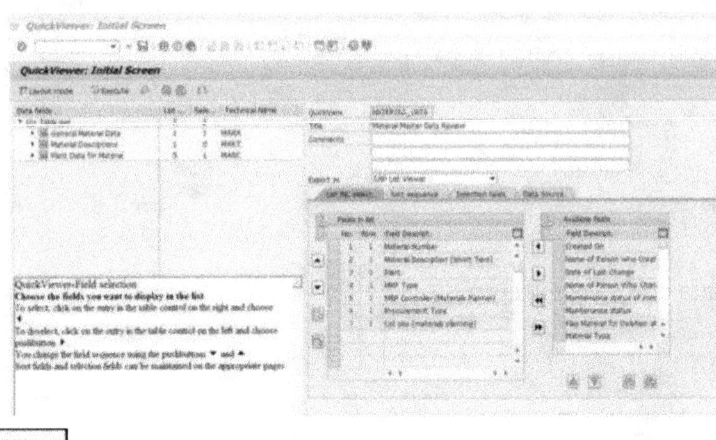

22. Click
23. Click Green Arrow Back.
24. Click Yes when this screen pops up.

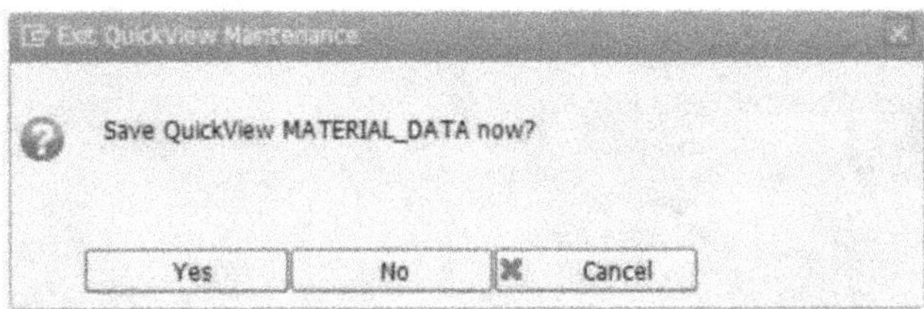

25. New Query appears in the list of queries.

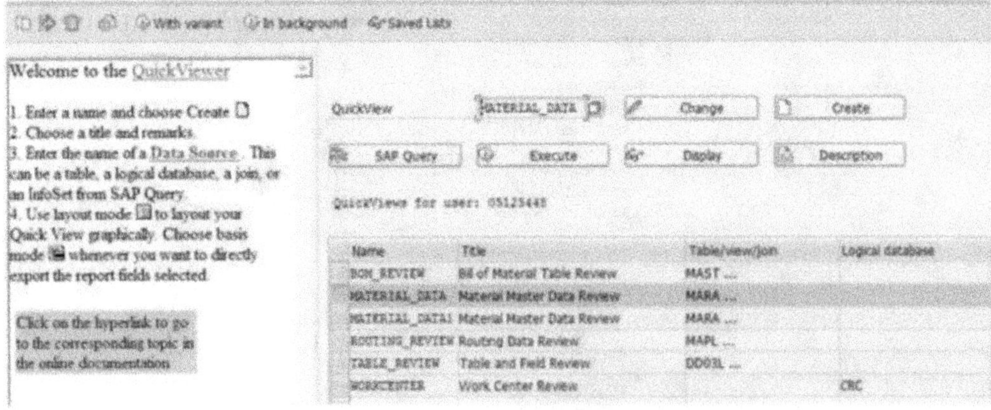

17.3. Other Table Joins which are useful

17.3.1. Table Information table join

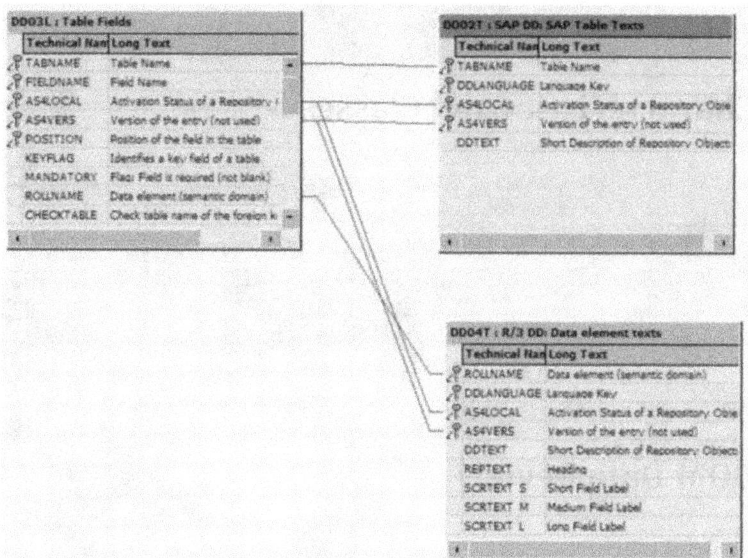

17.3.2. Material Master Data Review

17.3.2.1. Logical Data Base: MSM,

17.3.2.2. Table Joins MRP Data with storage location

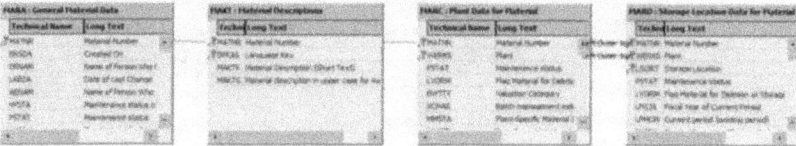

17.3.2.3. With Costing table

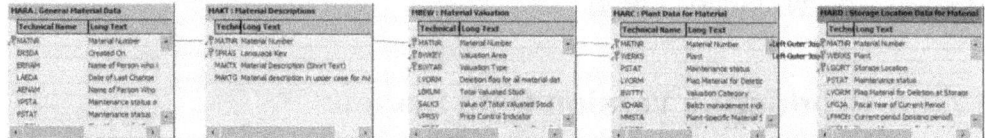

17.3.2.4. Material Master Data Sale Review

17.3.3. Characteristics and Classes

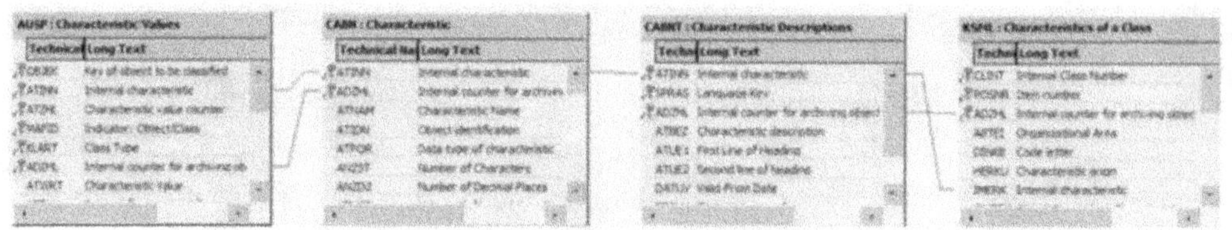

KLAH

17.3.4. BOM Data Review

17.3.4.1. Logical Data Base: CMC

17.3.4.2. Table Join

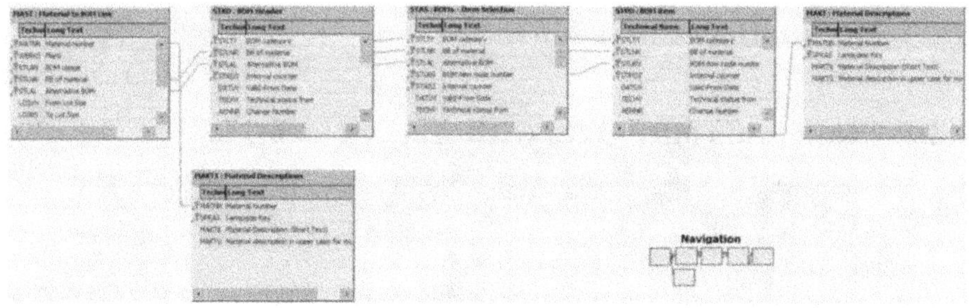

17.3.5. Routing Data Review

MAPL – PLKO – PLAS – PLFL - PLPO

17.3.6. Production Version Data Review

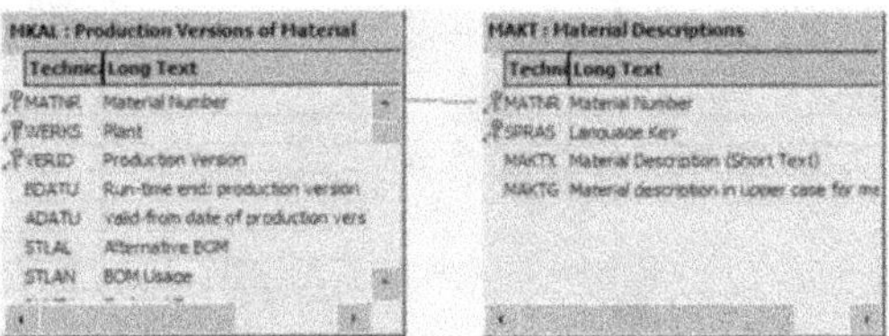

17.3.7. Work Center Data Reviews

17.3.7.1. Logical Data Base: CRC

17.3.7.2. Table Join

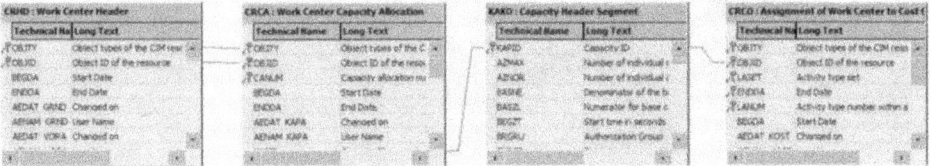

17.3.8. Handling Units with Values

ADD table MAKT for description.

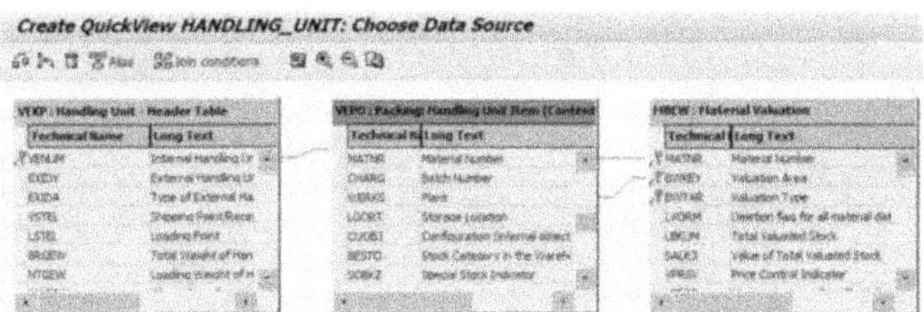

17.4.DEMO 3:

Ref:: Natesh Kumar Valmiki's artefact

SAP Query Initial Login steps through SQ01

1.	Sap Queries

Menu path	SAP menu-Tools-ABAP Workbench -Utilities-SAP Query - Queries
Transaction Code	SQ01 - Queries

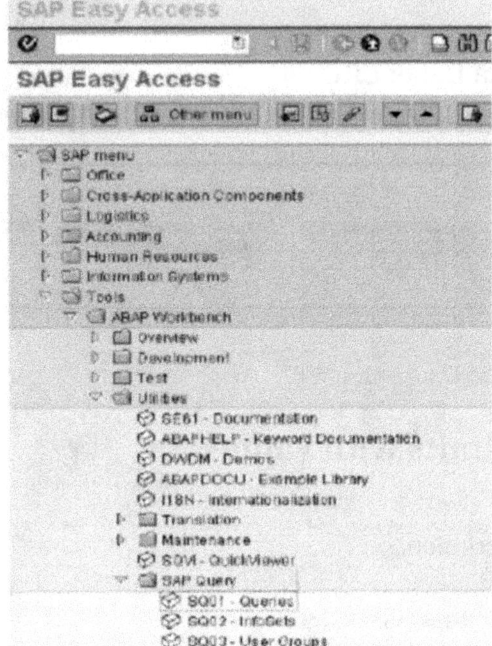

Now goto **Environment then select Query area.**

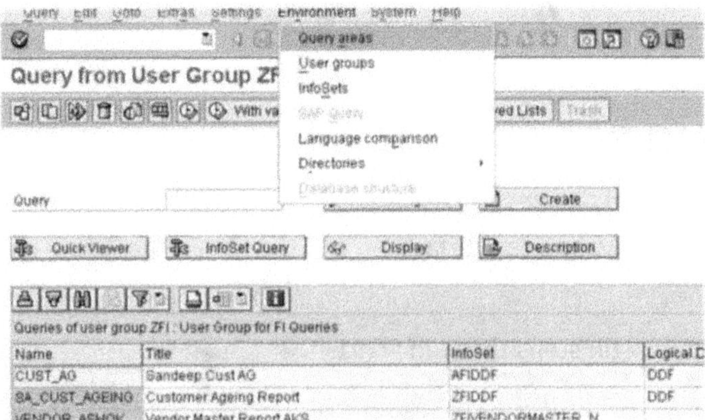

Select Standard Query area

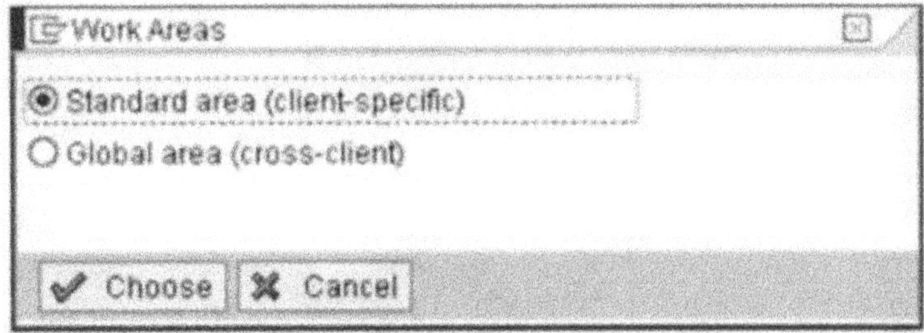

<u>Click on the "Other User Group"</u>

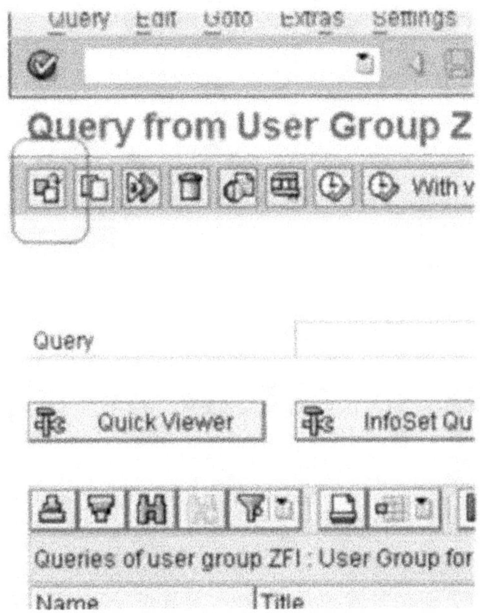

then select " ZFI User group of FI Queries".

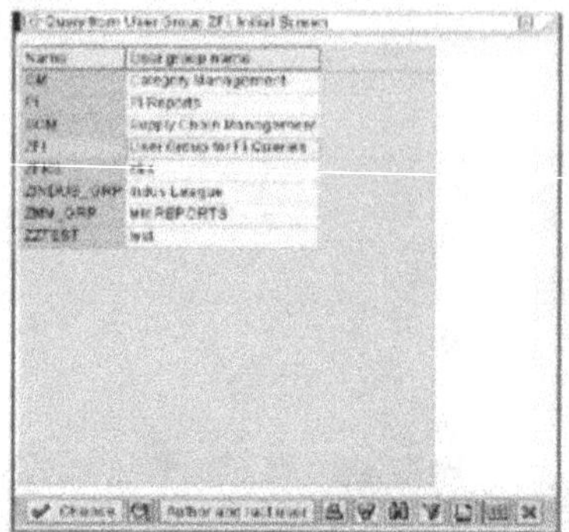

Note:Users who wish to view the reports of ZFI group must have their user IDs assigned to the user group

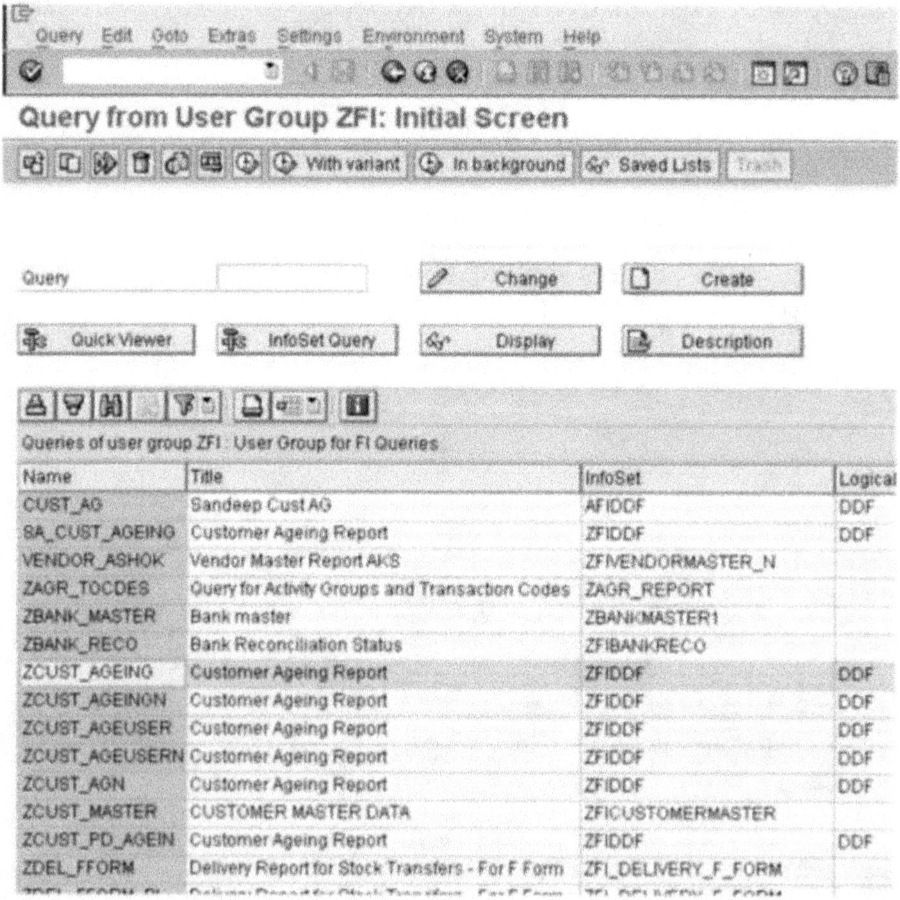

Query Edit Goto Extras Settings Environment System Help

Query from User Group ZFI: Initial Screen

With variant | In background | Saved Lists | Trash

Query [ ] Change | Create

Quick Viewer | InfoSet Query | Display | Description

Queries of user group ZFI : User Group for FI Queries

Name	Title	InfoSet	Logical
CUST_AG	Sandeep Cust AG	AFIDDF	DDF
SA_CUST_AGEING	Customer Ageing Report	ZFIDDF	DDF
VENDOR_ASHOK	Vendor Master Report AKS	ZFIVENDORMASTER_N	
ZAGR_TOCDES	Query for Activity Groups and Transaction Codes	ZAGR_REPORT	
ZBANK_MASTER	Bank master	ZBANKMASTER1	
ZBANK_RECO	Bank Reconciliation Status	ZFIBANKRECO	
ZCUST_AGEING	Customer Ageing Report	ZFIDDF	DDF
ZCUST_AGEINGN	Customer Ageing Report	ZFIDDF	DDF
ZCUST_AGEUSER	Customer Ageing Report	ZFIDDF	DDF
ZCUST_AGEUSERN	Customer Ageing Report	ZFIDDF	DDF
ZCUST_AGN	Customer Ageing Report	ZFIDDF	DDF
ZCUST_MASTER	CUSTOMER MASTER DATA	ZFICUSTOMERMASTER	
ZCUST_PD_AGEIN	Customer Ageing Report	ZFIDDF	DDF
ZDEL_FFORM	Delivery Report for Stock Transfers - For F Form	ZFI_DELIVERY_F_FORM	

Double click on query and then Executive(F8)

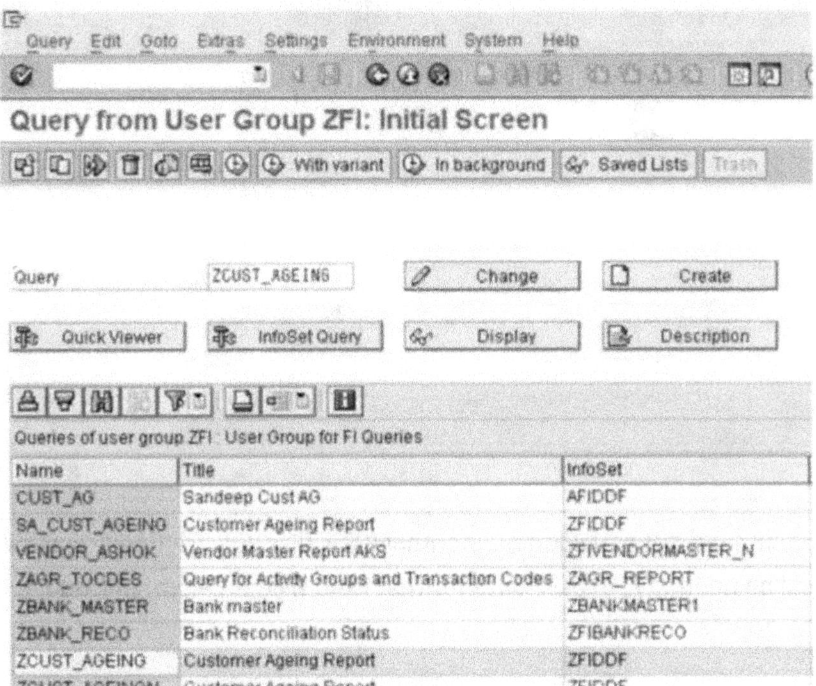

For ZDOC_STATS Query local fields have added.

SQ01:

First count has been added as mentioned below.

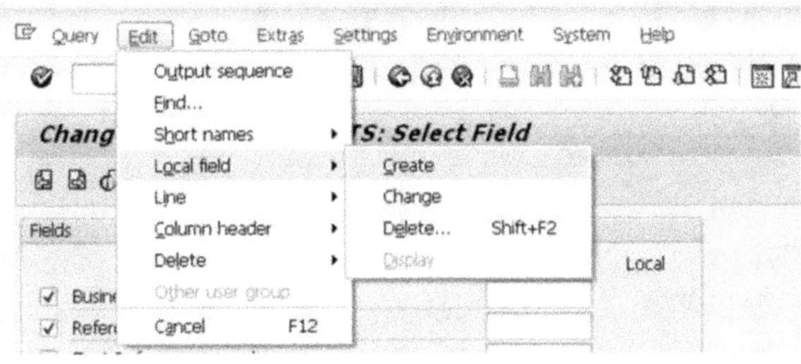

Count Logic will be as follows.

In below case count, we have added Total number of Document types.

Field definition

Short Name	COUNT
Field Description	COUNT
Heading	COUNT
Field group	Accounting Document Header

Properties

- ○ Same attributes as field
- ○ Text field — No. of Characters
- ● Calculation field — Number of Digits: 10 — Decimal Places
- ○ Date Field
- ○ Time Field
- ○ Symbol
- ○ Icon

Calculation Formula

- ● 1
- Condition
- ○ Input on Selection Screen — ☐ Mandatory

Complex calculation | Fields | Symbols

Next Count need to be divided on monthly Basis (E.g. July to June F year rule).
Logic will be need to give as **Month** for that Field (Filed is **Fiscal period I.e. MONAT**).

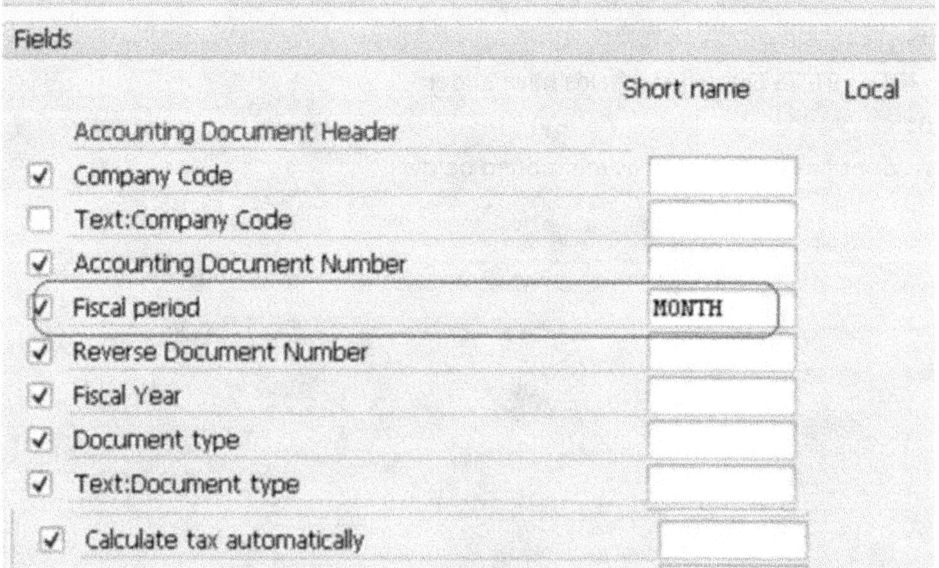

Next step need to give month wise as mentioned below.

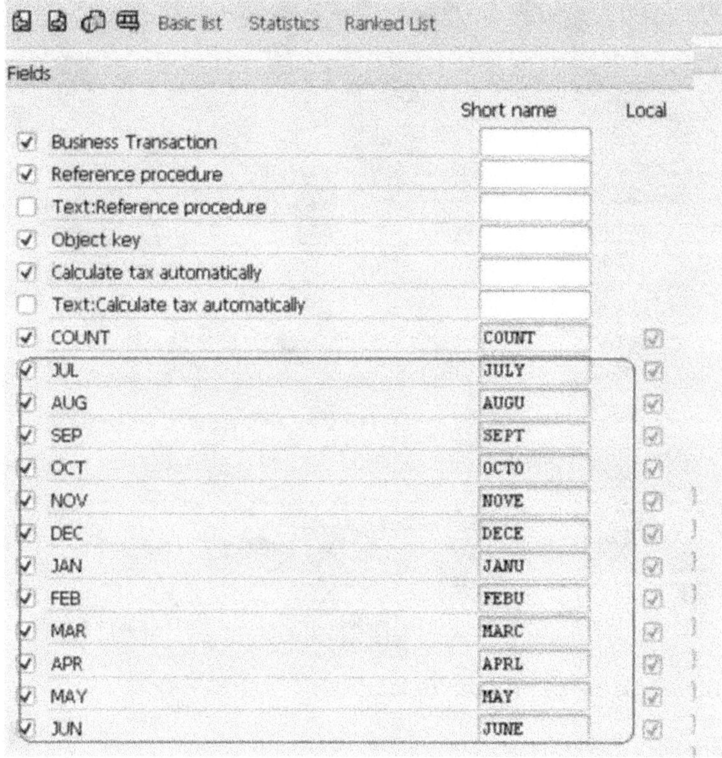

Logic for month is:

E.g.: July

Short Name JULY
Field Description JUL
Heading JUL
Field group Accounting Document Header
Properties
Same attributes as field
Text field No. of Characters
Calculation field Number of Digits 10 Decimal Places
Date Field
Time Field
Symbol
Icon
Calculation Formula
COUNT
Condition MONTH = '01'
Input on Selection Screen Mandatory

E.g.: August

Field definition

Short Name	AUGU
Field Description	AUG
Heading	AUG
Field group	Accounting Document Header

Properties

- ○ Same attributes as field
- ○ Text field — No. of Characters
- ● Calculation field — Number of Digits 10 — Decimal Places
- ○ Date Field
- ○ Time Field
- ○ Symbol
- ○ Icon

Calculation Formula

- ● COUNT
  - Condition: MONTH = '02'
- ○ Input on Selection Screen — Mandatory

Complex calculation | Fields | Symbols

Query out Put will be as mentioned below:

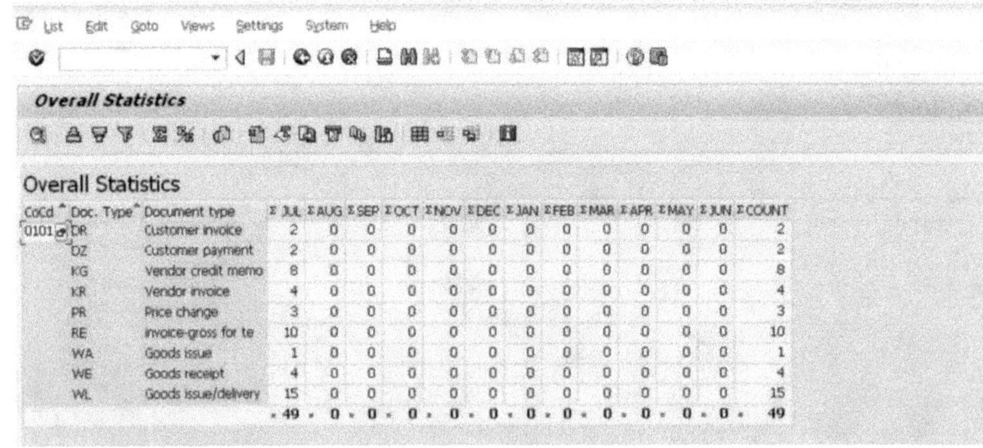

Overall Statistics

CoCd	Doc. Type	Document type	Σ JUL	Σ AUG	Σ SEP	Σ OCT	Σ NOV	Σ DEC	Σ JAN	Σ FEB	Σ MAR	Σ APR	Σ MAY	Σ JUN	Σ COUNT
0101	DR	Customer invoice	2	0	0	0	0	0	0	0	0	0	0	0	2
	DZ	Customer payment	2	0	0	0	0	0	0	0	0	0	0	0	2
	KG	Vendor credit memo	8	0	0	0	0	0	0	0	0	0	0	0	8
	KR	Vendor invoice	4	0	0	0	0	0	0	0	0	0	0	0	4
	PR	Price change	3	0	0	0	0	0	0	0	0	0	0	0	3
	RE	invoice-gross for te	10	0	0	0	0	0	0	0	0	0	0	0	10
	WA	Goods issue	1	0	0	0	0	0	0	0	0	0	0	0	1
	WE	Goods receipt	4	0	0	0	0	0	0	0	0	0	0	0	4
	WL	Goods issue/delivery	15	0	0	0	0	0	0	0	0	0	0	0	15
			• 49	• 0	• 0	• 0	• 0	• 0	• 0	• 0	• 0	• 0	• 0	• 0	• 49

Local Fields for ZCUST_AGE_BASE Query.

Customer Ageing Query.

In this case Base line date wise report has been prepared.

Baseline date for due date calculation NETDATE as given as mentioned:

Baseline date for due date calculation NETDATE

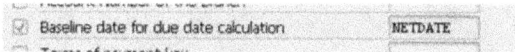

Local fieldshave added as mentioned below:

Key Date for Ageing KEYDATE

In below Name as KEY Date Field as NETDATE.

Field definition

Short Name KEYDATE
Field Description Key Date for Ageing
Heading Key Date (A)
Field group Secondary Index & Additions
Properties
Same attributes as field NETDATE
Text field No. of Characters
Calculation field Number of Digits Decimal Places
Date Field
Time Field
Symbol
Icon
Calculation Formula
Condition
Input on Selection Screen Mandatory
Complex calculation

DAYS DAYS

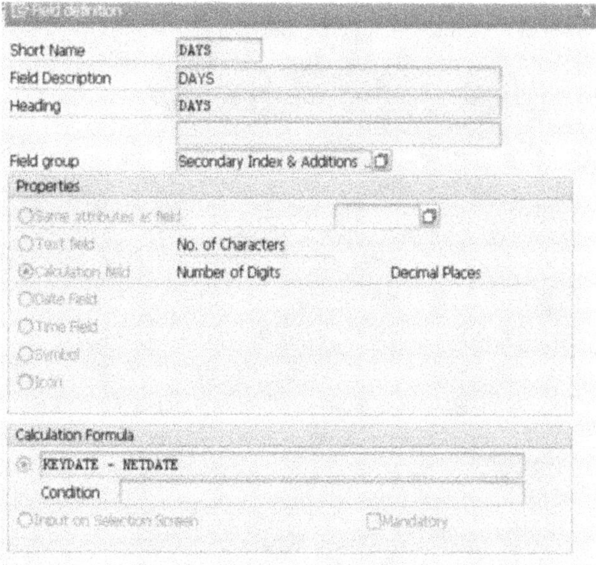

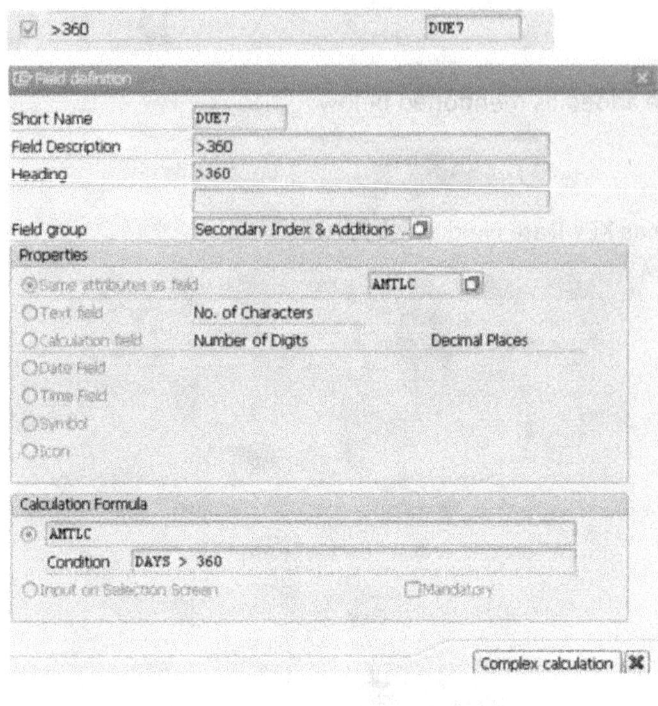
>360
DUE7
Field definition
Short Name
DUE7
Field Description
>360
Heading
>360
Field group
Secondary Index & Additions
Properties
Same attributes as field
AMTLC
Text field
No. of Characters
Calculation field
Number of Digits
Decimal Places
Date Field
Time Field
Symbol
Icon
Calculation Formula
AMTLC
Condition
DAYS > 360
Input on Selection Screen
Mandatory
Complex calculation

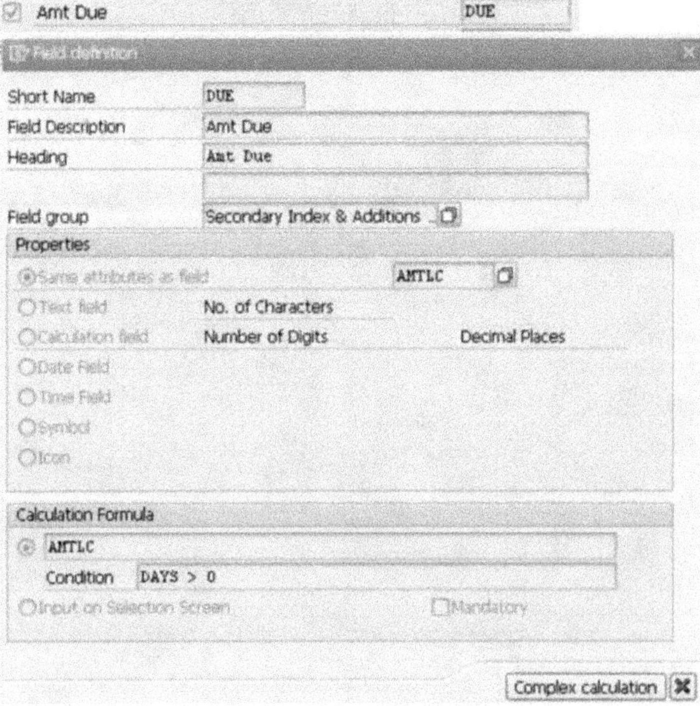
Amt Due
DUE
Field definition
Short Name
DUE
Field Description
Amt Due
Heading
Amt Due
Field group
Secondary Index & Additions
Properties
Same attributes as field
AMTLC
Text field
No. of Characters
Calculation field
Number of Digits
Decimal Places
Date Field
Time Field
Symbol
Icon
Calculation Formula
AMTLC
Condition
DAYS > 0
Input on Selection Screen
Mandatory
Complex calculation

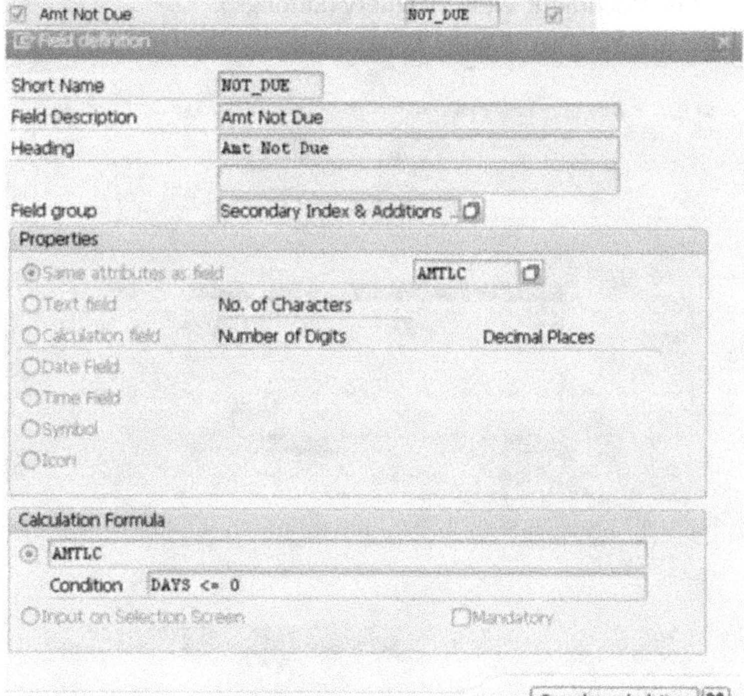

End Columns how to get:

....+....1....+....2....+....3....+....4....+....5....+....6....+....7....+....8....+....9....+..

Reference	DocumentNo	Bline date	Amt Not Due	1-30	31-60	6
Text:Customer Number 1 ABCDEFGHIJKLMNOPQRSTUVWXYZabcdefghi						
ABCDEFGHIJKLMNOP	ABCDEFGHIJ	1 .81.1990	1234567890,123.45	12345678		1
Total Customer Number ABCDEFGHIJ			1234567890,123.45	12345678		1
0			1234567890.123.45	12345678		1

Delete field
List options
List line options

Column break character need to select and select apply button, then columns will get as above mentioned.

Column break characte
Slash in front of list line
0 Space in front of thi line
0 Space after this line
Slash after list line
New output of line at page header
New page
Output only in connection with line n
Apply | Reset

Display Accounting Document View on Query (Settings).

SQ01--> Change mode—goto--Report Assignment.

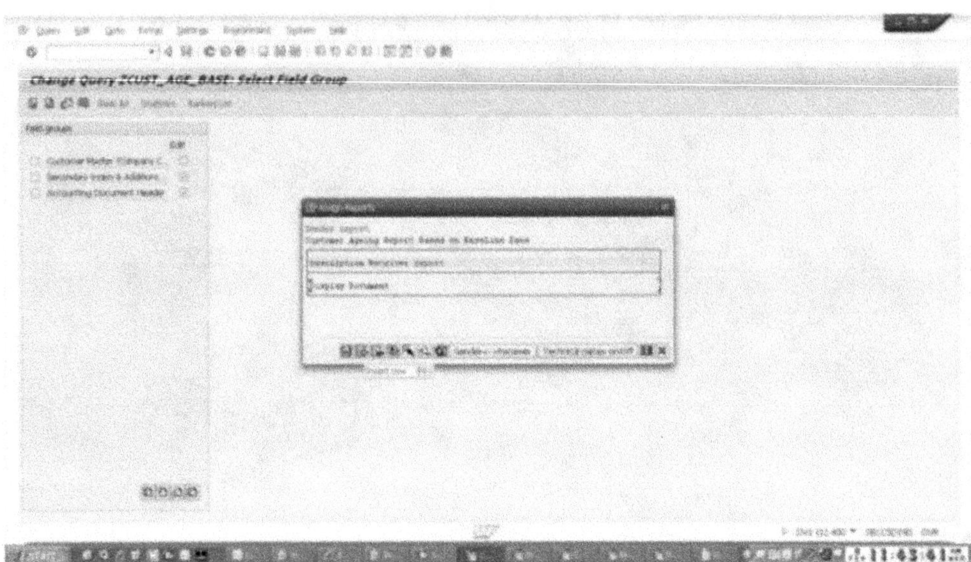

Select Insert Row button(F6).

Select other report type button.

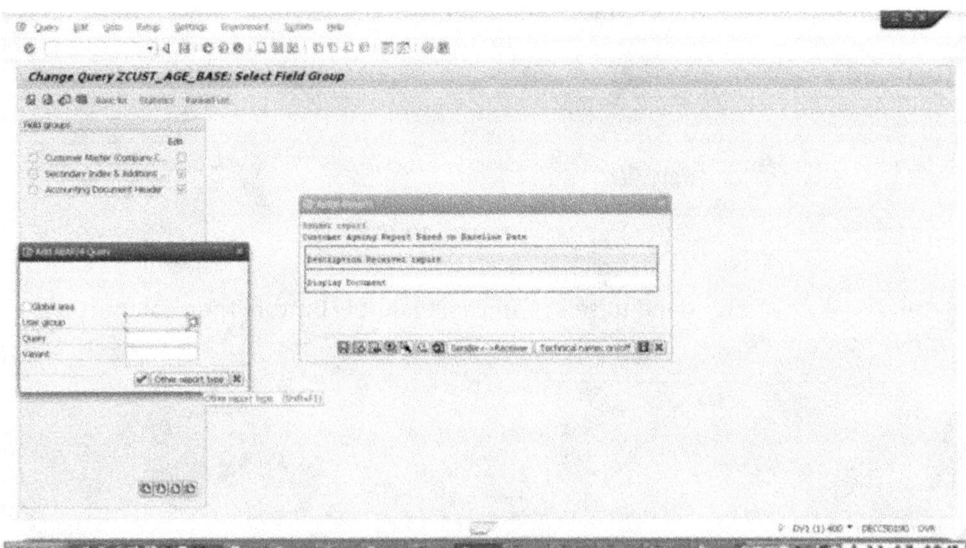

Select transaction:

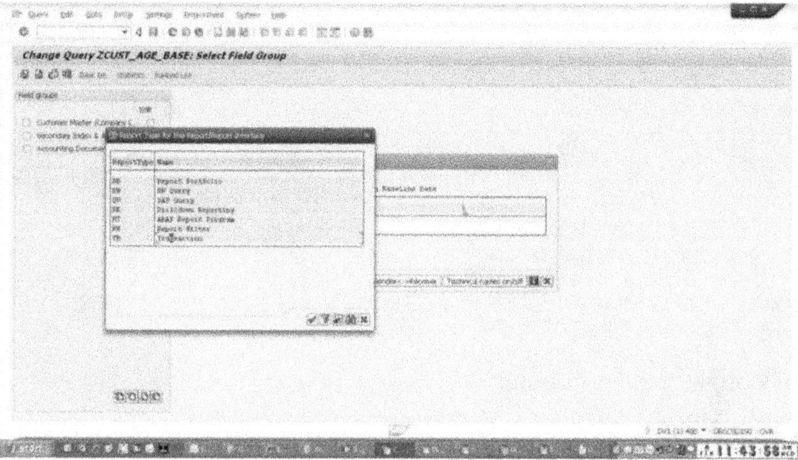

And give transaction.

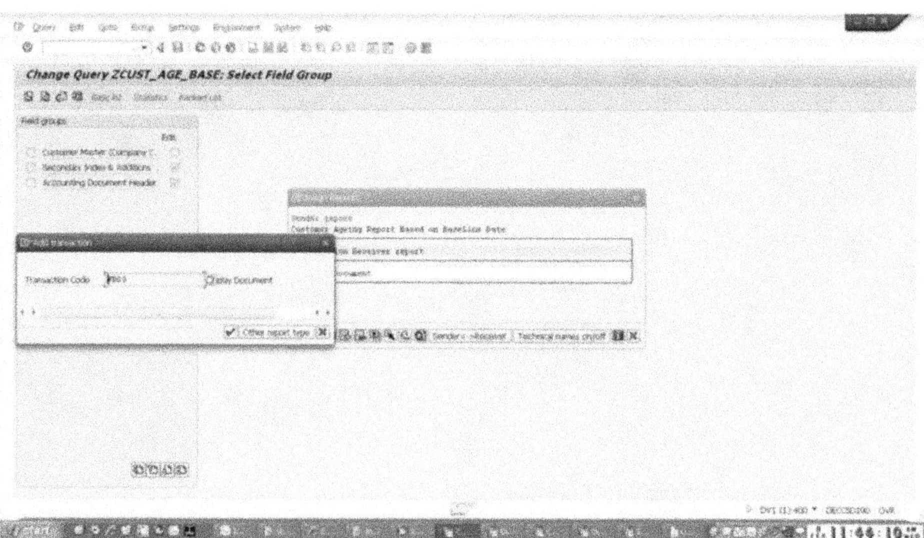

and save.

Result will be:

Total				0.00	0.00
Reference	DocumentNo	Bline date	Amt Not Due	1-30	31-
Text:Customer Number 1 PANTALOONS-CALCUTTA					
0246	1800000166	14.11.2011	0.00	0.00	0.
	100000052	30.11.2011	0.00	0.00	0.
104.00	1800000034	29.09.2011	0.00	0.00	0.
112.36-	1800000028	23.09.2011	0.00	0.00	0.
1800000026	1800000027	23.09.2011	0.00	0.00	0.
MESSAGE NO. F5A0	1800000026	23.09.2011	0.00	0.00	0.

Double click on document number.

Will get document overview.

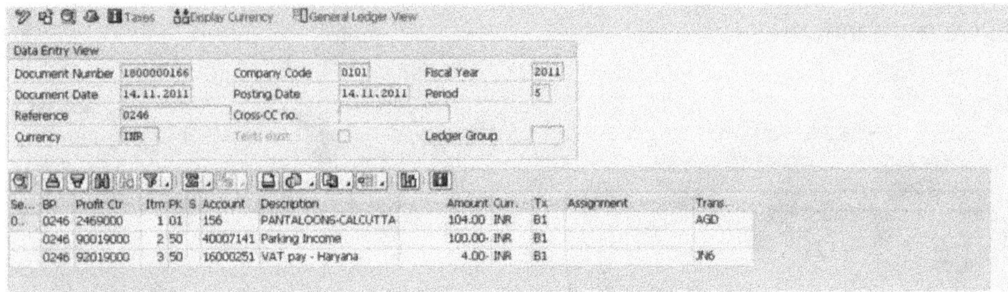

Taxes | Display Currency | General Ledger View

Data Entry View

Document Number	1800000166	Company Code	0101	Fiscal Year	2011
Document Date	14.11.2011	Posting Date	14.11.2011	Period	5
Reference	0246	Cross-CC no.			
Currency	INR	Texts exist		Ledger Group	

Se...	BP	Profit Ctr	Itm	PK	S	Account	Description	Amount	Curr.	Tx	Assignment	Trans.
0..	0246	2469000	1	01		156	PANTALOONS-CALCUTTA	104.00	INR	B1		AGD
	0246	90019000	2	50		40007141	Parking Income	100.00-	INR	B1		
	0246	92019000	3	50		16000251	VAT pay - Haryana	4.00-	INR	B1		JN6

CHAPTER 18

SAP ALE scenario development

Application Link Enabling (ALE) is a mechanism for the exchange of business data between loosely-coupled R/3 applications built by customers of SAP, the enterprise resource management program.

18.1. Introduction to ale development

To develop a new custom ALE scenario, comprises 5 steps:

1. Design and develop the custom IDoc with its segments and a new message type
2. Configure the ALE environment with the new IDoc and message type (customer model, partner profiles and linking IDoc to message type)
3. Develop the outbound process which does the following:
    - Populates the custom IDoc with control info and functional data
    - Sends the [Doc to the ALE layer for distribution
    - Updates status and handles errors
4. Configure the ALE inbound side (partner profiles with inbound process code)
5. Develop the inbound process which does the following:

Below is a pictorial representation of the flow of a complete ALE scenario from the sending system to the receiving system.

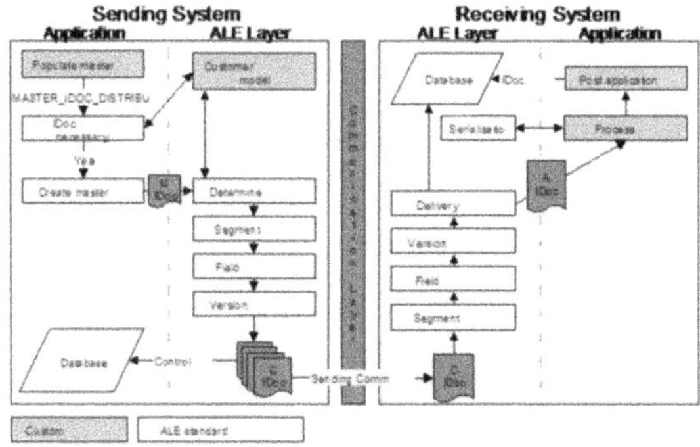

18.2. ALE Example

For the purposes of this example we 'Ain develop a small ALE scenario. nns scenario is described below. "Data is fetched from Z table on the sender system and inserted it in the Z table of Receiver system using ALEPDOC"

18.3. Settings on the Sender End

Table Creation T – Code SE11. The table contains data that is to be sent to Receiver.
ALE Configuration
T-Code – SALE

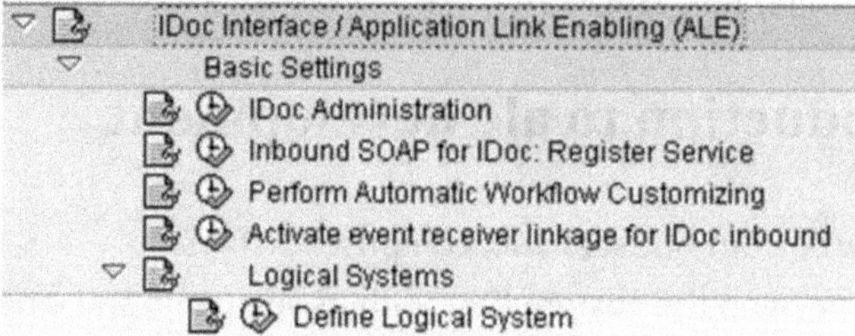

18.4. Defining Logical System

VY800 is our sender
PB080 is our receiver

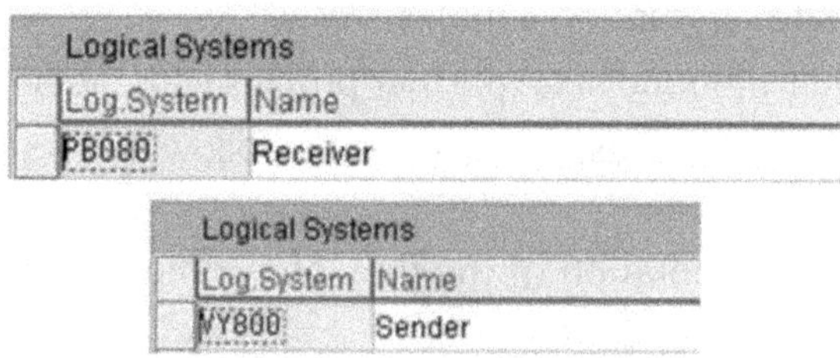

Assigning Client to Logical System

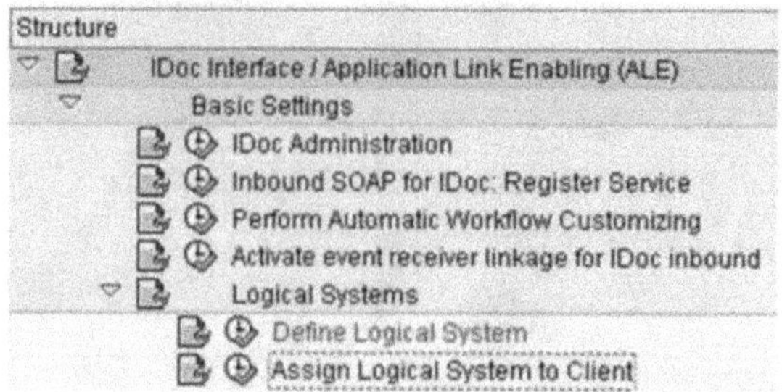

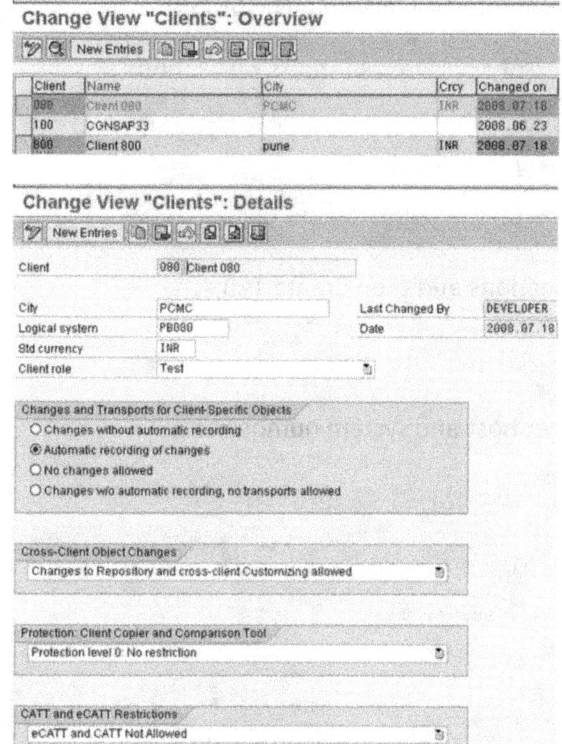
Change View "Clients": Overview
New Entries
Client | Name | City | Crcy | Changed on
000 | Client 000 | PCMC | INR | 2008.07.18
100 | CGNSAP33 | | | 2008.06.23
800 | Client 800 | pune | INR | 2008.07.18
Change View "Clients": Details
New Entries
Client 000 Client 000
City PCMC
Last Changed By DEVELOPER
Logical system PB000
Date 2008.07.18
Std currency INR
Client role Test
Changes and Transports for Client-Specific Objects
Changes without automatic recording
Automatic recording of changes
No changes allowed
Changes w/o automatic recording, no transports allowed
Cross-Client Object Changes
Changes to Repository and cross-client Customizing allowed
Protection: Client Copier and Comparison Tool
Protection level 0: No restriction
CATT and eCATT Restrictions
eCATT and CATT Not Allowed

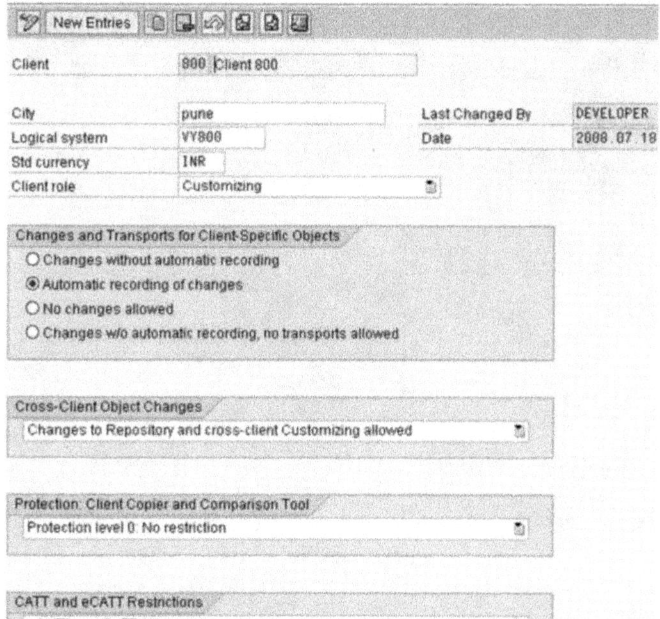
Change View "Clients": Details
New Entries
Client 800 Client 800
City pune
Last Changed By DEVELOPER
Logical system VY800
Date 2008.07.18
Std currency INR
Client role Customizing
Changes and Transports for Client-Specific Objects
Changes without automatic recording
Automatic recording of changes
No changes allowed
Changes w/o automatic recording, no transports allowed
Cross-Client Object Changes
Changes to Repository and cross-client Customizing allowed
Protection: Client Copier and Comparison Tool
Protection level 0: No restriction
CATT and eCATT Restrictions
eCATT and CATT Allowed

Defining Target System for RFC Calls (T-code – SM59)

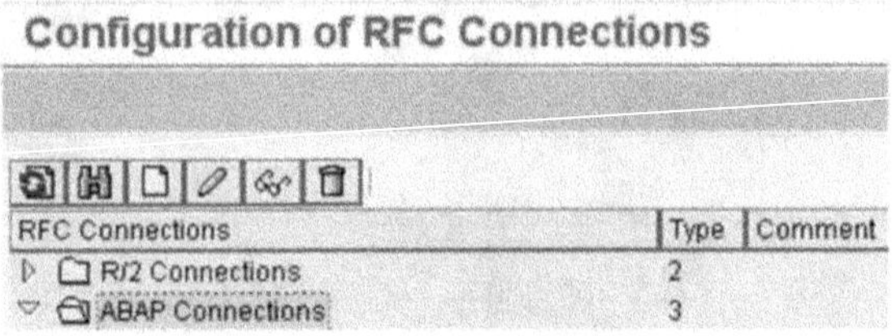

Click on ABAP Connections and then Create TAB

Step 1

We should give Target host and system number only.

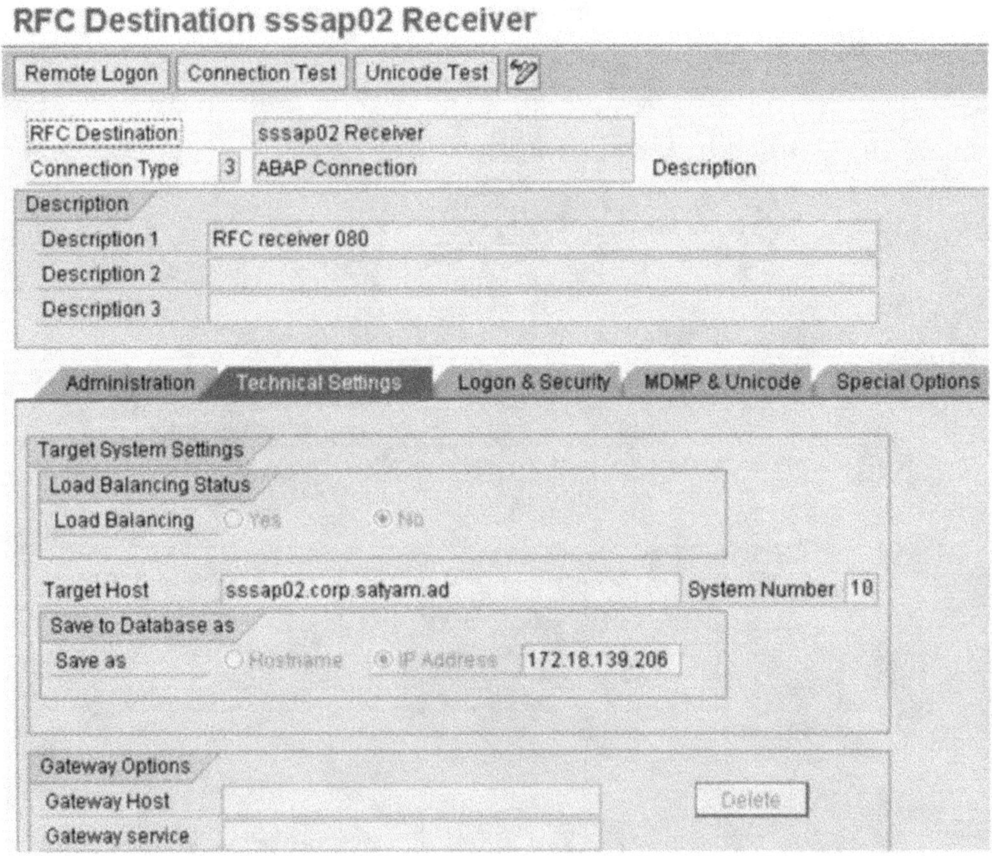

Defining Target System for RFC Calls (T-code – SM59)

Click on ABAP Connections and then Create TAB

Step 1

We should give Target host and system number only.

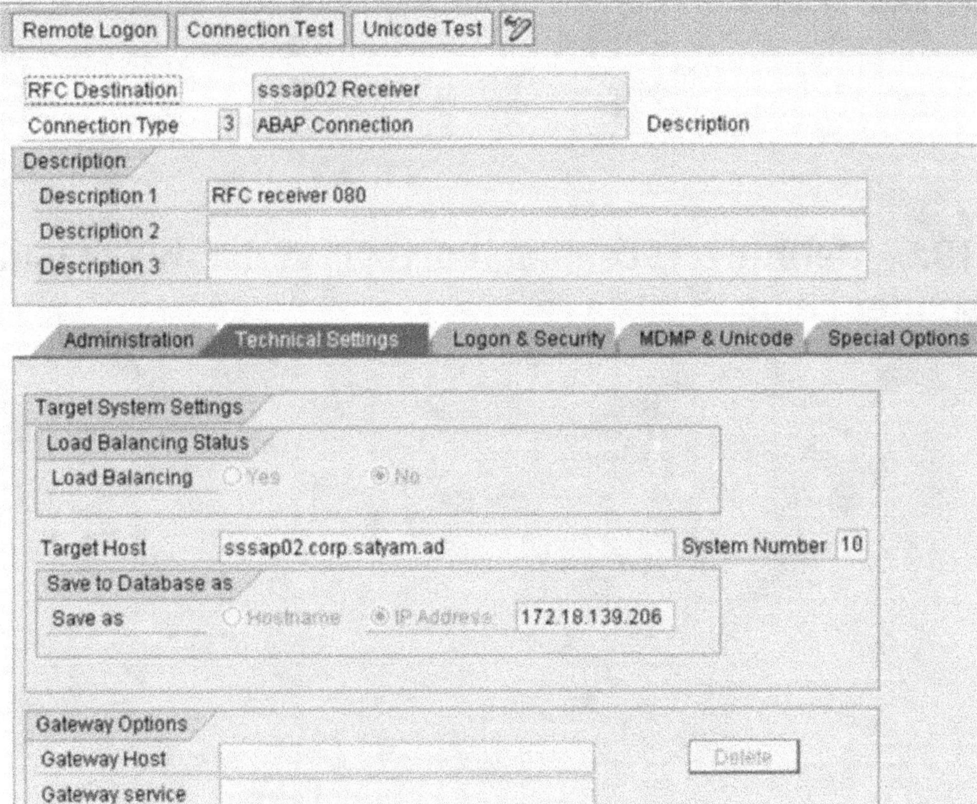

Step 2

RFC Destination sssap02 Receiver

Remote Logon | Connection Test | Unicode Test

RFC Destination: sssap02 Receiver
Connection Type: 3 ABAP Connection — Description

Description
Description 1: RFC receiver 080
Description 2:
Description 3:

Administration | Technical Settings | Logon & Security | MDMP & Unicode | Special Options

Security Options
Trusted System/Logon Screen Status
Trusted System
Status of Secure Protocol
Authorization for Destination

Logon
Language: EN
Client: 080
User: DEVELOPER
PW Status: saved

18.5. Defining receiving Port (T Code: WE21) in sender client

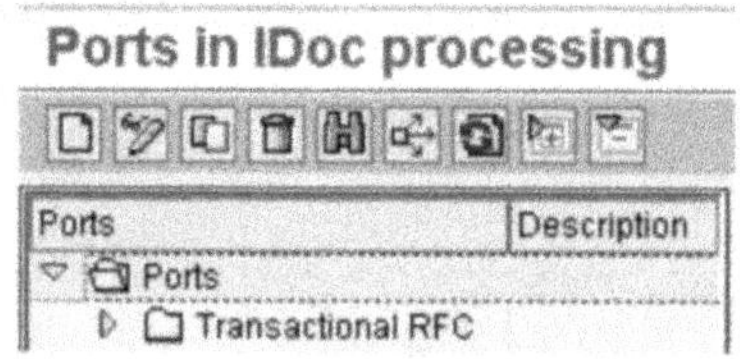

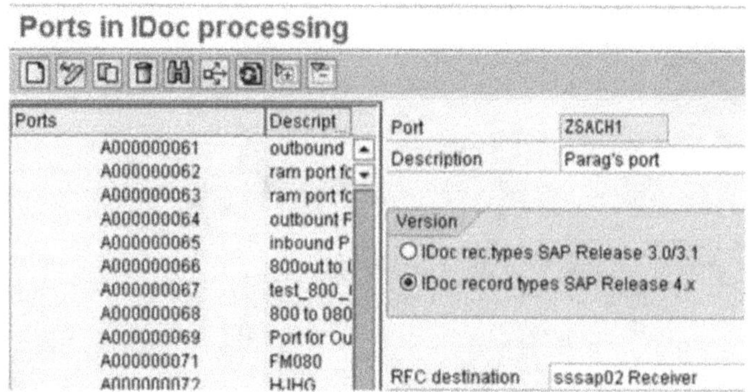

The sender system is connected to the receiver system through this Port.

18.6. Create Message type (T Code: WE81)

Display View "EDI: Logical Message Types": Overview

EDI Logical Message Types

Message Type	Short text
ZSACH1	ZVPY Message Type vikas

18.7. Create table (T code: SE11)

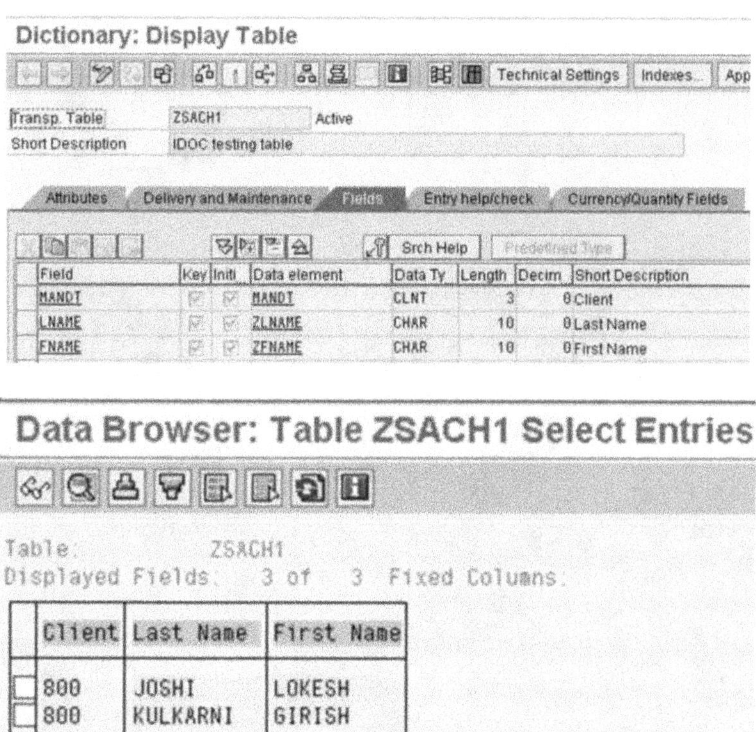

Dictionary: Display Table

Transp. Table: ZSACH1 Active

Short Description: IDOC testing table

Field	Key	Initi	Data element	Data Ty	Length	Decim	Short Description
MANDT	✓	✓	MANDT	CLNT	3	0	Client
LNAME	✓	✓	ZLNAME	CHAR	10	0	Last Name
FNAME	✓	✓	ZFNAME	CHAR	10	0	First Name

Data Browser: Table ZSACH1 Select Entries

Table: ZSACH1

Displayed Fields: 3 of 3 Fixed Columns:

Client	Last Name	First Name
800	JOSHI	LOKESH
800	KULKARNI	GIRISH

18.8. Defining the Z Segment type

T-code – WE31

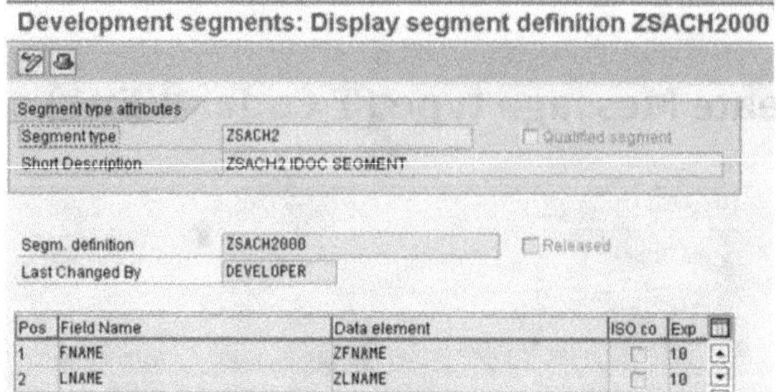

18.9. Defining the Basic Type

T Code WE30

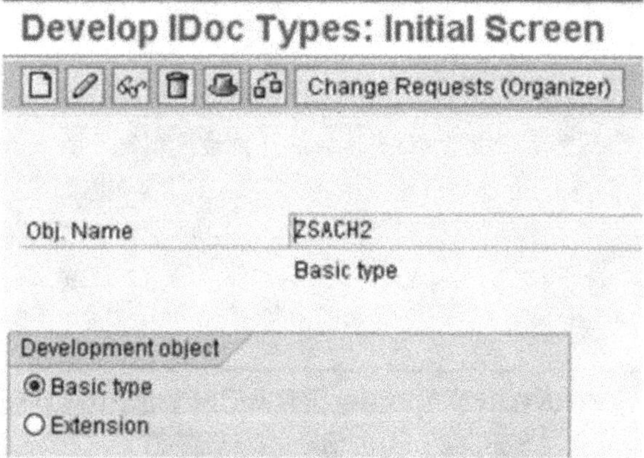

Click on Create.
Select Create new

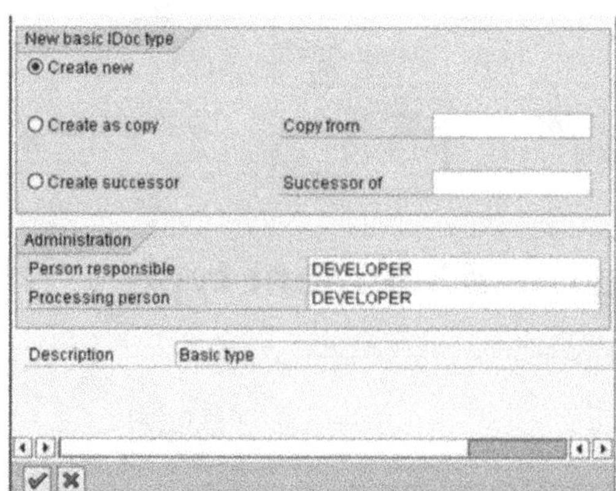

18.10. This will take you to next screen as follows

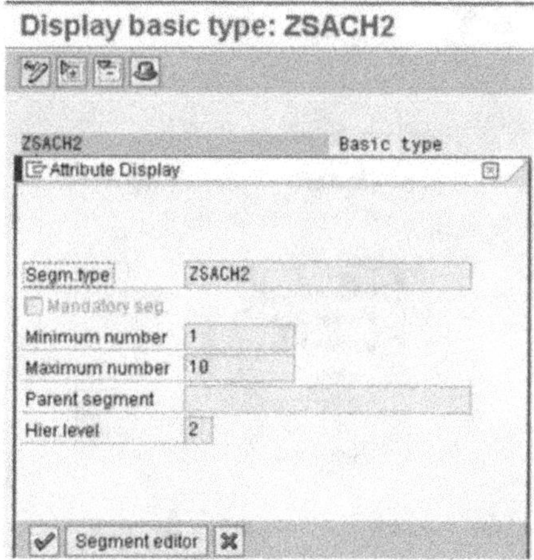

Here you have connected the basic type to the segment type.
Enter again and this will take you to screen as follows:

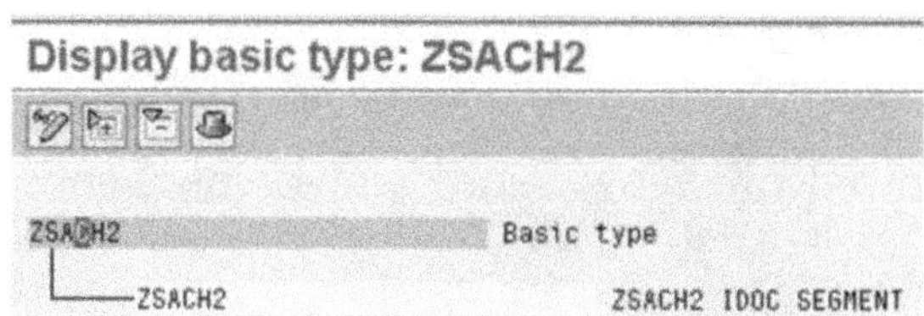

This shows the relation between the basic and the segment types.
Next you need to make the entry of the segment in the system table.
Next is the following entry which is required.

T Code: WE82

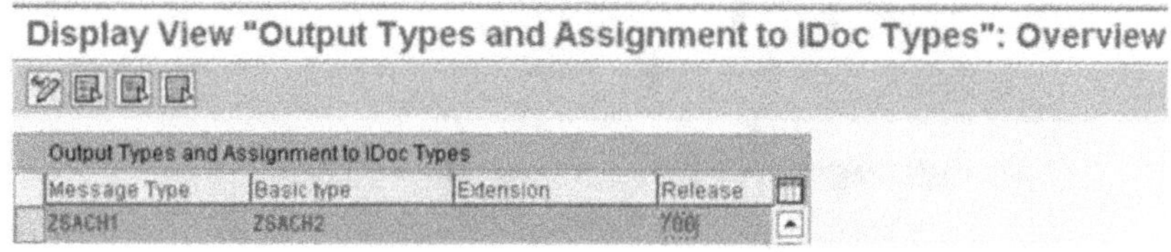

Here you are specifying the message type and the basic type and the release version.
This is all about the configuration you need to do on the sender side.
Now on the sender side you also need a program that will fetch the required data, couple it in the IDOC format and post it.

18.11. Defining Partner Profiles (WE20)

Click on partner type LS.
Click on create.

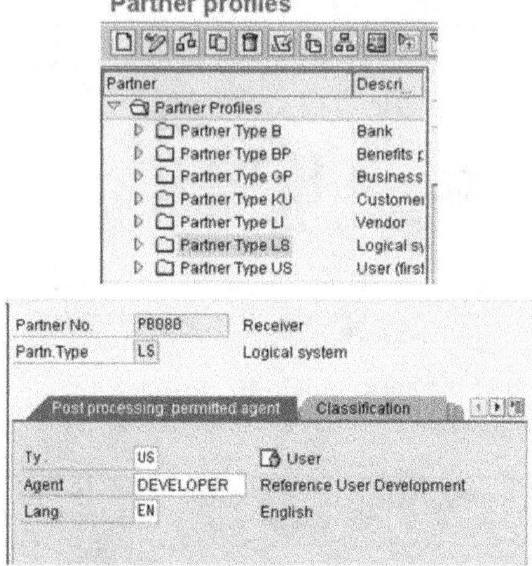

Save the entered data.
Create outbound parameters.
Since this is a sender we have to define only Outbound Parameters in this case.
For sender system we should have Message type 'SYNCH'

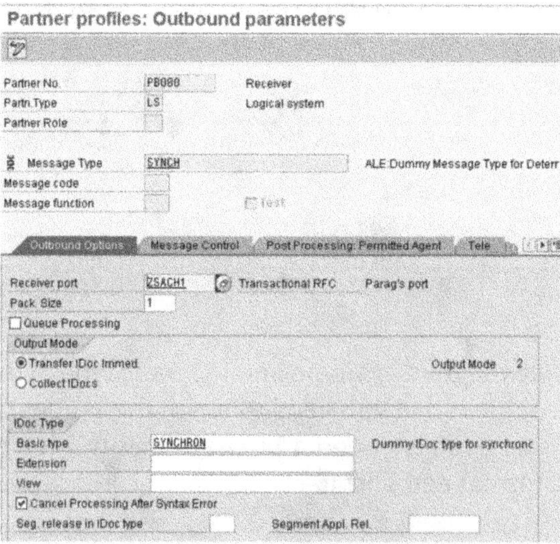

Partner profiles: Outbound parameters

Partner No.	PB080	Receiver	
Partn.Type	LS	Logical system	
Partner Role			
Message Type	ZSACH1		ZVPY Message Type vikas
Message code			
Message function		☐ Test	

Outbound Options | Message Control | Post Processing: Permitted Agent | Tele

Receiver port	ZSACH1	Transactional RFC	Parag's port
Pack. Size	1		

☐ Queue Processing

Output Mode

◉ Transfer IDoc Immed. Output Mode 2

○ Collect IDocs

IDoc Type

Basic type	ZSACH2	Basic type
Extension		
View		

☑ Cancel Processing After Syntax Error

Seg. release in IDoc type Segment Appl. Rel.

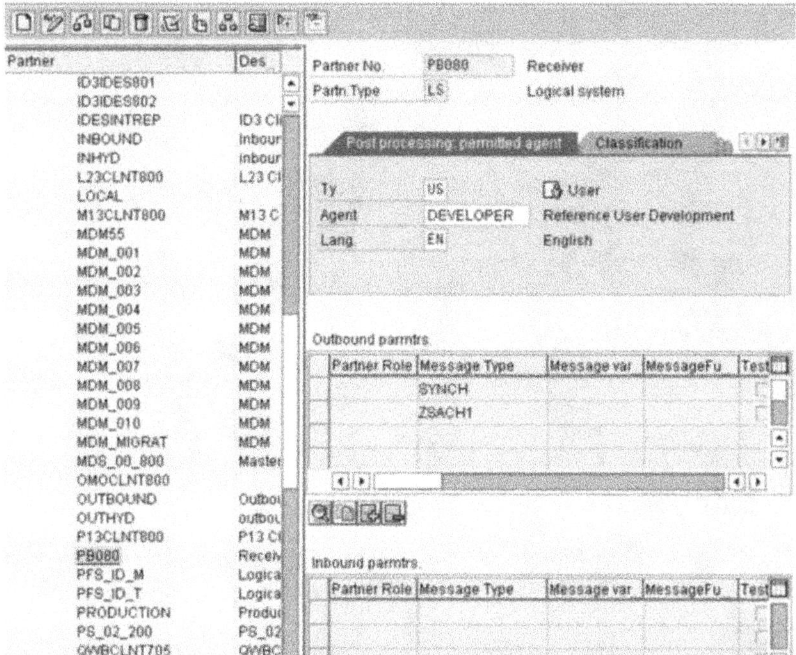

The partner for client 800(Sender) is the client 080 (Receiver).

2. Maintaining Distribution Model (T-Code BD64).

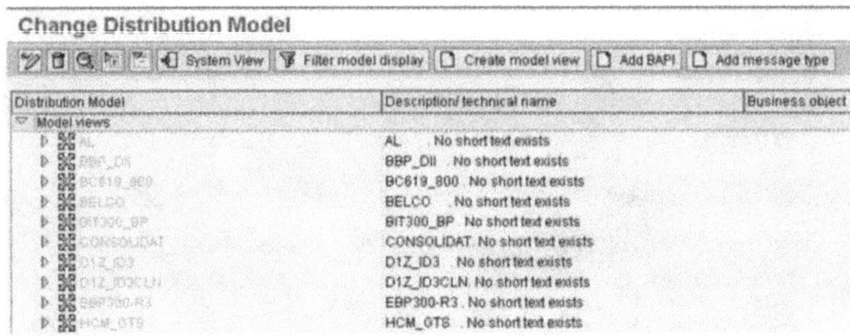

Click on Create model view

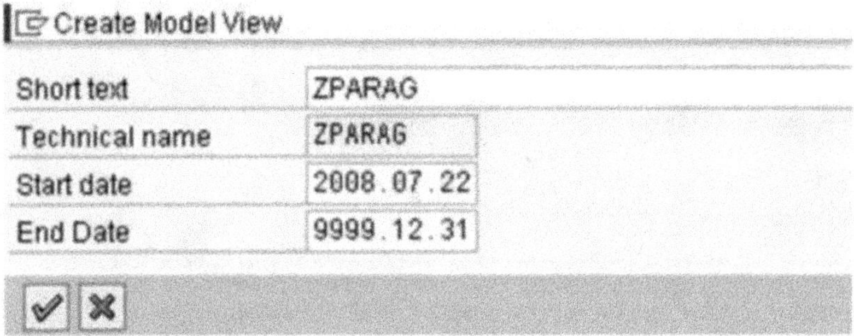

Click on Add message type

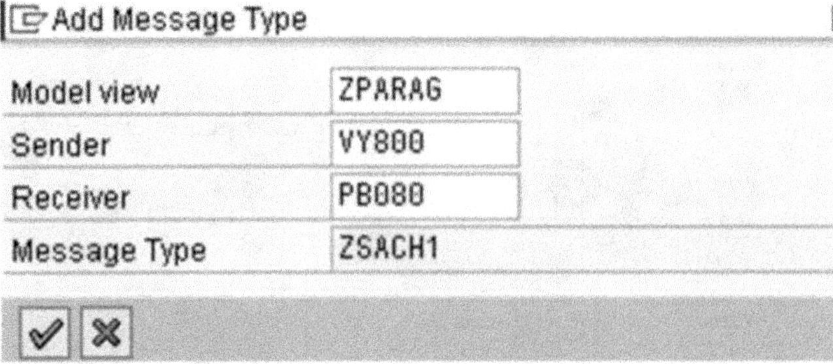

Change Distribution Model

System View | Filter model display | Create model view | Add BAPI | Add message type

Distribution Model	Description/ technical name	Business object
	HR_ORG_BW	
	ID3-->DEJ	
	ID3-DMJ	
	ID3 - DMK	
	ID3-DSZ	
	FICOTORPM	
	HRTORPM	
	IDES_GDS	
	VAR_KONF_2	
	MDMDEMO	
	MDM55	
	MEREP	
	MM-SUS	
	MMSUSTRAIN	
	PLMXXX	
	PRAC_MODEL	
	PRAC_VIEW	
	EBP_TO_R3	
	SMBONE	
	SMI	
	EX_MODEL	
	US_PDR	
ZPARAG	ZPARAG	
Sender	VY800	
Receiver	PB080	
ZSACH1	ZVPY Message Type vikas	

18.12. Now Distribute this Model View

Distribute it from Edit → Model View → Distribute.

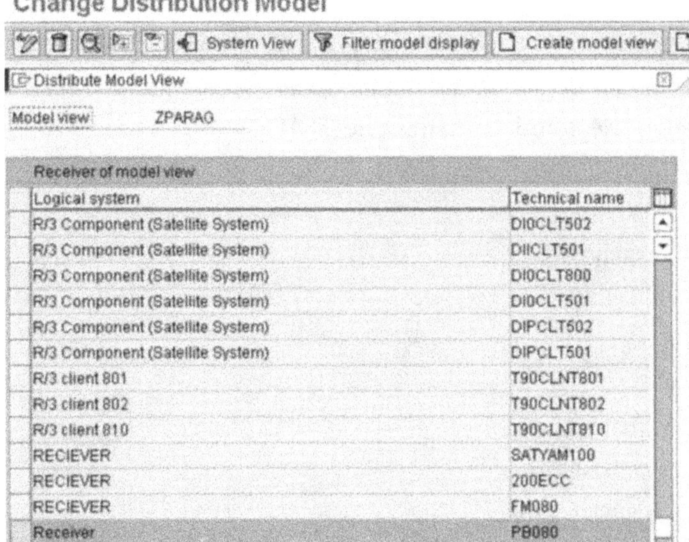

Change Distribution Model

System View | Filter model display | Create model view

Distribute Model View

Model view ZPARAG

Receiver of model view

Logical system	Technical name
R/3 Component (Satellite System)	DIOCLT502
R/3 Component (Satellite System)	DIICLT501
R/3 Component (Satellite System)	DIOCLT800
R/3 Component (Satellite System)	DIOCLT501
R/3 Component (Satellite System)	DIPCLT502
R/3 Component (Satellite System)	DIPCLT501
R/3 client 801	T90CLNT801
R/3 client 802	T90CLNT802
R/3 client 810	T90CLNT810
RECIEVER	SATYAM100
RECIEVER	200ECC
RECIEVER	FM080
Receiver	PB080

Click on 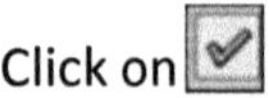

Log of Model View Distribution

Distribution of model view ZPARAG

Target system PB080	Model view ZPARAG has been changed

Create a program to fetch the data from table: ZSACH1.

T Code: SE38

Create new program: ZSACH_CUST_IDOC

```
*&---------------------------------------------------------------------*
*&Report ZSACH_CUST_IDOC
*&
*&---------------------------------------------------------------------*
*&
*&
*&---------------------------------------------------------------------*

report zsach_cust_idoc.

parameters:         p_logsys like tbdlst-logsys.

data: gen_segment like edidd-segnam value 'ZSACH2'.

data: control_dat like edidc,
    gen_data like zsach1.

tables: zsach1.

data: begin of inttab occurs 0,
      lname type zsach1-lname,
      fname type zsach1-fname,
    end of inttab.
```

```
data:
    int_edidd like edidd occurs 0 with header line,
    int_edidc like edidc occurs 0 with header line.


select * from zsach1 into corresponding fields of table inttab.

if sy-subrc ne 0.
  message 'no data' type 'I'.
  exit.
endif.


control_dat-mestyp = 'ZSACH1'.
control_dat-idoctp = 'ZSACH2'.
control_dat-rcvprt = 'LS'.
control_dat-rcvprn = p_logsys.



loop at inttab.
  gen_data-lname = inttab-lname.
  gen_data-fname = inttab-fname.
*  GEN_DATA-SSN = INTTAB-SSN.
*  GEN_DATA-DOB = INTTAB-DOB.

  int_edidd-segnam = gen_segment.
  int_edidd-sdata = gen_data.

  append int_edidd.
endloop.

call function 'MASTER_IDOC_DISTRIBUTE'
  exporting
```

```
    master_idoc_control              = control_dat
*   OBJ_TYPE                    = ''
*   CHNUM                       = ''
  tables
    communication_idoc_control        = int_edidc
    master_idoc_data                = int_edidd

 exceptions
   error_in_idoc_control            = 1
   error_writing_idoc_status          = 2
   error_in_idoc_data              = 3
   sending_logical_system_unknown      = 4
   others                      = 5

if sy-subrc <> 0.
message id sy-msgid type sy-msgty number sy-msgno.
else.
    loop at int_edidc.
    write :/ 'IDOC GENERATED', int_edidc-docnum.
  endloop.
  commit work.
endif.
```

Settings on the receiver side.

The ALE configuration is same as we did it on the sender side. The receiver specific differences are mentioned below.

T-Code – SALE

18.13.Steps

Defining Logical System (Same as sender)
Assigning Client to Logical System (Same as sender)

Defining Target System for RFC Calls (T-code – SM59) (Same as sender)

If we are doing the configuration in same server with different client, then we don't have to define Logical system as well as RFC call using SM59.

It is not required to create port (T Code: WE20) at receiving client as sending system is same

As this is cross client we don't have to create segment type, IDoc type as well as Message type. If we are using different server then we have to define Segment type (T Code: WE31), I Doc type (T Code: WE30) and Message type (T Code: WE81)

Create function module which will be assigned during partner profile creation in process code field.

T Code: SE37

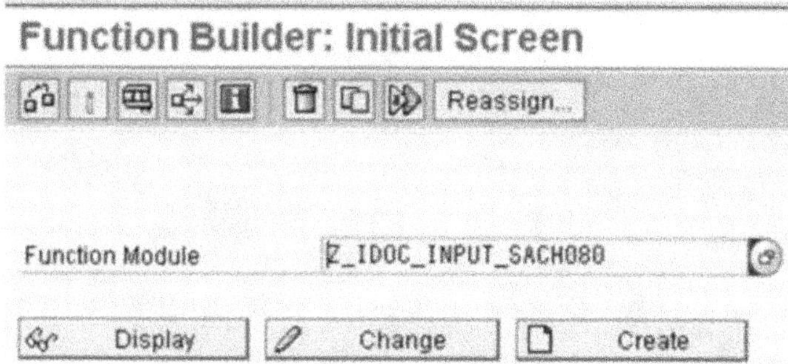

Function Module will look something as below:

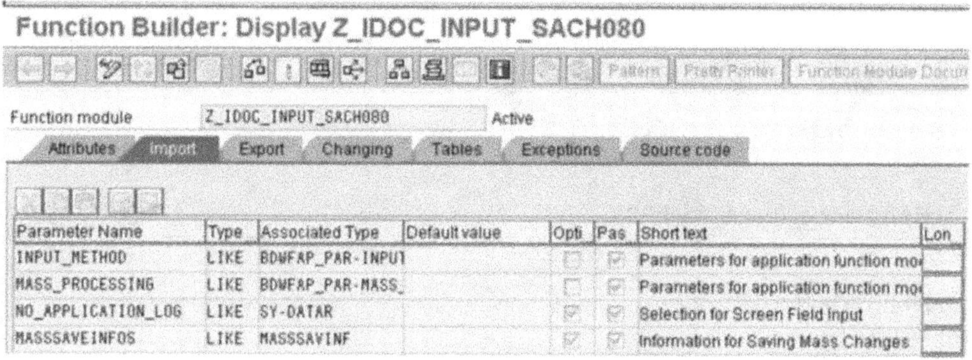

Parameter Name	Type	Associated Type	Default value	Opti	Pas	Short text	Lon
INPUT_METHOD	LIKE	BDWFAP_PAR-INPUT		☐	☑	Parameters for application function mo	
MASS_PROCESSING	LIKE	BDWFAP_PAR-MASS_		☐	☑	Parameters for application function mo	
NO_APPLICATION_LOG	LIKE	SY-DATAR		☑	☑	Selection for Screen Field Input	
MASSSAVEINFOS	LIKE	MASSSAVINF		☑	☑	Information for Saving Mass Changes	

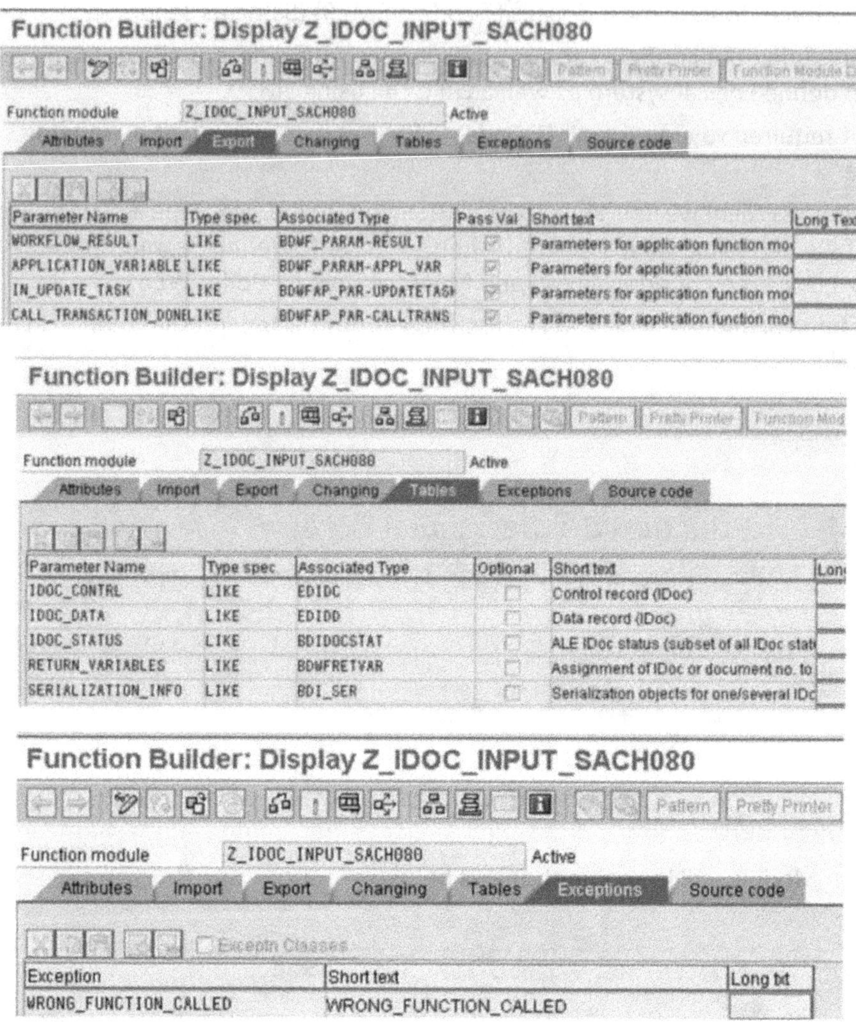

18.14. Source Code

```
function z_idoc_input_sach080.
*"----------------------------------------------------------------------
--Local Interface:
"" IMPORTING
""     VALUE(INPUTivlETHOD) LIKE BDWFAP_PAR-INPUTMETHD
""     VALUE(MASS_PROCESSING) LIKE BDWFAP_PAR-MASS_PROC
""     VALUE(NO_APPLICATION_LOG) LIKE SY-DATAR OPTIONAL VALUE(MASSSAVEINFOS)
```

```
     LIKE MASSSAVINF STRUCTURE MASSSAVINF
""   OPTIONAL
''' EXPORTING
""   VALUE(WORKFLOW_RESULT) LIKE BDWF_PARAM-RESULT
""   VALUE(APPLICATION_VARIABLE) LIKE BDWF_PARAM-APPL_VAR
"    VALUE(IN_UPDATE_TASK) LIKE BDWFAP_PAR-UPDATETASK
""   VALUE(CALL_TRANSACTION_DONE) LIKE BDWFAP_PAR-CALLTRANS
"" TABLES
""   IDOC_CONTRL STRUCTURE EDIDC
""   IDOCDATA STRUCTURE EDIDD
""   IDOC_STATUS STRUCTURE BDIDOCSTAT
""   RETURN VARIABLES STRUCTURE BDWFRETVAR
""   SERIALIZATION INFO STRUCTURE BDISER
"" EXCEPTIONS
""   WRONGFUNCTIONCALLED
"" ..........................................................................

include mbdconwf.
data: it_emp_data like zsach1 occurs 0 with header line.
data: gen_data like zsach1
workflow result = c_wf_result_ok.
data' counter type int4.

select count(`) from zsach1 into counter.
counter = counter + 1.
loop at idoc_contrl.

     if idoc_contrl-mestyp ne 'ZSACH1'.
         raise wrong_function_called.
     endif.
clear gen_data
refresh it_emp_data.

loop at idoc_data where docnum eq idoc_contrl-docnum
```

```
    if idoc_data-segnam = 'ZSACH2'

        gen_data = idoc_data-sdata.

        it_emp_data-mandt = counter.
        it_emp_data-lname = gen_data-lname
        it_emp_data-fname = gen_data-fname.

        counter = counter + 1.

        append it_emp_data.
    else.
        message 'ERROR' type 'I'.
    endif.

    endloop
endloop

insert zsach1 from table it_emp_data.
```

******* OPEN IDOC WITH INTENTION OF CHANGING IDOC CONTENTS**

```
call function 'EDI_DOCUMENT_OPEN_FOR_EDIT'
exporting
    document number                   = idoc_data-docnum
importing
    idoc_control                 = idoc_contrl
tables
    idoc_data            = idoc_data
exceptions
document_foreign_lock            = 1
document_not_exist     = 2
document_not_open                = 3
status_is_unable_for_changing = 4
```

```
others                    = 5.

******TRANSFER OF MANY CHANGED IDOC DATA RECORDS FOR ONE IDOC
call function 'EDI_CHANGE_DATA_SEGMENTS'

tables
      idoc_changed_data_range = idoc_data
exceptions
      idoc_not_open       = 1
data_record_not_exist  = 2
others              = 3.

******

data t_itab_edids40 like edi_ds40 occurs 0 with header line.
clear t_itab_edids40.
t_itab_edids40-docnum            = idoc_data-docnum.
t_itab_edids40-status   = '51'.
t_itab_edids40-repid              = sy-repid.
t_itab_edids40-tabnam ='EDI_DS'.
titabedids40-mandt                = sy-mandt.
t_itab_edids40-stamqu ='SAP'.
t_itab_edids40-stamid  ='B1'
t_itab_edids40-stamno = '999'.
t_itab_edids40-stapal   = 'Sold to changed to '.
l_itab_edids40-stapa2  = t_nevv_kunnr.
t_itab_edids40-logdat  = sy-datum.
t_itab_edids40-logtim  = sy-uzeit.

append t_itab_edids40.

******CLOSE DOC AND SAVE ALL CHANGES

call function 'EDI_DOCUMENT_CLOSE_EDIT'
```

```
exporting
        document number = idoc_data-docnum
        do commit              = 'X'
        doupdate  = 'X'
        writeallstatus          = 'X'
tables
        status records         = t_itabedids40
exceptions
        idoc_not_open      = 1
        db_error    = 2
        others          = 3.
endfunction.
```

Run Transaction BD51

Create entry for created function module

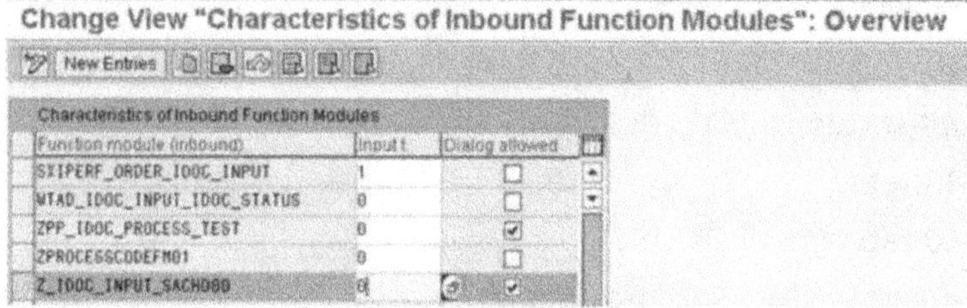

Note: 0 is for Mass processing and 1 is for Individual Input.

Run T Code: WE57

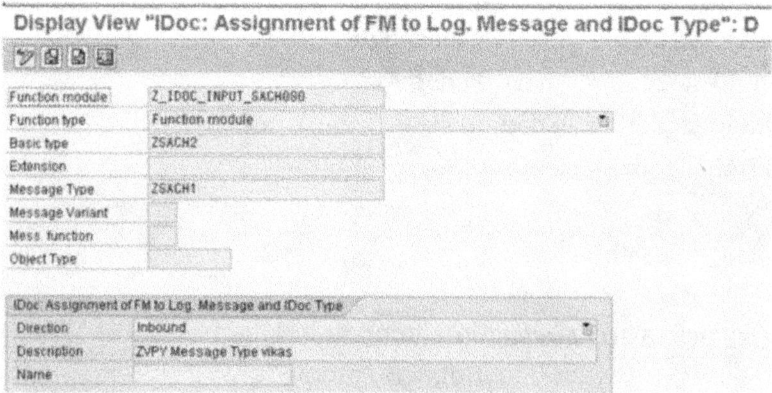

Above basic type and message type must be same as sender system.

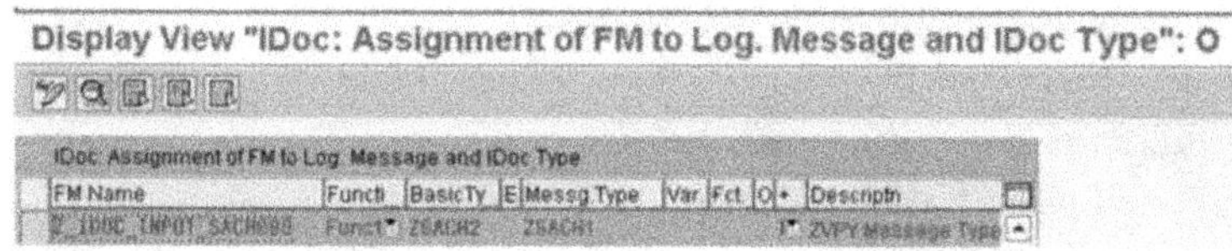

Create process code.

T Code: WE42.

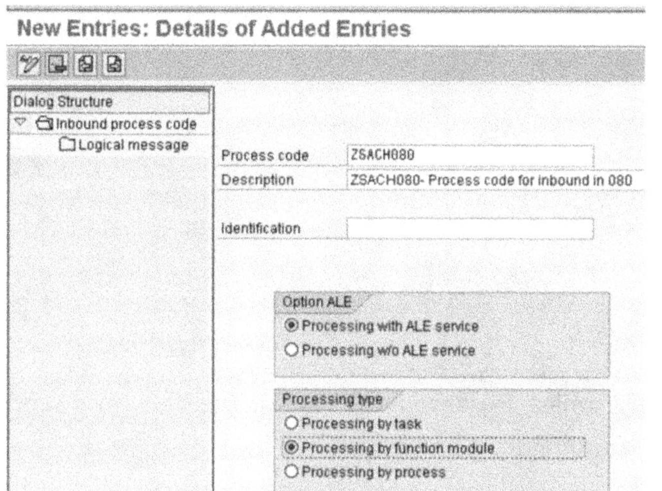

SAVE data.

Click on 

Change View "Function modules for inbound ALE-EDI": Details

Process code	ZSACH080
Module (inbound)	
Function Module	Z_IDOC_INPUT_SACH080
Maximum Number of Repeats	
IDoc packet	
Object Type	
End Event	
IDoc	
Object Type	
Start Event	
End event	
Success Event	
Application Object	
Object Type	
Start event	

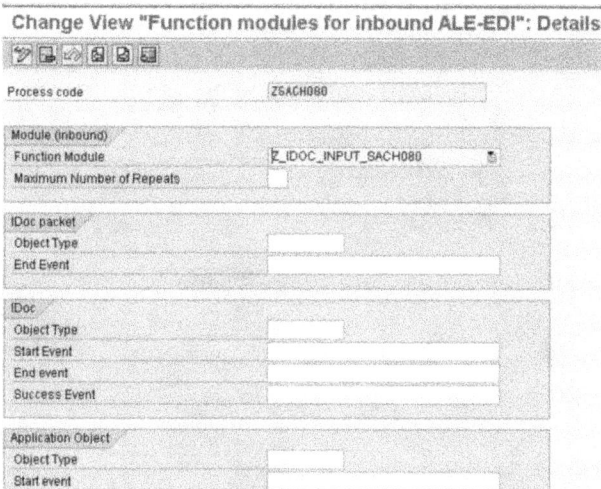

Function module is appearing in Identification field.

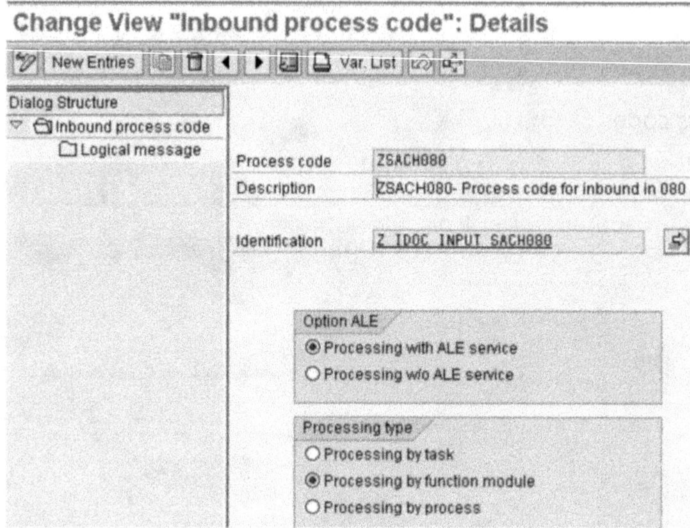

Defining partner Profiles- Here we are accepting the data from Sender system. Hence we nees to configure it as Inbound

T Code: WE20

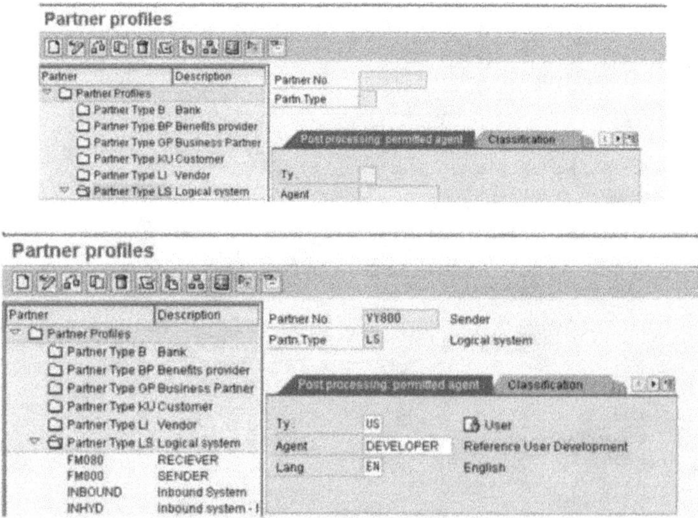

SAVE.

Define Inbound parameters. Here we have to assign process code in partner profile.

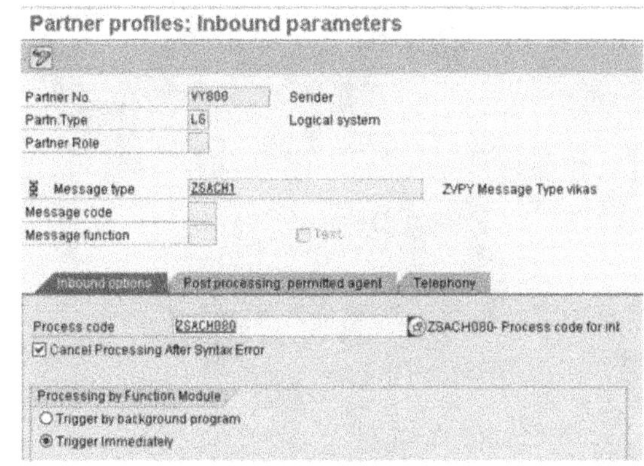

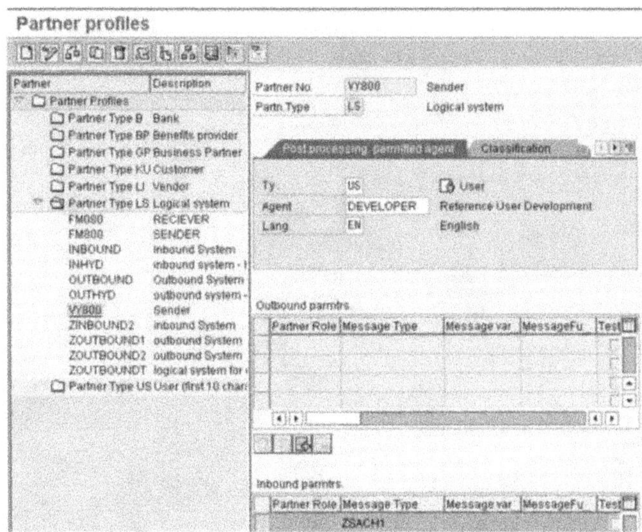

Here on the receiver end, we need to specify a process code at the time of defining the partner profile.

Process code is something that has the logic defined about what to be done after receiving the !do,

In our case, on receipt of the Idoc, we are updating the Z Table. I.e Inserting the data from the Idoc into the Z Table.

Running the Application

Sender system

T Code: SE38 Program: ZSACH_CUST_IDOC

Parag IDoc testing

P_LOGSYS PB080

Parag IDoc testing

Parag IDoc testing

IDOC GENERATED 0000000000768751

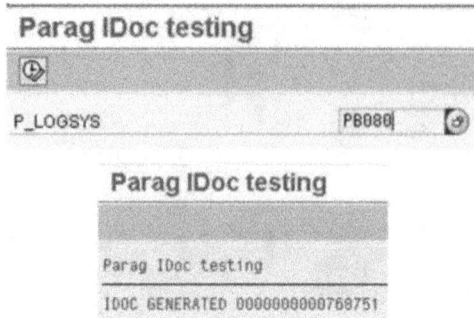

Checking the Idoc in Sender system.

T Code: WE05.

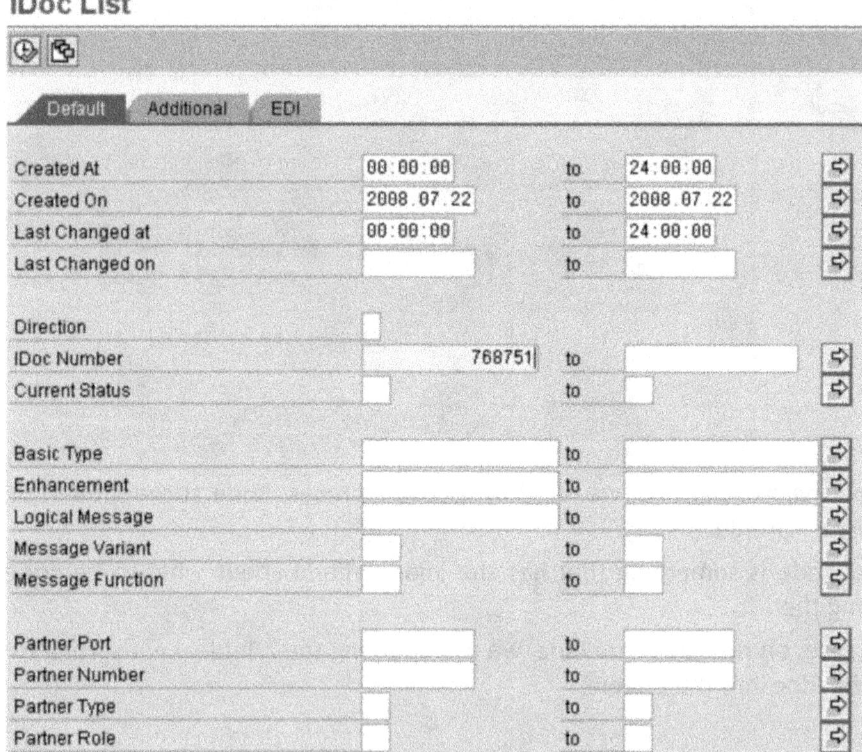

SAP

IDoc display
IDoc 0000000000768751
Control Rec.
Data records — Total number: 000002
ZSACH2 — Segment 000001
ZSACH2 — Segment 000002
Status records
30 — IDoc ready for dispatch
01 — IDoc generated

Technical short info

Direction	1	Outbox
Current status	30	
Basic type	ZSACH2	
Extension		
Message type	ZSACH1	
Partner No.	PB080	
Partn.Type	LS	
Port	ZSACH1	

Content of selected segment

Fld name	Fld cont.

Process IDoc.

T Code: BD87.

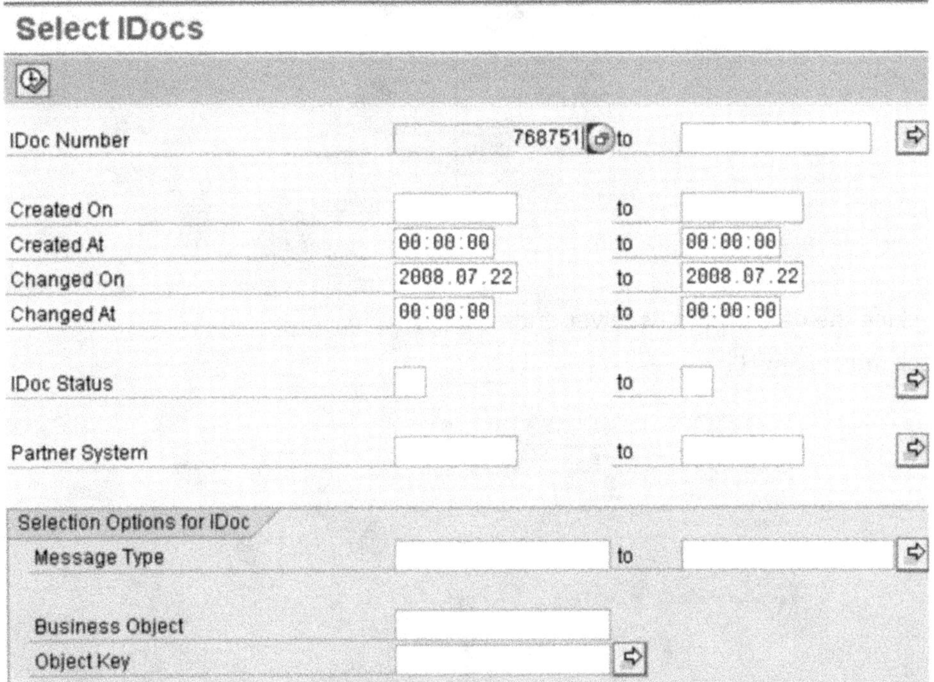

CLICK ON 

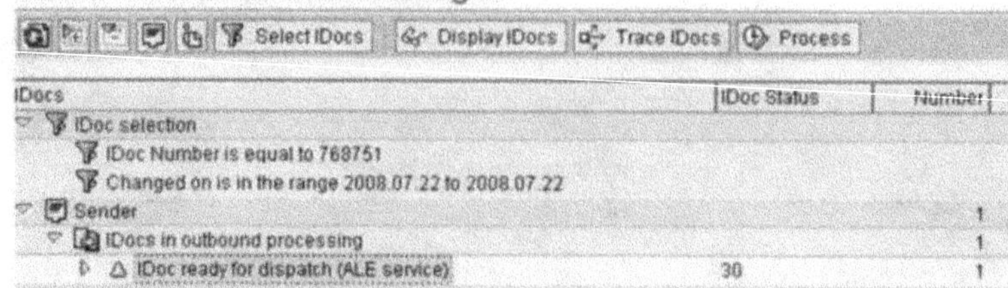

Click on Process

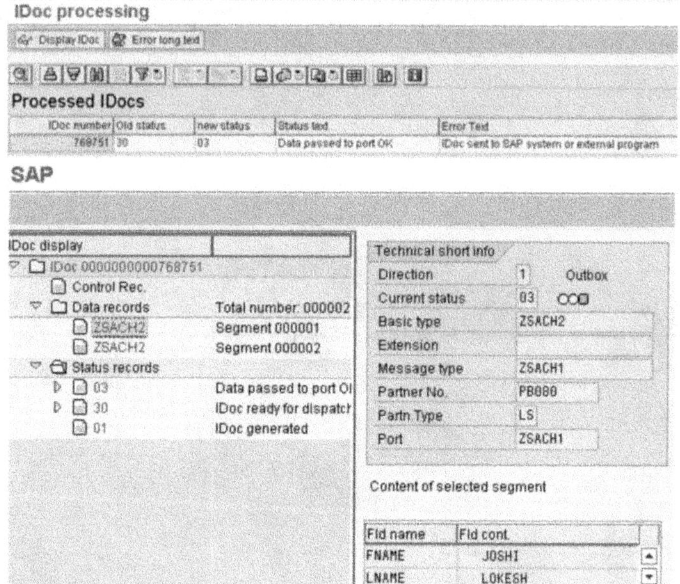

Checking the data on the Receiver end

Check table: ZSACH1

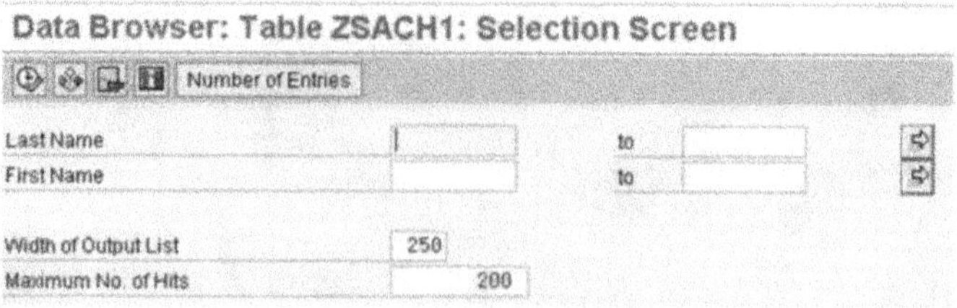

No table entries found for specified key

T-code: WE05

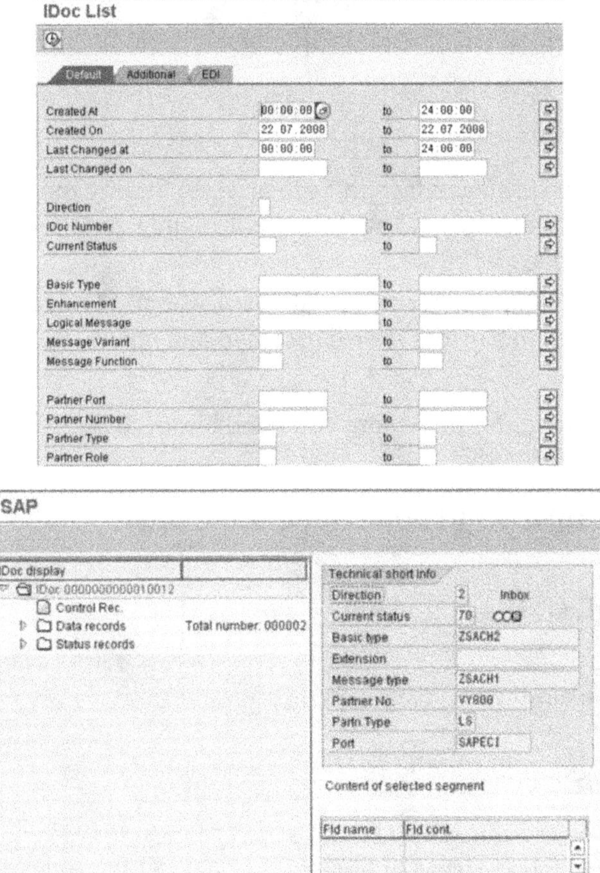

Checking the Database

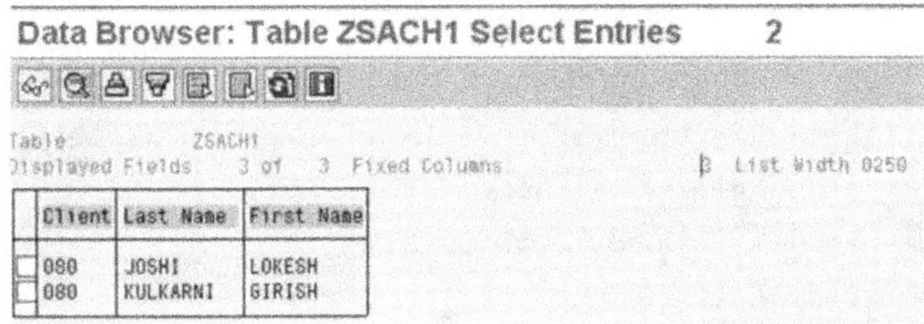

Client	Last Name	First Name
080	JOSHI	LOKESH
080	KULKARNI	GIRISH

This way, the data has come to the receiver end successfully.

Congratulations as You are IDoc expert now.

18.15. IDOC Outbound Error scenarios

18.15.1. Overview

This document can be used as a fast utility in order to localize the source of a problem and resolve it locally at source. The document is only confined to outbound idoc creation and sending.

The purpose of this document is to explain how ALE and EDI configuration is done within a R/3 box, and how errors are reprocessed and possibly escalated.

To read and understand this document you need basic SAP ALE skills.

18.15.2. Out bound Error categorization

18.15.2.1. IDOC status

These sections explain the IDOC statuses.

18.15.2.2. Error status

Most common errors are marked in Blue.

Status	SAP Description
02	Error passing data to port
04	Error within control information of EDI subsystem
05	Error during translation
07	Error during syntax check
09	Error during interchange handling
11	Error during dispatch
20	Error triggering EDI subsystem
21	Error passing data for test
23	Error during retransmission
25	Processing despite syntax error (outbound)

And.

26	Error during syntax check of IDoc (outbound)
27	Error in dispatch level (ALE service)
29	Error in ALE service
31	Error-no further processing
34	Error in control record of Idoc

18.15.3. Status to be processed

The list below contains status' in which the IDOC is awaiting to get processed. If an IDOC gets stuck in one of these statuses for too long (more than a few hours) this may indicate a potential problem.

Status	Direction	Description
30	Outbound	Idoc ready for dispatch (ALE service)

However, status 03 is a success status. It just has not been confirmed from the middleware or receiving SAP system yet.

18.15.4. Success status

The list below contains some successful IDOC statuses.

Status	Direction	Description
03	Outbound	Data passed to port OK
12	Outbound	Dispatch OK
41	Outbound	Application document created in target system

18.16. Common List of problems

18.16.1. Missing or faulty partner profiles

IDOC status 29 partner profile could be inactive or missing.

How to check partner profile is present or missing?

Transaction WE20. Check for partner you are interested to send the message. If it is not present, then one need to maintain the partner profile.

Example: We are trying to find if message type ADRMAS is maintained against the partner G15DVRH402.

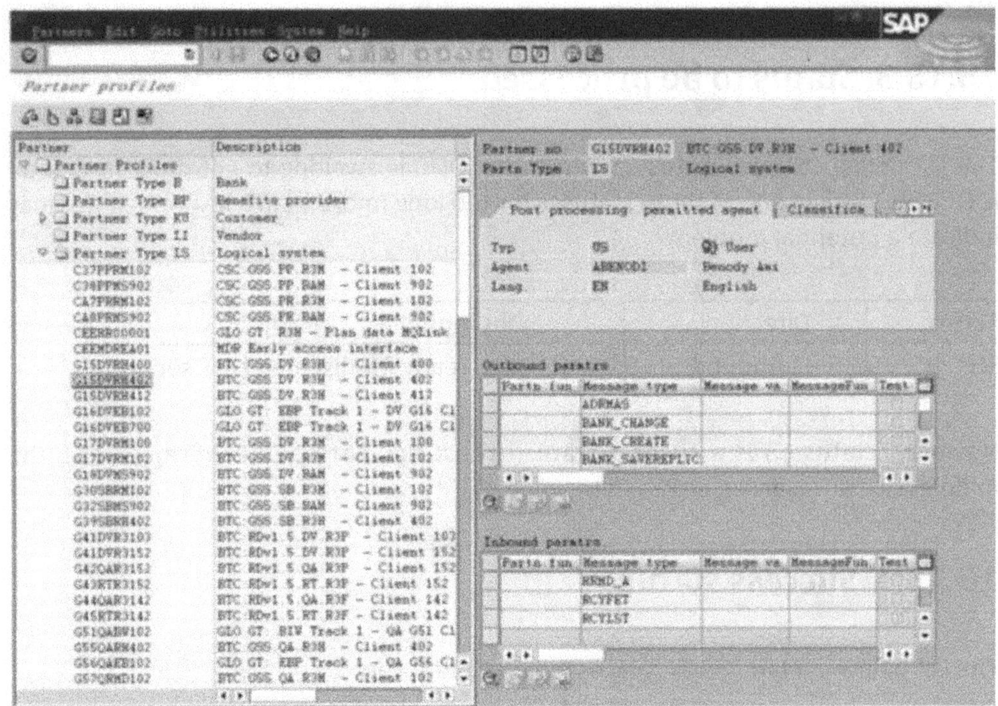

Some time it is difficult to find the partner profile, as it may be a long list of partners; in that case: Transaction SE16.

Table name: EDP13. (Partner Profile: Outbound)

Example: We are trying to find if message type ADRMAS is maintained against the partner G15DVRH402.

In Selection screen please input your Partner number to get the corresponding message type.

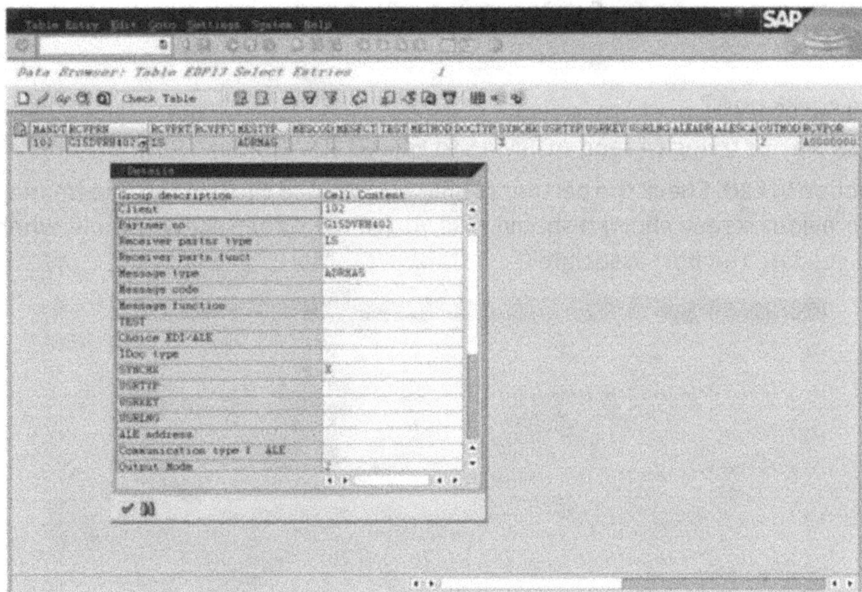

How to check Partner profile is Active or inactive?

Transaction **WE20.** Check for partner you are interested to send the message. If the partner profile is maintained, then go to the **classification tab** and check for the partner status, **it should be 'A'**.

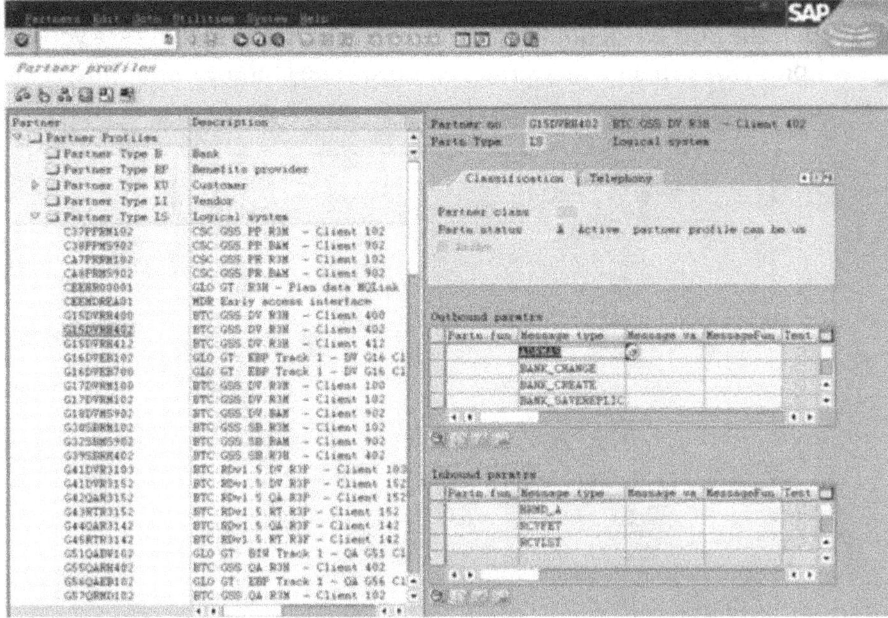

18.16.2. Missing or faulty ports.

How to check port?

Suppose we are trying to send ADRMAS to HR (G15DVRH402).

Transaction WE20. Check the partner profile and **double click on the line** (market blue in the previous screen short) It should take you to the screen shown below, where you should validate the port associated.

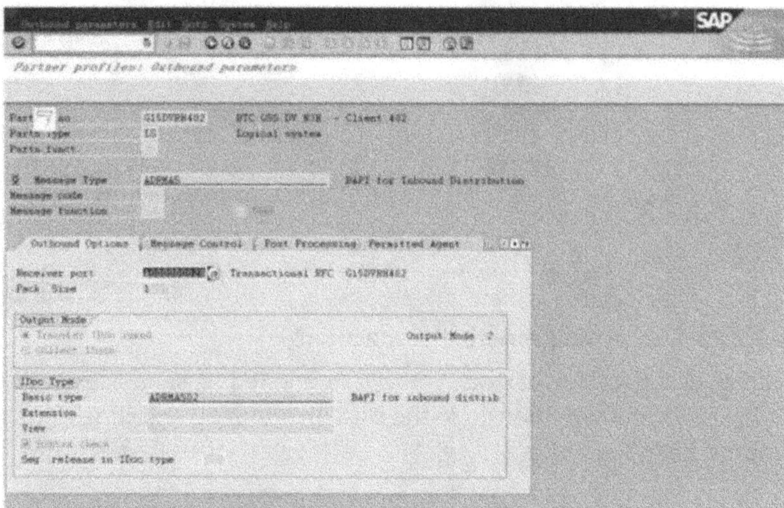

It may happen the port is not pointing to the correct system. In that case you need to change the port. You can also check the ports available in transaction WE21.

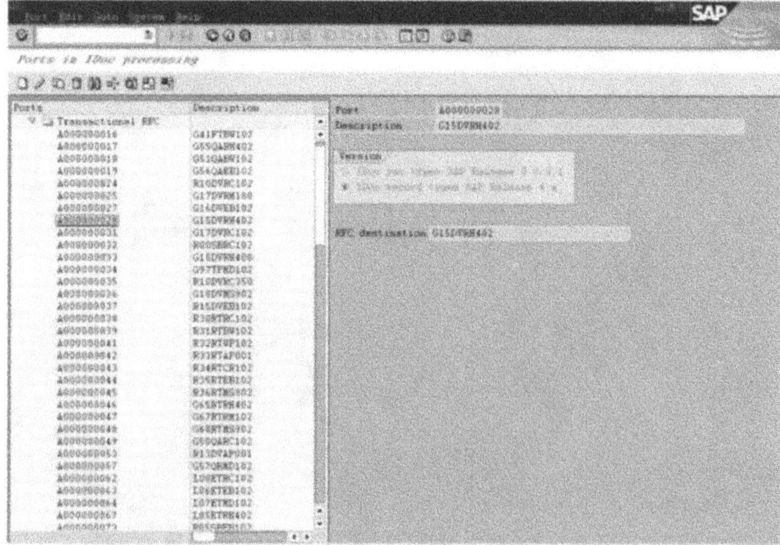

18.16.3. RFC destination related problem.

The port is associated with the RFC destination.

RFC calls that fail, or are recorded due to a heavy load on the system, end up in the RFC queue. Table ARFCSSTATE. Some entries in the RFC queue are IDOC related, some workflow related and others originate from various transactions that use cross systems communication.

Below is a list of common RFC errors.

18.16.3.1. "Transaction recorded"

This happens when the system is busy and is forced to record the function call instead of executing it.

18.16.3.2. "Transaction executing"

If a transaction is executing indefinitely, it is considered to be an error.

18.16.3.3. "RFC destination WORKFLOW_LOCAL does not exist"

This happens when the workflow configuration is not complete and the system tries to generate workflow events.

18.16.3.4. Name or password is incorrect. Please re-enter

The RFC destination has a faulty user name or password.

18.16.3.5. RFC destination XYZ does not exist

The port on the partner profile points to a faulty RFC destination.

18.16.3.6. Partner not reached (host ABC)

The receiving partner does not respond.

18.16.3.7. Connection to host XYZ timed out

The function call took too long to execute.

18.16.3.8. Program MQLINK123 not registered (This is for V 1.0 only)

The program used in the RFC destination (SM59) is wrong or has not been registered yet.

18.16.3.9. Program XXXXXX not registered" (This is for V 1.5 SAP BC)

18.16.3.10. Load distribution problems.

Sometimes the load distribution causes problems in RFC destinations. You can switch it off temporarily. Please note that this is a temporary solution, a request should be raised in MySap to set the load balancing in SM59 for the RFC connection, which is linked to your port in the previous step.

18.16.3.11. RFC destination missing

Check in SM59, provided you are given access. Contact BASIS team to resolve he problem.

18.16.4. Faulty Central User Administration (CUA) configuration.

For example, you might have to re-distribute the distribution model from the management station in transaction SCUA.

18.16.5. IDOC syntax errors.

This is due to the setting made in the partner profile one should not remove it to avoid the problem. It will cause problem at the receiving end.

IDOC status 26. If a system creates an IDOC extension that is unknown, or if a mandatory segment is missing or the IDOC was created with the wrong extension, or the some for the segments which was not supposed to be repeated has repeated itself.

18.16.5.1. Wrong extension.

Check for the extension maintained in the partner profile. For example, Message type HRMD_A, basic type HRMD_A05 with extension ZRMD_A0502 should be maintained as:

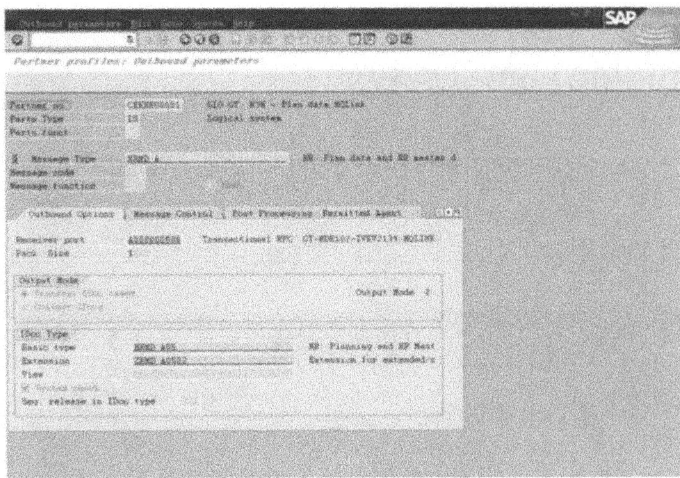

We need to check the settings in WE82; this should match with the settings in the partner profile.

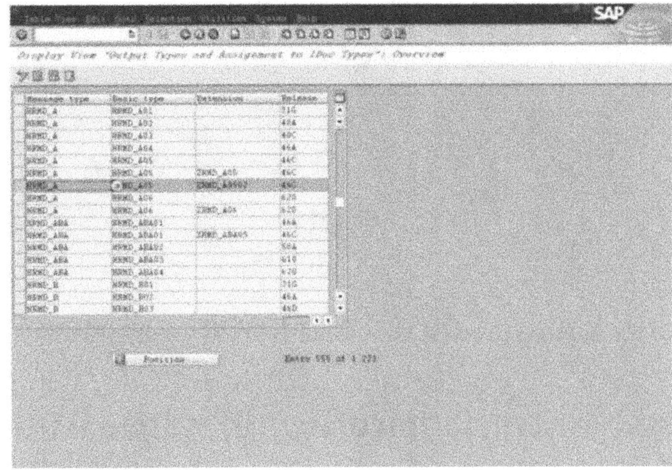

When all the settings are correct then there is a potential problem in the custom dev, Raise an alarm to the CD team.

18.16.6. Missing global company code configuration.

Raise a request to the Functional team to maintain it. IDOC status 29. If the cross system company code is not configured for the company code in the change pointer document, an IDOC is created but cannot be submitted.

18.16.7. Missing logical systems.

Check in transaction BD54, for the logical system, which you are interested to send.

Example screen shot below.

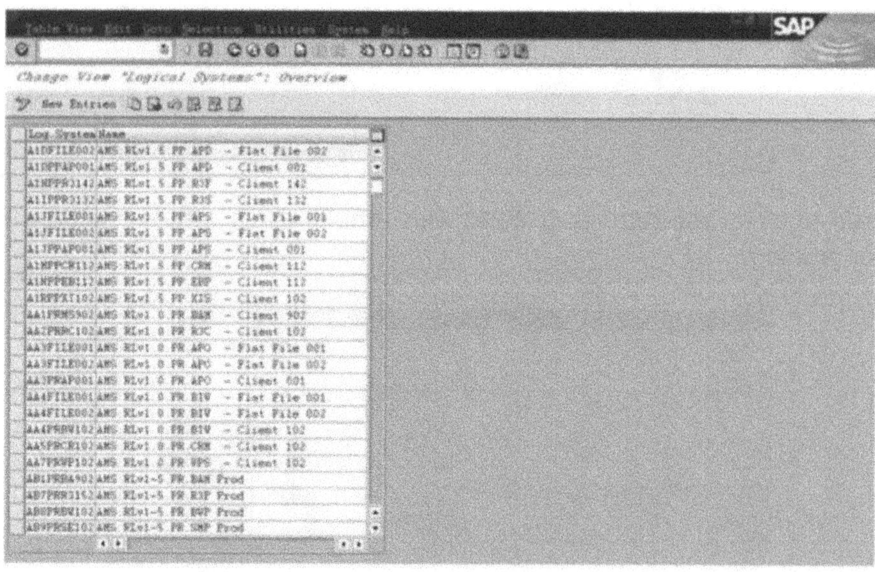

On not finding the system a request should be send to the BASIS team.

18.16.8. Missing association of logical system with the client. Or SCC4 transaction

Check the following: -

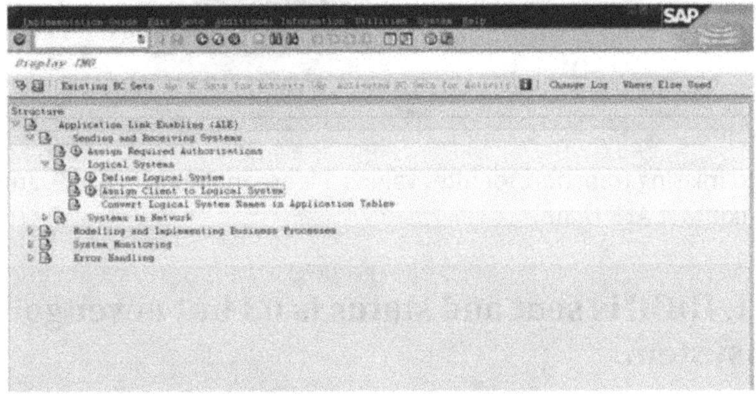

On not finding the entries, please inform the Basis team.

18.16.9. Problem related to batch jobs.

These are created by Basis, but the Cross Applications Support team creates the program variants.

Idocs never created irrespective of all the settings, then check the batch jobs (SM36/ SM35).

- The batch job is missing for that message type.
- Other processes that use all system resources or lock the tables have delayed the batch job.
- The batch job fails due to program errors in the function module that processes change pointers for that message type.
- The job fails due to unknown reasons, check the update log SM13.
- Sometimes job fails due to data issues or long date range issues.

Contact the ALE team for missing batch jobs. Contact the CD team for program error.

18.16.10. Object type yyyy not maintained for the message type xxxx

Please find the screen shot.

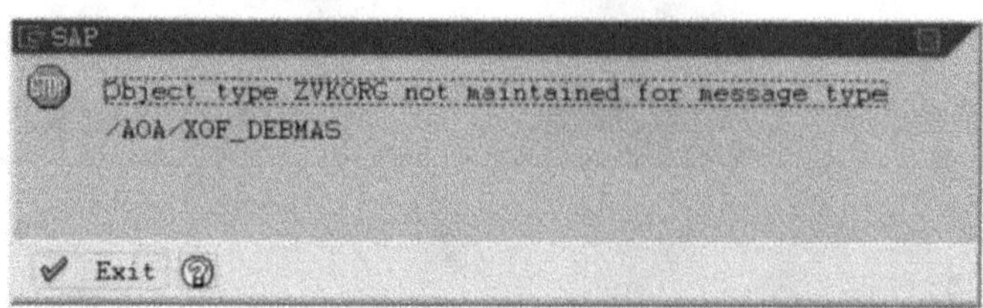

This is due to missing transport for filter values. Please maintain in BD59, and transport it. For help contact ALE team.

18.16.11. IDOC is sent and status is 03 but never goes out of the SAP system.

Also, in most components we do not execute BD75 (RBDMOIND – status conversion with successful tRFC execution)

Check BD75 transaction.

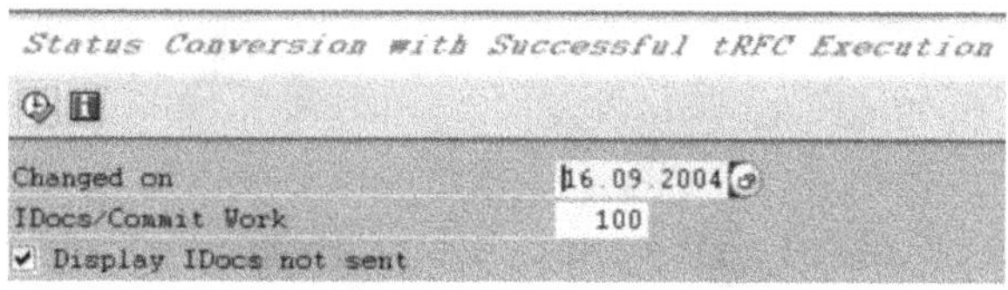

Press F8.

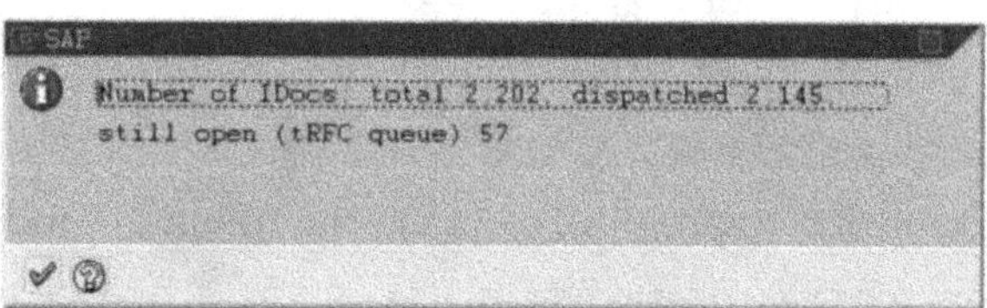

You can see the idocs still in the tRFC queue.

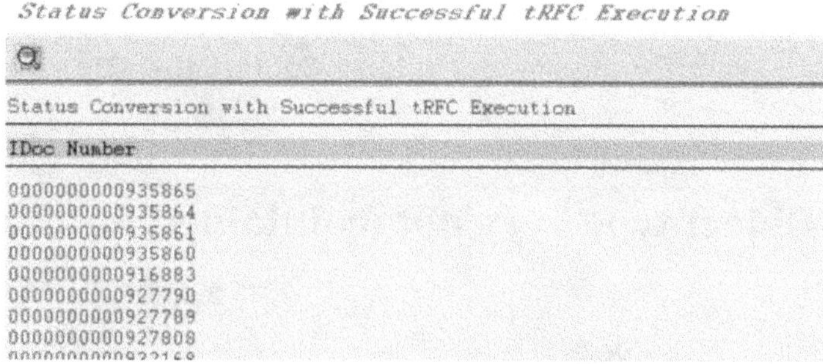

Double click on a line to get the details of the idoc.

You can check this in SM58 (Transactional RFC) also.

SKALRA	ARCHIV_CREATE_TABLE_MULT	NONE	16.09.2004	08:49:35	Error in HTTP Access: IF_HTTP_CLIENT->R
SKALRA	ARCHIV_CREATE_TABLE_MULT	NONE	16.09.2004	08:49:35	Error in HTTP Access: IF_HTTP_CLIENT->R

You may get message like program xxxxxxx not registered. Raise a request to the basis team to register the program.

18.17. Problem Specific to Master data distribution

18.17.1. Missing or faulty distribution models.

How to Check?

Transaction BD64.

Example: If we want to send message type ZMATMAS from G17DVRM102 to RD2DVR3172 then we need to click on the model, which has the structure as shown below:

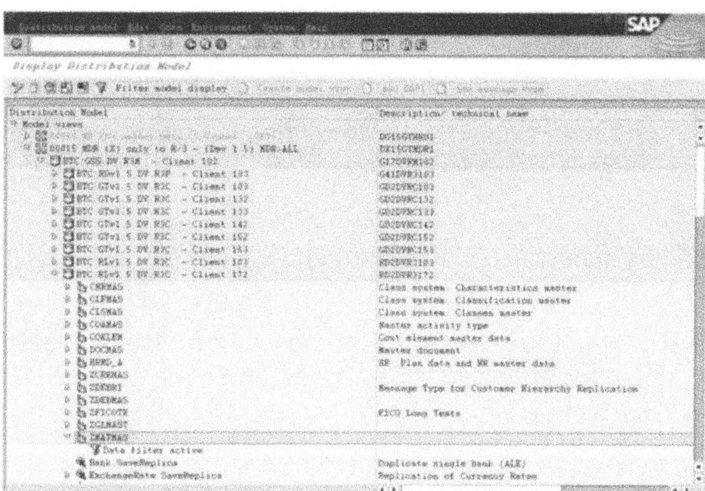

At times it is very difficult to find from BD64 if your model is maintained due to 100's of entries.

The alternate way is to run function module from **SE37 " ALE_MODEL_INFO_GET"**,with the search parameters namely **message type and receiving system name**.

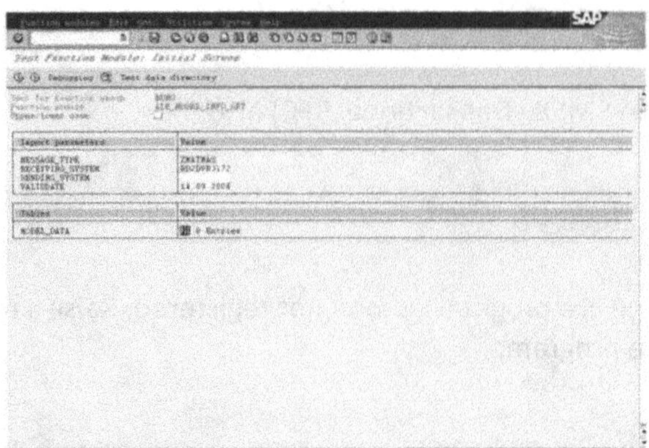

You will get the following information:

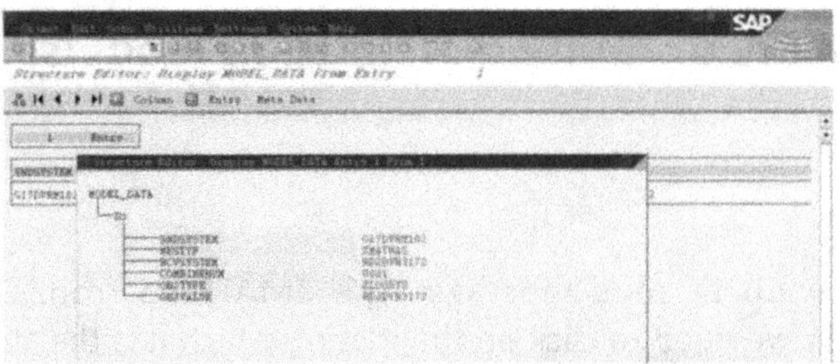

If the return is empty, then the model is not maintained. Raise a MySap Request to the ALE team.

Partner Profile, Ports, RFC destination and distribution model maintained but Idocs are not getting created! **Then check for the filters?**

Check for the filters maintained in the distribution model.

In the previous screenshot you can see a filter is maintained. The filter object is ZLOGSYS and the filter value is RD2DVR3172. So when the filed value is not RD2DVR3172, the communication idoc will not get created.

Another example of filters:

For Message type HRMD_A, sending system G17DVRM102 to receiving system GTEDVMQ001.

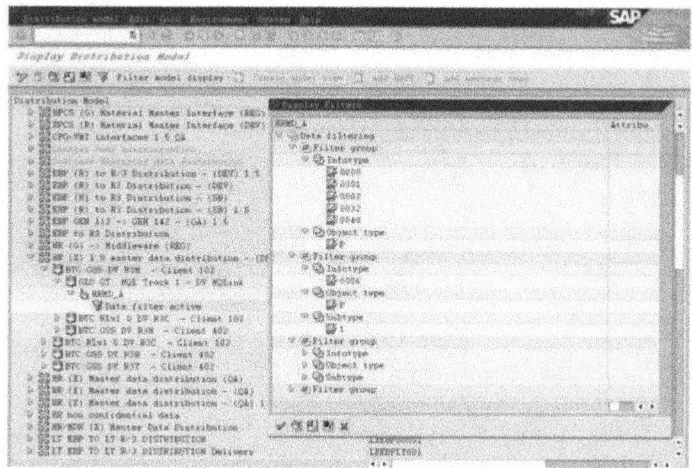

18.17.2. Change Pointer related problems

Nobody should execute this manually in Production, since you might disrupt serialization!

All unprocessed change pointers can be processed manually in BD21, or **in batch by creating a job in SM36.** If the processing still does not take place, there must be a technical error, like a faulty message type or function module.

If it turns out that the change pointers were lost due to a technical error or similar, you must inform the interface owner and possibly also distribute the affected master data objects through the standard master data distribution transactions **(BD10 - sending Material, BD12– sending Customersetc.).**

Check the global change pointer setting. **BD61. When the check box is off, change pointers will not get created for any message type from your system.** Contact ALE team to change it and transport it.

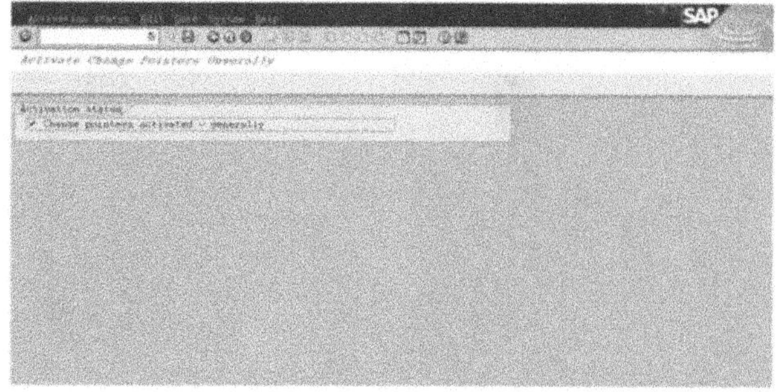

Check for individual message type settings. Transaction BD50.

The message type, which should create the change pointer entries, should be marked.

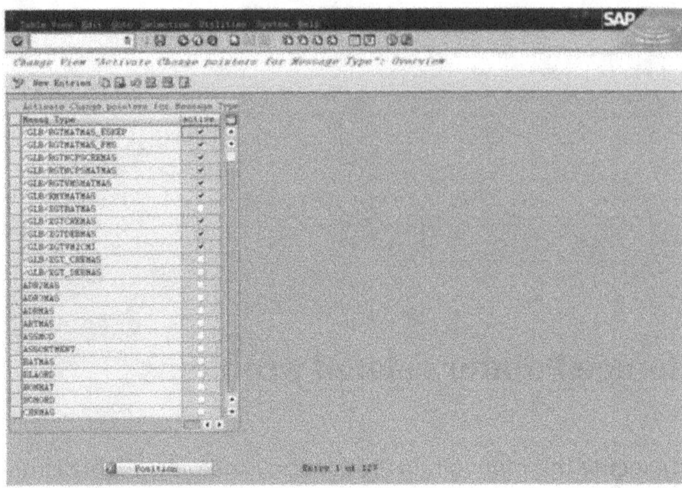

If this is not marked: Contact the ALE team, to change it and transport it.

We should get values in the view BDCPV, on changing the respective master data. But we are not.

Check BD52. The fields you have changed must be maintained here: Example of message type ZMATMAS.

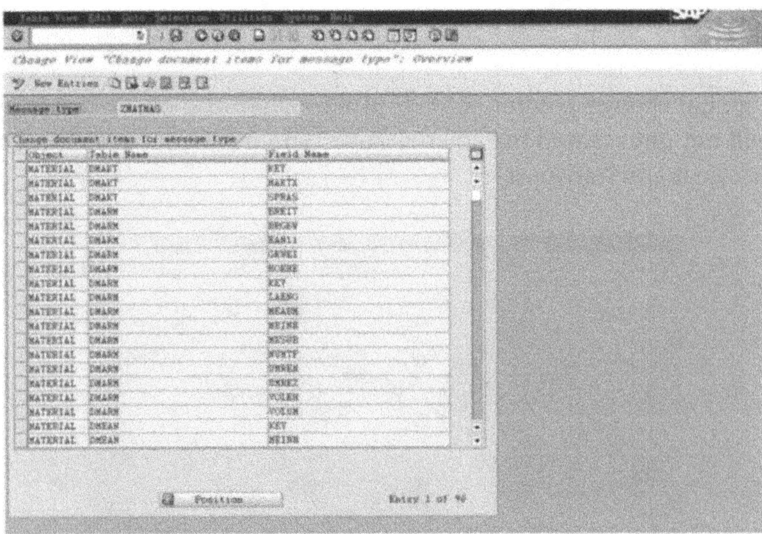

Contact CD team to maintain it and transport it again.

On running BD21 or RBDMIDOC the idoc is not getting created.(Don't do it in Production)

Check **BD60. The relevant message type should be configured with the function module, which creates the idoc.**

For example, message type /GLB/XGTVMICMI is associated with function module / GLB/XGT_MASTIDOC_VMICMI_SMD.

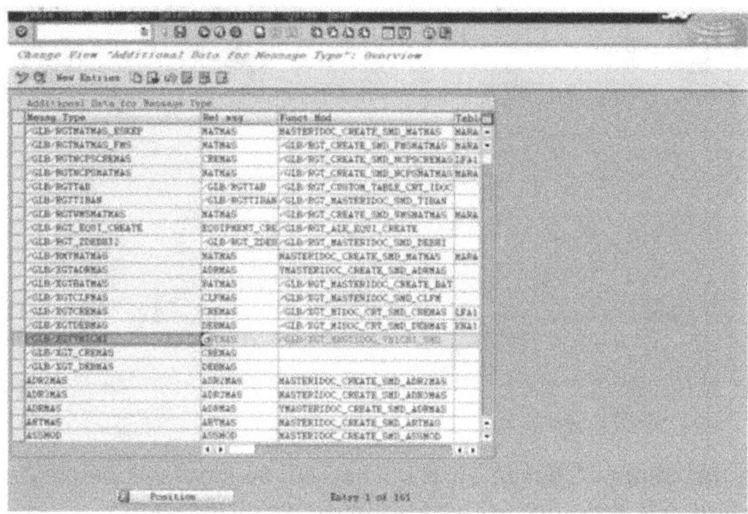

Inform the CD team to configure the same and transport it, provided it is not in place. If the entire is present then we should check distribution model, partner profiles.

18.18. Problem Specific to Transaction data distribution

This section cannot be generic - This is really specific to the type of transactional data we are intending to trigger.

Below section should be considered as an example scenario.

Generally, in most of the cases the idoc don't get created e.g. the communication idoc never getting created. It can be due to various reasons. We take up the most generic cases.

18.18.1. Idoc gets created on changing the document but not when we create a document or vice versa.

For example, when we create a Delivery: Dispatch order (SHPORD) and change it, we want an idoc to be created, but it is not happening.

Check the partner profile

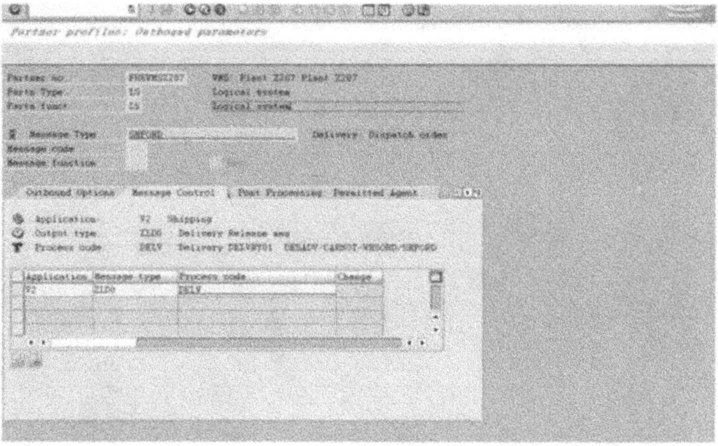

Please note the column "change", it is unchecked. So idocs will be created when an order is created, but it will not get created when we change it.

Resolution: One more line of entry is required as shown below.

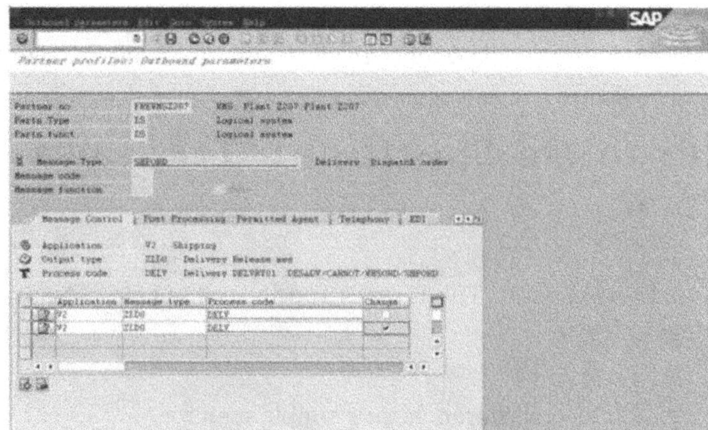

18.18.2. Condition record not maintained

Transaction nace.

(Continuing with the previous example)

Check the application V2 as it is maintained in your partner profile.

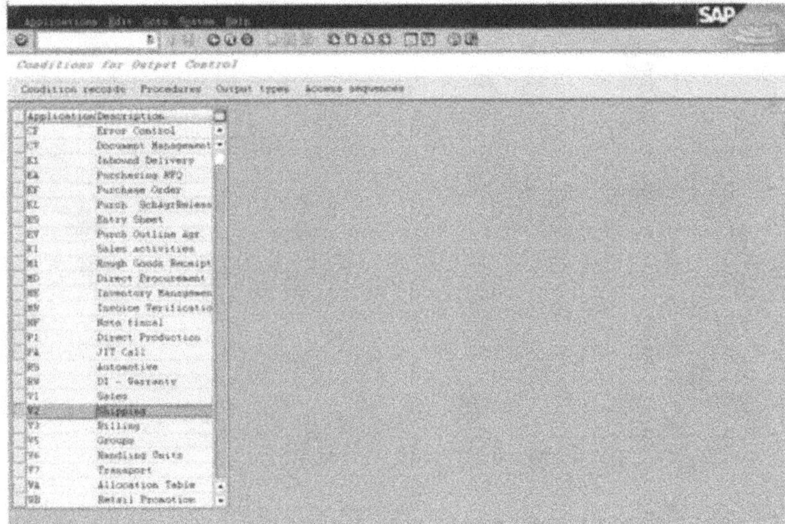

Click on condition record to get

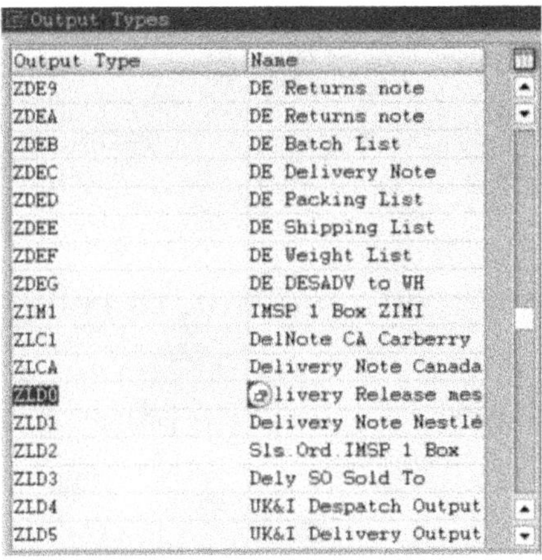

Output Types

Output Type	Name
ZDE9	DE Returns note
ZDEA	DE Returns note
ZDEB	DE Batch List
ZDEC	DE Delivery Note
ZDED	DE Packing List
ZDEE	DE Shipping List
ZDEF	DE Weight List
ZDEG	DE DESADV to WH
ZIM1	IMSP 1 Box ZIMI
ZLC1	DelNote CA Carberry
ZLCA	Delivery Note Canada
ZLD0	livery Release mes
ZLD1	Delivery Note Nestlé
ZLD2	Sls.Ord.IMSP 1 Box
ZLD3	Dely SO Sold To
ZLD4	UK&I Despatch Output
ZLD5	UK&I Delivery Output

Double click on ZLD0, as it is maintained in you partner profile.

Press enter to cross verify the values maintained against the partner.

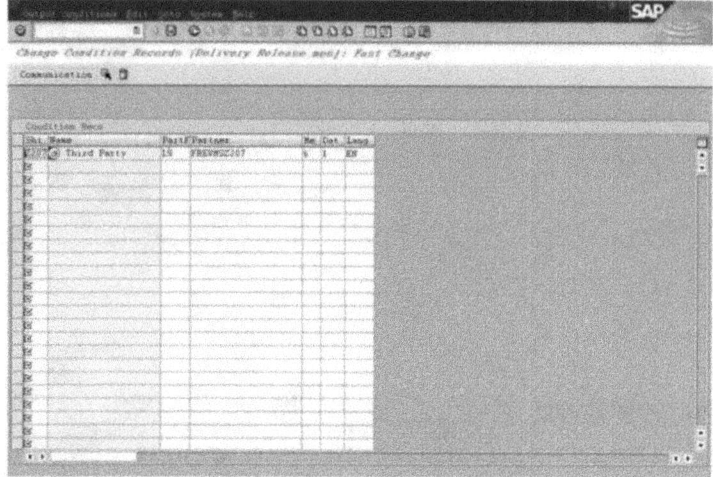

So this will get created against Shipping point Z200 and for partner FREWMSZ207 with medium EDI and periodically transferred.

For the shipping point, which is not maintained, the output type will not be proposed so the idoc will not get created. Contact the functional owner to arrange for the entries.

Alternate way to check. Go to the table NAST.

Give KAPPL = V2 and KSCHL = ZLDO (as per previous example). Check the entries in the field VSTAT:0 not processed, 1 Successfully processed, 2 Incorrectly processed.

18.18.3. Output not proposed due to requirement routine.

Check the requirement routine associated with your procedure in transaction NAST. (As per previous example).

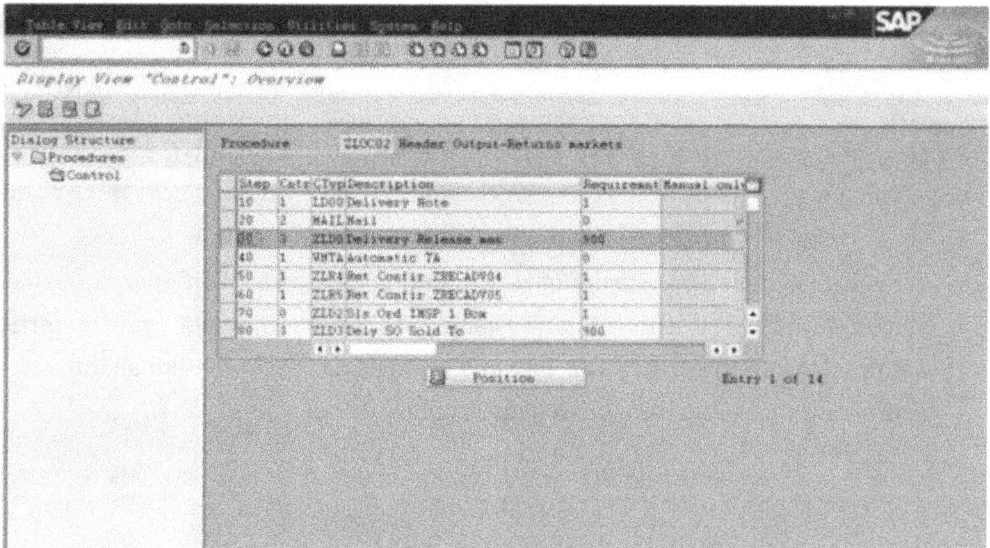

Pick up the requirement routine and go to transaction VOFM ->Requirements->Output control.

The requirement routine is 900 as per previous example. The CD team should check the code.

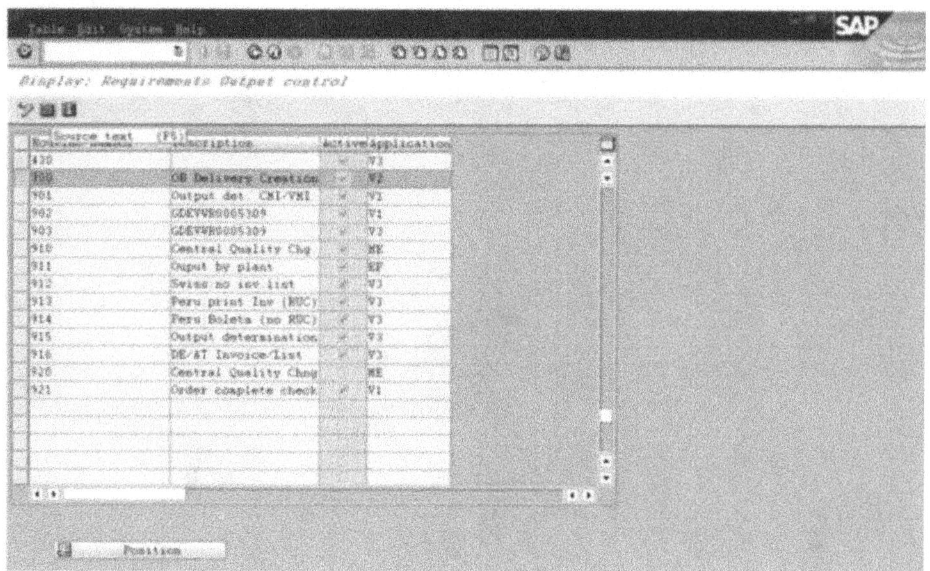

Specific scenarios

In one EDI outbound Interface mandatory Segment E1EDP28 was not Populating in Invoice (915538283) for Failed Idoc '1101942853'. We have Checked the Successful Idoc '1102061994' in EBI Within Segment 'E1EDP28' where the below field 'EXNUM' is populating fine for Invoice '915538398'.But for failed Idoc, 1101942853 for the Invoice '915538283' the field 'EXNUM' is being populated blank.So, this is not a Program Issue, this is Data Issue.

2. Whenever order or invoice or delivery is getting created by IDOC then some field values are missing or some quantity values are coming wrong or some materials are missing. It is due to program bug and we need to check whether all the logical expression operators have been used properly or not.

CHAPTER 19

LSMW

19.1 What is LSMW

LSMW stands for Legacy system migration workbench. It is a tool that supports the transfer of data from non-SAP systems to SAP. This can be a one-time transfer as well as a periodic one.
This also supports conversion of data of the legacy system in numerous way. The data can then be imported into SAP via batch input, direct input, BAPIs or IDocs.
Furthermore, the LSM Workbench provides a recording function that allows generating a "data migration object" to enable migration from any required transaction.
It is a component of the R/3 System and, therefore, is independent from the platform.

The data is loaded via the standard interfaces of the applications. This will include all checks that are run for online transactions. Invalid data will be rejected.

R/3 release 3.0F , 3.1x: version 1.0 of LSMW
R/3 release 4.0x, 4.5x , 4.6x : version 1.6 and 1.7 of LSMW

19.2 Core Functions of LSMW

- Importing legacy data from PC spreadsheet tables or sequential files.
- Converting data from its original (legacy system) format to the target (R\3) format.
- Importing the data using standard interfaces of R\3 (IDOC inbound processing, batch input , direct input).

19.3. Which data can be migrated using LSMW

- By means of standard transfer programs: a wide range of master data (e.g. G/L accounts , customer master , vendor master , material master) and transaction data (e.g. financial documents , sales order)

- By means of recording of transactions: further data objects (if the transaction can be run in batch input mode).

19.4. How LSMW works

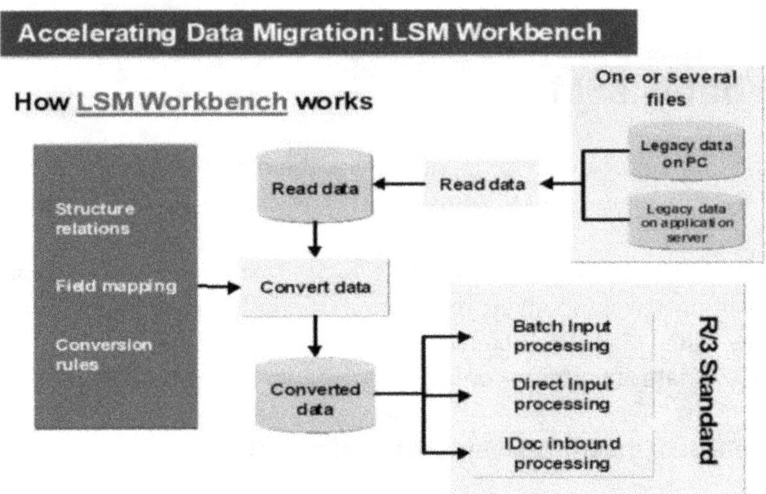

19.5. The main advantages of the LSM Workbench

- Part of R/3 and thus independent of individual platforms
- A variety of technical possibilities of data conversion:
- Data consistency due to standard import techniques:

  - o -Batch input
  - o -Direct input
  - o -BAPIs (Business Application Programming Interfaces)
  - o -IDocs (Intermediate Documents)

- Generation of the conversion program on the basis of defined rules
- Clear interactive process guide
- Interface for data in spreadsheet format

- Creation of data migration objects on the basis of recorded transactions
- Charge-free for SAP customers and SAP partners

Prior to using LSMW, it is recommended to perform some conceptual tasks.

19.6. Process Flow

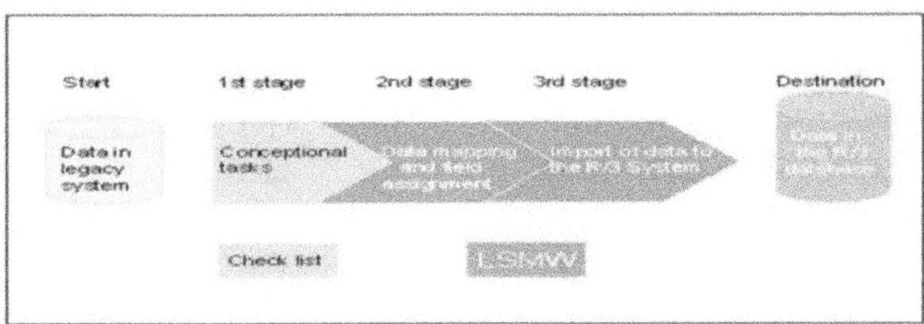

The following should be taken into account:

- Make sure that the R/3 Customizing has been completed.
- Analyse the data that exists in your legacy system (LS) and which of it (from a business point of view) will be required in the future as well.
- Identify the transaction(s) in the R/3 System that you want to use to transfer the data to this system.
- Process the respective transaction in R/3 manually using test data of the legacy system and note which fields must be filled. Maybe there are required fields that do not correspond to a data field in the legacy system. In this case, assigning a fixed value or constant or setting up a field as an optional field perhaps is useful for the data transfer.
- Carry out mapping on paper, that is, allocate the source fields and R/3 fields to each other. You can do this by using the object overview after you defined the object.
- Determine the conversion rule according to which the field contents of the source fields are to be converted into R/3 fields.
- Define the way in which the data is to be extracted from the non-SAP system. (Note: The LSMW does not extract any data itself.)
- Which format does the legacy data have? Decide which standard import technique you want to use, or if you should define an extra "object class" by means of recording.

- In case only a part of your legacy system is to be replaced with the R/3 System, you have to determine the functions that are to be covered by the R/3 System and those to be covered by the legacy system. If necessary, a concept of the data flows and interface architecture has to be created.

19.7. Objects of LSMW

Some objects that are of special significance for data migration with the LSMW are explained at the beginning of the documentation, even before the procedure for Migration of Legacy System Data Using LSMW is described.

- o Project
- o Sub project
- o Object
- o Structure relationships
- o Field assignments.

19.8. DEMO 1 - Step by Step LSMW Creation(Material Master) and Major tips/Precautions

LSMW stands for Legacy system migration workbench. It is a tool that supports the transfer of data from non-SAP systems to SAP. This can be a one-time transfer as well as a periodic one.

This also supports conversion of data of the legacy system in numerous way. The data can then be imported into SAP via batch input, direct input, BAPIs or IDocs.

Furthermore, the LSM Workbench provides a recording function that allows generating a "data migration object" to enable migration from any required transaction.

Step1: Creation of Project, Sub project and Object

Using Method "Batch Input recording"

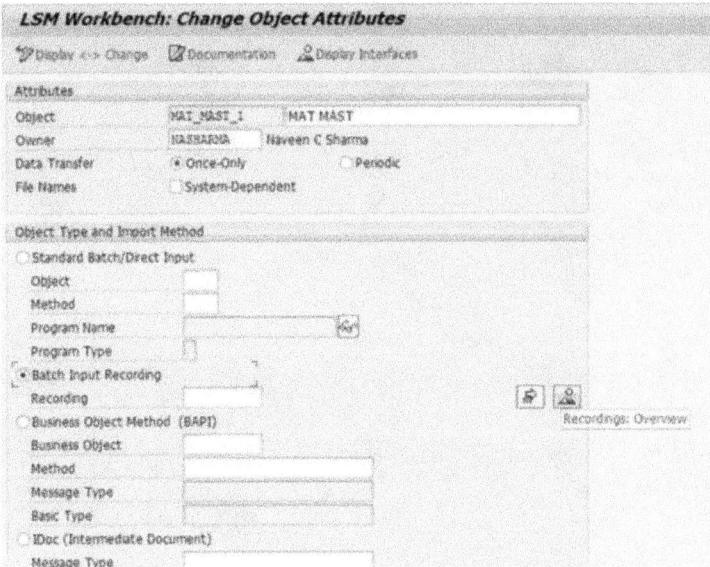

LSM Workbench: Change Object Attributes

Display <-> Change Documentation Display Interfaces

Attributes

Object MAT_MAST_1 MAT MAST

Owner NASHARMA Naveen C Sharma

Data Transfer Once-Only Periodic

File Names System-Dependent

Object Type and Import Method

Standard Batch/Direct Input

Object

Method

Program Name

Program Type

Batch Input Recording

Recording

Recordings: Overview

Business Object Method (BAPI)

Business Object

Method

Message Type

Basic Type

IDoc (Intermediate Document)

Message Type

Started the Recording Process – Recording Name and Description

Provide the Transaction Code.

Actual Recording of MM01.

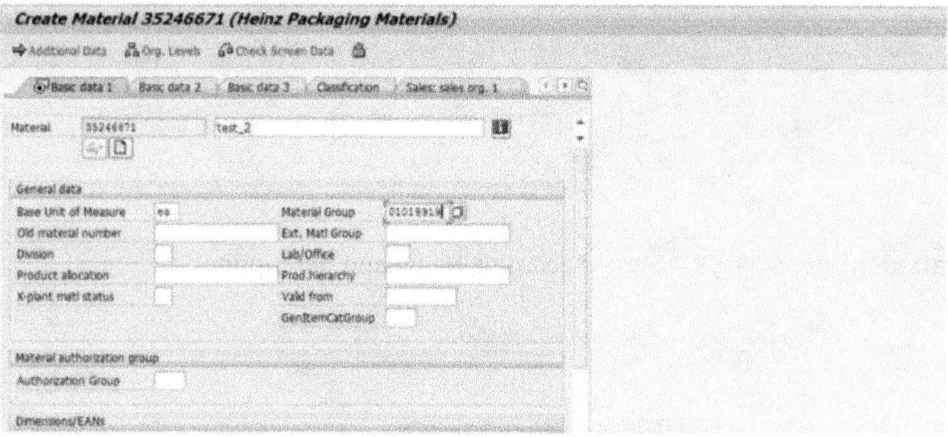

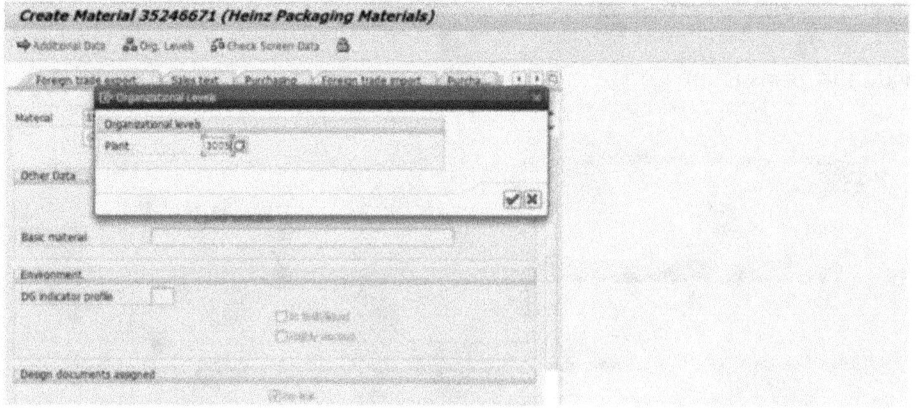

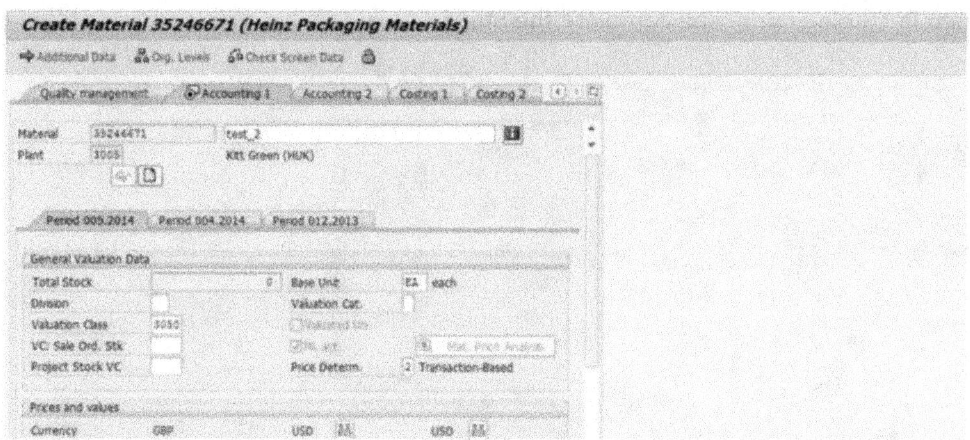

After Recording will come to this Screen wherein it shows the field name and Values.

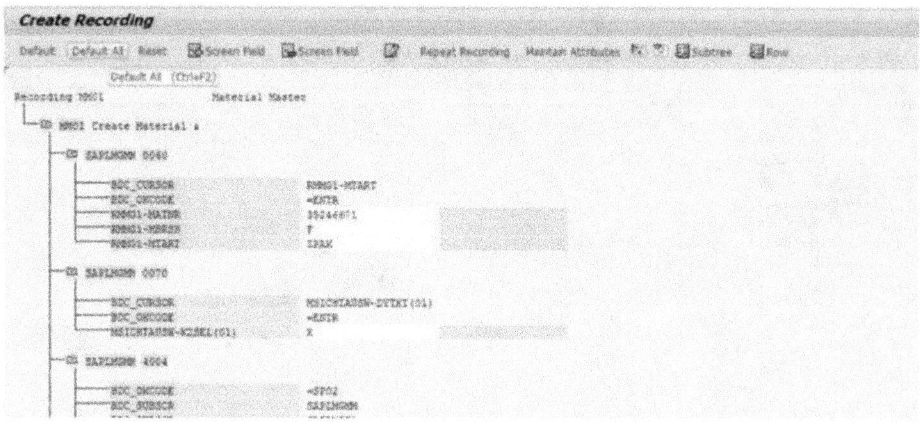

As a next step, should select option as “Default All”.

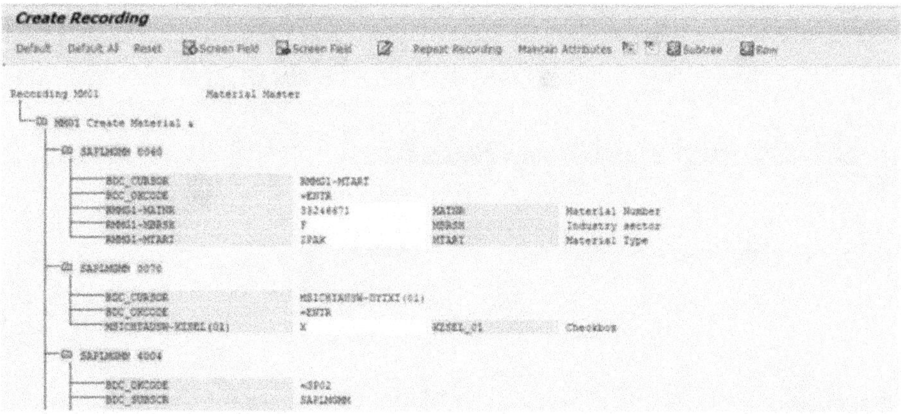

Then Recording name and complete the Step1.

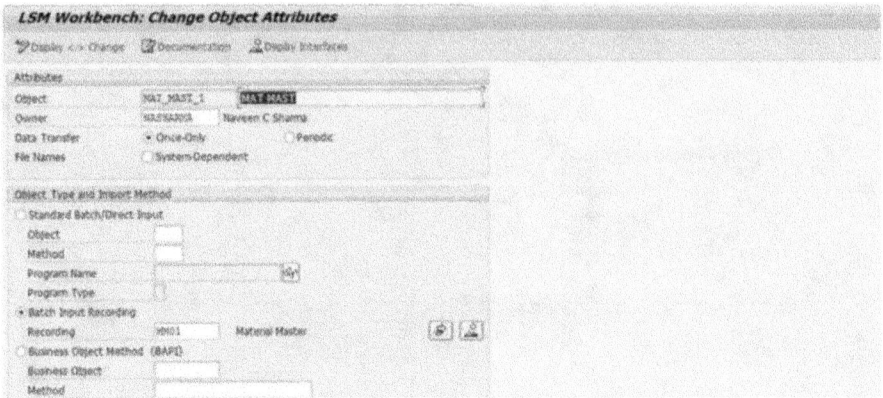

Step2: Maintain Source Structure

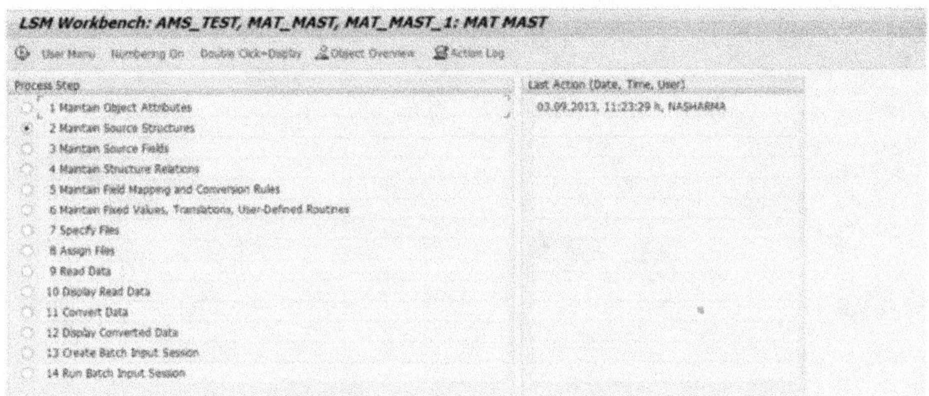

Creation of Source Structure – Provide the logical name.

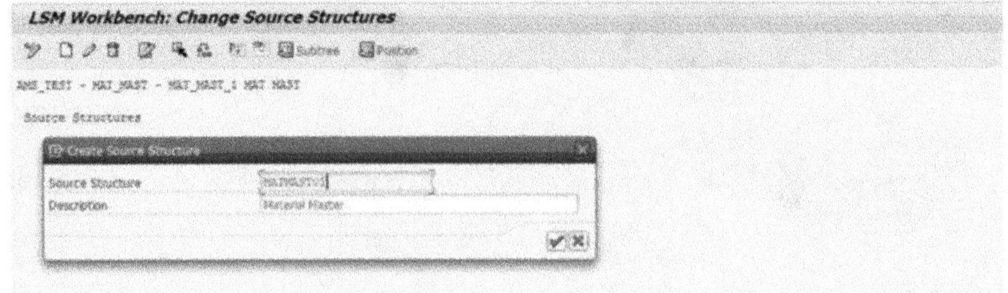

LSM Workbench: Change Source Structures

Subtree Position

AMS_TEST - MAT_MAST - MAT_MAST_1 MAT MAST

Source Structures

MATMAST01 Material Master

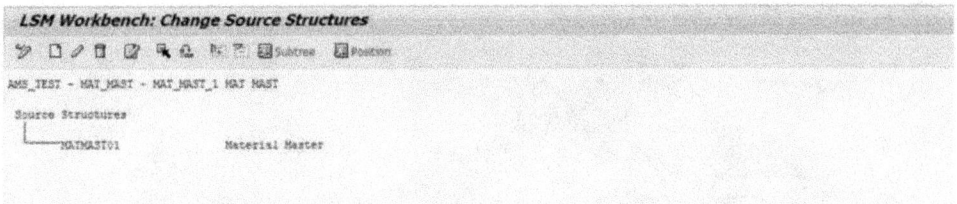

Step3: Maintain Source Field

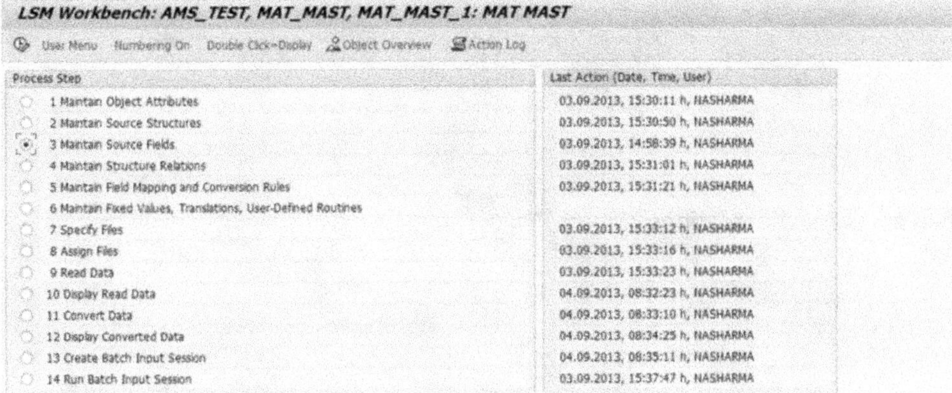

Take the field name from Step1 and maintain under table maintenance view.

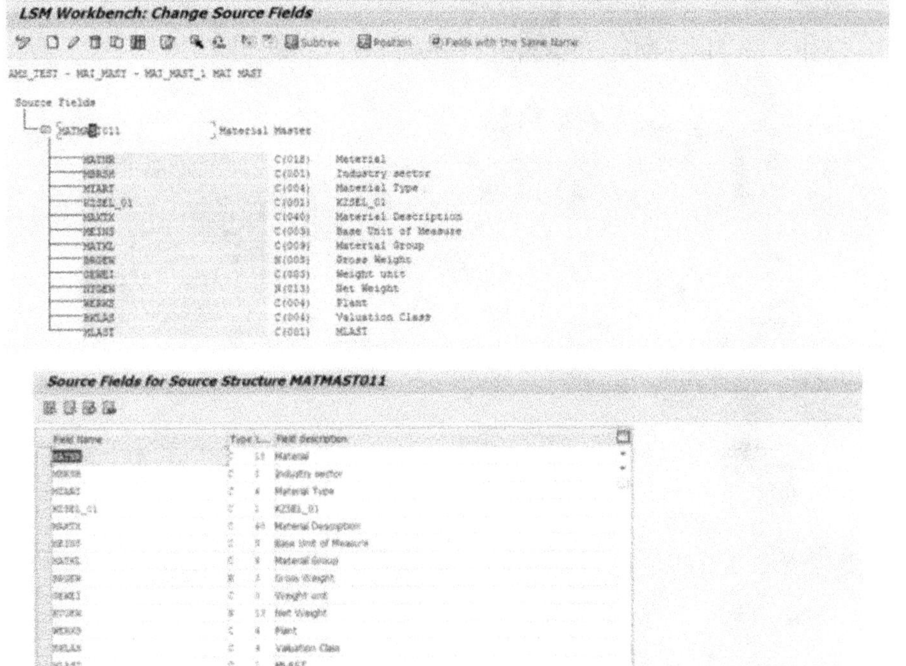

Step4: Maintain Structure Relations

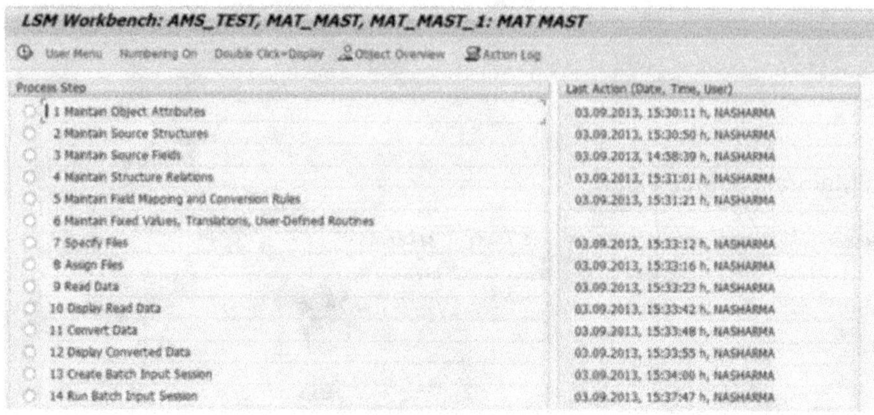

Open and save the relations.

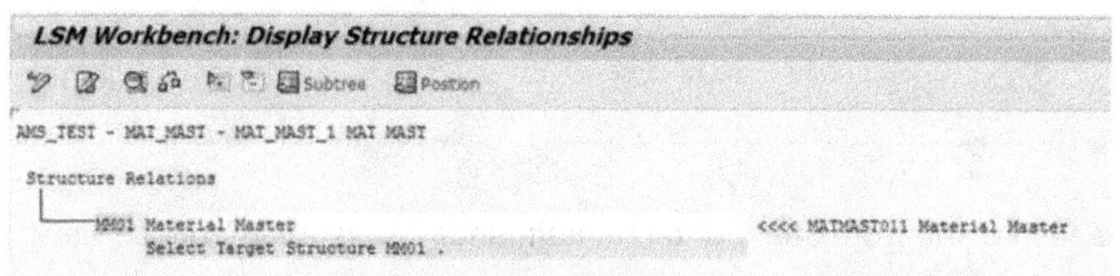

Step 5: Maintain Field Mapping and Conversion Rules

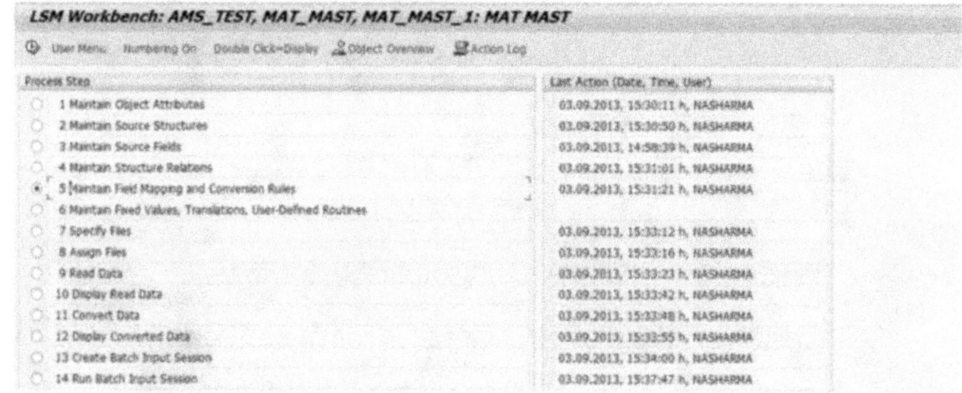

Take the Auto-Field mapping option and complete the Field mapping.

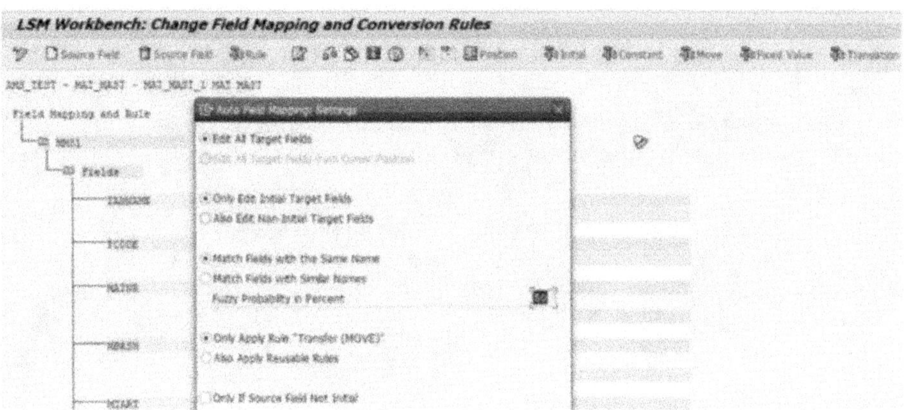

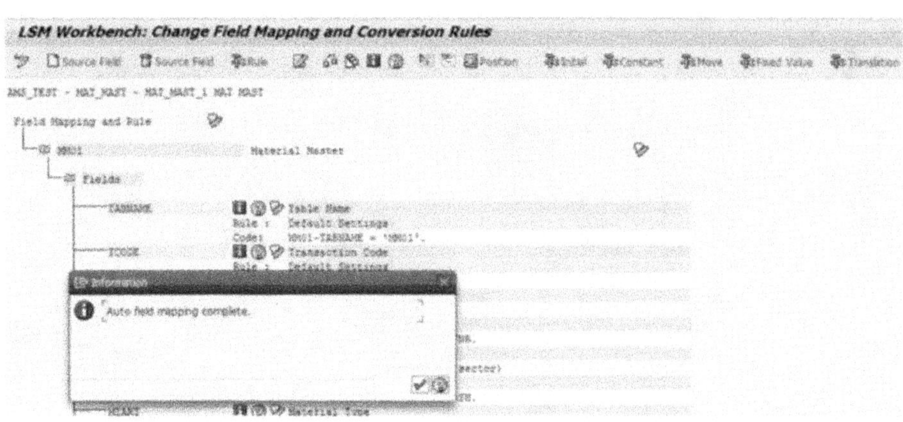

Step 6: Maintain Fixed Values, Translations, User-Defined Routines

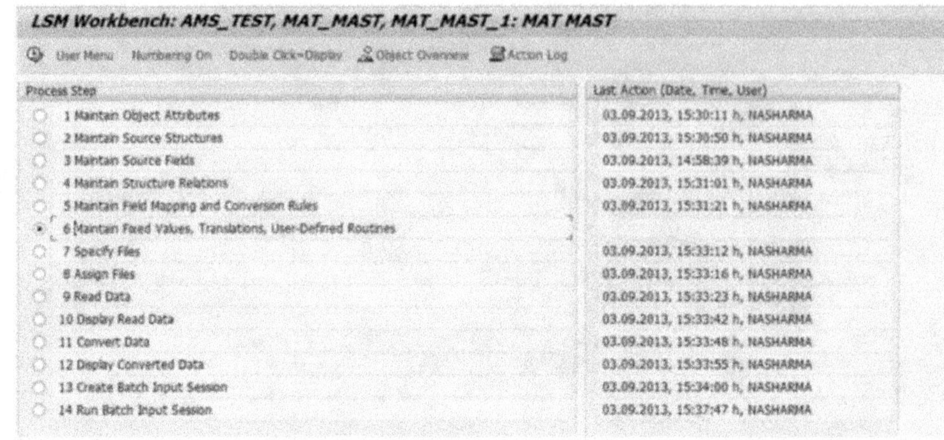

Process Step	Last Action (Date, Time, User)
1 Maintain Object Attributes	03.09.2013, 15:30:11 h, NASHARMA
2 Maintain Source Structures	03.09.2013, 15:30:50 h, NASHARMA
3 Maintain Source Fields	03.09.2013, 14:58:39 h, NASHARMA
4 Maintain Structure Relations	03.09.2013, 15:31:01 h, NASHARMA
5 Maintain Field Mapping and Conversion Rules	03.09.2013, 15:31:21 h, NASHARMA
6 Maintain Fixed Values, Translations, User-Defined Routines	
7 Specify Files	03.09.2013, 15:33:12 h, NASHARMA
8 Assign Files	03.09.2013, 15:33:16 h, NASHARMA
9 Read Data	03.09.2013, 15:33:23 h, NASHARMA
10 Display Read Data	03.09.2013, 15:33:42 h, NASHARMA
11 Convert Data	03.09.2013, 15:33:48 h, NASHARMA
12 Display Converted Data	03.09.2013, 15:33:55 h, NASHARMA
13 Create Batch Input Session	03.09.2013, 15:34:00 h, NASHARMA
14 Run Batch Input Session	03.09.2013, 15:37:47 h, NASHARMA

If want to fixed any value, please check.

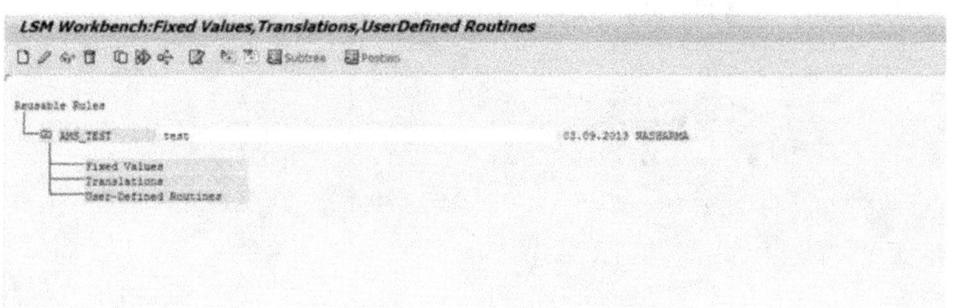

Step7: Specify Files

Process Step	Last Action (Date, Time, User)
1 Maintain Object Attributes	03.09.2013, 15:30:11 h, NASHARMA
2 Maintain Source Structures	03.09.2013, 15:30:50 h, NASHARMA
3 Maintain Source Fields	03.09.2013, 14:58:39 h, NASHARMA
4 Maintain Structure Relations	03.09.2013, 15:31:01 h, NASHARMA
5 Maintain Field Mapping and Conversion Rules	03.09.2013, 15:31:21 h, NASHARMA
6 Maintain Fixed Values, Translations, User-Defined Routines	
7 Specify Files	03.09.2013, 15:33:12 h, NASHARMA
8 Assign Files	03.09.2013, 15:33:16 h, NASHARMA
9 Read Data	03.09.2013, 15:33:23 h, NASHARMA
10 Display Read Data	03.09.2013, 15:33:42 h, NASHARMA
11 Convert Data	03.09.2013, 15:33:48 h, NASHARMA
12 Display Converted Data	03.09.2013, 15:33:55 h, NASHARMA
13 Create Batch Input Session	03.09.2013, 15:34:00 h, NASHARMA
14 Run Batch Input Session	03.09.2013, 15:37:47 h, NASHARMA

Select the file from Desktop.

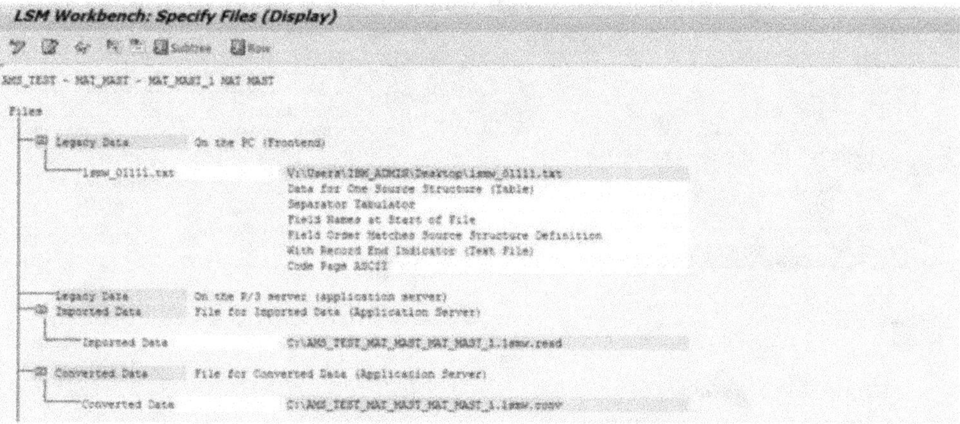

Step8: Assign Files

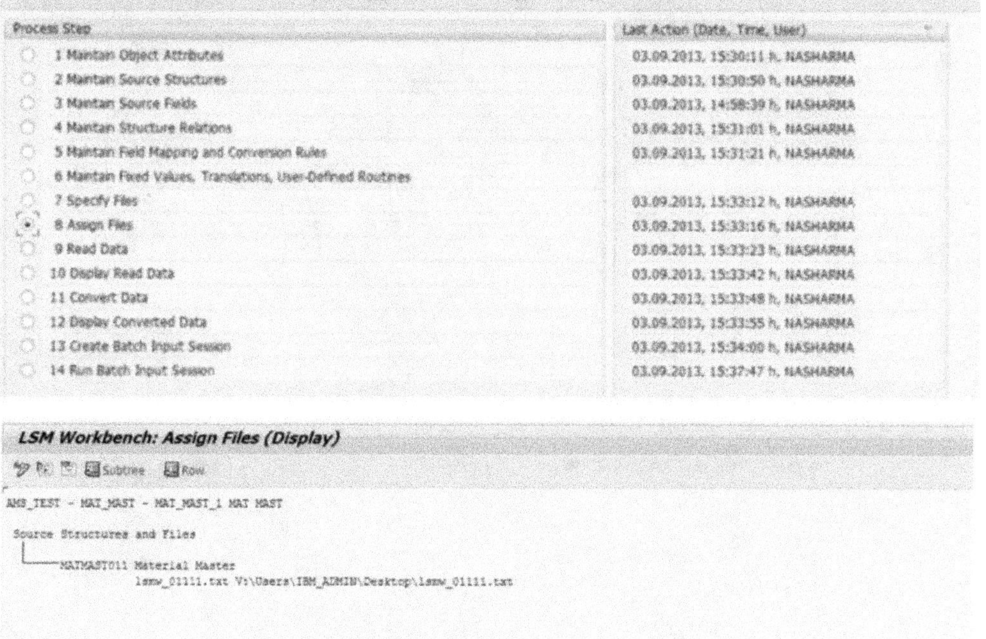

Step 10: Display Read Data

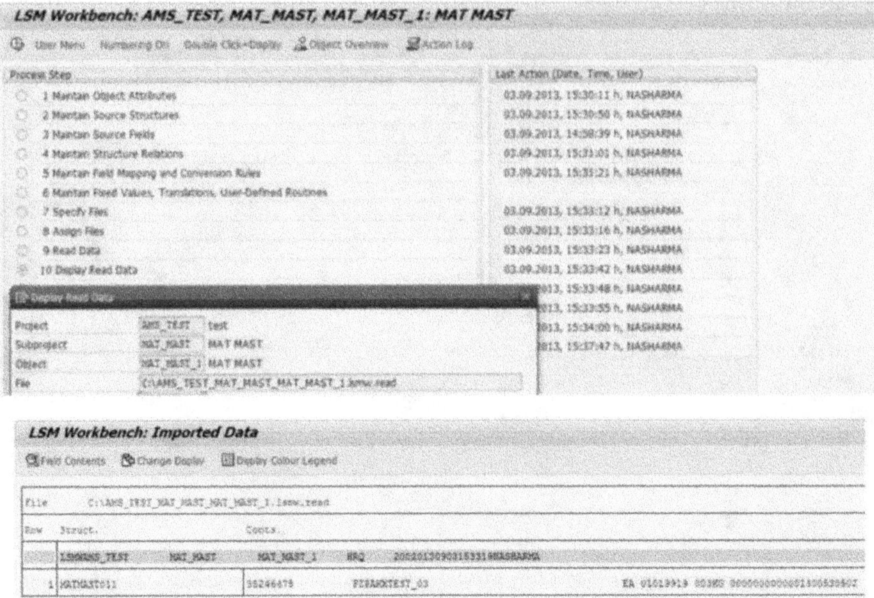

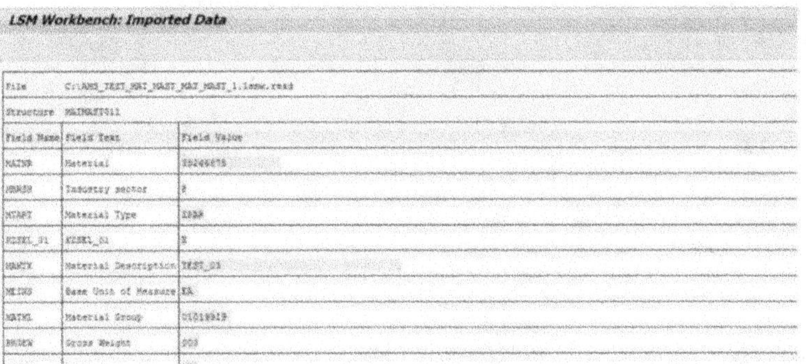

View the real data and check whether correct values are populating.

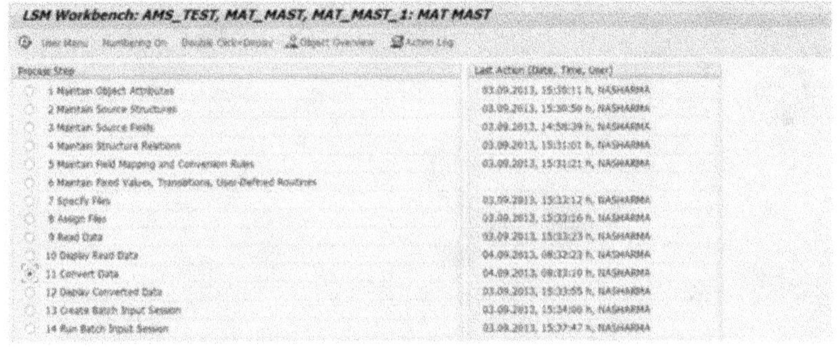

Step11: Convert Data

LSM Workbench: Convert Data For AMS_TEST, MAT_MAST, MAT_MAST_1

General Selection Parameter

Transaction Number [ ] to [ ]

LSM Workbench: Convert Data For AMS_TEST, MAT_MAST, MAT_MAST_1

```
LSM Workbench: Convert Data For AMS_TEST, MAT_MAST, MAT_MAST_1

04.09.2013 - 08:33:01

File Read:        C:\AMS_TEST_MAT_MAST_MAT_MAST_1.lsmw.read
File Written:     C:\AMS_TEST_MAT_MAST_MAT_MAST_1.lsmw.conv

Transactions Read:          1
Records Read:               1
Transactions Written:       1
Records Written:            1
```

Step12: Display Converted Data

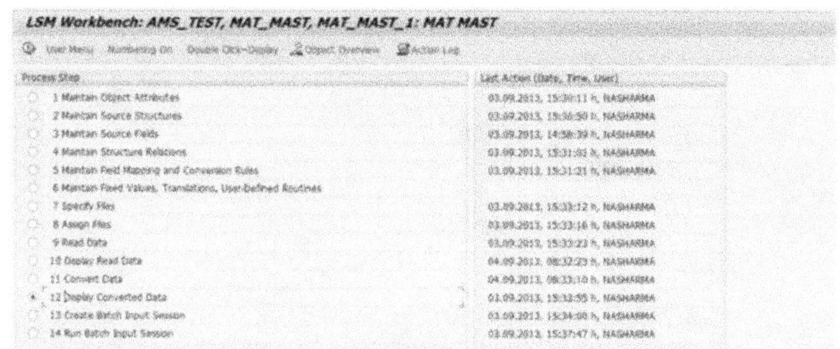

LSM Workbench: AMS_TEST, MAT_MAST, MAT_MAST_1: MAT MAST

User Menu   Numbering On   Double Click=Display   Object Overview   Action Log

Process Step	Last Action (Date, Time, User)
1 Maintain Object Attributes	03.09.2013, 15:30:11 h, NASHARMA
2 Maintain Source Structures	03.09.2013, 15:30:50 h, NASHARMA
3 Maintain Source Fields	03.09.2013, 14:58:39 h, NASHARMA
4 Maintain Structure Relations	03.09.2013, 15:31:01 h, NASHARMA
5 Maintain Field Mapping and Conversion Rules	03.09.2013, 15:31:21 h, NASHARMA
6 Maintain Fixed Values, Translations, User-Defined Routines	
7 Specify Files	03.09.2013, 15:33:12 h, NASHARMA
8 Assign Files	03.09.2013, 15:33:16 h, NASHARMA
9 Read Data	03.09.2013, 15:33:23 h, NASHARMA
10 Display Read Data	04.09.2013, 08:32:23 h, NASHARMA
11 Convert Data	04.09.2013, 08:33:10 h, NASHARMA
12 Display Converted Data	03.09.2013, 15:33:55 h, NASHARMA

Display Converted Data

Project	AMS_TEST	test
Subproject	MAT_MAST	MAT MAST
Object	MAT_MAST_1	MAT MAST
File	C:\AMS_TEST_MAT_MAST_MAT_MAST_1.lsmw.conv	
From Line		
To Line		

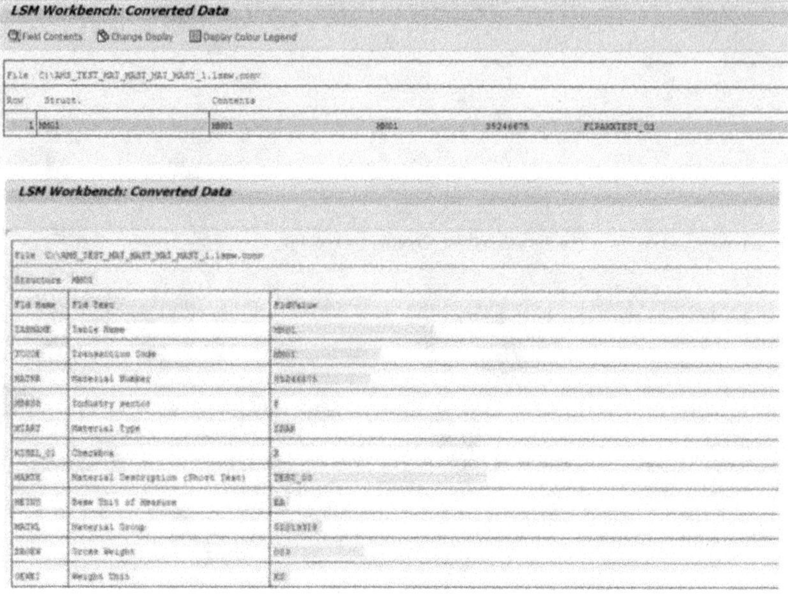

Step 13: Create Batch Input Session

LSM Workbench: AMS_TEST, MAT_MAST, MAT_MAST_1: MAT MAST

Process Step	Last Action (Date, Time, User)
1 Maintain Object Attributes	03.09.2013, 15:30:11 h, NASHARMA
2 Maintain Source Structures	03.09.2013, 15:30:50 h, NASHARMA
3 Maintain Source Fields	03.09.2013, 14:58:39 h, NASHARMA
4 Maintain Structure Relations	03.09.2013, 15:31:01 h, NASHARMA
5 Maintain Field Mapping and Conversion Rules	03.09.2013, 15:31:21 h, NASHARMA
6 Maintain Fixed Values, Translations, User-Defined Routines	
7 Specify Files	03.09.2013, 15:33:12 h, NASHARMA
8 Assign Files	03.09.2013, 15:33:16 h, NASHARMA
9 Read Data	03.09.2013, 15:33:23 h, NASHARMA
10 Display Read Data	04.09.2013, 08:32:23 h, NASHARMA
11 Convert Data	04.09.2013, 08:33:10 h, NASHARMA
12 Display Converted Data	04.09.2013, 08:34:25 h, NASHARMA
13 Create Batch Input Session	03.09.2013, 15:34:00 h, NASHARMA
14 Run Batch Input Session	03.09.2013, 15:37:47 h, NASHARMA

LSM Workbench: Generate Batch Input Folder

File Name (with Path)
Display Trans. per BI Folder
Name of Batch Input Folder(s) MAT_MAST_1
User ID
Keep batch input folder(s)?

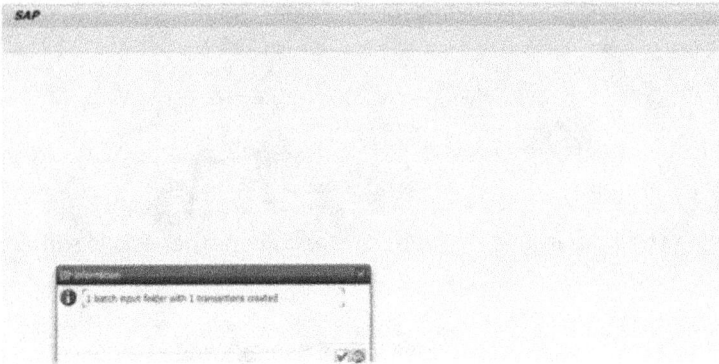

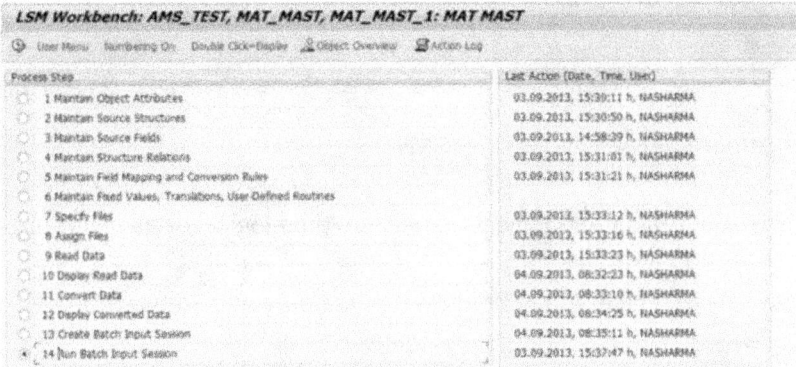

Step 14: Run Batch Input Session

LSM Workbench: AMS_TEST, MAT_MAST, MAT_MAST_1: MAT MAST

User Menu | Numbering On | Double Click=Display | Object Overview | Action Log

Process Step	Last Action (Date, Time, User)
1 Maintain Object Attributes	03.09.2013, 15:30:11 h, NASHARMA
2 Maintain Source Structures	03.09.2013, 15:30:50 h, NASHARMA
3 Maintain Source Fields	03.09.2013, 14:58:39 h, NASHARMA
4 Maintain Structure Relations	03.09.2013, 15:31:01 h, NASHARMA
5 Maintain Field Mapping and Conversion Rules	03.09.2013, 15:31:21 h, NASHARMA
6 Maintain Fixed Values, Translations, User-Defined Routines	
7 Specify Files	03.09.2013, 15:33:12 h, NASHARMA
8 Assign Files	03.09.2013, 15:33:16 h, NASHARMA
9 Read Data	03.09.2013, 15:33:23 h, NASHARMA
10 Display Read Data	04.09.2013, 08:32:23 h, NASHARMA
11 Convert Data	04.09.2013, 08:33:10 h, NASHARMA
12 Display Converted Data	04.09.2013, 08:34:25 h, NASHARMA
13 Create Batch Input Session	04.09.2013, 08:35:11 h, NASHARMA
14 Run Batch Input Session	03.09.2013, 15:37:47 h, NASHARMA

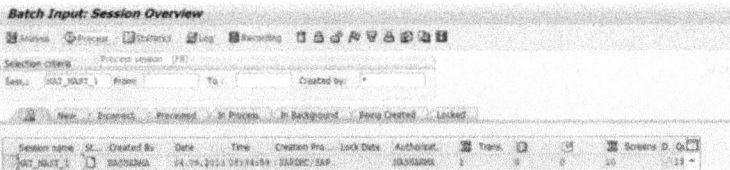

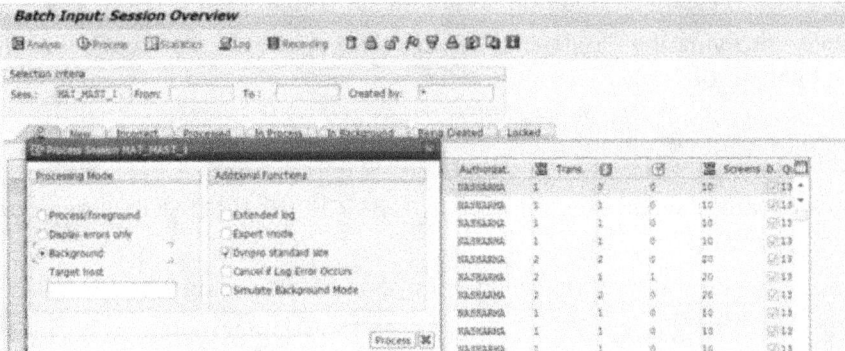

Batch Input: Session Overview

Analysis | Process | Statistics | Log | Recording

Selection criteria

Sess.: MAT_MAST_1 From: To: Created by: *

New | Incorrect | Processed | In Process | In Background | Being Created | Locked

Batch Input: Session Overview

Analysis | Process | Statistics | Log | Recording

Selection criteria

Sess.: MAT_MAST_1 From: To: Created by: *

Process Session MAT_MAST_1

Processing Mode: Process/foreground, Display errors only, Background, Target host

Additional Functions: Extended log, Expert mode, Dynpro standard size, Cancel if Log Error Occurs, Simulate Background Mode

Process

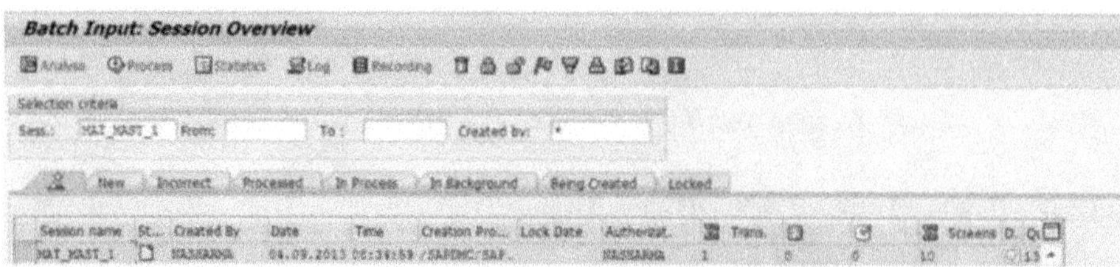

After scheduling the load in background, can verify whether Job is running or not.
Tcode: SM37

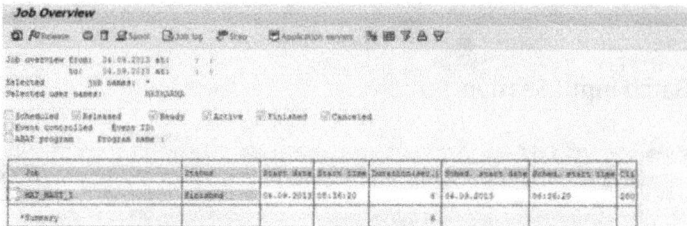

Major precautions/tips while making LSMW:

1. Project, Sub project and Object name should be logical or as per your project nomenclature.
2. Should have the clear idea about the upload data and Transaction.
3. While recording, data should be readily available.
4. Should avoid any types of warning while recording, which may create a problem.
5. After recording, should take the option as DEFAULT ALL, which will populate all the fields.
6. While generating the source field, you can take input from Step1 and provide the correct details for field type and length.
7. Field mapping can be done on automatic basis to avoid any conflict.
8. while specifying the file, should be very clear about the file type(Tab delimited etc.) and accordingly generate the file.
9. During read data step, please verify whether data is correct or not.
10. And re-verify the data at Display converted data.
11. Be very careful while executing the RUN BATCH INPUT SESSION. foreground or background etc.
12. If you execute this in background, then can verify by using tcode SM37.
13. Once the testing is successful, need to send the data template to business and get the data from them.
14. 1. LSMW can be moved by two ways:

a) Export/Import: Export the LSMW code and Import the same into the Production environment.

b) Transport request: Can move LSMW by Transport request as well.

15. While re-executing this LSMW, one needs to execute from Step7(SPECIFY FILE) onwards.

19.9. DEMO 2– Step by Step Guide for Using LSMW to Update Customer Master Records

Business Case:

As a part of reorganization and to better serve the customer needs, you are regrouping many of the customers. In SAP terms, you are changing the Sales Office, Sales Group and Customer Groups for specific Customer Master Records. Typically, you would maintain customer records with transaction XDO2 to update 'Sales View'. You would enter Customer Key (Customer No, Sales Organization, Distribution Channel, and Division) and update relevant fields on Sales View screen.

This document contains Step-by-step instructions to use LSMW to update Customer Master Records. It has two demonstration examples - one using Batch Recording and another using standard SAP Object.

LSMW to Update Customer Master Records with Transaction Recording

Call Legacy System Migration Workbench by entering transaction code LSMW. Every conversion task is grouped together as Project / Subproject / Object structure. Create a **Project** called **LSMW_DEMO** and a Subproject as CUSTOMERS and Object as CUST_REC as shown in below Figure.

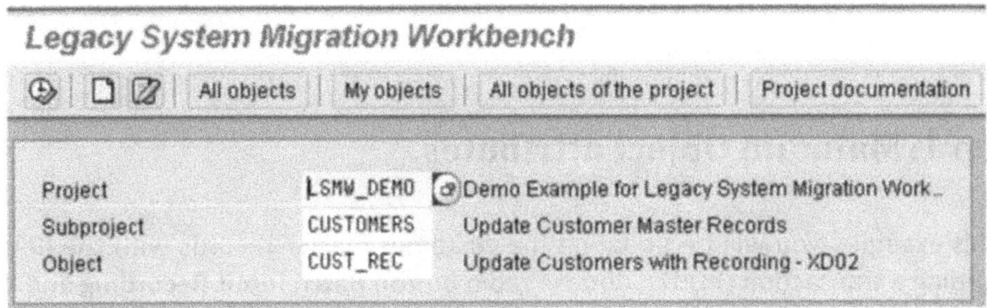

Conversion Task with Project, Subproject and Object

The main screen of LSMW provides wizard-like step-by-step tasks, as shown in figure below:

To complete your data conversion, you need to execute these steps in sequence. Once a step is executed, the cursor is automatically positioned to the next step.

Note that these steps may look different depending upon your **Personal menu** settings. You could make step numbers visible by 'Numbers on' icon or hidden by 'Numbers off' icon. You can execute a step by double-clicking on the row. Toggle icon `Doubleclick=Display' or 'Doubleclick=Edit, makes the step in 'display' mode or 'change' mode.

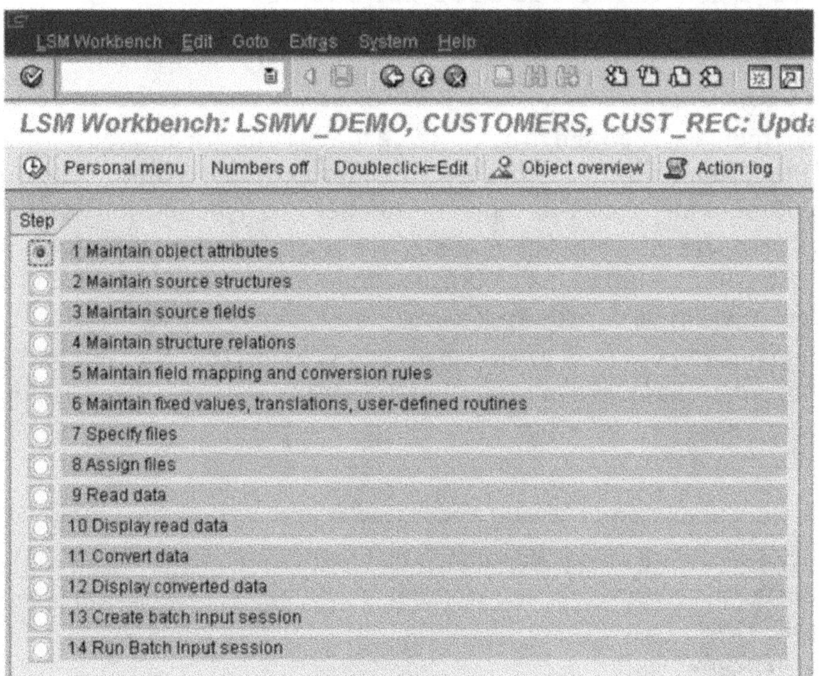

LSMW Wizard – initial screen

Step 1: Maintain Object attributes

In this example, you will be updating the customer master records with the help of recording a transaction (XD02). Choose radio button **Batch Input Recording** and click on the recording overview icon to record the R/3 transaction. Enter the **Recording** name as XD02_REC, the description as **Customer Master Updates Recording**, and the transaction code as XD02.

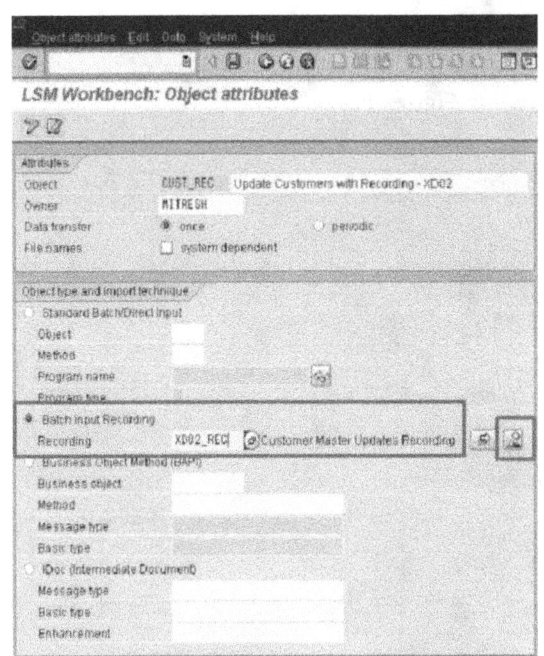

Object type 'Transaction Recording'

The system calls the transaction code XD02 and prompts you to complete the **Change Customer** transaction, as shown in Figure 4. Enter the key customer information (I entered customer number 1000, sales organization 1000, distribution channel 01, and division 00) and choose 'Sales' view within 'Sales area data'. Make changes to these three fields (I entered, sales office 1010, sales group 110, and customer group 01) and save the transaction.

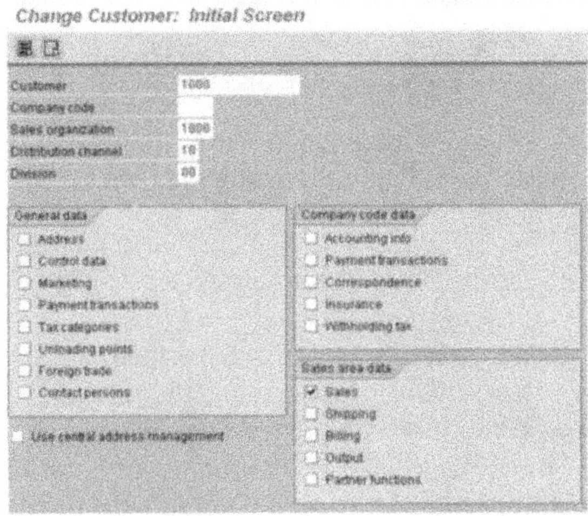

Transaction recording for Transaction Code 'XD02'

Once the transaction is completed, R/3 records the flow of screens and fields and saves the information, as shown in **Figure below**.

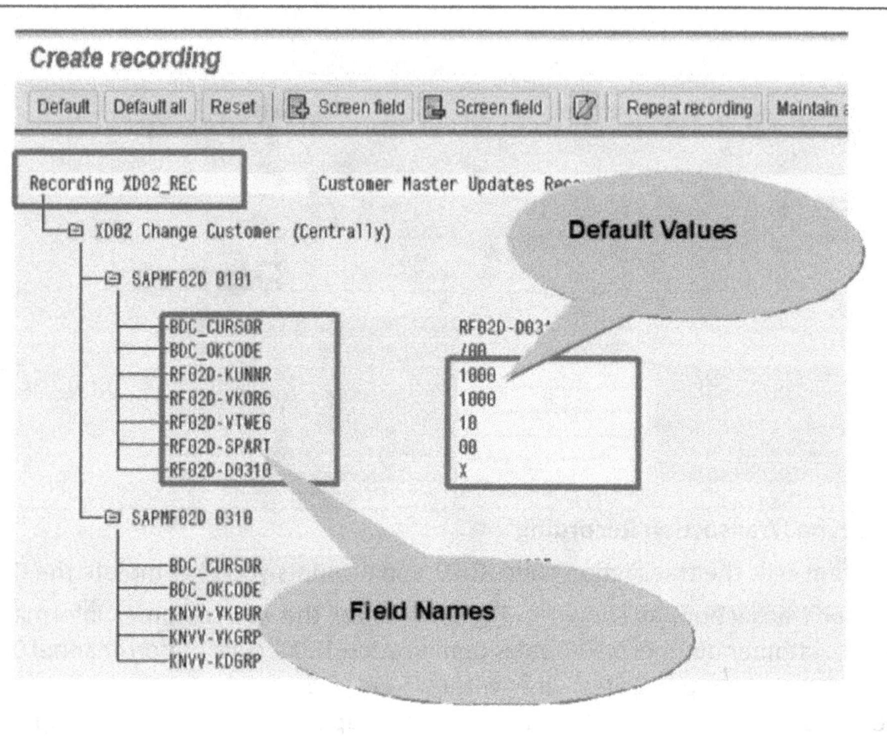

Transaction recording overview

Note that the fields are populated with default values. The values you entered when you recorded the transaction are set by default.

Note that if you have more fields in the recording than needed, you can remove them by clicking 'Remove Screen field' icon. Screen field

Observe that the transaction-recording process stores field names in a technical format. By pressing the F1 key on individual screen fields and then pressing the F9 key, the system displays technical names. You then can replace the technical names with descriptive names. Double-click on the field **RF02D-KUNNR** and enter the name as **KUNNR** and the description as **Customer Account Number** and remove the default value.

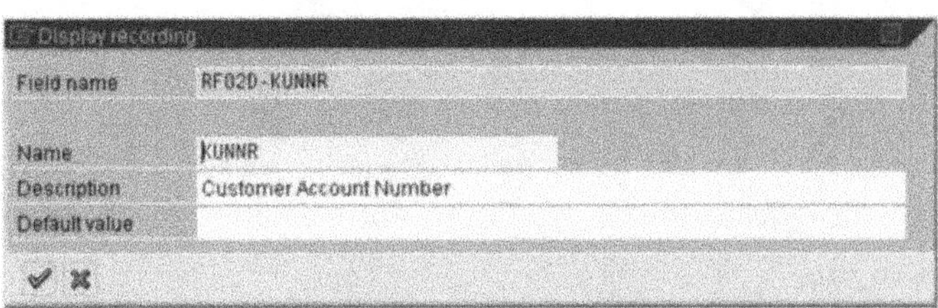

Field attributes

Similarly, double-click on all other fields with default values and make appropriate changes. Once you have made changes, the recording overview screen looks like what you see in **Figure below**.

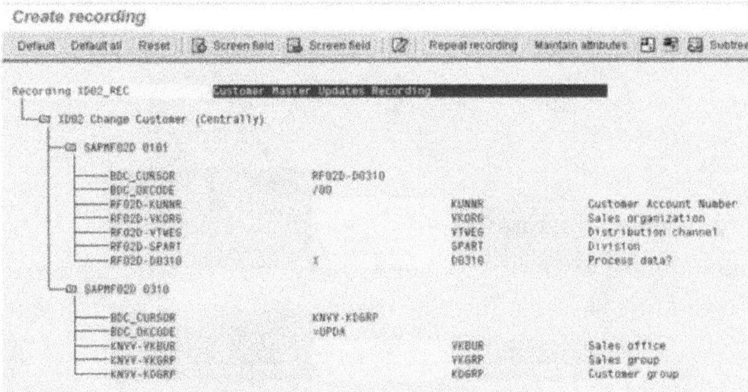

Transaction Recording Overview – with screen field attributes

Save your changes. When you go back to the initial screen, you will see that the initial screen steps have changed. Since you want to import data via the BDC method, the Direct Input and IDoc-related steps are hidden, as they are not relevant.

Step 2. Maintain Source Structures

Give a name and a description to the source structure.

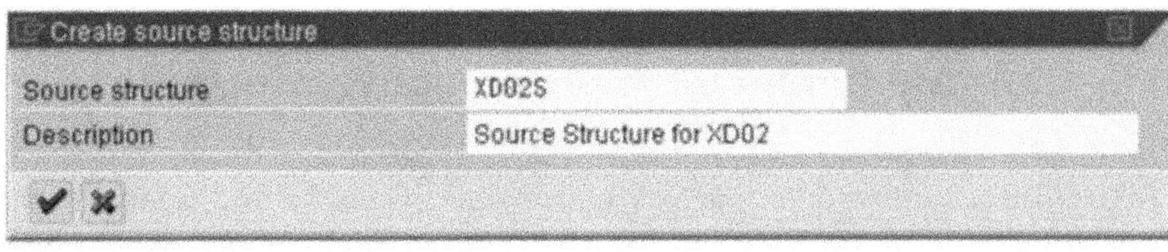

Source Structure

Step 3. Maintain Source Fields

In this step, you need to list what fields are present in the source structure. The easiest way is to click on 'Table Maintenance' icon to enter Fieldname, Type and Length for each field as shown:

Source fields of source structure XD02S

Field name	Type	L...	Field description
CUSTOMER	C	10	CUSTOMER
SALESORG	C	4	SALESORG
DISTCHANNEL	C	2	DISTCHANNEL
DIVISON	C	2	DIVISION
SALESOFFICE	C	4	SALESOFFICE
SALESGROUP	C	3	SALESGROUP
CUSTOMERGROUP	C	2	CUSTOMERGROUP

Source fields of source Structure

Note that your input file will have four fields as key fields and you need to update three fields in the system.

Step 4: Maintain Structure Relations

Execute a step to 'Maintain Structure Relations'. Since, there is only one Source and Target Structure, the relationship is defaulted automatically.

```
LSMW_DEMO - CUSTOMERS - CUST_REC Update Customers with Recording - XD02

 Structure relations
 └──XD02_REC Recording of XD02 Transaction                    <<<< XD02S Source Structure for XD02
          The target structure XD02_REC must be selected.
```

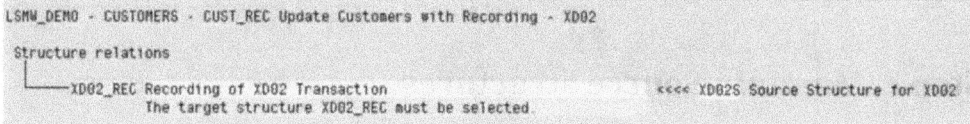

Structure Relation

Step 5: Maintain field mapping and conversion rules

Field **RF02D-D0310** represents that you chose 'Sales view' for the customer Master screen accordingly its value should be set to **X**. Keep your cursor on field RF02D-D0310 and click on Constant rule icon to choose the constant value of **'X'**.

If your source file already has the field value, you choose rule 'Source Field'.

Keep cursor on field 'KUNNR' and click on 'Assign Source field' icon to choose source field CUSTOMER from structure XD02S as shown in **Figure below**.

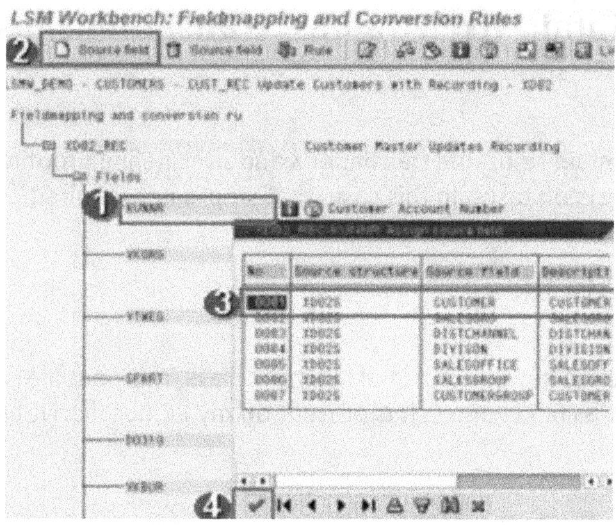

Assign source fields

Similarly, assign 'Source Field' rules to the remaining fields.

Once all the fields are mapped, you should have an overview screen as shown in **Figure below.**

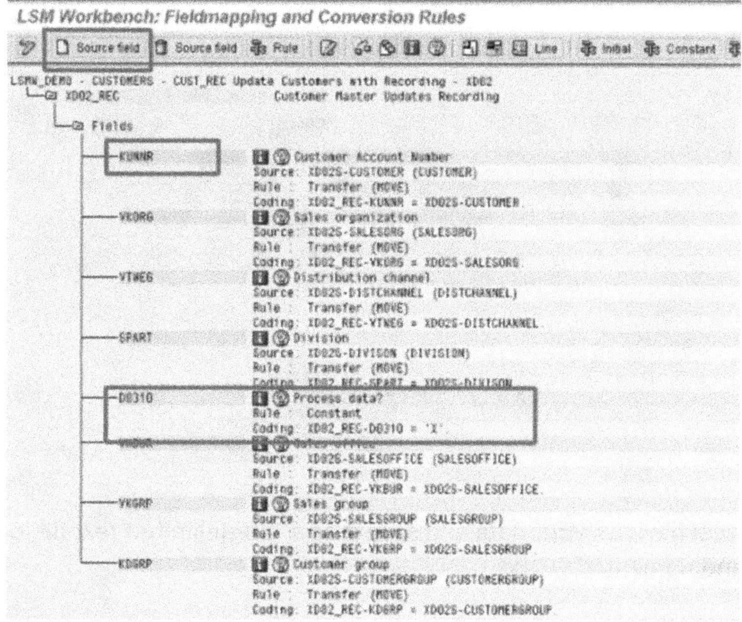

Field mapping and Conversion rules overview

Step 6: Maintain fixed values, translations, user-defined routines

You can also maintain re-usable translations and user-defined routines, which can be used across conversion tasks. In this case, that step is not required.

Step 7: Specify files

In this step, we define how the layout of the input file is. The input file is a [Tab] delimited with the first row as field names. It is present on my PC (local drive) as C:\XD02.txt.

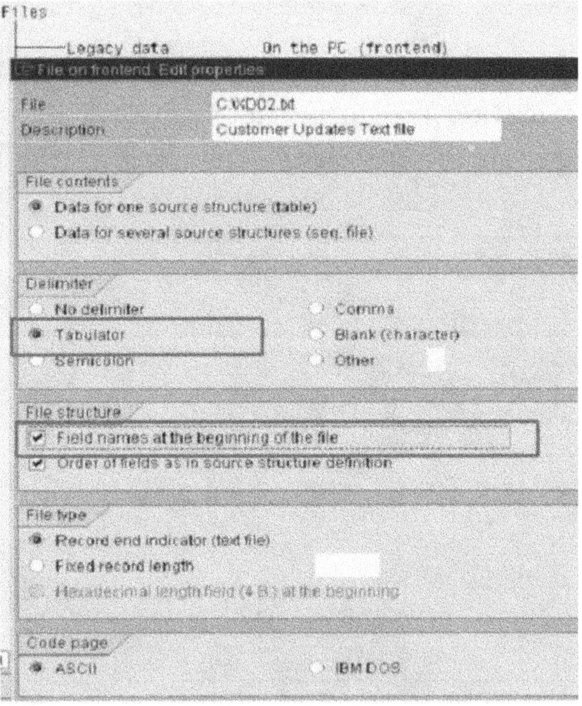

File attributes

Create an Excel file with your data and save it as a Tab-delimited text file on your local drive (C:\) and name it XD02.txt.

	A	B	C	D	E	F	G
1	Customer	SalesOrg	DistChnl	Division	SalesOff	SalesGrp	CustGrp
2	1000	1000	10	00	1010	110	01
3	1007	1000	10	00	1010	110	01
4	1008	1000	10	00	1010	110	01
5	1010	1000	10	00	1010	110	01
6	1020	1000	10	00	1010	110	01
7	1025	1000	10	00	1010	110	01
8	1026	1000	10	00	1010	110	01
9	1030	1000	10	00	1010	110	01
10	1040	1000	10	00	1010	110	01
11	1051	1000	10	00	1010	110	01

Source data in Excel file (saved as Tab delimited file)

Step 8: Assign files

Execute step 'Assign Files' and the system automatically defaults the filename to the source structure.

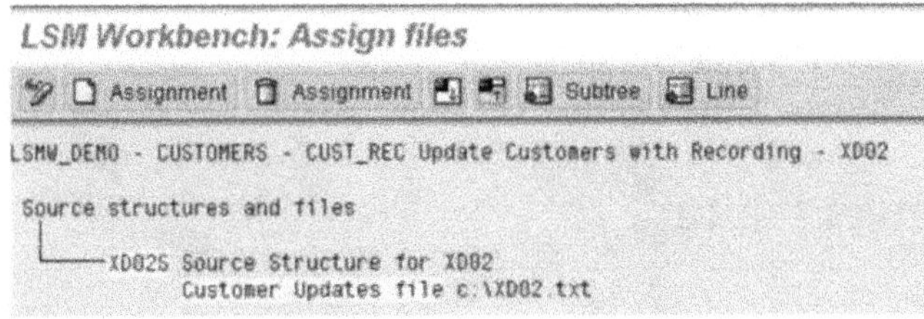

Assign file to Source Structure

Step 9: Read data

In this step, LSMW reads the data from the source file (from your PC's local drive). You have the option to read only selected rows and convert data values to Internal format.

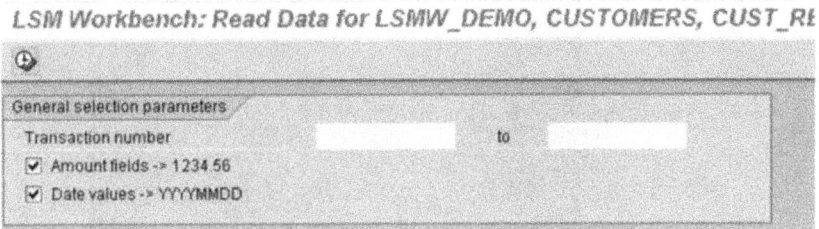

LSM Workbench: Read Data for LSMW_DEMO, CUSTOMERS, CUST_RE

General selection parameters

Transaction number to

☑ Amount fields -> 1234.56

☑ Date values -> YYYYMMDD

Read Data

Step 10: Display read data

This step is optional. If required, you can review the field contents for the rows of data read.

File name LSMW_DEMO_CUSTOMERS_CUST_REC.lsmw.read		
Structure XD02S		
Field name	Field text	Field value
CUSTOMER	CUSTOMER	1000
SALESORG	SALESORG	1000
DISTCHANNEL	DISTCHANNEL	10
DIVISION	DIVISION	00
SALESOFFICE	SALESOFFICE	1010
SALESGROUP	SALESGROUP	110
CUSTOMERGROUP	CUSTOMERGROUP	01

Display Read Data

Step 11: Convert data

This is the step that actually converts the source data (in source format) to a target format. Based on the conversion rules defined, source fields are mapped to target fields.

Step 12: Display Converted data

Again this is an optional step to view how the source data is converted to internal SAP format.

File name LSMW_DEMO_CUSTOMERS_CUST_REC.lsmw.conv		
Structure XD02_REC		
Field name	Field text	Field value
TABNAME	Table name	XD02_REC
TCODE	Transaction code	XD02
RF02D-KUNNR	Customer Number	1000
RF02D-VKORG	Sales Organization	1000
RF02D-VTWEG	Distribution Channel	10
RF02D-SPART	Division	00
RF02D-D0310	SalesView	X
KNVV-VKBUR	Sales Office	1010
KNVV-VKGRP	Sales Group	110
KNVV-KDGRP	Customer Group	01

Display Converted Data

Step 13: Create batch input session

Once the source data is converted in an internal format, you can create a batch session to process updates.

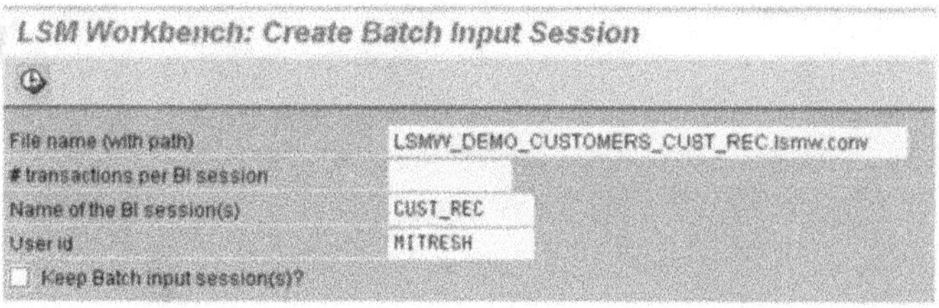

Create Batch Input Session

Step 14: Run Batch Input Session

You can execute the BDC session by Run Batch input session. Executing a batch input session is a standard SM35 transaction for managing BDC sessions.Once you have successfully executed the batch input session, the customer master records are updated in the system. You can confirm this by viewing the customer master records (XD03).

Note! Browsing thru these 14 steps, you may get a feeling that this is a very lengthy and time-consuming activity. However, for the purposes of demonstration, I have made it detailed. Although it looks lengthy, actually it takes hardly few hours from start-to-finish! After playing around with few simple LSMW scripts, you will find it so easy to change and create more complex ones.

19.9.1. LSMW to Update Customer Master Records with Standard Object

As an alternative to using 'Transaction Recording', you could also use a standard SAP object to update Customer Master Records. Business Object '0050' is already pre-defined in the system with standard Batch Input Interface Program 'RFBIDE00'.

Create an Object **CUST_OBJ** within Project as **LSMW_DEMO** and **Subproject** as **CUSTOMERS** as shown in **Figure below.**

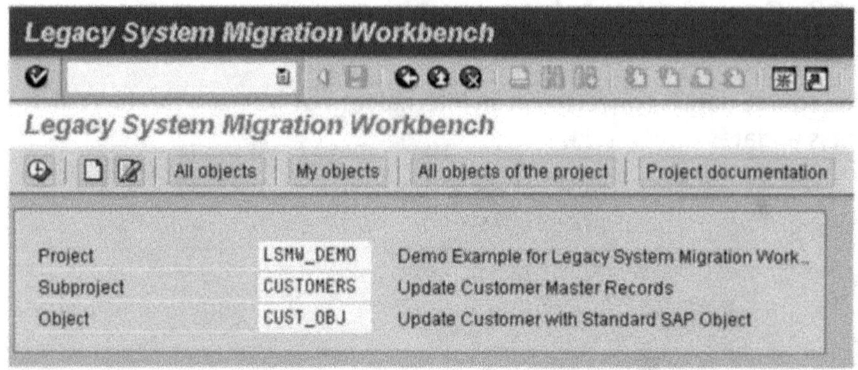

LSMW Object with Standard SAP Object

Note! For the Demo example 2, I will list only those steps that are different from the first demo example.

Step 1: Maintain Object attributes

You will be updating the customer master records with the help of Standard Batch Input; therefore, choose radio-button **Standard Batch/Direct Input** as shown below. Enter Object '0050' for Customer Master records and default method '0000' and click on Save.

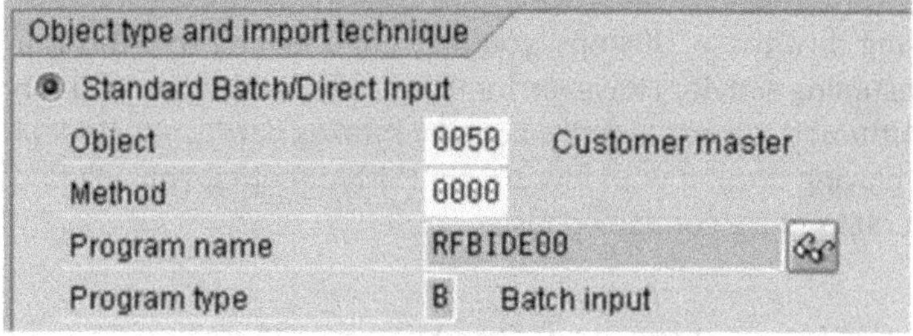

Standard Batch/Direct Input Object Attributes

Step 4: Maintain Structure Relations

Sales view of Customer Master is stored in table KNVV. Accordingly, you need to update structure BKNVV. However, in addition, the Standard Object '0050' also requires updates to BGR00, BKN00 and BKNA1 structures. (If you do not maintain Structure relations for mandatory entries, you might get a message such as 'Target structure BKNA1 needs a relation to a source structure'.)

Even though you don't want to update any fields in these structures, you need to create a relationship with source structures. In all, you need to create relationship for four target structures.

Create relationship between source structures XD02S with these target structures with icon 'Create Relationship' . Relationship

Keep Cursor on these four target structures and click on icon 'Create Relation' and structure relations are maintained as shown below:

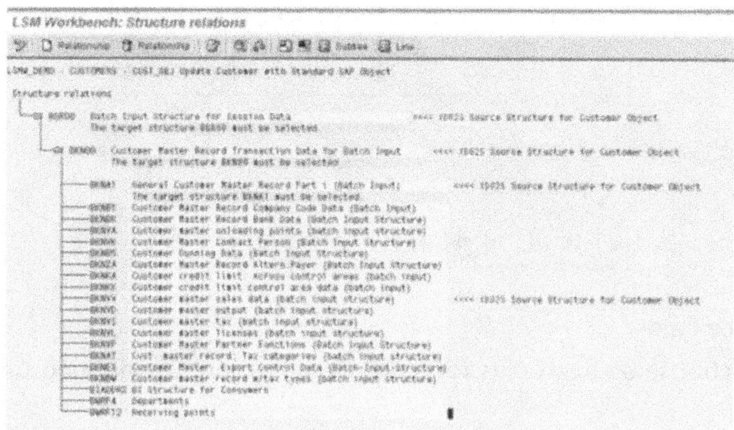

Structure Relation

Step 5: Maintain field mapping and conversion rules

-- Keep your cursor on 'TCODE' field and click on 'Insert Rule' icon Rule

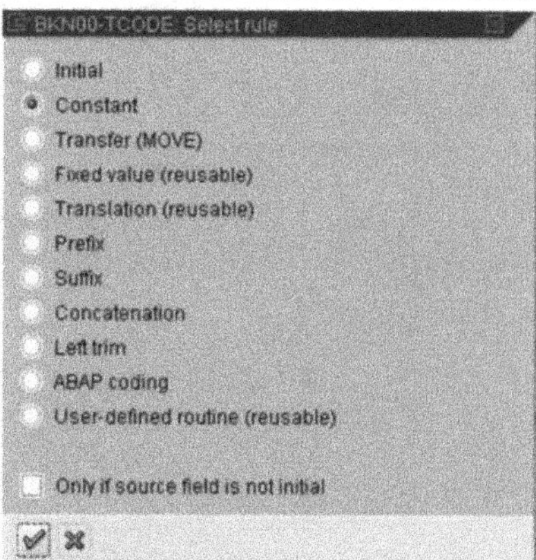

LSMW Conversion Rules

Choose radio button 'Constant' to enter value 'XD02' transaction code.

--Keep your cursor on field 'KUNNR' and click on 'Assign source field' icon Source field

Choose source field 'Customer' from source structure 'XD02S'.

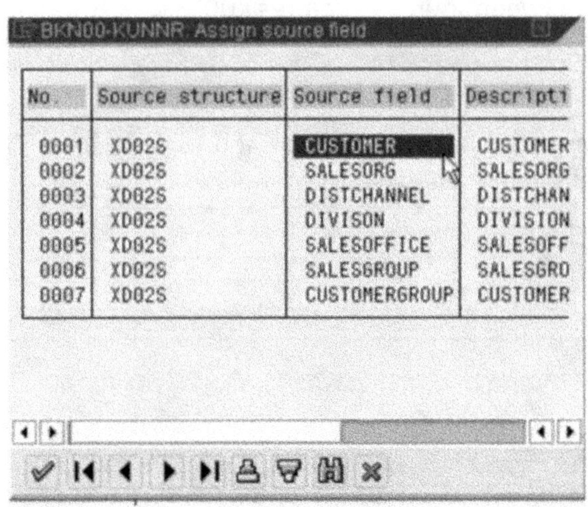

Assign Source fields

--Similarly, choose source fields for Sales Organization, Distribution Channel, and Division.

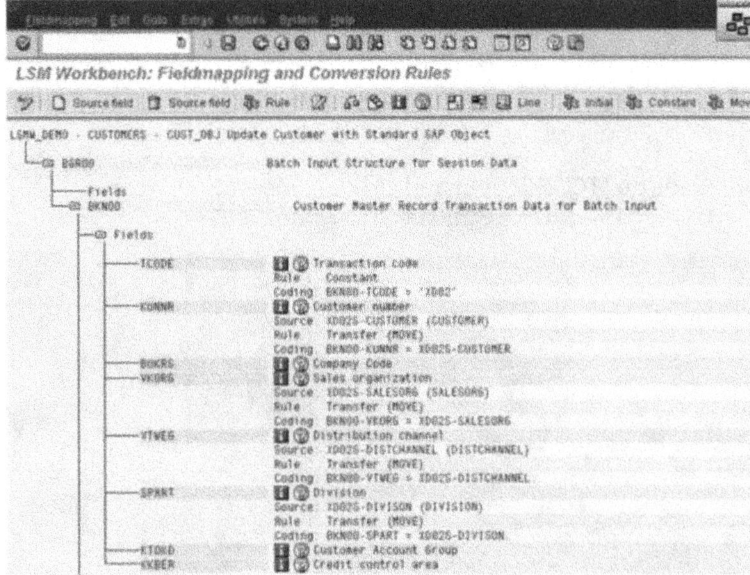

Field Mapping and Conversion Rules

--Scroll down to structure BKNVV fields and assign source fields to three fields Sales Office, Sales Group, and Customer Group.

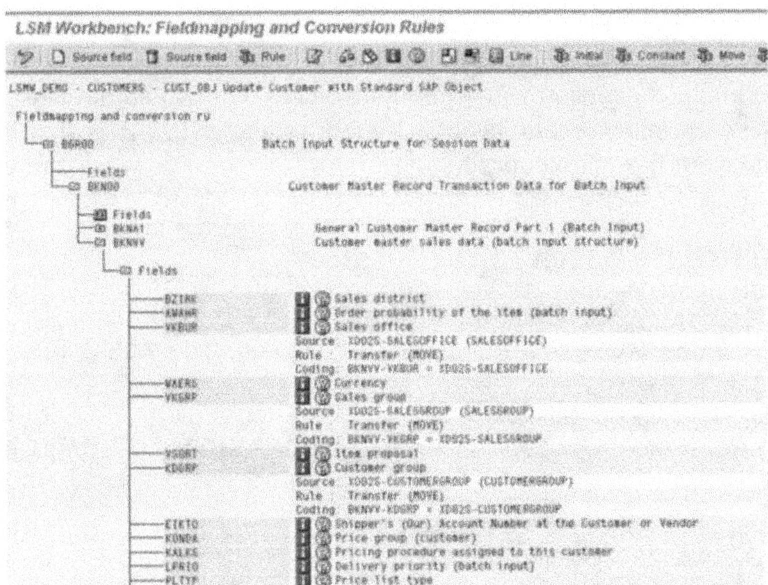

Field Mapping and Conversion Rules

Save and go back to main screen.

Step 12: Display Converted data

When you convert data, LSMW automatically converts into the appropriate structure layouts, as required by Standard program (RFBIDE00).

LSM Workbench: Display Converted Data

Field contents | Change display | Display color legenc

File name LSMW_DEMO_CUSTOMERS_CUST_OBJ.lsmw.conv

Line	Struktur	Conts.
1	BGR00	0CUST_OBJ 80
2	BKN00	1XD02
3	BKNA1	2BKNA1
4	BKNVV	2BKNVV

Converted data into multiple structures

Note that if you had only one record in source file, the converted file has four records.

Earlier, creating this input file, so that the standard interface program can read it, was a big nightmare, the primary reason being that it could have multiple record layouts. Even for a simple conversion with one input record, you would have to create this complex file with many record layouts. The advantage of LSMW is that it prepares these multi-layout files automatically.

Step 13: Create batch input session

Once source data is converted in internal format, you can create a BDC session to process the updates.

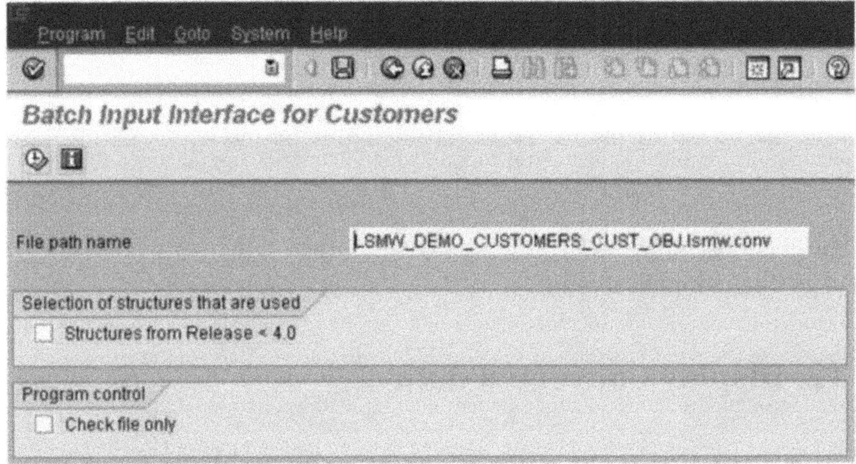

Create BDC Session

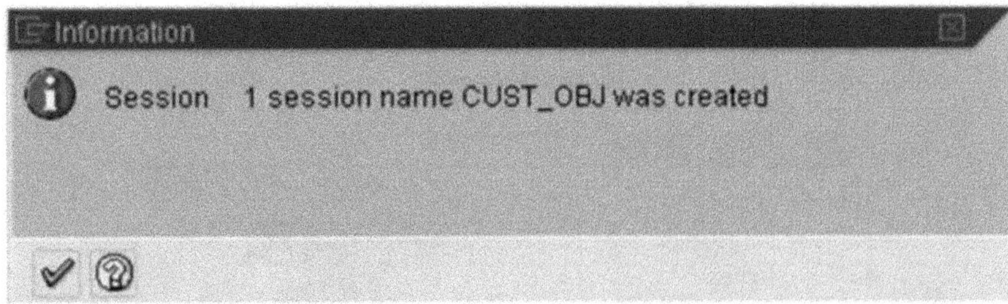

BDC Session 'CUST_OBJ' created

Summary

Once BDC session is processed successfully, SAP updates the customer master records with relevant changes. Review these specific customers (transaction code XD03) and confirm that the changes are correctly reflected in the master records.

19.10. DEMO 3 – LSMW Steps for GL upload

1. Go to LSMW screen in SAP.

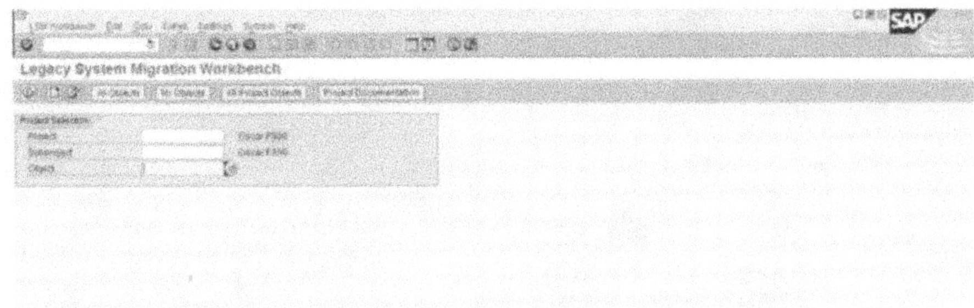

2. Create Project, Subproject and object name.

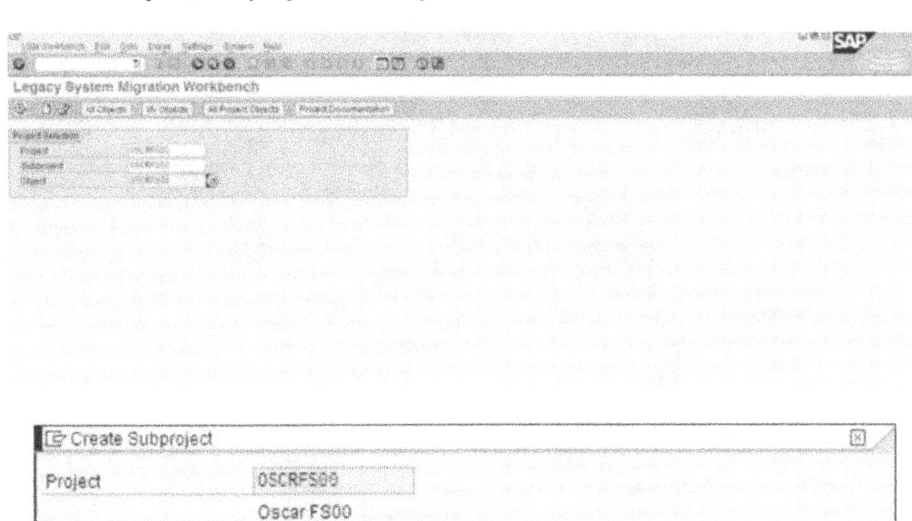

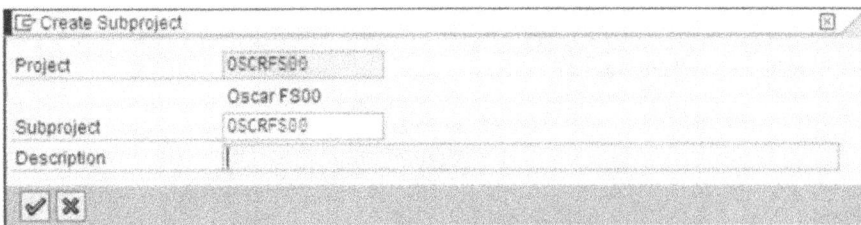

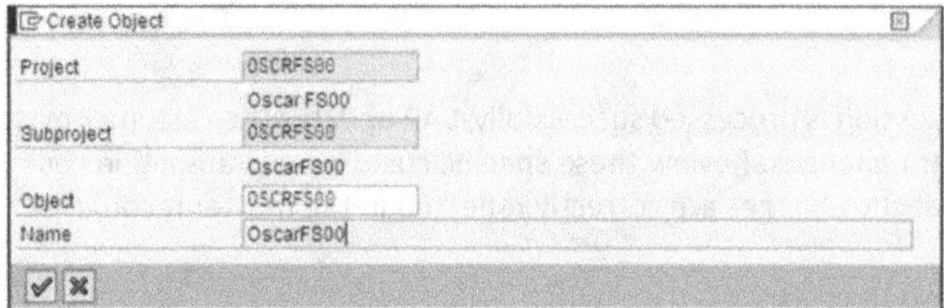

3. Go to Recordings (GOTO – Recordings).

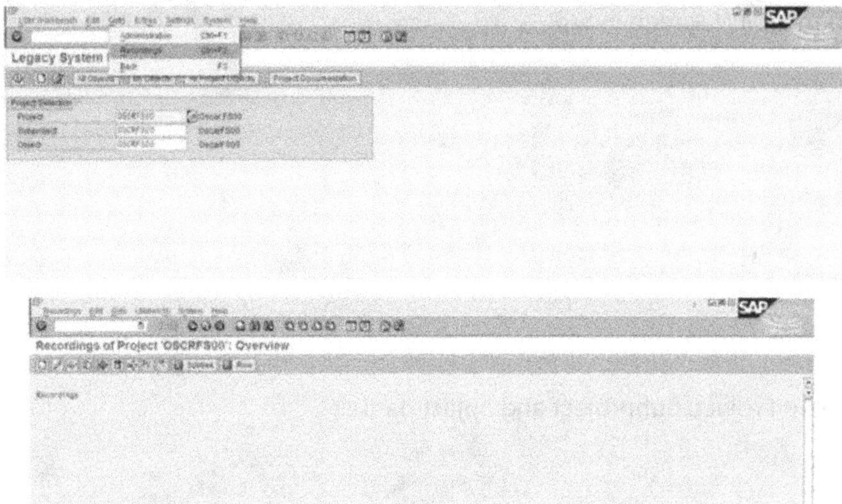

4. Create Recordings and enter the name of the recording.

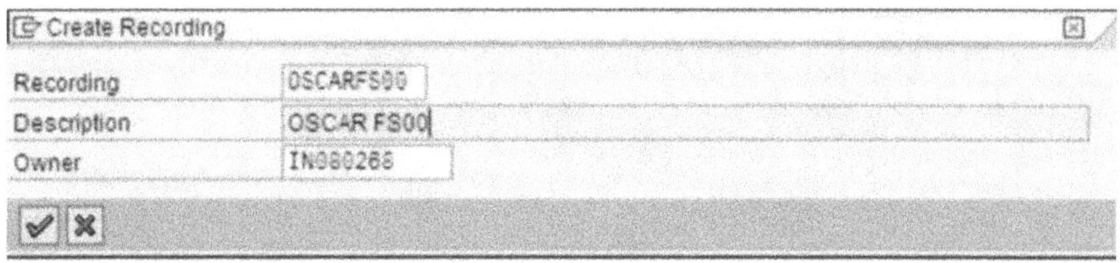

Click on tick button.

5. Enter the Transaction Code FS00.

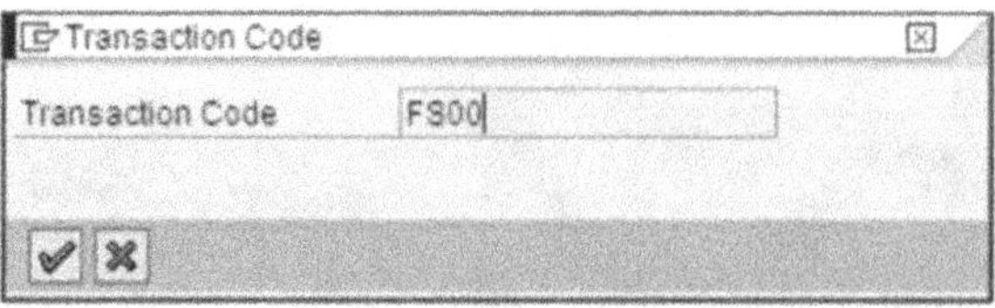

6. Create a dummy GL account to Record the steps of creating GL account.

a. Click on Create Button.

b. Enter the Details of the GL Account.

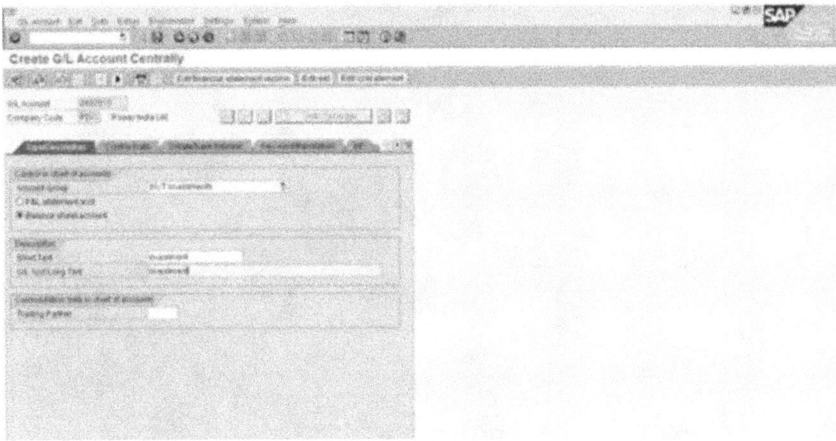

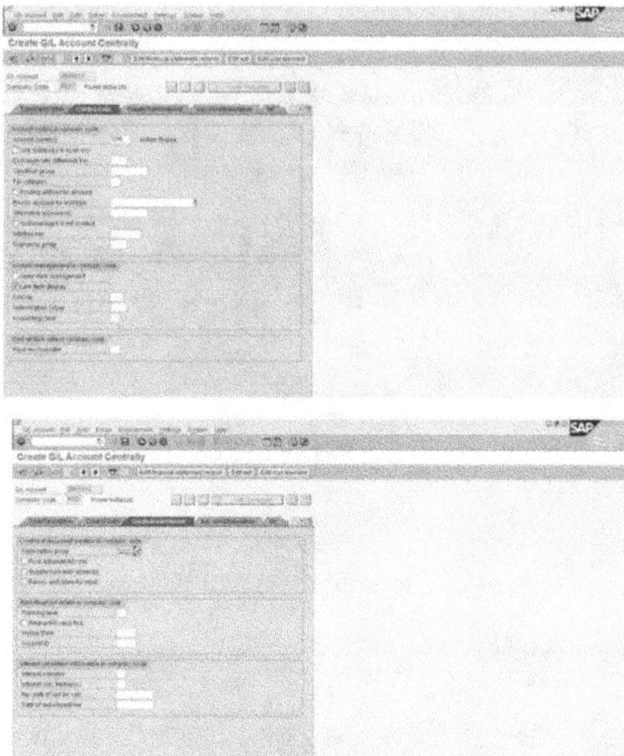

After all the details entered, click on Save Button to save the recordings.

The following screen is shown:

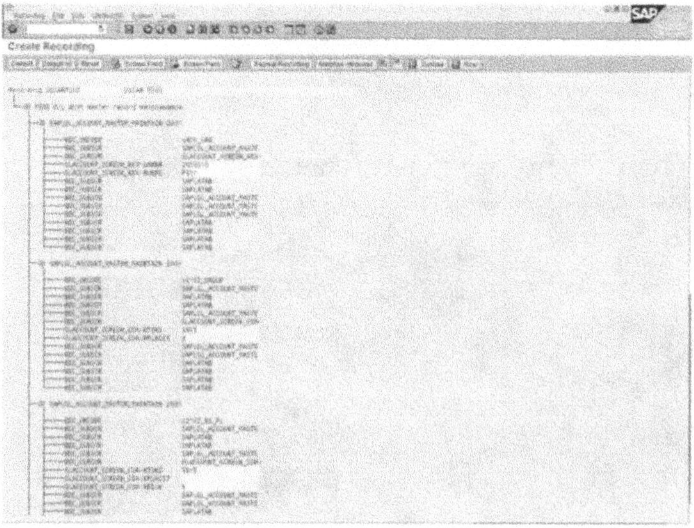

7. Click default All button to show the data.

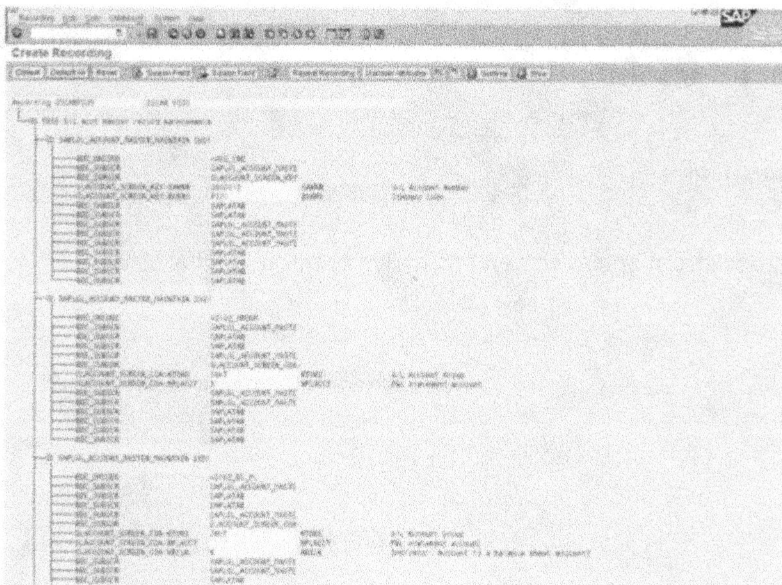

Click on Save button to save the data.

8. The details of this activity can be saved to a spreadsheet as follows:

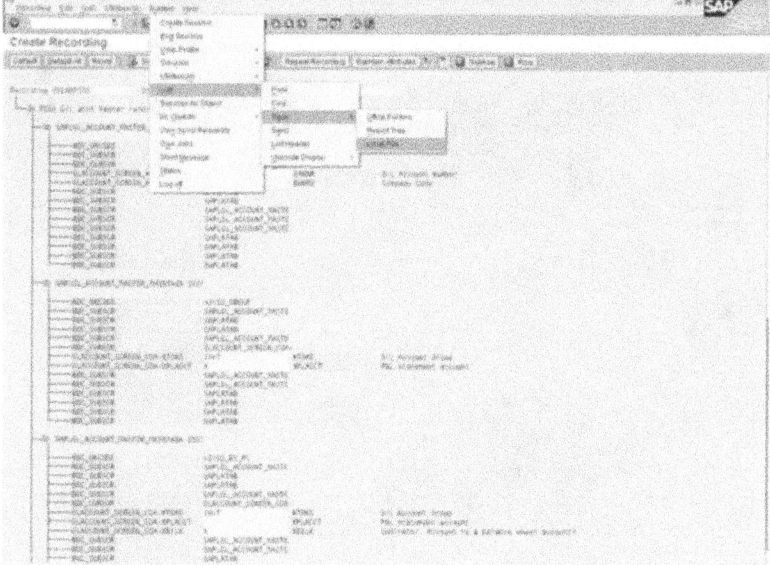

Save it to spreadsheet.

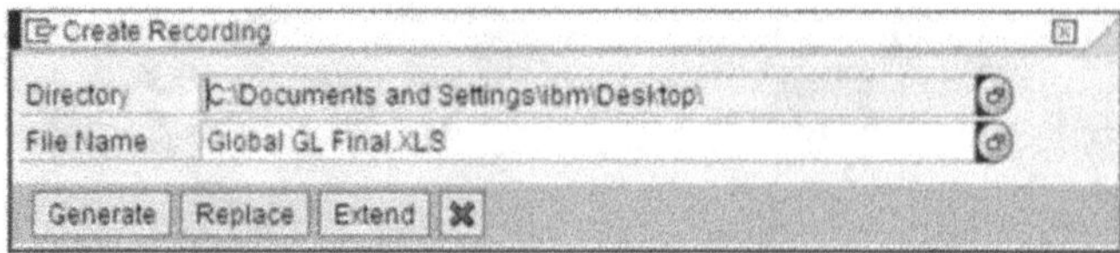

Press Generate Button.

9. Press back from above screen and arrive at the following screen.

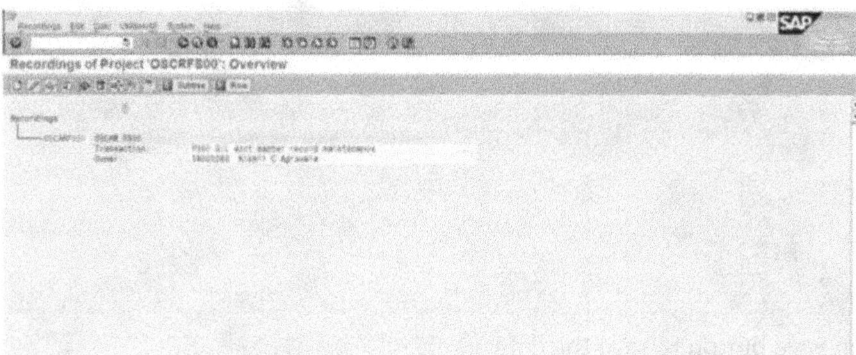

Press Back Button.

10. This screen comes after the execute button is clicked.

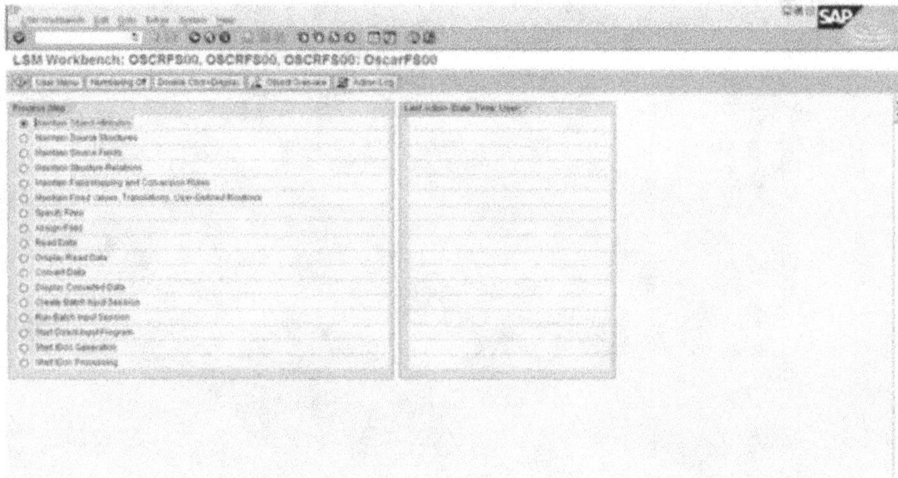

Maintain Object Attributes will be selected; press Execute button to proceed.

11.

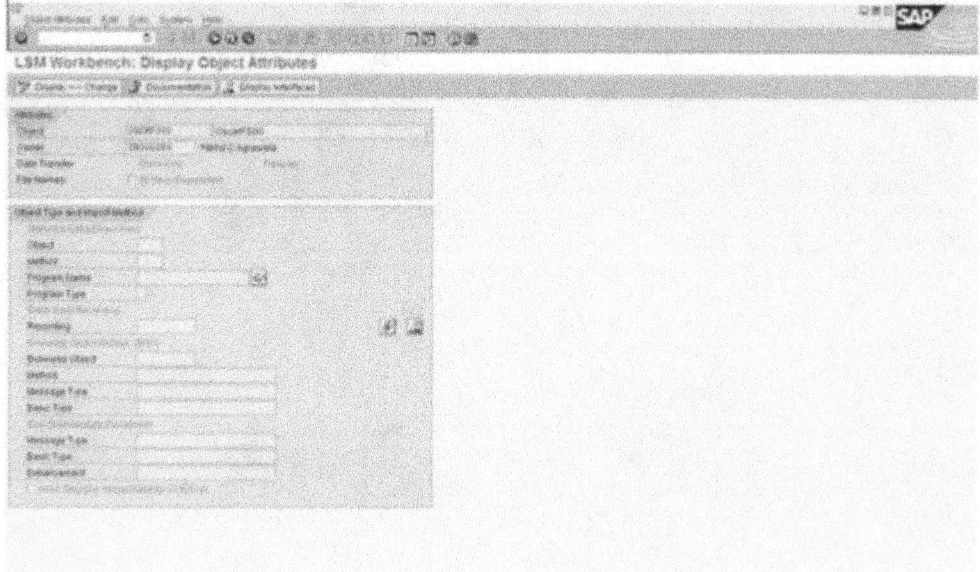

Click on Change – Display.

12.

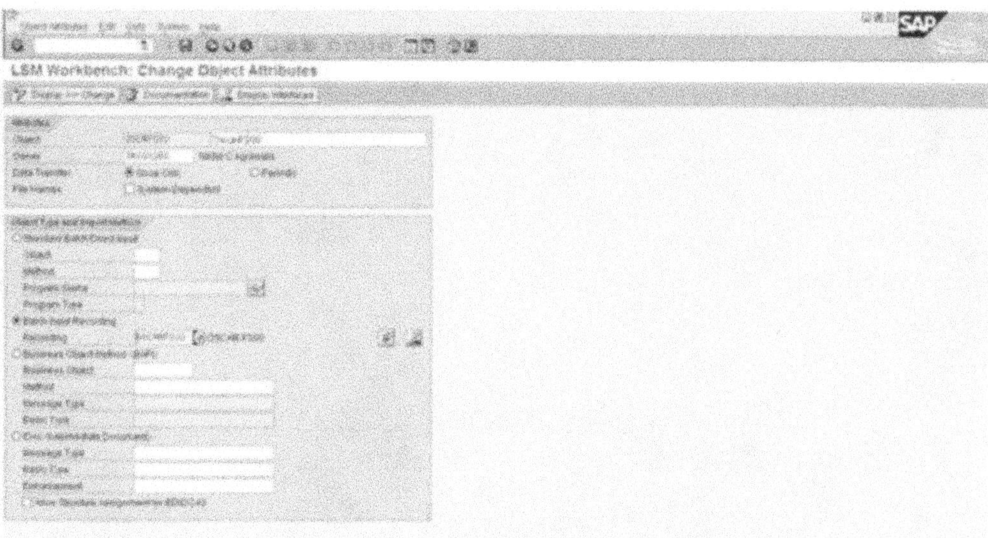

Press Save and Back button after completed.

11. Automatically Maintain Source Fields will be selected.

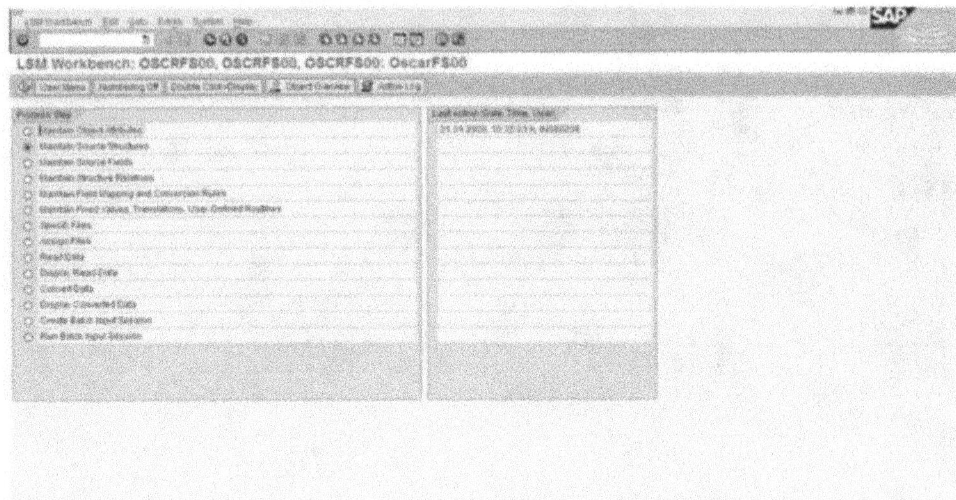

Press Execute Button.

15.

Press Edit button.

16.

Press Create Button.

This will ask for Source Structure and Description.

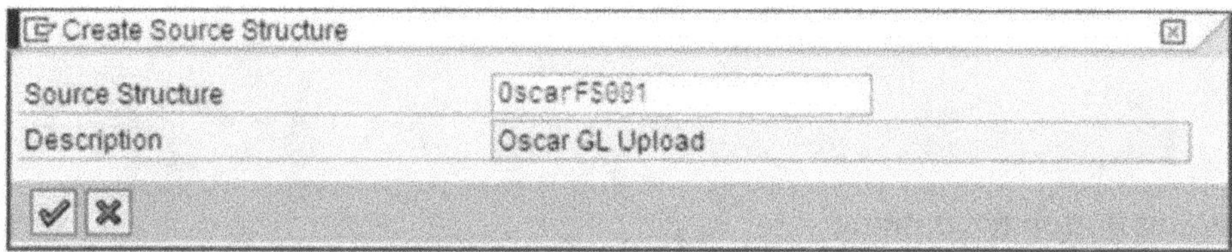

17.

Press Save and back button.

18. Maintain Source Fields will be selected automatically.

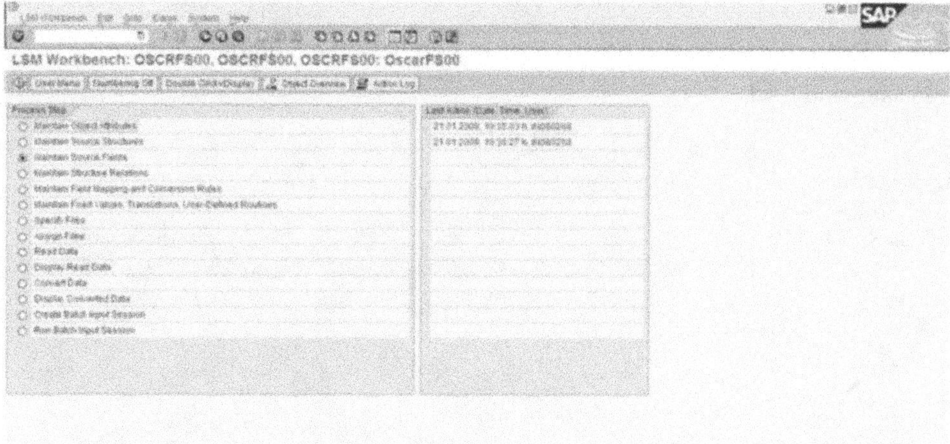

Press Execute button to continue.

19.

Press Edit Button to continue.

Then press Table Main Button to Proceed to the next step.

20.

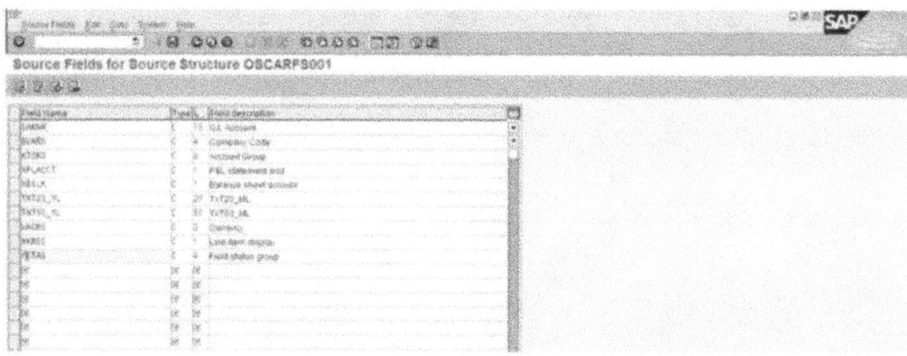

Enter all the parameters and press enter to populate the field description.

Press save and back.

21.

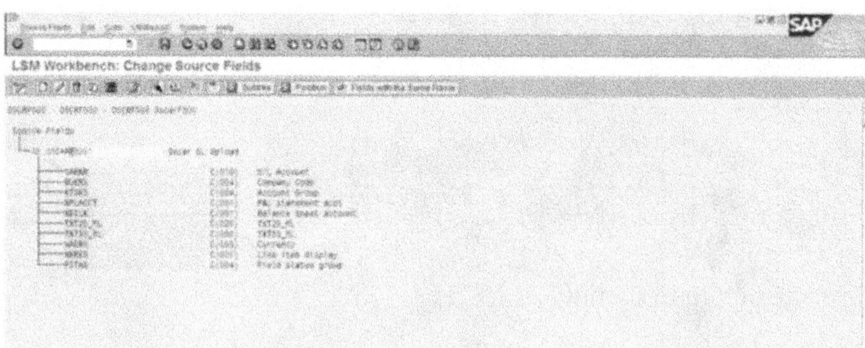

Press Save and back button.

22. Automatically Maintain Structure Relations will be selected.

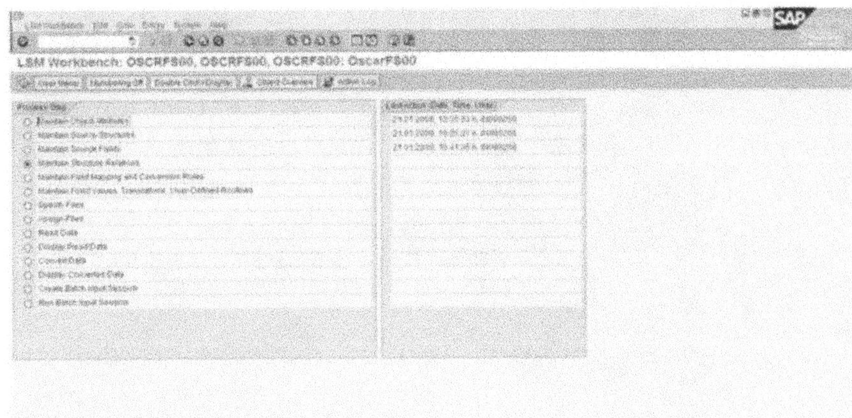

Press Execute button to proceed.

23.

Press Edit button.

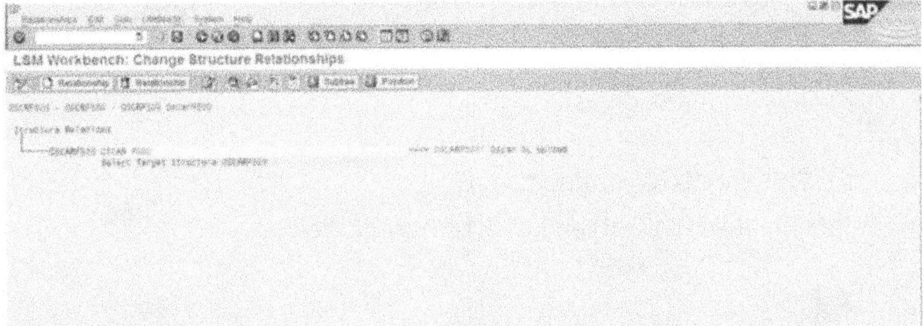

In this screen press save and back button to continue.

24. Automatically Maintain Field Mapping and Conversion Rules will be selected.

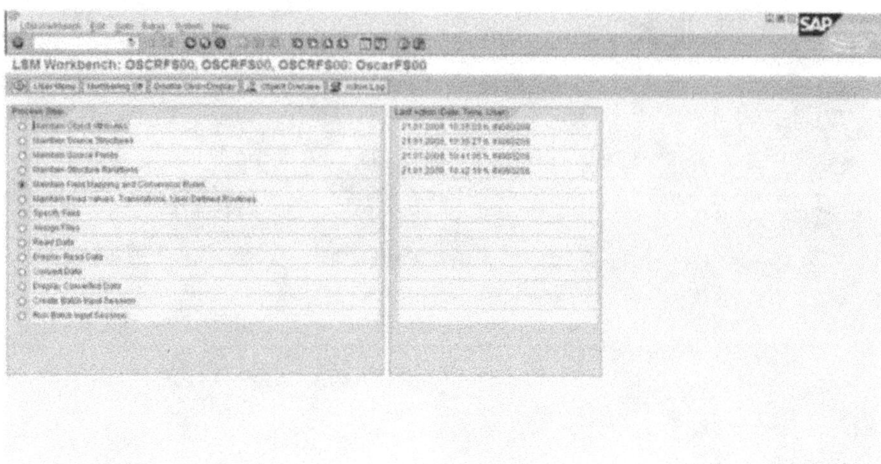

Press Execute button to continue.

25. This screen will be displayed:

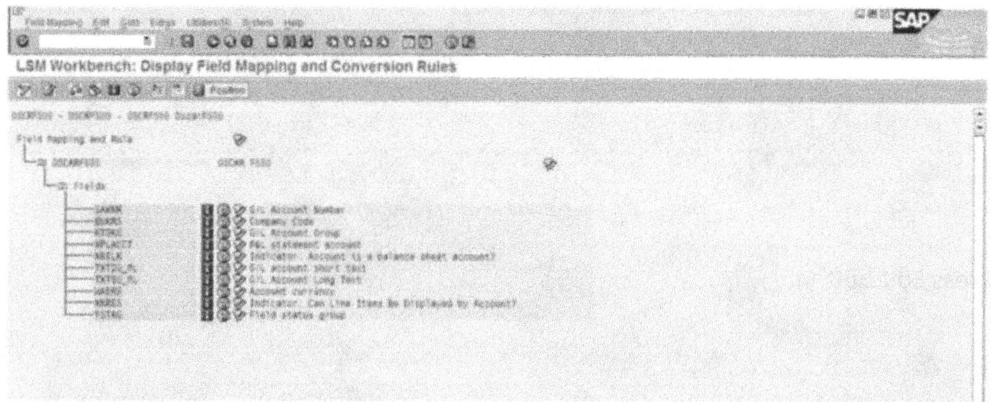

a. Press Edit button to continue.
b. Select the field (SAKNR) and click on Source Field.

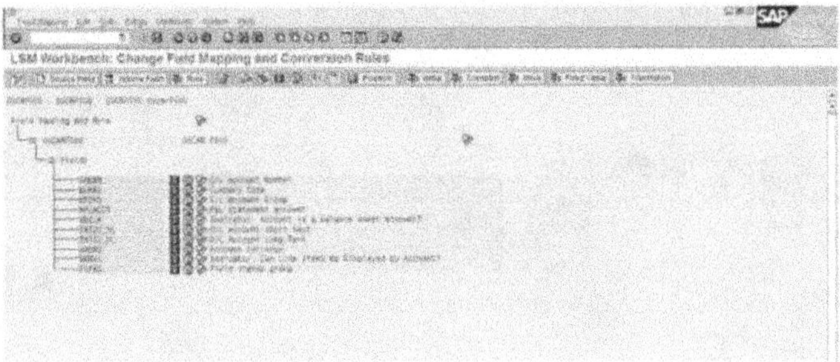

Double click to map and repeat for all fields.

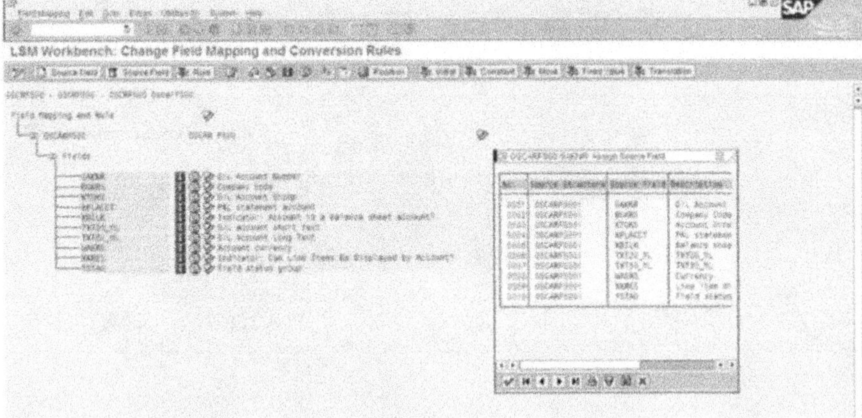

Press Save and Back button to continue.

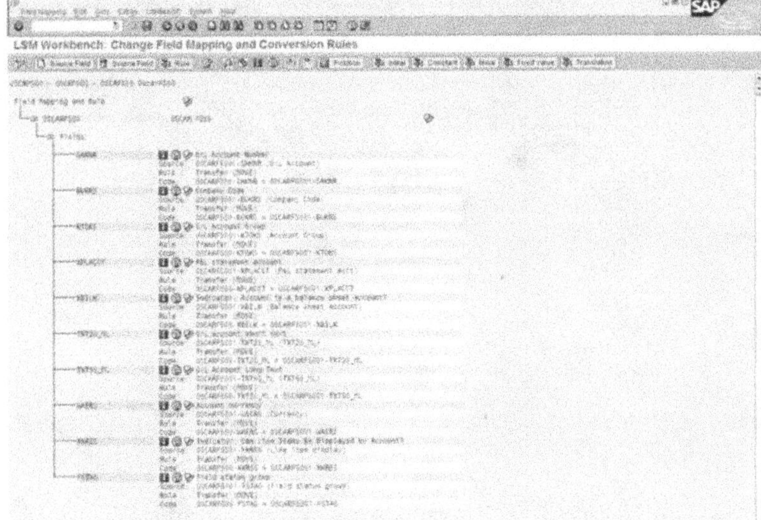

Continue the same steps for other Fields as well.

Otherwise auto mapping feature can be used.

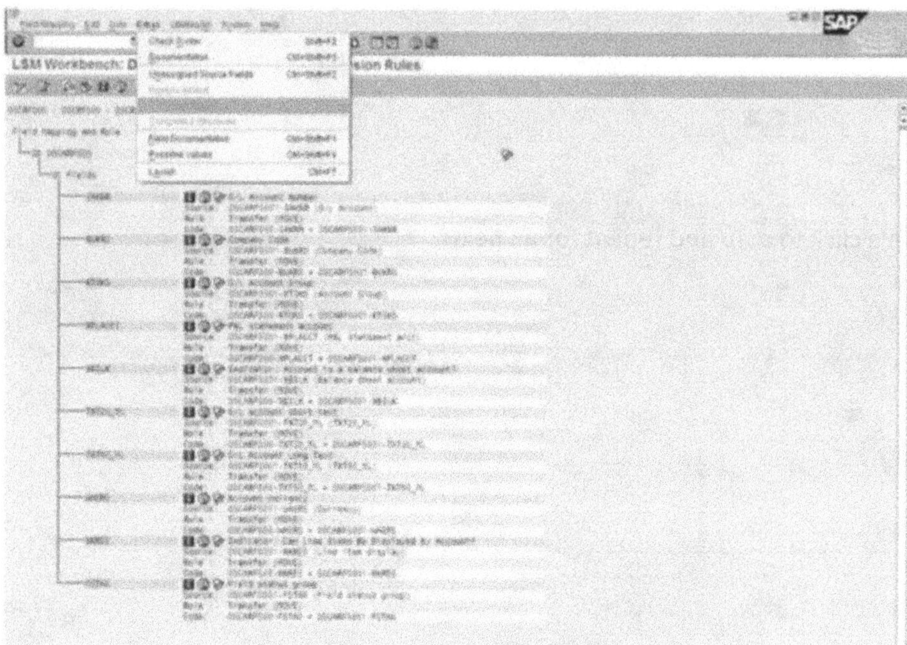

26. Automatically Maintain Fixed Values will be selected. This screen is not required to user can proceed to next screen of Specify Files.

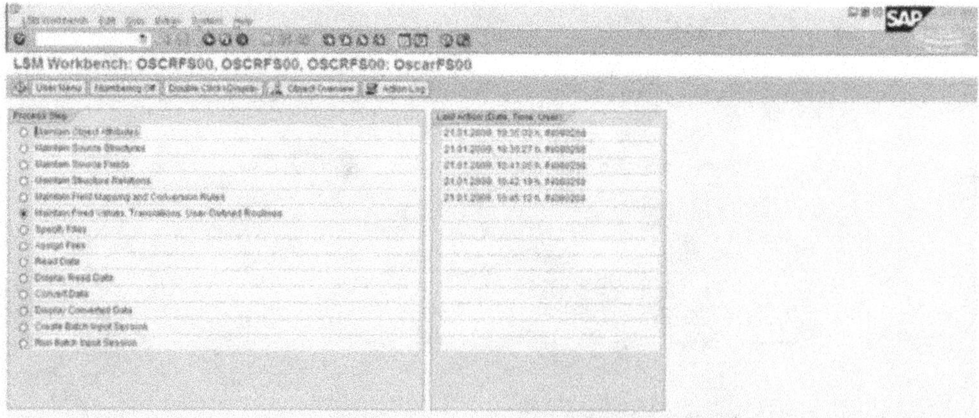

Press Back (this screen is not required).

27.

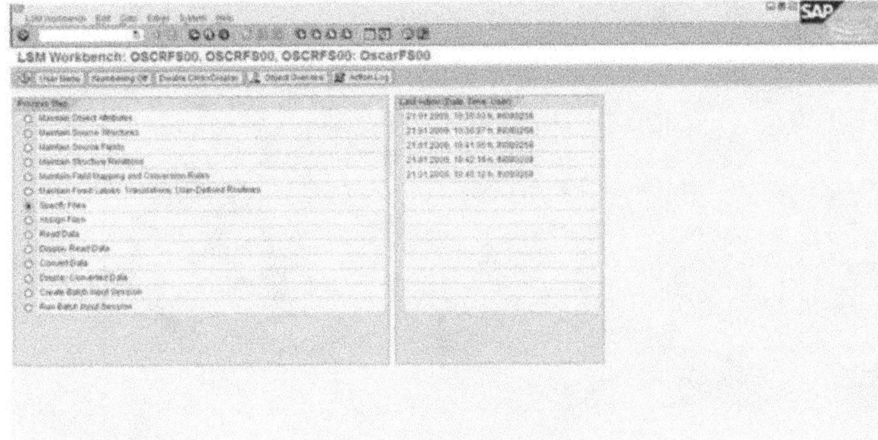

Press Execute Button.

28.

Press Edit Button.

29.

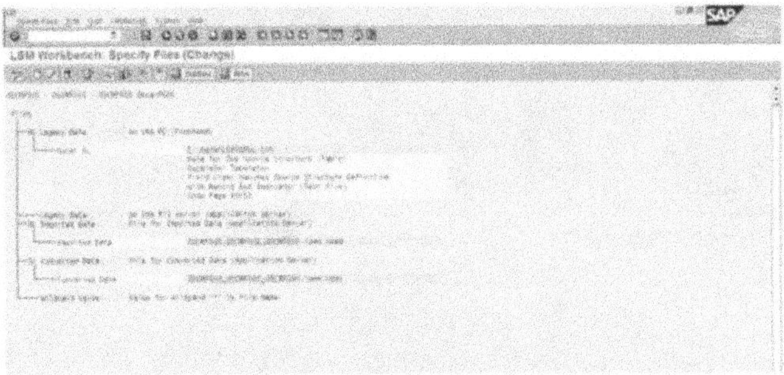

Double Click on Legacy Data and continue.

30. The following screen is being displayed.

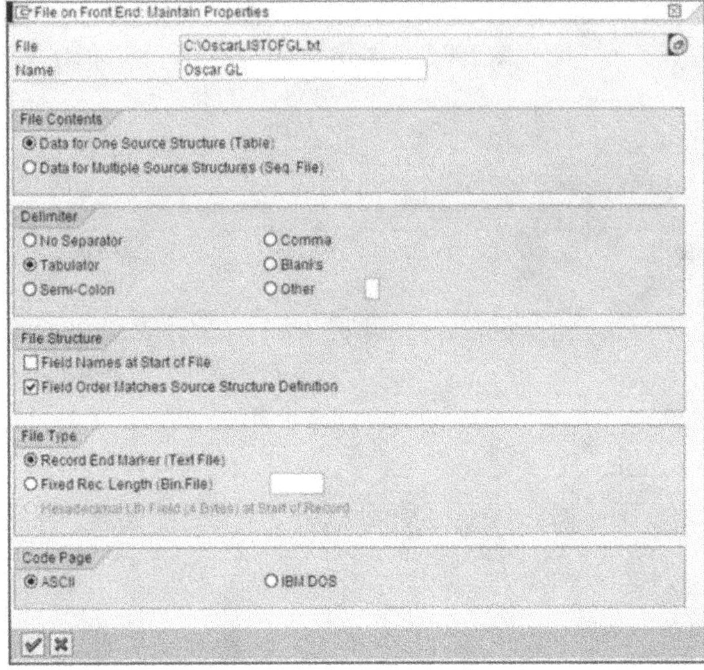

Select the file which need to be uploaded and enter the name of the file and check on Tabulator Delimiter.

31.

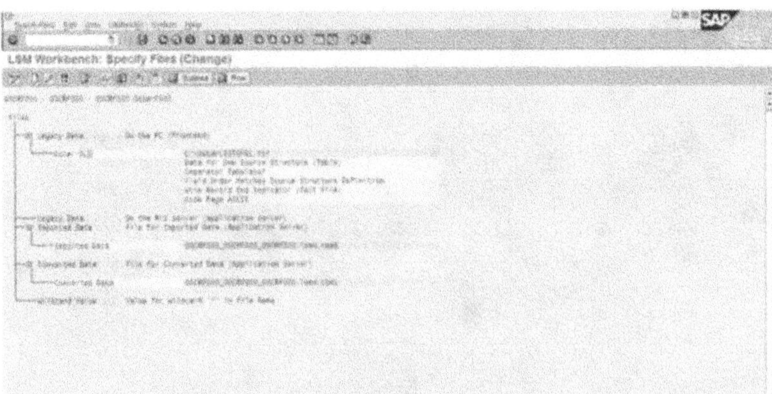

Press Save and Back button.

32. Automatically Assign Files is selected.

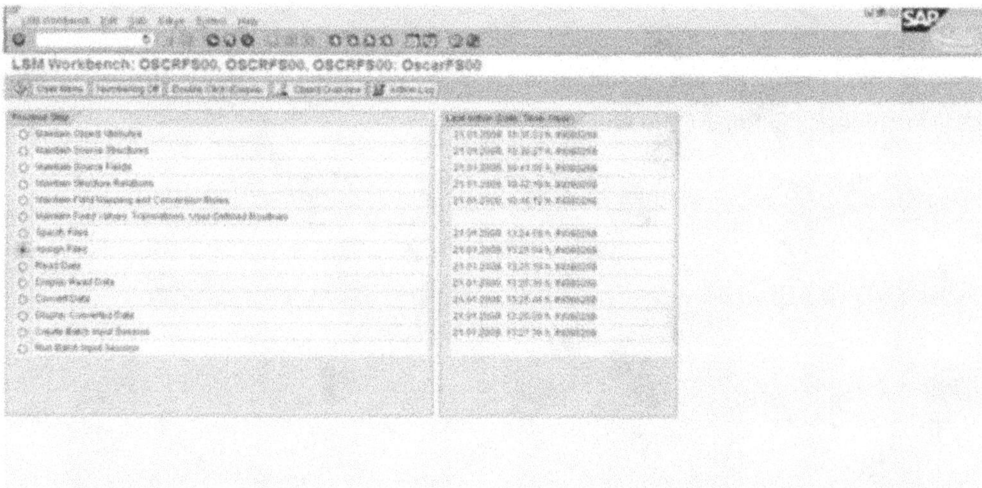

Press Execute button.

33. Press the edit button.

34. Press the save button and press on Back button.

35. Automatically Read Data will be selected.

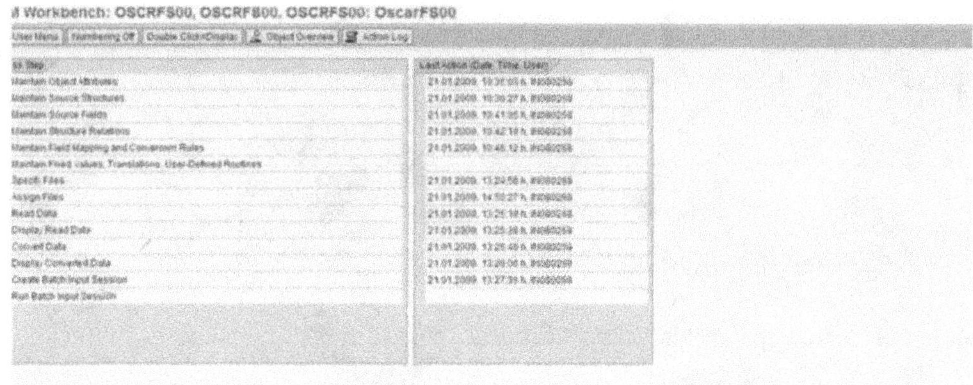

Press the execute button to continue.

36. Press Execute Button.

37. Check the details and press back button two times.

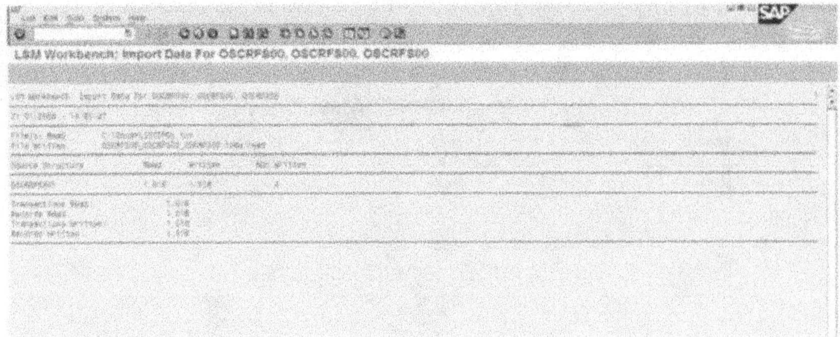

38. Automatically Display Read Data will be selected.

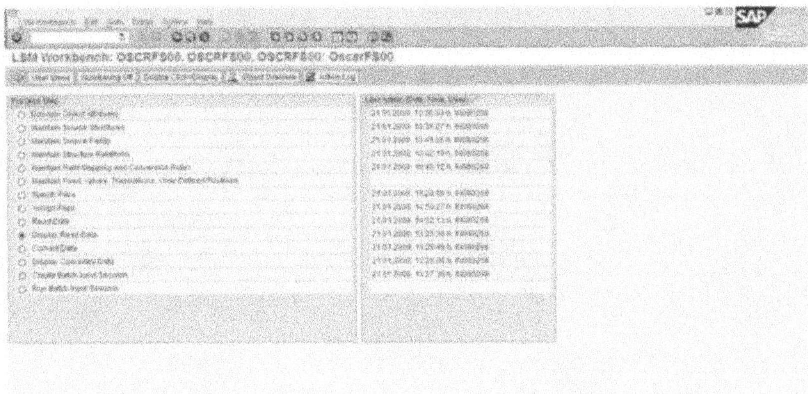

Press execute button.

39. Press tick button in the box to continue.

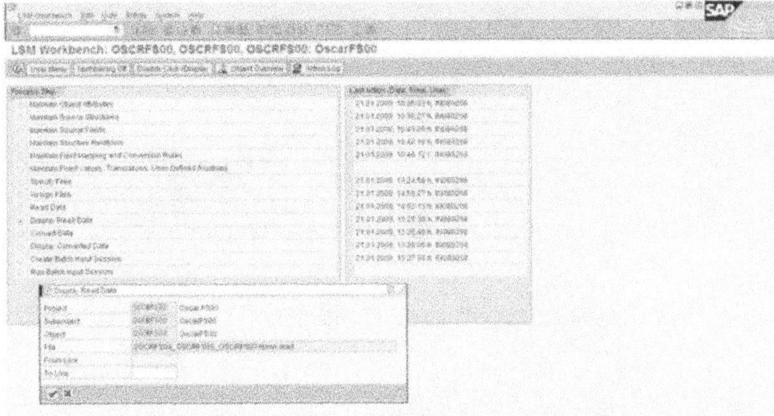

40. This will display all the data, user can check it and press back button to continue.

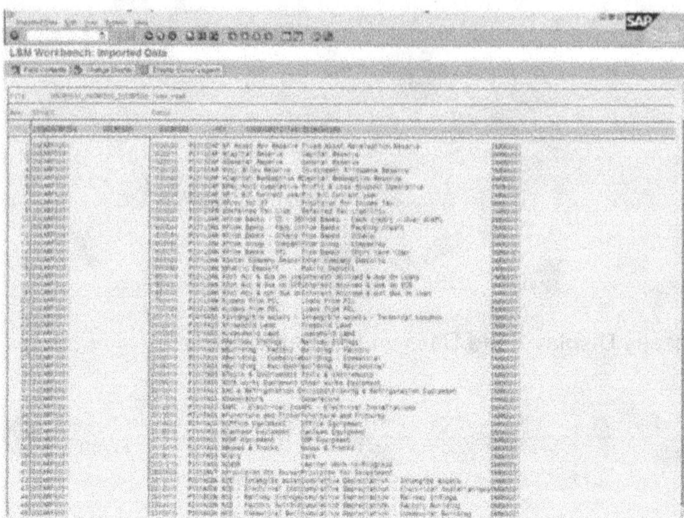

Double click on line item for confirmation of data to check the details of each line.

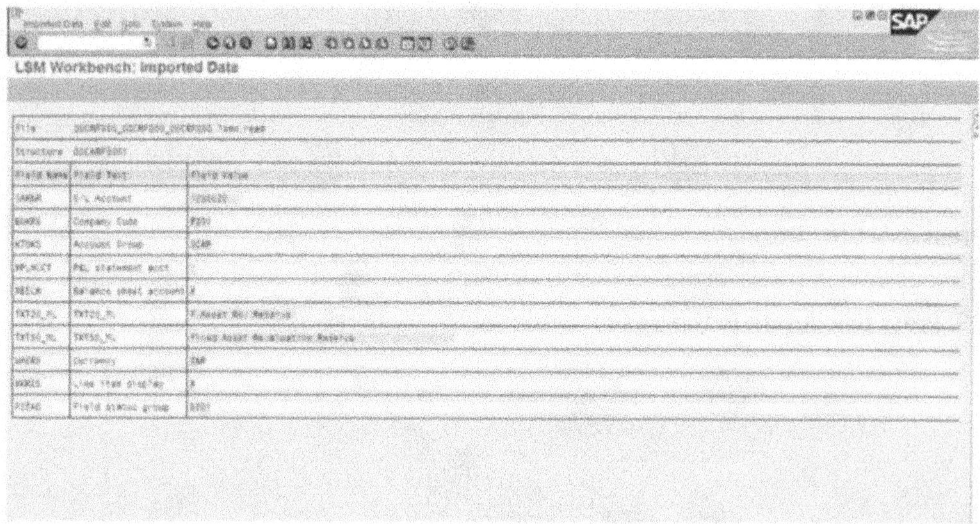

This shows the details of the line item. Press back to continue.

41. Automatically Convert Data will be selected.

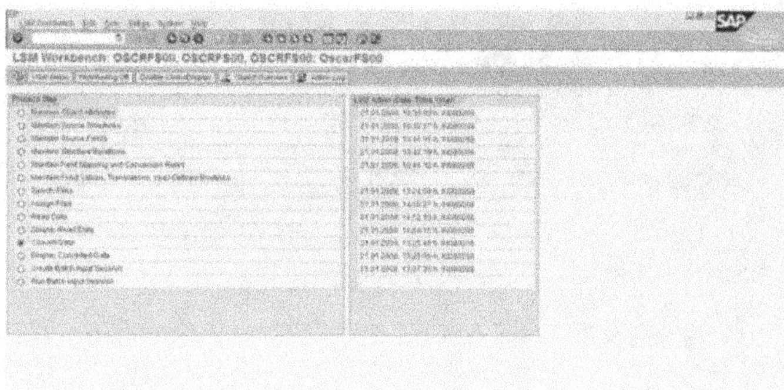

Press execute button to continue.

42.

Press execute button to continue.

43. This will confirm the data to be uploaded.

Press back button to continue.

44. Automatically Display Converted Data will be selected.

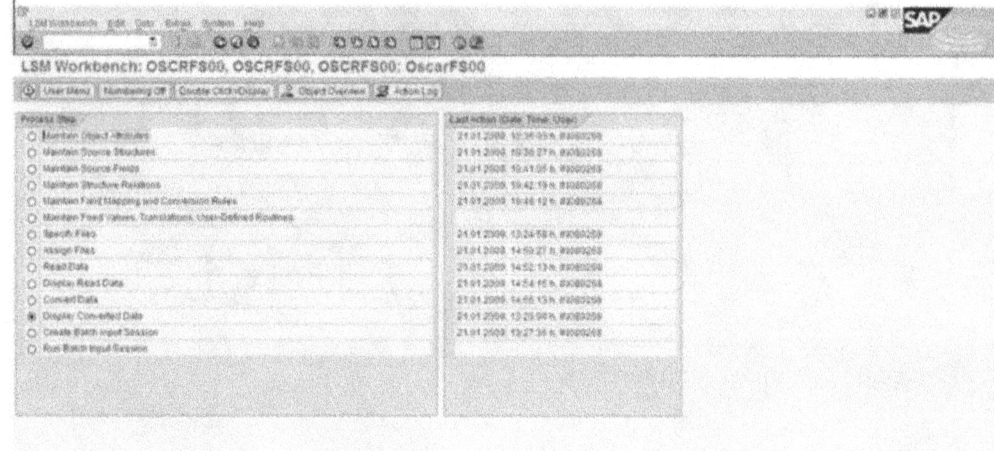

Press Execute button to continue.

45.

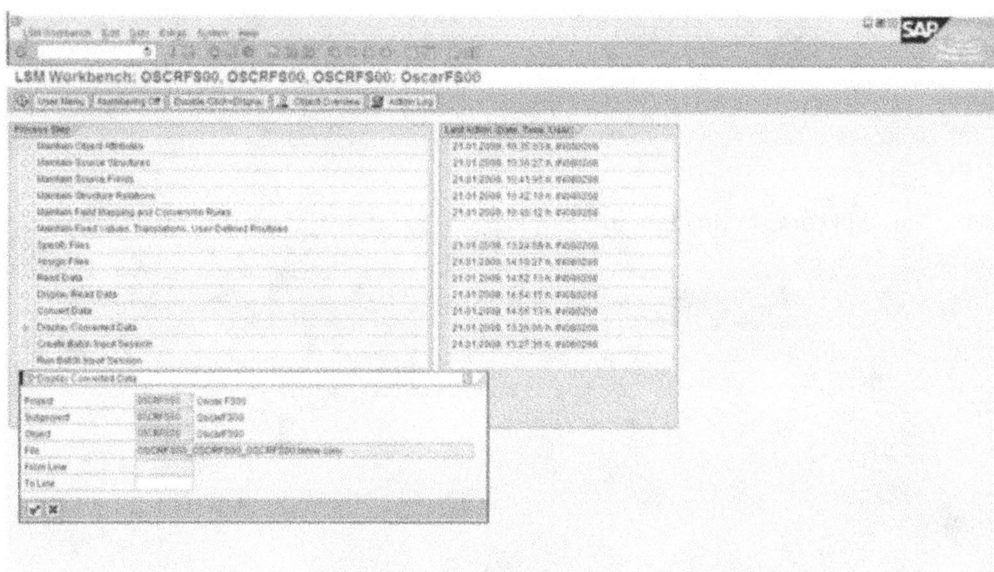

Press the tick button to continue.

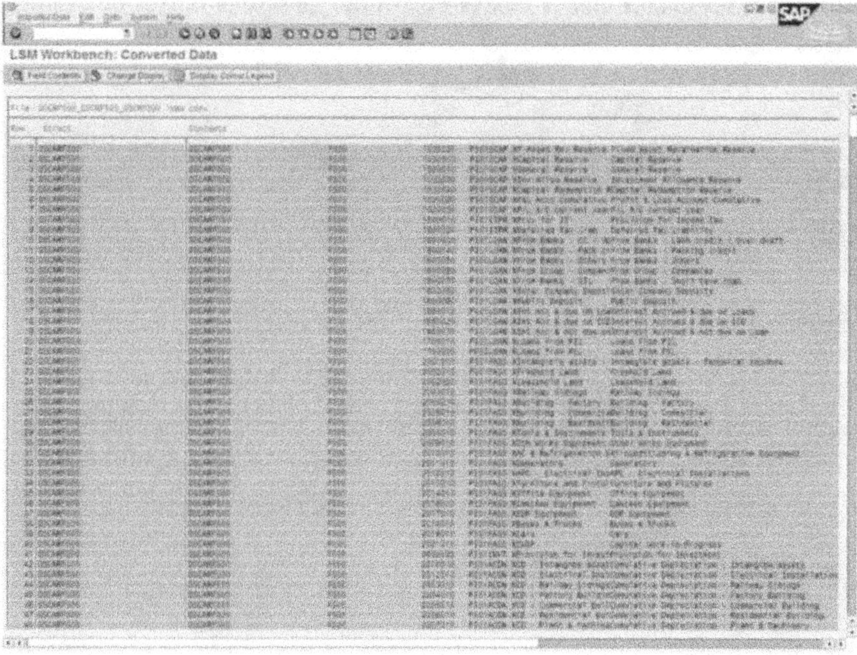

Double click on line item for confirmation of data.

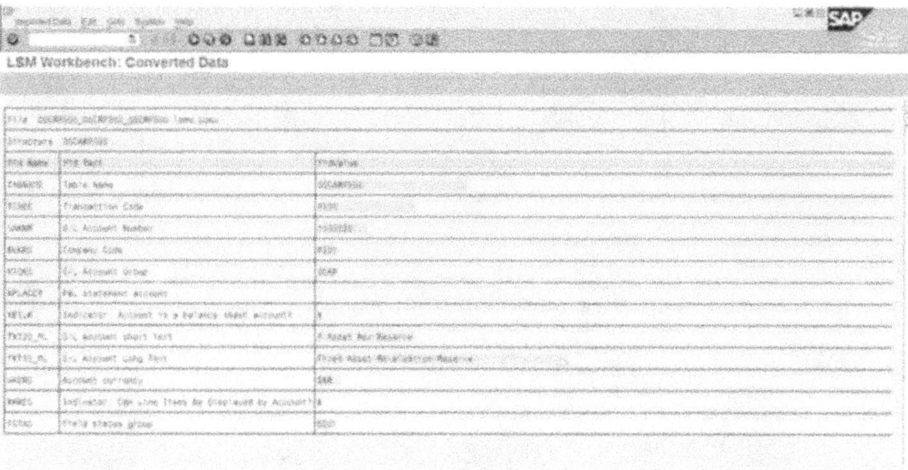

This shows the details of each line item.

Press back to continue.

46. Automatically Create Batch Input Session will be selected.

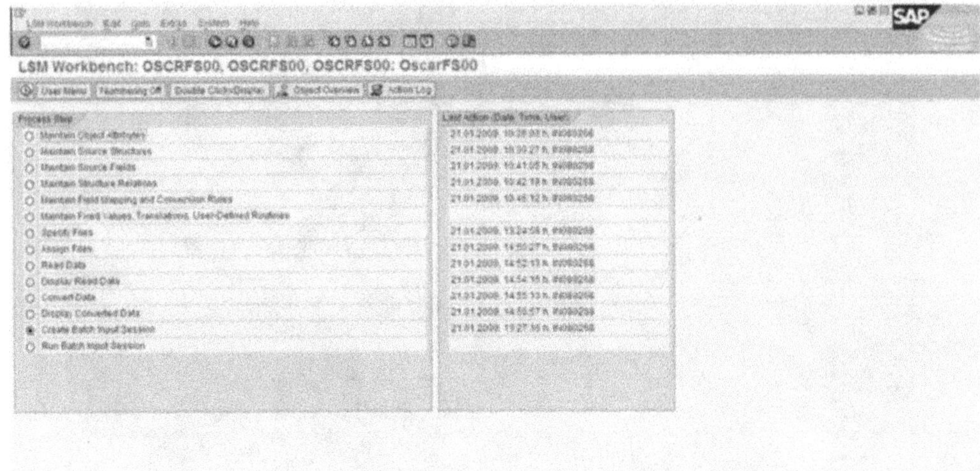

Press execute button to continue.

47. This screen will come.

Press execute button to create a batch input folder.

48.

Press tick button and continue for next step.

49. Automatically Run Batch Input Session will be selected.

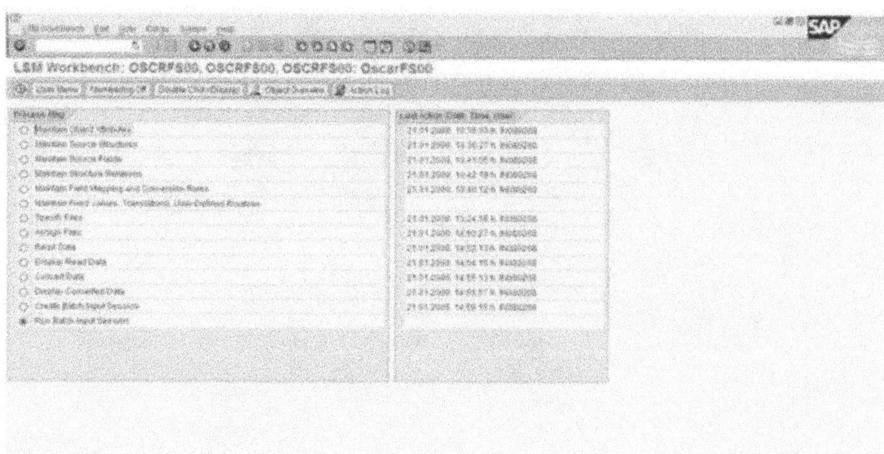

Press execute button to continue.

50. This screen is used to upload the data.

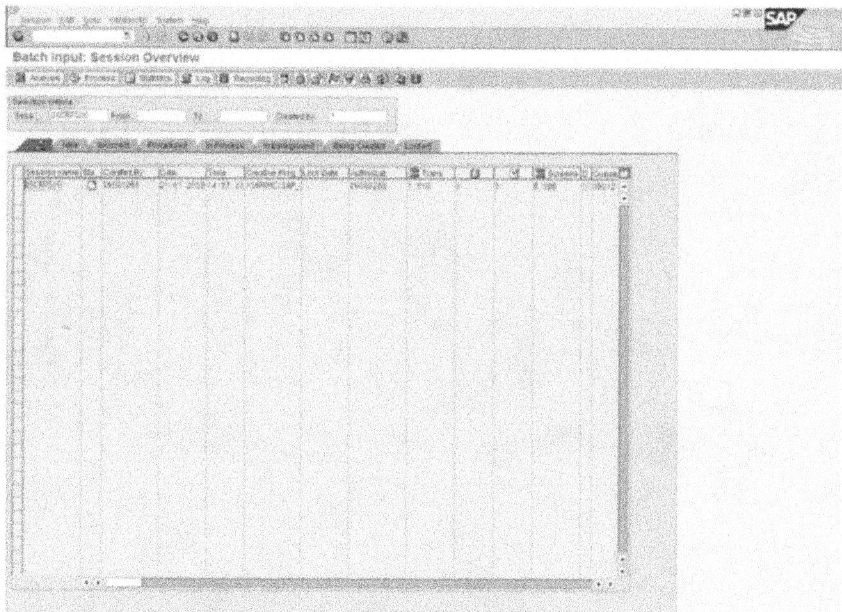

Select the line item and click Process button to upload the GLs from the text file.

51.

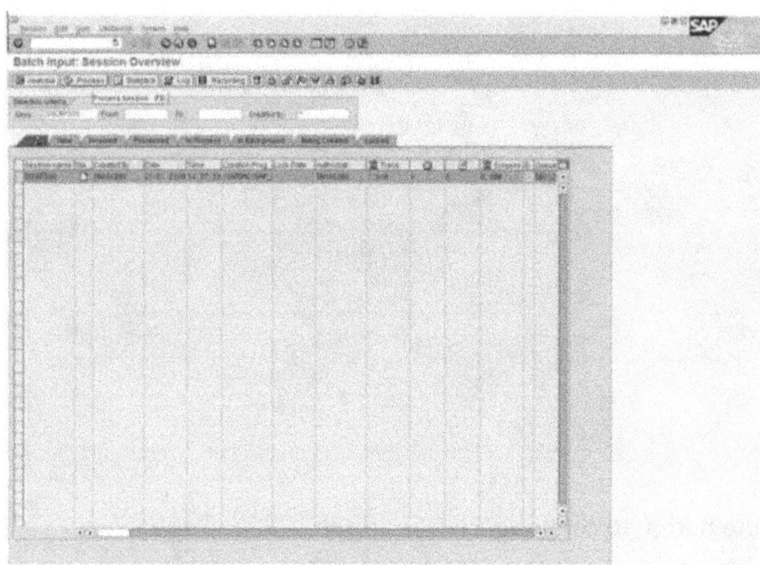

All the GLs are successfully created.

After the process is completed the above screen will be displayed. User can check the log file for any information required.

19.11. DEMO 4 – LSMW asset upload step by step testing

Goto TCode LSMW

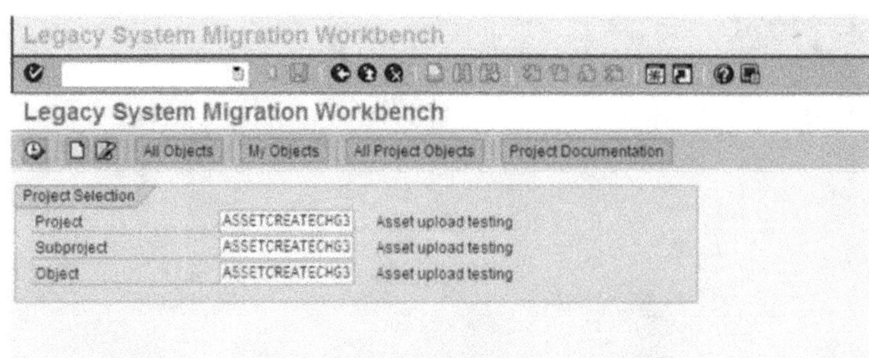

LSM Workbench: ASSETCREATECHG3, ASSETCREATECHG3, ASSETCREATECHG3: Asse
User Menu
Numbering Off
Double Click=Display
Object Overview
Action Log
Process Step
Maintain Object Attributes
Maintain Source Structures
Maintain Source Fields
Maintain Structure Relations
Maintain Field Mapping and Conversion Rules
Maintain Fixed Values, Translations, User-Defined Routines
Specify Files
Assign Files
Read Data
Display Read Data
Convert Data
Display Converted Data
Create Batch Input Session
Run Batch Input Session
Last Action (Date, Time, User)
17.02.2012, 22:16:49 h, SDASGUPTA
17.02.2012, 22:17:23 h, SDASGUPTA
17.02.2012, 22:18:15 h, SDASGUPTA
17.02.2012, 22:18:38 h, SDASGUPTA
17.02.2012, 22:19:22 h, SDASGUPTA
17.02.2012, 22:21:04 h, SDASGUPTA
17.02.2012, 22:21:20 h, SDASGUPTA
17.02.2012, 22:21:36 h, SDASGUPTA
17.02.2012, 22:21:43 h, SDASGUPTA
17.02.2012, 22:21:55 h, SDASGUPTA
17.02.2012, 22:22:02 h, SDASGUPTA
17.02.2012, 22:22:08 h, SDASGUPTA

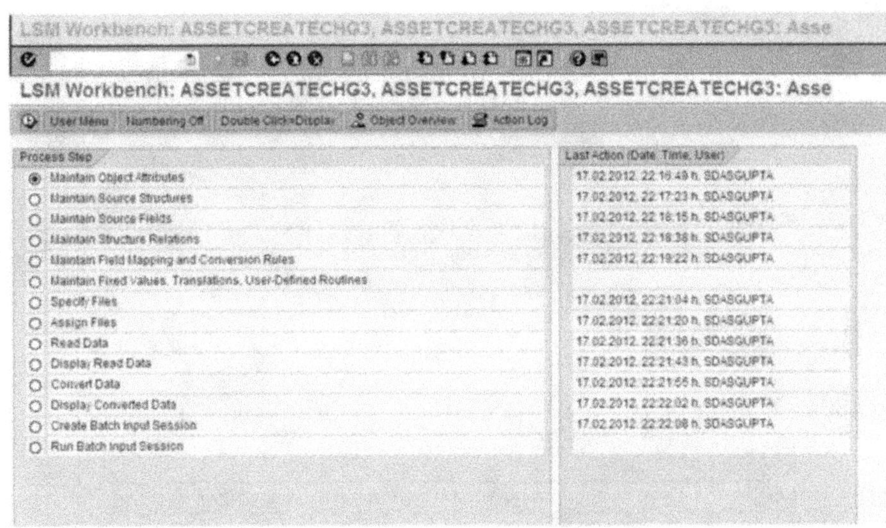

LSM Workbench: Change Object Attributes
Display <-> Change
Documentation
Display Interfaces
Attributes
Object
ASSETCREATECHG3
Asset upload testing
Owner
SDASGUPTA
Srijata Dasgupta
Data Transfer
Once-Only
Periodic
File Names
System-Dependent
Object Type and Import Method
Standard Batch/Direct Input
Object
Method
Program Name
Program Type
Batch Input Recording
Recording
ASSTTEST
Asset creation
Business Object Method (BAPI)
Business Object
Method
Message Type
Basic Type
IDoc (Intermediate Document)
Message Type
Basic Type
Enhancement
Allow Structure Assignment for EDIDC40

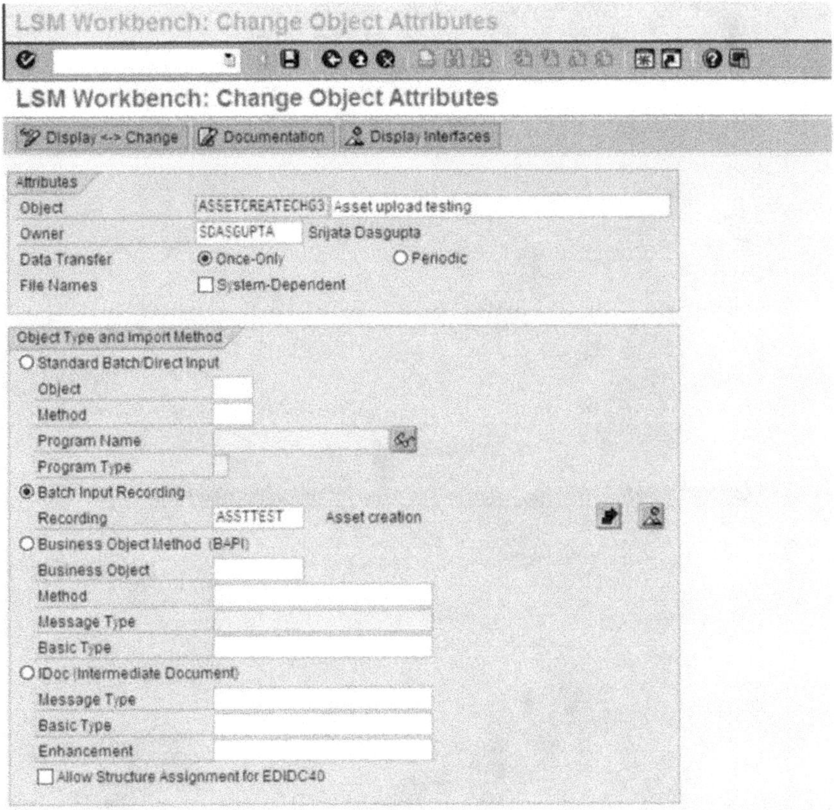

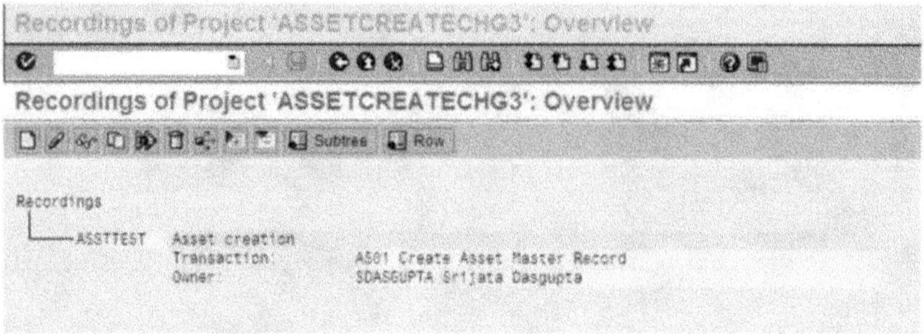

Recordings of Project 'ASSETCREATECHG3': Overview

Subtree Row

Recordings
ASSTTEST Asset creation
Transaction: AS01 Create Asset Master Record
Owner: SDASGUPTA Srijata Dasgupta

Repeat Recording

T-code AS01

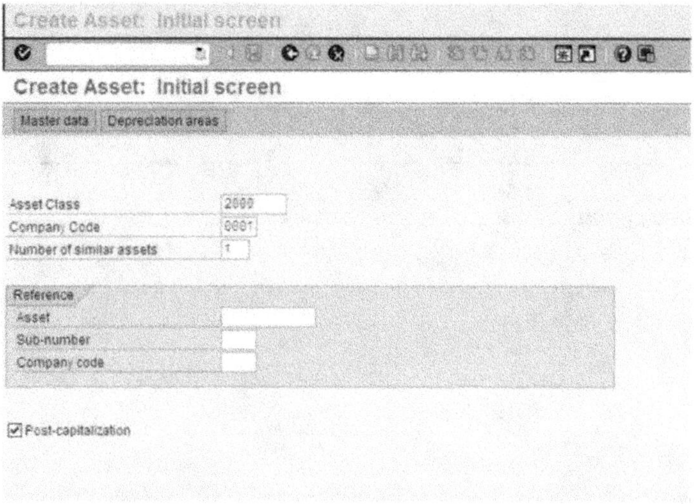

Create Asset: Initial screen

Master data Depreciation areas

Asset Class 2000
Company Code 0001
Number of similar assets 1

Reference
Asset
Sub-number
Company code

Post-capitalization

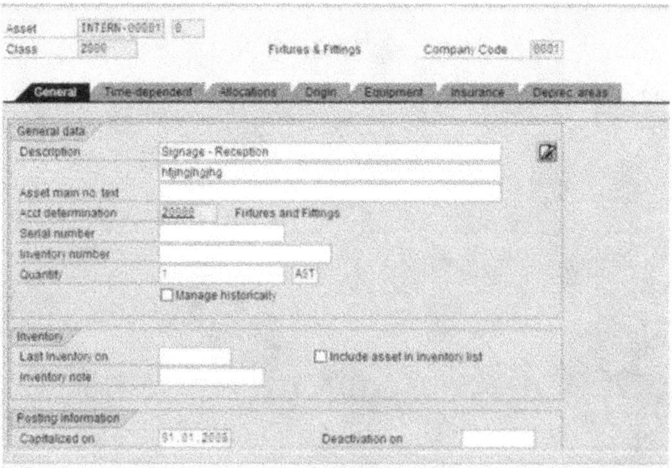

Asset INTERN-00001 0
Class 2000 Fixtures & Fittings Company Code 0001

General Time-dependent Allocations Origin Equipment Insurance Deprec. areas

General data
Description Signage - Reception
hfjhghjghg
Asset main no. text
Acct determination 20000 Fixtures and Fittings
Serial number
Inventory number
Quantity 1 AST
Manage historically

Inventory
Last inventory on
Include asset in inventory list
Inventory note

Posting information
Capitalized on 01.01.2005 Deactivation on

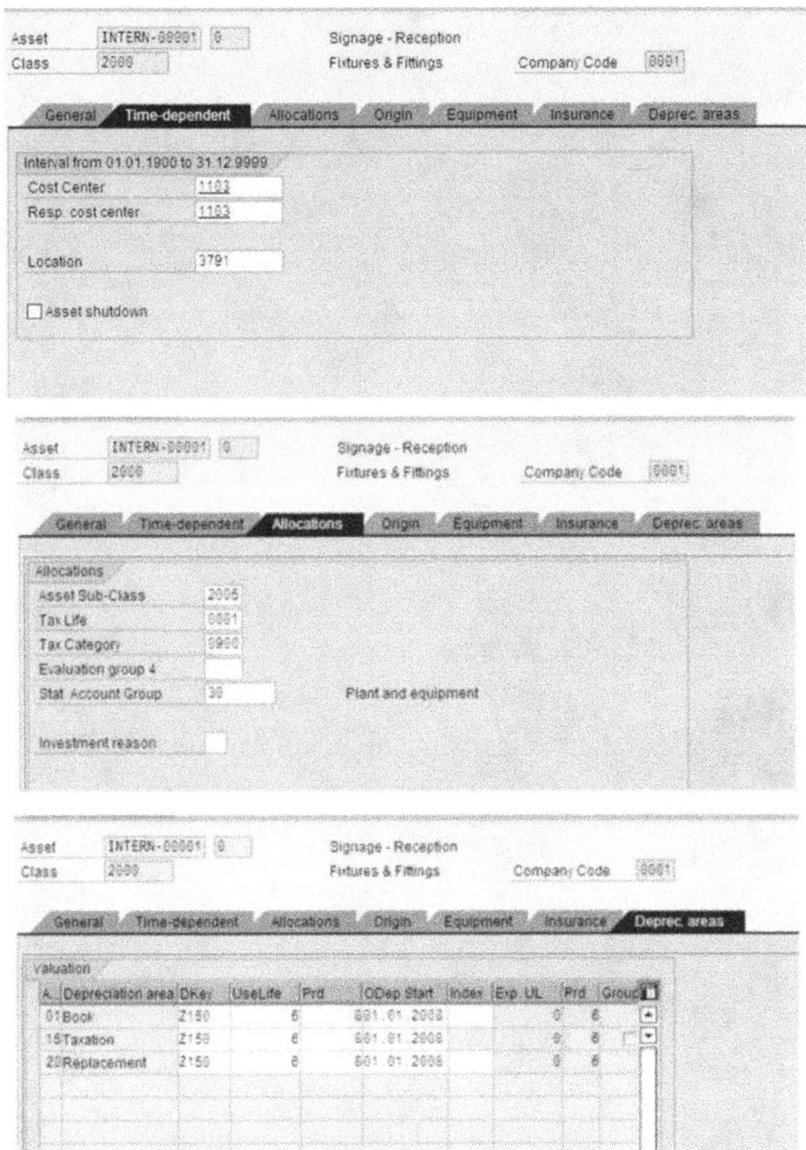

Double click on Dep Area 15.

Warning message comes as: Dep. key/useful life were changed. The system calculated new values.

We give the Gr Asset and Sub Asset in this screen and save.

Default All

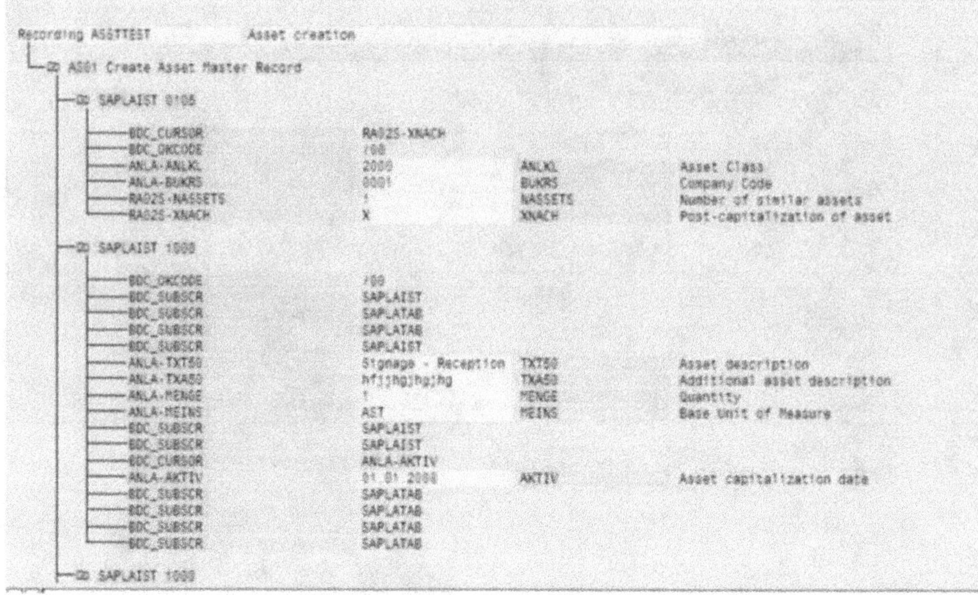
Recording ASSTTEST Asset creation
AS01 Create Asset Master Record
SAPLAIST 0105
BDC_CURSOR RA02S-XNACH
BDC_OKCODE /00
ANLA-ANLKL 2000 ANLKL Asset Class
ANLA-BUKRS 0001 BUKRS Company Code
RA02S-NASSETS 1 NASSETS Number of similar assets
RA02S-XNACH X XNACH Post-capitalization of asset
SAPLAIST 1000
BDC_OKCODE /00
BDC_SUBSCR SAPLAIST
BDC_SUBSCR SAPLATAB
BDC_SUBSCR SAPLATAB
BDC_SUBSCR SAPLAIST
ANLA-TXT50 Signage - Reception TXT50 Asset description
ANLA-TXA50 hfjjhgjhgjhg TXA50 Additional asset description
ANLA-MENGE 1 MENGE Quantity
ANLA-MEINS AST MEINS Base Unit of Measure
BDC_SUBSCR SAPLAIST
BDC_SUBSCR SAPLAIST
BDC_CURSOR ANLA-AKTIV
ANLA-AKTIV 01.01.2008 AKTIV Asset capitalization date
BDC_SUBSCR SAPLATAB
BDC_SUBSCR SAPLATAB
BDC_SUBSCR SAPLATAB
BDC_SUBSCR SAPLATAB
SAPLAIST 1000

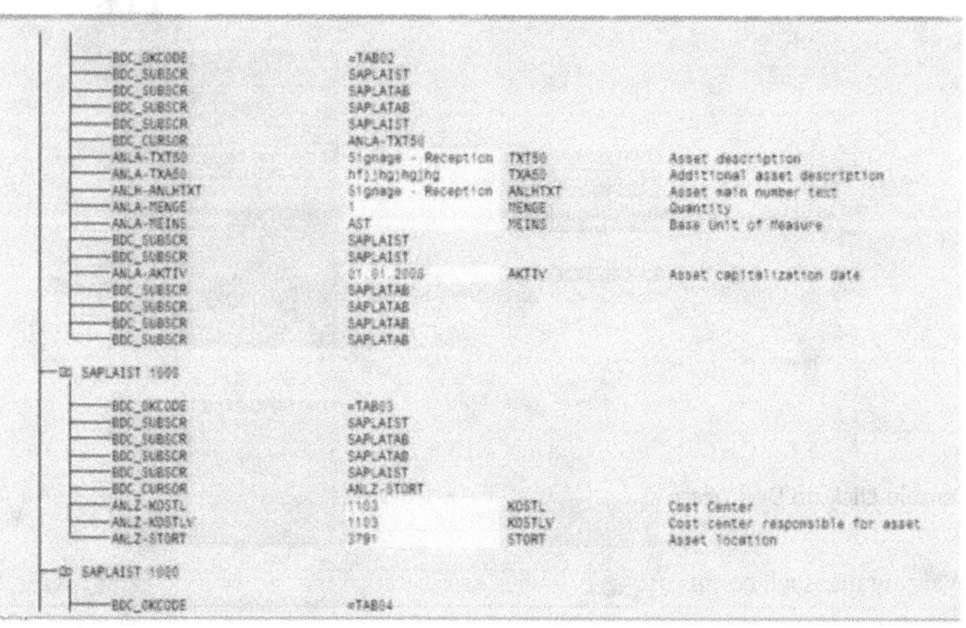
BDC_OKCODE =TAB02
BDC_SUBSCR SAPLAIST
BDC_SUBSCR SAPLATAB
BDC_SUBSCR SAPLATAB
BDC_SUBSCR SAPLAIST
BDC_CURSOR ANLA-TXT50
ANLA-TXT50 Signage - Reception TXT50 Asset description
ANLA-TXA50 hfjjhgjhgjhg TXA50 Additional asset description
ANLH-ANLHTXT Signage - Reception ANLHTXT Asset main number text
ANLA-MENGE 1 MENGE Quantity
ANLA-MEINS AST MEINS Base Unit of Measure
BDC_SUBSCR SAPLAIST
BDC_SUBSCR SAPLAIST
ANLA-AKTIV 01.01.2008 AKTIV Asset capitalization date
BDC_SUBSCR SAPLATAB
BDC_SUBSCR SAPLATAB
BDC_SUBSCR SAPLATAB
BDC_SUBSCR SAPLATAB
SAPLAIST 1000
BDC_OKCODE =TAB03
BDC_SUBSCR SAPLAIST
BDC_SUBSCR SAPLATAB
BDC_SUBSCR SAPLATAB
BDC_SUBSCR SAPLAIST
BDC_CURSOR ANLZ-STORT
ANLZ-KOSTL 1103 KOSTL Cost Center
ANLZ-KOSTLV 1103 KOSTLV Cost center responsible for asset
ANLZ-STORT 3791 STORT Asset location
SAPLAIST 1000
BDC_OKCODE =TAB04

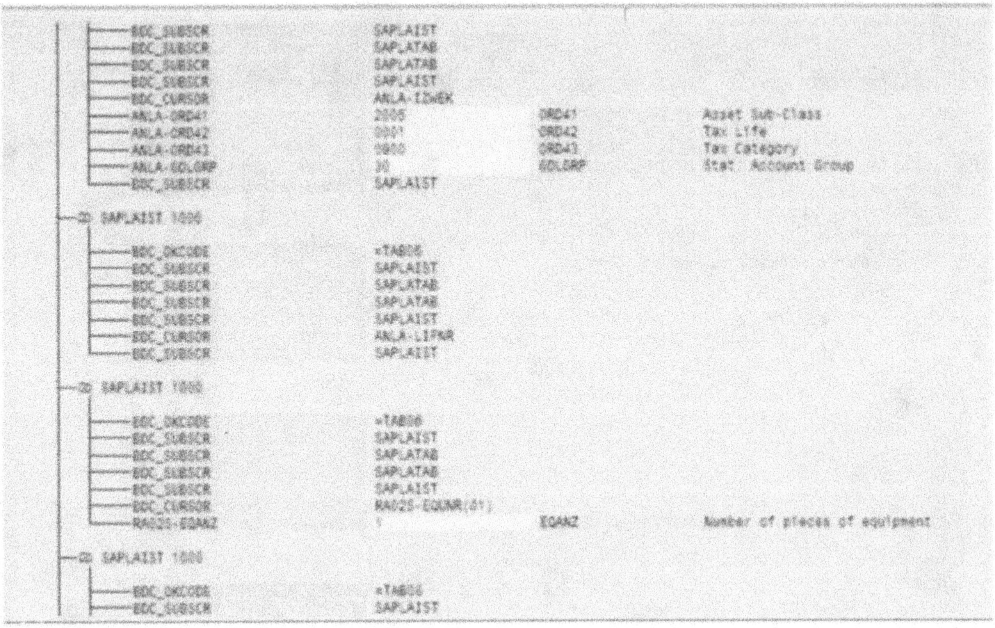

```
|    |----BDC_SUBSCR           SAPLAIST
|    |----BDC_SUBSCR           SAPLATAB
|    |----BDC_SUBSCR           SAPLATAB
|    |----BDC_SUBSCR           SAPLAIST
|    |----BDC_CURSOR           ANLA-IZWEK
|    |----ANLA-ORD41           2005            ORD41      Asset Sub-Class
|    |----ANLA-ORD42           0001            ORD42      Tax Life
|    |----ANLA-ORD43           9800            ORD43      Tax Category
|    |----ANLA-GDLGRP          30              GDLGRP     Stat. Account Group
|    |----BDC_SUBSCR           SAPLAIST
|
|--SAPLAIST 1000
|    |----BDC_OKCODE           =TABO5
|    |----BDC_SUBSCR           SAPLAIST
|    |----BDC_SUBSCR           SAPLATAB
|    |----BDC_SUBSCR           SAPLATAB
|    |----BDC_SUBSCR           SAPLAIST
|    |----BDC_CURSOR           ANLA-LIFNR
|    |----BDC_SUBSCR           SAPLAIST
|
|--SAPLAIST 1000
|    |----BDC_OKCODE           =TAB06
|    |----BDC_SUBSCR           SAPLAIST
|    |----BDC_SUBSCR           SAPLATAB
|    |----BDC_SUBSCR           SAPLATAB
|    |----BDC_SUBSCR           SAPLAIST
|    |----BDC_CURSOR           RA02S-EQUNR(01)
|    |----RA02S-EQANZ          1               EQANZ      Number of pieces of equipment
|
|--SAPLAIST 1000
|    |----BDC_OKCODE           =TAB06
|    |----BDC_SUBSCR           SAPLAIST
```

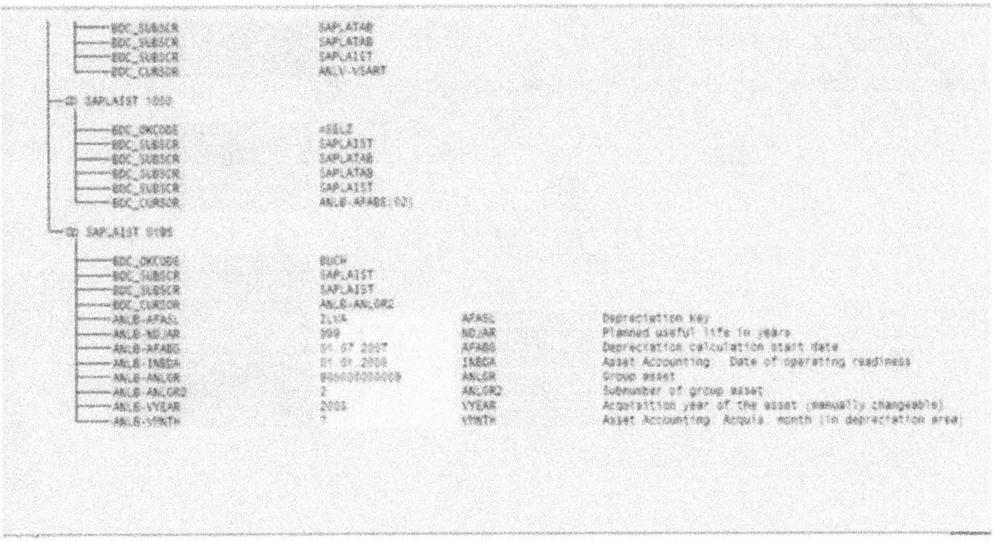

```
|    |----BDC_SUBSCR           SAPLATAB
|    |----BDC_SUBSCR           SAPLATAB
|    |----BDC_SUBSCR           SAPLAIST
|    |----BDC_CURSOR           ANLV-VSART
|
|--SAPLAIST 1000
|    |----BDC_OKCODE           =SELZ
|    |----BDC_SUBSCR           SAPLAIST
|    |----BDC_SUBSCR           SAPLATAB
|    |----BDC_SUBSCR           SAPLATAB
|    |----BDC_SUBSCR           SAPLAIST
|    |----BDC_CURSOR           ANLB-AFABE(02)
|
|--SAPLAIST 0195
     |----BDC_OKCODE           BUCH
     |----BDC_SUBSCR           SAPLAIST
     |----BDC_SUBSCR           SAPLAIST
     |----BDC_CURSOR           ANLB-ANLGR2
     |----ANLB-AFASL           ILVA           AFASL      Depreciation key
     |----ANLB-NDJAR           999            NDJAR      Planned useful life in years
     |----ANLB-AFABG           01.07.2007     AFABG      Depreciation calculation start date
     |----ANLB-INBDA           01.01.2008     INBDA      Asset Accounting: Date of operating readiness
     |----ANLB-ANLGR           000000000059   ANLGR      Group asset
     |----ANLB-ANLGR2          2              ANLGR2     Subnumber of group asset
     |----ANLB-VYEAR           2008           VYEAR      Acquisition year of the asset (manually changeable)
     |----ANLB-VMNTH           7              VMNTH      Asset Accounting: Acquis. month (in depreciation area)
```

Save.

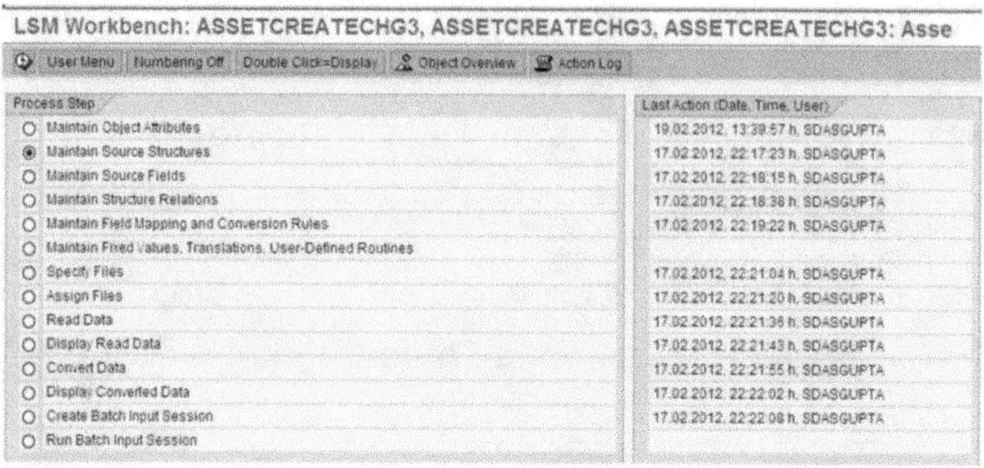

LSM Workbench: ASSETCREATECHG3, ASSETCREATECHG3, ASSETCREATECHG3: Asse

User Menu | Numbering Off | Double Click=Display | Object Overview | Action Log

Process Step	Last Action (Date, Time, User)
○ Maintain Object Attributes	19.02.2012, 13:39:57 h, SDASGUPTA
◉ Maintain Source Structures	17.02.2012, 22:17:23 h, SDASGUPTA
○ Maintain Source Fields	17.02.2012, 22:18:15 h, SDASGUPTA
○ Maintain Structure Relations	17.02.2012, 22:18:38 h, SDASGUPTA
○ Maintain Field Mapping and Conversion Rules	17.02.2012, 22:19:22 h, SDASGUPTA
○ Maintain Fixed Values, Translations, User-Defined Routines	
○ Specify Files	17.02.2012, 22:21:04 h, SDASGUPTA
○ Assign Files	17.02.2012, 22:21:20 h, SDASGUPTA
○ Read Data	17.02.2012, 22:21:36 h, SDASGUPTA
○ Display Read Data	17.02.2012, 22:21:43 h, SDASGUPTA
○ Convert Data	17.02.2012, 22:21:55 h, SDASGUPTA
○ Display Converted Data	17.02.2012, 22:22:02 h, SDASGUPTA
○ Create Batch Input Session	17.02.2012, 22:22:08 h, SDASGUPTA
○ Run Batch Input Session	

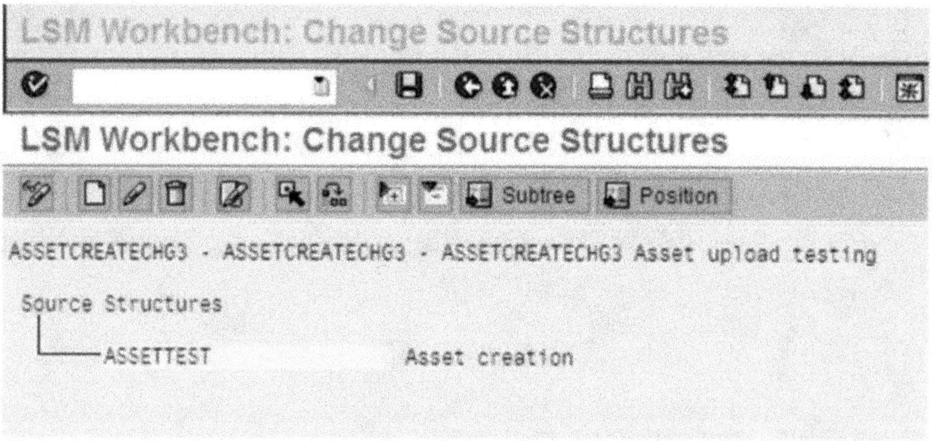

LSM Workbench: Change Source Structures

LSM Workbench: Change Source Structures

Subtree | Position

ASSETCREATECHG3 - ASSETCREATECHG3 - ASSETCREATECHG3 Asset upload testing

Source Structures
└── ASSETTEST Asset creation

Save.

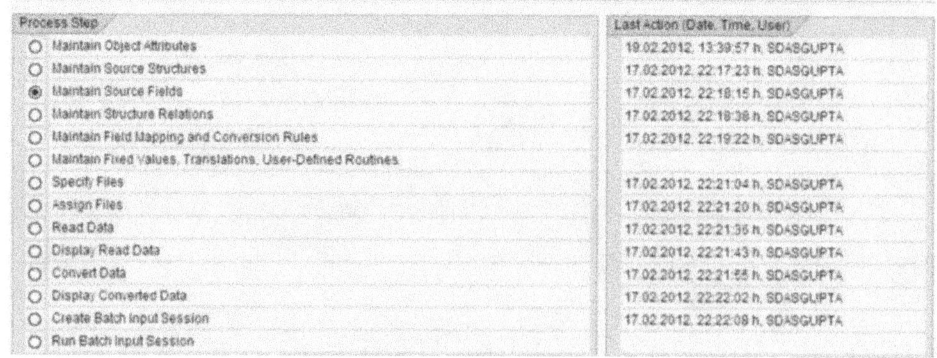

Process Step	Last Action (Date, Time, User)
○ Maintain Object Attributes	19.02.2012, 13:39:57 h, SDASGUPTA
○ Maintain Source Structures	17.02.2012, 22:17:23 h, SDASGUPTA
◉ Maintain Source Fields	17.02.2012, 22:18:15 h, SDASGUPTA
○ Maintain Structure Relations	17.02.2012, 22:18:38 h, SDASGUPTA
○ Maintain Field Mapping and Conversion Rules	17.02.2012, 22:19:22 h, SDASGUPTA
○ Maintain Fixed Values, Translations, User-Defined Routines	
○ Specify Files	17.02.2012, 22:21:04 h, SDASGUPTA
○ Assign Files	17.02.2012, 22:21:20 h, SDASGUPTA
○ Read Data	17.02.2012, 22:21:36 h, SDASGUPTA
○ Display Read Data	17.02.2012, 22:21:43 h, SDASGUPTA
○ Convert Data	17.02.2012, 22:21:55 h, SDASGUPTA
○ Display Converted Data	17.02.2012, 22:22:02 h, SDASGUPTA
○ Create Batch Input Session	17.02.2012, 22:22:08 h, SDASGUPTA
○ Run Batch Input Session	

ASSETCREATECHG3 - ASSETCREATECHG3 - ASSETCREATECHG3 Asset upload testing

Source Fields

ASSETTEST Asset creation

Field	Type	Description
BUKRS	C(010)	Company code
ANLKL	C(010)	Asset class
NASSETS	C(010)	Number of similar assets
XNACH	C(001)	Post capitalization
TXT50	C(030)	Description
MENGE	C(010)	Quantity
MEINS	C(010)	Base unit of measure
KOSTL	C(010)	Cost center
KOSTLV	C(010)	Resp. cost center
STORT	C(010)	Location
ORD41	C(010)	Asset Sub-class
ORD42	C(010)	Tax Life
ORD43	C(010)	Tax Category
CATPAVAL	C(010)	Parameter contents
NDJAR	C(010)	Useful life
AFASL	C(010)	Depreciation key
NDPER	C(010)	Usef.life in periods
AFASLTAX	C(010)	Depreciation key
NDJARTAX	C(010)	Useful life
NDPERTAX	C(010)	Usef.life in periods
IZWEK	C(010)	Investment reason
ANLHTXT	C(010)	Asset main no. text
SERNR	C(010)	Serial number
INVNR	C(010)	Inventory number
AKTIV	C(010)	Asset capitalization Date
ANLGR	C(010)	Group asset
ANLGR2	C(010)	Subnumber

Process Step	Last Action (Date, Time, User)
○ Maintain Object Attributes	19.02.2012, 13:39:57 h, SDASGUPTA
○ Maintain Source Structures	17.02.2012, 22:17:23 h, SDASGUPTA
○ Maintain Source Fields	17.02.2012, 22:18:15 h, SDASGUPTA
◉ Maintain Structure Relations	17.02.2012, 22:18:38 h, SDASGUPTA
○ Maintain Field Mapping and Conversion Rules	17.02.2012, 22:19:22 h, SDASGUPTA
○ Maintain Fixed Values, Translations, User-Defined Routines	
○ Specify Files	17.02.2012, 22:21:04 h, SDASGUPTA
○ Assign Files	17.02.2012, 22:21:20 h, SDASGUPTA
○ Read Data	17.02.2012, 22:21:36 h, SDASGUPTA
○ Display Read Data	17.02.2012, 22:21:43 h, SDASGUPTA
○ Convert Data	17.02.2012, 22:21:55 h, SDASGUPTA
○ Display Converted Data	17.02.2012, 22:22:02 h, SDASGUPTA
○ Create Batch Input Session	17.02.2012, 22:22:08 h, SDASGUPTA
○ Run Batch Input Session	

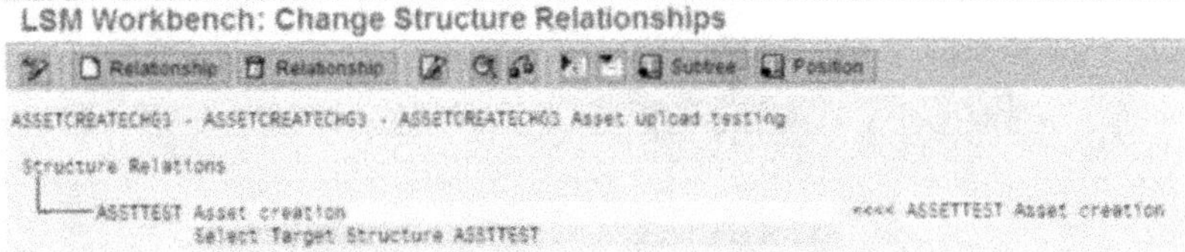

Save.

Process Step	Last Action (Date, Time, User)
○ Maintain Object Attributes	19.02.2012, 13:39:57 h, SDASGUPTA
○ Maintain Source Structures	17.02.2012, 22:17:23 h, SDASGUPTA
○ Maintain Source Fields	17.02.2012, 22:18:15 h, SDASGUPTA
○ Maintain Structure Relations	19.02.2012, 13:44:22 h, SDASGUPTA
◉ Maintain Field Mapping and Conversion Rules	17.02.2012, 22:19:22 h, SDASGUPTA
○ Maintain Fixed Values, Translations, User-Defined Routines	
○ Specify Files	17.02.2012, 22:21:04 h, SDASGUPTA
○ Assign Files	17.02.2012, 22:21:20 h, SDASGUPTA
○ Read Data	17.02.2012, 22:21:36 h, SDASGUPTA
○ Display Read Data	17.02.2012, 22:21:43 h, SDASGUPTA
○ Convert Data	17.02.2012, 22:21:55 h, SDASGUPTA
○ Display Converted Data	17.02.2012, 22:22:02 h, SDASGUPTA
○ Create Batch Input Session	17.02.2012, 22:22:08 h, SDASGUPTA
○ Run Batch Input Session	

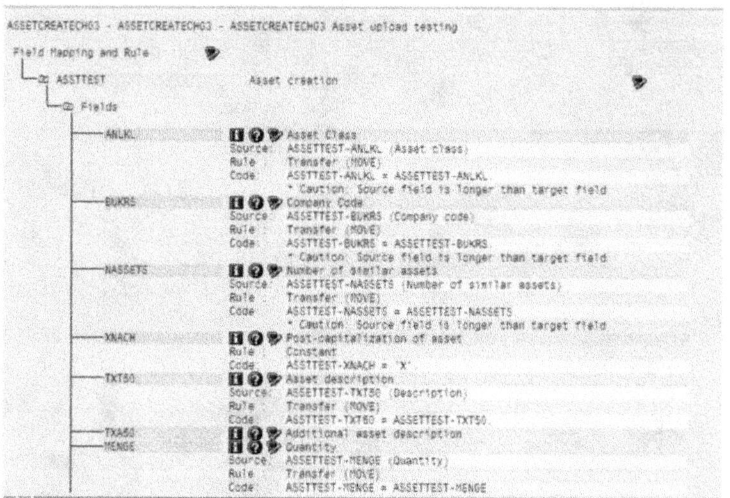

```
ASSETCREATECH03 - ASSETCREATECH03 - ASSETCREATECH03 Asset upload testing
Field Mapping and Rule
  ASSTTEST                      Asset creation
    Fields
      ANLKL      Asset Class
                 Source:  ASSETTEST-ANLKL (Asset class)
                 Rule  :  Transfer (MOVE)
                 Code:    ASSTTEST-ANLKL = ASSETTEST-ANLKL.
                          * Caution: Source field is longer than target field
      BUKRS      Company Code
                 Source:  ASSETTEST-BUKRS (Company code)
                 Rule  :  Transfer (MOVE)
                 Code:    ASSTTEST-BUKRS = ASSETTEST-BUKRS.
                          * Caution: Source field is longer than target field
      NASSETS    Number of similar assets
                 Source:  ASSETTEST-NASSETS (Number of similar assets)
                 Rule  :  Transfer (MOVE)
                 Code:    ASSTTEST-NASSETS = ASSETTEST-NASSETS.
                          * Caution: Source field is longer than target field
      XNACH      Post-capitalization of asset
                 Rule  :  Constant
                 Code:    ASSTTEST-XNACH = 'X'.
      TXT50      Asset description
                 Source:  ASSETTEST-TXT50 (Description)
                 Rule  :  Transfer (MOVE)
                 Code:    ASSTTEST-TXT50 = ASSETTEST-TXT50.
      TXA50      Additional asset description
      MENGE      Quantity
                 Source:  ASSETTEST-MENGE (Quantity)
                 Rule  :  Transfer (MOVE)
                 Code:    ASSTTEST-MENGE = ASSETTEST-MENGE.
```

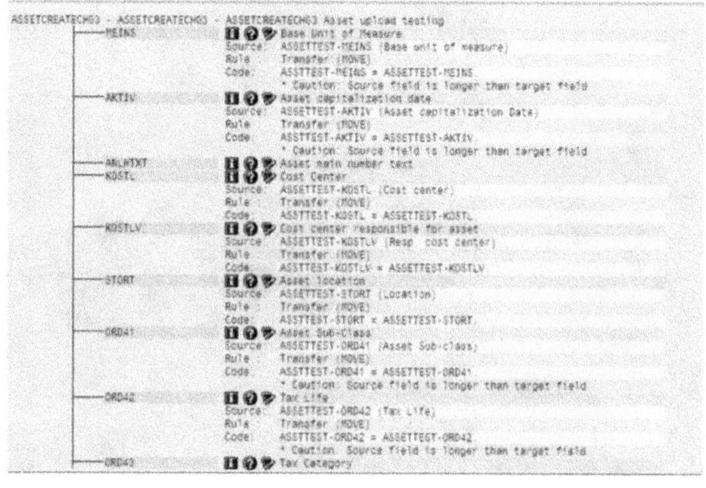

```
ASSETCREATECH03 - ASSETCREATECH03 - ASSETCREATECH03 Asset upload testing
      MEINS      Base Unit of Measure
                 Source:  ASSETTEST-MEINS (Base unit of measure)
                 Rule  :  Transfer (MOVE)
                 Code:    ASSTTEST-MEINS = ASSETTEST-MEINS.
                          * Caution: Source field is longer than target field
      AKTIV      Asset capitalization date
                 Source:  ASSETTEST-AKTIV (Asset capitalization Date)
                 Rule  :  Transfer (MOVE)
                 Code:    ASSTTEST-AKTIV = ASSETTEST-AKTIV.
                          * Caution: Source field is longer than target field
      ANLHTXT    Asset main number text
      KOSTL      Cost Center
                 Source:  ASSETTEST-KOSTL (Cost center)
                 Rule  :  Transfer (MOVE)
                 Code:    ASSTTEST-KOSTL = ASSETTEST-KOSTL.
      KOSTLV     Cost center responsible for asset
                 Source:  ASSETTEST-KOSTLV (Resp. cost center)
                 Rule  :  Transfer (MOVE)
                 Code:    ASSTTEST-KOSTLV = ASSETTEST-KOSTLV.
      STORT      Asset location
                 Source:  ASSETTEST-STORT (Location)
                 Rule  :  Transfer (MOVE)
                 Code:    ASSTTEST-STORT = ASSETTEST-STORT.
      ORD41      Asset Sub-Class
                 Source:  ASSETTEST-ORD41 (Asset Sub-class)
                 Rule  :  Transfer (MOVE)
                 Code:    ASSTTEST-ORD41 = ASSETTEST-ORD41.
                          * Caution: Source field is longer than target field
      ORD42      Tax Life
                 Source:  ASSETTEST-ORD42 (Tax Life)
                 Rule  :  Transfer (MOVE)
                 Code:    ASSTTEST-ORD42 = ASSETTEST-ORD42.
                          * Caution: Source field is longer than target field
      ORD43      Tax Category
```

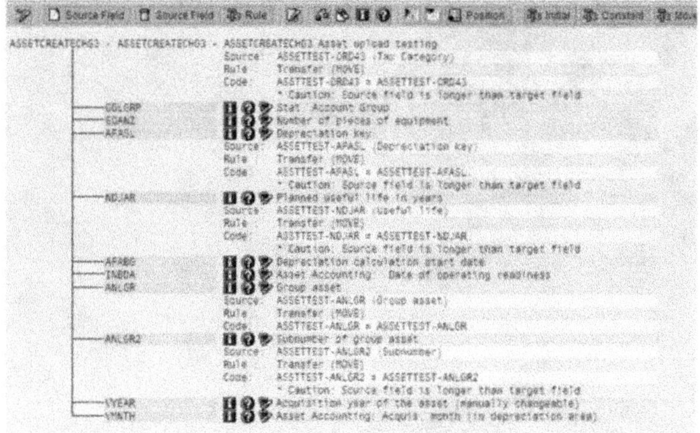

Save.

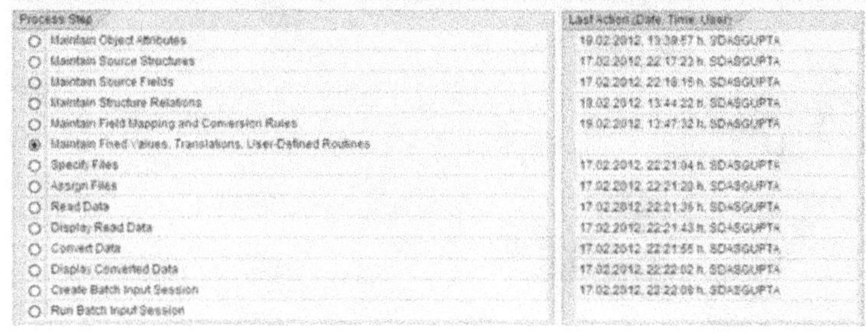

Process Step	Last Action (Date, Time, User)
○ Maintain Object Attributes	19.02.2012, 13:39:57 h, SDASGUPTA
○ Maintain Source Structures	17.02.2012, 22:17:23 h, SDASGUPTA
○ Maintain Source Fields	17.02.2012, 22:18:15 h, SDASGUPTA
○ Maintain Structure Relations	19.02.2012, 13:44:22 h, SDASGUPTA
○ Maintain Field Mapping and Conversion Rules	19.02.2012, 13:47:32 h, SDASGUPTA
◉ Maintain Fixed Values, Translations, User-Defined Routines	
○ Specify Files	17.02.2012, 22:21:04 h, SDASGUPTA
○ Assign Files	17.02.2012, 22:21:20 h, SDASGUPTA
○ Read Data	17.02.2012, 22:21:36 h, SDASGUPTA
○ Display Read Data	17.02.2012, 22:21:43 h, SDASGUPTA
○ Convert Data	17.02.2012, 22:21:55 h, SDASGUPTA
○ Display Converted Data	17.02.2012, 22:22:02 h, SDASGUPTA
○ Create Batch Input Session	17.02.2012, 22:22:08 h, SDASGUPTA
○ Run Batch Input Session	

```
Reusable Rules
└─ ASSETCREATECHG3 Asset upload testing                17.02.2012 SDASGUPTA
      ├──Fixed Values
      ├──Translations
      └──User-Defined Routines
```

Save.

Process Step	Last Action (Date, Time, User)
○ Maintain Object Attributes	19.02.2012, 13:39:57 h, SDASGUPTA
○ Maintain Source Structures	17.02.2012, 22:17:23 h, SDASGUPTA
○ Maintain Source Fields	17.02.2012, 22:18:15 h, SDASGUPTA
○ Maintain Structure Relations	19.02.2012, 13:44:22 h, SDASGUPTA
○ Maintain Field Mapping and Conversion Rules	19.02.2012, 13:47:32 h, SDASGUPTA
○ Maintain Fixed Values, Translations, User-Defined Routines	
◉ Specify Files	17.02.2012, 22:21:04 h, SDASGUPTA
○ Assign Files	17.02.2012, 22:21:20 h, SDASGUPTA
○ Read Data	17.02.2012, 22:21:36 h, SDASGUPTA
○ Display Read Data	17.02.2012, 22:21:43 h, SDASGUPTA
○ Convert Data	17.02.2012, 22:21:55 h, SDASGUPTA
○ Display Converted Data	17.02.2012, 22:22:02 h, SDASGUPTA
○ Create Batch Input Session	17.02.2012, 22:22:08 h, SDASGUPTA
○ Run Batch Input Session	

```
ASSETCREATECHG3 - ASSETCREATECHG3 - ASSETCREATECHG3 Asset upload testing

Files
 ├─ Legacy Data          On the PC (Frontend)
 │   └──Asset creation with Gr Assets  C:\RACV\Asset Creation template.txt
 │                                     Data for One Source Structure (Table)
 │                                     Separator Tabulator
 │                                     Field Names at Start of File
 │                                     With Record End Indicator (Text File)
 │                                     Code Page ASCII
 ├──Legacy Data          On the R/3 server (application server)
 ├─ Imported Data        File for Imported Data (Application Server)
 │   └──Imported Data                  ASSETCREATECHG3.lsmw.read
 ├─ Converted Data       File for Converted Data (Application Server)
 │   └──Converted Data                 ASSETCREATECHG3.lsmw.conv
 └──Wildcard Value       Value for Wildcard '*' in File Name
```

Save.

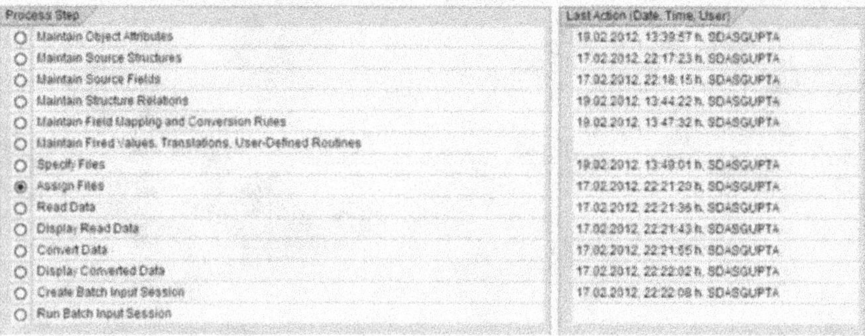

Process Step	Last Action (Date, Time, User)
○ Maintain Object Attributes	19.02.2012, 13:39:57 h, SDASGUPTA
○ Maintain Source Structures	17.02.2012, 22:17:23 h, SDASGUPTA
○ Maintain Source Fields	17.02.2012, 22:18:15 h, SDASGUPTA
○ Maintain Structure Relations	19.02.2012, 13:44:22 h, SDASGUPTA
○ Maintain Field Mapping and Conversion Rules	19.02.2012, 13:47:32 h, SDASGUPTA
○ Maintain Fixed Values, Translations, User-Defined Routines	
○ Specify Files	19.02.2012, 13:49:01 h, SDASGUPTA
◉ Assign Files	17.02.2012, 22:21:29 h, SDASGUPTA
○ Read Data	17.02.2012, 22:21:36 h, SDASGUPTA
○ Display Read Data	17.02.2012, 22:21:43 h, SDASGUPTA
○ Convert Data	17.02.2012, 22:21:55 h, SDASGUPTA
○ Display Converted Data	17.02.2012, 22:22:02 h, SDASGUPTA
○ Create Batch Input Session	17.02.2012, 22:22:08 h, SDASGUPTA
○ Run Batch Input Session	

```
ASSETCREATECHG3 - ASSETCREATECHG3 - ASSETCREATECHG3 Asset upload testing

Source Structures and Files
 └──ASSETTEST Asset creation
              Asset creation with Gr Assets C:\RACV\Asset Creation template.txt
```

Save.

Process Step	Last Action (Date, Time, User)
○ Maintain Object Attributes	19.02.2012, 13:39:57 h, SDASGUPTA
○ Maintain Source Structures	17.02.2012, 22:17:23 h, SDASGUPTA
○ Maintain Source Fields	17.02.2012, 22:18:15 h, SDASGUPTA
○ Maintain Structure Relations	19.02.2012, 13:44:22 h, SDASGUPTA
○ Maintain Field Mapping and Conversion Rules	19.02.2012, 13:47:32 h, SDASGUPTA
○ Maintain Fixed Values, Translations, User-Defined Routines	
○ Specify Files	19.02.2012, 13:49:01 h, SDASGUPTA
○ Assign Files	19.02.2012, 13:49:35 h, SDASGUPTA
◉ Read Data	17.02.2012, 22:21:36 h, SDASGUPTA
○ Display Read Data	17.02.2012, 22:21:43 h, SDASGUPTA
○ Convert Data	17.02.2012, 22:21:55 h, SDASGUPTA
○ Display Converted Data	17.02.2012, 22:22:02 h, SDASGUPTA
○ Create Batch Input Session	17.02.2012, 22:22:08 h, SDASGUPTA
○ Run Batch Input Session	

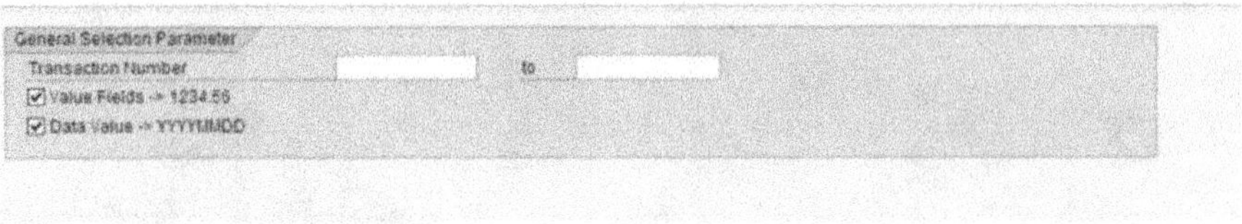

General Selection Parameter
Transaction Number [ ] to [ ]
☑ Value Fields -> 1234.56
☑ Data Value -> YYYYMMDD

Execute.

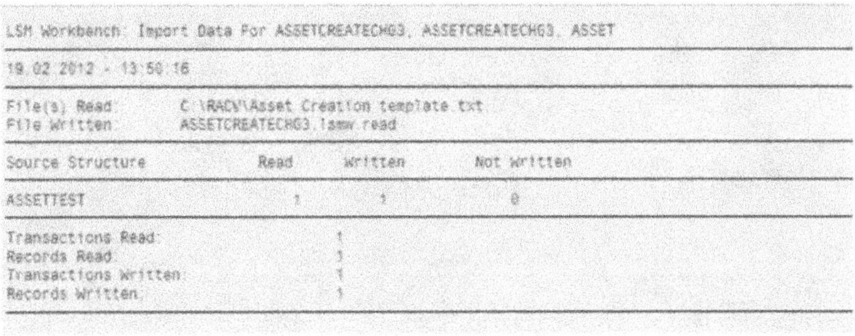

```
LSM Workbench: Import Data For ASSETCREATECHG3, ASSETCREATECHG3, ASSET

19.02.2012 - 13:50:16

File(s) Read:      C:\RACV\Asset Creation template.txt
File Written:      ASSETCREATECHG3.lsmw.read

Source Structure          Read      Written       Not Written

ASSETTEST                    1         1              0

Transactions Read:                 1
Records Read:                      1
Transactions Written:              1
Records Written:                   1
```

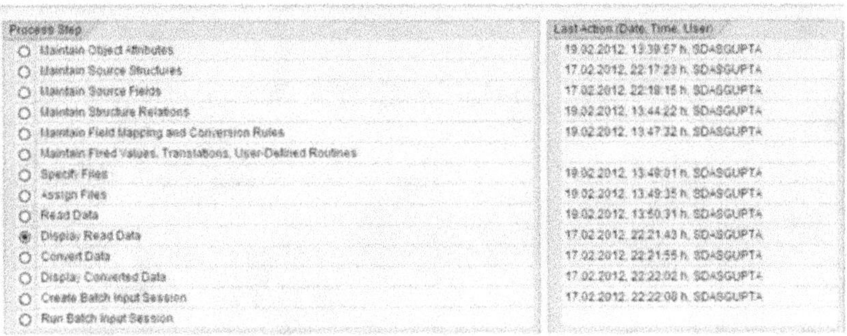

Process Step	Last Action (Date, Time, User)
○ Maintain Object Attributes	19.02.2012, 13:39:57 h, SDASGUPTA
○ Maintain Source Structures	17.02.2012, 22:17:23 h, SDASGUPTA
○ Maintain Source Fields	17.02.2012, 22:18:15 h, SDASGUPTA
○ Maintain Structure Relations	19.02.2012, 13:44:22 h, SDASGUPTA
○ Maintain Field Mapping and Conversion Rules	19.02.2012, 13:47:32 h, SDASGUPTA
○ Maintain Fixed Values, Translations, User-Defined Routines	
○ Specify Files	19.02.2012, 13:48:01 h, SDASGUPTA
○ Assign Files	19.02.2012, 13:49:35 h, SDASGUPTA
○ Read Data	19.02.2012, 13:50:31 h, SDASGUPTA
◉ Display Read Data	17.02.2012, 22:21:43 h, SDASGUPTA
○ Convert Data	17.02.2012, 22:21:55 h, SDASGUPTA
○ Display Converted Data	17.02.2012, 22:22:02 h, SDASGUPTA
○ Create Batch Input Session	17.02.2012, 22:22:08 h, SDASGUPTA
○ Run Batch Input Session	

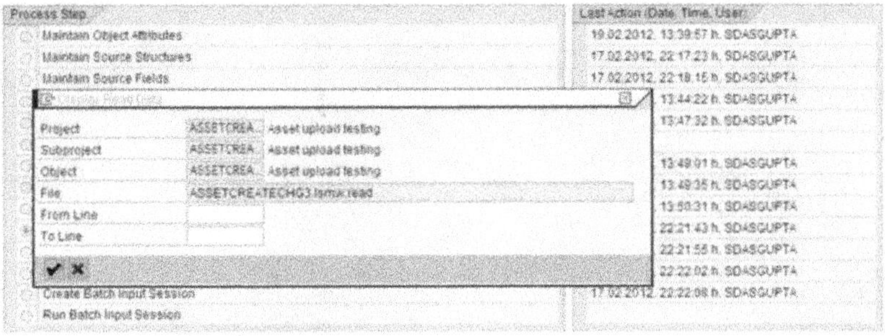

Display Read Data

Project	ASSETCREA...	Asset upload testing
Subproject	ASSETCREA...	Asset upload testing
Object	ASSETCREA...	Asset upload testing
File	ASSETCREATECHG3.lsmw.read	
From Line		
To Line		

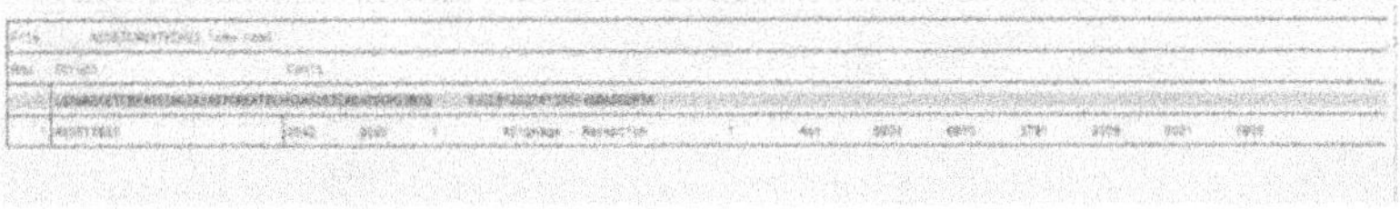

✔ ✖

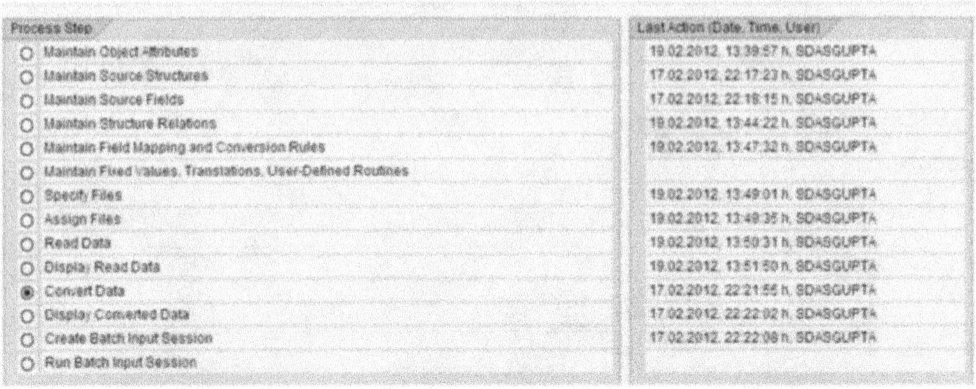

Process Step	Last Action (Date, Time, User)
○ Maintain Object Attributes	19.02.2012, 13:39:57 h, SDASGUPTA
○ Maintain Source Structures	17.02.2012, 22:17:23 h, SDASGUPTA
○ Maintain Source Fields	17.02.2012, 22:18:15 h, SDASGUPTA
○ Maintain Structure Relations	19.02.2012, 13:44:22 h, SDASGUPTA
○ Maintain Field Mapping and Conversion Rules	19.02.2012, 13:47:32 h, SDASGUPTA
○ Maintain Fixed Values, Translations, User-Defined Routines	
○ Specify Files	19.02.2012, 13:49:01 h, SDASGUPTA
○ Assign Files	19.02.2012, 13:49:35 h, SDASGUPTA
○ Read Data	19.02.2012, 13:50:31 h, SDASGUPTA
○ Display Read Data	19.02.2012, 13:51:50 h, SDASGUPTA
◉ Convert Data	17.02.2012, 22:21:55 h, SDASGUPTA
○ Display Converted Data	17.02.2012, 22:22:02 h, SDASGUPTA
○ Create Batch Input Session	17.02.2012, 22:22:08 h, SDASGUPTA
○ Run Batch Input Session	

General Selection Parameter

Transaction Number ______ to ______

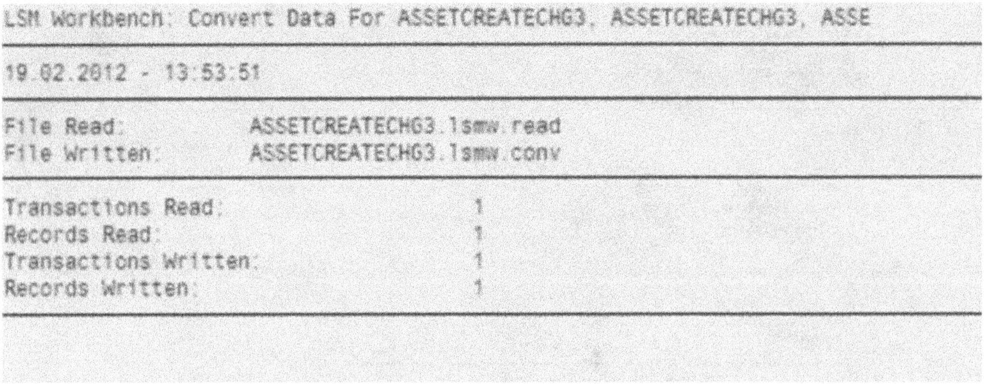

LSM Workbench: Convert Data For ASSETCREATECHG3, ASSETCREATECHG3, ASSE

19.02.2012 - 13:53:51

File Read: ASSETCREATECHG3.lsmw.read
File Written: ASSETCREATECHG3.lsmw.conv

Transactions Read: 1
Records Read: 1
Transactions Written: 1
Records Written: 1

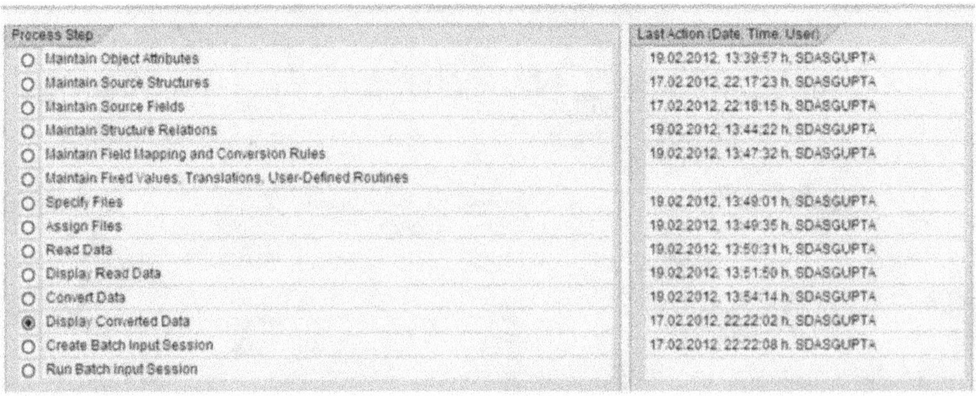

Process Step	Last Action (Date, Time, User)
○ Maintain Object Attributes	19.02.2012, 13:39:57 h, SDASGUPTA
○ Maintain Source Structures	17.02.2012, 22:17:23 h, SDASGUPTA
○ Maintain Source Fields	17.02.2012, 22:18:15 h, SDASGUPTA
○ Maintain Structure Relations	19.02.2012, 13:44:22 h, SDASGUPTA
○ Maintain Field Mapping and Conversion Rules	19.02.2012, 13:47:32 h, SDASGUPTA
○ Maintain Fixed Values, Translations, User-Defined Routines	
○ Specify Files	19.02.2012, 13:49:01 h, SDASGUPTA
○ Assign Files	19.02.2012, 13:49:35 h, SDASGUPTA
○ Read Data	19.02.2012, 13:50:31 h, SDASGUPTA
○ Display Read Data	19.02.2012, 13:51:50 h, SDASGUPTA
○ Convert Data	19.02.2012, 13:54:14 h, SDASGUPTA
◉ Display Converted Data	17.02.2012, 22:22:02 h, SDASGUPTA
○ Create Batch Input Session	17.02.2012, 22:22:08 h, SDASGUPTA
○ Run Batch Input Session	

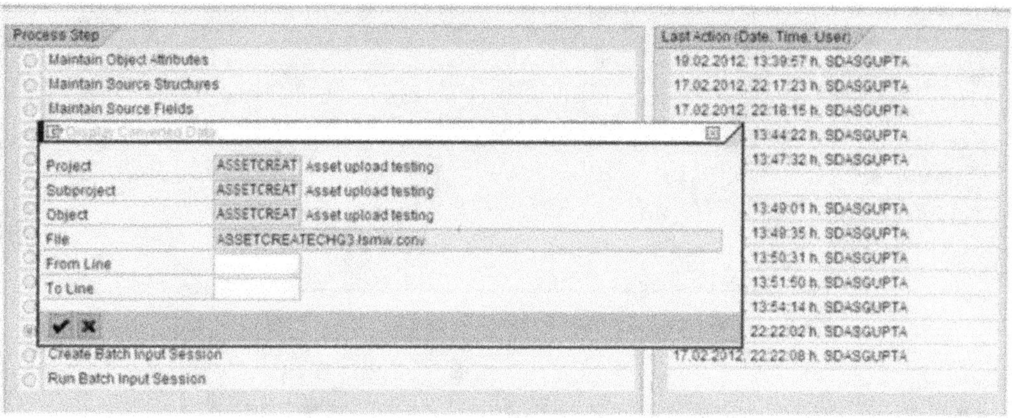

Process Step	Last Action (Date, Time, User)
Maintain Object Attributes	19.02.2012, 13:39:57 h, SDASGUPTA
Maintain Source Structures	17.02.2012, 22:17:23 h, SDASGUPTA
Maintain Source Fields	17.02.2012, 22:18:15 h, SDASGUPTA
	13:44:22 h, SDASGUPTA
	13:47:32 h, SDASGUPTA
	13:49:01 h, SDASGUPTA
	13:49:35 h, SDASGUPTA
	13:50:31 h, SDASGUPTA
	13:51:50 h, SDASGUPTA
	13:54:14 h, SDASGUPTA
	22:22:02 h, SDASGUPTA
Create Batch Input Session	17.02.2012, 22:22:08 h, SDASGUPTA
Run Batch Input Session	

Display Converted Data

Project	ASSETCREAT	Asset upload testing
Subproject	ASSETCREAT	Asset upload testing
Object	ASSETCREAT	Asset upload testing
File	ASSETCREATECHG3.lsmw.conv	
From Line		
To Line		

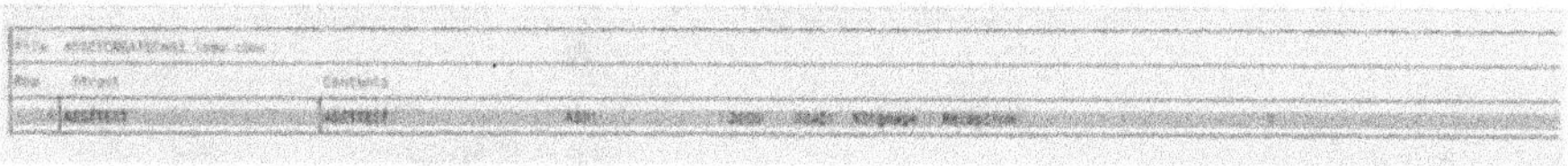

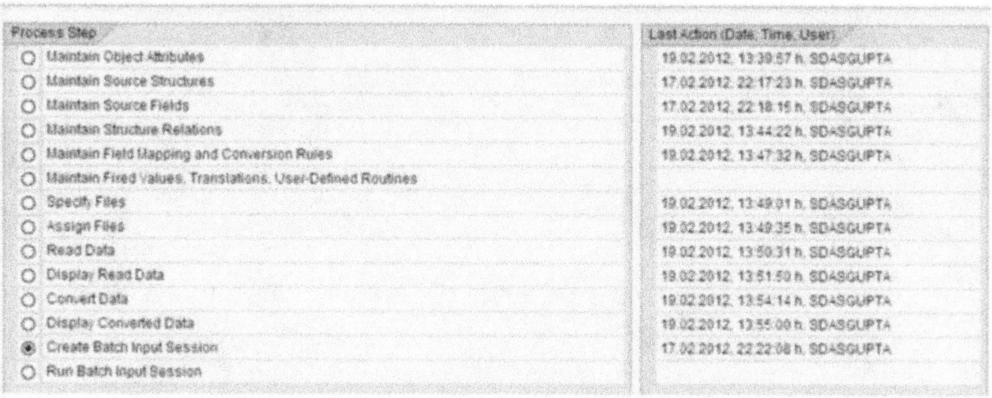

Process Step	Last Action (Date, Time, User)
Maintain Object Attributes	19.02.2012, 13:39:57 h, SDASGUPTA
Maintain Source Structures	17.02.2012, 22:17:23 h, SDASGUPTA
Maintain Source Fields	17.02.2012, 22:18:15 h, SDASGUPTA
Maintain Structure Relations	19.02.2012, 13:44:22 h, SDASGUPTA
Maintain Field Mapping and Conversion Rules	19.02.2012, 13:47:32 h, SDASGUPTA
Maintain Fixed Values, Translations, User-Defined Routines	
Specify Files	19.02.2012, 13:49:01 h, SDASGUPTA
Assign Files	19.02.2012, 13:49:35 h, SDASGUPTA
Read Data	19.02.2012, 13:50:31 h, SDASGUPTA
Display Read Data	19.02.2012, 13:51:50 h, SDASGUPTA
Convert Data	19.02.2012, 13:54:14 h, SDASGUPTA
Display Converted Data	19.02.2012, 13:55:00 h, SDASGUPTA
Create Batch Input Session	17.02.2012, 22:22:08 h, SDASGUPTA
Run Batch Input Session	

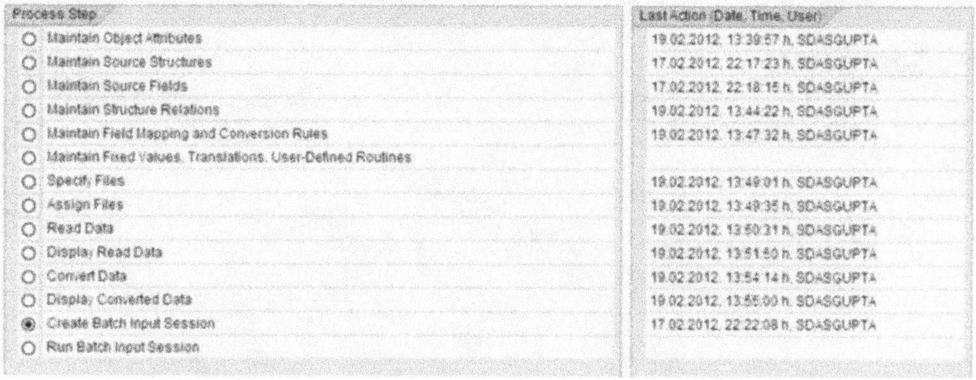

Process Step	Last Action (Date, Time, User)
Maintain Object Attributes	19.02.2012, 13:39:57 h, SDASGUPTA
Maintain Source Structures	17.02.2012, 22:17:23 h, SDASGUPTA
Maintain Source Fields	17.02.2012, 22:18:15 h, SDASGUPTA
Maintain Structure Relations	19.02.2012, 13:44:22 h, SDASGUPTA
Maintain Field Mapping and Conversion Rules	19.02.2012, 13:47:32 h, SDASGUPTA
Maintain Fixed Values, Translations, User-Defined Routines	
Specify Files	19.02.2012, 13:49:01 h, SDASGUPTA
Assign Files	19.02.2012, 13:49:35 h, SDASGUPTA
Read Data	19.02.2012, 13:50:31 h, SDASGUPTA
Display Read Data	19.02.2012, 13:51:50 h, SDASGUPTA
Convert Data	19.02.2012, 13:54:14 h, SDASGUPTA
Display Converted Data	19.02.2012, 13:55:00 h, SDASGUPTA
Create Batch Input Session	17.02.2012, 22:22:08 h, SDASGUPTA
Run Batch Input Session	

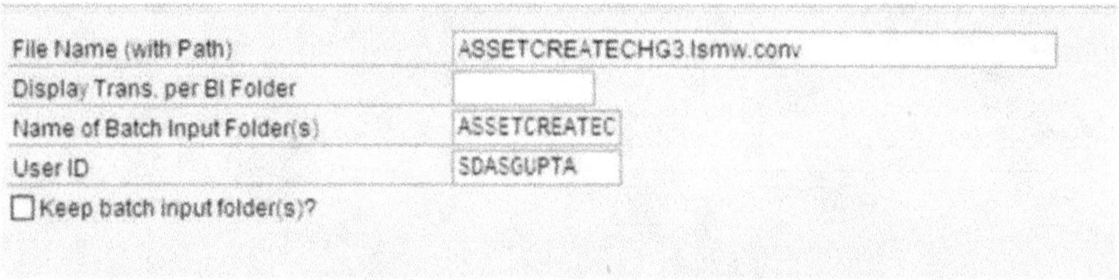

File Name (with Path)	ASSETCREATECHG3.lsmw.conv
Display Trans. per BI Folder	
Name of Batch Input Folder(s)	ASSETCREATEC
User ID	SDASGUPTA

☐ Keep batch input folder(s)?

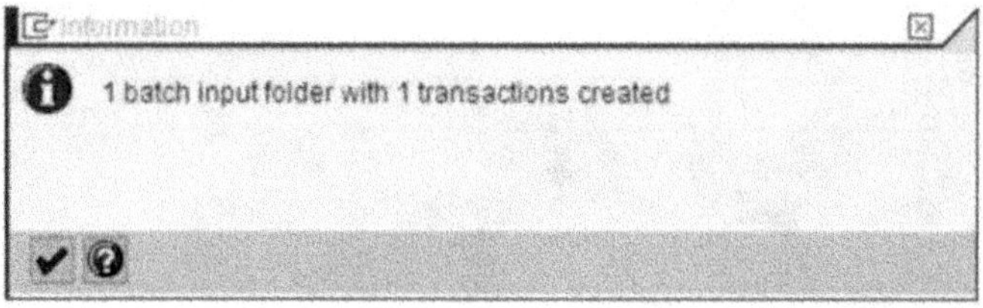

Information

1 batch input folder with 1 transactions created

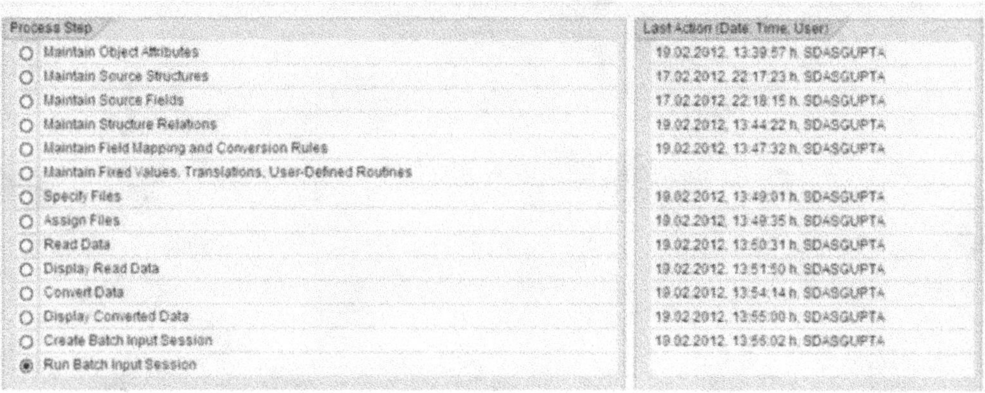

Process Step	Last Action (Date, Time, User)
○ Maintain Object Attributes	19.02.2012, 13:39:57 h, SDASGUPTA
○ Maintain Source Structures	17.02.2012, 22:17:23 h, SDASGUPTA
○ Maintain Source Fields	17.02.2012, 22:18:15 h, SDASGUPTA
○ Maintain Structure Relations	19.02.2012, 13:44:22 h, SDASGUPTA
○ Maintain Field Mapping and Conversion Rules	19.02.2012, 13:47:32 h, SDASGUPTA
○ Maintain Fixed Values, Translations, User-Defined Routines	
○ Specify Files	19.02.2012, 13:49:01 h, SDASGUPTA
○ Assign Files	19.02.2012, 13:49:35 h, SDASGUPTA
○ Read Data	19.02.2012, 13:50:31 h, SDASGUPTA
○ Display Read Data	19.02.2012, 13:51:50 h, SDASGUPTA
○ Convert Data	19.02.2012, 13:54:14 h, SDASGUPTA
○ Display Converted Data	19.02.2012, 13:55:00 h, SDASGUPTA
○ Create Batch Input Session	19.02.2012, 13:56:02 h, SDASGUPTA
◉ Run Batch Input Session	

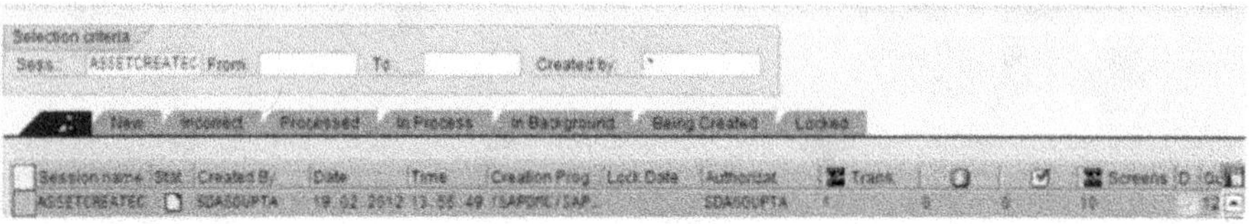

Selection criteria

Sess.: ASSETCREATEC From: To: Created by: *

New | Incorrect | Processed | In Process | In Background | Being Created | Locked

Session name	Stat	Created By	Date	Time	Creation Prog	Lock Date	Authorizat.	Trans.			Screens	D	Q
ASSETCREATEC		SDASGUPTA	19.02.2012	13:55:49	/SAPDMC/SAP...		SDASGUPTA	1	0	0	10		12

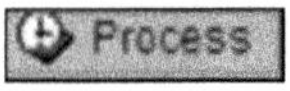

Process

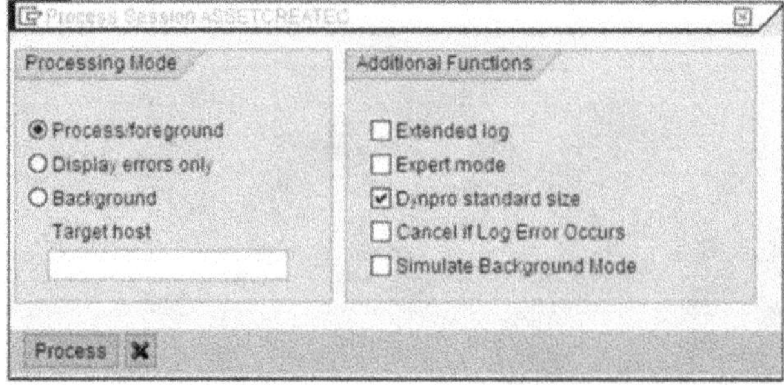

Asset Class 2000
Company Code 0042
Number of similar assets 1

Reference
Asset
Sub-number
Company code

Post-capitalization

Create Asset: Initial screen
OK-Code
/00

Asset INTERN-00001 0
Class 2000 Fixtures & Fittings Company Code 0042

General | Time-dependent | Allocations | Origin | Equipment | Insuranc

Acct determination 20000 Fixtures and Fittings
Serial number
Inventory number
Quantity 1 Ast
Manage historically

Inventory
Last inventory on
Include asset in inventory list
Inventory note

Posting information
Capitalized on 01.04.2011
Deactivation on

Create Asset: Post-capitalization
OK-Code
/00

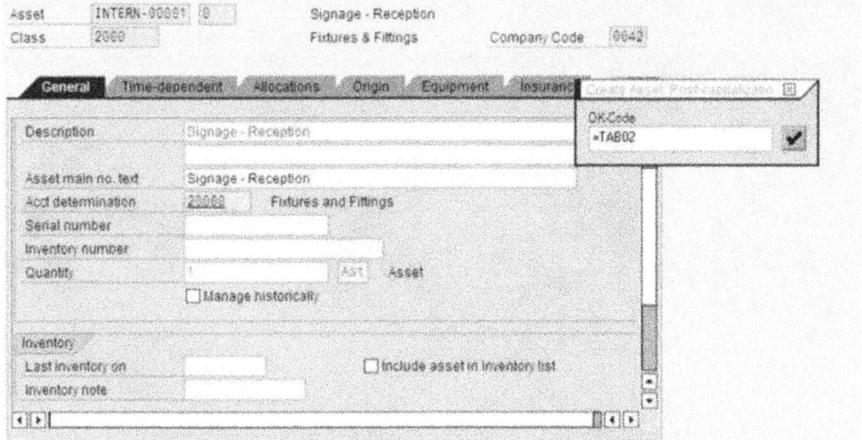

Asset INTERN-00001 0 Signage - Reception
Class 2000 Fixtures & Fittings Company Code 0042

General | Time-dependent | Allocations | Origin | Equipment | Insuranc

Create Asset: Post-capitalizatio

OK-Code
=TAB03

Interval from 01.01.1900 to 31.12.9999

Cost Center 6600
Resp. cost center 6600

Location 3791

Asset shutdown

Asset INTERN-00001 0 Signage - Reception
Class 2000 Fixtures & Fittings Company Code 0042

General | Time-dependent | Allocations | Origin | Equipment | Insuranc

Create Asset: Post-capitalizatio

OK-Code
=TAB04

Allocations

Asset Sub-Class 2005
Tax Life 0001
Tax Category 0900
Evaluation group 4
Stat. Account Group 30 Plant and equipment

Investment reason

Investment support measures

Key	Description

Asset INTERN-00001 0 Signage - Reception
Class 2000 Fixtures & Fittings Company Code 0042

General | Time-dependent | Allocations | Origin | Equipment | Insuranc

Create Asset: Post-capitalizatio

OK-Code
=TAB05

Origin

Vendor
Manufacturer
Asset purch. new
Purchased used
Country of origin
Type name

Original asset Acq. on
Orig. Acquis. Year
Original value AUD
In-house prod.perc.

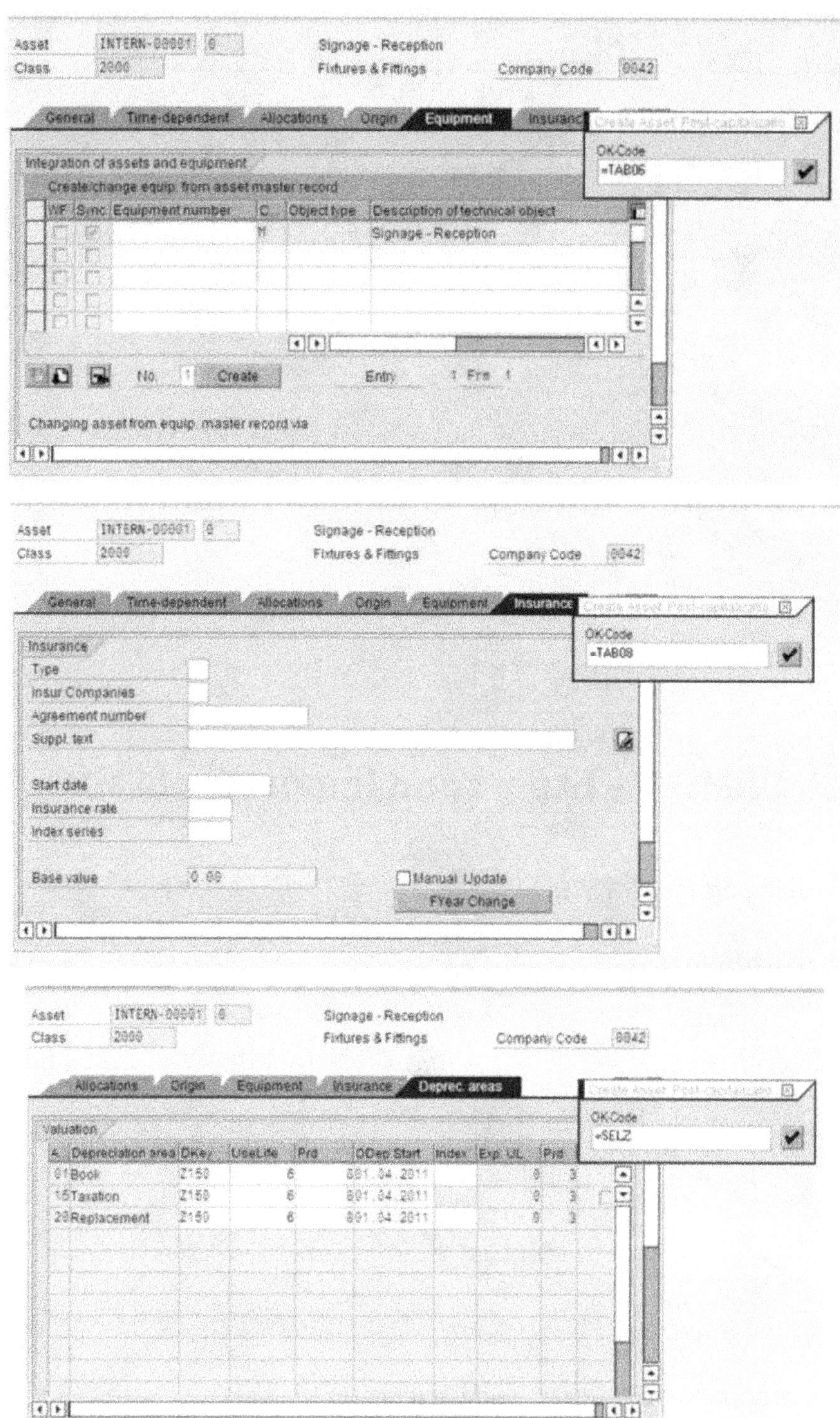
Asset INTERN-00001 0
Class 2000
Signage - Reception
Fixtures & Fittings
Company Code 0042
General
Time-dependent
Allocations
Origin
Equipment
Insurance
Create Asset: Post-capitalizatio
OK-Code
=TAB06
Integration of assets and equipment
Create/change equip. from asset master record
WF
Sync
Equipment number
C.
Object type
Description of technical object
Signage - Reception
No.
Create
Entry
Changing asset from equip. master record via
OK-Code
=TAB08
Insurance
Type
Insur.Companies
Agreement number
Suppl. text
Start date
Insurance rate
Index series
Base value
0.00
Manual Update
FYear Change
Deprec. areas
OK-Code
=SELZ
Valuation
Depreciation area
DKey
UseLife
Prd
ODep Start
Index
Exp. UL
Prd
01 Book
Z150
15 Taxation
20 Replacement
001.04.2011

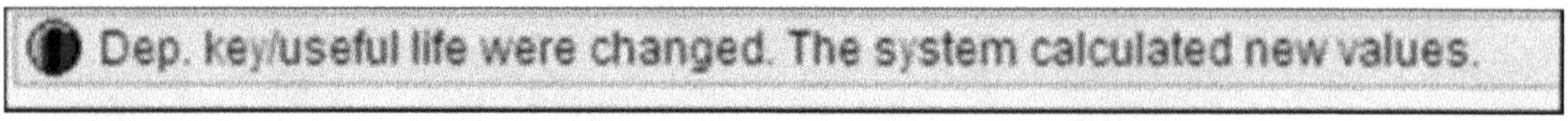

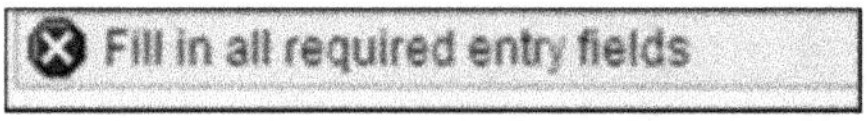

Dep. key/useful life were changed. The system calculated new values.

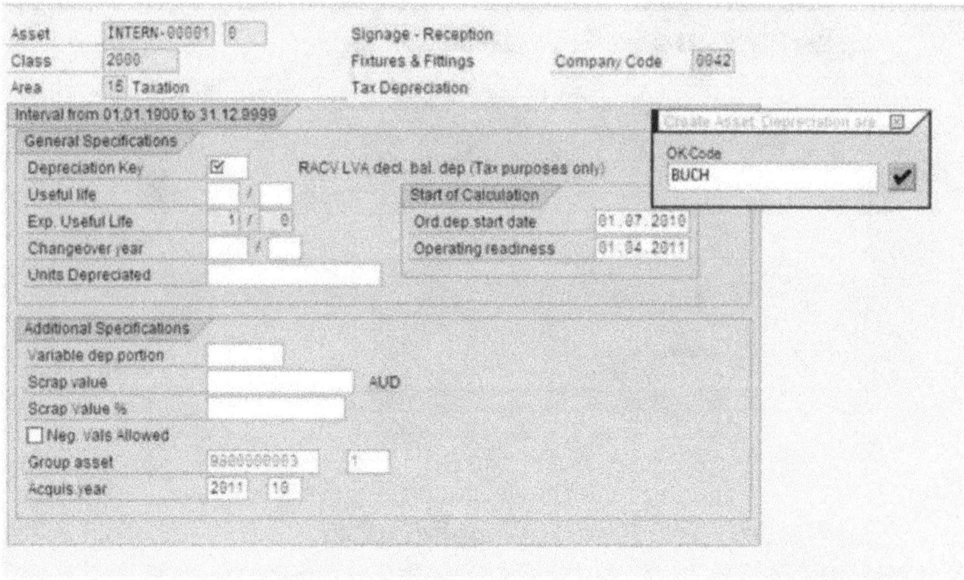

Asset INTERN-00001 0 Signage - Reception
Class 2000 Fixtures & Fittings Company Code 0042
Area 15 Taxation Tax Depreciation

Interval from 01.01.1900 to 31.12.9999

General Specifications
Depreciation Key RACV LVA decl. bal. dep (Tax purposes only)
Useful life /
Exp. Useful Life 1 / 0
Changeover year /
Units Depreciated

Start of Calculation
Ord.dep.start date 01.07.2010
Operating readiness 01.04.2011

Create Asset Depreciation are
OK-Code
BUCH

Additional Specifications
Variable dep portion
Scrap value AUD
Scrap value %
Neg. vals Allowed
Group asset 0000000003 1
Acquis.year 2011 10

Fill in all required entry fields

19.12. DEMO 5 – Export and Import for LSMW

Export and import for LSMW.

Go to Lsmw. Sample example in DEV-400.

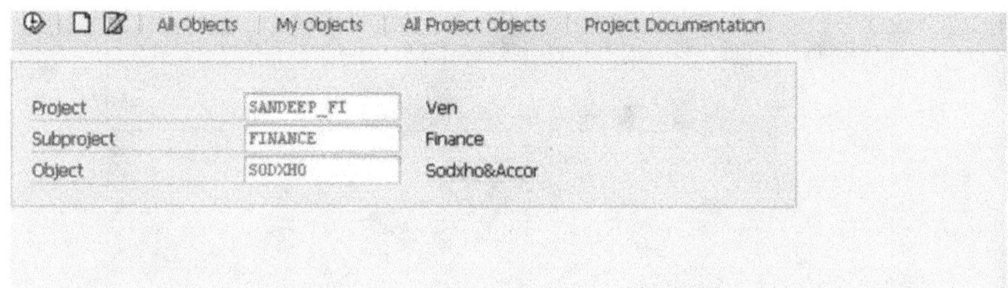

Select export option from Extras, below screens you will get it.

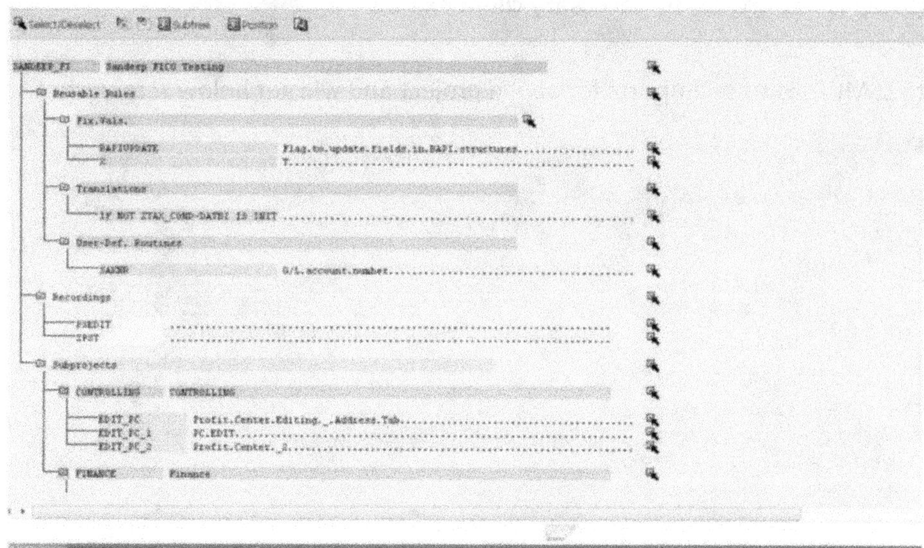

Next step: Deselect unnecessary sub projects and objects and select necessary subproject and object as mentioned below. Example if I want to export only GLTOGL object with FINANCE Subproject as mentioned below.

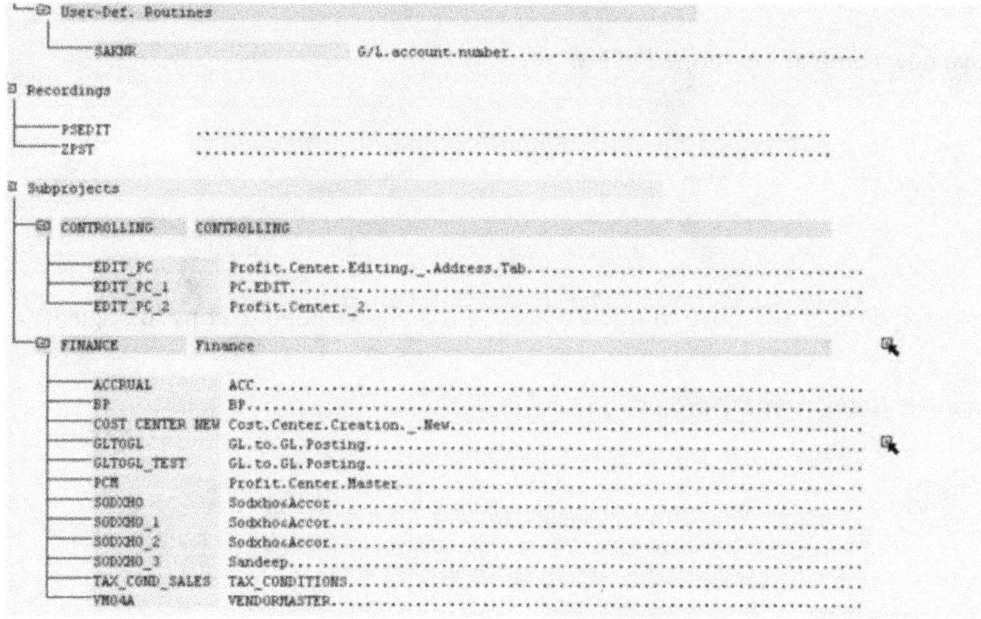

And select export option or F8 and File will save under c drive.

Next step is Import: Go to necessary client ex PD1

Go to LSMW-- Extras-- Imports for above project and will get below screen shot.

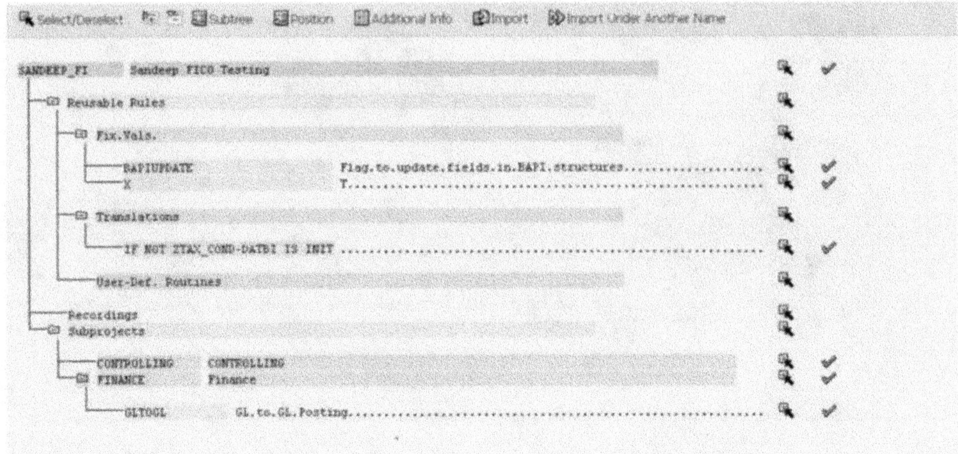

Next step: Deselect unnecessary sub projects and objects and select necessary subproject and object as mentioned below. And select import under another name or F8.

Give new name as mentioned below:

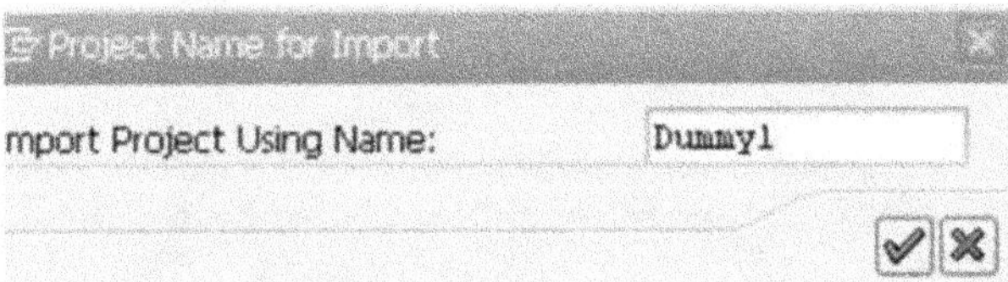

Selected objects will move to Above1 and from there we need to copy to original1.

Example Nateshkumar2 project.

Goto

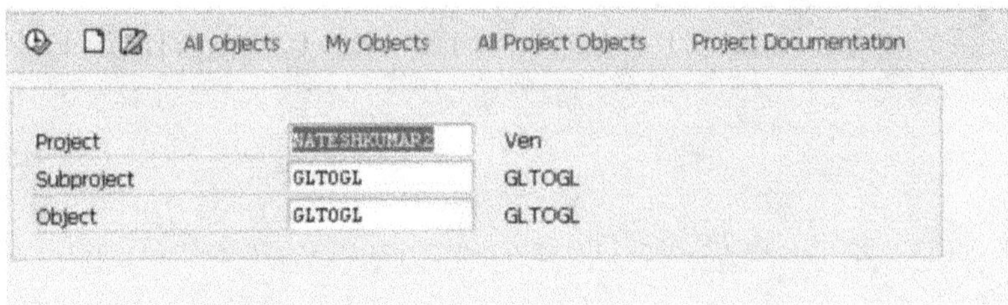

Goto-- administration

Select dummy project, subproject and object.

keep curser on respective object select copy option, get below screen. (Ctrl F4)

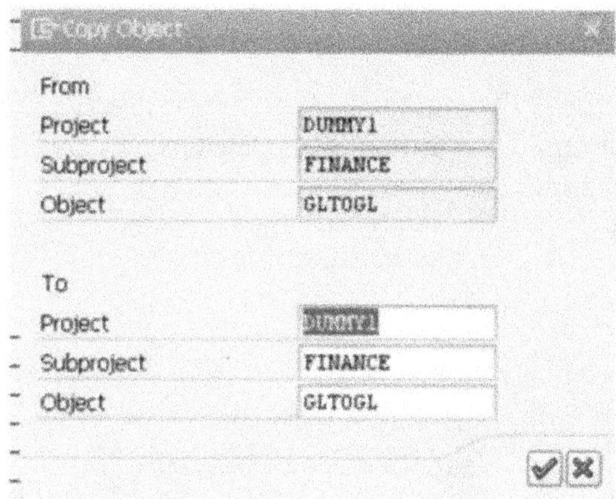

Changes to original project.

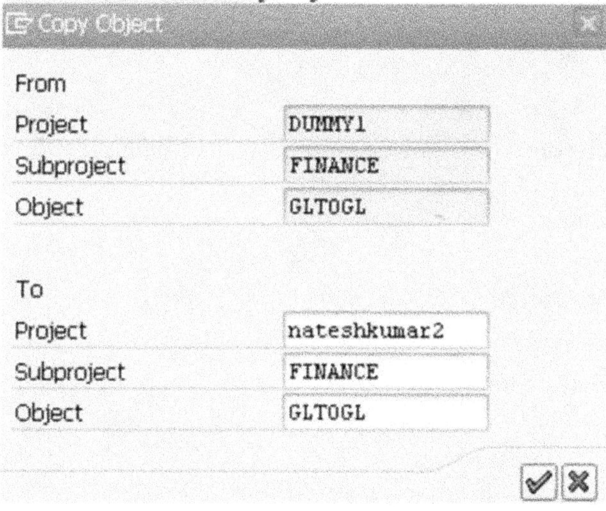

CHAPTER 20

Step by Step guide to configure Fiori Launchpad Tiles for Fiori Transactional App

This document lists down the detailed steps for configuring Fiori Launchpad Tiles for Fiori Transactional App using Catalogs and Groups. For this document, I am using below listed standard app.

App Name Application ID	Make Bank Transfers
UI5 App Name	F0691
	FIN_CASHTRAN /sap/bc/ui5_ui5/sap/fin_cashtran
Odata Service Standard SAP Roles	FCLM_BT_SRV
	PERP_FCLM_BTBAL_SRV
	SAP_FIN_BANKTRANS_APP

Login to the SAP NetWeaver Gateway System with admin user ID.

Create Launchpad Role:

* Execute Transaction LPD_CUST.
* Click on "New Launchpad".
* Enter the following details in the popup.
    Role: ZFINCASH
    Instance: TRANSACTIONAL

Description: Make Bank Transfer LPD Role

* Click on Yes if asked “Are you sure that you don’t need a namespace”

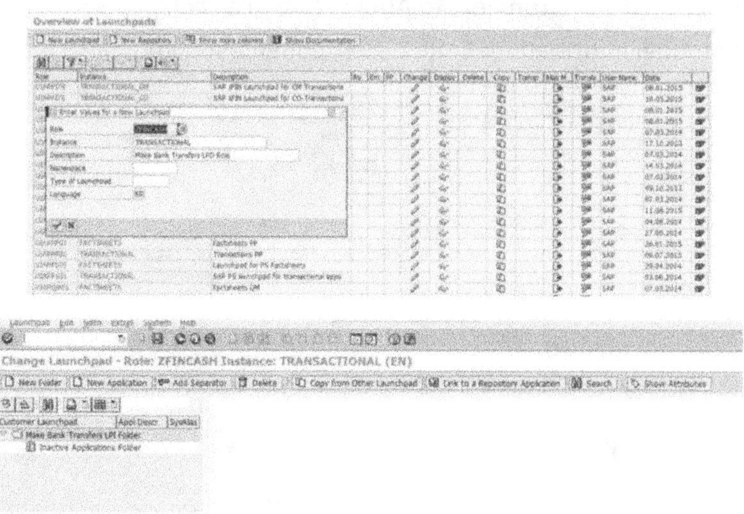

Create an Application in Launchpad Role

* Click on “New Application”
* Enter the Details below:

  Link – application name

  The URL is composite of:

  /sap/bc/ui5_ui5/sap/ + <your_bsp_name>

Here, our app URL is: /sap/bc/ui5_ui5/sap/fin_cashtran

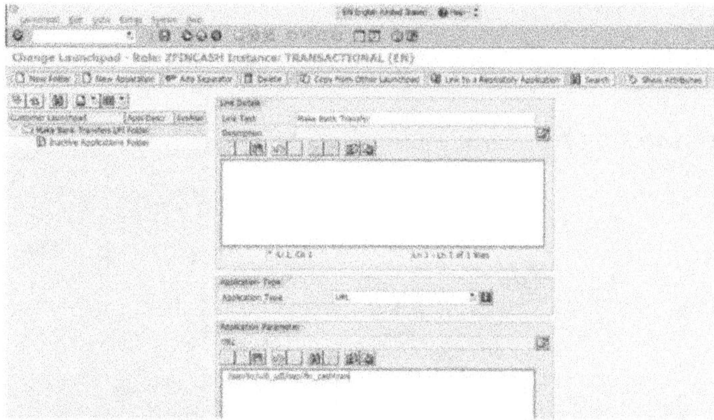

Click on button "Show Advanced (Optional) Parameters.

- Click on the "Edit" button next to Application Alias field, Enter: ZFINCASHAlias.
- Edit Additional Information: SAPUI5.Component=you.app.namespace SAPUI5. Component=fin.cash.transfercash.
  Tip: get namespace from here:

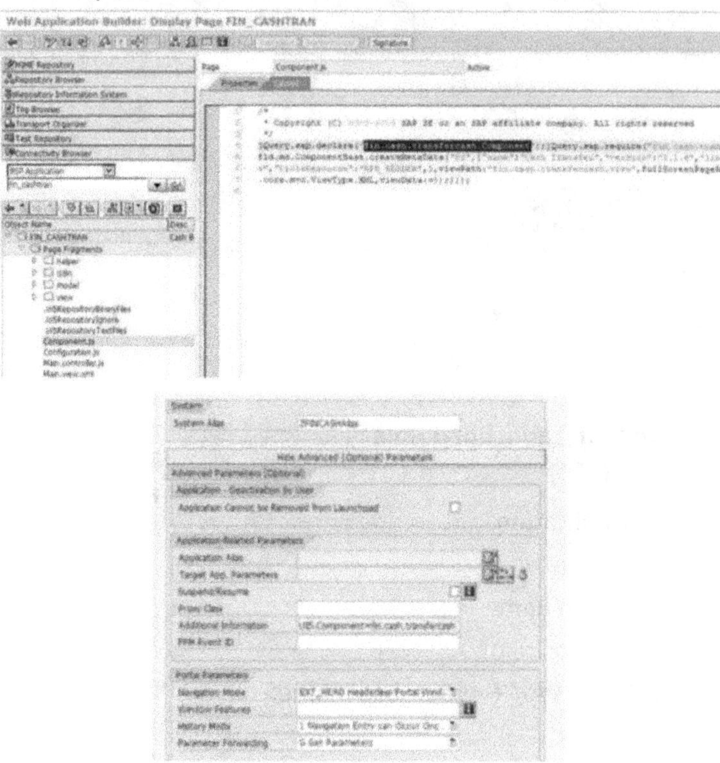

- Click on "Save" button

Create Semantic Object

- Execute transaction /n/UI2/SEMOBJ.

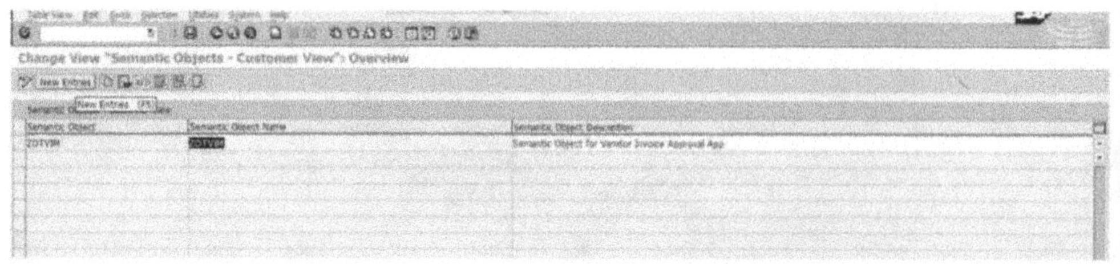

* Click on “New Entries” button.
* Enter the following: Semantic Object: ZFINCASH Object Name: ZFINCASH

Object Description: Semantic Object for make bank transfer.

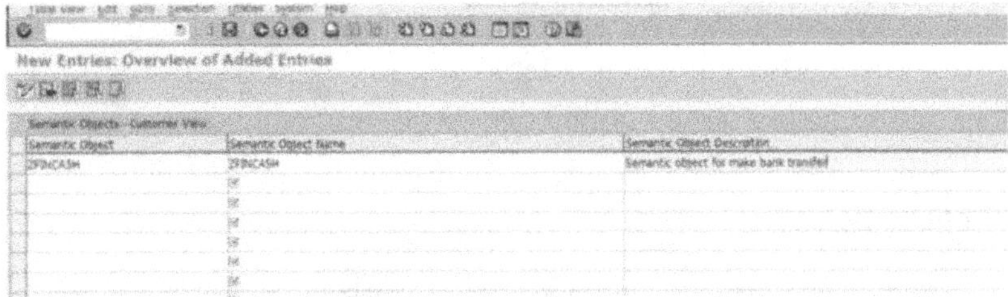

* Click on “Save” button.
* Choose your transport request and click on.

Launch Fiori Launchpad Designer

* Launch the Fiori Launchpad Designer url with admin id: http://<yourservername>:<port>/sap/bc/ui5_ui5/sap/arsrvc_upb_admn/main.html

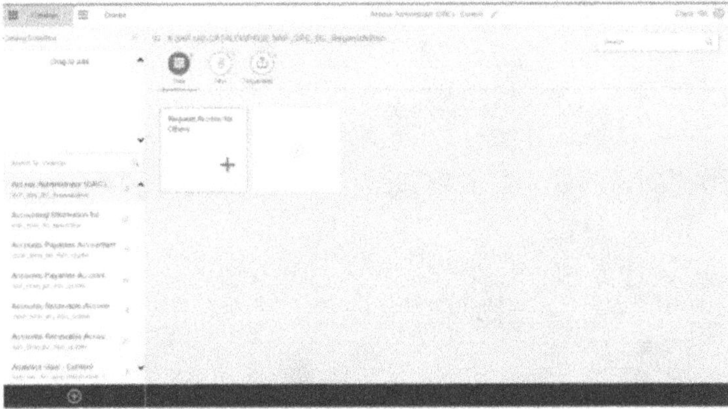

Create a Catalog

* Click on “plus” bar under “Catalogs” tab.

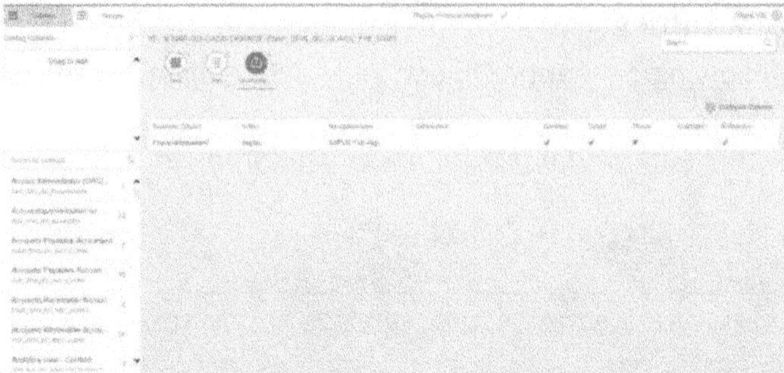

2. Enter Title and ID.

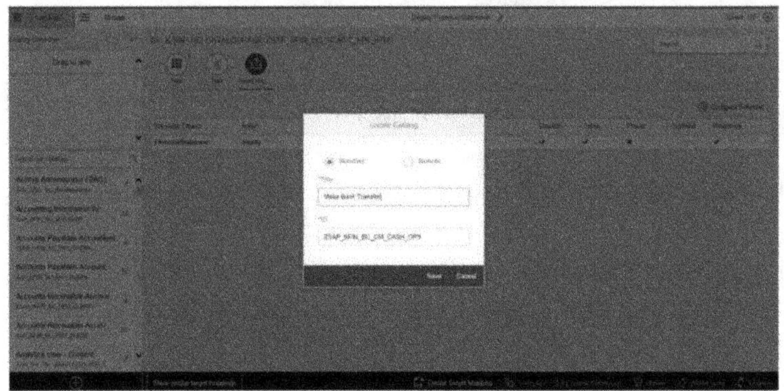

3. Click on Save, Catalog is now created.

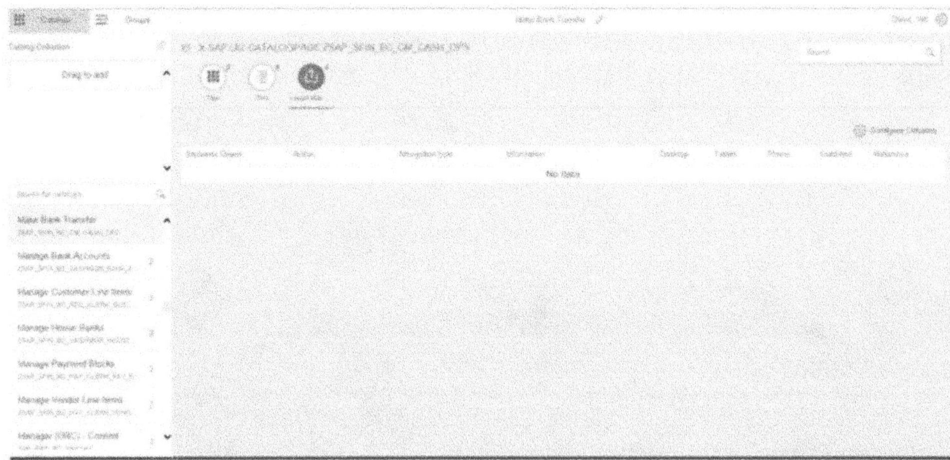

Create Target Mapping

* Click “Target Mapping” icon to switch Switch IconTabBar to Target Mapping table.
* Click “Create Target Mapping” button.

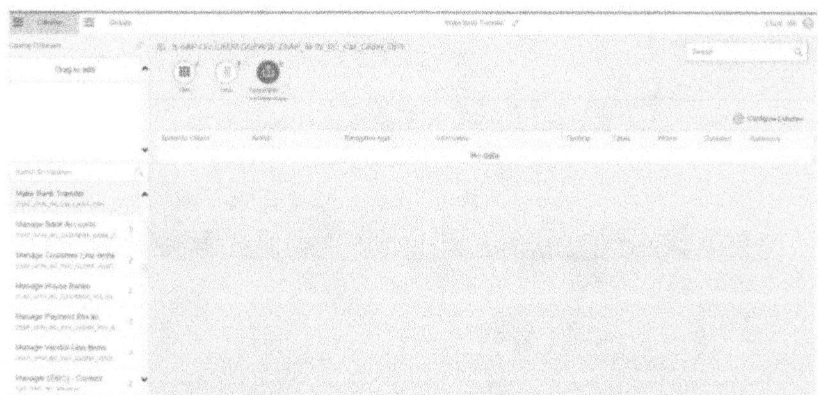

* Under Target, enter:
  Application Type
  Launchpad Role:

  Launchpad Instance:
  TRANSACTIONAL Application Alias:

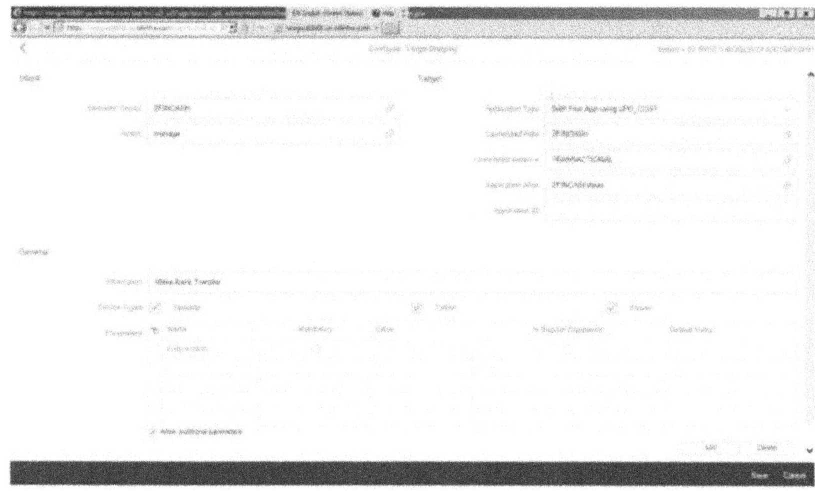

4. Click on Save to save your Target Mapping.

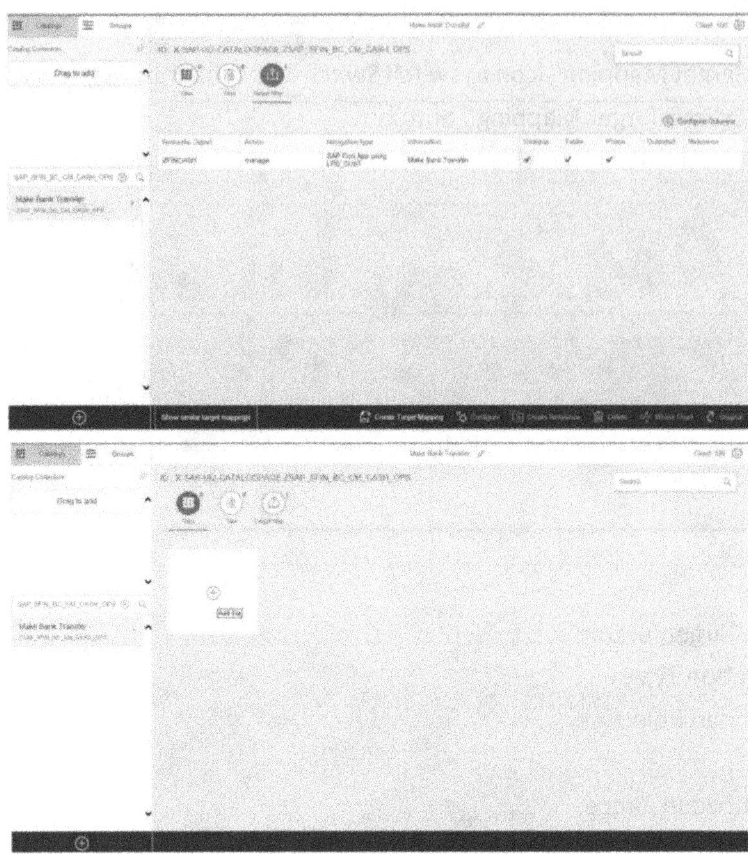

Create Static Tile

* Click on the “plus” tile of Detail Page.
* Click on “App Launcher - Static” tile to create a Target Mapping.

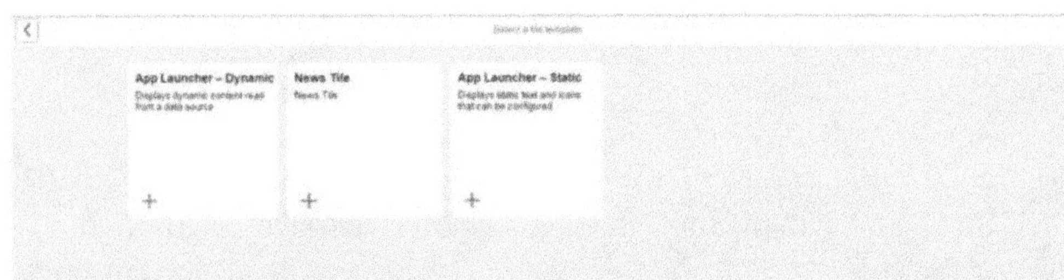

3. Click on the Static tile you just created.

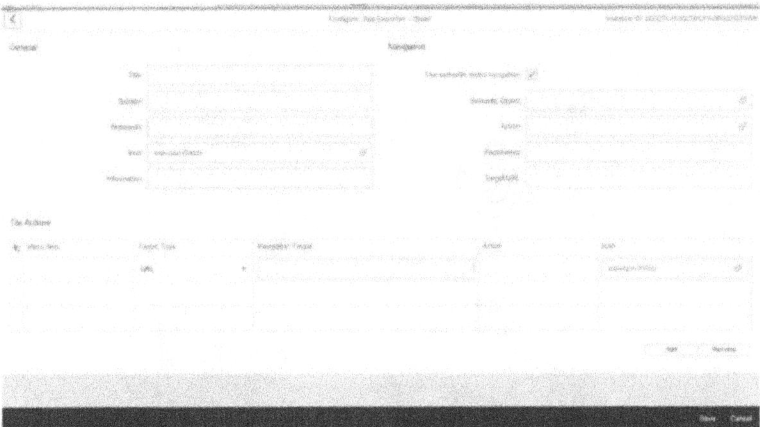

4. Enter the details as shown in screen shot.

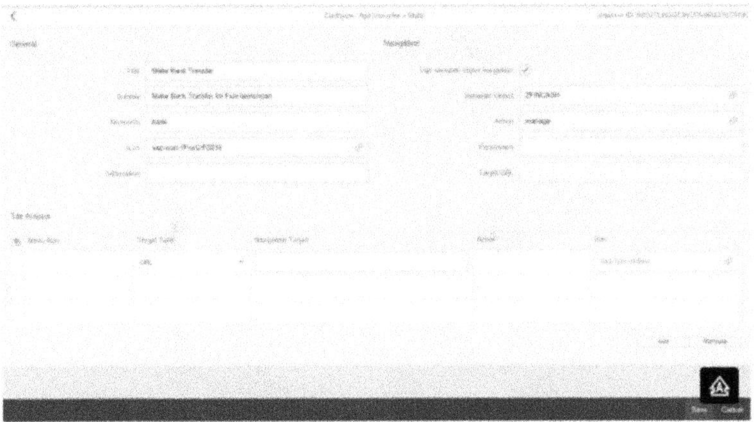

5. Save it, then we have now created a Static tile.

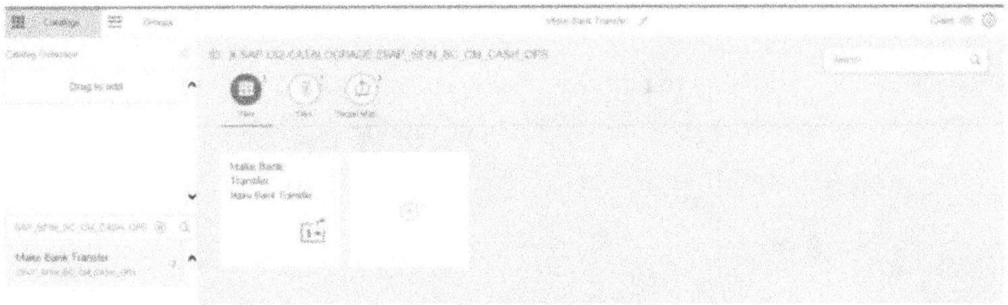

Create a Group

* Click on "plus" bar under "Group" tab. Enter Title and ID.

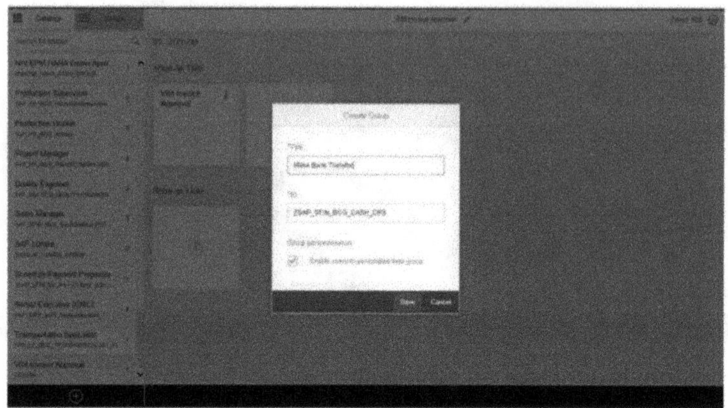

* Click on Save, your Group is now created.

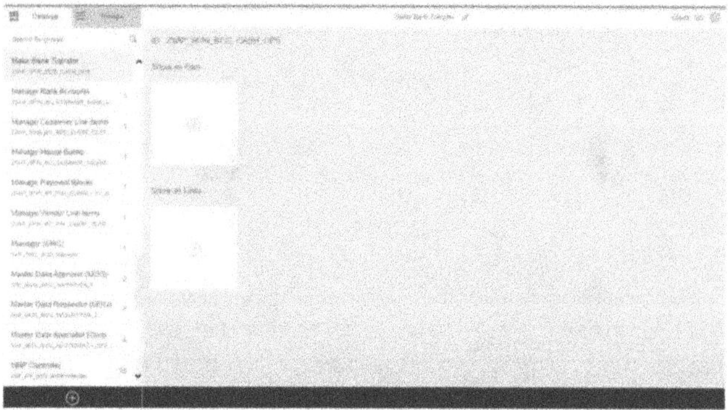

Add Catalog to Group

* Click on the "plus" tile to add the catalog you created to the group.
* Click on value helper to to lookup for your catalog.

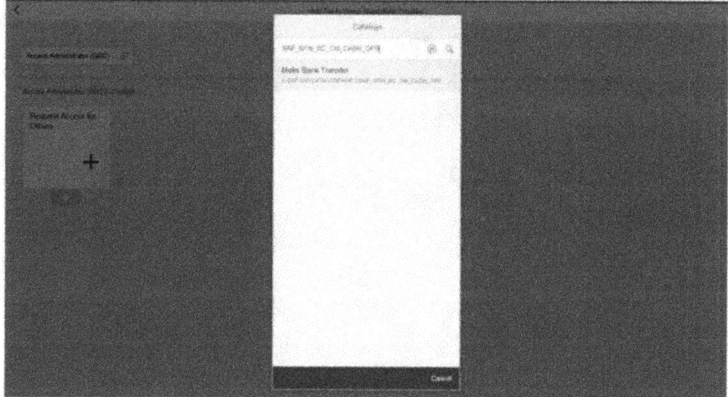

* You can filter and lookup for your catalog and click on it to choose.
* Click on the "+" plus button to add the catalog to the group.

5. You have now created a Group and added the catalog to it.

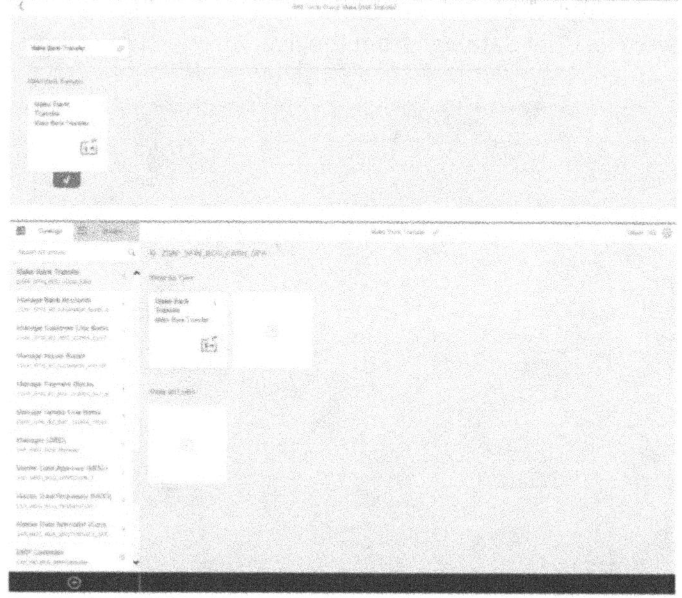

Create PFCG Role for Catalog and Group

1. Execute Transaction PFCG
   * Enter Role Name:
     Click on "Single Role" button
   * Enter Description:
     Click "save" button

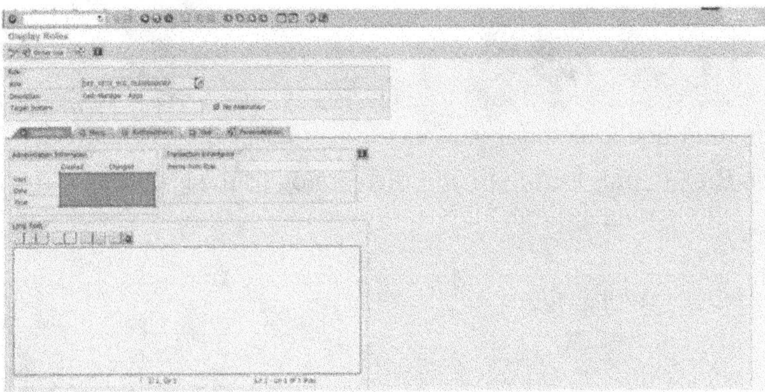

Add Tile Catalog to Role

* Click on the "Menu" Tab.
* Add Transaction (Click on the Arrow and not the button).
* Choose "SAP Fiori Tile Catalog" from the list.

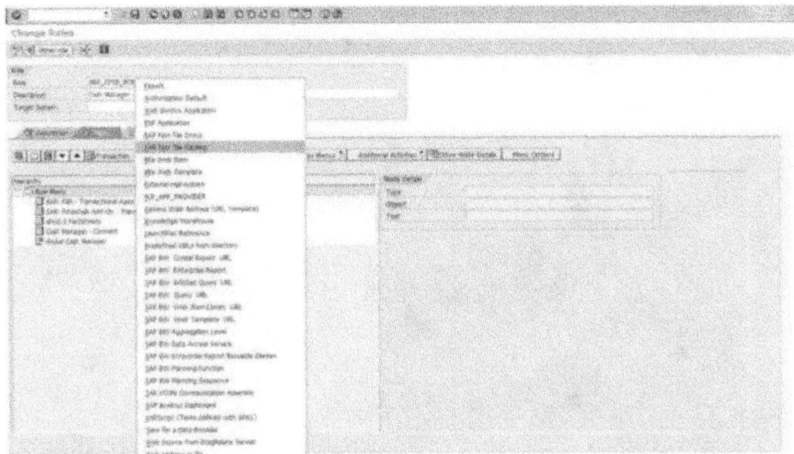

4. Enter your Catalog ID and click on "ok" (you can choose Catalog ID by value helper).

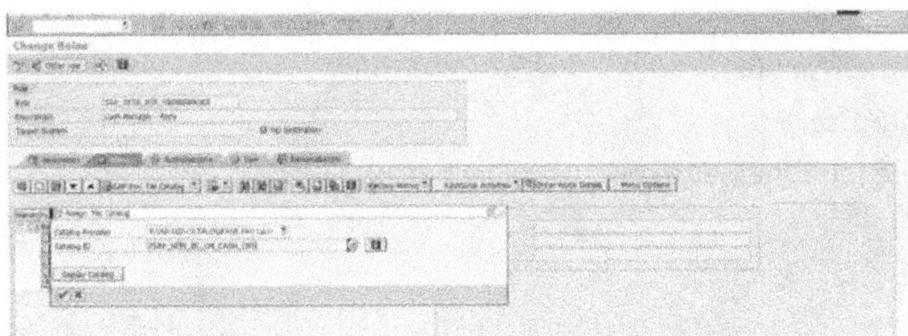

Add Group to Single Role

1. Click on the "SAP Fiori Tile Group" (Click on the Arrow and not the button).

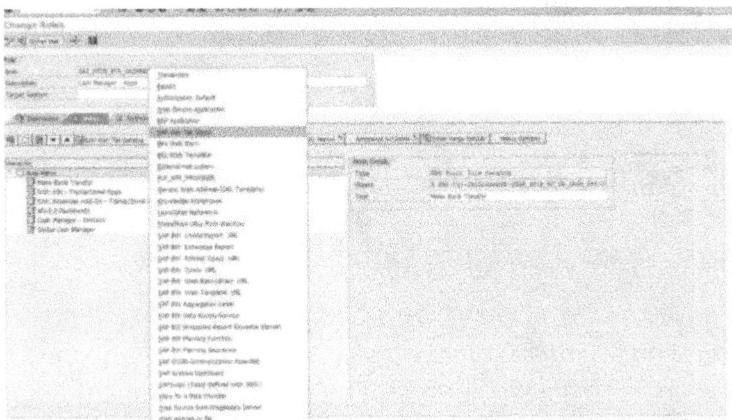

2. Choose Group from the list.
3. Enter the Group ID and click on "ok".

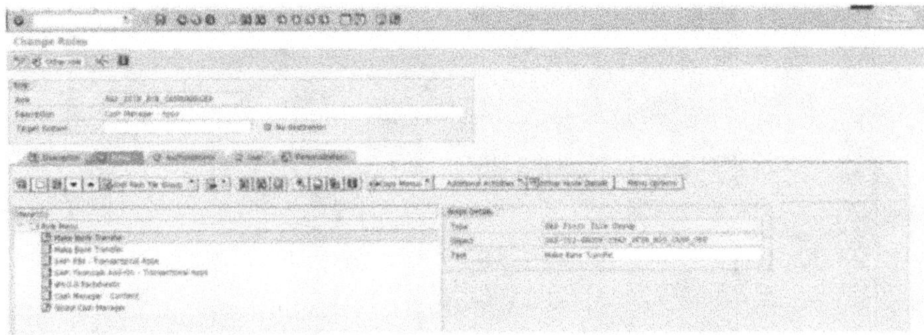

Add User to Single Role

1. Click on the User Tab.
2. Enter your User Id.
   (use value input helper to add users by batch)

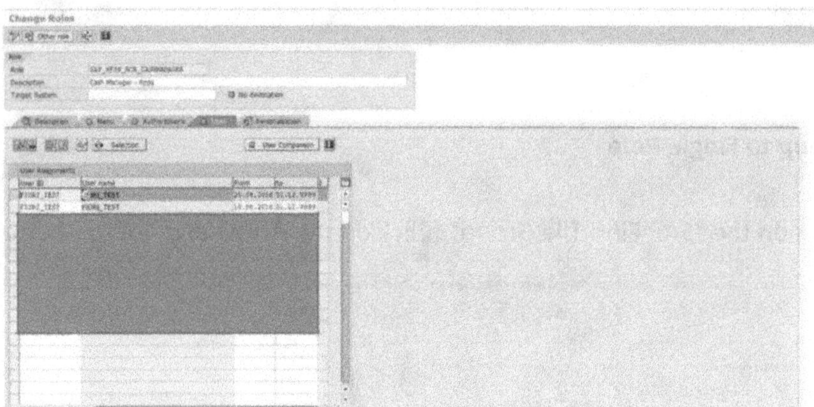

3. Click on "Save" to save the role.

Test Launchpad

Test URL:
http://<yourservername>:<port>/sap/bc/ui5_ui5/ui2/ushell/shells/abap/Fiorilaunchpad.html

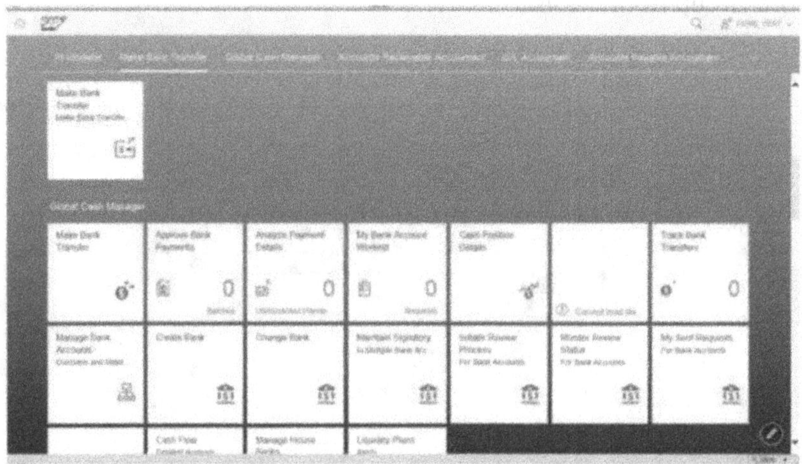

CHAPTER 21

SAP UI5

SAPUI5 (SAP user interface for HTML 5) is a collection of libraries that developers can use to build desktop and mobile applications that run in a browser. With SAP's SAPUI5 JavaScript toolkit, developers can build SAP web applications using HTML5 web development standards.

21.1. How does SAP UI5 work

To begin, you must understand SAPUI5's primary, underlying develop concept. SAPUI5 supports the Model View Controller (MVC) concept, "a software architectural pattern for implementing user interfaces". As a developer, you are encouraged to use the MVC to keep the data model handling, the UI design and the application logic separate. This helps in facilitating UI development in addition to modifying the different parts.

Model: This is the part that is accountable for the management, retrieval, and updating of the data that is being viewed in your application.

View: This part is accountable for interpreting and rendering the initial UI. The view in the context of SAPUI5, generates the presentation to the user based on changes in the model.

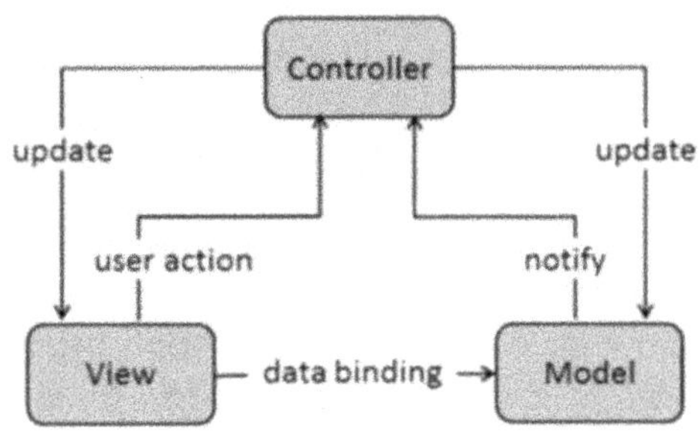

What does a view look like? Well, in its directory, views are in stored in the "view" folder and names of XML views always end with *.view.xml (as you'll see below).

Controller: This is one of the most important parts. This is the part that is accountable for separating the view logic from the data logic. The Controller responds to user interaction and "view events" by adjusting the view and the model. The controller is essentially sending commands to the model to update it's state, like editing a document in a word processing application. Similar to views, Controllers carry the same name as the related view (if there is a 1:1 relationship). Controller names always end with *controller.js (as you'll see below).

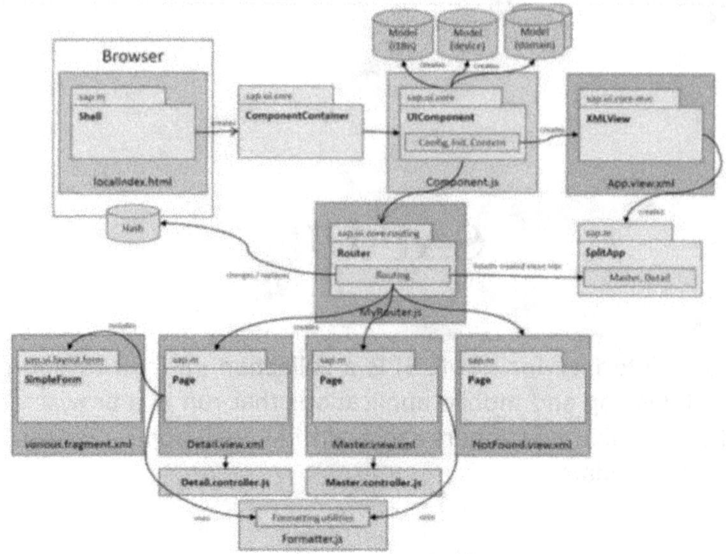

21.2. DEMO 1 - Building Your First SAP UI5 Application using Eclipse IDE

Ref: Anoop S.E Artifact

21.2.1. Overview

21.2.1.1. What Is SAP UI5

SAPUI5 (SAP user interface for HTML 5) is a collection of libraries that developers can use to build desktop and mobile applications that run in a browser. With SAP's SAPUI5 JavaScript toolkit, developers can build SAP web applications using HTML5 web development standards.

21.2.1.2. Architecture

Development scenario and architecture of the entire sample application developed in this document is illustrated in below. It focuses on UI and service definition using the corresponding IDE tools.

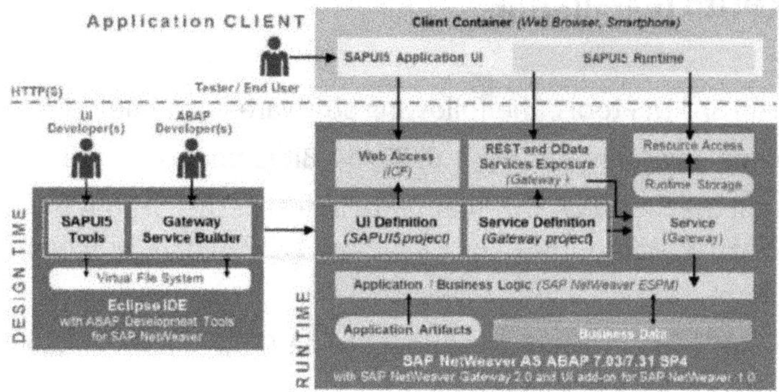

21.2.1.3. Features

- well-designed API, easy to consume and use
- extensible UI component model, including tooling support
- high performance, SAP product standard compliant
- powerful theming support based on CSS
- provides Ajax capabilities
- Based on open standards like OpenAjax, CSS, HTML 5, etc.
- using and including the popular jQuery library

21.2.1.4. Libraries

- sap.ui.commons – For buttons, standard control. Commonly used for web applications.
- sap.m – most common library used for mobile devices.
- sap.ui.table – Table control
- sap.makit -SAPUI5 library contains the makit charts.

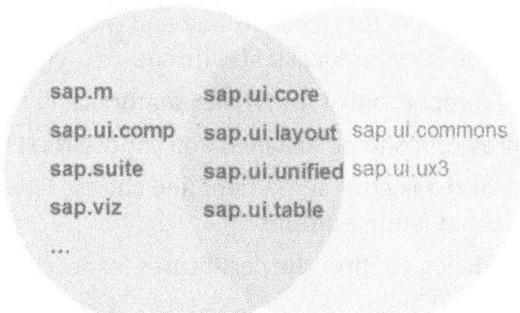

sap.m
sap.ui.comp
sap.suite
sap.viz
...
sap.ui.core
sap.ui.layout
sap.ui.unified
sap.ui.table
sap.ui.commons
sap.ui.ux3

21.2.1.5. SAPUI5 Installation

To install and run SAPUIS tools, the following software has to be installed:

- Java Runtime environment: JRE 1.6, 32/64-Bit (same as Eclipse)

  If you install the SAPUIS ABAP Team Provider together with ASAP development tools for SAP NetWeaver in a version below 1.0 Patch 07, you need to use the 32 Bit versions
- SAPUI5 ABAP Team Provider to connect to an ABAP backend system on SAP NetWeaver 7.3 EHP1 or 7.40

  If you want to use the SAPUIS ABAP Team Provider to connect to an ABAP backend system, the following additional prerequisites are required:
- User interface add-on for SAP NetWeaver 1.0 support package 04
- AiE Communication Framework

  The AIE Communication Framework is part of the ABAP development tools for SAP NetWeaver. Install the complete AMP development tools according to the installation procedure in the Installation Guide for the ABAP Development Tools, see SAP Note 1950493.
- Eclipse Kepler; Eclipse Indigo and Juno are not supported.
- Operating system: Windows XP, Vista, 7 (32- or 64-8it), 8/8.1

21.2.1.6. Installation Process for SAPUI5 Tools

To install SAPUI5 tools, proceed as follows:

- Launch your Eclipse workbench.
- Open the installation wizard by choosing **Help → Install New Software** .
- In the Work with field of the installation wizard, specify the target directory of the package.

To add the new installation directory, choose Add and then choose Archive to specify the location. Enter a name for your local software site.

- Select all UI development toolkit for HTML5 features and choose **Next.**
- Review the feature groups to be installed and choose **Next.**
- Accept the terms of the license agreement and choose Finish to initiate the installation of selected feature groups.
- In the Certificates dialog confirm the certificates from Eclipse.org and SAP with OK.

- To apply the changes of the installation procedure, restart the Eclipse workbench.
- To check, whether the installation has been successful, proceed as follows:

For SAPUI5 application development open the Eclipse IDE and choose **File →New → Other ... →SAPUI5 Application Development →Application Project** . If the installation has been successful, the New Application Project wizard opens.

For the SAPUI5 ABAP repository team provider open the Eclipse IDE and choose **File →New → Other ... →SAPUI5 Application Development →Application Project** . Select the new project and choose **Context Menu →Team →Share Project**... . If the installation has been successful, SAPUI5 ABAP Repository appears in the list

21.2.1.7. Model View Controller (MVC)

The Model View Controller (MVC) concept is used in SAPUI5 to separate the representation of information from the user interaction. This separation facilitates development and the changing of parts independently.

Model, view, and controller are assigned the following roles:

- The view is responsible for defining and rendering the UI.
- The model manages the application data.
- The controller reacts to view events and user interaction by modifying the view and model.

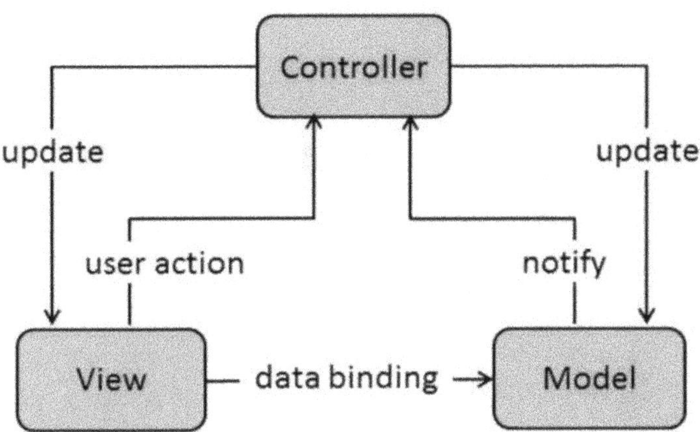

The purpose of data binding in the UI is to separate the definition of the user interface (view), the data visualized by the application (model), and the code for the business logic for processing the data (controller). The separation has the following advantages: It provides better readability, maintainability, and extensibility and it allows you to change the view without touching the underlying business logic and to define several views of the same data.

Views and controllers often form a 1:1 relationship, but it is also possible to have controllers without a UI, these controllers are called application controllers. It is also possible to create views without controllers. From a technical position, a view is a SAPUI5 control and can have or inherit a SAMS model.

View and controller represent reusable units, and distributed development is highly supported.

21.2.1.8. Hello World! Application

Start your Eclipse IDE to create your SAPUI application.

1. Start the New SAPUI5 Application Project wizard in the Eclipse by choosing New→Other →SAPUI5 Application Development →Application Project.

Enter the project name and choose the Library and press button 'Next'.

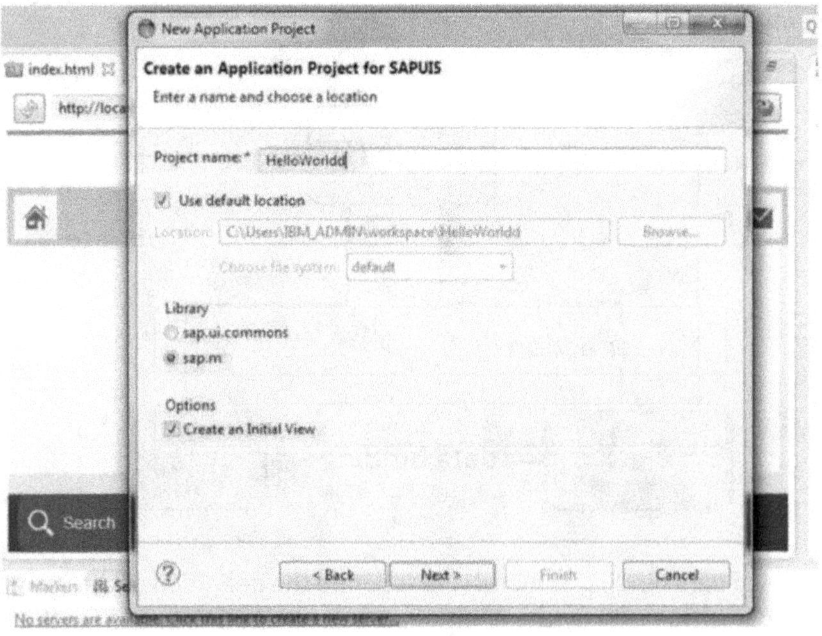

2. Input the name of your View and select the view type. Once done, Press button 'Finish'.

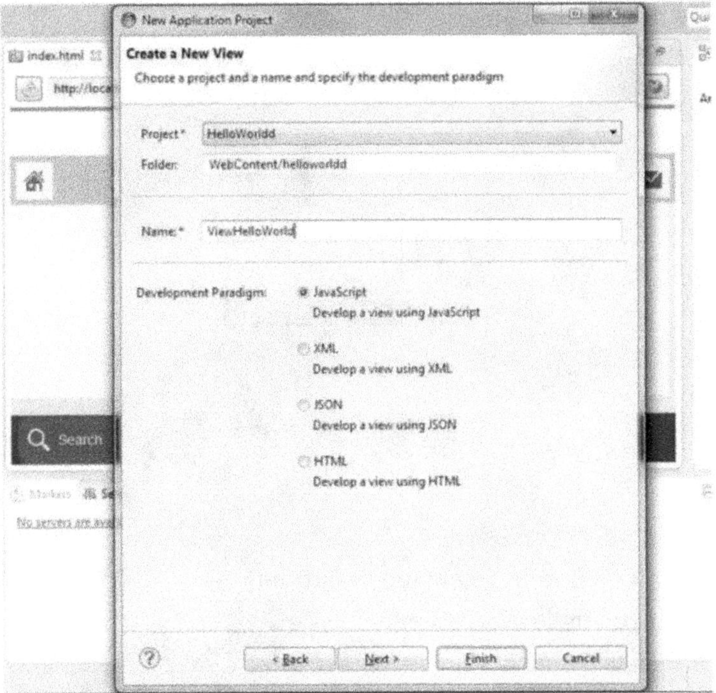

After finishing, your project wizard will open. You can see three default sections:

a. Index.html – where all your UI5 components will be placed at.
b. View.
c. Controller.

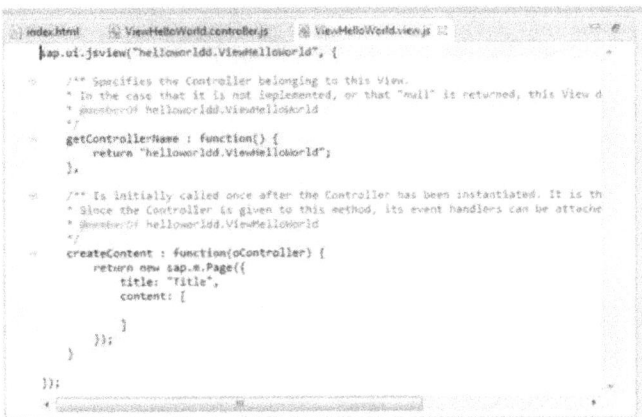

```
index.html    ViewHelloWorld.controller.js    ViewHelloWorld.view.js

sap.ui.jsview("helloworldd.ViewHelloWorld", {

    /** Specifies the Controller belonging to this View.
    * In the case that it is not implemented, or that "null" is returned, this View d
    * @memberOf helloworldd.ViewHelloWorld
    */
    getControllerName : function() {
        return "helloworldd.ViewHelloWorld";
    },

    /** Is initially called once after the Controller has been instantiated. It is th
    * Since the Controller is given to this method, its event handlers can be attache
    * @memberOf helloworldd.ViewHelloWorld
    */
    createContent : function(oController) {
        return new sap.m.Page({
            title: "Title",
            content: [

            ]
        });
    }

});
```

Now let us move on to creating the Hello world app.

1. Create a Button in your view.

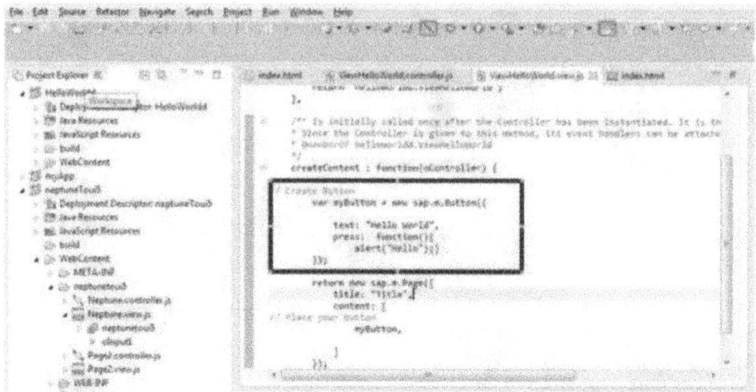

Code:

```
// Create Button
        var myButton = new sap.m.Button({
        text: "Hello World",
        press:  function() {
                alert("Hello");}
  });
```

2. Now place the button in your UI5 Page.

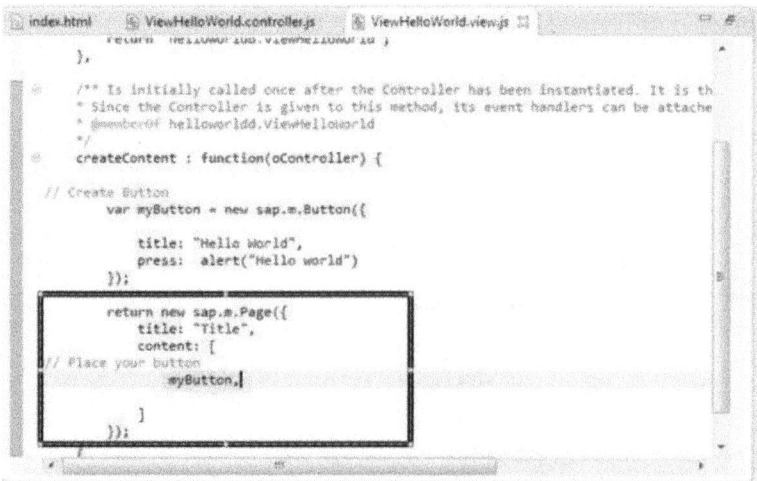

```
index.html    ViewHelloWorld.controller.js    ViewHelloWorld.view.js
    },

    /** Is initially called once after the Controller has been instantiated. It is th
    * Since the Controller is given to this method, its event handlers can be attache
    * @memberOf helloworldd.ViewHelloWorld
    */
    createContent : function(oController) {

// Create Button
        var myButton = new sap.m.Button({

            title: "Hello World",
            press:  alert("Hello world")
        });

        return new sap.m.Page({
            title: "Title",
            content: [
// Place your button
                myButton,

            ]
        });
```

3. Run your application by following the below steps:

   a. Rigt click on your project name.
   b. Clik on 'Run As'.
   c. Click on 'Web App Preview'.

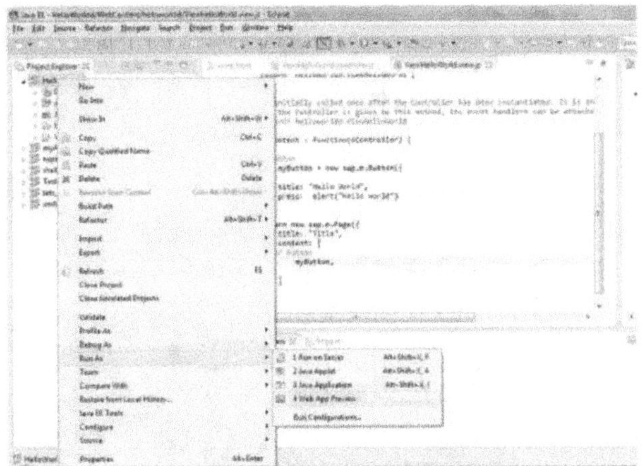

4. Now your application will open in new window.

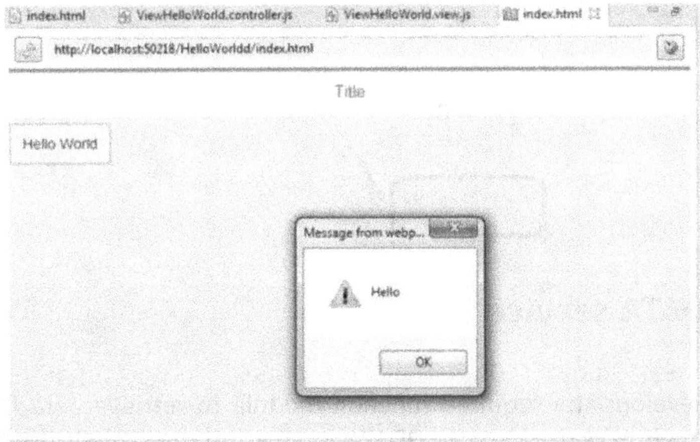

21.3. DEMO 2 - Developing Journal entry application using UI5

Ref: Ashfaq Ahmed's Artifact - Reading and displaying drop-down values from ODATA service

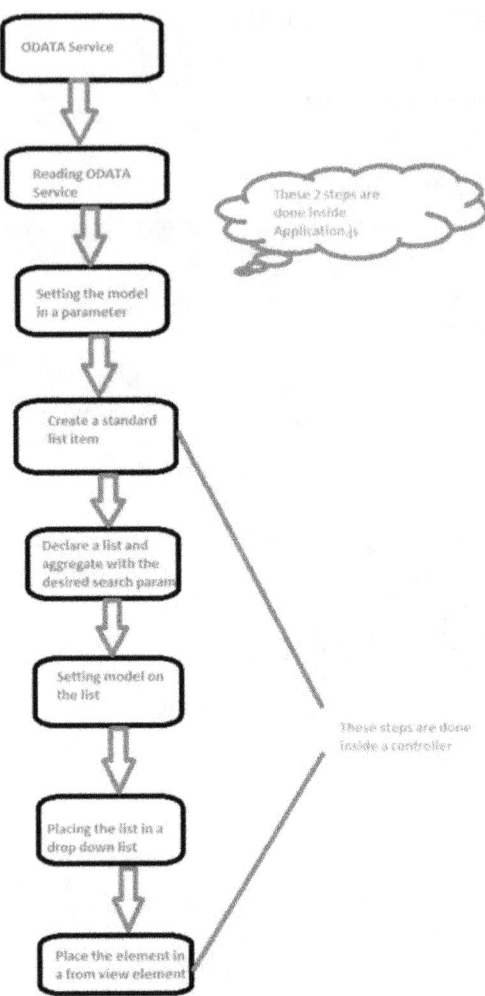

21.3.1. ODATA service

ABAP team develops the required function module to retrieve data from backend tables. The data is packaged into an ODATA service and the same is used by the UI to read and display values in the front end.

The link which is shared with a UI5 developer should contain a list of collection. When each collection is traversed then data pertaining to the collection is retrieved.

The initial ODATA service looks as follows:

When one goes to the HeaderTextSetcollection he can see the following values:

As shown in the above screen there is a list of combinations of Description and Reasoncode. These can be used to read and display adequate drop down data.

We will discuss in detail how to read the ODATA in a UI5 application.

21.3.2. Configuring Application.js

The application.js is a file which is present in all UI5 application. This file is used to declare global parameters which will be used throughout an application.

In the init() function of the application.js read the ODATA service URL. Create an ODATA model and place the values retrieved in this parameter.

Sample code attached:

```
var Model_base =
" http://xxxxxxx:8014/sap/opu/odata/sap/zfi_je_appln_search_help_srv/?sap-client=110";
this._oModel = new sap.ui.model.odata.ODataModel(this.getODataUrlPrefix(Model_base), true);
```

```
sap.ui.getCore().setModel(this._oModel, "valuehelpmodel");
```

The "valuehelpmodel" parameter stores the ODATA model and would be used later in the application.

We have used a function called getODataUrlPrefix to take care of cross browser issue while retrieving data from an ODATA service.

The function looks as follows:

```
var sOrigin = window.location.protocol+ "//"+ window.location.hostname+ (window.location.port ? ":"+ window.location.port : "");
if (!jQuery.sap.startsWith(sServiceUrl, sOrigin)) {
                    return "proxy/" + sServiceUrl.replace("://", "/");
                          } else {
                    return sServiceUrl.substring(sOrigin.length);
                          }
```

The above method appends "proxy/" to the ODATA URL based on the place where this URL is called, i.e. based on its origin.

21.3.3. Preparing drop down data in controller class

- **Create a Standard list item in the controller class**

  ```
  var oItemTemplateHdTxt = new sap.m.StandardListItem({title : "{Description}"});
  ```

- **Declare a sap.m.List**

  The sap.m.list mentions the name of the collection (marked in RED below) which needs to be read from the ODATA service and also the parameters which needs to be retrieved from the collection (marked in BROWN below).

  ```
  A> this.oHdTxtList = new sap.m.List( {
      mode: "SingleSelectLeft",
      includeItemInSelection: true,
      select: (jQuery.proxy(this.onHdTxtListChanged,
      this))
      });
  ```

```
B>  this.oHdTxtList.bindAggregation("items", {
                path: "/HeaderTextSet",
                template: oItemTemplateHdTxt,
                parameters: {
                                "select": "Description,Reasoncode"
                                }
                        });
C>  this.oHdTxtSelPop = new sap.m.Popover({placement : sap.m.PlacementType.
Bottom,
title: this.oBundle.getText("HEADER"),
content: [ this.oHdTxtList ]
});
this.oHdTxtSelPop.addStyleClass("cjeSelPop");
```

- **Reading ODATA model and setting ODATA model**

  Read ODATA model and set the model as a parameter in the header text list created.

  ```
  this.oModel = sap.ui.getCore().getModel("valuehelpmodel");
  this.oHdTxtList.setModel(this.oModel);
  ```

- **Place the drop down list created in a form**

  Create a form and place the drop down list in the same.

  ```
  new sap.ui.commons.form.FormElement(
  {
  label : "{i18n>HEADER}",
  fields: [ new sap.m.Button(
  {
  id: "JECJE_TXA_HEADER",
  text: "",
  icon: "sap-icon://down",
  press: jQuery.proxy(this.onHdTxtBtnSelectPress, this)}) ]
  ```

  The onHdTxtBtnSelectPressmethod opens the drop-down box created in the form of a pop-up (sap.m.Popover - this.oHdTxtSelPop). User can select the desired value.

The function looks as follows:

```
if (this.oHdTxtSelPop.isOpen()) {
this.oHdTxtSelPop.close();
} else {
this.oHdTxtSelPop.openBy(evt.getSource());
if (!this.oHdTxtList.getSelectedItem()) {
this.oHdTxtList.setSelectedItem(this.oHdTxtList.getItems()[0]);
                }
        }
```

The end drop-down looks like:

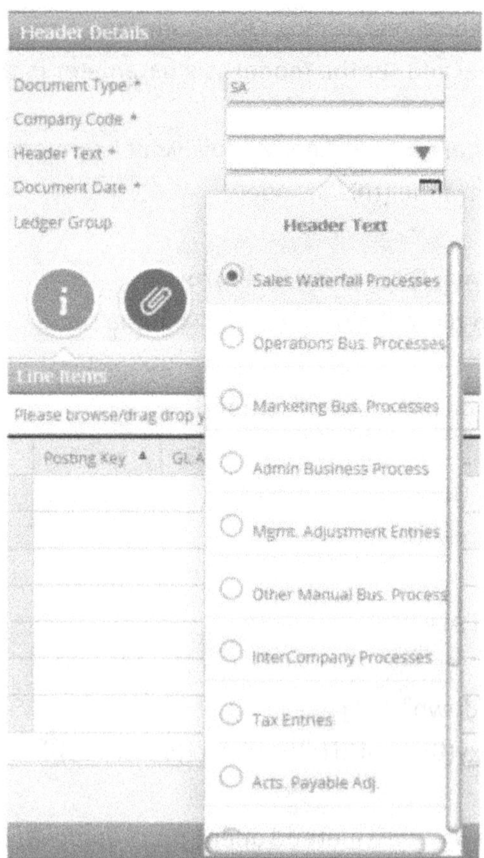

21.4. Creating a journal entry

21.5. Logical Infrastructure

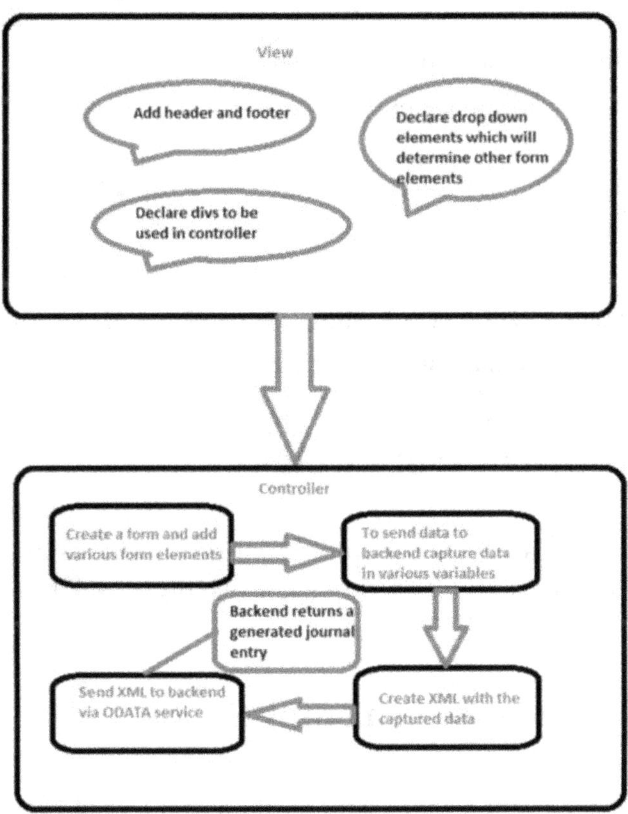

21.6. Creating view class

We will create a HTML view of the component. Let us name is “CreateJournalEntry.view.html”. In this we define the static header and footer components along with some “div” elements which will be used later in the controller.

21.6.1. A typical header element would look like

```
<div data-sap-ui-aggregation="customHeader">
```

```
<div data-sap-ui-type="sap.m.Bar">
<div data-sap-ui-aggregation="contentRight">
<div data-sap-ui-type="sap.m.Button" id="CJE_BTNBACK"
      data-enabled="true" data-icon="sap-icon://nav-back" data-press="onBack"
      data-text="Back"></div>

<div data-sap-ui-aggregation="contentMiddle">
<div data-sap-ui-type="sap.m.Label" data-text="{i18n>LR_CREATE_JE}"></div>
</div>
</div>
</div>
```

We have defined:

1. A back button. On clicking the button, the user is taken back to home screen
2. A static label mentioning the purpose of this page.

21.7. Creating controller class

The controller class initializes the control elements to be used in view, takes care of the flow of the application and controls the logic within the view. It has 2 main methods, namely onInit() and onNavigate().

21.7.1. Steps take care in a onInit().

In this function we declare various variable which will be initialized once and used through the application. For e.g. the drop down control list which we have discussed earlier in the section can be declared in this class.

Next we will declare a single or multiple forms to build up the view.

» Declare a form as **new sap.ui.commons.form.Form**

» A form can hold multiple form containers(**sap.ui.commons.form.FormContainer**). The form containers are used to bundle up few form elements to make the design as per the requirements

» A form container can have enumerable form elements (**sap.ui.commons.form. FormElement**). Each form element can either hold a text field, date, search help or combo box control based on the requirements. A typical text field control is place inside a form element as follows:

```
new sap.ui.commons.form.FormElement(
    {
        label : "{i18n>DOCUMENT_TYPE}",
        fields : [ new sap.ui.commons.TextField(
            {
                id : "JECJE_TXA_DOC_TYPE",
                required : true,
                maxLength : 2
            }) ],
        layoutData : new sap.ui.commons.layout.ResponsiveFlowLayoutData(
            {
                linebreak: true,
                margin: false
            })
    })
```

Note we have defined a responsive layout to design the element in the lines of responsive design.

After the form has been built we place the form in a 'div' which was declared in the view class. We use the following syntax: - oForm1.placeAt("SJEDiv")

After the view has been defined the application looks as follows:

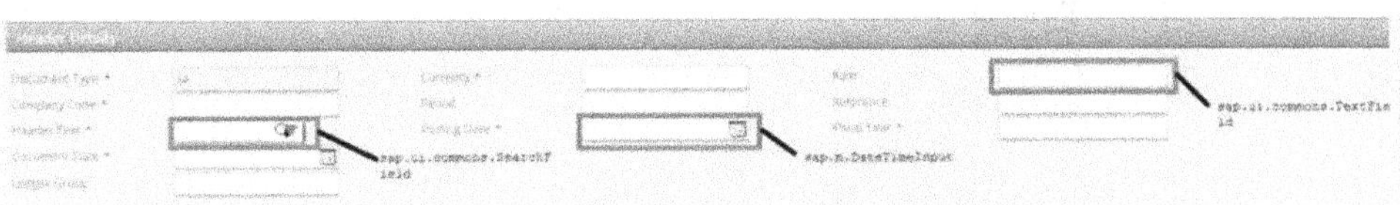

21.8. Sending data to backend

After the view has been created we have to handle the mechanism to send data to backend system. After the user has entered all the required values he clicks on a button. Let us call this button as "Send".

21.8.1. On clicking the send button the each data is read and an XML is created in the desired format.

The XML would look like:

```
var sBody = "<?xml version=\"1.0\" encoding=\"UTF-8\"?><atom:entry"
                  + " xmlns:atom=\"http://www.w3.org/2005/Atom\""
                  + " xmlns:d=\"http://schemas.microsoft.com/ado/2007/08/
dataservices\""
                  + " xmlns:m=\"http://schemas.microsoft.com/ado/2007/08/
dataservices/metadata\">"
                  + "<atom:content type=\"application/xml\"><m:properties>";

    sBody += "<d:COMP_CODE>" + compCode + "</d:COMP_CODE>";
    sBody += "<d:FI_DOC>0</d:FI_DOC>";
    sBody += "<d:FISCAL_YEAR>" + finyear + "</d:FISCAL_YEAR>";
    sBody += "<d:REQ_ACTION>SUB</d:REQ_ACTION>";
    sBody += "<d:JE_TYPE>" + jeType + "</d:JE_TYPE>";
sBody += "</m:properties></atom:content>";
```

21.8.2. Create a XML http request and call a "POST" method on the required ODATA service.

21.8.3.Set the required request headers before making the call, for e.g. "Cache-Control" can be set as "no-store,no-cache"

21.8.3. Before sending the XML payload a CSRF token is retrieved to make a secure connection

21.8.4. Once the CSRF token is received the ODATA service is called

21.8.5. If the activity is completed successfully; for e.g. creating journal entry, then we call a success call back method which was defined in the controller. The success callback method carries out the next series of steps which need to be followed. For instance we can show a message toast (sap.m.MessageToast) to display confirmation message to the user.

21.8.6. If the journal entry is not created successfully then an error message would be sent by the backend. Generally, the error message would be in the form of a JSON. An error call back method is called in the similar way as success call back and user is intimated about the error message.

We can parse and show the error messages using the following code:

```
var aErrors = new Array();

var error1 = new sap.ui.commons.Message( {
type : sap.ui.commons.MessageType.Error,
      text : response.error.message.value
                                          });

      aErrors.push(error1);

      for ( var i = 0; i < response.error.innererror.errordetails.length; i++) {

            var error = new sap.ui.commons.Message(
                                          {
```

```
type : sap.ui.commons.MessageType.Error,
text : response.error.innererror.errordetails[i].message
});

aErrors.push(error);

}

this.msgBar.addMessages(aErrors);
```

21.9. Displaying a journal entry

After we have created a journal entry we would like to view the journal entry details.

- o We need to declare controller and view classes for display journal entry.
- o Add similar view elements as Create Journal entry
- o Call the ODATA service to read journal entry application data. Use “ajax” to make a call to the ODATA service and retrieve the result.

A code snippet to call the ODATA service is as follows:

```
$.ajax( {
url : XXXXXXXX,
jsonpCallback : 'getJSON',
contentType : "application/json",
dataType : 'json',
success : function(data, textStatus, jqXHR) {
},
error : function(jqXHR, textStatus,errorThrown) {
}
});
```

If the ODATA service has been called successfully then the code inside the successblock would be called.

In the success block we would read the JSON data and populate various display controls nwith the required data.

```
var oModelHeader = new sap.ui.model.json.JSONModel();
oModelHeader.setData(data);
sap.ui.getCore().setModel(oModelHeader);
aDataFI_DOC = oModelHeader.getProperty("/d/FI_DOC");
```

The above code shows how we read "FI_DOC" field from the returned JSON. We can read other fields similarly and display in the front end.

21.10. DEMO - Sending attachment to backend using UI5

Ref: Ashfaq Ahmed's Artefact

Logical Infrastructure

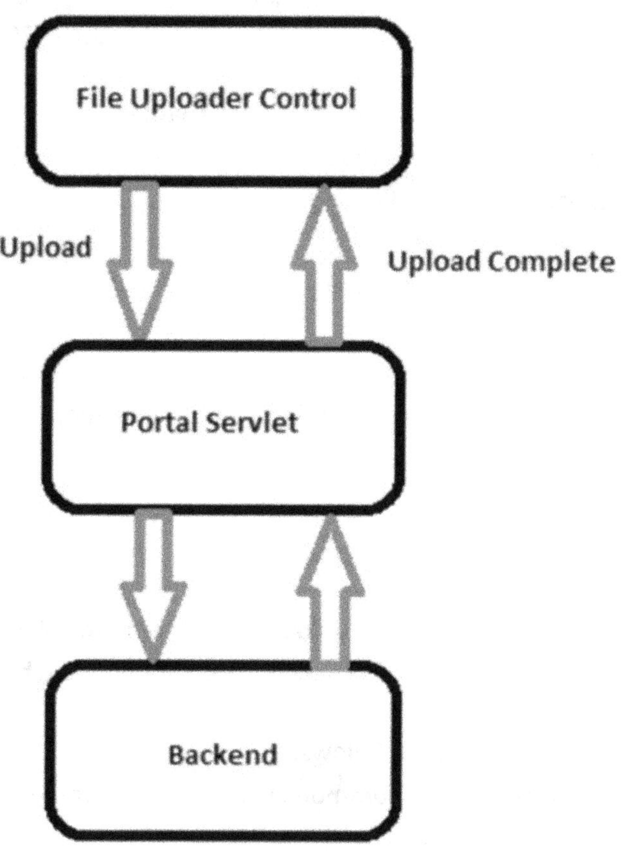

21.10.1. Using file browser control to send attachment to portal servlet

- **Declare a FileUploader control**

  The FileUploader uses uploadUrl to define the servlet URL which would be called and uploadComplete function. The uploadComplete method would be called once the attachments have been successfully saved by the servlet.

  A code snippet would look as follows:

```
new sap.ui.commons.FileUploader(
                    "fLoad",
                            {
                                        id : "uLoad",
                      uploadUrl : XXXX,
                          uploadComplete : function(        oEvent) {},
                                              width : "209px"
                                              })
```

- **Read the file and place it in a local storage variable**

```
var file = document.getElementById("fLoad-fu").files[0];
   reader.onload = (function(file) {
          return function(e) {
                var result = e.target.result;
                var oEntry = {};
                oEntry.Name = file.name;
                localStorage.setItem('FILE1', file.name);
                };

          })(file);
reader.readAsDataURL(file);
```

- **Call the upload method of the file uploader at the required place in your program. Before calling an upload method declare the parameters which is required to be passed to the servlet.**

  1. A parameter is declared as follows:

```
var param4 = new sap.ui.commons.FileUploaderParameter();
param4.setName("FI_DOC");
param4.setValue(fiDoc);
```

This creates a parameter name "FI_DOC" and value "fiDoc".

2. Retrieve the declared file uploader control.
   var finput = sap.ui.getCore().getElementById("fLoad");
3. Add the parameters in the controller.
   finput.addParameter(param4);
4. Call the rerender and upload function to call the servlet.
   finput.rerender();
   finput.upload();

21.10.2. Portal servlet to get the attachment details from UI5 and send it to Backend via JCA call

- Servlet to get the required details like FI_DOC,COMP_CODE etc from SAP UI5 application as POST request

A code snippet would look as follows:

```
{
   FileItem item = (FileItem)iterator.next();
   if(item.isFormField())
   {
      String fieldname = item.getFieldName();
      String fieldvalue = item.getString();
      if(fieldname.equals("COMP_CODE"))
         compCodeParam = fieldvalue;
      else
      if(fieldname.equals("FI_DOC"))
         fiDocParam = fieldvalue;
      else
      if(fieldname.equals("FISCAL_YEAR"))
         fiscalYearParam = fieldvalue;
      else
      if(fieldname.equals("namesOfControls"))
         namesOfControls = fieldvalue;
   }
```

```
}
```

- Since multiple attachment is being handled so we are getting the array of nameOfControls

```
String controlNames[] = namesOfControls.split("\\|");
        for(int i = 0; i < controlNames.length; i++)
        {
           String controlName = controlNames[i];
        }
```

- File contents is taken into file input stream and set to the table input parameter as 1024-byte array.

```
InputStream fileContent = item.getInputStream();
        IRecordSet table = (IRecordSet)sf.getStructure(function.getParameter("FILE_
        CONTENT").getStructure());
              byte bytes[] = new byte[1024];
              for(int read = 0; (read = fileContent.read(bytes)) != -1;)
              {
                 table.insertRow();
                 table.setBytes("LINE", bytes);
              }
```

- Other import parameters like COMP_CODE,FI_DOC,FISCAL_YEAR etc. are being set to the backend structure

```
inputRecord.put("FILE_CONTENT", table);
          IRecord structure = (IRecord)sf.getStructure(function.getParameter("IM_
          FILE_DATA").getStructure());
              structure.setString("COMP_CODE", compCodeParam);
              structure.setString("FI_DOC", fiDocParam);
              structure.setInt("FISCAL_YEAR", Integer.parseInt(fiscalYearParam));
```

- Different MIME Type are defined inside the servlet.

```
MIME_TYPES = new MimetypesFileTypeMap();
    MIME_TYPES.addMimeTypes("application/msword doc dot DOC DOT");
    MIME_TYPES.addMimeTypes("application/octet-stream bin BIN");
    MIME_TYPES.addMimeTypes("application/pdf pdf PDF");
```

- Prepare the code to initiate the JCA call to execute the BAPI to send the attachment to backend.

  A code snippet would look as follows:

```
ix = connection.createInteractionEx();
  IInteractionSpec ixSpec = ix.getInteractionSpec();
  ixSpec.setPropertyValue("Name", bapiName);
IFunction function = connection.getFunctionsMetaData().getFunction(bapiName);
  RecordFactory rf = ix.getRecordFactory();
  IStructureFactory sf = ix.retrieveStructureFactory();
  MappedRecord inputRecord = rf.createMappedRecord("input");
  HttpServletRequest servletRequest = request.getServletRequest();
  for(Iterator iterator = items.iterator(); iterator.hasNext();)
```

- Execute the BAPI with all the required details

```
MappedRecord outputRecord = (MappedRecord)ix.execute(ixSpec, inputRecord);
```

- Get the BAPI response as output

```
String outputParameters = profile.getProperty("com.ibm.OutputParameters");
  String parameters[] = outputParameters.split(",");
```

- Output parameters are converted into JSON format to be used by SAP UI5 application

  A code snippet would look as follows:

```
        IRecordSet recordSet = (IRecordSet)result;
        IRecordMetaData rmd = recordSet.retrieveMetaData();
        int columnCount = rmd.getColumnCount();
```

```
JSONArray jsonMetaData = new JSONArray();
for(int c = 0; c < columnCount; c++)
  try
  {
    JSONObject jsonHeaderField = new JSONObject();
    jsonHeaderField.put("name", rmd.getColumnName(c));
    jsonHeaderField.put("label", rmd.getColumnLabel(c));
  }
```

21.10.3. RFC function Module at Backend

It is normal function module to be created at backend to take the binary stream as an input.

Use the standard FM-ARCHIVOBJECT_CREATE_TABLE and archive the binary data which comes from the portal into content server.

Use the standard FM ARCHIV_CONNECTION_INSERT to link the archive object id to FI document no.

www.ingramcontent.com/pod-product-compliance
Lightning Source LLC
Chambersburg PA
CBHW052057230326
41599CB00054B/3020